PS
3529
N5
A6
1982
v.1

O'Neill

The plays of Eugene O'Neill

THE PLAYS OF
EUGENE O'NEILL
VOLUME I

ANNA CHRISTIE

BEYOND THE HORIZON

THE EMPEROR JONES

THE HAIRY APE

THE GREAT GOD BROWN

THE STRAW

DYNAMO

DAYS WITHOUT END

THE ICEMAN COMETH

THE PLAYS
OF
EUGENE
O'NEILL
VOLUME I

THE MODERN LIBRARY · NEW YORK

CONTENTS

"ANNA CHRISTIE"

A Play in Four Acts

CHARACTERS

"JOHNNY-THE-PRIEST"

TWO LONGSHOREMEN

A POSTMAN

LARRY, *bartender*

CHRIS CHRISTOPHERSON, *captain of the barge "Simeon Winthrop"*

MARTHY OWEN

ANNA CHRISTOPHERSON, *Chris's daughter*

THREE MEN OF A STEAMER'S CREW

MAT BURKE, *a stoker*

JOHNSON, *deckhand on the barge*

SCENES

ACT ONE

"Johnny-the-Priest's" saloon near the water front, New York City.

ACT TWO

The barge, "Simeon Winthrop," at anchor in the harbor of Province-town, Mass. Ten days later.

ACT THREE

Cabin of the barge, at dock in Boston. A week later.

ACT FOUR

The same. Two days later.

"ANNA CHRISTIE"

ACT ONE

Scene—"Johnny-the-Priest's" *saloon near South Street, New York City. The stage is divided into two sections, showing a small back room on the right. On the left, forward, of the barroom, a large window looking out on the street. Beyond it, the main entrance—a double swinging door. Farther back, another window. The bar runs from left to right nearly the whole length of the rear wall. In back of the bar, a small showcase displaying a few bottles of case goods, for which there is evidently little call. The remainder of the rear space in front of the large mirrors is occupied by half-barrels of cheap whisky of the "nickel-a-shot" variety, from which the liquor is drawn by means of spigots. On the right is an open doorway leading to the back room. In the back room are four round wooden tables with five chairs grouped about each. In the rear, a family entrance opening on a side street.*

It is late afternoon of a day in fall.

As the curtain rises, JOHNNY *is discovered.* "JOHNNY-THE-PRIEST" *deserves his nickname. With his pale, thin, clean-shaven face, mild blue eyes and white hair, a cassock would seem more suited to him than the apron he wears. Neither his voice nor his general manner dispel this illusion which has made him a personage of the water front. They are soft and bland. But beneath all his mildness one senses the man behind the mask—cynical, callous, hard as nails. He is lounging at ease behind the bar, a pair of spectacles on his nose, reading an evening paper.*

Two longshoremen enter from the street, wearing their working

3

aprons, the button of the union pinned conspicuously on the caps pulled sideways on their heads at an aggressive angle.

FIRST LONGSHOREMAN. (*as they range themselves at the bar*) Gimme a shock. Number Two. (*He tosses a coin on the bar.*)

SECOND LONGSHOREMAN. Same here. (*JOHNNY sets two glasses of barrel whiskey before them.*)

FIRST LONGSHOREMAN. Here's luck! (*The other nods. They gulp down their whisky.*)

SECOND LONGSHOREMAN. (*putting money on the bar*) Give us another.

FIRST LONGSHOREMAN. Gimme a scoop this time—lager and porter. I'm dry.

SECOND LONGSHOREMAN. Same here. (*JOHNNY draws the lager and porter and sets the big, foaming schooners before them. They drink down half the contents and start to talk together hurriedly in low tones. The door on the left is swung open and LARRY enters. He is a boyish, red-cheeked, rather good-looking young fellow of twenty or so.*)

LARRY. (*nodding to JOHNNY—cheerily*) Hello, boss.

JOHNNY. Hello, Larry. (*With a glance at his watch*) Just on time. (*LARRY goes to the right behind the bar, takes off his coat, and puts on an apron.*)

FIRST LONGSHOREMAN. (*abruptly*) Let's drink up and get back to it. (*They finish their drinks and go out left. THE POSTMAN enters as they leave. He exchanges nods with JOHNNY and throws a letter on the bar.*)

THE POSTMAN. Addressed care of you, Johnny. Know him?

JOHNNY. (*picks up the letter, adjusting his spectacles. LARRY comes and peers over his shoulders. JOHNNY reads very slowly*) Christopher Christopherson.

THE POSTMAN. (*helpfully*) Square-head name.

LARRY. Old Chris—that's who.

4

JOHNNY. Oh, sure. I was forgetting Chris carried a hell of a name like that. Letters come here for him sometimes before, I remember now. Long time ago, though.

THE POSTMAN. It'll get him all right then?

JOHNNY. Sure thing. He comes here whenever he's in port.

THE POSTMAN. (*turning to go*) Sailor, eh?

JOHNNY. (*with a grin*) Captain of a coal barge.

THE POSTMAN. (*laughing*) Some job! Well, s'long.

JOHNNY. S'long. I'll see he gets it. (THE POSTMAN *goes out.* JOHNNY *scrutinizes the letter*) You got good eyes, Larry. Where's it from?

LARRY. (*after a glance*) St. Paul. That'll be in Minnesota, I'm thinkin'. Looks like a woman's writing, too, the old divil!

JOHNNY. He's got a daughter somewheres out West, I think he told me once. (*He puts the letter on the cash register*) Come to think of it, I ain't seen old Chris in a dog's age. (*Putting his overcoat on, he comes around the end of the bar*) Guess I'll be gettin' home. See you tomorrow.

LARRY. Good-night to ye, boss. (*As* JOHNNY *goes toward the street door, it is pushed open and* CHRISTOPHER CHRISTOPHERSON *enters. He is a short, squat, broad-shouldered man of about fifty, with a round, weather-beaten, red face from which his light blue eyes peer short-sightedly, twinkling with a simple good humor. His large mouth, overhung by a thick, drooping, yellow mustache, is childishly self-willed and weak, of an obstinate kindliness. A thick neck is jammed like a post into the heavy trunk of his body. His arms with their big, hairy, freckled hands, and his stumpy legs terminating in large flat feet, are awkwardly short and muscular. He walks with a clumsy, rolling gait. His voice, when not raised in a hollow boom, is toned down to a sly, confidential half-whisper with something vaguely plaintive in its quality. He is dressed in a wrinkled, ill-fitting dark suit of shore clothes, and wears a faded cap of gray cloth over his mop of grizzled, blond hair. Just now his face beams with a too-blissful hap-*

piness, and he has evidently be°n drinking. He reaches his hand out to JOHNNY.)

CHRIS. Hello, Yohnny! Have drink on me. Come on, Larry. Give us drink. Have one yourself. (*Putting his hand in his pocket*) Ay gat money—plenty money.

JOHNNY. (*shakes* CHRIS *by the hand*) Speak of the devil. We was just talkin' about you.

LARRY. (*coming to the end of the bar*) Hello, Chris. Put it there. (*They shake hands.*)

CHRIS. (*beaming*) Give us drink.

JOHNNY. (*with a grin*) You got a half-snootful now. Where'd you get it?

CHRIS. (*grinning*) Oder fallar on oder barge—Irish fallar—he gat bottle vhisky and we drank it, yust us two. Dot vhisky gat kick, by yingo! Ay yust come ashore. Give us drink, Larry. Ay vas little drunk, not much. Yust feel good. (*He laughs and commences to sing in a nasal, high-pitched quaver.*)

"My Yosephine, come board de ship. Long time Ay vait for you.
De moon, she shi-i-i-ine. She looka yust like you.
Tchee-tchee, tchee-tchee, tchee-tchee, tchee-tchee."

(*To the accompaniment of this last he waves his hand as if he were conducting an orchestra.*)

JOHNNY. (*with a laugh*) Same old Yosie, eh Chris?

CHRIS. You don't know good song when you hear him. Italian fallar on oder barge, he learn me dat. Give us drink. (*He throws change on the bar.*)

LARRY. (*with a professional air*) What's your pleasure, gentlemen?

JOHNNY. Small beer, Larry.

CHRIS. Vhisky—Number Two.

LARRY. (*as he gets their drinks*) I'll take a cigar on you.

CHRIS. (*lifting his glass*) Skoal! (*He drinks.*)

6

JOHNNY. Drink hearty.

CHRIS. (*immediately*) Have oder drink.

JOHNNY. No. Some other time. Got to go home now. So you've just landed? Where are you in from this time?

CHRIS. Norfolk. Ve make slow voyage—dirty vedder—yust fog, fog, fog, all bloody time! (*There is an insistent ring from the doorbell at the family entrance in the back room.* CHRIS *gives a start—hurriedly*) Ay go open, Larry. Ay forgat. It was Marthy. She come with me. (*He goes into the back room.*)

LARRY. (*with a chuckle*) He's still got that same cow livin' with him, the old fool!

JOHNNY. (*with a grin*) A sport, Chris is. Well, I'll beat it home. S'long. (*He goes to the street door.*)

LARRY. So long, boss.

JOHNNY. Oh—don't forget to give him his letter.

LARRY. I won't. (JOHNNY *goes out. In the meantime,* CHRIS *has opened the family-entrance door, admitting* MARTHY. *She might be forty or fifty. Her jowly, mottled face, with its thick red nose, is streaked with interlacing purple veins. Her thick, gray hair is piled anyhow in a greasy mop on top of her round head. Her figure is flabby and fat; her breath comes in wheezy gasps; she speaks in a loud, mannish voice, punctuated by explosions of hoarse laughter. But there still twinkles in her bloodshot blue eyes a youthful lust for life which hard usage has failed to stifle, a sense of humor mocking, but good-tempered. She wears a man's cap, double-breasted man's jacket, and a grimy, calico skirt. Her bare feet are encased in a man's brogans several sizes too large for her, which gives her a shuffling, wobbly gait.*)

MARTHY. (*grumblingly*) What yuh tryin' to do, Dutchy—keep me standin' out there all day? (*She comes forward and sits at the table in the right corner, front.*)

CHRIS. (*mollifyingly*) Ay'm sorry, Marthy. Ay talk to Yohnny. Ay forgat. What you goin' take for drink?

MARTHY. (*appeased*) Gimme a scoop of lager an' ale.

CHRIS. Ay go bring him back. (*He returns to the bar*) Lager and ale for Marthy, Larry. Vhisky for me. (*He throws change on the bar.*)

LARRY. Right you are. (*Then remembering, he takes the letter from in back of the bar*) Here's a letter for you—from St. Paul, Minnesota —and a lady's writin'. (*He grins.*)

CHRIS. (*quickly—taking it*) Oh, den it come from my daughter, Anna. She live dere. (*He turns the letter over in his hands uncertainly*) Ay don't gat letter from Anna—must be a year.

LARRY. (*jokingly*) That's a fine fairy tale to be tellin'—your daughter! Sure I'll bet it's some bum.

CHRIS. (*soberly*) No. Dis come from Anna. (*Engrossed by the letter in his hand—uncertainly*) By golly, Ay tank Ay'm too drunk for read dis letter from Anna. Ay tank Ay sat down for a minute. You bring drinks in back room, Larry. (*He goes into the room on right.*)

MARTHY. (*angrily*) Where's my lager an' ale, yuh big stiff?

CHRIS. (*preoccupied*) Larry bring him. (*He sits down opposite her. LARRY brings in the drinks and sets them on the table. He and MARTHY exchange nods of recognition. LARRY stands looking at CHRIS curiously. MARTHY takes a long draught of her schooner and heaves a huge sigh of satisfaction, wiping her mouth with the back of her hand. CHRIS stares at the letter for a moment—slowly opens it, and, squinting his eyes, commences to read laboriously, his lips moving as he spells out the words. As he reads his face lights up with an expression of mingled joy and bewilderment.*)

LARRY. Good news?

MARTHY. (*her curiosity also aroused*) What's that yuh got—a letter, fur Gawd's sake?

CHRIS. (*pauses for a moment, after finishing the letter, as if to let the news sink in—then suddenly pounds his fist on the table with happy excitement*) Py yiminy! Yust tank, Anna say she's comin' here right avay! She gat sick on yob in St. Paul, she say. It's short letter, don't tal me much more'n dat. (*Beaming*) Py golly, dat's good news all at one time for ole fallar! (*Then turning to MARTHY, rather shame-*

facedly) You know, Marthy, Ay've tole you Ay don't see my Anna since she vas little gel in Sveden five year ole.

MARTHY. How old'll she be now?

CHRIS. She must be—lat me see—she must be twenty year ole, py Yo!

LARRY. (*surprised*) You've not seen her in fifteen years?

CHRIS. (*suddenly growing somber—in a low tone*) No. Ven she vas little gel, Ay vas bo'sum on vindjammer. Ay never gat home only few time dem year. Ay'm fool sailor fallar. My voman—Anna's mother—she gat tired vait all time Sveden for me ven Ay don't never come. She come dis country, bring Anna, dey go out Minnesota, live with her cousins on farm. Den ven her mo'der die ven Ay vas on voyage, Ay tank it's better dem cousins keep Anna. Ay tank it's better Anna live on farm, den she don't know dat ole davil, sea, she don't know fa'der like me.

LARRY. (*with a wink at MARTHY*) This girl, now, 'll be marryin' a sailor herself, likely. It's in the blood.

CHRIS. (*suddenly springing to his feet and smashing his fist on the table in a rage*) No, py God! She don't do dat!

MARTHY. (*grasping her schooner hastily—angrily*) Hey, look out, yuh nut! Wanta spill my suds for me?

LARRY. (*amazed*) Oho, what's up with you? Ain't you a sailor yourself now, and always been?

CHRIS. (*slowly*) Dat's yust vhy Ay say it. (*Forcing a smile*) Sailor vas all right fallar, but not for marry gel. No. Ay know dat. Anna's mo'der, she know it, too.

LARRY. (*as CHRIS remains sunk in gloomy reflection*) When is your daughter comin'? Soon?

CHRIS. (*roused*) Py yiminy, Ay forgat. (*Reads through the letter hurriedly*) She say she come right avay, dat's all.

LARRY. She'll maybe be comin' here to look for you, I s'pose. (*He returns to the bar, whistling. Left alone with MARTHY, who stares at him with a twinkle of malicious humor in her eyes, CHRIS suddenly becomes desperately ill at ease. He fidgets, then gets up hurriedly.*)

9

CHRIS. Ay gat speak with Larry. Ay be right back. (*Mollifyingly*) Ay bring you oder drink.

MARTHY. (*emptying her glass*) Sure. That's me. (*As he retreats with the glass she guffaws after him derisively.*)

CHRIS. (*to* LARRY *in an alarmed whisper*) Py yingo, Ay gat dat Marthy shore off barge before Anna come! Anna raise hell if she find dat out. Marthy raise hell, too, for go, py golly!

LARRY. (*with a chuckle*) Serve ye right, ye old divil—havin' a woman at your age!

CHRIS. (*scratching his head in a quandary*) You tal me lie for tal Marthy, Larry, so's she gat off barge quick.

LARRY. She knows your daughter's comin'. Tell her to get the hell out of it.

CHRIS. No. Ay don't like make her feel bad.

LARRY. You're an old mush! Keep your girl away from the barge, then. She'll likely want to stay ashore anyway. (*Curiously*) What does she work at, your Anna?

CHRIS. She stay on dem cousins' farm 'til two year ago. Dan she gat yob nurse gel in St. Paul. (*Then shaking his head resolutely*) But Ay don't vant for her gat yob now. Ay vant for her stay with me.

LARRY. (*scornfully*) On a coal barge! She'll not like that, I'm thinkin'.

MARTHY. (*shouts from next room*) Don't I get that bucket o' suds, Dutchy?

CHRIS. (*startled—in apprehensive confusion*) Yes, Ay come, Marthy.

LARRY. (*drawing the lager and ale, hands it to* CHRIS—*laughing*) Now you're in for it! You'd better tell her straight to get out!

CHRIS. (*shaking in his boots*) Py golly. (*He takes her drink in to* MARTHY *and sits down at the table. She sips it in silence.* LARRY *moves quietly close to the partition to listen, grinning with expectation.* CHRIS *seems on the verge of speaking, hesitates, gulps down his whisky desperately as if seeking for courage. He attempts to whistle a few bars of "Yosephine" with careless bravado, but the whistle peters out fu-*

tilely. MARTHY *stares at him keenly, taking in his embarrassment with a malicious twinkle of amusement in her eye.* CHRIS *clears his throat*) Marthy—

MARTHY. (*aggressively*) Wha's that? (*Then, pretending to fly into a rage, her eyes enjoying* CHRIS' *misery*) I'm wise to what's in back of your nut, Dutchy. Yuh want to git rid o' me, huh?—now she's comin'. Gimme the bum's rush ashore, huh? Lemme tell yuh, Dutchy, there ain't a square-head workin' on a boat man enough to git away with that. Don't start nothin' yuh can't finish!

CHRIS. (*miserably*) Ay don't start nutting, Marthy.

MARTHY. (*glares at him for a second—then cannot control a burst of laughter*) Ho-ho! Yuh're a scream, Square-head—an honest-ter-Gawd knockout! Ho-ho! (*She wheezes, panting for breath.*)

CHRIS. (*with childish pique*) Ay don't see nutting for laugh at.

MARTHY. Take a slant in the mirror and yuh'll see. Ho-ho! (*Recovering from her mirth—chuckling, scornfully*) A square-head tryin' to kid Marthy Owen at this late day!—after me campin' with barge men the last twenty years. I'm wise to the game, up, down, and sideways. I ain't been born and dragged up on the water front for nothin'. Think I'd make trouble, huh? Not me! I'll pack up me duds an' beat it. I'm quittin' yuh, get me? I'm tellin' yuh I'm sick of stickin' with yuh, and I'm leavin' yuh flat, see? There's plenty of other guys on other barges waitin' for me. Always was, I always found. (*She claps the astonished* CHRIS *on the back*) So cheer up, Dutchy! I'll be offen the barge before she comes. You'll be rid o' me for good—and me o' you—good riddance for both of us. Ho-ho!

CHRIS. (*seriously*) Ay don' tank dat. You vas good gel, Marthy.

MARTHY. (*grinning*) Good girl? Aw, can the bull! Well, yuh treated me square, yuhself. So it's fifty-fifty. Nobody's sore at nobody. We're still good fren's, huh? (LARRY *returns to the bar.*)

CHRIS. (*beaming now that he sees his troubles disappearing*) Yes, py golly.

MARTHY. That's the talkin'! In all my time I tried never to split with a guy with no hard feelin's. But what was yuh so scared about—that I'd kick up a row? That ain't Marthy's way. (*Scornfully*) Think I'd break my heart to loose yuh? Commit suicide, huh? Ho-ho! Gawd! The world's full o' men if that's all I'd worry about! (*Then with a grin, after emptying her glass*) Blow me to another scoop, huh? I'll drink your kid's health for yuh.

CHRIS. (*eagerly*) Sure tang. Ay go gat him. (*He takes the two glasses into the bar*) Oder drink. Same for both.

LARRY. (*getting the drinks and putting them on the bar*) She's not such a bad lot, that one.

CHRIS. (*jovially*) She's good gel, Ay tal you! Py golly, Ay calabrate now! Give me vhisky here at bar, too. (*He puts down money.* LARRY *serves him*) You have drink, Larry.

LARRY. (*virtuously*) You know I never touch it.

CHRIS. You don't know what you miss. Skoal! (*He drinks—then begins to sing loudly*).

"My Yosephine, come board de ship—"

(*He picks up the drinks for* MARTHY *and himself and walks unsteadily into the back room, singing.*)

"De moon, she shi-i-i-ine. She looks yust like you.
Tchee-tchee, tchee-tchee, tchee-tchee, tchee- tchee."

MARTHY. (*grinning, hands to ears*) Gawd!

CHRIS. (*sitting down*) Ay'm good singer, yes? Ve drink, eh? Skoal! Ay calabrate! (*He drinks*) Ay calabrate 'cause Anna's coming home. You know, Marthy, Ay never write for her to come, 'cause Ay tank Ay'm no good for her. But all time Ay hope like hell some day she vant for see me and den she come. And dat's vay it happen now, py yimminy! (*His face beaming*) What you tank she look like, Marthy? Ay bet you she's fine, good, strong gel, pooty like hell! Living on farm

made her like dat. And Ay bet you some day she marry good, steady
land fallar here in East, have home all her own, have kits—and dan
Ay'm ole grandfader, py golly! And Ay go visit dem every time Ay gat
in port near! (*Bursting with joy*) By yimminy crickens, Ay calabrate
dat! (*Shouts*) Bring oder drink, Larry! (*He smashes his fist on the
table with a bang.*)

LARRY. (*coming in from bar—irritably*) Easy there! Don't be
breakin' the table, you old goat!

CHRIS. (*by way of reply, grins foolishly and begins to sing*)

"My Yosephine, come board de ship—"

MARTHY. (*touching* CHRIS' *arm persuasively*) You're soused to the
ears, Dutchy. Go out and put a feed into you. It'll sober you up. (*Then
as* CHRIS *shakes his head obstinately*) Listen, yuh old nut! Yuh don't
know what time your kid's liable to show up. Yuh want to be sober
when she comes, don't yuh?

CHRIS. (*aroused—gets unsteadily to his feet*) Py golly, yes.

LARRY. That's good sense for you. A good beef stew'll fix you. Go
round the corner.

CHRIS. All right. Ay be back soon, Marthy. (CHRIS *goes through the
bar and out the street door.*)

LARRY. He'll come round all right with some grub in him.

MARTHY. Sure. (LARRY *goes back to the bar and resumes his newspaper.* MARTHY *sips what is left of her schooner reflectively. There is
the ring of the family-entrance bell.* LARRY *comes to the door and
opens it a trifle—then, with a puzzled expression, pulls it wide.* ANNA
CHRISTOPHERSON *enters. She is a tall, blond, fully-developed girl of
twenty, handsome after a large, Viking-daughter fashion but now run
down in health and plainly showing all the outward evidences of
belonging to the world's oldest profession. Her youthful face is already
hard and cynical beneath its layer of make-up. Her clothes are the*

tawdry finery of peasant stock turned prostitute. She comes and sinks wearily in a chair by the table, left front.)

ANNA. Gimme a whisky—ginger ale on the side. (*Then, as* LARRY *turns to go, forcing a winning smile at him*) And don't be stingy, baby.

LARRY. (*sarcastically*) Shall I serve it in a pail?

ANNA. (*with a hard laugh*) That suits me down to the ground. (LARRY *goes into the bar. The two women size each other up with frank stares.* LARRY *comes back with the drink which he sets before* ANNA *and returns to the bar again.* ANNA *downs her drink at a gulp. Then, after a moment, as the alcohol begins to rouse her, she turns to* MARTHY *with a friendly smile*) Gee, I needed that bad, all right, all right!

MARTHY. (*nodding her head sympathetically*) Sure—yuh look all in. Been on a bat?

ANNA. No—traveling—day and a half on the train. Had to sit up all night in the dirty coach, too. Gawd, I thought I'd never get here!

MARTHY. (*with a start—looking at her intently*) Where'd yuh come from, huh?

ANNA. St. Paul—out in Minnesota.

MARTHY. (*staring at her in amazement—slowly*) So—yuh're— (*She suddenly bursts out into hoarse, ironical laughter*) Gawd!

ANNA. All the way from Minnesota, sure. (*Flaring up*) What you laughing at? Me?

MARTHY. (*hastily*) No, honest, kid. I was thinkin' of somethin' else.

ANNA. (*mollified—with a smile*) Well, I wouldn't blame you, at that. Guess I do look rotten—yust out of the hospital two weeks. I'm going to have another 'ski. What d'you say? Have something on me?

MARTHY. Sure I will. T'anks. (*She calls*) Hey, Larry! Little service! (*He comes in.*)

ANNA. Same for me.

MARTHY. Same here. (LARRY *takes their glasses and goes out.*)

ANNA. Why don't you come sit over here, be sociable. I'm a dead stranger in this burg—and I ain't spoke a word with no one since day before yesterday.

MARTHY. Sure thing. (*She shuffles over to* ANNA's *table and sits down opposite her.* LARRY *brings the drinks and* ANNA *pays him.*)

ANNA. Skoal! Here's how! (*She drinks.*)

MARTHY. Here's luck! (*She takes a gulp from her schooner.*)

ANNA. (*taking a package of Sweet Caporal cigarettes from her bag*) Let you smoke in here, won't they?

MARTHY. (*doubtfully*) Sure. (*Then with evident anxiety*) On'y trow it away if yuh hear someone comin'.

ANNA. (*lighting one and taking a deep inhale*) Gee, they're fussy in this dump, ain't they? (*She puffs, staring at the table top.* MARTHY *looks her over with a new penetrating interest, taking in every detail of her face.* ANNA *suddenly becomes conscious of this appraising stare—resentfully*) Ain't nothing wrong with me, is there? You're looking hard enough.

MARTHY. (*irritated by the other's tone—scornfully*) Ain't got to look much. I got your number the minute you stepped in the door.

ANNA. (*her eyes narrowing*) Ain't you smart! Well, I got yours, too, without no trouble. You're me forty years from now. That's you! (*She gives a hard laugh.*)

MARTHY. (*angrily*) Is that so? Well, I'll tell you straight, kiddo, that Marthy Owen never— (*She catches herself up short—with a grin*) What are you and me scrappin' over? Let's cut it out, huh? Me, I don't want no hard feelin's with no one. (*Extending her hand*) Shake and forget it, huh?

ANNA. (*shakes her hand gladly*) Only too glad to. I ain't looking for trouble. Let's have 'nother. What d'you say?

MARTHY. (*shaking her head*) Not for mine. I'm full up. And you— Had anythin' to eat lately?

ANNA. Not since this morning on the train.

MARTHY. Then yuh better go easy on it, hadn't yuh?

ANNA. (*after a moment's hesitation*) Guess you're right. I got to meet someone, too. But my nerves is on edge after that rotten trip.

MARTHY. Yuh said yuh was just outa the hospital?

ANNA. Two weeks ago. (*Leaning over to* MARTHY *confidentially*) The joint I was in out in St. Paul got raided. That was the start. The judge give all us girls thirty days. The others didn't seem to mind being in the cooler much. Some of 'em was used to it. But me, I couldn't stand it. It got my goat right—couldn't eat or sleep or nothing. I never could stand being caged up nowheres. I got good and sick and they had to send me to the hospital. It was nice there. I was sorry to leave it, honest!

MARTHY. (*after a slight pause*) Did yuh say yuh got to meet someone here?

ANNA. Yes. Oh, not what you mean. It's my Old Man I got to meet. Honest! It's funny, too. I ain't seen him since I was a kid—don't even know what he looks like—yust had a letter every now and then. This was always the only address he give me to write him back. He's yanitor of some building here now—used to be a sailor.

MARTHY. (*astonished*) Janitor!

ANNA. Sure. And I was thinking maybe, seeing he ain't never done a thing for me in my life, he might be willing to stake me to a room and eats till I get rested up. (*Wearily*) Gee, I sure need that rest! I'm knocked out. (*Then resignedly*) But I ain't expecting much from him. Give you a kick when you're down, that's what all men do. (*With sudden passion*) Men, I hate 'em—all of 'em! And I don't expect he'll turn out no better than the rest. (*Then with sudden interest*) Say, do you hang out around this dump much?

MARTHY. Oh, off and on.

ANNA. Then maybe you know him—my Old Man—or at least seen him?

MARTHY. It ain't old Chris, is it?

ANNA. Old Chris?

MARTHY. Chris Christopherson, his full name is.

ANNA. (*excitedly*) Yes, that's him! Anna Christopherson—that's my real name—only out there I called myself Anna Christie. So you know him, eh?

MARTHY. (*evasively*) Seen him about for years.

ANNA. Say, what's he like, tell me, honest?

MARTHY. Oh, he's short and—

ANNA. (*impatiently*) I don't care what he looks like. What kind is he?

MARTHY. (*earnestly*) Well, yuh can bet your life, kid, he's as good an old guy as ever walked on two feet. That goes!

ANNA. (*pleased*) I'm glad to hear it. Then you think's he'll stake me to that rest cure I'm after?

MARTHY. (*emphatically*) Surest thing you know. (*Disgustedly*) But where'd yuh get the idea he was a janitor?

ANNA. He wrote me he was himself.

MARTHY. Well, he was lyin'. He ain't. He's captain of a barge—five men under him.

ANNA. (*disgusted in her turn*) A barge? What kind of a barge?

MARTHY. Coal, mostly.

ANNA. A coal barge! (*with a harsh laugh*) If that ain't a swell job to find your long lost Old Man working at! Gee, I knew something'd be bound to turn out wrong—always does with me. That puts my idea of his giving me a rest on the bum.

MARTHY. What d'yuh mean?

ANNA. I s'pose he lives on the boat, don't he?

MARTHY. Sure. What about it? Can't you live on it, too?

ANNA. (*scornfully*) Me? On a dirty coal barge! What d'you think I am?

MARTHY. (*resentfully*) What d'yuh know about barges, huh? Bet yuh ain't never seen one. That's what comes of his bringing yuh up inland—away from the old devil sea—where yuh'd be safe—Gawd! (*The irony of it strikes her sense of humor and she laughs hoarsely.*)

ANNA. (*angrily*) His bringing me up! Is that what he tells people!

I like his nerve! He let them cousins of my Old Woman's keep me on their farm and work me to death like a dog.

MARTHY. Well, he's got queer notions on some things. I've heard him say a farm was the best place for a kid.

ANNA. Sure. That's what he'd always answer back—and a lot of crazy stuff about staying away from the sea—stuff I couldn't make head or tail to. I thought he must be nutty.

MARTHY. He is on that one point. (*Casually*) So yuh didn't fall for life on the farm, huh?

ANNA. I should say not! The old man of the family, his wife, and four sons—I had to slave for all of 'em. I was only a poor relation, and they treated me worse than they dare treat a hired girl. (*After a moment's hesitation—somberly*) It was one of the sons—the youngest—started me—when I was sixteen. After that, I hated 'em so I'd killed 'em all if I'd stayed. So I run away—to St. Paul.

MARTHY. (*who has been listening sympathetically*) I've heard Old Chris talkin' about your bein' a nurse girl out there. Was that all a bluff yuh put up when yuh wrote him?

ANNA. Not on your life, it wasn't. It was true for two years. I didn't go wrong all at one jump. Being a nurse girl was yust what finished me. Taking care of other people's kids, always listening to their bawling and crying, caged in, when you're only a kid yourself and want to go out and see things. At last I got the chance—to get into that house. And you bet your life I took it! (*Defiantly*) And I ain't sorry neither. (*After a pause—with bitter hatred*) It was all men's fault—the whole business. It was men on the farm ordering and beating me—and giving me the wrong start. Then when I was a nurse, it was men again hanging around, bothering me, trying to see what they could get. (*She gives a hard laugh*) And now it's men all the time. Gawd, I hate 'em all, every mother's son of 'em! Don't you?

MARTHY. Oh, I dunno. There's good ones and bad ones, kid. You've just had a run of bad luck with 'em, that's all. Your Old Man, now—old Chris—he's a good one.

ANNA. (*skeptically*) He'll have to show me.

MARTHY. Yuh kept right on writing him yuh was a nurse girl still, even after yuh was in the house, didn't yuh?

ANNA. Sure. (*Cynically*) Not that I think he'd care a darn.

MARTHY. Yuh're all wrong about him, kid. (*Earnestly*) I know Old Chris well for a long time. He's talked to me 'bout you lots o' times. He thinks the world o' you, honest he does.

ANNA. Aw, quit the kiddin'!

MARTHY. Honest! Only, he's a simple old guy, see? He's got nutty notions. But he means well, honest. Listen to me, kid— (*She is interrupted by the opening and shutting of the street door in the bar and by hearing* CHRIS' *voice*) Ssshh!

ANNA. What's up?

CHRIS. (*who has entered the bar. He seems considerably sobered up*) Py golly, Larry, dat grub taste good. Marthy in back?

LARRY. Sure—and another tramp with her. (CHRIS *starts for the entrance to the back room.*)

MARTHY. (*to* ANNA *in a hurried, nervous whisper*) That's him now. He's comin' in here. Brace up!

ANNA. Who? (CHRIS *opens the door.*)

MARTHY. (*as if she were greeting him for the first time*) Why hello, Old Chris. (*Then before he can speak, she shuffles hurriedly past him into the bar, beckoning him to follow her*) Come here. I wanta tell yuh somethin'. (*He goes out to her. She speaks hurriedly in a low voice*) Listen! I'm goin' to beat it down to the barge—pack up me duds and blow. That's her in there—your Anna—just come—waitin' for yuh. Treat her right, see? She's been sick. Well, s'long! (*She goes into the back room—to* ANNA) S'long, kid. I gotta beat it now. See yuh later.

ANNA. (*nervously*) So long. (MARTHY *goes quickly out of the family entrance.*)

LARRY. (*looking at the stupefied* CHRIS *curiously*) Well, what's up now?

CHRIS. (*vaguely*) Nutting—nutting. (*He stands before the door to the back room in an agony of embarrassed emotion—then he forces himself to a bold decision, pushes open the door and walks in. He stands there, casts a shy glance at Anna, whose brilliant clothes, and, to him, high-toned appearance, awe him terribly. He looks about him with pitiful nervousness as if to avoid the appraising look with which she takes in his face, his clothes, etc.—his voice seeming to plead for her forbearance*) Anna!

ANNA. (*acutely embarrassed in her turn*) Hello—father. She told me it was you. I yust got here a little while ago.

CHRIS. (*goes slowly over to her chair*) It's good—for see you—after all dem years, Anna. (*He bends down over her. After an embarrassed struggle they manage to kiss each other.*)

ANNA. (*a trace of genuine feeling in her voice*) It's good to see you, too.

CHRIS. (*grasps her arms and looks into her face—then overcome by a wave of fierce tenderness*) Anna lilla! Anna lilla! (*Takes her in his arms.*)

ANNA. (*shrinks away from him, half frightened*) What's that— Swedish? I don't know it. (*Then as if seeking relief from the tension in a voluble chatter*) Gee, I had an awful trip coming here. I'm all in. I had to sit up in a dirty coach all night—couldn't get no sleep, hardly —and then I had a hard job finding this place. I never been in New York before, you know, and—

CHRIS. (*who has been staring down at her face admiringly, not hearing what she says—impulsively*) You know you was awful pooty gel, Anna? Ay bet all men see you fall in love with you, py yiminy!

ANNA. (*repelled—harshly*) Cut it! You talk same as they all do.

CHRIS. (*hurt—humbly*) Ain't no harm for your fader talk dat vay, Anna.

ANNA. (*forcing a short laugh*) No—course not. Only—it's funny to see you and not remember nothing. You're like—a stranger.

CHRIS. (*sadly*) Ay s'pose. Ay never come home only few times ven you vas kit in Sveden. You don't remember dat?

ANNA. No. (*Resentfully*) But why didn't you never come home them days? Why didn't you never come out West to see me?

CHRIS. (*slowly*) Ay tank, after your mo'der die, ven Ay vas avay on voyage, it's better for you you don't never see me! (*He sinks down in the chair opposite her dejectedly—then turns to her—sadly*) Ay don't know, Anna, vhy Ay never come home Sveden in ole year. Ay vant come home end of every voyage. Ay vant see your mo'der, your two bro'der before dey vas drowned, you ven you vas born—but—Ay—don't go. Ay sign on oder ships—go South America, go Australia, go China, go every port all over world many times—but Ay never go aboard ship sail for Sveden. Ven Ay gat money for pay passage home as passenger den— (*He bows his head guiltily*) Ay forgat and Ay spend all money. Ven Ay tank again, it's too late. (*He sighs*) Ay don't know why but dat's vay with most sailor fallar, Anna. Dat ole davil sea make dem crazy fools with her dirty tricks. It's so.

ANNA. (*who has watched him keenly while he has been speaking—with a trace of scorn in her voice*) Then you think the sea's to blame for everything, eh? Well, you're still workin' on it, ain't you, spite of all you used to write me about hating it. That dame was here told me you was captain of a coal barge—and you wrote me you was yanitor of a building!

CHRIS. (*embarrassed but lying glibly*) Oh, Ay vork on land long time as yanitor. Yust short time ago Ay got dis yob cause Ay vas sick, need open air.

ANNA. (*sceptically*) Sick? You? You'd never think it.

CHRIS. And, Anna, dis ain't real sailor yob. Dis ain't real boat on sea. She's yust ole tub—like piece of land with house on it dat float. Yob on her ain't sea yob. No. Ay don't gat yob on sea, Anna, if Ay die first. Ay swear dat ven your mo'der die. Ay keep my word, py yingo!

ANNA. (*perplexed*) Well, I can't see no difference. (*Dismissing the subject*) Speaking of being sick, I been there myself—yust out of the hospital two weeks ago.

CHRIS. (*immediately all concern*) You Anna? Py golly! (*Anxiously*) You feel better now, dough, don't you? You look little tired, dat's all!

ANNA. (*wearily*) I am. Tired to death. I need a long rest and I don't see much chance of getting it.

CHRIS. What you mean, Anna?

ANNA. Well, when I made up my mind to come to see you, I thought you was a yanitor—that you'd have a place where, maybe, if you didn't mind having me, I could visit a while and rest up—till I felt able to get back on the job again.

CHRIS. (*eagerly*) But Ay gat place, Anna—nice place. You rest all you want, py yiminy! You don't never have to vork as nurse gel no more. You stay with me, py golly!

ANNA. (*surprised and pleased by his eagerness—with a smile*) Then you're really glad to see me—honest?

CHRIS. (*pressing one of her hands in both of his*) Anna, Ay like see you like hell, Ay tal you! And don't you talk no more about gatting yob. You stay with me. Ay don't see you for long time, you don't forgat dat. (*His voice trembles*) Ay'm gatting ole. Ay gat no one in vorld but you.

ANNA. (*touched—embarrassed by this unfamiliar emotion*) Thanks. It sounds good to hear someone—talk to me that way. Say, though— if you're so lonely—it's funny—why ain't you ever married again?

CHRIS. (*shaking his head emphatically—after a pause*) Ay love your mo'der too much for ever do dat, Anna.

ANNA. (*impressed—slowly*) I don't remember nothing about her. What was she like? Tell me.

CHRIS. Ay tal you all about everytang—and you tal me all tangs happen to you. But not here now. Dis ain't good place for young gel, anyway. Only no good sailor fallar come here for gat drunk. (*He gets to his feet quickly and picks up her bag*) You come with me, Anna. You need lie down, gat rest.

22

ANNA. (*half rises to her feet, then sits down again*) Where're you going?

CHRIS. Come. Ve gat on board.

ANNA. (*disappointedly*) On board your barge, you mean? (*Dryly*) Nix for mine! (*Then seeing his crestfallen look—forcing a smile*) Do you think that's a good place for a young girl like me—a coal barge?

CHRIS. (*dully*) Yes, Ay tank. (*He hesitates—then continues more and more pleadingly*) You don't know how nice it's on barge, Anna. Tug come and ve gat towed out on voyage—yust water all round, and sun, and fresh air, and good grub for make you strong, healthy gel. You see many tangs you don't see before. You gat moonlight at night, maybe; see steamer pass; see schooner make sail—see everytang dat's pooty. You need take rest like dat. You work too hard for young gel already. You need vacation, yes!

ANNA. (*who has listened to him with a growing interest—with an uncertain laugh*) It sounds good to hear you tell it. I'd sure like a trip on the water, all right. It's the barge idea has me stopped. Well, I'll go down with you and have a look—and maybe I'll take a chance. Gee, I'd do anything once.

CHRIS. (*picks up her bag again*) Ve go, eh?

ANNA. What's the rush? Wait a second. (*Forgetting the situation for a moment, she relapses into the familiar form and flashes one of her winning trade smiles at him*) Gee, I'm thirsty.

CHRIS. (*sets down her bag immediately—hastily*) Ay'm sorry, Anna. What you tank you like for drink, eh?

ANNA. (*promptly*) I'll take a— (*Then suddenly reminded—confusedly*) I don't know. What'a they got here?

CHRIS. (*with a grin*) Ay don't tank dey got much fancy drink for young gel in dis place, Anna. Yinger ale—sas'prilla, maybe.

ANNA. (*forcing a laugh herself*) Make it sas, then.

CHRIS. (*coming up to her—with a wink*) Ay tal you, Anna, ve calabrate, yes—dis one time because ve meet after many year. (*In a half whisper, embarrassedly*) Dey gat good port vine, Anna. It's good for

23

you, Ay tank—little bit—for give you appetite. It ain't strong, neider.
One glass don't go to your head, Ay promise.

ANNA. (*with a half hysterical laugh*) All right. I'll take port.

CHRIS. Ay go gat him. (*He goes out to the bar. As soon as the door
closes,* ANNA *starts to her feet.*)

ANNA. (*picking up her bag—half-aloud—stammeringly*) Gawd, I
can't stand this! I better beat it. (*Then she lets her bag drop, stumbles
over to her chair again, and covering her face with her hands, begins
to sob.*)

LARRY. (*putting down his paper as* CHRIS *comes up—with a grin*)
Well, who's the blonde?

CHRIS. (*proudly*) Dat vas Anna, Larry.

LARRY. (*in amazement*) Your daughter, Anna? (CHRIS *nods.* LARRY
lets a long, low whistle escape him and turns away embarrassedly.)

CHRIS. Don't you tank she vas pooty gel, Larry?

LARRY. (*rising to the occasion*) Sure! A peach!

CHRIS. You bet you! Give me drink for take back—one port vine for
Anna—she calabrate dis one time with me—and small beer for me.

LARRY. (*as he gets the drinks*) Small beer for you, eh? She's reform-
in' you already.

CHRIS. (*pleased*) You bet! (*He takes the drinks. As she hears him
coming,* ANNA *hastily dries her eyes, tries to smile.* CHRIS *comes in and
sets the drinks down on the table—stares at her for a second anxiously
—patting her hand*) You look tired, Anna. Vell, Ay make you take
good long rest now. (*Picking up his beer*) Come, you drink vine. It
put new life in you. (*She lifts her glass—he grins*) Skoal, Anna! You
know dat Svedish word?

ANNA. Skoal! (*downing her port at a gulp like a drink of whisky—
her lips trembling*) Skoal? Guess I know that word, all right, all
right!

CURTAIN

24

ACT TWO

SCENE—*Ten days later. The stern of the deeply-laden barge, "Simeon Winthrop," at anchor in the outer harbor of Provincetown, Mass. It is ten o'clock at night. Dense fog shrouds the barge on all sides, and she floats motionless in a calm. A lantern set up on an immense coil of thick hawser sheds a dull, filtering light on objects near it—the heavy steel bits for making fast the tow lines, etc. In the rear is the cabin, its misty windows glowing wanly with the light of a lamp inside. The chimney of the cabin stove rises a few feet above the roof. The doleful tolling of bells, on Long Point, on ships at anchor breaks the silence at regular intervals.*

As the curtain rises, ANNA *is discovered standing near the coil of rope on which the lantern is placed. She looks healthy, transformed, the natural color has come back to her face. She has on a black oilskin coat, but wears no hat. She is staring out into the fog astern with an expression of awed wonder. The cabin door is pushed open and* CHRIS *appears. He is dressed in yellow oilskins—coat, pants, sou'wester—and wears high seaboots.*

CHRIS. (*the glare from the cabin still in his eyes, peers blinkingly astern*) Anna! (*Receiving no reply, he calls again, this time with apparent apprehension*) Anna!

ANNA. (*with a start—making a gesture with her hand as if to impose silence—in a hushed whisper*) Yes, here I am. What d'you want?

CHRIS. (*walks over to her solicitously*) Don't you come turn in, Anna? It's late—after four bells. It ain't good for you stay out here in fog, Ay tank.

ANNA. Why not? (*With a trace of strange exultation*) I love this fog! Honest! It's so— (*She hesitates, groping for a word*) Funny and still. I feel as if I was—out of things altogether.

25

CHRIS. (*spitting disgustedly*) Fog's vorst one of her dirty tricks, py yingo!

ANNA. (*with a short laugh*) Beefing about the sea again? I'm getting so's I love it, the little I've seen.

CHRIS (*glancing at her moodily*) Dat's foolish talk, Anna. You see her more, you don't talk dat vay. (*Then seeing her irritation, he hastily adopts a more cheerful tone*) But Ay'm glad you like it on barge. Ay'm glad it makes you feel good again. (*With a placating grin*) You like live like dis alone with ole fa'der, eh?

ANNA. Sure I do. Everything's been so different from anything I ever come across before. And now—this fog— Gee, I wouldn't have missed it for nothing. I never thought living on ships was so different from land. Gee, I'd yust love to work on it, honest I would, if I was a man. I don't wonder you always been a sailor.

CHRIS. (*vehemently*) Ay ain't sailor, Anna. And dis ain't real sea. You only see nice part. (*Then as she doesn't answer, he continues hopefully*) Vell, fog lift in morning, Ay tank.

ANNA. (*the exultation again in her voice*) I love it! I don't give a rap if it never lifts! (CHRIS *fidgets from one foot to the other worriedly.* ANNA *continues slowly, after a pause*) It makes me feel clean—out here—'s if I'd taken a bath.

CHRIS. (*after a pause*) You better go in cabin read book. Dat put you to sleep.

ANNA. I don't want to sleep. I want to stay out here—and think about things.

CHRIS. (*walks away from her toward the cabin—then comes back*) You act funny tonight, Anna.

ANNA. (*her voice rising angrily*) Say, what're you trying to do—make things rotten? You been kind as kind can be to me and I certainly appreciate it—only don't spoil it all now. (*Then, seeing the hurt expression on her father's face, she forces a smile*) Let's talk of something else. Come. Sit down here. (*She points to the coil of rope.*)

CHRIS. (*sits down beside her with a sigh*) It's gatting pooty late in night, Anna. Must be near five bells.

ANNA. (*interestedly*) Five bells? What time is that?

CHRIS. Half past ten.

ANNA. Funny I don't know nothing about sea talk—but those cousins was always talking crops and that stuff. Gee, wasn't I sick of it—and of them!

CHRIS. You don't like live on farm, Anna?

ANNA. I've told you a hundred times I hated it. (*Decidedly*) I'd rather have one drop of ocean than all the farms in the world! Honest! And you wouldn't like a farm, neither. Here's where you belong. (*She makes a sweeping gesture seaward*) But not on a coal barge. You belong on a real ship, sailing all over the world.

CHRIS. (*moodily*) Ay've done dat many year, Anna, when Ay vas dam fool.

ANNA. (*disgustedly*) Oh, rats! (*After a pause she speaks musingly*) Was the men in our family always sailors—as far back as you know about?

CHRIS. (*shortly*) Yes. Dam fools! All men in our village on coast, Sveden, go to sea. Ain't nutting else for dem to do. My fa'der die on board ship in Indian Ocean. He's buried at sea. Ay don't never know him only little bit. Den my tree bro'der, older'n me, dey go on ships. Den Ay go, too. Den my mo'der she's left all 'lone. She die pooty quick after dat—all 'lone. Ve vas all avay on voyage when she die. (*He pauses sadly*) Two my bro'der dey gat lost on fishing boat same like your bro'ders vas drowned. My oder bro'der, he save money, give up sea, den he die home in bed. He's only one dat ole davil don't kill. (*Defiantly*) But me, Ay bet you Ay die ashore in bed, too!

ANNA. Were all of 'em yust plain sailors?

CHRIS. Able body seaman, most of dem. (*With a certain pride*) Dey vas all smart seaman, too—A one. (*Then after hesitating a moment—shyly*) Ay vas bo'sun.

ANNA. Bo'sun?

27

CHRIS. Dat's kind of officer.

ANNA. Gee, that was fine. What does he do?

CHRIS. (*after a second's hesitation, plunged into gloom again by his fear of her enthusiasm*) Hard vork all time. It's rotten, Ay tal you, for go to sea. (*Determined to disgust her with sea life—volubly*) Dey're all fool fallar, dem fallar in our family. Dey all vork rotten yob on sea for nutting, don't care nutting but yust gat big pay day in pocket, gat drunk, gat robbed, ship avay again on oder voyage. Dey don't come home. Dey don't do anytang like good man do. And dat ole davil, sea, sooner, later she svallow dem up.

ANNA. (*with an excited laugh*) Good sports, I'd call 'em. (*Then hastily*) But say—listen—did all the women of the family marry sailors?

CHRIS. (*eagerly—seeing a chance to drive home his point*) Yes—and it's bad on dem like hell vorst of all. Dey don't see deir men only once in long while. Dey set and vait all 'lone. And vhen deir boys grow up, go to sea, dey sit and vait some more. (*Vehemently*) Any gel marry sailor, she's crazy fool! Your mo'der she tal you same tang if she vas alive. (*He relapses into an attitude of somber brooding.*)

ANNA. (*after a pause—dreamily*) Funny! I do feel sort of—nutty, tonight. I feel old.

CHRIS. (*mystified*) Ole?

ANNA. Sure—like I'd been living a long, long time—out here in the fog. (*Frowning perplexedly*) I don't know how to tell you yust what I mean. It's like I'd come home after a long visit away some place. It all seems like I'd been here before lots of times—on boats—in this same fog. (*With a short laugh*) You must think I'm off my base.

CHRIS. (*gruffly*) Anybody feel funny dat vay in fog.

ANNA. (*persistently*) But why d'you s'pose I feel so—so—like I'd found something I'd missed and been looking for—'s if this was the right place for me to fit in? And I seem to have forgot—everything that's happened—like it didn't matter no more. And I feel clean, somehow—like you feel yust after you've took a bath. And I feel

28

happy for once—yes, honest!—happier than I ever been anywhere before! (*As* CHRIS *makes no comment but a heavy sigh, she continues wonderingly*) It's nutty for me to feel that way, don't you think?

CHRIS. (*a grim foreboding in his voice*) Ay tank Ay'm damn fool for bring you on voyage, Anna.

ANNA. (*impressed by his tone*) You talk—nutty tonight yourself. You act 's if you was scared something was going to happen.

CHRIS. Only God know dat, Anna.

ANNA. (*half-mockingly*) Then it'll be Gawd's will, like the preachers say—what does happen.

CHRIS. (*starts to his feet with fierce protest*) No! Dat ole davil, sea, she ain't God! (*In the pause of silence that comes after his defiance a hail in a man's husky, exhausted voice comes faintly out of the fog to port*) "Ahoy!" (CHRIS *gives a startled exclamation.*)

ANNA. (*jumping to her feet*) What's that?

CHRIS. (*who has regained his composure—sheepishly*) Py golly, dat scare me for minute. It's only some fallar hail, Anna—loose his course in fog. Must be fisherman's power boat. His engine break down, Ay guess. (*The "ahoy" comes again through the wall of fog, sounding much nearer this time.* CHRIS *goes over to the port bulwark*) Sound from dis side. She come in from open sea. (*He holds his hands to his mouth, megaphone-fashion, and shouts back*) Ahoy, dere! Vhat's trouble?

THE VOICE. (*this time sounding nearer but up forward toward the bow*) Heave a rope when we come alongside. (*Then irritably*) Where are ye, ye scut?

CHRIS. Ay hear dem rowing. Dey come up by bow, Ay tank. (*Then shouting out again*) Dis vay!

THE VOICE. Right ye are! (*There is a muffled sound of oars in oarlocks.*)

ANNA. (*half to herself—resentfully*) Why don't that guy stay where he belongs?

CHRIS. (*hurriedly*) Ay go up bow. All hands asleep 'cepting fallar on vatch. Ay gat heave line to dat fallar. (*He picks up a coil of rope and hurries off toward the bow.* ANNA *walks back toward the extreme stern as if she wanted to remain as much isolated as possible. She turns her back on the proceedings and stares out into the fog.* THE VOICE *is heard again shouting "Ahoy" and* CHRIS *answering "Dis vay." Then there is a pause—the murmur of excited voices—then the scuffling of feet.* CHRIS *appears from around the cabin to port. He is supporting the limp form of a man dressed in dungarees, holding one of the man's arms around his neck. The deckhand,* JOHNSON, *a young blond Swede, follows him, helping along another exhausted man similar fashion.* ANNA *turns to look at them.* CHRIS *stops for a second— volubly*) Anna! You come help, vill you? You find vhisky in cabin. Dese fallars need drink for fix dem. Dey vas near dead.

ANNA. (*hurrying to him*) Sure—but who are they? What's the trouble?

CHRIS. Sailor fallars. Deir steamer gat wrecked. Dey been five days in open boat—four fallars—only one left able stand up. Come, Anna. (*She precedes him into the cabin, holding the door open while he and* JOHNSON *carry in their burdens. The door is shut, then opened again as* JOHNSON *comes out.* CHRIS' *voice shouts after him*) Go gat oder fallar, Yohnson.

JOHNSON. Yes, sir. (*He goes. The door is closed again.* MAT BURKE *stumbles in around the port side of the cabin. He moves slowly, feeling his way uncertainly, keeping hold of the port bulwark with his right hand to steady himself. He is stripped to the waist, has on nothing but a pair of dirty dungaree pants. He is a powerful, broad-chested six-footer, his face handsome in a hard, rough, bold, defiant way. He is about thirty, in the full power of his heavy-muscled, immense strength. His dark eyes are bloodshot and wild from sleeplessness. The muscles of his arms and shoulders are lumped in knots and bunches, the veins of his forearms stand out like blue cords. He finds his way to the coil of hawser and sits down on it facing the cabin, his back bowed, head in his hands, in an attitude of spent weariness.*)

BURKE. (*talking aloud to himself*) Row, ye divil! Row! (*Then lifting his head and looking about him*) What's this tub? Well, we're safe anyway—with the help of God. (*He makes the sign of the cross mechanically.* JOHNSON *comes along the deck to port, supporting the fourth man, who is babbling to himself incoherently.* BURKE *glances at him disdainfully*) Is it losing the small wits ye iver had, ye are? Deck-scrubbing scut! (*They pass him and go into the cabin, leaving the door open.* BURKE *sags forward wearily*) I'm bate out—bate out entirely.

ANNA. (*comes out of the cabin with a tumbler quarter-full of of whisky in her hand. She gives a start when she sees* BURKE *so near her, the light from the open door falling full on him. Then, overcoming what is evidently a feeling of repulsion, she comes up beside him*) Here you are. Here's a drink for you. You need it, I guess.

BURKE. (*lifting his head slowly—confusedly*) Is it dreaming I am?

ANNA. (*half smiling*) Drink it and you'll find it ain't no dream.

BURKE. To hell with the drink—but I'll take it just the same. (*He tosses it down*) Ahah! I'm needin' that—and 'tis fine stuff. (*Looking up at her with frank, grinning admiration*) But 'twasn't the booze I meant when I said, was I dreaming. I thought you was some mermaid out of the sea come to torment me. (*He reaches out to feel of her arm*) Aye, rale flesh and blood, divil a less.

ANNA. (*coldly—stepping back from him*) Cut that.

BURKE. But tell me, isn't this a barge I'm on—or isn't it?

ANNA. Sure.

BURKE. And what is a fine handsome woman the like of you doing on this scow?

ANNA. (*coldly*) Never you mind. (*Then half amused in spite of herself*) Say, you're a great one, honest—starting right in kidding after what you been through.

BURKE. (*delighted—proudly*) Ah, it was nothing—aisy for a rale man with guts to him, the like of me. (*He laughs*) All in the day's work, darlin'. (*Then, more seriously but still in a boastful tone, con-*

31

fidentially) But I won't be denying 'twas a damn narrow squeak. We'd all ought to be with Davy Jones at the bottom of the sea, be rights. And only for me, I'm telling you, and the great strength and guts is in me, we'd be being scoffed by the fishes this minute!

ANNA. (*contemptuously*) Gee, you hate yourself, don't you? (*Then turning away from him indifferently*) Well, you'd better come in and lie down. You must want to sleep.

BURKE. (*stung—rising unsteadily to his feet with chest out and head thrown back—resentfully*) Lie down and sleep, is it? Divil a wink I'm after having for two days and nights and divil a bit I'm needing now. Let you not be thinking I'm the like of them three weak scuts come in the boat with me. I could lick the three of them sitting down with one hand tied behind me. They may be bate out, but I'm not—and I've been rowing the boat with them lying in the bottom not able to raise a hand for the last two days we was in it. (*Furiously, as he sees this is making no impression on her*) And I can lick all hands on this tub, wan be wan, tired as I am!

ANNA. (*sarcastically*) Gee, ain't you a hard guy! (*Then, with a trace of sympathy, as she notices him swaying from weakness*) But never mind that fight talk. I'll take your word for all you've said. Go on and sit down here, anyway, if I can't get you to come inside. (*He sits down weakly*) You're all in, you might as well own up to it.

BURKE. (*fiercely*) The hell I am!

ANNA. (*coldly*) Well, be stubborn then for all I care. And I must say I don't care for your language. The men I know don't pull that rough stuff when ladies are around.

BURKE. (*getting unsteadily to his feet again—in a rage*) Ladies! Ho-ho! Divil mend you! Let you not be making game of me. What would ladies be doing on this bloody hulk? (*As ANNA attempts to go to the cabin, he lurches into her path*) Aisy, now! You're not the old square-head's woman, I suppose you'll be telling me next—living in his cabin with him, no less! (*Seeing the cold, hostile expression on ANNA's face, he suddenly changes his tone to one of boisterous jovial-*

ity) But I do be thinking iver since the first look my eyes took at you, that it's a fool you are to be wasting yourself—a fine, handsome girl —on a stumpy runt of a man like the old Swede. There's too many strapping great lads on the sea would give their heart's blood for one kiss of you!

ANNA. (*scornfully*) Lads like you, eh?

BURKE (*grinning*) Ye take the words out o' my mouth. I'm the proper lad for you, if it's meself do be saying it. (*With a quick movement he puts his arms about her waist*) Whisht, now, me daisy! Himself's in the cabin. It's wan of your kisses I'm needing to take the tiredness from me bones. Wan kiss, now! (*He presses her to him and attempts to kiss her.*)

ANNA. (*struggling fiercely*) Leggo of me, you big mutt! (*She pushes him away with all her might.* BURKE, *weak and tottering, is caught off his guard. He is thrown down backward and, in falling, hits his head a hard thump against the bulwark. He lies there still, knocked out for the moment.* ANNA *stands for a second, looking down at him frightenedly. Then she kneels down beside him and raises his head to her knee, staring into his face anxiously for some sign of life.*)

BURKE. (*stirring a bit—mutteringly*) God stiffen it! (*He opens his eyes and blinks up at her with vague wonder.*)

ANNA. (*letting his head sink back on the deck, rising to her feet with a sigh of relief*) You're coming to all right, eh? Gee, I was scared for a moment I'd killed you.

BURKE. (*with difficulty rising to a sitting position—scornfully*) Killed, is it? It'd take more than a bit of a blow to crack my thick skull. (*Then looking at her with the most intense admiration*) But, glory be, it's a power of strength is in them two fine arms of yours. There's not a man in the world can say the same as you, that he seen Mat Burke lying at his feet and him dead to the world.

ANNA. (*rather remorsefully*) Forget it. I'm sorry it happened, see? (*Burke rises and sits on bench. Then severely*) Only you had no right to be getting fresh with me. Listen, now, and don't go getting any

33

more wrong notions. I'm on this barge because I'm making a trip with my father. The captain's my father. Now you know.

BURKE. The old square—the old Swede, I mean?

ANNA. Yes.

BURKE. (*rising—peering at her face*) Sure I might have known it, if I wasn't a bloody fool from birth. Where else'd you get that fine yellow hair is like a golden crown on your head?

ANNA. (*with an amused laugh*) Say, nothing stops you, does it? (*Then attempting a severe tone again*) But don't you think you ought to be apologizing for what you said and done yust a minute ago, instead of trying to kid me with that mush?

BURKE. (*indignantly*) Mush! (*Then bending forward toward her with very intense earnestness*) Indade and I will ask your pardon a thousand times—and on my knees, if ye like. I didn't mean a word of what I said or did. (*Resentful again for a second*) But divil a woman in all the ports of the world has iver made a great fool of me that way before!

ANNA. (*with amused sarcasm*) I see. You mean you're a lady-killer and they all fall for you.

BURKE. (*offended—passionately*) Leave off your fooling! 'Tis that is after getting my back up at you. (*Earnestly*) 'Tis no lie I'm telling you about the women. (*Ruefully*) Though it's a great jackass I am to be mistaking you, even in anger, for the like of them cows on the waterfront is the only women I've met up with since I was growed to a man. (*As* ANNA *shrinks away from him at this, he hurries on pleadingly*) I'm a hard, rough man and I'm not fit, I'm thinking, to be kissing the shoe-soles of a fine, dacent girl the like of yourself. 'Tis only the ignorance of your kind made me see you wrong. So you'll forgive me, for the love of God, and let us be friends from this out. (*Passionately*) I'm thinking I'd rather be friends with you than have my wish for anything else in the world. (*He holds out his hand to her shyly.*)

ANNA. (*looking queerly at him, perplexed and worried, but moved and pleased in spite of herself—takes his hand uncertainly*) Sure.

BURKE. (*with boyish delight*) God bless you! (*In his excitement he squeezes her hand tight.*)

ANNA. Ouch!

BURKE. (*hastily dropping her hand—ruefully*) Your pardon, Miss. 'Tis a clumsy ape I am. (*Then simply—glancing down his arm proudly*) It's great power I have in my hand and arm, and I do be forgetting it at times.

ANNA. (*nursing her crushed hand and glancing at his arm, not without a trace of his own admiration*) Gee, you're some strong, all right.

BURKE. (*delighted*) It's no lie, and why shouldn't I be, with me shoveling a million tons of coal in the stokeholes of ships since I was a lad only. (*He pats the coil of hawser invitingly*) Let you sit down, now, Miss, and I'll be telling you a bit of myself, and you'll be telling me a bit of yourself, and in an hour we'll be as old friends as if we was born in the same house. (*He pulls at her sleeve shyly*) Sit down now, if you plaze.

ANNA. (*with a half laugh*) Well— (*She sits down*) But we won't talk about me, see? You tell me about yourself and about the wreck.

BURKE. (*flattered*) I'll tell you, surely. But can I be asking you one question, Miss, has my head in a puzzle?

ANNA. (*guardedly*) Well—I dunno—what is it?

BURKE. What is it you do when you're not taking a trip with the Old Man? For I'm thinking a fine girl the like of you ain't living always on this tub.

ANNA. (*uneasily*) No—of course I ain't. (*She searches his face suspiciously, afraid there may be some hidden insinuation in his words. Seeing his simple frankness, she goes on confidently*) Well, I'll tell you. I'm a governess, see? I take care of kids for people and learn them things.

BURKE. (*impressed*) A governess, is it? You must be smart, surely.

ANNA. But let's not talk about me. Tell me about the wreck, like you promised me you would.

BURKE. (*importantly*) 'Twas this way, Miss. Two weeks out we ran into the divil's own storm, and she sprang wan hell of a leak up for'ard. The skipper was hoping to make Boston before another blow would finish her, but ten days back we met up with another storm the like of the first, only worse. Four days we was in it with green seas raking over her from bow to stern. That was a terrible time, God help us. (*Proudly*) And if 'twasn't for me and my great strength, I'm telling you—and it's God's truth—there'd been mutiny itself in the stokehole. 'Twas me held them to it, with a kick to wan and a clout to another, and they not caring a damn for the engineers any more, but fearing a clout of my right arm more than they'd fear the sea itself. (*He glances at her anxiously, eager for her approval.*)

ANNA. (*concealing a smile—amused by this boyish boasting of his*) You did some hard work, didn't you?

BURKE. (*promptly*) I did that! I'm a divil for sticking it out when them that's weak give up. But much good it did anyone! 'Twas a mad, fightin' scramble in the last seconds with each man for himself. I disremember how it come about, but there was the four of us in wan boat and when we was raised high on a great wave I took a look about and divil a sight there was of ship or men on top of the sea.

ANNA. (*in a subdued voice*) Then all the others was drowned?

BURKE. They was, surely.

ANNA. (*with a shudder*) What a terrible end!

BURKE. (*turns to her*) A terrible end for the like of them swabs does live on land, maybe. But for the like of us does be roaming the seas, a good end, I'm telling you—quick and clane.

ANNA. (*struck by the word*) Yes, clean. That's yust the word for—all of it—the way it makes me feel.

BURKE. The sea, you mean? (*Interestedly*) I'm thinking you have a bit of it in your blood, too. Your Old Man wasn't only a barge rat—begging your pardon—all his life, by the cut of him.

ANNA. No, he was bo'sun on sailing ships for years. And all the men on both sides of the family have gone to sea as far back as he remembers, he says. All the women have married sailors, too.

BURKE. (*with intense satisfaction*) Did they, now? They had spirit in them. It's only on the sea you'd find rale men with guts is fit to wed with fine, high-tempered girls (*Then he adds half-boldly*) the like of yourself.

ANNA. (*with a laugh*) There you go kiddin' again. (*Then seeing his hurt expression—quickly*) But you was going to tell me about yourself. You're Irish, of course I can tell that.

BURKE. (*stoutly*) Yes, thank God, though I've not seen a sight of it in fifteen years.

ANNA. (*thoughtfully*) Sailors never do go home hardly, do they? That's what my father was saying.

BURKE. He wasn't telling no lie. (*With sudden melancholy*) It's a hard and lonesome life, the sea is. The only women you'd meet in the ports of the world who'd be willing to speak you a kind word isn't women at all. You know the kind I mane, and they're a poor, wicked lot, God forgive them. They're looking to steal the money from you only.

ANNA. (*her face averted—rising to her feet—agitatedly*) I think—I guess I'd better see what's doing inside.

BURKE. (*afraid he has offended her—beseechingly*) Don't go, I'm saying! Is it I've given you offense with my talk of the like of them? Don't heed it at all! I'm clumsy in my wits when it comes to talking proper with a girl the like of you. And why wouldn't I be? Since the day I left home for to go to sea punching coal, this is the first time I've had a word with a rale, dacent woman. So don't turn your back on me now, and we beginning to be friends.

ANNA. (*turning to him again—forcing a smile*) I'm not sore at you, honest.

BURKE. (*gratefully*) God bless you!

ANNA. (*changing the subject abruptly*) But if you honestly think the sea's such a rotten life, why don't you get out of it?

BURKE. (*surprised*) Work on land, is it? (*She nods. He spits scorn-*

fully) Digging spuds in the muck from dawn to dark, I suppose? (*Vehemently*) I wasn't made for it, Miss.

ANNA. (*with a laugh*) I thought you'd say that.

BURKE. (*argumentatively*) But there's good jobs and bad jobs at sea, like there'd be on land. I'm thinking if it's in the stokehole of a proper liner I was, I'd be able to have a little house and be home to it wan week out of four. And I'm thinking that maybe then I'd have the luck to find a fine dacent girl—the like of yourself, now—would be willing to wed with me.

ANNA. (*turning away from him with a short laugh—uneasily*) Why sure. Why not?

BURKE. (*edging up close to her—exultantly*) Then you think a girl the like of yourself might maybe not mind the past at all but only be seeing the good herself put in me?

ANNA. (*in the same tone*) Why, sure.

BURKE. (*passionately*) She'd not be sorry for it, I'd take my oath! 'Tis no more drinking and roving about I'd be doing then, but giving my pay day into her hand and staying at home with her as meek as a lamb each night of the week I'd be in port.

ANNA. (*moved in spite of herself and troubled by this half-concealed proposal—with a forced laugh*) All you got to do is find the girl.

BURKE. I have found her!

ANNA. (*half-frightenedly—trying to laugh it off*) You have? When? I thought you was saying—

BURKE. (*boldly and forcefully*) This night. (*Hanging his head —humbly*) If she'll be having me. (*Then raising his eyes to hers— simply*) 'Tis you I mean.

ANNA. (*is held by his eyes for a moment—then shrinks back from him with a strange, broken laugh*) Say—are you—going crazy? Are you trying to kid me? Proposing—to me!—for Gawd's sake!—on such short acquaintance? (CHRIS *comes out of the cabin and stands staring blinkingly astern. When he makes out* ANNA *in such intimate proximity to this strange sailor, an angry expression comes over his face.*)

BURKE. (*following her—with fierce, pleading insistence*) I'm telling you there's the will of God in it that brought me safe through the storm and fog to the wan spot in the world where you was! Think of that now, and isn't it queer—

CHRIS. Anna! (*He comes toward them, raging, his fists clenched*) Anna, you gat in cabin, you hear!

ANNA. (*all her emotions immediately transformed into resentment at his bullying tone*) Who d'you think you're talking to—a slave?

CHRIS. (*hurt—his voice breaking—pleadingly*) You need gat rest, Anna. You gat sleep. (*She does not move. He turns on* BURKE *furiously*) What you doing here, you sailor fallar? You ain't sick like oders. You gat in fo'c's'tle. Dey give you bunk. (*Threateningly*) You hurry, Ay tal you!

ANNA. (*impulsively*) But he is sick. Look at him. He can hardly stand up.

BURKE. (*straightening and throwing out his chest—with a bold laugh*) Is it giving me orders ye are, me bucko? Let you look out, then! With wan hand, weak as I am, I can break ye in two and fling the pieces over the side—and your crew after you. (*Stopping abruptly*) I was forgetting. You're her Old Man and I'd not raise a fist to you for the world. (*His knees sag, he wavers and seems about to fall.* ANNA *utters an exclamation of alarm and hurries to his side.*)

ANNA. (*taking one of his arms over her shoulder*) Come on in the cabin. You can have my bed if there ain't no other place.

BURKE. (*with jubilant happiness—as they proceed toward the cabin*) Glory be to God, is it holding my arm about your neck you are! Anna! Anna! Sure it's a sweet name is suited to you.

ANNA. (*guiding him carefully*) Sssh! Sssh!

BURKE. Whisht, is it? Indade, and I'll not. I'll be roaring it out like a fog horn over the sea! You're the girl of the world and we'll be marrying soon and I don't care who knows it!

ANNA. (*as she guides him through the cabin door*) Ssshh! Never mind that talk. You go to sleep. (*They go out of sight in the cabin.*

CHRIS, *who has been listening to* BURKE's *last words with open-mouthed amazement stands looking after them desperately.*)

CHRIS. (*turns suddenly and shakes his fist out at the sea—with bitter hatred*) Dat's your dirty trick, damn ole davil, you! (*Then in a frenzy of rage*) But, py God, you don't do dat! Not while Ay'm living! No, py God, you don't!

CURTAIN

ACT THREE

S cene—*The interior of the cabin on the barge "Simeon Winthrop"
(at dock in Boston)—a narrow, low-ceilinged compartment the
walls of which are painted a light brown with white trimmings. In the
rear on the left, a door leading to the sleeping quarters. In the far left
corner, a large locker-closet, painted white, on the door of which a
mirror hangs on a nail. In the rear wall, two small square windows
and a door opening out on the deck toward the stern. In the right wall,
two more windows looking out on the port deck. White curtains, clean
and stiff, are at the windows. A table with two cane-bottomed chairs
stands in the center of the cabin. A dilapidated wicker rocker, painted
brown, is also by the table.*

*It is afternoon of a sunny day about a week later. From the harbor
and docks outside, muffled by the closed door and windows, comes the
sound of steamers' whistles and the puffing snort of the donkey engines of some ship unloading nearby.*

As the curtain rises, chris *and* anna *are discovered.* anna *is seated
in the rocking-chair by the table, with a newspaper in her hands. She
is not reading but staring straight in front of her. She looks unhappy,
troubled, frowningly concentrated on her thoughts.* chris *wanders
about the room, casting quick, uneasy side glances at her face, then
stopping to peer absent-mindedly out of the window. His attitude
betrays an overwhelming, gloomy anxiety which has him on tenter-
hooks. He pretends to be engaged in setting things ship-shape, but this
occupation is confined to picking up some object, staring at it stupidly
for a second, then aimlessly putting it down again. He clears his throat
and starts to sing to himself in a low, doleful voice: "My Yosephine,
come board de ship. Long time Ay vait for you."*

ANNA. (*turning on him, sarcastically*) I'm glad someone's feeling good. (*Wearily*) Gee, I sure wish we was out of this dump and back in New York.

CHRIS. (*with a sigh*) Ay'm glad vhen ve sail again, too. (*Then, as she makes no comment, he goes on with a ponderous attempt at sarcasm*) Ay don't see vhy you don't like Boston, dough. You have good time here, Ay tank. You go ashore all time, every day and night veek ve've been here. You go to movies, see show, gat all kinds fun— (*His eyes hard with hatred*) All with that damn Irish fallar!

ANNA. (*with weary scorn*) Oh, for heaven's sake, are you off on that again? Where's the harm in his taking me around? D'you want me to sit all day and night in this cabin with you—and knit? Ain't I got a right to have as good a time as I can?

CHRIS. It ain't right kind of fun—not with that fallar, no.

ANNA. I been back on board every night by eleven, ain't I? (*Then struck by some thought—looks at him with keen suspicion—with rising anger*) Say, look here, what d'you mean by what you yust said?

CHRIS. (*hastily*) Nutting but what Ay say, Anna.

ANNA. You said "ain't right" and you said it funny. Say, listen here, you ain't trying to insinuate that there's something wrong between us, are you?

CHRIS. (*horrified*) No, Anna! No, Ay svear to God, Ay never tank dat!

ANNA. (*mollified by his very evident sincerity—sitting down again*) Well, don't you never think it neither if you want me ever to speak to you again. (*Angrily again*) If I ever dreamt you thought that, I'd get the hell out of this barge so quick you couldn't see me for dust.

CHRIS. (*soothingly*) Ay wouldn't never dream— (*Then after a second's pause, reprovingly*) You vas gatting learn to swear. Dat ain't nice for young gel, you tank?

ANNA. (*with a faint trace of a smile*) Excuse me. You ain't used to such language, I know. (*Mockingly*) That's what your taking me to sea has done for me.

CHRIS. (*indignantly*) No, it ain't me. It's dat damn sailor fallar learn you bad tangs.

ANNA. He ain't a sailor. He's a stoker.

CHRIS. (*forcibly*) Dat vas million times vorse, Ay tal you! Dem fallars dat vork below shoveling coal vas de dirtiest, rough gang of no-good fallars in vorld!

ANNA. I'd hate to hear you say that to Mat.

CHRIS. Oh, Ay tal him same tang. You don't gat it in head Ay'm scared of him yust 'cause he vas stronger'n Ay vas. (*Menacingly*) You don't gat for fight with fists with dem fallars. Dere's oder vay for fix him.

ANNA. (*glancing at him with sudden alarm*) What d'you mean?

CHRIS. (*sullenly*) Nutting.

ANNA. You'd better not. I wouldn't start no trouble with him if I was you. He might forget some time that you was old and my father —and then you'd be out of luck.

CHRIS. (*with smoldering hatred*) Vell, yust let him! Ay'm ole bird maybe, but Ay bet Ay show him trick or two.

ANNA. (*suddenly changing her tone—persuasively*) Aw come on, be good. What's eating you, anyway? Don't you want no one to be be nice to me except yourself?

CHRIS. (*placated—coming to her—eagerly*) Yes, Ay do, Anna— only not fallar on sea. But Ay like for you marry steady fallar got good yob on land. You have little home in country all your own—

ANNA. (*rising to her feet—brusquely*) Oh, cut it out! (*Scornfully*) Little home in the country! I wish you could have seen the little home in the country where you had me in jail till I was sixteen! (*With rising irritation*) Some day you're going to get me so mad with that talk, I'm going to turn loose on you and tell you—a lot of things that'll open your eyes.

CHRIS. (*alarmed*) Ay don't vant—

ANNA. I know you don't; but you keep on talking yust the same.

CHRIS. Ay don't talk no more den, Anna.

43

ANNA. Then promise me you'll cut out saying nasty things about Mat Burke every chance you get.

CHRIS. (*evasive and suspicious*) Vhy? You like dat fallar—very much, Anna?

ANNA. Yes, I certainly do! He's a regular man, no matter what faults he's got. One of his fingers is worth all the hundreds of men I met out there—inland.

CHRIS. (*his face darkening*) Maybe you tank you love him, den?

ANNA. (*defiantly*) What of it if I do?

CHRIS. (*scowling and forcing out the words*) Maybe—you tank you —marry him?

ANNA. (*shaking her head*) No! (CHRIS' *face lights up with relief.* ANNA *continues slowly, a trace of sadness in her voice*) If I'd met him four years ago—or even two years ago—I'd have jumped at the chance, I tell you that straight. And I would now—only he's such a simple guy—a big kid—and I ain't got the heart to fool him. (*She breaks off suddenly*) But don't never say again he ain't good enough for me. It's me ain't good enough for him.

CHRIS. (*snorts scornfully*) Py yiminy, you go crazy, Ay tank!

ANNA. (*with a mournful laugh*) Well, I been thinking I was myself the last few days. (*She goes and takes a shawl from a hook near the door and throws it over her shoulders*) Guess I'll take a walk down to the end of the dock for a minute and see what's doing. I love to watch the ships passing. Mat'll be along before long, I guess. Tell him where I am, will you?

CHRIS. (*despondently*) All right, Ay tal him. (ANNA *goes out the doorway on rear.* CHRIS *follows her out and stands on the deck outside for a moment looking after her. Then he comes back inside and shuts the door. He stands looking out of the window—mutters—"Dirty ole davil, you." Then he goes to the table, sets the cloth straight mechanically, picks up the newspaper* ANNA *has let fall to the floor and sits down in the rocking-chair. He stares at the paper for a while, then puts it on table, holds his head in his hands and sighs drearily. The noise of a man's heavy footsteps comes from the deck outside and there is a loud knock on the door.* CHRIS *starts, makes a move as if to get up and go to the door, then thinks better of it and sits still. The knock is repeated—then as no answer comes, the door is flung open and* MAT BURKE *appears.* CHRIS *scowls at the intruder and his hand instinctively goes back to the sheath knife on his hip.* BURKE *is dressed up—wears a cheap blue suit, a striped cotton shirt with a black tie, and black shoes newly shined. His face is beaming with good humor.*)

BURKE. (*as he sees* CHRIS—*in a jovial tone of mockery*) Well, God bless who's here! (*He bends down and squeezes his huge form through the narrow doorway*) And how is the world treating you this afternoon, Anna's father?

CHRIS. (*sullenly*) Pooty goot—if it ain't for some fallars.

BURKE. (*with a grin*) Meaning me, do you? (*He laughs*) Well, if you ain't the funny old crank of a man! (*Then soberly*) Where's herself? (CHRIS *sits dumb, scowling, his eyes averted.* BURKE *is irritated by this silence*) Where's Anna, I'm after asking you?

CHRIS. (*hesitating—then grouchily*) She go down end of dock.

BURKE. I'll be going down to her, then. But first I'm thinking I'll take this chance when we're alone to have a word with you. (*He sits down opposite* CHRIS *at the table and leans over toward him*) And that word is soon said. I'm marrying your Anna before this day is out, and you might as well make up your mind to it whether you like it or no.

CHRIS. (*glaring at him with hatred and forcing a scornful laugh*) Ho-ho! Dat's easy for say!

BURKE. You mean I won't? (*Scornfully*) Is it the like of yourself will stop me, are you thinking?

CHRIS. Yes, Ay stop it if it come to vorst.

BURKE. (*with scornful pity*) God help you!

CHRIS. But ain't no need for me do dat. Anna—

BURKE. (*smiling confidently*) Is it Anna you think will prevent me?

CHRIS. Yes.

45

BURKE. And I'm telling you she'll not. She knows I'm loving her, and she loves me the same, and I know it.

CHRIS. Ho-ho! She only have fun. She make big fool of you, dat's all!

BURKE. (*unshaken—pleasantly*) That's a lie in your throat, divil mend you!

CHRIS. No, it ain't lie. She tal me yust before she go out she never marry fallar like you.

BURKE. I'll not believe it. 'Tis a great old liar you are, and a divil to be making a power of trouble if you had your way. But 'tis not trouble I'm looking for, and me sitting down here. (*Earnestly*) Let us be talking it out now as man to man. You're her father, and wouldn't it be a shame for us to be at each other's throats like a pair of dogs, and I married with Anna? So out with the truth, man alive. What is it you're holding against me at all?

CHRIS. (*a bit placated, in spite of himself, by* BURKE's *evident sincerity—but puzzled and suspicious*) Vell—Ay don't vant for Anna gat married. Listen, you fallar. Ay'm a ole man. Ay don't see Anna for fifteen year. She vas all Ay gat in vorld. And now ven she come on first trip—you tank Ay vant her leave me 'lone again?

BURKE. (*heartily*) Let you not be thinking I have no heart at all for the way you'd be feeling.

CHRIS. (*astonished and encouraged—trying to plead persuasively*) Den you do right tang, eh? You ship away again, leave Anna alone. (*Cajolingly*) Big fallar like you dat's on sea, he don't need vife. He gat new gel in every port, you know dat.

BURKE. (*angrily for a second*) God stiffen you! (*Then controlling himself—calmly*) I'll not be giving you the lie on that. But divil take you, there's a time comes to every man, on sea or land, that isn't a born fool, when he's sick of the lot of them cows, and wearing his heart out to meet up with a fine dacent girl, and have a home to call his own and be rearing up children in it. 'Tis small use you're asking me to leave Anna. She's the wan woman of the world for me, and I can't live without her now, I'm thinking.

CHRIS. You forgat all about her in one veek out of port, Ay bet you!

BURKE. You don't know the like I am. Death itself wouldn't make me forget her. So let you not be making talk to me about leaving her. I'll not, and be damned to you! It won't be so bad for you as you'd make out at all. She'll be living here in the States, and her married to me. And you'd be seeing her often so—a sight more often than ever you saw her the fifteen years she was growing up in the West. It's quare you'd be the one to be making great trouble about her leaving you when you never laid eyes on her once in all them years.

CHRIS. (guiltily) Ay tought it vas better Anna stay away, grow up inland where she don't ever know ole davil, sea.

BURKE. (scornfully) Is it blaming the sea for your troubles ye are again, God help you? Well, Anna knows it now. 'Twas in her blood, anyway.

CHRIS. And Ay don't vant she ever know no-good fallar on sea—

BURKE. She knows one now.

CHRIS. (banging the table with his fist—furiously) Dat's yust it! Dat's yust what you are—no-good, sailor fallar! You tank Ay lat her life be made sorry by you like her mo'der's vas by me! No, Ay svear! She don't marry you if Ay gat kill you first!

BURKE. (looks at him a moment, in astonishment—then laughing uproariously) Ho-ho! Glory be to God, it's bold talk you have for a stumpy runt of a man!

CHRIS. (threateningly) Vell—you see!

BURKE. (with grinning defiance) I'll see, surely! I'll see myself and Anna married this day, I'm telling you. (Then with contemptuous exasperation) It's quare fool's blather you have about the sea done this and the sea done that. You'd ought to be 'shamed to be saying the like, and you an old sailor yourself. I'm after hearing a lot of it from you and a lot more that Anna's told me you do be saying to her, and I'm thinking it's a poor weak thing you are, and not a man at all!

CHRIS. (*darkly*) You see if Ay'm man—maybe quicker'n you tank.

BURKE. (*contemptuously*) Yerra, don't be boasting. I'm thinking 'tis out of your wits you've got with fright of the sea. You'd be wishing Anna married to a farmer, she told me. That'd be a swate match, surely! Would you have a fine girl the like of Anna lying down at nights with a muddy scut stinking of pigs and dung? Or would you have her tied for life to the like of them skinny, shriveled swabs does be working in cities?

CHRIS. Dat's lie, you fool!

BURKE. 'Tis not. 'Tis your own mad notions I'm after telling. But you know the truth in your heart, if great fear of the sea has made you a liar and coward itself. (*Pounding the table*) The sea's the only life for a man with guts in him isn't afraid of his own shadow! 'Tis only on the sea he's free, and him roving the face of the world, seeing all things, and not giving a damn for saving up money, or stealing from his friends, or any of the black tricks that a landlubber'd waste his life on. 'Twas yourself knew it once, and you a bo'sun for years.

CHRIS. (*sputtering with rage*) You vas crazy fool, Ay tal you!

BURKE. You've swallowed the anchor. The sea give you a clout once, knocked you down, and you're not man enough to get up for another, but lie there for the rest of your life howling bloody murder. (*Proudly*) Isn't it myself the sea has nearly drowned, and me battered and bate till I was that close to hell I could hear the flames roaring, and never a groan out of me till the sea gave up and it seeing the great strength and guts of a man was in me?

CHRIS. (*scornfully*) Yes, you vas hell of fallar, hear you tal it!

BURKE. (*angrily*) You'll be calling me a liar once too often, me old bucko! Wasn't the whole story of it and my picture itself in the newspapers of Boston a week back? (*Looking* CHRIS *up and down belittlingly*) Sure I'd like to see you in the best of your youth do the like of what I done in the storm and after. 'Tis a mad lunatic, screeching with fear, you'd be this minute!

CHRIS. Ho-ho! You vas young fool! In ole years when Ay was on windyammer, Ay vas through hundred storms vorse'n dat! Ships vas ships den—and men dat sail on dem vas real men. And now what you gat on steamers? You gat fallars on deck don't know ship from mudscow. (*With a meaning glance at* BURKE) and below deck you gat fallars yust know how for shovel coal—might yust as vell vork on coal wagon ashore!

BURKE. (*stung—angrily*) Is it casting insults at the men in the stokehole ye are, ye old ape? God stiffen you! Wan of them is worth any ten stock-fish-swilling square-heads ever shipped on a windbag!

CHRIS. (*his face working with rage, his hand going back to the sheath-knife on his hip*) Irish svine, you!

BURKE. (*tauntingly*) Don't ye like the Irish, ye old baboon? 'Tis that you're needing in your family, I'm telling you—an Irishman and a man of the stokehole—to put guts in it so that you'll not be having grandchildren would be fearful cowards and jackasses the like of yourself!

CHRIS. (*half rising from his chair—in a voice choked with rage*) You look out!

BURKE. (*watching him intently—a mocking smile on his lips*) And it's that you'll be having, no matter what you'll do to prevent; for Anna and me'll be married this day, and no old fool the like of you will stop us when I've made up my mind.

CHRIS. (*with a hoarse cry*) You don't! (*He throws himself at* BURKE, *knife in hand, knocking his chair over backwards.* BURKE *springs to his feet quickly in time to meet the attack. He laughs with the pure love of battle. The old Swede is like a child in his hands.* BURKE *does not strike or mistreat him in any way, but simply twists his right hand behind his back and forces the knife from his fingers. He throws the knife into a far corner of the room—tauntingly.*)

BURKE. Old men is getting childish shouldn't play with knives. (*Holding the struggling* CHRIS *at arm's length—with a sudden rush of anger, drawing back his fist*) I've half a mind to hit you a great clout will put sense in your square head. Kape off me now, I'm warning you! (*He gives* CHRIS *a push with the flat of his hand which sends the old Swede staggering back against the cabin wall, where he remains standing, panting heavily, his eyes fixed on* BURKE *with hatred, as if he were only collecting his strength to rush at him again.*)

BURKE. (*warningly*) Now don't be coming at me again, I'm saying, or I'll flatten you on the floor with a blow, if 'tis Anna's father you are itself! I've no patience left for you. (*Then with an amused laugh*) Well, 'tis a bold old man you are just the same, and I'd never think it was in you to come tackling me alone. (*A shadow crosses the cabin windows. Both men start.* ANNA *appears in the doorway.*)

ANNA. (*with pleased surprise as she sees* BURKE) Hello, Mat. Are you here already? I was down— (*She stops, looking from one to the other, sensing immediately that something has happened*) What's up? (*Then noticing the overturned chair—in alarm*) How'd that chair get knocked over? (*Turning on* BURKE *reproachfully*) You ain't been fighting with him, Mat—after you promised?

BURKE. (*his old self again*) I've not laid a hand on him, Anna. (*He goes and picks up the chair, then turning on the still-questioning* ANNA—*with a reassuring smile*) Let you not be worried at all. 'Twas only a bit of an argument we was having to pass the time till you'd come.

ANNA. It must have been some argument when you got to throwing chairs. (*She turns on* CHRIS) Why don't you say something? What was it about?

CHRIS. (*relaxing at last—avoiding her eyes—sheepishly*) Ve vas talking about ships and fallars on sea.

ANNA. (*with a relieved smile*) Oh—the old stuff, eh?

BURKE. (*suddenly seeming to come to a bold decision—with a defiant grin at* CHRIS) He's not after telling you the whole of it. We was arguing about you mostly.

ANNA. (*with a frown*) About me?

BURKE. And we'll be finishing it out right here and now in your presence if you're willing. (*He sits down at the left of table.*)

50

ANNA. (*uncertainly—looking from him to her father*) Sure. Tell me what it's all about.

CHRIS. (*advancing toward the table—protesting to* BURKE) No! You don't do dat, you! You tal him you don't vant for hear him talk, Anna.

ANNA. But I do. I want this cleared up.

CHRIS. (*miserably afraid now*) Vell, not now, anyvay. You vas going ashore, yes? You ain't got time—

ANNA. (*firmly*) Yes, right here and now. (*She turns to* BURKE) You tell me, Mat, since he don't want to.

BURKE. (*draws a deep breath—then plunges in boldly*) The whole of it's in a few words only. So's he'd make no mistake, and him hating the sight of me, I told him in his teeth I loved you. (*Passionately*) And that's God truth, Anna, and well you know it!

CHRIS. (*scornfully—forcing a laugh*) Ho-ho! He tal same tang to gel every port he go!

ANNA. (*shrinking from her father with repulsion—resentfully*) Shut up, can't you? (*Then to* BURKE—*feelingly*) I know it's true, Mat. I don't mind what he says.

BURKE. (*humbly grateful*) God bless you!

ANNA. And then what?

BURKE. And then— (*Hesitatingly*) And then I said— (*He looks at her pleadingly*) I said I was sure—I told him I thought you have a bit of love for me, too. (*Passionately*) Say you do, Anna! Let you not destroy me entirely, for the love of God! (*He grasps both her hands in his two.*)

ANNA. (*deeply moved and troubled—forcing a trembling laugh*) So you told him that, Mat? No wonder he was mad. (*Forcing out the words*) Well, maybe it's true, Mat. Maybe I do. I been thinking and thinking—I didn't want to, Mat, I'll own up to that—I tried to cut it out—but— (*She laughs helplessly*) I guess I can't help it anyhow. So I guess I do, Mat. (*Then with a sudden joyous defiance*) Sure I do! What's the use of kidding myself different? Sure I love you, Mat!

CHRIS. (*with a cry of pain*) Anna! (*He sits crushed.*)

BURKE. (*with a great depth of sincerity in his humble gratitude*) God be praised!

ANNA. (*assertively*) And I ain't never loved a man in my life before, you can always believe that—no matter what happens.

BURKE. (*goes over to her and puts his arms around her*) Sure I do be believing ivery word you iver said or iver will say. And 'tis you and me will be having a grand, beautiful life together to the end of our days! (*He tries to kiss her. At first she turns away her head—then, overcome by a fierce impulse of passionate love, she takes his head in both her hands and holds his face close to hers, staring into his eyes. Then she kisses him full on the lips.*)

ANNA. (*pushing him away from her—forcing a broken laugh*) Good-by. (*She walks to the doorway in rear—stands with her back toward them, looking out. Her shoulders quiver once or twice as if she were fighting back her sobs.*)

BURKE. (*too much in the seventh heaven of bliss to get any correct interpretation of her word—with a laugh*) Good-by, is it? The divil you say! I'll be coming back at you in a second for more of the same! (*To* CHRIS, *who has quickened to instant attention at his daughter's good-by and has looked back at her with a stirring of foolish hope in his eyes*) Now, me old bucko, what'll you be saying? You heard the words from her own lips. Confess I've bate you. Own up like a man when you're bate fair and square. And here's my hand to you— (*Holds out his hand*) And let you take it and we'll shake and forget what's over and done, and be friends from this out.

CHRIS. (*with implacable hatred*) Ay don't shake hands with you fallar—not vhile Ay live!

BURKE. (*offended*) The back of my hand to you then, if that suits you better. (*Growling*) 'Tis a rotten bad loser you are, divil mend you!

CHRIS. Ay don't lose. (*Trying to be scornful and self-convincing*) Anna say she like you little bit but you don't hear her say she marry you, Ay bet. (*At the sound of her name* ANNA *has turned round to them. Her face is composed and calm again, but it is the dead calm of despair.*)

BURKE. (*scornfully*) No, and I wasn't hearing her say the sun is shining either.

CHRIS. (*doggedly*) Dat's all right. She don't say it, yust same.

ANNA. (*quietly—coming forward to them*) No, I didn't say it, Mat.

CHRIS. (*eagerly*) Dere! You hear!

BURKE. (*misunderstanding her—with a grin*) You're waiting till you do be asked, you mane? Well, I'm asking you now. And we'll be married this day, with the help of God!

ANNA. (*gently*) You heard what I said, Mat—after I kissed you?

BURKE. (*alarmed by something in her manner*) No—I disremember.

ANNA. I said good-by. (*Her voice trembling*) That kiss was for good-by, Mat.

BURKE. (*terrified*) What d'you mane?

ANNA. I can't marry you, Mat—and we've said good-by. That's all.

CHRIS. (*unable to hold back his exultation*) Ay know it! Ay know dat vas so!

BURKE. (*jumping to his feet—unable to believe his ears*) Anna! Is it making game of me you'd be? 'Tis a quare time to joke with me, and don't be doing it, for the love of God.

ANNA. (*looking him in the eyes steadily*) D'you think I'd kid you? No, I'm not joking, Mat. I mean what I said.

BURKE. Ye don't! Ye can't! 'Tis mad you are, I'm telling you!

ANNA. (*fixedly*) No, I'm not.

BURKE. (*desperately*) But what's come over you so sudden? You was saying you loved me—

ANNA. I'll say that as often as you want me to. It's true.

BURKE. (*bewilderedly*) Then why—what, in the divil's name— Oh, God help me, I can't make head or tail to it at all!

ANNA. Because it's the best way out I can figure, Mat. (*Her voice*

53

catching) I been thinking it over and thinking it over day and night all week. Don't think it ain't hard on me, too, Mat.

BURKE. For the love of God, tell me then, what is it that's preventing you wedding me when the two of us has love? (*Suddenly getting an idea and pointing at* CHRIS—*exasperatedly*) Is it giving heed to the like of that old fool ye are, and him hating me and filling your ears full of bloody lies against me?

CHRIS. (*getting to his feet—raging triumphantly before* ANNA *has a chance to get in a word*) Yes, Anna believe me, not you! She know her old fa'der don't lie like you.

ANNA. (*turning on her father angrily*) You sit down, d'you hear? Where do you come in butting in and making things worse? You're like a devil, you are! (*Harshly*) Good Lord, and I was beginning to like you, beginning to forget all I've got held up against you!

CHRIS. (*crushed feebly*) You ain't got nutting for hold against me, Anna.

ANNA. Ain't I yust! Well, lemme tell you— (*She glances at* BURKE *and stops abruptly*) Say, Mat, I'm s'prised at you. You didn't think anything he'd said—

BURKE. (*glumly*) Sure, what else would it be?

ANNA. Think I've ever paid any attention to all his crazy bull? Gee, you must take me for a five-year-old kid.

BURKE. (*puzzled and beginning to be irritated at her too*) I don't know how to take you, with your saying this one minute and that the next.

ANNA. Well, he has nothing to do with it.

BURKE. Then what is it has? Tell me, and don't keep me waiting and sweating blood.

ANNA. (*resolutely*) I can't tell you—and I won't. I got a good reason —and that's all you need to know. I can't marry you, that's all there is to it. (*Distractedly*) So, for Gawd's sake, let's talk of something else.

BURKE. I'll not! (*Then fearfully*) Is it married to someone else you are—in the West maybe?

ANNA. (*vehemently*) I should say not.

BURKE. (*regaining his courage*) To the divil with all other reasons then. They don't matter with me at all. (*He gets to his feet confidently, assuming a masterful tone*) I'm thinking you're the like of them women can't make up their mind till they're drove to it. Well, then, I'll make up your mind for you bloody quick. (*He takes her by the arms, grinning to soften his serious bullying*) We've had enough of talk! Let you be going into your room now and be dressing in your best and we'll be going ashore.

CHRIS. (*aroused—angrily*) No, py God, she don't do that! (*Takes hold of her arm.*)

ANNA. (*who has listened to* BURKE *in astonishment. She draws away from him, instinctively repelled by his tone, but not exactly sure if he is serious or not—a trace of resentment in her voice*) Say, where do you get that stuff?

BURKE. (*imperiously*) Never mind, now! Let you go get dressed, I'm saying. (*Then turning to* CHRIS) We'll be seeing who'll win in the end—me or you.

CHRIS. (*to* ANNA—*also in an authoritative tone*) You stay right here, Anna, you hear! (ANNA *stands looking from one to the other of them as if she thought they had both gone crazy. Then the expression of her face freezes into the hardened sneer of her experience.*)

BURKE. (*violently*) She'll not! She'll do what I say! You've had your hold on her long enough. It's my turn now.

ANNA. (*with a hard laugh*) Your turn? Say, what am I, anyway?

BURKE. 'Tis not what you are, 'tis what you're going to be this day— and that's wedded to me before night comes. Hurry up now with your dressing.

CHRIS. (*commandingly*) You don't do one tang he say, Anna! (ANNA *laughs mockingly.*)

BURKE. She will, so!

CHRIS. Ay tal you she don't! Ay'm her fa'der.

BURKE. She will in spite of you. She's taking my orders from this out, not yours.

ANNA. (*laughing again*) Orders is good!

BURKE. (*turning to her impatiently*) Hurry up now, and shake a leg. We've no time to be wasting. (*Irritated as she doesn't move*) Do you hear what I'm telling you?

CHRIS. You stay dere, Anna!

ANNA. (*at the end of her patience—blazing out at them passionately*) You can go to hell, both of you! (*There is something in her tone that makes them forget their quarrel and turn to her in a stunned amazement.* ANNA *laughs wildly*) You're just like all the rest of them—you two! Gawd, you'd think I was a piece of furniture! I'll show you! Sit down now! (*As they hesitate—furiously*) Sit down and let me talk for a minute. You're all wrong, see? Listen to me! I'm going to tell you something—and then I'm going to beat it. (*To* BURKE—*with a harsh laugh*) I'm going to tell you a funny story, so pay attention. (*Pointing to* CHRIS) I've been meaning to turn it loose on him every time he'd get my goat with his bull about keeping me safe inland. I wasn't going to tell you, but you forced me into it. What's the dif? It's all wrong anyway, and you might as well get cured that way as any other. (*With hard mocking*) Only don't forget what you said a minute ago about it not mattering to you what other reason I got so long as I wasn't married to no one else.

BURKE. (*manfully*) That's my word, and I'll stick to it!

ANNA. (*laughing bitterly*) What a chance! You make me laugh, honest! Want to bet you will? Wait 'n see! (*She stands at the table rear, looking from one to the other of the two men with her hard, mocking smile. Then she begins, fighting to control her emotion and speak calmly*) First thing is, I want to tell you two guys something. You was going on 's if one of you had got to own me. But nobody owns me, see?—'cepting myself. I'll do what I please and no man, I don't give a hoot who he is, can tell me what to do! I ain't asking either of you for a living. I can make it myself—one way or other.

I'm my own boss. So put that in your pipe and smoke it! You and your orders!

BURKE. (*protestingly*) I wasn't meaning it that way at all and well you know it. You've no call to be raising this rumpus with me. (*Pointing to* CHRIS) 'Tis him you've a right—

ANNA. I'm coming to him. But you—you did mean it that way, too. You sounded—yust like all the rest. (*Hysterically*) But, damn it, shut up! Let me talk for a change!

BURKE. 'Tis quare, rough talk, that—for a dacent girl the like of you!

ANNA. (*with a hard laugh*) Decent? Who told you I was? (CHRIS *is sitting with bowed shoulders, his head in his hands. She leans over in exasperation and shakes him violently by the shoulder*) Don't go to sleep, Old Man! Listen here, I'm talking to you now!

CHRIS. (*straightening up and looking about as if he were seeking a way to escape—with frightened foreboding in his voice*) Ay don't vant for hear it. You vas going out of head, Ay tank, Anna.

ANNA. (*violently*) Well, living with you is enough to drive anyone off their nut. Your bunk about the farm being so fine! Didn't I write you year after year how rotten it was and what a dirty slave them cousins made of me? What'd you care? Nothing! Not even enough to come out and see me! That crazy bull about wanting to keep me away from the sea don't go down with me! You yust didn't want to be bothered with me! You're like all the rest of 'em!

CHRIS. (*feebly*) Anna! It ain't so—

ANNA. (*not heeding his interruption—revengefully*) But one thing I never wrote you. It was one of them cousins that you think is such nice people—the youngest son—Paul—that started me wrong. (*Loudly*) It wasn't none of my fault. I hated him worse'n hell and he knew it. But he was big and strong—(*Pointing to Burke*)—like you!

BURKE. (*half springing to his feet—his fists clenched*) God blarst it! (*He sinks slowly back in his chair again, the knuckles showing white*

57

on his clenched hands, his face tense with the effort to suppress his grief and rage.)

CHRIS. (*in a cry of horrified pain*) Anna!

ANNA. (*to him—seeming not to have heard their interruptions*) That was why I run away from the farm. That was what made me get a yob as nurse girl in St. Paul. (*With a hard, mocking laugh*) And you think that was a nice yob for a girl, too, don't you? (*Sarcastically*) With all them nice inland fellers yust looking for a chance to marry me, I s'pose. Marry me? What a chance! They wasn't looking for marrying. (*As* BURKE *lets a groan of fury escape him—desperately*) I'm owning up to everything fair and square. I was caged in, I tell you—yust like in yail—taking care of other people's kids—listening to 'em bawling and crying day and night—when I wanted to be out—and I was lonesome—lonesome as hell! (*With a sudden weariness in her voice*) So I give up finally. What was the use? (*She stops and looks at the two men. Both are motionless and silent.* CHRIS *seems in a stupor of despair, his house of cards fallen about him.* BURKE's *face is livid with the rage that is eating him up, but he is too stunned and bewildered yet to find a vent for it. The condemnation she feels in their silence goads* ANNA *into a harsh, strident defiance*) You don't say nothing—either of you—but I know what you're thinking. You're like all the rest! (*To* CHRIS—*furiously*) And who's to blame for it, me or you? If you'd even acted like a man—if you'd even had been a regular father and had me with you—maybe things would be different!

CHRIS. (*in agony*) Don't talk dat vay, Anna! Ay go crazy! Ay von't listen! (*Puts his hands over his ears.*)

ANNA. (*infuriated by his action—stridently*) You will too listen! (*She leans over and pulls his hands from his ears—with hysterical rage*) You—keeping me safe inland—I wasn't no nurse girl the last two years—I lied when I wrote you—I was in a house, that's what!—yes, that kind of a house—the kind sailors like you and Mat goes to in port—and your nice inland men, too—and all men, God damn 'em!

I hate 'em! Hate 'em! (*She breaks into hysterical sobbing, throwing herself into the chair and hiding her face in her hands on the table. The two men have sprung to their feet.*)

CHRIS. (*whimpering like a child*) Anna! Anna! It's lie! It's lie! (*He stands wringing his hands together and begins to weep.*)

BURKE. (*his whole great body tense like a spring—dully and gropingly*) So that's what's in it!

ANNA. (*raising her head at the sound of his voice—with extreme mocking bitterness*) I s'pose you remember your promise, Mat? No other reason was to count with you so long as I wasn't married already. So I s'pose you want me to get dressed and go ashore, don't you? (*She laughs*) Yes, you do!

BURKE. (*on the verge of his outbreak—stammeringly*) God stiffen you!

ANNA. (*trying to keep up her hard, bitter tone, but gradually letting a note of pitiful pleading creep in*) I s'pose if I tried to tell you I wasn't—that—no more you'd believe me, wouldn't you? Yes, you would! And if I told you that yust getting out in this barge, and being on the sea had changed me and made me feel different about things, 's if all I'd been through wasn't me and didn't count and was yust like it never happened—you'd laugh, wouldn't you? And you'd die laughing sure if I said that meeting you that funny way that night in the fog, and afterwards seeing that you was straight goods stuck on me, had got me to thinking for the first time, and I sized you up as a different kind of man—a sea man as different from the ones on land as water is from mud—and that was why I got stuck on you, too. I wanted to marry you and fool you, but I couldn't. Don't you see how I've changed? I couldn't marry you with you believing a lie—and I was ashamed to tell you the truth—till the both of you forced my hand, and I seen you was the same as all the rest. And now, give me a bawling out and beat it, like I can tell you're going to. (*She stops, looking at* BURKE. *He is silent, his face averted, his features beginning to work with fury. She pleads passionately*) Will you believe it if I tell

59

you that loving you has made me—clean? It's the straight goods, honest? (*Then as he doesn't reply—bitterly*) Like hell you will! You're like all the rest!

BURKE. (*blazing out—turning on her in a perfect frenzy of rage—his voice trembling with passion*) The rest, is it? God's curse on you! Clane, is it? You slut, you, I'll be killing you now! (*He picks up the chair on which he has been sitting and, swinging it high over his shoulder, springs toward her.* CHRIS *rushes forward with a cry of alarm, trying to ward off the blow from his daughter.* ANNA *looks up into* BURKE's *eyes with the fearlessness of despair.* BURKE *checks himself, the chair held in the air.*)

CHRIS. (*wildly*) Stop, you crazy fool! You vant for murder her?

ANNA. (*pushing her father away brusquely, her eyes still holding* BURKE's) Keep out of this, you! (*To* BURKE—*dully*) Well, ain't you got the nerve to do it? Go ahead! I'll be thankful to you, honest. I'm sick of the whole game.

BURKE. (*throwing the chair away into a corner of the room—helplessly*) I can't do it, God help me, and your two eyes looking at me. (*Furiously*) Though I do be thinking I'd have a good right to smash your skull like a rotten egg. Was there iver a woman in the world had the rottenness in her that you have, and was there iver a man the like of me was made the fool of the world, and me thinking thoughts about you, and having great love for you, and dreaming dreams of the fine life we'd have when we'd be wedded! (*His voice high pitched in a lamentation that is like a keen*) Yerra, God help me! I'm destroyed entirely and my heart is broken in bits! I'm asking God Himself, was it for this He'd have me roaming the earth since I was a lad only, to come to black shame in the end, where I'd be giving a power of love to a woman is the same as others you'd meet in any hooker-shanty in port, with red gowns on them and paint on their grinning mugs, would be sleeping with any man for a dollar or two!

ANNA. (*in a scream*) Don't, Mat! For Gawd's sake! (*Then raging and pounding on the table with her hands*) Get out of here! Leave me alone! Get out of here!

BURKE. (*his anger rushing back on him*) I'll be going, surely! And I'll be drinking sloos of whisky will wash that black kiss of yours off my lips; and I'll be getting dead rotten drunk so I'll not remember if 'twas iver born you was at all; and I'll be shipping away on some boat will take me to the other end of the world where I'll never see your face again! (*He turns toward the door.*)

CHRIS. (*who has been standing in a stupor—suddenly grasping* BURKE *by the arm—stupidly*) No, you don't go. Ay tank maybe it's better Anna marry you now.

BURKE. (*shaking* CHRIS *off—furiously*) Lave go of me, ye old ape! Marry her, is it? I'd see her roasting in hell first! I'm shipping away out of this, I'm telling you! (*Pointing to* ANNA—*passionately*) And my curse on you and the curse of Almighty God and all the Saints! You've destroyed me this day and may you lie awake in the long nights, tormented with thoughts of Mat Burke and the great wrong you've done him!

ANNA. (*in anguish*) Mat! (*But he turns without another word and strides out of the doorway.* ANNA *looks after him wildly, starts to run after him, then hides her face in her outstretched arms, sobbing.* CHRIS *stands in a stupor, staring at the floor.*)

CHRIS. (*after a pause, dully*) Ay tank Ay go ashore, too.

ANNA. (*looking up, wildly*) Not after him! Let him go! Don't you dare—

CHRIS. (*somberly*) Ay go for gat drink.

ANNA. (*with a harsh laugh*) So I'm driving you to drink, too, eh? I s'pose you want to get drunk so's you can forget—like him?

CHRIS. (*bursting out angrily*) Yes, Ay vant! You tank Ay like hear dem tangs? (*Breaking down—weeping*) Ay tank you vasn't dat kind of gel, Anna.

ANNA. (*mockingly*) And I s'pose you want me to beat it, don't you? You don't want me here disgracing you, I s'pose?

CHRIS. No, you stay here! (*Goes over and pats her on the shoulder, the tears running down his face*) Ain't your fault, Anna, Ay know dat. (*She looks up at him, softened. He bursts into rage*) It's dat ole davil, sea, do this to me! (*He shakes his fist at the door*) It's her dirty tricks! It vas all right on barge with yust you and me. Den she bring dat Irish fallar in fog, she make you like him, she make you fight with me all time! If dat Irish fallar don't never come, you don't never tal me dem tangs, Ay don't never know, and everytang's all right. (*He shakes his fist again*) Dirty ole davil!

ANNA. (*with spent weariness*) Oh, what's the use? Go on ashore and get drunk.

CHRIS. (*goes into room on left and gets his cap. He goes to the door, silent and stupid—then turns*) You vait here, Anna?

ANNA. (*dully*) Maybe—and maybe not. Maybe I'll get drunk, too. Maybe I'll— But what the hell do you care what I do? Go on and beat it. (CHRIS *turns stupidly and goes out.* ANNA *sits at the table, staring straight in front of her.*)

CURTAIN

ACT FOUR

Scene—*Same as Act Three, about nine o'clock of a foggy night two days later. The whistles of steamers in the harbor can be heard. The cabin is lighted by a small lamp on the table. A suitcase stands in the middle of the floor.* ANNA *is sitting in the rocking-chair. She wears a hat, is all dressed up as in Act One. Her face is pale, looks terribly tired and worn, as if the two days just past had been ones of suffering and sleepless nights. She stares before her despondently, her chin in her hands. There is a timid knock on the door in rear.* ANNA *jumps to her feet with a startled exclamation and looks toward the door with an expression of mingled hope and fear.*

ANNA. (*faintly*) Come in. (*Then summoning her courage—more resolutely*) Come in. (*The door is opened and* CHRIS *appears in the doorway. He is in a very bleary, bedraggled condition, suffering from the aftereffects of his drunk. A tin pail full of foaming beer is in his hand. He comes forward, his eyes avoiding* ANNA's. *He mutters stupidly*) It's foggy.

ANNA. (*looking him over with contempt*) So you come back at last, did you? You're a fine looking sight! (*Then jeeringly*) I thought you'd beaten it for good on account of the disgrace I'd brought on you.

CHRIS. (*wincing—faintly*) Don't say dat, Anna, please! (*He sits in a chair by the table, setting down the can of beer, holding his head in his hands.*)

ANNA. (*looks at him with a certain sympathy*) What's the trouble? Feeling sick?

CHRIS. (*dully*) Inside my head feel sick.

ANNA. Well, what d'you expect after being soused for two days?

63

(*Resentfully*) It serves you right. A fine thing—you leaving me alone on this barge all that time!

CHRIS. (*humbly*) Ay'm sorry, Anna.

ANNA. (*scornfully*) Sorry!

CHRIS. But Ay'm not sick inside head vay you mean. Ay'm sick from tank too much about you, about me.

ANNA. And how about me? D'you suppose I ain't been thinking, too?

CHRIS. Ay'm sorry, Anna. (*He sees her bag and gives a start*) You pack your bag, Anna? You vas going—?

ANNA. (*forcibly*) Yes, I was going right back to what you think.

CHRIS. Anna!

ANNA. I went ashore to get a train for New York. I'd been waiting and waiting 'till I was sick of it. Then I changed my mind and decided not to go today. But I'm going first thing tomorrow, so it'll all be the same in the end.

CHRIS. (*raising his head—pleadingly*) No, you never do dat, Anna!

ANNA. (*with a sneer*) Why not, I'd like to know?

CHRIS. You don't never gat to do—dat vay—no more, Ay tal you. Ay fix dat up all right.

ANNA. (*suspiciously*) Fix what up?

CHRIS. (*not seeming to have heard her question—sadly*) You vas vaiting, you say? You vasn't vaiting for me, Ay bet.

ANNA. (*callously*) You'd win.

CHRIS. For dat Irish fallar?

ANNA. (*defiantly*) Yes—if you want to know! (*Then with a forlorn laugh*) If he did come back it'd only be 'cause he wanted to beat me up or kill me, I suppose. But even if he did, I'd rather have him come than not show up at all. I wouldn't care what he did.

CHRIS. Ay guess it's true you vas in love with him all right.

ANNA. You guess!

CHRIS. (*turning to her earnestly*) And Ay'm sorry for you like hell he don't come, Anna!

ANNA. (*softened*) Seems to me you've changed your tune a lot.

CHRIS. Ay've been tanking, and Ay guess it vas all my fault—all bad tangs dat happen to you. (*Pleadingly*) You try for not hate me, Anna. Ay'm crazy ole fool, dat's all.

ANNA. Who said I hated you?

CHRIS. Ay'm sorry for everytang Ay do wrong for you, Anna. Ay vant for you be happy all rest of your life for make up! It make you happy marry dat Irish fallar, Ay vant it, too.

ANNA. (*dully*) Well, there ain't no chance. But I'm glad you think different about it, anyway.

CHRIS. (*supplicatingly*) And you tank—maybe—you forgive me sometime?

ANNA. (*with a wan smile*) I'll forgive you right now.

CHRIS. (*seizing her hand and kissing it—brokenly*) Anna lilla! Anna lilla!

ANNA. (*touched but a bit embarrassed*) Don't bawl about it. There ain't nothing to forgive, anyway. It ain't your fault, and it ain't mine, and it ain't his neither. We're all poor nuts, and things happen, and we yust get mixed in wrong, that's all.

CHRIS. (*eagerly*) You say right tang, Anna, py golly! It ain't nobody's fault! (*Shaking his fist*) It's dat ole davil, sea!

ANNA. (*with an exasperated laugh*) Gee, won't you ever can that stuff? (CHRIS *relapses into injured silence. After a pause* ANNA *continues curiously*) You said a minute ago you'd fixed something up—about me. What was it?

CHRIS. (*after a hesitating pause*) Ay'm shipping avay on sea again, Anna.

ANNA. (*astounded*) You're—what?

CHRIS. Ay sign on steamer sail tomorrow. Ay gat my ole yob—bo'sun. (ANNA *stares at him. As he goes on, a bitter smile comes over her face*) Ay tank dat's best tang for you. Ay only bring you bad luck, Ay tank. Ay make your mo'der's life sorry. Ay don't vant make yours dat way, but Ay do yust same. Dat ole davil, sea, she make me Yonah

65

man ain't no good for nobody. And Ay tank now it ain't no use fight with sea. No man dat live going to beat her, py yingo!

ANNA. (*with a laugh of helpless bitterness*) So that's how you've fixed me, is it?

CHRIS. Yes, Ay tank if dat ole davil gat me back she leave you alone den.

ANNA. (*bitterly*) But, for Gawd's sake, don't you see you're doing the same thing you've always done? Don't you see—? (*But she sees the look of obsessed stubborness on her father's face and gives it up helplessly*) But what's the use of talking? You ain't right, that's what. I'll never blame you for nothing no more. But how you could figure out that was fixing me—!

CHRIS. Dat ain't all. Ay gat dem fallars in steamship office to pay you all money coming to me every month vhile Ay'm avay.

ANNA. (*with a hard laugh*) Thanks. But I guess I won't be hard up for no small change.

CHRIS. (*hurt—humbly*) It ain't much, Ay know, but it's plenty for keep you so you never gat go back—

ANNA. (*shortly*) Shut up, will you? We'll talk about it later, see?

CHRIS. (*after a pause—ingratiatingly*) You like Ay go ashore look for dat Irish fallar, Anna?

ANNA. (*angrily*) Not much! Think I want to drag him back?

CHRIS. (*after a pause—uncomfortably*) Py golly, dat booze don't go vell. Give me fever, Ay tank. Ay feel hot like hell. (*He takes off his coat and lets it drop on the floor. There is a loud thud.*)

ANNA. (*with a start*) What you got in your pocket, for Pete's sake— a ton of lead? (*She reaches down, takes the coat and pulls out a re-volver—looks from it to him in amazement*) A gun? What were you doing with this?

CHRIS. (*sheepishly*) Ay forget. Ain't nothing. Ain't loaded, anyvay.

ANNA. (*breaking it open to make sure—then closing it again—look-ing at him suspiciously*) That ain't telling me why you got it?

CHRIS. Ay'm ole fool. Ay got it when Ay go ashore first. Ay tank den it's all fault of dat Irish fallar.

ANNA. (*with a shudder*) Say, you're crazier than I thought. I never dreamt you'd go that far.

CHRIS. (*quickly*) Ay don't. Ay gat better sense right avay. Ay don't never buy bullets even. It ain't his fault, Ay know.

ANNA. (*still suspicious of him*) Well, I'll take care of this for a while, loaded or not. (*She puts it in the drawer of table and closes the drawer.*)

CHRIS. (*placatingly*) Throw it overboard if you vant. Ay don't care. (*Then after a pause*) Py golly, Ay tank Ay go lie down. Ay feel sick. (ANNA *takes a magazine from the table.* CHRIS *hesitates by her chair*) We talk again before Ay go, yes?

ANNA. (*dully*) Where's this ship going to?

CHRIS. Cape Town. Dat's in South Africa. She's British steamer called "Londonderry." (*He stands hesitatingly—finally blurts out*) Anna—you forgive me sure?

ANNA. (*wearily*) Sure I do. You ain't to blame. You're yust—what you are—like me.

CHRIS. (*pleadingly*) Den—you lat me kiss you again once?

ANNA. (*raising her face—forcing a wan smile*) Sure. No hard feelings.

CHRIS. (*kisses her brokenly*) Anna lilla! Ay— (*He fights for words to express himself, but finds none—miserably—with a sob*) Ay can't say it. Good-night, Anna.

ANNA. Good-night. (*He picks up the can of beer and goes slowly into the room on left, his shoulders bowed, his head sunk forward dejectedly. He closes the door after him.* ANNA *turns over the pages of the magazine, trying desperately to banish her thoughts by looking at the pictures. This fails to distract her, and flinging the magazine back on the table, she springs to her feet and walks about the cabin distractedly, clenching and unclenching her hands. She speaks aloud to herself in a tense, trembling voice*) Gawd, I can't stand this much longer! What am I waiting for anyway?—like a damn fool! (*She laughs helplessly, then checks herself abruptly, as she hears the sound of heavy footsteps on the deck outside. She appears to recognize these and her face lights up with joy. She gasps*) Mat! (*A strange terror seems suddenly to seize her. She rushes to the table, takes the revolver out of drawer and crouches down in the corner, left, behind the cupboard. A moment later the door is flung open and* MAT BURKE *appears in the doorway. He is in bad shape—his clothes torn and dirty, covered with sawdust as if he had been groveling or sleeping on barroom floors. There is a red bruise on his forehead over one of his eyes, another over one cheekbone, his knuckles are skinned and raw—plain evidence of the fighting he has been through on his "bat." His eyes are bloodshot and heavy-lidded, his face has a bloated look. But beyond these appearances—the results of heavy drinking—there is an expression in his eyes of wild mental turmoil, of impotent animal rage baffled by its own abject misery.*)

BURKE. (*peers blinkingly about the cabin—hoarsely*) Let you not be hiding from me, whoever's here—though 'tis well you know I'd have a right to come back and murder you. (*He stops to listen. Hearing no sound, he closes the door behind him and comes forward to the table. He throws himself into the rocking-chair—despondently*) There's no one here, I'm thinking, and 'tis a great fool I am to be coming. (*With a sort of dumb, uncomprehending anguish*) Yerra, Mat Burke, 'tis a great jackass you've become and what's got into you at all, at all? She's gone out of this long ago, I'm telling you, and you'll never see her face again. (ANNA *stands up, hesitating, struggling between joy and fear.* BURKE's *eyes fall on* ANNA's *bag. He leans over to examine it*) What's this? (*Joyfully*) It's hers. She's not gone! But where is she? Ashore? (*Darkly*) What would she be doing ashore on this rotten night? (*His face suddenly convulsed with grief and rage*) 'Tis that, is it? Oh, God's curse on her! (*Raging*) I'll wait 'till she comes and choke her dirty life out. (ANNA *starts, her face grows hard. She steps into the room, the revolver in her right hand by her side.*)

ANNA. (*in a cold, hard tone*) What are you doing here?

BURKE. (*wheeling about with a terrified gasp*) Glory be to God!
(*They remain motionless and silent for a moment, holding each
other's eyes.*)

ANNA. (*in the same hard voice*) Well, can't you talk?

BURKE. (*trying to fall into an easy, careless tone*) You've a year's
growth scared out of me, coming at me so sudden and me thinking
I was alone.

ANNA. You've got your nerve butting in here without knocking or
nothing. What d'you want?

BURKE. (*airily*) Oh, nothing much. I was wanting to have a last
word with you, that's all. (*He moves a step toward her.*)

ANNA. (*sharply—raising the revolver in her hand*) Careful now.
Don't try getting too close. I heard what you said you'd do to me.

BURKE. (*noticing the revolver for the first time*) Is it murdering
me you'd be now, God forgive you? (*Then with a contemptuous
laugh*) Or is it thinking I'd be frightened by that old tin whistle?
(*He walks straight for her.*)

ANNA. (*wildly*) Look out, I tell you!

BURKE. (*who has come so close that the revolver is almost
touching his chest*) Let you shoot, then! (*Then with sudden wild
grief*) Let you shoot, I'm saying, and be done with it! Let you
end me with a shot and I'll be thanking you, for it's a rotten dog's
life I've lived the past two days since I've known what you are, 'til
I'm after wishing I was never born at all!

ANNA. (*overcome—letting the revolver drop to the floor, as if her
fingers had no strength to hold it—hysterically*) What d'you want
coming here? Why don't you beat it? Go on! (*She passes him and
sinks down in the rocking-chair.*)

BURKE. (*following her—mournfully*) 'Tis right you'd be asking
why did I come. (*Then angrily*) 'Tis because 'tis a great weak fool
of the world I am, and me tormented with the wickedness you'd
told of yourself, and drinking oceans of booze that'd make me forget.

69

Forget? Divil a word I'd forget, and your face grinning always in front of my eyes, awake or asleep, 'til I do be thinking a madhouse is the proper place for me.

ANNA. (*glancing at his hands and face—scornfully*) You look like you ought to be put away some place. Wonder you wasn't pulled in. You been scrapping, too, ain't you?

BURKE. I have—with every scut would take off his coat to me! (*Fiercely*) And each time I'd be hitting one a clout in the mug, it wasn't his face I'd be seeing at all, but yours, and me wanting to drive you a blow would knock you out of this world where I wouldn't be seeing or thinking more of you.

ANNA. (*her lips trembling pitifully*) Thanks!

BURKE. (*walking up and down—distractedly*) That's right, make game of me! Oh, I'm a great coward surely, to be coming back to speak with you at all. You've a right to laugh at me.

ANNA. I ain't laughing at you, Mat.

BURKE. (*unheeding*) You to be what you are, and me to be Mat Burke, and me to be drove back to look at you again! 'Tis black shame is on me!

ANNA. (*resentfully*) Then get out. No one's holding you!

BURKE. (*bewilderedly*) And me to listen to that talk from a woman like you and be frightened to close her mouth with a slap! Oh, God help me, I'm a yellow coward for all men to spit at! (*Then furiously*) But I'll not be getting out of this 'till I've had me word. (*Raising his fist threateningly*) And let you look out how you'd drive me! (*Letting his fist fall helplessly*) Don't be angry now! I'm raving like a real lunatic, I'm thinking, and the sorrow you put on me has my brains drownded in grief. (*Suddenly bending down to her and grasping her arm intensely*) Tell me it's a lie, I'm saying! That's what I'm after coming to hear you say.

ANNA. (*dully*) A lie? What?

BURKE. (*with passionate entreaty*) All the badness you told me two days back. Sure it must be a lie! You was only making game of me, wasn't you? Tell me 'twas a lie, Anna, and I'll be saying prayers of thanks on my two knees to the Almighty God!

ANNA. (*terribly shaken—faintly*) I can't, Mat. (*As he turns away—imploringly*) Oh, Mat, won't you see that no matter what I was I ain't that any more? Why, listen! I packed up my bag this afternoon and went ashore. I'd been waiting here all alone for two days, thinking maybe you'd come back—thinking maybe you'd think over all I'd said—and maybe—oh, I don't know what I was hoping! But I was afraid to even go out of the cabin for a second, honest—afraid you might come and not find me here. Then I gave up hope when you didn't show up and I went to the railroad station. I was going to New York. I was going back—

BURKE. (*hoarsely*) God's curse on you!

ANNA. Listen, Mat! You hadn't come, and I'd gave up hope. But—in the station—I couldn't go. I'd bought my ticket and everything. (*She takes the ticket from her dress and tries to hold it before his eyes*) But I got to thinking about you—and I couldn't take the train—I couldn't! So I come back here—to wait some more. Oh, Mat, don't you see I've changed? Can't you forgive what's dead and gone—and forget it?

BURKE. (*turning on her—overcome by rage again*) Forget, is it? I'll not forget 'til my dying day, I'm telling you, and me tormented with thoughts. (*In a frenzy*) Oh, I'm wishing I had wan of them fornenst me this minute and I'd beat him with my fists 'til he'd be a bloody corpse! I'm wishing the whole lot of them will roast in hell 'til the Judgment Day—and yourself along with them, for you're as bad as they are.

ANNA. (*shuddering*) Mat! (*Then after a pause—in a voice of dead, stony calm*) Well, you've had your say. Now you better beat it.

BURKE. (*starts slowly for the door—hesitates—then after a pause*) And what'll you be doing?

ANNA. What difference does it make to you?

BURKE. I'm asking you!

ANNA. (*in the same tone*) My bag's packed and I got my ticket. I'll go to New York tomorrow.

BURKE. (*helplessly*) You mean—you'll be doing the same again?

ANNA. (*stonily*) Yes.

BURKE. (*in anguish*) You'll not! Don't torment me with that talk! 'Tis a she-divil you are sent to drive me mad entirely!

ANNA. (*her voice breaking*) Oh, for Gawd's sake, Mat, leave me alone! Go away! Don't you see I'm licked? Why d'you want to keep on kicking me?

BURKE. (*indignantly*) And don't you deserve the worst I'd say, God forgive you?

ANNA. All right. Maybe I do. But don't rub it in. Why ain't you done what you said you was going to? Why ain't you got that ship was going to take you to the other side of the earth where you'd never see me again?

BURKE. I have.

ANNA. (*startled*) What—then you're going—honest?

BURKE. I signed on today at noon, drunk as I was—and she's sailing tomorrow.

ANNA. And where's she going to?

BURKE. Cape Town.

ANNA. (*the memory of having heard that name a little while before coming to her—with a start, confusedly*) Cape Town? Where's that? Far away?

BURKE. 'Tis at the end of Africa. That's far for you.

ANNA. (*forcing a laugh*) You're keeping your word all right, ain't you? (*After a slight pause—curiously*) What's the boat's name?

BURKE. The "Londonderry."

ANNA. (*it suddenly comes to her that this is the same ship her father is sailing on*) The "Londonderry"! It's the same— Oh, this is too much! (*With wild, ironical laughter*) Ha-ha-ha!

BURKE. What's up with you now?

ANNA. Ha-ha-ha! It's funny, funny! I'll die laughing!

BURKE. (*irritated*) Laughing at what?

ANNA. It's a secret. You'll know soon enough. It's funny. (*Controlling herself—after a pause—cynically*) What kind of a place is this Cape Town? Plenty of dames there, I suppose?

BURKE. To hell with them! That I may never see another woman to my dying hour!

ANNA. That's what you say now, but I'll bet by the time you get there you'll have forgot all about me and start in talking the same old bull you talked to me to the first one you meet.

BURKE. (*offended*) I'll not, then! God mend you, is it making me out to be the like of yourself you are, and you taking up with this one and that all the years of your life?

ANNA. (*angrily assertive*) Yes, that's yust what I do mean! You been doing the same thing all your life, picking up a new girl in every port. How're you any better than I was?

BURKE. (*thoroughly exasperated*) Is it no shame you have at all? I'm a fool to be wasting talk on you and you hardened in badness. I'll go out of this and lave you alone forever. (*He starts for the door—then stops to turn on her furiously*) And I suppose 'tis the same lies you told them all before that you told to me?

ANNA. (*indignantly*) That's a lie! I never did!

BURKE. (*miserably*) You'd be saying that, anyway.

ANNA. (*forcibly, with growing intensity*) Are you trying to accuse me—of being in love—really in love—with them?

BURKE. I'm thinking you were, surely.

ANNA. (*furiously, as if this were the last insult—advancing on him threateningly*) You mutt, you! I've stood enough from you. Don't you dare! (*With scornful bitterness*) Love 'em! Oh, my Gawd! You damn thick-head! Love 'em? (*Savagely*) I hated 'em, I tell you! Hated 'em, hated 'em, hated 'em! And may Gawd strike me dead this minute and my mother, too, if she was alive, if I ain't telling you the honest truth!

BURKE. (*immensely pleased by her vehemence—a light beginning to*

73

break over his face—but still uncertain, torn between doubt and the desire to believe—helplessly) If I could only be believing you now!

ANNA. (*distractedly*) Oh, what's the use? What's the use of me talking? What's the use of anything? (*Pleadingly*) Oh, Mat, you mustn't think that for a second! You mustn't! Think all the other bad about me you want to, and I won't kick, 'cause you've a right to. But don't think that! (*On the point of tears*) I couldn't bear it! It'd be yust too much to know you was going away where I'd never see you again—thinking that about me!

BURKE. (*after an inward struggle—tensely—forcing out the words with difficulty*) If I was believing—that you'd never had love for any other man in the world but me—I could be forgetting the rest, maybe.

ANNA. (*with a cry of joy*) Mat!

BURKE. (*slowly*) If 'tis truth you're after telling, I'd have a right, maybe, to believe you'd changed—and that I'd changed you myself 'til the thing you'd been all your life wouldn't be you any more at all.

ANNA. (*hanging on his words—breathlessly*) Oh, Mat! That's what I been trying to tell you all along!

BURKE. (*simply*) For I've a power of strength in me to lead men the way I want, and women, too, maybe, and I'm thinking I'd change you to a new woman entirely, so I'd never know, or you either, what kind of woman you'd been in the past at all.

ANNA. Yes, you could, Mat! I know you could!

BURKE. And I'm thinking 'twasn't your fault, maybe, but having that old ape for a father that left you to grow up alone, made you what you was. And if I could be believing 'tis only me you—

ANNA. (*distractedly*) You got to believe it, Mat! What can I do? I'll do anything, anything you want to prove I'm not lying!

BURKE. (*suddenly seems to have a solution. He feels in the pocket of his coat and grasps something—solemnly*) Would you be willing to swear an oath, now—a terrible, fearful oath would send your soul to the divils in hell if you was lying?

ANNA. (*eagerly*) Sure, I'll swear, Mat—on anything!

74

BURKE. (*takes a small, cheap old crucifix from his pocket and holds it up for her to see*) Will you swear on this?

ANNA. (*reaching out for it*) Yes. Sure I will. Give it to me.

BURKE. (*holding it away*) 'Tis a cross was given me by my mother, God rest her soul. (*He makes the sign of the cross mechanically*) I was a lad only, and she told me to keep it by me if I'd be waking or sleeping and never lose it, and it'd bring me luck. She died soon after. But I'm after keeping it with me from that day to this, and I'm telling you there's great power in it, and 'tis great bad luck it's saved me from and me roaming the seas, and I having it tied round my neck when my last ship sunk, and it bringing me safe to land when the others went to their death. (*Very earnestly*) And I'm warning you now, if you'd swear an oath on this, 'tis my old woman herself will be looking down from Hivin above, and praying Almighty God and the Saints to put a great curse on you if she'd hear you swearing a lie!

ANNA. (*awed by his manner—superstitiously*) I wouldn't have the nerve—honest—if it was a lie. But it's the truth and I ain't scared to swear. Give it to me.

BURKE. (*handing it to her—almost frightenedly, as if he feared for her safety*) Be careful what you'd swear, I'm saying.

ANNA. (*holding the cross gingerly*) Well—what do you want me to swear? You say it.

BURKE. Swear I'm the only man in the world ivir you felt love for.

ANNA. (*looking into his eyes steadily*) I swear it.

BURKE. And that you'll be forgetting from this day all the badness you've done and never do the like of it again.

ANNA. (*forcibly*) I swear it! I swear it by God!

BURKE. And may the blackest curse of God strike you if you're lying. Say it now!

ANNA. And may the blackest curse of God strike me if I'm lying!

BURKE. (*with a stupendous sigh*) Oh, glory be to God, I'm after believing you now! (*He takes the cross from her hand, his face beaming with joy, and puts it back in his pocket. He puts his arm about her waist and is about to kiss her when he stops, appalled by some terrible doubt.*)

ANNA. (*alarmed*) What's the matter with you?

BURKE. (*with sudden fierce questioning*) Is it Catholic ye are?

ANNA. (*confused*) No. Why?

BURKE. (*filled with a sort of bewildered foreboding*) Oh, God, help me! (*With a dark glance of suspicion at her*) There's some divil's trickery in it, to be swearing an oath on a Catholic cross and you wan of the others.

ANNA. (*distractedly*) Oh, Mat, don't you believe me?

BURKE. (*miserably*) If it isn't a Catholic you are—

ANNA. I ain't nothing. What's the difference? Didn't you hear me swear?

BURKE. (*passionately*) Oh, I'd a right to stay away from you—but I couldn't! I was loving you in spite of it all and wanting to be with you, God forgive me, no matter what you are. I'd go mad if I'd not have you! I'd be killing the world— (*He seizes her in his arms and kisses her fiercely.*)

ANNA. (*with a gasp of joy*) Mat!

BURKE. (*suddenly holding her away from him and staring into her eyes as if to probe into her soul—slowly*) If your oath is no proper oath at all, I'll have to be taking your naked word for it and have you anyway, I'm thinking—I'm needing you that bad!

ANNA. (*hurt—reproachfully*) Mat! I swore, didn't I?

BURKE. (*defiantly, as if challenging fate*) Oath or no oath, 'tis no matter. We'll be wedded in the morning, with the help of God. (*Still more defiantly*) We'll be happy now, the two of us, in spite of the divil! (*He crushes her to him and kisses her again. The door on the left is pushed open and* CHRIS *appears in the doorway. He stands blinking at them. At first the old expression of hatred of* BURKE *comes into his eyes instinctively. Then a look of resignation and relief takes its place. His face lights up with a sudden happy thought. He turns back into the bedroom—reappears immediately with the tin can of beer in his hand—grinning.*)

CHRIS. Ve have drink on this, py golly! (*They break away from each other with startled exclamations.*)

BURKE. (*explosively*) God stiffen it! (*He takes a step toward* CHRIS *threateningly.*)

ANNA. (*happily—to her father*) That's the way to talk! (*With a laugh*) And say, it's about time for you and Mat to kiss and make up. You're going to be shipmates on the "Londonderry," did you know it?

BURKE. (*astounded*) Shipmates— Has himself—

CHRIS. (*equally astounded*) Ay vas bo'sun on her.

BURKE. The divil! (*Then angrily*) You'd be going back to sea and leaving her alone, would you?

ANNA. (*quickly*) It's all right, Mat. That's where he belongs, and I want him to go. You got to go, too; we'll need the money. (*With a laugh, as she gets the glasses*) And as for me being alone, that runs in the family, and I'll get used to it. (*Pouring out their glasses*) I'll get a little house somewhere and I'll make a regular place for you two to come back to,—wait and see. And now you drink up and be friends.

BURKE. (*happily—but still a bit resentful against the old man*) Sure! (*Clinking his glass against* CHRIS') Here's luck to you! (*He drinks.*)

CHRIS. (*subdued—his face melancholy*) Skoal. (*He drinks.*)

BURKE. (*to* ANNA, *with a wink*) You'll not be lonesome long. I'll see to that, with the help of God. 'Tis himself here will be having a grandchild to ride on his foot, I'm telling you!

ANNA. (*turning away in embarrassment*) Quit the kidding now. (*She picks up her bag and goes into the room on left. As soon as she is gone* BURKE *relapses into an attitude of gloomy thought.* CHRIS *stares at his beer absent-mindedly. Finally* BURKE *turns on him.*)

BURKE. Is it any religion at all you have, you and your Anna?

CHRIS. (*surprised*) Vhy, yes. Ve vas Lutheran in ole country.

BURKE. (*horrified*) Luthers, is it? (*Then with a grim resignation, slowly, aloud to himself*) Well, I'm damned then surely. Yerra, what's the difference? 'Tis the will of God, anyway.

CHRIS. (*moodily preoccupied with his own thoughts—speaks with somber premonition as* ANNA *re-enters from the left*) It's funny. It's queer, yes—you and me shipping on same boat dat vay. It ain't right. Ay don't know—it's dat funny vay ole davil sea do her vorst dirty tricks, yes. It's so. (*He gets up and goes back and, opening the door, stares out into the darkness.*)

BURKE. (*nodding his head in gloomy acquiescence—with a great sigh*) I'm fearing maybe you have the right of it for once, divil take you.

ANNA. (*forcing a laugh*) Gee, Mat, you ain't agreeing with him, are you? (*She comes forward and puts her arm about his shoulder—with a determined gaiety*) Aw say, what's the matter? Cut out the gloom. We're all fixed now, ain't we, me and you? (*Pours out more beer into his glass and fills one for herself—slaps him on the back*) Come on! Here's to the sea, no matter what! Be a game sport and drink to that! Come on! (*She gulps down her drink.* BURKE *banishes his superstitious premonitions with a defiant jerk of his head, grins up at her, and drinks to her toast.*)

CHRIS. (*looking out into the night—lost in his somber preoccupation—shakes his head and mutters*) Fog, fog, fog, all bloody time. You can't see vhere you vas going, no. Only dat ole davil, sea—she knows! (*The two stare at him. From the harbor comes the muffled, mournful wail of steamers' whistles.*)

CURTAIN

BEYOND THE HORIZON

A Play in Three Acts

CHARACTERS

JAMES MAYO, *a farmer*
KATE MAYO, *his wife*
CAPTAIN DICK SCOTT, *of the bark "Sunda," her brother*
ANDREW MAYO } *sons of* JAMES MAYO
ROBERT MAYO }
RUTH ATKINS
MRS. ATKINS, *her widowed mother*
MARY
BEN, *a farm hand*
DOCTOR FAWCETT

SCENES

ACT ONE

Scene I: The Road. Sunset of a day in Spring.
Scene II: The Farm House. The same night.

ACT TWO

(Three years later)
Scene I: The Farm House. Noon of a Summer day.
Scene II: The top of a hill on the farm overlooking the sea. The following day.

ACT THREE

(Five years later)
Scene I: The Farm House. Dawn of a day in late Fall.
Scene II: The Road. Sunrise.

BEYOND THE HORIZON

ACT ONE—SCENE ONE

A SECTION of *country highway. The road runs diagonally from the left, forward, to the right, rear, and can be seen in the distance winding toward the horizon like a pale ribbon between the low, rolling hills with their freshly plowed fields clearly divided from each other, checkerboard fashion, by the lines of stone walls and rough snake fences.*

The forward triangle cut off by the road is a section of a field from the dark earth of which myriad bright-green blades of fall-sown rye are sprouting. A straggling line of piled rocks, too low to be called a wall, separates this field from the road.

To the rear of the road is a ditch with a sloping, grassy bank on the far side. From the center of this an old, gnarled apple tree, just budding into leaf, strains its twisted branches heavenwards, black against the pallor of distance. A snake-fence sidles from left to right along the top of the bank, passing beneath the apple tree.

The hushed twilight of a day in May is just beginning. The horizon hills are still rimmed by a faint line of flame, and the sky above them glows with the crimson flush of the sunset. This fades gradually as the action of the scene progresses.

At the rise of the curtain, ROBERT MAYO *is discovered sitting on the fence. He is a tall, slender young man of twenty-three. There is a touch of the poet about him expressed in his high forehead and wide, dark eyes. His features are delicate and refined, leaning to weakness in the mouth and chin. He is dressed in gray corduroy trousers pushed into high laced boots, and a blue flannel shirt with a bright colored tie. He is reading a book by the fading sunset light. He shuts this, keeping a finger in to mark the place, and turns his head toward the horizon, gazing out over the fields and hills. His lips move as if he were reciting something to himself.*

His brother ANDREW *comes along the road from the right, returning from his work in the fields. He is twenty-seven years old, an opposite type to* ROBERT—*husky, sun-bronzed, handsome in a large-featured, manly fashion—a son of the soil, intelligent in a shrewd way, but with nothing of the intellectual about him. He wears overalls, leather boots, a gray flannel shirt open at the neck, and a soft, mud-stained hat pushed back on his head. He stops to talk to* ROBERT, *leaning on the hoe he carries.*

ANDREW. (*seeing* ROBERT *has not noticed his presence—in a loud shout*) Hey there! (ROBERT *turns with a start. Seeing who it is, he smiles*) Gosh, you do take the prize for day-dreaming! And I see you've toted one of the old books along with you. (*He crosses the ditch and sits on the fence near his brother*) What is it this time—poetry, I'll bet. (*He reaches for the book*) Let me see.

ROBERT. (*handing it to him rather reluctantly*) Look out you don't get it full of dirt.

ANDREW. (*glancing at his hands*) That isn't dirt—it's good clean earth. (*He turns over the pages. His eyes read something and he gives an exclamation of disgust*) Hump! (*With a provoking grin at his brother he reads aloud in a doleful, sing-song voice*) "I have loved wind and light and the bright sea. But holy and most sacred night, not as I love and have loved thee." (*He hands the book back*) Here! Take it and bury it. I suppose it's that year in college gave you a liking for that kind of stuff. I'm darn glad I stopped at High School, or maybe I'd been crazy too. (*He grins and slaps* ROBERT *on the back affectionately*) Imagine me reading poetry and plowing at the same time. The team'd run away, I'll bet.

ROBERT. (*laughing*) Or picture me plowing.

ANDREW. You should have gone back to college last fall, like I know you wanted to. You're fitted for that sort of thing—just as I ain't.

ROBERT. You know why I didn't go back, Andy. Pa didn't like the idea, even if he didn't say so; and I know he wanted the money to use improving the farm. And besides, I'm not keen on being a student, just because you see me reading books all the time. What I want to do now is keep on moving so that I won't take root in any one place.

ANDREW. Well, the trip you're leaving on tomorrow will keep you moving all right. (*At this mention of the trip they both fall silent. There is a pause. Finally* ANDREW *goes on, awkwardly, attempting to speak casually*) Uncle says you'll be gone three years.

ROBERT. About that, he figures.

ANDREW. (*moodily*) That's a long time.

ROBERT. Not so long when you come to consider it. You know the "Sunda" sails around the Horn for Yokohama first, and that's a long voyage on a sailing ship; and if we go to any of the other places Uncle Dick mentions—India, or Australia, or South Africa, or South America—they'll be long voyages, too.

ANDREW. You can have all those foreign parts for all of me. (*After a pause*) Ma's going to miss you a lot, Rob.

ROBERT. Yes—and I'll miss her.

ANDREW. And Pa ain't feeling none too happy to have you go—though he's been trying not to show it.

ROBERT. I can see how he feels.

ANDREW. And you can bet that I'm not giving any cheers about it. (*He puts one hand on the fence near* ROBERT.)

ROBERT. (*putting one hand on top of* ANDREW's *with a gesture almost of shyness*) I know that, too, Andy.

ANDREW. I'll miss you as much as anybody, I guess. You see, you and I ain't like most brothers—always fighting and separated a lot of the time, while we've always been together—just the two of us. It's different with us. That's why it hits so hard, I guess.

ROBERT. (*with feeling*) It's just as hard for me, Andy—believe that!

83

I hate to leave you and the old folks—but—I feel I've got to. There's something calling me— (*He points to the horizon*) Oh, I can't just explain it to you, Andy.

ANDREW. No need to, Rob. (*Angry at himself*) Hell! You want to go—that's all there is to it; and I wouldn't have you miss this chance for the world.

ROBERT. It's fine of you to feel that way, Andy.

ANDREW. Huh! I'd be a nice son-of-a-gun if I didn't, wouldn't I? When I know how you need this sea trip to make a new man of you —in the body, I mean—and give you your full health back.

ROBERT. (*a trifle impatiently*) All of you seem to keep harping on my health. You were so used to seeing me lying around the house in the old days that you never will get over the notion that I'm a chronic invalid. You don't realize how I've bucked up in the past few years. If I had no other excuse for going on Uncle Dick's ship but just my health, I'd stay right here and start in plowing.

ANDREW. Can't be done. Farming ain't your nature. There's all the difference shown in just the way us two feel about the farm. You— well, you like the home part of it, I expect; but as a place to work and grow things, you hate it. Ain't that right?

ROBERT. Yes, I suppose it is. For you it's different. You're a Mayo through and through. You're wedded to the soil. You're as much a product of it as an ear of corn is, or a tree. Father is the same. This farm is his life-work, and he's happy in knowing that another Mayo, inspired by the same love, will take up the work where he leaves off. I can understand your attitude, and Pa's; and I think it's wonderful and sincere. But I—well, I'm not made that way.

ANDREW. No, you ain't; but when it comes to understanding, I guess I realize that you've got your own angle of looking at things.

ROBERT. (*musingly*) I wonder if you do, really.

ANDREW. (*confidently*) Sure I do. You've seen a bit of the world, enough to make the farm seem small, and you've got the itch to see it all.

84

ROBERT. It's more than that, Andy.

ANDREW. Oh, of course. I know you're going to learn navigation, and all about a ship, so's you can be an officer. That's natural, too. There's fair pay in it, I expect, when you consider that you've always got a home and grub thrown in; and if you're set on traveling, you can go anywhere you're a mind to without paying fare.

ROBERT. (*with a smile that is half sad*) It's more than that, Andy.

ANDREW. Sure it is. There's always a chance of a good thing coming your way in some of those foreign ports or other. I've heard there are great opportunities for a young fellow with his eyes open in some of those new countries that are just being opened up. (*Jovially*) I'll bet that's what you've been turning over in your mind under all your quietness! (*He slaps his brother on the back with a laugh*) Well, if you get to be a millionaire all of a sudden, call 'round once in a while and I'll pass the plate to you. We could use a lot of money right here on the farm without hurting it any.

ROBERT. (*forced to laugh*) I've never considered that practical side of it for a minute, Andy.

ANDREW. Well, you ought to.

ROBERT. No, I oughtn't. (*Pointing to the horizon—dreamily*) Supposing I was to tell you that it's just Beauty that's calling me, the beauty of the far off and unknown, the mystery and spell of the East which lures me in the books I've read, the need of the freedom of great wide spaces, the joy of wandering on and on—in quest of the secret which is hidden over there, beyond the horizon? Suppose I told you that was the one and only reason for my going?

ANDREW. I should say you were nutty.

ROBERT. (*frowning*) Don't, Andy. I'm serious.

ANDREW. Then you might as well stay here, because we've got all you're looking for right on this farm. There's wide space enough, Lord knows; and you can have all the sea you want by walking a mile down to the beach; and there's plenty of horizon to look at, and beauty enough for anyone, except in the winter. (*He grins*) As for

85

the mystery and spell, I haven't met 'em yet, but they're probably lying around somewheres. I'll have you understand this is a first class farm with all the fixings. (*He laughs.*)

ROBERT. (*joining in the laughter in spite of himself*) It's no use talking to you, you chump!

ANDREW. You'd better not say anything to Uncle Dick about spells and things when you're on the ship. He'll likely chuck you overboard for a Jonah. (*He jumps down from fence*) I'd better run along. I've got to wash up some as long as Ruth's Ma is coming over for supper.

ROBERT. (*pointedly—almost bitterly*) And Ruth.

ANDREW. (*confused—looking everywhere except at* ROBERT—*trying to appear unconcerned*) Yes, Ruth'll be staying too. Well, I better hustle, I guess, and— (*He steps over the ditch to the road while he is talking.*)

ROBERT. (*who appears to be fighting some strong inward emotion—impulsively*) Wait a minute, Andy! (*He jumps down from the fence*) There is something I want to— (*He stops abruptly, biting his lips, his face coloring.*)

ANDREW. (*facing him; half-defiantly*) Yes?

ROBERT. (*confusedly*) No— never mind— it doesn't matter, it was nothing.

ANDREW. (*after a pause, during which he stares fixedly at* ROBERT's *averted face*) Maybe I can guess— what you were going to say— but I guess you're right not to talk about it. (*He pulls* ROBERT's *hand from his side and grips it tensely; the two brothers stand looking into each other's eyes for a minute*) We can't help those things, Rob. (*He turns away, suddenly releasing* ROBERT's *hand*) You'll be coming along shortly, won't you?

ROBERT. (*dully*) Yes.

ANDREW. See you later, then. (*He walks off down the road to the left.* ROBERT *stares after him for a moment; then climbs to the fence rail again, and looks out over the hills, an expression of deep grief on his face. After a moment or so,* RUTH *enters hurriedly from the left.*

She is a healthy, blonde, out-of-door girl of twenty, with a graceful, slender figure. Her face, though inclined to roundness, is undeniably pretty, its large eyes of a deep blue set off strikingly by the sun-bronzed complexion. Her small, regular features are marked by a certain strength—an underlying, stubborn fixity of purpose hidden in the frankly-appealing charm of her fresh youthfulness. She wears a simple white dress but no hat.)

RUTH. (*seeing him*) Hello, Rob!

ROBERT. (*startled*) Hello, Ruth!

RUTH. (*jumps the ditch and perches on the fence beside him*) I was looking for you.

ROBERT. (*pointedly*) Andy just left here.

RUTH. I know. I met him on the road a second ago. He told me you were here. (*Tenderly playful*) I wasn't looking for Andy, Smarty, if that's what you mean. I was looking for *you*.

ROBERT. Because I'm going away tomorrow?

RUTH. Because your mother was anxious to have you come home and asked me to look for you. I just wheeled Ma over to your house.

ROBERT. (*perfunctorily*) How is your mother?

RUTH. (*a shadow coming over her face*) She's about the same. She never seems to get any better or any worse. Oh, Rob, I do wish she'd try to make the best of things that can't be helped.

ROBERT. Has she been nagging at you again?

RUTH. (*nods her head, and then breaks forth rebelliously*) She never stops nagging. No matter what I do for her she finds fault. If only Pa was still living— (*She stops as if ashamed of her outburst*) I suppose I shouldn't complain this way. (*She sighs*) Poor Ma, Lord knows it's hard enough for her. I suppose it's natural to be cross when you're not able ever to walk a step. Oh, I'd like to be going away some place —like you!

ROBERT. It's hard to stay—and equally hard to go, sometimes.

RUTH. There! If I'm not the stupid body! I swore I wasn't going to speak about your trip—until after you'd gone; and there I go, first thing!

ROBERT. Why didn't you want to speak of it?

RUTH. Because I didn't want to spoil this last night you're here. Oh, Rob, I'm going to—we're all going to miss you so awfully. Your mother is going around looking as if she'd burst out crying any minute. You ought to know how I feel. Andy and you and I—why it seems as if we'd always been together.

ROBERT. (*with a wry attempt at a smile*) You and Andy will still have each other. It'll be harder for me without anyone.

RUTH. But you'll have new sights and new people to take your mind off; while we'll be here with the old, familiar place to remind us every minute of the day. It's a shame you're going—just at this time, in spring, when everything is getting so nice. (*With a sigh*) I oughtn't to talk that way when I know going's the best thing for you. You're bound to find all sorts of opportunities to get on, your father says.

ROBERT. (*heatedly*) I don't give a damn about that! I wouldn't take a voyage across the road for the best opportunity in the world of the kind Pa thinks of. (*He smiles at his own irritation*) Excuse me, Ruth, for getting worked up over it; but Andy gave me an overdose of the practical considerations.

RUTH. (*slowly, puzzled*) Well, then, if it isn't— (*With sudden intensity*) Oh, Rob, why *do* you want to go?

ROBERT. (*turning to her quickly, in surprise—slowly*) Why do you ask that, Ruth?

RUTH. (*dropping her eyes before his searching glance*) Because— (*Lamely*) It seems such a shame.

ROBERT. (*insistently*) Why?

RUTH. Oh, because—everything.

ROBERT. I could hardly back out now, even if I wanted to. And I'll be forgotten before you know it.

RUTH. (*indignantly*) You won't! I'll never forget— (*She stops and turns away to hide her confusion.*)

88

ROBERT. (*softly*) Will you promise me that?

RUTH. (*evasively*) Of course. It's mean of you to think that any of us would forget so easily.

ROBERT. (*disappointedly*) Oh!

RUTH. (*with an attempt at lightness*) But you haven't told me your reason for leaving yet?

ROBERT. (*moodily*) I doubt if you'll understand. It's difficult to explain, even to myself. Either you feel it, or you don't. I can remember being conscious of it first when I was only a kid—you haven't forgotten what a sickly specimen I was then, in those days, have you?

RUTH. (*with a shudder*) Let's not think about them.

ROBERT. You'll have to, to understand. Well, in those days, when Ma was fixing meals, she used to get me out of the way by pushing my chair to the west window and telling me to look out and be quiet. That wasn't hard. I guess I was always quiet.

RUTH. (*compassionately*) Yes, you always were—and you suffering so much, too!

ROBERT. (*musingly*) So I used to stare out over the fields to the hills, out there—(*He points to the horizon*) and somehow after a time I'd forget any pain I was in, and start dreaming. I knew the sea was over beyond those hills,—the folks had told me—and I used to wonder what the sea was like, and try to form a picture of it in my mind. (*With a smile*) There was all the mystery in the world to me then about that—far-off sea—and there still is! It called to me then just as it does now. (*After a slight pause*) And other times my eyes would follow this road, winding off into the distance, toward the hills, as if it, too, was searching for the sea. And I'd promise myself that when I grew up and was strong, I'd follow that road, and it and I would find the sea together. (*With a smile*) You see, my making this trip is only keeping that promise of long ago.

RUTH. (*charmed by his low, musical voice telling the dreams of his childhood*) Yes, I see.

ROBERT. Those were the only happy moments of my life then, dreaming there at the window. I liked to be all alone—those times. I got to know all the different kinds of sunsets by heart. And all those sunsets took place over there—(*He points*) beyond the horizon. So gradually I came to believe that all the wonders of the world happened on the other side of those hills. There was the home of the good fairies who performed beautiful miracles. I believed in fairies then. (*With a smile*) Perhaps I still do believe in them. Anyway, in those days they were real enough, and sometimes I could actually hear them calling to me to come out and play with them, dance with them down the road in the dusk in a game of hide-and-seek to find out where the sun was hiding himself. They sang their little songs to me, songs that told of all the wonderful things they had in their home on the other side of the hills; and they promised to show me all of them, if I'd only come, come! But I couldn't come then, and I used to cry sometimes and Ma would think I was in pain. (*He breaks off suddenly with a laugh*) That's why I'm going now, I suppose. For I can still hear them calling. But the horizon is as far away and as luring as ever. (*He turns to her— softly*) Do you understand now, Ruth?

RUTH. (*spellbound, in a whisper*) Yes.

ROBERT. You feel it then?

RUTH. Yes, yes, I do! (*Unconsciously she snuggles close against his side. His arm steals about her as if he were not aware of the action*) Oh, Rob, how could I help feeling it? You tell things so beautifully!

ROBERT. (*suddenly realizing that his arm is around her, and that her head is resting on his shoulder, gently takes his arm away.* RUTH, *brought back to herself, is overcome with confusion*) So now you know why I'm going. It's for that reason—that and one other.

RUTH. You've another? Then you must tell me that, too.

ROBERT. (*looking at her searchingly. She drops her eyes before his gaze*) I wonder if I ought to! You'll promise not to be angry—whatever it is?

RUTH. (*softly, her face still averted*) Yes, I promise.

ROBERT. (*simply*) I love you. That's the other reason.

RUTH. (*hiding her face in her hands*) Oh, Rob!

ROBERT. I wasn't going to tell you, but I feel I have to. It can't matter now that I'm going so far away, and for so long—perhaps forever. I've loved you all these years, but the realization never came 'til I agreed to go away with Uncle Dick. Then I thought of leaving you, and the pain of that thought revealed to me in a flash—that I loved you, had loved you as long as I could remember. (*He gently pulls one of* RUTH's *hands away from her face*) You mustn't mind my telling you this, Ruth. I realize how impossible it all is—and I understand; for the revelation of my own love seemed to open my eyes to the love of others. I saw Andy's love for you—and I knew that you must love him.

RUTH. (*breaking out stormily*) I don't! I don't love Andy! I don't! (ROBERT *stares at her in stupid astonishment.* RUTH *weeps hysterically*) Whatever—put such a fool notion into—into your head? (*She suddenly throws her arms about his neck and hides her head on his shoulder*) Oh, Rob! Don't go away! Please! You mustn't, now! You can't! I won't let you! It'd break my—my heart!

ROBERT. (*the expression of stupid bewilderment giving way to one of overwhelming joy. He presses her close to him—slowly and tenderly*) Do you mean that—that you love me?

RUTH. (*sobbing*) Yes, yes—of course I do—what d'you s'pose? (*She lifts up her head and looks into his eyes with a tremulous smile*) You stupid thing! (*He kisses her*) I've loved you right along.

ROBERT. (*mystified*) But you and Andy were always together!

RUTH. Because you never seemed to want to go any place with me. You were always reading an old book, and not paying any attention to me. I was too proud to let you see I cared because I thought the year you had away to college had made you stuck-up, and you thought yourself too educated to waste any time on me.

ROBERT. (*kissing her*) And I was thinking— (*With a laugh*) What fools we've both been!

RUTH. (*overcome by a sudden fear*) You won't go away on the trip, will you, Rob? You'll tell them you can't go on account of me, won't you? You can't go now! You can't!

ROBERT. (*bewildered*) Perhaps—you can come too.

RUTH. Oh, Rob, don't be so foolish. You know I can't. Who'd take care of ma? Don't you see I couldn't go—on her account? (*She clings to him imploringly*) Please don't go—not now. Tell them you've decided not to. They won't mind. I know your mother and father'll be glad. They'll all be. They don't want you to go so far away from them. Please, Rob! We'll be so happy here together where it's natural and we know things. Please tell me you won't go!

ROBERT. (*face to face with a definite, final decision, betrays the conflict going on within him*) But—Ruth—I—Uncle Dick—

RUTH. He won't mind when he knows it's for your happiness to stay. How could he? (*As ROBERT remains silent she bursts into sobs again*) Oh, Rob! And you said—you loved me!

ROBERT. (*conquered by this appeal—an irrevocable decision in his voice*) I won't go, Ruth. I promise you. There! Don't cry! (*He presses her to him, stroking her hair tenderly. After a pause he speaks with happy hopefulness*) Perhaps after all Andy was right—righter than he knew—when he said I could find all the things I was seeking for here, at home on the farm. I think love must have been the secret—the secret that called to me from over the world's rim—the secret beyond every horizon; and when I did not come, it came to me. (*He clasps RUTH to him fiercely*) Oh, Ruth, our love is sweeter than any distant dream! (*He kisses her passionately and steps to the ground, lifting RUTH in his arms and carrying her to the road where he puts her down.*)

RUTH. (*with a happy laugh*) My, but you're strong!

ROBERT. Come! We'll go and tell them at once.

RUTH. (*dismayed*) Oh, no, don't, Rob, not 'til after I've gone. There'd be bound to be such a scene with them all together.

ROBERT. (*kissing her—gayly*) As you like—little Miss Common Sense!

RUTH. Let's go, then. (*She takes his hand, and they start to go off left.* ROBERT *suddenly stops and turns as though for a last look at the hills and the dying sunset flush.*)

ROBERT. (*looking upward and pointing*) See! The first star. (*He bends down and kisses her tenderly*) Our star!

RUTH. (*in a soft murmur*) Yes. Our very own star. (*They stand for a moment looking up at it, their arms around each other. Then* RUTH *takes his hand again and starts to lead him away*) Come, Rob, let's go. (*His eyes are fixed again on the horizon as he half turns to follow her.* RUTH *urges*) We'll be late for supper, Rob.

ROBERT. (*shakes his head impatiently, as though he were throwing off some disturbing thought—with a laugh*) All right. We'll run then. Come on! (*They run off laughing as the curtain falls.*)

ACT ONE—SCENE TWO

THE *small sitting room of the Mayo farmhouse about nine o'clock same night. On the left, two windows looking out on the fields. Against the wall between the windows, an old-fashioned walnut desk. In the left corner, rear, a sideboard with a mirror. In the rear wall to the right of the sideboard, a window looking out on the road. Next to the window a door leading out into the yard. Farther right, a black horsehair sofa, and another door opening on a bedroom. In the corner, a straight-backed chair. In the right wall, near the middle, an open doorway leading to the kitchen. Farther forward a double-heater stove with coal scuttle, etc. In the center of the newly-carpeted floor, an oak dining-room table with a red cover. In the center of the table, a large oil reading lamp. Four chairs, three rockers with crocheted tidies on their backs, and one straight-backed, are placed about the table. The walls are papered a dark red with a scrolly-figured pattern. Everything in the room is clean, well-kept, and in its exact place, yet*

93

there is no suggestion of primness about the whole. Rather the atmosphere is one of the orderly comfort of a simple, hard-earned prosperity, enjoyed and maintained by the family as a unit.

JAMES MAYO, *his wife, her brother,* CAPTAIN DICK SCOTT, *and* ANDREW *are discovered.* MAYO *is his son* ANDREW *over again in body and face— an* ANDREW *sixty-five years old with a short, square, white beard.* MRS. MAYO *is a slight, round-faced, rather prim-looking woman of fifty-five who had once been a school teacher. The labors of a farmer's wife have bent but not broken her, and she retains a certain refinement of movement and expression foreign to the* MAYO *part of the family. Whatever of resemblance* ROBERT *has to his parents may be traced to her. Her brother, the* CAPTAIN, *is short and stocky, with a weather-beaten, jovial face and a white mustache—a typical old salt, loud of voice and given to gesture. He is fifty-eight years old.*

JAMES MAYO *sits in front of the table. He wears spectacles, and a farm journal which he has been reading lies in his lap. The* CAPTAIN *leans forward from a chair in the rear, his hands on the table in front of him.* ANDREW *is tilted back on the straight-backed chair to the left, his chin sunk forward on his chest, staring at the carpet, preoccupied and frowning.*

As the Curtain rises the CAPTAIN *is just finishing the relation of some sea episode. The others are pretending an interest which is belied by the absent-minded expressions on their faces.*

THE CAPTAIN. (*chuckling*) And that mission woman, she hails me on the dock as I was acomin' ashore, and she says—with her silly face all screwed up serious as judgment—"Captain," she says, "would you be so kind as to tell me where the sea-gulls sleeps at nights?" Blow me if them warn't her exact words! (*He slaps the table with the palms of his hands and laughs loudly. The others force smiles*) Ain't that just like a fool woman's question? And I looks at her serious as I could. "Ma'm," says I, "I couldn't rightly answer that question. I ain't never seed a sea-gull in his bunk yet. The next time I hears one snorin'," I says, "I'll make a note of where he's turned in, and write you a letter 'bout it." And then she calls me a fool real spiteful and tacks away from me quick. (*He laughs again uproariously*) So I got rid of her that way. (*The others smile but immediately relapse into expressions of gloom again.*)

MRS. MAYO. (*absent-mindedly—feeling that she has to say something*) But when it comes to that, where *do* sea-gulls sleep, Dick?

SCOTT. (*slapping the table*) Ho! Ho! Listen to her, James. 'Nother one! Well, if that don't beat all hell—'scuse me for cussin', Kate.

MAYO. (*with a twinkle in his eyes*) They unhitch their wings, Katey, and spreads 'em out on a wave for a bed.

SCOTT. And then they tells the fish to whistle to 'em when it's time to turn out. Ho! Ho!

MRS. MAYO. (*with a forced smile*) You men folks are too smart to live, aren't you? (*She resumes her knitting.* MAYO *pretends to read his paper;* ANDREW *stares at the floor.*)

SCOTT. (*looks from one to the other of them with a puzzled air. Finally he is unable to bear the thick silence a minute longer, and blurts out*) You folks look as if you was settin' up with a corpse. (*With exaggerated concern*) God A'mighty, there ain't anyone dead, be there?

MAYO. (*sharply*) Don't play the dunce, Dick! You know as well as we do there ain't no great cause to be feelin' chipper.

SCOTT. (*argumentatively*) And there ain't no cause to be wearin' mourning, either, I can make out.

MRS. MAYO. (*indignantly*) How can you talk that way, Dick Scott, when you're taking our Robbie away from us, in the middle of the night, you might say, just to get on that old boat of yours on time! I think you might wait until morning when he's had his breakfast.

SCOTT. (*appealing to the others hopelessly*) Ain't that a woman's way o' seein' things for you? God A'mighty, Kate, I can't give orders to the tide that it's got to be high just when it suits me to have it. I ain't gettin' no fun out o' missing sleep and leavin' here at six bells myself.

(*Protestingly*) And the "Sunda" ain't an old ship—leastways, not very old—and she's good's she ever was.

MRS. MAYO. (*her lips trembling*) I wish Robbie weren't going.

MAYO. (*looking at her over his glasses—consolingly*) There, Katey!

MRS. MAYO. (*rebelliously*) Well, I *do* wish he wasn't!

SCOTT. You shouldn't be taking it so hard, 's far as I kin see. This vige'll make a man of him. I'll see to it he learns how to navigate, 'n' study for a mate's c'tificate right off—and it'll give him a trade for the rest of his life, if he wants to travel.

MRS. MAYO. But I don't want him to travel all his life. You've got to see he comes home when this trip is over. Then he'll be all well, and he'll want to—to marry—(ANDREW *sits forward in his chair with an abrupt movement*)—and settle down right here. (*She stares down at the knitting in her lap—after a pause*) I never realized how hard it was going to be for me to have Robbie go—or I wouldn't have considered it a minute.

SCOTT. It ain't no good goin' on that way, Kate, now it's all settled.

MRS. MAYO. (*on the verge of tears*) It's all right for *you* to talk. You've never had any children. You don't know what it means to be parted from them—and Robbie my youngest, too. (ANDREW *frowns and fidgets in his chair.*)

ANDREW. (*suddenly turning to them*) There's one thing none of you seem to take into consideration—that Rob wants to go. He's dead set on it. He's been dreaming over this trip ever since it was first talked about. It wouldn't be fair to him not to have him go. (*A sudden uneasiness seems to strike him*) At least, not if he still feels the same way about it he did when he was talking to me this evening.

MAYO. (*with an air of decision*) Andy's right, Katey. That ends all argyment, you can see that. (*Looking at his big silver watch*) Wonder what's happened to Robert? He's been gone long enough to wheel the widder to home, certain. He can't be out dreamin' at the stars his last night.

MRS. MAYO. (*a bit reproachfully*) Why didn't you wheel Mrs. At-

96

kins back tonight, Andy? You usually do when she and Ruth come over.

ANDREW. (*avoiding her eyes*) I thought maybe Robert wanted to tonight. He offered to go right away when they were leaving.

MRS. MAYO. He only wanted to be polite.

ANDREW. (*gets to his feet*) Well, he'll be right back, I guess. (*He turns to his father*) Guess I'll go take a look at the black cow, Pa—see if she's ailing any.

MAYO. Yes—better had, son. (ANDREW *goes into the kitchen on the right.*)

SCOTT. (*as he goes out—in a low tone*) There's the boy that would make a good, strong sea-farin' man—if he'd a mind to.

MAYO. (*sharply*) Don't you put no such fool notions in Andy's head, Dick—or you 'n' me's goin' to fall out. (*Then he smiles*) You couldn't tempt him, no ways. Andy's a Mayo bred in the bone, and he's a born farmer, and a damn good one, too. He'll live and die right here on this farm, like I expect to. (*With proud confidence*) And he'll make this one of the slickest, best-payin' farms in the state, too, afore he gits through!

SCOTT. Seems to me it's a pretty slick place right now.

MAYO. (*shaking his head*) It's too small. We need more land to make it amount to much, and we ain't got the capital to buy it. (ANDREW *enters from the kitchen. His hat is on, and he carries a lighted lantern in his hand. He goes to the door in the rear leading out.*)

ANDREW. (*opens the door and pauses*) Anything else you can think of to be done, Pa?

MAYO. No, nothin' I know of. (ANDREW *goes out, shutting the door.*)

MRS. MAYO. (*after a pause*) What's come over Andy tonight, I wonder? He acts so strange.

MAYO. He does seem sort o' glum and out of sorts. It's 'count o' Robert leavin', I s'pose. (*To* SCOTT) Dick, you wouldn't believe how them boys o' mine sticks together. They ain't like most brothers.

They've been thick as thieves all their lives, with nary a quarrel I kin remember.

scott. No need to tell me that. I can see how they take to each other.

mrs. mayo. (*pursuing her train of thought*) Did you notice, James, how queer everyone was at supper? Robert seemed stirred up about something; and Ruth was so flustered and giggly; and Andy sat there dumb, looking as if he'd lost his best friend; and all of them only nibbled at their food.

mayo. Guess they was all thinkin' about tomorrow, same as us.

mrs. mayo. (*shaking her head*) No. I'm afraid somethin's happened —somethin' else.

mayo. You mean—'bout Ruth?

mrs. mayo. Yes.

mayo. (*after a pause—frowning*) I hope her and Andy ain't had a serious fallin'-out. I always sorter hoped they'd hitch up together sooner or later. What d'you say, Dick? Don't you think them two'd pair up well?

scott. (*nodding his head approvingly*) A sweet, wholesome couple they'd make.

mayo. It'd be a good thing for Andy in more ways than one. I ain't what you'd call calculatin' generally, and I b'lieve in lettin' young folks run their affairs to suit themselves; but there's advantages for both o' them in this match you can't overlook in reason. The Atkins farm is right next to ourn. Jined together they'd make a jim-dandy of a place, with plenty o' room to work in. And bein' a widder with only a daughter, and laid up all the time to boot, Mrs. Atkins can't do nothin' with the place as it ought to be done. She needs a man, a first-class farmer, to take hold o' things; and Andy's just the one.

mrs. mayo. (*abruptly*) I don't think Ruth loves Andy.

mayo. You don't? Well, maybe a woman's eyes is sharper in such things, but—they're always together. And if she don't love him now, she'll likely come around to it in time. (*As* MRS. MAYO *shakes her head*) You seem mighty fixed in your opinion, Katey. How d'you know?

MRS. MAYO. It's just—what I feel.

MAYO. (*a light breaking over him*) You don't mean to say— (MRS. MAYO *nods.* MAYO *chuckles scornfully*) Shucks! I'm losin' my respect for your eyesight, Katey. Why, Robert ain't got no time for Ruth, 'cept as a friend!

MRS. MAYO. (*warningly*) Sss-h-h! (*The door from the yard opens, and* ROBERT *enters. He is smiling happily, and humming a song to himself, but as he comes into the room an undercurrent of nervous uneasiness manifests itself in his bearing.*)

MAYO. So here you be at last! (ROBERT *comes forward and sits on* ANDY's *chair.* MAYO *smiles slyly at his wife*) What have you been doin' all this time—countin' the stars to see if they all come out right and proper?

ROBERT. There's only one I'll ever look for any more, Pa.

MAYO. (*reproachfully*) You might've even not wasted time lookin' for that one—your last night.

MRS. MAYO. (*as if she were speaking to a child*) You ought to have worn your coat a sharp night like this, Robbie.

SCOTT. (*disgustedly*) God A'mighty, Kate, you treat Robert as if he was one year old!

MRS. MAYO. (*notices* ROBERT'S *nervous uneasiness*) You look all worked up over something, Robbie. What is it?

ROBERT. (*swallowing hard, looks quickly from one to the other of them—then begins determinedly*) Yes, there *is* something—something I must tell you—all of you. (*As he begins to talk* ANDREW *enters quietly from the rear, closing the door behind him, and setting the lighted lantern on the floor. He remains standing by the door, his arms folded, listening to* ROBERT *with a repressed expression of pain on his face.* ROBERT *is so much taken up with what he is going to say that he does not notice* ANDREW's *presence*) Something I discovered only this evening—very beautiful and wonderful—something I did not take

99

into consideration previously because I hadn't dared to hope that such happiness could ever come to me. (*Appealingly*) You must all remember that fact, won't you?

MAYO. (*frowning*) Let's get to the point, son.

ROBERT. (*with a trace of defiance*) Well, the point is this, Pa: I'm not going—I mean—I can't go tomorrow with Uncle Dick—or at any future time, either.

MRS. MAYO. (*with a sharp sigh of joyful relief*) Oh, Robbie, I'm so glad!

MAYO. (*astounded*) You ain't serious, be you, Robert? (*Severely*) Seems to me it's a pretty late hour in the day for you to be upsettin' all your plans so sudden!

ROBERT. I asked you to remember that until this evening I didn't know myself. I had never dared to dream—

MAYO. (*irritably*) What is this foolishness you're talkin' of?

ROBERT. (*flushing*) Ruth told me this evening that—she loved me. It was after I'd confessed I loved her. I told her I hadn't been conscious of my love until after the trip had been arranged, and I realized it would mean—leaving her. That was the truth. I *didn't* know until then. (*As if justifying himself to the others*) I hadn't intended telling her anything but—suddenly—I felt I must. I didn't think it would matter, because I was going away. And I thought she loved—someone else. (*Slowly—his eyes shining*) And then she cried and said it was I she'd loved all the time, but I hadn't seen it.

MRS. MAYO. (*rushes over and throws her arms about him*) I knew it! I was just telling your father when you came in—and, oh, Robbie, I'm so happy you're not going!

ROBERT. (*kissing her*) I knew you'd be glad, Ma.

MAYO. (*bewilderedly*) Well, I'll be damned! You do beat all for gettin' folks' minds all tangled up, Robert. And Ruth too! Whatever got into her of a sudden? Why, I was thinkin'—

MRS. MAYO. (*hurriedly—in a tone of warning*) Never mind what you were thinking, James. It wouldn't be any use telling us that now.

(*Meaningly*) And what you were hoping for turns out just the same almost, doesn't it?

MAYO. (*thoughtfully—beginning to see this side of the argument*) Yes; I suppose you're right, Katey. (*Scratching his head in puzzlement*) But how it ever come about! It do beat anything ever I heard. (*Finally he gets up with a sheepish grin and walks over to* ROBERT) We're glad you ain't goin', your Ma and I, for we'd have missed you terrible, that's certain and sure; and we're glad you've found happiness. Ruth's a fine girl and'll make a good wife to you.

ROBERT. (*much moved*) Thank you, Pa. (*He grips his father's hand in his.*)

ANDREW. (*his face tense and drawn comes forward and holds out his hand, forcing a smile*) I guess it's my turn to offer congratulations, isn't it?

ROBERT. (*with a startled cry when his brother appears before him so suddenly*) Andy! (*Confused*) Why—I—I didn't see you. Were you here when—

ANDREW. I heard everything you said; and here's wishing you every happiness, you and Ruth. You both deserve the best there is.

ROBERT. (*taking his hand*) Thanks, Andy, it's fine of you to— (*His voice dies away as he sees the pain in* ANDREW's *eyes.*)

ANDREW. (*giving his brother's hand a final grip*) Good luck to you both! (*He turns away and goes back to the rear where he bends over the lantern, fumbling with it to hide his emotion from the others.*)

MRS. MAYO. (*to the* CAPTAIN, *who has been too flabbergasted by* ROBERT's *decision to say a word*) What's the matter, Dick? Aren't you going to congratulate Robbie?

SCOTT. (*embarrassed*) Of course I be! (*He gets to his feet and shakes* ROBERT's *hand, muttering a vague*) Luck to you, boy. (*He stands beside* ROBERT *as if he wanted to say something more but doesn't know how to go about it.*)

ROBERT. Thanks, Uncle Dick.

scott. So you're not acomin' on the "Sunda" with me? (*His voice indicates disbelief.*)

robert. I can't, Uncle—not now. I wouldn't miss it for anything in the world under any other circumstances. (*He sighs unconsciously*) But you see I've found—a bigger dream. (*Then with joyous high spirits*) I want you all to understand one thing—I'm not going to be a loafer on your hands any longer. This means the beginning of a new life for me in every way. I'm going to settle right down and take a real interest in the farm, and do my share. I'll prove to you, Pa, that I'm as good a Mayo as you are—or Andy, when I want to be.

mayo. (*kindly but skeptically*) That's the right spirit, Robert. Ain't none of us doubts your willin'ness, but you ain't never learned—

robert. Then I'm going to start learning right away, and you'll teach me, won't you?

mayo. (*mollifyingly*) Of course I will, boy, and be glad to, only you'd best go easy at first.

scott. (*who has listened to this conversation in mingled consternation and amazement*) You don't mean to tell me you're going to let him stay, do you, James?

mayo. Why, things bein' as they be, Robert's free to do as he's a mind to.

mrs. mayo. *Let him!* The very idea!

scott. (*more and more ruffled*) Then all I got to say is, you're a soft, weak-willed critter to be permittin' a boy—and women, too—to be layin' your course for you wherever they damn pleases.

mayo. (*slyly amused*) It's just the same with me as 'twas with you, Dick. You can't order the tides on the seas to suit you, and I ain't pretendin' I can reg'late love for young folks.

scott. (*scornfully*) Love! They ain't old enough to know love when they sight it! Love! I'm ashamed of you, Robert, to go lettin' a little huggin' and kissin' in the dark spile your chances to make a man out o' yourself. It ain't common sense—no siree, it ain't—not by a hell of a sight! (*He pounds the table with his fists in exasperation.*)

MRS. MAYO. (*laughing provokingly at her brother*) A fine one you
are to be talking about love, Dick—an old cranky bachelor like you.
Goodness sakes!

SCOTT. (*exasperated by their joking*) I've never been a damn fool like
most, if that's what you're steerin' at.

MRS. MAYO. (*tauntingly*) Sour grapes, aren't they, Dick? (*She laughs.
ROBERT and his father chuckle.* SCOTT *sputters with annoyance*) Good
gracious, Dick, you do act silly, flying into a temper over nothing.

SCOTT. (*indignantly*) Nothin'! You talk as if I wasn't concerned
nohow in this here business. Seems to me I've got a right to have my
say. Ain't I made all arrangements with the owners and stocked up
with some special grub all on Robert's account?

ROBERT. You've been fine, Uncle Dick; and I appreciate it. Truly.

MAYO. 'Course; we all does, Dick.

SCOTT. (*unplacated*) I've been countin' sure on havin' Robert for
company on this vige—to sorta talk to and show things to, and teach,
kinda, and I got my mind so set on havin' him I'm goin' to be double
lonesome this vige. (*He pounds on the table, attempting to cover up
this confession of weakness*) Darn all this silly lovin' business, anyway. (*Irritably*) But all this talk ain't tellin' me what I'm to do with
that sta'b'd cabin I fixed up. It's all painted white, an' a bran new
mattress on the bunk, 'n' new sheets 'n' blankets 'n' things. And Chips
built in a book-case so's Robert could take his books along—with a
slidin' bar fixed across't it, mind, so's they couldn't fall out no matter
how she rolled. (*With excited consternation*) What d'you suppose
my officers is goin' to think when there's no one comes aboard to oc-
cupy that sta'b'd cabin? And the men what did the work on it—
what'll *they* think? (*He shakes his finger indignantly*) They're liable
as not to suspicion it was a *woman* I'd planned to ship along, and that
she gave me the go-by at the last moment! (*He wipes his perspiring
brow in anguish at this thought*) Gawd A'mighty! They're only
lookin' to have the laugh on me for something like that. They're liable
to b'lieve anything, those fellers is!

MAYO. (*with a wink*) Then there's nothing to it but for you to get right out and hunt up a wife somewheres for that spick 'n' span cabin. She'll have to be a pretty one, too, to match it. (*He looks at his watch with exaggerated concern*) You ain't got much time to find her, Dick.

SCOTT. (*as the others smile—sulkily*) You kin go to thunder, Jim Mayo!

ANDREW. (*comes forward from where he has been standing by the door, rear, brooding. His face is set in a look of grim determination*) You needn't worry about that spare cabin, Uncle Dick, if you've a mind to take me in Robert's place.

ROBERT. (*turning to him quickly*) Andy! (*He sees at once the fixed resolve in his brother's eyes, and realizes immediately the reason for it—in consternation*) Andy, you mustn't!

ANDREW. You've made your decision, Rob, and now I've made mine. You're out of this, remember.

ROBERT. (*hurt by his brother's tone*) But Andy—

ANDREW. Don't interfere, Rob—that's all I ask. (*Turning to his uncle*) You haven't answered my question, Uncle Dick.

SCOTT. (*clearing his throat, with an uneasy side glance at* JAMES MAYO *who is staring at his elder son as if he thought he had suddenly gone mad*) O' course, I'd be glad to have you, Andy.

ANDREW. It's settled then. I can pack the little I want to take in a few minutes.

MRS. MAYO. Don't be a fool, Dick. Andy's only joking you.

SCOTT. (*disgruntedly*) It's hard to tell who's jokin' and who's not in this house.

ANDREW. (*firmly*) I'm not joking, Uncle Dick. (*As* SCOTT *looks at him uncertainly*) You needn't be afraid I'll go back on my word.

ROBERT. (*hurt by the insinuation he feels in* ANDREW's *tone*) Andy! That isn't fair!

MAYO. (*frowning*) Seems to me this ain't no subject to joke over— not for Andy.

104

ANDREW. (*facing his father*) I agree with you, Pa, and I tell you again, once and for all, that I've made up my mind to go.

MAYO. (*dumbfounded—unable to doubt the determination in* AN-DREW's *voice—helplessly*) But why, son? Why?

ANDREW. (*evasively*) I've always wanted to go.

ROBERT. Andy!

ANDREW. (*half angrily*) You shut up, Rob! (*Turning to his father again*) I didn't ever mention it because as long as Rob was going I knew it was no use; but now Rob's staying on here, there isn't any reason for me not to go.

MAYO. (*breathing hard*) No reason? Can you stand there and say that to me, Andrew?

MRS. MAYO. (*hastily—seeing the gathering storm*) He doesn't mean a word of it, James.

MAYO. (*making a gesture to her to keep silence*) Let me talk, Katey. (*In a more kindly tone*) What's come over you so sudden, Andy? You know's well as I do that it wouldn't be fair o' you to run off at a moment's notice right now when we're up to our necks in hard work.

ANDREW. (*avoiding his eyes*) Rob'll hold his end up as soon as he learns.

MAYO. Robert was never cut out for a farmer, and you was.

ANDREW. You can easily get a man to do my work.

MAYO. (*restraining his anger with an effort*) It sounds strange to hear you, Andy, that I always thought had good sense, talkin' crazy like that. (*Scornfully*) Get a man to take your place! You ain't been workin' here for no hire, Andy, that you kin give me your notice to quit like you've done. The farm is your'n as well as mine. You've always worked on it with that understanding; and what you're sayin' you intend doin' is just skulkin' out o' your rightful responsibility.

ANDREW. (*looking at the floor—simply*) I'm sorry, Pa. (*After a slight pause*) It's no use talking any more about it.

MRS. MAYO. (*in relief*) There! I knew Andy'd come to his senses!

ANDREW. Don't get the wrong idea, Ma. I'm not backing out.

MAYO. You mean you're goin' in spite of—everythin'?

ANDREW. Yes. I'm going. I've got to. (*He looks at his father defiantly*) I feel I oughtn't to miss this chance to go out into the world and see things, and—I want to go.

MAYO. (*with bitter scorn*) So—you want to go out into the world and see thin's? (*His voice raised and quivering with anger*) I never thought I'd live to see the day when a son o' mine'd look me in the face and tell a bare-faced lie! (*Bursting out*) You're a liar, Andy Mayo, and a mean one to boot!

MRS. MAYO. James!

ROBERT. Pa!

SCOTT. Steady there, Jim!

MAYO. (*waving their protests aside*) He is and he knows it.

ANDREW. (*his face flushed*) I won't argue with you, Pa. You can think as badly of me as you like.

MAYO. (*shaking his finger at* ANDY, *in a cold rage*) You know I'm speakin' truth—that's why you're afraid to argy! You lie when you say you want to go 'way—and see thin's! You ain't got no likin' in the world to go. I've watched you grow up, and I know your ways, and they're my ways. You're runnin' against your own nature, and you're goin' to be a'mighty sorry for it if you do. 'S if I didn't know your real reason for runnin' away! And runnin' away's the only words to fit it. You're runnin' away 'cause you're put out and riled 'cause your own brother's got Ruth 'stead o' you, and—

ANDREW. (*his face crimson—tensely*) Stop, Pa! I won't stand hearing that—not even from you!

MRS. MAYO. (*rushing to* ANDY *and putting her arms about him protectingly*) Don't mind him, Andy dear. He don't mean a word he's saying! (ROBERT *stands rigidly, his hands clenched, his face contracted by pain.* SCOTT *sits dumbfounded and open-mouthed.* ANDREW *soothes his mother who is on the verge of tears.*)

MAYO. (*in angry triumph*) It's the truth, Andy Mayo! And you ought to be bowed in shame to think of it!

106

ROBERT. (*protestingly*) Pa!

MRS. MAYO. (*coming from* ANDREW *to his father; puts her hands on his shoulders as though to try to push him back in the chair from which he has risen*) Won't you be still, James? Please won't you?

MAYO. (*looking at* ANDREW *over his wife's shoulder—stubbornly*) The truth—God's truth!

MRS. MAYO. Sh-h-h! (*She tries to put a finger across his lips, but he twists his head away.*)

ANDREW. (*who has regained control over himself*) You're wrong, Pa, it isn't truth. (*With defiant assertiveness*) I don't love Ruth. I never loved her, and the thought of such a thing never entered my head.

MAYO. (*with an angry snort of disbelief*) Hump! You're pilin' lie on lie.

ANDREW. (*losing his temper—bitterly*) I suppose it'd be hard for you to explain anyone's wanting to leave this blessed farm except for some outside reason like that. But I'm sick and tired of it—whether you want to believe me or not—and that's why I'm glad to get a chance to move on.

ROBERT. Andy! Don't! You're only making it worse.

ANDREW. (*sulkily*) I don't care. I've done my share of work here. I've earned my right to quit when I want to. (*Suddenly overcome with anger and grief; with rising intensity*) I'm sick and tired of the whole damn business. I hate the farm and every inch of ground in it. I'm sick of digging in the dirt and sweating in the sun like a slave without getting a word of thanks for it. (*Tears of rage starting to his eyes—hoarsely*) I'm through, through for good and all; and if Uncle Dick won't take me on his ship, I'll find another. I'll get away somewhere, somehow.

MRS. MAYO. (*in a frightened voice*) Don't you answer him, James. He doesn't know what he's saying. Don't say a word to him 'til he's in his right senses again. Please James, don't—

MAYO. (*pushes her away from him; his face is drawn and pale with the violence of his passion. He glares at* ANDREW *as if he hated him*) You dare to—you dare to speak like that to me? You talk like that 'bout this farm—the Mayo farm—where you was born—you—you— (*He clenches his fist above his head and advances threateningly on* ANDREW) You damned whelp!

MRS. MAYO. (*with a shriek*) James! (*She covers her face with her hands and sinks weakly into* MAYO's *chair.* ANDREW *remains standing motionless, his face pale and set.*)

SCOTT. (*starting to his feet and stretching his arms across the table toward* MAYO) Easy there, Jim!

ROBERT. (*throwing himself between father and brother*) Stop! Are you mad?

MAYO. (*grabs* ROBERT's *arm and pushes him aside—then stands for a moment gasping for breath before* ANDREW. *He points to the door with a shaking finger*) Yes—go!—go!— You're no son o' mine—no son o' mine! You can go to hell if you want to! Don't let me find you here—in the mornin'—or—or—I'll *throw* you out!

ROBERT. Pa! For God's sake! (MRS. MAYO *bursts into noisy sobbing.*)

MAYO. (*he gulps convulsively and glares at* ANDREW) You go—to-morrow mornin'—and by God—don't come back—don't dare come back—by God, not while I'm livin'—or I'll—I'll— (*He shakes over his muttered threat and strides toward the door rear, right.*)

MRS. MAYO. (*rising and throwing her arms around him—hysterically*) James! James! Where are you going?

MAYO. (*incoherently*) I'm goin'—to bed, Katey. It's late, Katey—it's late. (*He goes out.*)

MRS. MAYO. (*following him, pleading hysterically*) James! Take back what you've said to Andy. James! (*She follows him out.* ROBERT *and the* CAPTAIN *stare after them with horrified eyes.* ANDREW *stands rigidly looking straight in front of him, his fists clenched at his sides.*)

SCOTT. (*the first to find his voice—with an explosive sigh*) Well, if he ain't the devil himself when he's roused! You oughtn't to have talked to him that way, Andy, 'bout the damn farm, knowin' how touchy he is about it. (*With another sigh*) Well, you won't mind what he's said in anger. He'll be sorry for it when he's calmed down a bit.

ANDREW. (*in a dead voice*) You don't know him. (*Defiantly*) What's said is said and can't be unsaid; and I've chosen.

ROBERT. (*with violent protest*) Andy! You can't go! This is all so stupid—and terrible!

ANDREW. (*coldly*) I'll talk to you in a minute, Rob. (*Crushed by his brother's attitude* ROBERT *sinks down into a chair, holding his head in his hands.*)

SCOTT. (*comes and slaps* ANDREW *on the back*) I'm damned glad you're shippin' on, Andy. I like your spirit, and the way you spoke up to him. (*Lowering his voice to a cautious whisper*) The sea's the place for a young feller like you that isn't half dead 'n' alive. (*He gives* ANDY *a final approving slap*) You 'n' me'll get along like twins, see if we don't. I'm goin' aloft to turn in. Don't forget to pack your dunnage. And git some sleep, if you kin. We'll want to sneak out extra early b'fore they're up. It'll do away with more argyments. Robert can drive us down to the town, and bring back the team. (*He goes to the door in the rear, left*) Well, good night.

ANDREW. Good night. (SCOTT *goes out. The two brothers remain silent for a moment. Then* ANDREW *comes over to his brother and puts a hand on his back. He speaks in a low voice, full of feeling*) Buck up, Rob. It ain't any use crying over spilt milk; and it'll all turn out for the best—let's hope. It couldn't be helped—what's happened.

ROBERT. (*wildly*) But it's a lie, Andy, a lie!

ANDREW. Of course it's a lie. You know it and I know it,—but that's all ought to know it.

ROBERT. Pa'll never forgive you. Oh, the whole affair is so senseless —and tragic. Why did you think you must go away?

ANDREW. You know better than to ask that. You know why. (*Fiercely*) I can wish you and Ruth all the good luck in the world, and I do, and I mean it; but you can't expect me to stay around here and watch you two together, day after day—and me alone. I couldn't stand it—not after all the plans I'd made to happen on this place thinking—(*His voice breaks*) thinking she cared for me.

ROBERT. (*putting a hand on his brother's arm*) God! It's horrible! I feel so guilty—to think that I should be the cause of your suffering, after we've been such pals all our lives. If I could have foreseen what'd happen, I swear to you I'd have never said a word to Ruth. I swear I wouldn't have, Andy!

ANDREW. I know you wouldn't; and that would've been worse, for Ruth would've suffered then. (*He pats his brother's shoulder*) It's best as it is. It had to be, and I've got to stand the gaff, that's all. Pa'll see how I felt—after a time. (*As* ROBERT *shakes his head*)—and if he don't—well, it can't be helped.

ROBERT. But think of Ma! God, Andy, you can't go! You can't!

ANDREW. (*fiercely*) I've got to go—to get away! I've got to, I tell you. I'd go crazy here, bein' reminded every second of the day what a fool I'd made of myself. I've got to get away and try and forget, if I can. And I'd hate the farm if I stayed, hate it for bringin' things back. I couldn't take interest in the work any more, work with no purpose in sight. Can't you see what a hell it'd be? You love her too, Rob. Put yourself in my place, and remember I haven't stopped loving her, and couldn't if I was to stay. Would that be fair to you or to her? Put yourself in my place. (*He shakes his brother fiercely by the shoulder*) What'd you do then? Tell me the truth! You love her. What'd you do?

ROBERT. (*chokingly*) I'd—I'd go, Andy! (*He buries his face in his hands with a shuddering sob*) God!

ANDREW. (*seeming to relax suddenly all over his body—in a low, steady voice*) Then you know why I got to go; and there's nothing more to be said.

ROBERT. (*in a frenzy of rebellion*) Why did this have to happen to us? It's damnable! (*He looks about him wildly, as if his vengeance were seeking the responsible fate.*)

ANDREW. (*soothingly—again putting his hands on his brother's shoulder*) It's no use fussing any more, Rob. It's done. (*Forcing a smile*) I guess Ruth's got a right to have who she likes. She made a good choice—and God bless her for it!

ROBERT. Andy! Oh, I wish I could tell you half I feel of how fine you are!

ANDREW. (*interrupting him quickly*) Shut up! Let's go to bed. I've got to be up long before sun-up. You, too, if you're going to drive us down.

ROBERT. Yes. Yes.

ANDREW. (*turning down the lamp*) And I've got to pack yet. (*He yawns with utter weariness*) I'm as tired as if I'd been plowing twenty-four hours at a stretch. (*Dully*) I feel—dead. (ROBERT *covers his face again with his hands.* ANDREW *shakes his head as if to get rid of his thoughts, and continues with a poor attempt at cheery briskness*) I'm going to douse the light. Come on. (*He slaps his brother on the back.* ROBERT *does not move.* ANDREW *bends over and blows out the lamp. His voice comes from the darkness*) Don't sit there mourning, Rob. It'll all come out in the wash. Come and get some sleep. Everything'll turn out all right in the end. (ROBERT *can be heard stumbling to his feet, and the dark figures of the two brothers can be seen groping their way toward the doorway in the rear as the curtain falls.*)

ACT TWO—SCENE ONE

S AME *as Act One, Scene Two. Sitting room of the farmhouse about half past twelve in the afternoon of a hot, sun-baked day in mid-summer, three years later. All the windows are open, but no breeze stirs the soiled white curtains. A patched screen door is in the rear. Through it the yard can be seen, its small stretch of lawn divided by the dirt path leading to the door from the gate in the white picket fence which borders the road.*

The room has changed, not so much in its outward appearance as in its general atmosphere. Little significant details give evidence of carelessness, of inefficiency, of an industry gone to seed. The chairs appear shabby from lack of paint; the table cover is spotted and askew; holes show in the curtains; a child's doll, with one arm gone, lies under the table; a hoe stands in a corner; a man's coat is flung on the couch in the rear; the desk is cluttered up with odds and ends; a number of books are piled carelessly on the sideboard. The noon enervation of the sultry, scorching day seems to have penetrated indoors, causing even inanimate objects to wear an aspect of despondent exhaustion.

A place is set at the end of the table, left, for someone's dinner. Through the open door to the kitchen comes the clatter of dishes being washed, interrupted at intervals by a woman's irritated voice and the peevish whining of a child.

At the rise of the curtain MRS. MAYO *and* MRS. ATKINS *are discovered sitting facing each other,* MRS. MAYO *to the rear,* MRS. ATKINS *to the right of the table.* MRS. MAYO's *face has lost all character, disintegrated, become a weak mask wearing a helpless, doleful expression of being constantly on the verge of comfortless tears. She speaks in an uncertain voice, without assertiveness, as if all power of willing had deserted her.* MRS. ATKINS *is in her wheel chair. She is a thin, pale-faced, unintelligent-looking woman of about forty-eight, with hard, bright eyes.*

*A victim of partial paralysis for many years, condemned to be pushed
from day to day of her life in a wheel chair, she has developed the selfish, irritable nature of the chronic invalid. Both women are dressed
in black.* MRS. ATKINS *knits nervously as she talks. A ball of unused
yarn, with needles stuck through it, lies on the table before* MRS. MAYO.

MRS. ATKINS. (*with a disapproving glance at the place set on the
table*) Robert's late for his dinner again, as usual. I don't see why Ruth
puts up with it, and I've told her so. Many's the time I've said to her,
"It's about time you put a stop to his nonsense. Does he suppose you're
runnin' a hotel—with no one to help with things?" But she don't pay
no attention. She's as bad as he is, a'most—thinks she knows better
than an old, sick body like me.

MRS. MAYO. (*dully*) Robbie's always late for things. He can't help
it, Sarah.

MRS. ATKINS. (*with a snort*) Can't help it! How you do go on, Kate,
findin' excuses for him! Anybody can help anything they've a mind
to—as long as they've got health, and ain't rendered helpless like me
— (*She adds as a pious afterthought*)—through the will of God.

MRS. MAYO. Robbie can't.

MRS. ATKINS. Can't! It do make me mad, Kate Mayo, to see folks that
God gave all the use of their limbs to potterin' round and wastin'
time doin' everything the wrong way—and me powerless to help
and at their mercy, you might say. And it ain't that I haven't pointed
the right way to 'em. I've talked to Robert thousands of times and
told him how things ought to be done. You know that, Kate Mayo.
But d'you s'pose he takes any notice of what I say? Or Ruth, either—
my own daughter? No, they think I'm a crazy, cranky old woman,
half dead a'ready, and the sooner I'm in the grave and out o' their
way the better it'd suit them.

MRS. MAYO. You mustn't talk that way, Sarah. They're not as wicked
as that. And you've got years and years before you.

MRS. ATKINS. You're like the rest, Kate. You don't know how near the end I am. Well, at least I can go to my eternal rest with a clear conscience. I've done all a body could do to avert ruin from this house. On their heads be it!

MRS. MAYO. (*with hopeless indifference*) Things might be worse. Robert never had any experience in farming. You can't expect him to learn in a day.

MRS. ATKINS. (*snappily*) He's had three years to learn, and he's gettin' worse 'stead of better. Not on'y your place but mine too is driftin' to rack and ruin, and I can't do nothin' to prevent.

MRS. MAYO. (*with a spark of assertiveness*) You can't say but Robbie works hard, Sarah.

MRS. ATKINS. What good's workin' hard if it don't accomplish anythin', I'd like to know?

MRS. MAYO. Robbie's had bad luck against him.

MRS. ATKINS. Say what you've a mind to, Kate, the proof of the puddin's in the eatin'; and you can't deny that things have been goin' from bad to worse ever since your husband died two years back.

MRS. MAYO. (*wiping tears from her eyes with her handkerchief*) It was God's will that he should be taken.

MRS. ATKINS. (*triumphantly*) It was God's punishment on James Mayo for the blasphemin' and denyin' of God he done all his sinful life! (MRS. MAYO *begins to weep softly*) There, Kate, I shouldn't be remindin' you, I know. He's at peace, poor man, and forgiven, let's pray.

MRS. MAYO. (*wiping her eyes—simply*) James was a good man.

MRS. ATKINS. (*ignoring this remark*) What I was sayin' was that since Robert's been in charge things've been goin' down hill steady. You don't know *how* bad they are. Robert don't let on to you what's happenin'; and you'd never see it yourself if 'twas under your nose. But, thank the Lord, Ruth still comes to me once in a while for advice when she's worried near out of her senses by his goin's-on. Do you know what she told me last night? But I forgot, she said not to tell you—still I think you've got a right to know, and it's my duty not to let such things go on behind your back.

MRS. MAYO. (*wearily*) You can tell me if you want to.

MRS. ATKINS. (*bending over toward her—in a low voice*) Ruth was almost crazy about it. Robert told her he'd have to mortgage the farm —said he didn't know how he'd pull through 'til harvest without it, and he can't get money any other way. (*She straightens up—indignantly*) Now what do you think of your Robert?

MRS. MAYO. (*resignedly*) If it has to be—

MRS. ATKINS. You don't mean to say you're goin' to sign away your farm, Kate Mayo—after me warnin' you?

MRS. MAYO. I'll do what Robbie says is needful.

MRS. ATKINS. (*holding up her hands*) Well, of all the foolishness!— well, it's your farm, not mine, and I've nothin' more to say.

MRS. MAYO. Maybe Robbie'll manage till Andy gets back and sees to things. It can't be long now.

MRS. ATKINS. (*with keen interest*) Ruth says Andy ought to turn up any day. When does Robert figger he'll get here?

MRS. MAYO. He says he can't calculate exactly on account o' the "Sunda" being a sail boat. Last letter he got was from England, the day they were sailing for home. That was over a month ago, and Robbie thinks they're overdue now.

MRS. ATKINS. We can give praise to God then that he'll be back in the nick o' time. He ought to be tired of travelin' and anxious to get home and settle down to work again.

MRS. MAYO. Andy *has* been working. He's head officer on Dick's boat, he wrote Robbie. You know that.

MRS. ATKINS. That foolin' on ships is all right for a spell, but he must be right sick of it by this.

MRS. MAYO. (*musingly*) I wonder if he's changed much. He used to be so fine-looking and strong. (*With a sigh*) Three years! It seems more like three hundred. (*Her eyes filling—piteously*) Oh, if James could only have lived 'til he came back—and forgiven him!

MRS. ATKINS. He never would have—not James Mayo! Didn't he keep his heart hardened against him till the last in spite of all you and Robert did to soften him?

MRS. MAYO. (*with a feeble flash of anger*) Don't you dare say that! (*Brokenly*) Oh, I know deep down in his heart he forgave Andy, though he was too stubborn ever to own up to it. It was that brought on his death—breaking his heart just on account of his stubborn pride. (*She wipes her eyes with her handkerchief and sobs.*)

MRS. ATKINS. (*piously*) It was the will of God. (*The whining crying of the child sounds from the kitchen.* MRS. ATKINS *frowns irritably*) Drat that young one! Seems as if she cries all the time on purpose to set a body's nerves on edge.

MRS. MAYO. (*wiping her eyes*) It's the heat upsets her. Mary doesn't feel any too well these days, poor little child!

MRS. ATKINS. She gets it right from her Pa—bein' sickly all the time. You can't deny Robert was always ailin' as a child. (*She sighs heavily*) It was a crazy mistake for them two to get married. I argyed against it at the time, but Ruth was so spelled with Robert's wild poetry notions she wouldn't listen to sense. Andy was the one would have been the match for her.

MRS. MAYO. I've often thought since it might have been better the other way. But Ruth and Robbie seem happy enough together.

MRS. ATKINS. At any rate it was God's work—and His will be done. (*The two women sit in silence for a moment.* RUTH *enters from the kitchen, carrying in her arms her two-year-old daughter,* MARY, *a pretty but sickly and anemic-looking child with a tear-stained face.* RUTH *has aged appreciably. Her face has lost its youth and freshness. There is a trace in her expression of something hard and spiteful. She sits in the rocker in front of the table and sighs wearily. She wears a gingham dress with a soiled apron tied around her waist.*)

RUTH. Land sakes, if this isn't a scorcher! That kitchen's like a furnace. Phew! (*She pushes the damp hair back from her forehead.*)

MRS. MAYO. Why didn't you call me to help with the dishes?

RUTH. (*shortly*) No. The heat in there'd kill you.

MARY. (*sees the doll under the table and struggles on her mother's lap*) Dolly, Mama! Dolly!

RUTH. (*pulling her back*) It's time for your nap. You can't play with Dolly now.

MARY. (*commencing to cry whiningly*) Dolly!

MRS. ATKINS. (*irritably*) Can't you keep that child still? Her racket's enough to split a body's ears. Put her down and let her play with the doll if it'll quiet her.

RUTH. (*lifting* MARY *to the floor*) There! I hope you'll be satisfied and keep still. (MARY *sits down on the floor before the table and plays with the doll in silence.* RUTH *glances at the place set on the table*) It's a wonder Rob wouldn't try to get to meals on time once in a while.

MRS. MAYO. (*dully*) Something must have gone wrong again.

RUTH. (*wearily*) I s'pose so. Something's always going wrong these days, it looks like.

MRS. ATKINS. (*snappily*) It wouldn't if you possessed a bit of spunk. The idea of you permittin' him to come in to meals at all hours— and you doin' the work! I never heard of such a thin'. You're too easy goin', that's the trouble.

RUTH. Do stop your nagging at me, Ma! I'm sick of hearing you. I'll do as I please about it; and thank you for not interfering. (*She wipes her moist forehead—wearily*) Phew! It's too hot to argue. Let's talk of something pleasant. (*Curiously*) Didn't I hear you speaking about Andy a while ago?

MRS. MAYO. We were wondering when he'd get home.

RUTH. (*brightening*) Rob says any day now he's liable to drop in and surprise us—him and the Captain. It'll certainly look natural to see him around the farm again.

MRS. ATKINS. Let's hope the farm'll look more natural, too, when he's had a hand at it. The way thin's are now!

RUTH. (*irritably*) Will you stop harping on that, Ma? We all know things aren't as they might be. What's the good of your complaining all the time?

MRS. ATKINS. There, Kate Mayo! Ain't that just what I told you? I can't say a word of advice to my own daughter even, she's that stubborn and self-willed.

RUTH. (*putting her hands over her ears—in exasperation*) For goodness sakes, Ma!

MRS. MAYO. (*dully*) Never mind. Andy'll fix everything when he comes.

RUTH. (*hopefully*) Oh, yes, I know he will. He always did know just the right thing ought to be done. (*With weary vexation*) It's a shame for him to come home and have to start in with things in such a topsy-turvy.

MRS. MAYO. Andy'll manage.

RUTH. (*sighing*) I s'pose it isn't Rob's fault things go wrong with him.

MRS. ATKINS. (*scornfully*) Hump! (*She fans herself nervously*) Land o' Goshen, but it's bakin' in here! Let's go out in under the trees in back where there's a breath of fresh air. Come, Kate. (MRS. MAYO *gets up obediently and starts to wheel the invalid's chair toward the screen door*) You better come too, Ruth. It'll do you good. Learn him a lesson and let him get his own dinner. Don't be such a fool.

RUTH. (*going and holding the screen door open for them—listlessly*) He wouldn't mind. He doesn't eat much. But I can't go anyway. I've got to put baby to bed.

MRS. ATKINS. Let's go, Kate. I'm boilin' in here. (MRS. MAYO *wheels her out and off left.* RUTH *comes back and sits down in her chair.*)

RUTH. (*mechanically*) Come and let me take off your shoes and stockings, Mary, that's a good girl. You've got to take your nap now. (*The child continues to play as if she hadn't heard, absorbed in her doll. An eager expression comes over* RUTH's *tired face. She glances toward the door furtively—then gets up and goes to the desk. Her movements indicate a guilty fear of discovery. She takes a letter from a pigeon-hole and retreats swiftly to her chair with it. She opens the envelope and reads the letter with great interest, a flush of excitement coming to her cheeks.* ROBERT *walks up the path and opens the screen door quietly and comes into the room. He, too, has aged. His shoulders are stooped as if under too great a burden. His eyes are dull and lifeless, his face burned by the sun and unshaven for days. Streaks of sweat have smudged the layer of dust on his cheeks. His lips drawn down at the corners give him a hopeless, resigned expression. The three years have accentuated the weakness of his mouth and chin. He is dressed in overalls, laced boots, and a flannel shirt open at the neck.*)

ROBERT. (*throwing his hat over on the sofa—with a great sigh of exhaustion*) Phew! The sun's hot today! (RUTH *is startled. At first she makes an instinctive motion as if to hide the letter in her bosom. She immediately thinks better of this and sits with the letter in her hands looking at him with defiant eyes. He bends down and kisses her.*)

RUTH. (*feeling of her cheek—irritably*) Why don't you shave? You look awful.

ROBERT. (*indifferently*) I forgot—and it's too much trouble this weather.

MARY. (*throwing aside her doll, runs to him with a happy cry*) Dada! Dada!

ROBERT. (*swinging her up above his head—lovingly*) And how's this little girl of mine this hot day, eh?

MARY. (*screeching happily*) Dada! Dada!

RUTH. (*in annoyance*) Don't do that to her! You know it's time for her nap and you'll get her all waked up; then I'll be the one that'll have to sit beside her till she falls asleep.

ROBERT. (*sitting down in the chair on the left of table and cuddling* MARY *on his lap*) You needn't bother. I'll put her to bed.

RUTH. (*shortly*) You've got to get back to your work, I s'pose.

ROBERT. (*with a sigh*) Yes, I was forgetting. (*He glances at the open letter on* RUTH's *lap*) Reading Andy's letter again? I should think you'd know it by heart by this time.

119

RUTH. (*coloring as if she'd been accused of something—defiantly*) I've got a right to read it, haven't I? He says it's meant for all of us.

ROBERT. (*with a trace of irritation*) Right? Don't be so silly. There's no question of right. I was only saying that you must know all that's in it after so many readings.

RUTH. Well, I don't. (*She puts the letter on the table and gets wearily to her feet*) I s'pose you'll be wanting your dinner now.

ROBERT. (*listlessly*) I don't care. I'm not hungry.

RUTH. And here I been keeping it hot for you!

ROBERT. (*irritably*) Oh, all right then. Bring it in and I'll try to eat.

RUTH. I've got to get her to bed first. (*She goes to lift* MARY *off his lap*) Come, dear. It's after time and you can hardly keep your eyes open now.

MARY. (*crying*) No, no! (*Appealing to her father*) Dada! No!

RUTH. (*accusingly to* ROBERT) There! Now see what you've done! I told you not to—

ROBERT. (*shortly*) Let her alone, then. She's all right where she is. She'll fall asleep on my lap in a minute if you'll stop bothering her.

RUTH. (*hotly*) She'll not do any such thing! She's got to learn to mind me! (*Shaking her finger at* MARY) You naughty child! Will you come with Mama when she tells you for your own good?

MARY. (*clinging to her father*) No, Dada!

RUTH. (*losing her temper*) A good spanking's what you need, my young lady—and you'll get one from me if you don't mind better, d'you hear? (MARY *starts to whimper frightenedly.*)

ROBERT. (*with sudden anger*) Leave her alone! How often have I told you not to threaten her with whipping? I won't have it. (*Soothing the wailing* MARY) There! There, little girl! Baby mustn't cry. Dada won't like you if you do. Dada'll hold you and you must promise to go to sleep like a good little girl. Will you when Dada asks you?

MARY. (*cuddling up to him*) Yes, Dada.

RUTH. (*looking at them, her pale face set and drawn*) A fine one you are to be telling folks how to do things! (*She bites her lips. Hus-*

band and wife look into each other's eyes with something akin to hatred in their expressions; then RUTH *turns away with a shrug of affected indifference*) All right, take care of her then, if you think it's so easy. (*She walks away into the kitchen.*)

ROBERT. (*smoothing* MARY's *hair—tenderly*) We'll show Mama you're a good little girl, won't we?

MARY. (*crooning drowsily*) Dada, Dada.

ROBERT. Let's see: Does your mother take off your shoes and stockings before your nap?

MARY. (*nodding with half-shut eyes*) Yes, Dada.

ROBERT. (*taking off her shoes and stockings*) We'll show Mama we know how to do those things, won't we? There's one old shoe off— and there's the other old shoe—and here's one old stocking—and there's the other old stocking. There we are, all nice and cool and comfy. (*He bends down and kisses her*) And now will you promise to go right to sleep if Dada takes you to bed? (MARY *nods sleepily*) That's the good little girl. (*He gathers her up in his arms carefully and carries her into the bedroom. His voice can be heard faintly as he lulls the child to sleep.* RUTH *comes out of the kitchen and gets the plate from the table. She hears the voice from the room and tiptoes to the door to look in. Then she starts for the kitchen but stands for a moment thinking, a look of ill-concealed jealousy on her face. At a noise from inside she hurriedly disappears into the kitchen. A moment later* ROBERT *re-enters. He comes forward and picks up the shoes and stockings which he shoves carelessly under the table. Then, seeing no one about, he goes to the sideboard and selects a book. Coming back to his chair, he sits down and immediately becomes absorbed in reading.* RUTH *returns from the kitchen bringing his plate heaped with food, and a cup of tea. She sets those before him and sits down in her former place.* ROBERT *continues to read, oblivious to the food on the table.*)

RUTH. (*after watching him irritably for a moment*) For heaven's sakes, put down that old book! Don't you see your dinner's getting cold?

ROBERT. (*closing his book*) Excuse me, Ruth. I didn't notice. (*He picks up his knife and fork and begins to eat gingerly, without appetite.*)

RUTH. I should think you might have some feeling for me, Rob, and not always be late for meals. If you think it's fun sweltering in that oven of a kitchen to keep things warm for you, you're mistaken.

ROBERT. I'm sorry, Ruth, really I am. Something crops up every day to delay me. I mean to be here on time.

RUTH. (*with a sigh*) Mean-tos don't count.

ROBERT. (*with a conciliating smile*) Then punish me, Ruth. Let the food get cold and don't bother about me.

RUTH. I'd have to wait just the same to wash up after you.

ROBERT. But I can wash up.

RUTH. A nice mess there'd be then!

ROBERT. (*with an attempt at lightness*) The food is lucky to be able to get cold this weather. (*As RUTH doesn't answer or smile he opens his book and resumes his reading, forcing himself to take a mouthful of food every now and then. RUTH stares at him in annoyance.*)

RUTH. And besides, you've got your own work that's got to be done.

ROBERT. (*absent-mindedly, without taking his eyes from the book*) Yes, of course.

RUTH. (*spitefully*) Work you'll never get done by reading books all the time.

ROBERT. (*shutting the book with a snap*) Why do you persist in nagging at me for getting pleasure out of reading? Is it because— (*He checks himself abruptly.*)

RUTH. (*coloring*) Because I'm too stupid to understand them, I s'pose you were going to say.

ROBERT. (*shame-facedly*) No—no. (*In exasperation*) Why do you goad me into saying things I don't mean? Haven't I got my share of troubles trying to work this cursed farm without your adding to

122

them? You know how hard I've tried to keep things going in spite of bad luck—

RUTH. (*scornfully*) Bad luck!

ROBERT. And my own very apparent unfitness for the job, I was going to add; but you can't deny there's been bad luck to it, too. Why don't you take things into consideration? Why can't we pull together? We used to. I know it's hard on you also. Then why can't we help each other instead of hindering?

RUTH. (*sullenly*) I do the best I know how.

ROBERT. (*gets up and puts his hand on her shoulder*) I know you do. But let's both of us try to do better. We can both improve. Say a word of encouragement once in a while when things go wrong, even if it is my fault. You know the odds I've been up against since Pa died. I'm not a farmer. I've never claimed to be one. But there's nothing else I can do under the circumstances, and I've got to pull things through somehow. With your help, I can do it. With you against me— (*He shrugs his shoulders. There is a pause. Then he bends down and kisses her hair—with an attempt at cheerfulness*) So you promise that; and I'll promise to be here when the clock strikes—and anything else you tell me to. Is it a bargain?

RUTH. (*dully*) I s'pose so. (*They are interrupted by the sound of a loud knock at the kitchen door*) There's someone at the kitchen door. (*She hurries out. A moment later she reappears*) It's Ben.

ROBERT. (*frowning*) What's the trouble now, I wonder? (*In a loud voice*) Come on in here, Ben. (BEN *slouches in from the kitchen. He is a hulking, awkward young fellow with a heavy, stupid face and shifty, cunning eyes. He is dressed in overalls, boots, etc., and wears a broad-brimmed hat of coarse straw pushed back on his head*) Well, Ben, what's the matter?

BEN. (*drawlingly*) The mowin' machine's bust.

ROBERT. Why, that can't be. The man fixed it only last week.

BEN. It's bust just the same.

ROBERT. And can't you fix it?

BEN. No. Don't know what's the matter with the goll-darned thing. 'Twon't work, anyhow.

ROBERT. (*getting up and going for his hat*) Wait a minute and I'll go look it over. There can't be much the matter with it.

BEN. (*impudently*) Don't make no diff'rence t' me whether there be or not. I'm quittin'.

ROBERT. (*anxiously*) You don't mean you're throwing up your job here?

BEN. That's what! My month's up today and I want what's owin' t' me.

ROBERT. But why are you quitting now, Ben, when you know I've so much work on hand? I'll have a hard time getting another man at such short notice.

BEN. That's for you to figger. I'm quittin'.

ROBERT. But what's your reason? You haven't any complaint to make about the way you've been treated, have you?

BEN. No. 'Tain't that. (*Shaking his finger*) Look-a-here. I'm sick o' being made fun at, that's what; an' I got a job up to Timms' place; an' I'm quittin' here.

ROBERT. Being made fun of? I don't understand you. Who's making fun of you?

BEN. They all do. When I drive down with the milk in the mornin' they all laughs and jokes at me—that boy up to Harris' and the new feller up to Slocum's, and Bill Evans down to Meade's, and all the rest on 'em.

ROBERT. That's a queer reason for leaving me flat. Won't they laugh at you just the same when you're working for Timms?

BEN. They wouldn't dare to. Timms is the best farm hereabouts. They was laughin' at me for workin' for *you*, that's what! "How're things up to the Mayo place?" they hollers every mornin'. "What's Robert doin' now—pasturin' the cattle in the cornlot? Is he seasonin' his hay with rain this year, same as last?" they shouts. "Or is he inventin' some 'lectrical milkin' engine to fool them dry cows o' his into givin' hard cider?" (*Very much ruffled*) That's like they talks; and I ain't goin' to put up with it no longer. Everyone's always knowed me as a first-class hand hereabouts, and I ain't wantin' 'em to get no different notion. So I'm quittin' you. And I wants what's comin' to me.

ROBERT. (*coldly*) Oh, if that's the case, you can go to the devil. You'll get your money tomorrow when I get back from town—not before!

BEN. (*turning to doorway to kitchen*) That suits me. (*As he goes out he speaks back over his shoulder*) And see that I do get it, or there'll be trouble. (*He disappears and the slamming of the kitchen door is heard.*)

ROBERT. (*as* RUTH *comes from where she has been standing by the doorway and sits down dejectedly in her old place*) The stupid damn fool! And now what about the haying? That's an example of what I'm up against. No one can say I'm responsible for that.

RUTH. He wouldn't dare act that way with anyone else! (*Spitefully, with a glance at* ANDREW's *letter on the table*) It's lucky Andy's coming back.

ROBERT. (*without resentment*) Yes, Andy'll see the right thing to do in a jiffy. (*With an affectionate smile*) I wonder if the old chump's changed much? He doesn't seem to from his letters, does he? (*Shaking his head*) But just the same I doubt if he'll want to settle down to a humdrum farm life, after all he's been through.

RUTH. (*resentfully*) Andy's not like you. He likes the farm.

ROBERT. (*immersed in his own thoughts—enthusiastically*) Gad, the things he's seen and experienced! Think of the places he's been! All the wonderful far places I used to dream about! God, how I envy him! What a trip! (*He springs to his feet and instinctively goes to the window and stares out at the horizon.*)

RUTH. (*bitterly*) I s'pose you're sorry now you didn't go?

ROBERT. (*too occupied with his own thoughts to hear her—vindictively*) Oh, those cursed hills out there that I used to think promised me so much! How I've grown to hate the sight of them! They're like

125

the walls of a narrow prison yard shutting me in from all the freedom and wonder of life! (*He turns back to the room with a gesture of loathing*) Sometimes I think if it wasn't for you, Ruth, and—(*His voice softening*)—little Mary, I'd chuck everything up and walk down the road with just one desire in my heart—to put the whole rim of the world between me and those hills, and be able to breathe freely once more! (*He sinks down into his chair and smiles with bitter self-scorn*) There I go dreaming again—my old fool dreams.

RUTH. (*in a low, repressed voice—her eyes smoldering*) You're not the only one!

ROBERT. (*buried in his own thoughts—bitterly*) And Andy, who's had the chance—what has he got out of it? His letters read like the diary of a—of a farmer! "We're in Singapore now. It's a dirty hole of a place and hotter than hell. Two of the crew are down with fever and we're short-handed on the work. I'll be damn glad when we sail again, although tacking back and forth in these blistering seas is a rotten job too!" (*Scornfully*) That's about the way he summed up his impressions of the East.

RUTH. (*her repressed voice trembling*) You needn't make fun of Andy.

ROBERT. When I think—but what's the use? You know I wasn't making fun of Andy personally, but his attitude toward things is—

RUTH. (*her eyes flashing—bursting into uncontrollable rage*) You was too making fun of him! And I ain't going to stand for it! You ought to be ashamed of yourself! (ROBERT *stares at her in amazement. She continues furiously*) A fine one to talk about anyone else—after the way you've ruined everything with your lazy loafing!—and the stupid way you do things!

ROBERT. (*angrily*) Stop that kind of talk, do you hear?

RUTH. You findin' fault—with your own brother who's ten times the man you ever was or ever will be! You're jealous, that's what! Jealous because he's made a man of himself, while you're nothing but a—but a— (*She stutters incoherently, overcome by rage.*)

126

ROBERT. Ruth! Ruth! You'll be sorry for talking like that.

RUTH. I won't! I won't never be sorry! I'm only saying what I've been thinking for years.

ROBERT. (*aghast*) Ruth! You can't mean that!

RUTH. What do you think—living with a man like you—having to suffer all the time because you've never been man enough to work and do things like other people. But no! You never own up to that. You think you're so much better than other folks, with your college education, where you never learned a thing, and always reading your stupid books instead of working. I s'pose you think I ought to be *proud* to be your wife—a poor, ignorant thing like me! (*Fiercely*) But I'm not. I hate it! I hate the sight of you. Oh, if I'd only known! If I hadn't been such a fool to listen to your cheap, silly, poetry talk that you learned out of books! If I could have seen how you were in your true self—like you are now—I'd have killed myself before I'd have married you! I was sorry for it before we'd been together a month. I knew what you were really like—when it was too late.

ROBERT. (*his voice raised loudly*) And now—I'm finding out what you're really like—what a—a creature I've been living with. (*With a harsh laugh*) God! It wasn't that I haven't guessed how mean and small you are—but I've kept on telling myself that I must be wrong— like a fool!—like a damned fool!

RUTH. You were saying you'd go out on the road if it wasn't for me. Well, you can go, and the sooner the better! I don't care! I'll be glad to get rid of you! The farm'll be better off too. There's been a curse on it ever since you took hold. So go! Go and be a tramp like you've always wanted. It's all you're good for. I can get along without you, don't you worry. (*Exulting fiercely*) Andy's coming back, don't forget that! He'll attend to things like they should be. He'll show what a man can do! I don't need you. Andy's coming!

ROBERT. (*they are both standing.* ROBERT *grabs her by the shoulders and glares into her eyes*) What do you mean? (*He shakes her vio-*

lently) What are you thinking of? What's in your evil mind, you—you— (*His voice is a harsh shout.*)

RUTH. (*in a defiant scream*) Yes, I do mean it! I'd say it if you was to kill me! I do love Andy. I do! I do! I always loved him. (*Exultantly*) And he loves me! He loves me! I know he does. He always did! And you know he did, too! So go! Go if you want to!

ROBERT. (*throwing her away from him. She staggers back against the table—thickly*) You—you slut! (*He stands glaring at her as she leans back, supporting herself by the table, gasping for breath. A loud frightened whimper sounds from the awakened child in the bedroom. It continues. The man and woman stand looking at one another in horror, the extent of their terrible quarrel suddenly brought home to them. A pause. The noise of a horse and carriage comes from the road before the house. The two, suddenly struck by the same premonition, listen to it breathlessly, as to a sound heard in a dream. It stops. They hear* ANDY'S *voice from the road shouting a long hail—"Ahoy there!"*)

RUTH. (*with a strangled cry of joy*) Andy! Andy! (*She rushes and grabs the knob of the screen door, about to fling it open.*)

ROBERT. (*in a voice of command that forces obedience*) Stop! (*He goes to the door and gently pushes the trembling* RUTH *away from it. The child's crying rises to a louder pitch*) I'll meet Andy. You better go in to Mary, Ruth. (*She looks at him defiantly for a moment, but there is something in his eyes that makes her turn and walk slowly into the bedroom.*)

ANDY'S VOICE. (*in a louder shout*) Ahoy there, Rob!

ROBERT. (*in an answering shout of forced cheeriness*) Hello, Andy! (*He opens the door and walks out as the curtain falls.*)

ACT TWO—SCENE TWO

THE *top of a hill on the farm. It is about eleven o'clock the next morning. The day is hot and cloudless. In the distance the sea can be seen.*

The top of the hill slopes downward slightly toward the left. A big boulder stands in the center toward the rear. Further right, a large oak tree. The faint trace of a path leading upward to it from the left foreground can be detected through the bleached, sun-scorched grass.

ROBERT *is discovered sitting on the boulder, his chin resting on his hands, staring out toward the horizon seaward. His face is pale and haggard, his expression one of utter despondency.* MARY *is sitting on the grass near him in the shade, playing with her doll, singing happily to herself. Presently she casts a curious glance at her father, and, propping her doll up against the tree, comes over and clambers to his side.*

MARY. (*pulling at his hand—solicitously*) Dada sick?

ROBERT. (*looking at her with a forced smile*) No, dear. Why?

MARY. Play wif Mary.

ROBERT. (*gently*) No, dear, not today. Dada doesn't feel like playing today.

MARY. (*protestingly*) Yes, Dada!

ROBERT. No, dear. Dada does feel sick—a little. He's got a bad headache.

MARY. Mary see. (*He bends his head. She pats his hair*) Bad head.

ROBERT. (*kissing her—with a smile*) There! It's better now, dear, thank you. (*She cuddles up close against him. There is a pause during which each of them looks out seaward. Finally* ROBERT *turns to her tenderly*) Would you like Dada to go away?—far, far away?

MARY. (*tearfully*) No! No! No, Dada, no!

ROBERT. Don't you like Uncle Andy—the man that came yesterday —not the old man with the white mustache—the other?

MARY. Mary loves Dada.

ROBERT. (*with fierce determination*) He won't go away, baby. He was only joking. He couldn't leave his little Mary. (*He presses the child in his arms.*)

MARY. (*with an exclamation of pain*) Oh! Hurt!

ROBERT. I'm sorry, little girl. (*He lifts her down to the grass*) Go play with Dolly, that's a good girl; and be careful to keep in the shade. (*She reluctantly leaves him and takes up her doll again. A moment later she points down the hill to the left.*)

MARY. Mans, Dada.

ROBERT. (*looking that way*) It's your Uncle Andy. (*A moment later* ANDREW *comes up from the left, whistling cheerfully. He has changed but little in appearance, except for the fact that his face has been deeply bronzed by his years in the tropics; but there is a decided change in his manner. The old easy-going good-nature seems to have been partly lost in a breezy, business-like briskness of voice and gesture. There is an authoritative note in his speech as though he were accustomed to give orders and have them obeyed as a matter of course. He is dressed in the simple blue uniform and cap of a merchant ship's officer.*)

ANDREW. Here you are, eh?

ROBERT. Hello, Andy.

ANDREW. (*going over to* MARY) And who's this young lady I find you all alone with, eh? Who's this pretty young lady? (*He tickles the laughing, squirming* MARY, *then lifts her up at arm's length over his head*) Upsy—daisy! (*He sets her down on the ground again*) And there you are! (*He walks over and sits down on the boulder beside* ROBERT *who moves to one side to make room for him*) Ruth told me I'd probably find you up top-side here; but I'd have guessed it, any-way. (*He digs his brother in the ribs affectionately*) Still up to your old tricks, you old beggar! I can remember how you used to come up here to mope and dream in the old days.

ROBERT. (*with a smile*) I come up here now because it's the coolest place on the farm. I've given up dreaming.

ANDREW. (*grinning*) I don't believe it. You can't have changed that much. (*After a pause—with boyish enthusiasm*) Say, it sure brings back old times to be up here with you having a chin all by our lonesomes again. I feel great being back home.

ROBERT. It's great for us to have you back.

ANDREW. (*after a pause—meaningly*) I've been looking over the old place with Ruth. Things don't seem to be—

ROBERT. (*his face flushing—interrupts his brother shortly*) Never mind the damn farm! Let's talk about something interesting. This is the first chance I've had to have a word with you alone. Tell me about your trip.

ANDREW. Why, I thought I told you everything in my letters.

ROBERT. (*smiling*) Your letters were—sketchy, to say the least.

ANDREW. Oh, I know I'm no author. You needn't be afraid of hurting my feelings. I'd rather go through a typhoon again than write a letter.

ROBERT. (*with eager interest*) Then you were through a typhoon?

ANDREW. Yes—in the China sea. Had to run before it under bare poles for two days. I thought we were bound down for Davy Jones, sure. Never dreamed waves could get so big or the wind blow so hard. If it hadn't been for Uncle Dick being such a good skipper we'd have gone to the sharks, all of us. As it was we came out minus a main topmast and had to beat back to Hong-Kong for repairs. But I must have written you all this.

ROBERT. You never mentioned it.

ANDREW. Well, there was so much dirty work getting things shipshape again I must have forgotten about it.

ROBERT. (*looking at* ANDREW—*marveling*) Forget a typhoon? (*With*

131

a trace of scorn) You're a strange combination, Andy. And is what you've told me all you remember about it?

ANDREW. Oh, I could give you your bellyful of details if I wanted to turn loose on you. It was all-wool-and-a-yard-wide-Hell, I'll tell you. You ought to have been there. I remember thinking about you at the worst of it, and saying to myself: "This'd cure Rob of them ideas of his about the beautiful sea, if he could see it." And it would have too, you bet! (*He nods emphatically.*)

ROBERT. (*dryly*) The sea doesn't seem to have impressed you very favorably.

ANDREW. I should say it didn't! I'll never set foot on a ship again if I can help it—except to carry me some place I can't get to by train.

ROBERT. But you studied to become an officer!

ANDREW. Had to do something or I'd gone mad. The days were like years. (*He laughs*) And as for the East you used to rave about—well, you ought to see it, and *smell* it! One walk down one of their filthy narrow streets with the tropic sun beating on it would sicken you for life with the "wonder and mystery" you used to dream of.

ROBERT. (*shrinking from his brother with a glance of aversion*) So all you found in the East was a stench?

ANDREW. *A* stench! Ten thousand of them!

ROBERT. But you did like some of the places, judging from your letters—Sydney, Buenos Aires—

ANDREW. Yes, Sydney's a good town. (*Enthusiastically*) But Buenos Aires—there's the place for you. Argentine's a country where a fellow has a chance to make good. You're right I like it. And I'll tell you, Rob, that's right where I'm going just as soon as I've seen you folks a while and can get a ship. I can get a berth as second officer, and I'll jump the ship when I get there. I'll need every cent of the wages Uncle's paid me to get a start at something in B. A.

ROBERT. (*staring at his brother—slowly*) So you're not going to stay on the farm?

ANDREW. Why sure not! Did you think I was? There wouldn't be any sense. One of us is enough to run this little place.

ROBERT. I suppose it does seem small to you now.

ANDREW. (*not noticing the sarcasm in* ROBERT'S *tone*) You've no idea, Rob, what a splendid place Argentine is. I had a letter from a marine insurance chap that I'd made friends with in Hong-Kong to his brother, who's in the grain business in Buenos Aires. He took quite a fancy to me, and what's more important, he offered me a job if I'd come back there. I'd have taken it on the spot, only I couldn't leave Uncle Dick in the lurch, and I'd promised you folks to come home. But I'm going back there, you bet, and then you watch me get on! (*He slaps* ROBERT *on the back*) But don't you think it's a big chance, Rob?

ROBERT. It's fine—for you, Andy.

ANDREW. We call this a farm—but you ought to hear about the farms down there—ten square miles where we've got an acre. It's a new country where big things are opening up—and I want to get in on something big before I die. I'm no fool when it comes to farming, and I know something about grain. I've been reading up a lot on it, too, lately. (*He notices* ROBERT'S *absent-minded expression and laughs*) Wake up, you old poetry bookworm, you! I know my talking about business makes you want to choke me, doesn't it?

ROBERT. (*with an embarrassed smile*) No, Andy, I—I just happened to think of something else. (*Frowning*) There've been lots of times lately that I wished I had some of your faculty for business.

ANDREW. (*soberly*) There's something I want to talk about, Rob.— the farm. You don't mind, do you?

ROBERT. No.

ANDREW. I walked over it this morning with Ruth—and she told me about things— (*Evasively*) I could see the place had run down; but you mustn't blame yourself. When luck's against anyone—

ROBERT. Don't, Andy! It *is* my fault. You know it as well as I do. The best I've ever done was to make ends meet.

ANDREW. (*after a pause*) I've got over a thousand saved, and you can have that.

ROBERT. (*firmly*) No. You need that for your start in Buenos Aires.

ANDREW. I don't. I can—

ROBERT. (*determinedly*) No, Andy! Once and for all, no! I won't hear of it!

ANDREW. (*protestingly*) You obstinate old son of a gun!

ROBERT. Oh, everything'll be on a sound footing after harvest. Don't worry about it.

ANDREW. (*doubtfully*) Maybe. (*After a pause*) It's too bad Pa couldn't have lived to see things through. (*With feeling*) It cut me up a lot—hearing he was dead. He never—softened up, did he—about me, I mean?

ROBERT. He never understood, that's a kinder way of putting it. He does now.

ANDREW. (*after a pause*) You've forgotten all about what—caused me to go, haven't you, Rob? (ROBERT *nods but keeps his face averted*) I was a slushier damn fool in those days than you were. But it was an act of Providence I did go. It opened my eyes to how I'd been fooling myself. Why, I'd forgotten all about—that—before I'd been at sea six months.

ROBERT. (*turns and looks into* ANDREW'S *eyes searchingly*) You're speaking of—Ruth?

ANDREW. (*confused*) Yes. I didn't want you to get false notions in your head, or I wouldn't say anything. (*Looking* ROBERT *squarely in the eyes*) I'm telling you the truth when I say I'd forgotten long ago. It don't sound well for me, getting over things so easy, but I guess it never really amounted to more than a kid idea I was letting rule me. I'm certain now I never was in love—I was getting fun out of thinking I was—and being a hero to myself. (*He heaves a great sigh of relief*) There! Gosh, I'm glad that's off my chest. I've been feeling sort of awkward ever since I've been home, thinking of what you two might think. (*A trace of appeal in his voice*) You've got it all straight now, haven't you, Rob?

ROBERT. (*in a low voice*) Yes, Andy.

ANDREW. And I'll tell Ruth, too, if I can get up the nerve. She must feel kind of funny having me round—after what used to be—and not knowing how I feel about it.

ROBERT. (*slowly*) Perhaps—for her sake—you'd better not tell her.

ANDREW. For her sake? Oh, you mean she wouldn't want to be reminded of my foolishness? Still, I think it'd be worse if—

ROBERT. (*breaking out—in an agonized voice*) Do as you please, Andy; but for God's sake, let's not talk about it! (*There is a pause. ANDREW stares at ROBERT in hurt stupefaction. ROBERT continues after a moment in a voice which he vainly attempts to keep calm*) Excuse me, Andy. This rotten headache has my nerves shot to pieces.

ANDREW. (*mumbling*) It's all right, Rob—long as you're not sore at me.

ROBERT. Where did Uncle Dick disappear to this morning?

ANDREW. He went down to the port to see to things on the "Sunda." He said he didn't know exactly when he'd be back. I'll have to go down and tend to the ship when he comes. That's why I dressed up in these togs.

MARY. (*pointing down to the hill to the left*) See! Mama! Mama! (*She struggles to her feet. RUTH appears at left. She is dressed in white, shows she has been fixing up. She looks pretty, flushed and full of life.*)

MARY. (*running to her mother*) Mama!

RUTH. (*kissing her*) Hello, dear! (*She walks toward the rock and addresses ROBERT coldly*) Jake wants to see you about something. He finished working where he was. He's waiting for you at the road.

ROBERT. (*getting up—wearily*) I'll go down right away. (*As he looks at RUTH, noting her changed appearance, his face darkens with pain.*)

RUTH. And take Mary with you, please. (*To MARY*) Go with Dada, that's a good girl. Grandma has your dinner 'most ready for you.

ROBERT. (*shortly*) Come, Mary!

MARY. (*taking his hand and dancing happily beside him*) Dada! Dada! (*They go down the hill to the left.* RUTH *looks after them for a moment, frowning—then turns to* ANDY *with a smile*) I'm going to sit down. Come on, Andy. It'll be like old times. (*She jumps lightly to the top of the rock and sits down*) It's so fine and cool up here after the house.

ANDREW. (*half-sitting on the side of the boulder*) Yes. It's great.

RUTH. I've taken a holiday in honor of your arrival. (*Laughing excitedly*) I feel so free I'd like to have wings and fly over the sea. You're a man. You can't know how awful and stupid it is—cooking and washing dishes all the time.

ANDREW. (*making a wry face*) I can guess.

RUTH. Besides, your mother just insisted on getting your first dinner to home, she's that happy at having you back. You'd think I was planning to poison you the flurried way she shooed me out of the kitchen.

ANDREW. That's just like Ma, bless her!

RUTH. She's missed you terrible. We all have. And you can't deny the farm has, after what I showed you and told you when we was looking over the place this morning.

ANDREW. (*with a frown*) Things are run down, that's a fact! It's too darn hard on poor old Rob.

RUTH. (*scornfully*) It's his own fault. He never takes any interest in things.

ANDREW. (*reprovingly*) You can't blame him. He wasn't born for it; but I know he's done his best for your sake and the old folks and the little girl.

RUTH. (*indifferently*) Yes, I suppose he has. (*Gaily*) But thank the Lord, all those days are over now. The "hard luck" Rob's always blaming won't last long when you take hold, Andy. All the farm's ever needed was someone with the knack of looking ahead and preparing for what's going to happen.

ANDREW. Yes, Rob hasn't got that. He's frank to own up to that himself. I'm going to try and hire a good man for him—an experienced farmer—to work the place on a salary and percentage. That'll take it off of Rob's hands, and he needn't be worrying himself to death any more. He looks all worn out, Ruth. He ought to be careful.

RUTH. (*absent-mindedly*) Yes, I s'pose. (*Her mind is filled with premonitions by the first part of his statement*) Why do you want to hire a man to oversee things? Seems as if now that you're back it wouldn't be needful.

ANDREW. Oh, of course I'll attend to everything while I'm here. I mean after I'm gone.

RUTH. (*as if she couldn't believe her ears*) Gone!

ANDREW. Yes. When I leave for the Argentine again.

RUTH. (*aghast*) You're going away to sea!

ANDREW. Not to sea, no; I'm through with the sea for good as a job. I'm going down to Buenos Aires to get in the grain business.

RUTH. But—that's far off—isn't it?

ANDREW. (*easily*) Six thousand miles more or less. It's quite a trip. (*With enthusiasm*) I've got a peach of a chance down there, Ruth. Ask Rob if I haven't. I've just been telling him all about it.

RUTH. (*a flush of anger coming over her face*) And didn't he try to stop you from going?

ANDREW. (*in surprise*) No, of course not. Why?

RUTH. (*slowly and vindictively*) That's just like him—not to.

ANDREW. (*resentfully*) Rob's too good a chum to try and stop me when he knows I'm set on a thing. And he could see just as soon's I told him what a good chance it was.

RUTH. (*dazedly*) And you're bound on going?

ANDREW. Sure thing. Oh, I don't mean right off. I'll have to wait for a ship sailing there for quite a while, likely. Anyway, I want to stay to home and visit with you folks a spell before I go.

RUTH. (*dumbly*) I s'pose. (*With sudden anguish*) Oh, Andy, you can't go! You can't. Why we've all thought—we've all been hoping and praying you was coming home to stay, to settle down on the farm and see to things. You mustn't go! Think of how your Ma'll take on if you go—and how the farm'll be ruined if you leave it to Rob to look after. You can see that.

ANDREW. (*frowning*) Rob hasn't done so bad. When I get a man to direct things the farm'll be safe enough.

RUTH. (*insistently*) But your Ma—think of her.

ANDREW. She's used to me being away. She won't object when she knows it's best for her and all of us for me to go. You ask Rob. In a couple of years down there, I'll make my pile, see if I don't; and then I'll come back and settle down and turn this farm into the crackiest place in the whole state. In the meantime, I can help you both from down there. (*Earnestly*) I tell you, Ruth, I'm going to make good right from the minute I land, if working hard and a determination to get on can do it; and I *know* they can! (*Excitedly—in a rather boastful tone*) I tell you, I feel ripe for bigger things than settling down here. The trip did that for me, anyway. It showed me the world is a larger proposition than ever I thought it was in the old days. I couldn't be content any more stuck here like a fly in molasses. It all seems trifling, somehow. You ought to be able to understand what I feel.

RUTH. (*dully*) Yes—I s'pose I ought. (*After a pause—a sudden suspicion forming in her mind*) What did Rob tell you—about me?

ANDREW. Tell? About you? Why, nothing.

RUTH. (*staring at him intensely*) Are you telling me the truth, Andy Mayo? Didn't he say—I— (*She stops confusedly.*)

ANDREW. (*surprised*) No, he didn't mention you, I can remember. Why? What made you think he did?

RUTH. (*wringing her hands*) Oh, I wish I could tell if you're lying or not!

ANDREW. (*indignantly*) What're you talking about? I didn't used to lie to you, did I? And what in the name of God is there to lie for?

RUTH. (*still unconvinced*) Are you sure—will you swear—it isn't the

138

reason— (*She lowers her eyes and half turns away from him*) The same reason that made you go last time that's driving you away again? 'Cause if it is—I was going to say—you mustn't go—on that account. (*Her voice sinks to a tremulous, tender whisper as she finishes.*)

ANDREW. (*confused—forces a laugh*) Oh, is *that* what you're driving at? Well, you needn't worry about that no more— (*Soberly*) I don't blame you, Ruth, feeling embarrassed having me around again, after the way I played the dumb fool about going away last time.

RUTH. (*her hope crushed—with a gasp of pain*) Oh, Andy!

ANDREW. (*misunderstanding*) I know I oughtn't to talk about such foolishness to you. Still I figure it's better to get it out of my system so's we three can be together same's years ago, and not be worried thinking one of us might have the wrong notion.

RUTH. Andy! Please! Don't!

ANDREW. Let me finish now that I've started. It'll help clear things up. I don't want you to think once a fool always a fool, and be upset all the time I'm here on my fool account. I want you to believe I put all that silly nonsense back of me a long time ago—and now—it seems —well—as if you'd always been my sister, that's what, Ruth.

RUTH. (*at the end of her endurance—laughing hysterically*) For God's sake, Andy—won't you please stop talking! (*She again hides her face in her hands, her bowed shoulders trembling.*)

ANDREW. (*ruefully*) Seem's if I put my foot in it whenever I open my mouth today. Rob shut me up with almost the same words when I tried speaking to him about it.

RUTH. (*fiercely*) You told him—what you've told me?

ANDREW. (*astounded*) Why sure! Why not?

RUTH. (*shuddering*) Oh, my God!

ANDREW. (*alarmed*) Why? Shouldn't I have?

RUTH. (*hysterically*) Oh, I don't care what you do! I don't care! Leave me alone! (*ANDREW gets up and walks down the hill to the left, embarrassed, hurt, and greatly puzzled by her behavior.*)

ANDREW. (*after a pause—pointing down the hill*) Hello! Here they

139

come back—and the Captain's with them. How'd he come to get back so soon, I wonder? That means I've got to hustle down to the port and get on board. Rob's got the baby with him. (*He comes back to the boulder.* RUTH *keeps her face averted from him*) Gosh, I never saw a father so tied up in a kid as Rob is! He just watches every move she makes. And I don't blame him. You both got a right to feel proud of her. She's surely a little winner. (*He glances at* RUTH *to see if this very obvious attempt to get back in her good graces is having any effect*) I can see the likeness to Rob standing out all over her, can't you? But there's no denying she's your young one, either. There's something about her eyes—

RUTH. (*piteously*) Oh, Andy, I've a headache! I don't want to talk! Leave me alone, won't you please?

ANDREW. (*stands staring at her for a moment—then walks away saying in a hurt tone*) Everybody hereabouts seems to be on edge today. I begin to feel as if I'm not wanted around. (*He stands near the path, left, kicking at the grass with the toe of his shoe. A moment later* CAPTAIN DICK SCOTT *enters, followed by* ROBERT *carrying* MARY. *The* CAPTAIN *seems scarcely to have changed at all from the jovial, booming person he was three years before. He wears a uniform similar to* AN-DREW'S. *He is puffing and breathless from his climb and mops wildly at his perspiring countenance.* ROBERT *casts a quick glance at* ANDREW, *noticing the latter's discomfited look, and then turns his eyes on* RUTH *who, at their approach, has moved so her back is toward them, her chin resting on her hands as she stares out seaward.*)

MARY. Mama! Mama! (ROBERT *puts her down and she runs to her mother.* RUTH *turns and grabs her up in her arms with a sudden fierce tenderness, quickly turning away again from the others. During the following scene she keeps* MARY *in her arms.*)

SCOTT. (*wheezily*) Phew! I got great news for you, Andy. Let me get my wind first. Phew! God A'mighty, mountin' this damned hill is worser'n goin' aloft to the skys'l yard in a blow. I got to lay to a while. (*He sits down on the grass, mopping his face.*)

ANDREW. I didn't look for you this soon, Uncle.

SCOTT. I didn't figger it, neither; but I run across a bit o' news down to the Seamen's Home made me 'bout ship and set all sail back here to find you.

ANDREW. (*eagerly*) What is it, Uncle?

SCOTT. Passin' by the Home I thought I'd drop in an 'let 'em know I'd be lackin' a mate next trip count o' your leavin.' Their man in charge o' the shippin' asked after you 'special curious. "Do you think he'd consider a berth as Second on a steamer, Captain?" he asks. I was going to say no when I thinks o' you wantin' to get back down south to the Plate agen; so I asks him: "What is she and where's she bound?" "She's the 'El Paso,' a brand new tramp," he says, "and she's bound for Buenos Aires."

ANDREW. (*his eyes lighting up—excitedly*) Gosh, that is luck! When does she sail?

SCOTT. Tomorrow mornin'. I didn't know if you'd want to ship away agen so quick an' I told him so. "Tell him I'll hold the berth open for him until late this afternoon," he says. So there you be, an' you can make your own choice.

ANDREW. I'd like to take it. There may not be another ship for Buenos Aires with a vacancy in months. (*His eyes roving from ROB-ERT to RUTH and back again—uncertainly*) Still—damn it all—tomorrow morning *is* soon. I wish she wasn't leaving for a week or so. That'd give me a chance—it seems hard to go right away again when I've just got home. And yet it's a chance in a thousand— (*Appealing to* ROBERT) What do you think, Rob? What would you do?

ROBERT. (*forcing a smile*) He who hesitates, you know. (*Frowning*) It's a piece of good luck thrown in your way—and—I think you owe it to yourself to jump at it. But don't ask me to decide for you.

RUTH. (*turning to look at* ANDREW—*in a tone of fierce resentment*) Yes, go, Andy! (*She turns quickly away again. There is a moment of embarrassed silence.*)

ANDREW. (*thoughtfully*) Yes, I guess I will. It'll be the best thing for all of us in the end, don't you think so, Rob? (ROBERT *nods but remains silent.*)

SCOTT. (*getting to his feet*) Then, that's settled.

ANDREW. (*now that he has definitely made a decision his voice rings with hopeful strength and energy*) Yes, I'll take the berth. The sooner I go the sooner I'll be back, that's a certainty; and I won't come back with empty hands next time. You bet I won't!

SCOTT. You ain't got so much time, Andy. To make sure you'd best leave here soon's you kin. I got to get right back aboard. You'd best come with me.

ANDREW. I'll go to the house and repack my bag right away.

ROBERT. (*quietly*) You'll both be here for dinner, won't you?

ANDREW. (*worriedly*) I don't know. Will there be time? What time is it now, I wonder?

ROBERT. (*reproachfully*) Ma's been getting dinner especially for you, Andy.

ANDREW. (*flushing—shamefacedly*) Hell! And I was forgetting! Of course I'll stay for dinner if I missed every damned ship in the world. (*He turns to the* CAPTAIN—*briskly*) Come on, Uncle. Walk down with me to the house and you can tell me more about this berth on the way. I've got to pack before dinner. (*He and the* CAPTAIN *start down to the left.* ANDREW *calls back over his shoulder*) You're coming soon, aren't you, Rob?

ROBERT. Yes. I'll be right down. (ANDREW *and the* CAPTAIN *leave.* RUTH *puts* MARY *on the ground and hides her face in her hands. Her shoulders shake as if she were sobbing.* ROBERT *stares at her with a grim, somber expression.* MARY *walks backward toward* ROBERT, *her wondering eyes fixed on her mother.*)

MARY. (*her voice vaguely frightened, taking her father's hand*) Dada, Mama's cryin', Dada.

ROBERT. (*bending down and stroking her hair—in a voice he endeavors to keep from being harsh*) No, she isn't, little girl. The sun hurts her eyes, that's all. Are'nt you beginning to feel hungry, Mary?

MARY. (*decidedly*) Yes, Dada.

ROBERT. (*meaningly*) It must be your dinner time now.

RUTH. (*in a muffled voice*) I'm coming, Mary. (*She wipes her eyes quickly and, without looking at* ROBERT, *comes and takes* MARY's *hand—in a dead voice*) Come on and I'll get your dinner for you. (*She walks out left, her eyes fixed on the ground, the skipping* MARY *tugging at her hand.* ROBERT *waits a moment for them to get ahead and then slowly follows as the curtain falls.*)

ACT THREE—SCENE ONE

S AME *as Act Two, Scene One—The sitting room of the farmhouse about six o'clock in the morning of a day toward the end of October five years later. It is not yet dawn, but as the action progresses the darkness outside the windows gradually fades to gray.*

The room, seen by the light of the shadeless oil lamp with a smoky chimney which stands on the table, presents an appearance of decay, of dissolution. The curtains at the windows are torn and dirty and one of them is missing. The closed desk is gray with accumulated dust as if it had not been used in years. Blotches of dampness disfigure the wall paper. Threadbare trails, leading to the kitchen and outer doors, show in the faded carpet. The top of the coverless table is stained with the imprints of hot dishes and spilt food. The rung of one rocker has been clumsily mended with a piece of plain board. A brown coating of rust covers the unblacked stove. A pile of wood is stacked up carelessly against the wall by the stove.

The whole atmosphere of the room, contrasted with that of former years, is one of an habitual poverty too hopelessly resigned to be any longer ashamed or even conscious of itself.

At the rise of the curtain RUTH *is discovered sitting by the stove, with hands outstretched to the warmth as if the air in the room were damp and cold. A heavy shawl is wrapped about her shoulders, half-concealing her dress of deep mourning. She has aged horribly. Her pale, deeply-lined face has the stony lack of expression of one to whom nothing more can ever happen, whose capacity for emotion has been exhausted. When she speaks her voice is without timbre, low and monotonous. The negligent disorder of her dress, the slovenly arrangement of her hair, now streaked with gray, her muddied shoes run down at the heel, give full evidence of the apathy in which she lives.*

144

Her mother is asleep in her wheel chair beside the stove toward the rear, wrapped up in a blanket.

There is a sound from the open bedroom door in the rear as if someone were getting out of bed. RUTH *turns in that direction with a look of dull annoyance. A moment later* ROBERT *appears in the doorway, leaning weakly against it for support. His hair is long and unkempt, his face and body emaciated. There are bright patches of crimson over his cheek bones and his eyes are burning with fever. He is dressed in corduroy pants, a flannel shirt, and wears worn carpet slippers on his bare feet.*

RUTH. (*dully*) S-s-s-h! Ma's asleep.

ROBERT. (*speaking with an effort*) I won't wake her. (*He walks weakly to a rocker by the side of the table and sinks down in it exhausted.*)

RUTH. (*staring at the stove*) You better come near the fire where it's warm.

ROBERT. No. I'm burning up now.

RUTH. That's the fever. You know the doctor told you not to get up and move round.

ROBERT. (*irritably*) That old fossil! He doesn't know anything. Go to bed and stay there—that's his only prescription.

RUTH. (*indifferently*) How are you feeling now?

ROBERT. (*buoyantly*) Better! Much better than I've felt in ages. Really I'm fine now—only very weak. It's the turning point, I guess. From now on I'll pick up so quick I'll surprise you—and no thanks to that old fool of a country quack, either.

RUTH. He's always tended to us.

ROBERT. Always helped us to die, you mean! He "tended" to Pa and Ma and— (*His voice breaks*) and to—Mary.

RUTH. (*dully*) He did the best he knew, I s'pose. (*After a pause*) Well, Andy's bringing a specialist with him when he comes. That ought to suit you.

ROBERT. (*bitterly*) Is that why you're waiting up all night?

145

RUTH. Yes.

ROBERT. For Andy?

RUTH. (*without a trace of feeling*) Somebody had got to. It's only right for someone to meet him after he's been gone five years.

ROBERT. (*with bitter mockery*) Five years! It's a long time.

RUTH. Yes.

ROBERT. (*meaningly*) To *wait!*

RUTH. (*indifferently*) It's past now.

ROBERT. Yes, it's past. (*After a pause*) Have you got his two telegrams with you? (RUTH *nods*) Let me see them, will you? My head was so full of fever when they came I couldn't make head or tail to them. (*Hastily*) But I'm feeling fine now. Let me read them again. (RUTH *takes them from the bosom of her dress and hands them to him.*)

RUTH. Here. The first one's on top.

ROBERT. (*opening it*) New York. "Just landed from steamer. Have important business to wind up here. Will be home as soon as deal is completed." (*He smiles bitterly*) Business first was always Andy's motto. (*He reads*) "Hope you are all well. Andy." (*He repeats ironically*) "Hope you are all well!"

RUTH. (*dully*) He couldn't know you'd been took sick till I answered that and told him.

ROBERT. (*contritely*) Of course he couldn't. I'm a fool. I'm touchy about nothing lately. Just what did you say in your reply?

RUTH. (*inconsequentially*) I had to send it collect.

ROBERT. (*irritably*) What did you say was the matter with me?

RUTH. I wrote you had lung trouble.

ROBERT. (*flying into a petty temper*) You *are* a fool! How often have I explained to you that it's *pleurisy* is the matter with me. You can't seem to get it in your head that the pleura is outside the lungs, not in them!

RUTH. (*callously*) I only wrote what Doctor Smith told me.

ROBERT. (*angrily*) He's a damned ignoramus!

146

RUTH. (*dully*) Makes no difference. I had to tell Andy something, didn't I?

ROBERT. (*after a pause, opening the other telegram*) He sent this last evening. Let's see. (*He reads*) "Leave for home on midnight train. Just received your wire. Am bringing specialist to see Rob. Will motor to farm from Port." (*He calculates*) What time is it now?

RUTH. Round six, must be.

ROBERT. He ought to be here soon. I'm glad he's bringing a doctor who knows something. A specialist will tell you in a second that there's nothing the matter with my lungs.

RUTH. (*stolidly*) You've been coughing an awful lot lately.

ROBERT. (*irritably*) What nonsense! For God's sake, haven't you ever had a bad cold yourself? (RUTH *stares at the stove in silence.* ROBERT *fidgets in his chair. There is a pause. Finally* ROBERT's *eyes are fixed on the sleeping* MRS. ATKINS) Your mother is lucky to be able to sleep so soundly.

RUTH. Ma's tired. She's been sitting up with me most of the night.

ROBERT. (*mockingly*) Is she waiting for Andy, too? (*There is a pause.* ROBERT *sighs*) I couldn't get to sleep to save my soul. I counted ten million sheep if I counted one. No use! I gave up trying finally and just laid there in the dark thinking. (*He pauses, then continues in a tone of tender sympathy*) I was thinking about you, Ruth—of how hard these last years must have been for you. (*Appealingly*) I'm sorry, Ruth.

RUTH. (*in a dead voice*) I don't know. They're past now. They were hard on all of us.

ROBERT. Yes; on all of us but Andy. (*With a flash of sick jealousy*) Andy's made a big success of himself—the kind he wanted. (*Mockingly*) And now he's coming home to let us admire his greatness. (*Frowning—irritably*) What am I talking about? My brain must be sick, too. (*After a pause*) Yes, these years have been terrible for both of us. (*His voice is lowered to a trembling whisper*) Especially the last eight months since Mary—died. (*He forces back a sob with a*

147

convulsive shudder—then breaks out in a passionate agony) Our last hope of happiness! I could curse God from the bottom of my soul—if there was a God! (*He is racked by a violent fit of coughing and hurriedly puts his handkerchief to his lips.*)

RUTH. (*without looking at him*) Mary's better off—being dead.

ROBERT. (*gloomily*) We'd all be better off for that matter. (*With a sudden exasperation*) You tell that mother of yours she's got to stop saying that Mary's death was due to a weak constitution inherited from me. (*On the verge of tears of weakness*) It's got to stop, I tell you!

RUTH. (*sharply*) S-h-h! You'll wake her; and then she'll nag at me—not you.

ROBERT. (*coughs and lies back in his chair weakly—a pause*) It's all because your mother's down on me for not begging Andy for help.

RUTH. (*resentfully*) You might have. He's got plenty.

ROBERT. How can *you* of all people think of taking money from *him?*

RUTH. (*dully*) I don't see the harm. He's your own brother.

ROBERT. (*shrugging his shoulders*) What's the use of talking to you? Well, I couldn't. (*Proudly*) And I've managed to keep things going, thank God. You can't deny that without help I've succeeded in— (*He breaks off with a bitter laugh*) My God, what am I boasting of? Debts to this one and that, taxes, interest unpaid! I'm a fool! (*He lies back in his chair closing his eyes for a moment, then speaks in a low voice*) I'll be frank, Ruth. I've been an utter failure, and I've dragged you with me. I couldn't blame you in all justice—for hating me.

RUTH. (*without feeling*) I don't hate you. It's been my fault too, I s'pose.

ROBERT. No. You couldn't help loving—Andy.

RUTH. (*dully*) I don't love anyone.

ROBERT. (*waving her remark aside*) You needn't deny it. It doesn't matter. (*After a pause—with a tender smile*) Do you know, Ruth,

148

what I've been dreaming back there in the dark? (*With a short laugh*) I was planning our future when I get well. (*He looks at her with appealing eyes as if afraid she will sneer at him. Her expression does not change. She stares at the stove. His voice takes on a note of eagerness*) After all, why shouldn't we have a future? We're young yet. If we can only shake off the curse of this farm! It's the farm that's ruined our lives, damn it! And now that Andy's coming back— I'm going to sink my foolish pride, Ruth! I'll borrow the money from him to give us a good start in the city. We'll go where people live instead of stagnating, and start all over again. (*Confidently*) I won't be the failure there that I've been here, Ruth. You won't need to be ashamed of me there. I'll prove to you the reading I've done can be put to some use. (*Vaguely*) I'll write, or something of that sort. I've always wanted to write. (*Pleadingly*) You'll want to do that, won't you, Ruth?

RUTH. (*dully*) There's Ma.

ROBERT. She can come with us.

RUTH. She wouldn't.

ROBERT. (*angrily*) So that's your answer! (*He trembles with violent passion. His voice is so strange that* RUTH *turns to look at him in alarm*) You're lying, Ruth! Your mother's just an excuse. You want to stay here. You think that because Andy's coming back that— (*He chokes and has an attack of coughing.*)

RUTH. (*getting up—in a frightened voice*) What's the matter? (*She goes to him*) I'll go with you, Rob. Stop that coughing for goodness' sake! It's awful bad for you. (*She soothes him in dull tones*) I'll go with you to the city—soon's you're well again. Honest I will, Rob, I promise! (ROB *lies back and closes his eyes. She stands looking down at him anxiously*) Do you feel better now?

ROBERT. Yes. (RUTH *goes back to her chair. After a pause he opens his eyes and sits up in his chair. His face is flushed and happy*) Then you *will* go, Ruth?

RUTH. Yes.

ROBERT. (*excitedly*) We'll make a new start, Ruth—just you and I. Life owes us some happiness after what we've been through. (*Vehemently*) It must! Otherwise our suffering would be meaningless—and that is unthinkable.

RUTH. (*worried by his excitement*) Yes, yes, of course, Rob, but you mustn't—

ROBERT. Oh, don't be afraid. I feel completely well, really I do—now that I can hope again. Oh if you knew how glorious it feels to have something to look forward to! Can't you feel the thrill of it, too—the vision of a new life opening up after all the horrible years?

RUTH. Yes, yes, but do be—

ROBERT. Nonsense! I won't be careful. I'm getting back all my strength. (*He gets lightly to his feet*) See! I feel light as a feather. (*He walks to her chair and bends down to kiss her smilingly*) One kiss—the first in years, isn't it?—to greet the dawn of a new life together.

RUTH. (*submitting to his kiss—worriedly*) Sit down, Rob, for goodness' sake!

ROBERT. (*with tender obstinacy—stroking her hair*) I won't sit down. You're silly to worry. (*He rests one hand on the back of her chair*) Listen. All our suffering has been a test through which we had to pass to prove ourselves worthy of a finer realization. (*Exultingly*) And we did pass through it! It hasn't broken us! And now the dream is to come true! Don't you see?

RUTH. (*looking at him with frightened eyes as if she thought he had gone mad*) Yes, Rob, I see; but won't you go back to bed now and rest?

ROBERT. No. I'm going to see the sun rise. It's an augury of good fortune. (*He goes quickly to the window in the rear left, and pushing the curtains aside, stands looking out.* RUTH *springs to her feet and comes quickly to the table, left, where she remains watching* ROBERT *in a tense, expectant attitude. As he peers out his body seems gradually to sag, to grow limp and tired. His voice is mournful as he speaks*) No sun yet. It isn't time. All I can see is the black rim of the damned hills outlined against a creeping grayness. (*He turns around; letting the curtains fall back, stretching a hand out to the wall to support himself. His false strength of a moment has evaporated leaving his face drawn and hollow-eyed. He makes a pitiful attempt to smile*) That's not a very happy augury, is it? But the sun'll come— soon. (*He sways weakly.*)

RUTH. (*hurrying to his side and supporting him*) Please go to bed, won't you, Rob? You don't want to be all wore out when the specialist comes, do you?

ROBERT. (*quickly*) No. That's right. He mustn't think I'm sicker than I am. And I feel as if I could sleep now— (*Cheerfully*) a good, sound, restful sleep.

RUTH. (*helping him to the bedroom door*) That's what you need most. (*They go inside. A moment later she reappears calling back*) I'll shut this door so's you'll be quiet. (*She closes the door and goes quickly to her mother and shakes her by the shoulder*) Ma! Ma! Wake up!

MRS. ATKINS. (*coming out of her sleep with a start*) Glory be! What's the matter with you?

RUTH. It was Rob. He's just been talking to me out here. I put him back to bed. (*Now that she is sure her mother is awake her fear passes and she relapses into dull indifference. She sits down in her chair and stares at the stove—dully*) He acted—funny; and his eyes looked so—so wild like.

MRS. ATKINS. (*with asperity*) And is that all you woke me out of a sound sleep for, and scared me near out of my wits?

RUTH. I was afraid. He talked so crazy. I couldn't quiet him. I didn't want to be alone with him that way. Lord knows what he might do.

MRS. ATKINS. (*scornfully*) Humph! A help I'd be to you and me not able to move a step! Why didn't you run and get Jake?

RUTH. (*dully*) Jake isn't here. He quit last night. He hasn't been paid in three months.

MRS. ATKINS. (*indignantly*) I can't blame him. What decent person'd want to work on a place like this? (*With sudden exasperation*) Oh, I wish you'd never married that man!

RUTH. (*wearily*) You oughtn't to talk about him now when he's sick in his bed.

MRS. ATKINS. (*working herself into a fit of rage*) You know very well, Ruth Mayo, if it wasn't for me helpin' you on the sly out of my savin's, you'd both been in the poor house—and all 'count of his pigheaded pride in not lettin' Andy know the state thin's were in. A nice thin' for me to have to support him out of what I'd saved for my last days—and me an invalid with no one to look to!

RUTH. Andy'll pay you back, Ma. I can tell him so's Rob'll never know.

MRS. ATKINS. (*with a snort*) What'd Rob think you and him was livin' on, I'd like to know?

RUTH. (*dully*) He didn't think about it, I s'pose. (*After a slight pause*) He said he'd made up his mind to ask Andy for help when he comes. (*As a clock in the kitchen strikes six*) Six o'clock. Andy ought to get here directly.

MRS. ATKINS. D'you think this special doctor'll do Rob any good?

RUTH. (*hopelessly*) I don't know. (*The two women remain silent for a time staring dejectedly at the stove.*)

MRS. ATKINS. (*shivering irritably*) For goodness' sake put some wood on that fire. I'm most freezin'!

RUTH. (*pointing to the door in the rear*) Don't talk so loud. Let him sleep if he can. (*She gets wearily from the chair and puts a few pieces of wood in the stove*) This is the last of the wood. I don't know who'll cut more now that Jake's left. (*She sighs and walks to the window in the rear, left, pulls the curtains aside, and looks out*) It's getting gray out. (*She comes back to the stove*) Looks like it'd be a nice day. (*She stretches out her hands to warm them*) Must've

152

been a heavy frost last night. *We're paying for the spell of warm weather we've been having. (The throbbing whine of a motor sounds from the distance outside.)*

MRS. ATKINS. *(sharply)* S-h-h! Listen! Ain't that an auto I hear?

RUTH. *(without interest)* Yes. It's Andy, I s'pose.

MRS. ATKINS. *(with nervous irritation)* Don't sit there like a silly goose. Look at the state of this room! What'll this strange doctor think of us? Look at that lamp chimney all smoke! Gracious sakes, Ruth—

RUTH. *(indifferently)* I've got a lamp all cleaned up in the kitchen.

MRS. ATKINS. *(peremptorily)* Wheel me in there this minute. I don't want him to see me looking a sight. I'll lay down in the room the other side. You don't need me now and I'm dead for sleep. *(RUTH wheels her mother off right. The noise of the motor grows louder and finally ceases as the car stops on the road before the farmhouse. RUTH returns from the kitchen with a lighted lamp in her hand which she sets on the table beside the other. The sound of footsteps on the path is heard—then a sharp rap on the door. RUTH goes and opens it. ANDREW enters, followed by DOCTOR FAWCETT carrying a small black bag. ANDREW has changed greatly. His face seems to have grown highstrung, hardened by the look of decisiveness which comes from being constantly under a strain where judgments on the spur of the moment are compelled to be accurate. His eyes are keener and more alert. There is even a suggestion of ruthless cunning about them. At present, however, his expression is one of tense anxiety. DOCTOR FAW-CETT is a short, dark, middle-aged man with a Vandyke beard. He wears glasses.)*

RUTH. Hello, Andy! I've been waiting—

ANDREW. *(kissing her hastily)* I got here as soon as I could. *(He throws off his cap and heavy overcoat on the table, introducing RUTH and the DOCTOR as he does so. He is dressed in an expensive business suit and appears stouter)* My sister-in-law, Mrs. Mayo—Doctor Fawcett. (*They bow to each other silently.* ANDREW *casts a quick glance about the room*) Where's Rob?

RUTH. (*pointing*) In there.

ANDREW. I'll take your coat and hat, Doctor. (*As he helps the* DOCTOR *with his things*) Is he very bad, Ruth?

RUTH. (*dully*) He's been getting weaker.

ANDREW. Damn! This way, Doctor. Bring the lamp, Ruth. (*He goes into the bedroom, followed by the* DOCTOR *and* RUTH *carrying the clean lamp.* RUTH *reappears almost immediately closing the door behind her, and goes slowly to the outside door, which she opens, and stands in the doorway looking out. The sound of* ANDREW'S *and* ROBERT'S *voices comes from the bedroom. A moment later* ANDREW *re-enters, closing the door softly. He comes forward and sinks down in the rocker on the right of table, leaning his head on his hand. His face is drawn in a shocked expression of great grief. He sighs heavily, staring mournfully in front of him.* RUTH *turns and stands watching him. Then she shuts the door and returns to her chair by the stove, turning it so she can face him.*)

ANDREW. (*glancing up quickly—in a harsh voice*) How long has this been going on?

RUTH. You mean—how long has he been sick?

ANDREW. (*shortly*) Of course! What else?

RUTH. It was last summer he had a bad spell first, but he's been ailin' ever since Mary died—eight months ago.

ANDREW. (*harshly*) Why didn't you let me know—cable me? Do you want him to die, all of you? I'm damned if it doesn't look that way! (*His voice breaking*) Poor old chap! To be sick in this out-of-the-way hole without anyone to attend to him but a country quack! It's a damned shame!

RUTH. (*dully*) I wanted to send you word once, but he only got mad when I told him. He was too proud to ask anything, he said.

ANDREW. Proud? To ask *me*? (*He jumps to his feet and paces nervously back and forth*) I can't understand the way you've acted.

Didn't you see how sick he was getting? Couldn't you realize—why, I nearly dropped in my tracks when I saw him! He looks— (*He shudders*) terrible! (*With fierce scorn*) I suppose you're so used to the idea of his being delicate that you took his sickness as a matter of course. God, if I'd only known!

RUTH. (*without emotion*) A letter takes some time to get where you were—and we couldn't afford to telegraph. We owed everyone already, and I couldn't ask Ma. She'd been giving me money out of her savings till she hadn't much left. Don't say anything to Rob about it. I never told him. He'd only be mad at me if he knew. But I had to, because—God knows how we'd have got on if I hadn't.

ANDREW. You mean to say— (*His eyes seemed to take in the poverty-stricken appearance of the room for the first time*) You sent that telegram to me collect. Was it because— (RUTH *nods silently.* ANDREW *pounds on the table with his fist*) Good God! And all this time I've been—why I've had everything! (*He sits down in his chair and pulls it close to* RUTH's *impulsively*) But—I can't get it through my head. Why? Why? What has happened? How did it ever come about? Tell me!

RUTH. (*dully*) There's nothing much to tell. Things kept getting worse, that's all—and Rob didn't seem to care. He never took any interest since way back when your Ma died. After that he got men to take charge, and they nearly all cheated him—he couldn't tell— and left one after another. Then after Mary died he didn't pay no heed to anything any more—just stayed indoors and took to reading books again. So I had to ask Ma if she wouldn't help us some.

ANDREW. (*surprised and horrified*) Why, damn it, this is frightful! Rob must be mad not to have let me know. Too proud to ask help of *me!* What's the matter with him in God's name? (*A sudden, horrible suspicion entering his mind*) Ruth! Tell me the truth. His mind hasn't gone back on him, has it?

RUTH. (*dully*) I don't know. Mary's dying broke him up terrible— but he's used to her being gone by this, I s'pose.

ANDREW. (*looking at her queerly*) Do you mean to say *you're* used to it?

RUTH. (*in a dead tone*) There's a time comes—when you don't mind any more—anything.

ANDREW. (*looks at her fixedly for a moment—with great pity*) I'm sorry, Ruth—if I seemed to blame you. I didn't realize— The sight of Rob lying in bed there, so gone to pieces—it made me furious at everyone. Forgive me, Ruth.

RUTH. There's nothing to forgive. It doesn't matter.

ANDREW. (*springing to his feet again and pacing up and down*) Thank God I came back before it was too late. This doctor will know exactly what to do. That's the first thing to think of. When Rob's on his feet again we can get the farm working on a sound basis once more. I'll see to that—before I leave.

RUTH. You're going away again?

ANDREW. I've got to.

RUTH. You wrote Rob you was coming back to stay this time.

ANDREW. I expected to—until I got to New York. Then I learned certain facts that make it necessary. (*With a short laugh*) To be candid, Ruth, I'm not the rich man you've probably been led to believe by my letters—not now. I was when I wrote them. I made money hand over fist as long as I stuck to legitimate trading; but I wasn't content with that. I wanted it to come easier, so like all the rest of the idiots, I tried speculation. Oh, I won all right! Several times I've been almost a millionaire—on paper—and then come down to earth again with a bump. Finally the strain was too much. I got disgusted with myself and made up my mind to get out and come home and forget it and really live again. (*He gives a harsh laugh*) And now comes the funny part. The day before the steamer sailed I saw what I thought was a chance to become a millionaire again. (*He snaps his fingers*) That easy! I plunged. Then, before things broke, I left—I was so confident I couldn't be wrong. But when I landed in New York—I wired you I had business to wind up, didn't I? Well, it was the business that wound me up! (*He smiles grimly, pacing up and down, his hands in his pockets.*)

RUTH. (*dully*) You found—you'd lost everything?

ANDREW. (*sitting down again*) Practically. (*He takes a cigar from his pocket, bites the end off, and lights it*) Oh, I don't mean I'm dead broke. I've saved ten thousand from the wreckage, maybe twenty. But that's a poor showing for five years' hard work. That's why I'll have to go back. (*Confidently*) I can make it up in a year or so down there—and I don't need but a shoestring to start with. (*A weary expression comes over his face and he sighs heavily*) I wish I didn't have to. I'm sick of it all.

RUTH. It's too bad—things seem to go wrong so.

ANDREW. (*shaking off his depression—briskly*) They might be much worse. There's enough left to fix the farm O. K. before I go. I won't leave 'til Rob's on his feet again. In the meantime I'll make things fly around here. (*With satisfaction*) I need a rest, and the kind of rest I need is hard work in the open—just like I used to do in the old days. (*Stopping abruptly and lowering his voice cautiously*) Not a word to Rob about my losing money! Remember that, Ruth! You can see why. If he's grown so touchy he'd never accept a cent if he thought I was hard up; see?

RUTH. Yes, Andy. (*After a pause, during which* ANDREW *puffs at his cigar abstractedly, his mind evidently busy with plans for the future, the bedroom door is opened and* DOCTOR FAWCETT *enters, carrying a bag. He closes the door quietly behind him and comes forward, a grave expression on his face.* ANDREW *springs out of his chair.*)

ANDREW. Ah, Doctor! (*He pushes a chair between his own and* RUTH's) Won't you have a chair?

FAWCETT. (*glancing at his watch*) I must catch the nine o'clock back to the city. It's imperative. I have only a moment. (*Sitting down and clearing his throat—in a perfunctory, impersonal voice*) The case of your brother, Mr. Mayo, is— (*He stops and glances at* RUTH *and says meaningly to* ANDREW) Perhaps it would be better if you and I—

157

RUTH. (*with dogged resentment*) I know what you mean, Doctor. (*Dully*) Don't be afraid I can't stand it. I'm used to bearing trouble by this; and I can guess what you've found out. (*She hesitates for a moment—then continues in a monotonous voice*) Rob's going to die.

ANDREW. (*angrily*) Ruth!

FAWCETT. (*raising his hand as if to command silence*) I am afraid my diagnosis of your brother's condition forces me to the same conclusion as Mrs. Mayo's.

ANDREW. (*groaning*) But, Doctor, surely—

FAWCETT. (*calmly*) Your brother hasn't long' to live—perhaps a few days, perhaps only a few hours. It's a marvel that he's alive at this moment. My examination revealed that both of his lungs are terribly affected.

ANDREW. (*brokenly*) Good God! (RUTH *keeps her eyes fixed on her lap in a trance-like stare.*)

FAWCETT. I am sorry I have to tell you this. If there was anything that could be done—

ANDREW. There isn't anything?

FAWCETT. (*shaking his head*) It's too late. Six months ago there might have—

ANDREW. (*in anguish*) But if we were to take him to the mountains —or to Arizona—or—

FAWCETT. That might have prolonged his life six months ago. (ANDREW *groans*) But now— (*He shrugs his shoulders significantly.*)

ANDREW. (*appalled by a sudden thought*) Good heavens, you haven't told him this, have you, Doctor?

FAWCETT. No. I lied to him. I said a change of climate— (*He looks at his watch again nervously*) I must leave you. (*He gets up.*)

ANDREW. (*getting to his feet—insistently*) But there must still be some chance—

FAWCETT. (*as if he were reassuring a child*) There is always that last chance—the miracle. (*He puts on his hat and coat—bowing to* RUTH) Good-by, Mrs. Mayo.

158

RUTH. (*without raising her eyes—dully*) Good-by.

ANDREW. (*mechanically*) I'll walk to the car with you, Doctor. (*They go out of the door.* RUTH *sits motionlessly. The motor is heard starting and the noise gradually recedes into the distance.* ANDREW *re-enters and sits down in his chair, holding his head in his hands*) Ruth! (*She lifts her eyes to his*) Hadn't we better go in and see him? God! I'm afraid to! I know he'll read it in my face. (*The bedroom door is noiselessly opened and* ROBERT *appears in the doorway. His cheeks are flushed with fever, and his eyes appear unusually large and brilliant.* ANDREW *continues with a groan*) It can't be, Ruth. It can't be as hopeless as he said. There's always a fighting chance. We'll take Rob to Arizona. He's *got* to get well. There *must* be a chance!

ROBERT. (*in a gentle tone*) Why must there, Andy? (RUTH *turns and stares at him with terrified eyes.*)

ANDREW. (*whirling around*) Rob! (*Scoldingly*) What are you doing out of bed? (*He gets up and goes to him*) Get right back now and obey the Doc, or you're going to get a licking from me!

ROBERT. (*ignoring these remarks*) Help me over to the chair, please, Andy.

ANDREW. Like hell I will! You're going right back to bed, that's where you're going, and stay there! (*He takes hold of* ROBERT's *arm.*)

ROBERT. (*mockingly*) Stay there 'til I die, eh, Andy? (*Coldly*) Don't behave like a child. I'm sick of lying down. I'll be more rested sitting up. (*As* ANDREW *hesitates—violently*) I swear I'll get out of bed every time you put me there. You'll have to sit on my chest, and that wouldn't help my health any. Come on, Andy. Don't play the fool. I want to talk to you, and I'm going to. (*With a grim smile*) A dying man has some rights, hasn't he?

ANDREW. (*with a shudder*) Don't talk that way, for God's sake! I'll only let you sit down if you'll promise that. Remember. (*He helps* ROBERT *to the chair between his own and* RUTH's) Easy now! There you are! Wait, and I'll get a pillow for you. (*He goes into the*

159

bedroom. ROBERT *looks at* RUTH *who shrinks away from him in terror.* ROBERT *smiles bitterly.* ANDREW *comes back with the pillow which he places behind* ROBERT'S *back)* How's that?

ROBERT. (*with an affectionate smile*) Fine! Thank you! (*As* ANDREW *sits down*) Listen, Andy. You've asked me not to talk—and I won't after I've made my position clear. (*Slowly*) In the first place I know I'm dying. (RUTH *bows her head and covers her face with her hands. She remains like this all during the scene between the two brothers.*)

ANDREW. Rob! That isn't so!

ROBERT. (*wearily*) It *is* so! Don't lie to me. After Ruth put me to bed before you came, I saw it clearly for the first time. (*Bitterly*) I'd been making plans for our future—Ruth's and mine—so it came hard at first—the realization. Then when the doctor examined me, I knew—although he tried to lie about it. And then to make sure I listened at the door to what he told you. So don't mock me with fairy tales about Arizona, or any such rot as that. Because I'm dying is no reason you should treat me as an imbecile or a coward. Now that I'm sure what's happening I can say Kismet to it with all my heart. It was only the silly uncertainty that hurt. (*There is a pause.* ANDREW *looks around in impotent anguish, not knowing what to say.* ROBERT *regards him with an affectionate smile.*)

ANDREW. (*finally blurts out*) It isn't foolish. You *have* got a chance. If you heard all the Doctor said that ought to prove it to you.

ROBERT. Oh, you mean when he spoke of the miracle? (*Dryly*) I don't believe in miracles—in my case. Besides, I know more than any doctor on earth *could* know—because I *feel* what's coming. (*Dismissing the subject*) But we've agreed not to talk of it. Tell me about yourself, Andy. That's what I'm interested in. Your letters were too brief and far apart to be illuminating.

ANDREW. I meant to write oftener.

ROBERT. (*with a faint trace of irony*) I judge from them you've accomplished all you set out to do five years ago?

ANDREW. That isn't much to boast of.

ROBERT. (*surprised*) Have you really, honestly reached that conclusion?

ANDREW. Well, it doesn't seem to amount to much now.

ROBERT. But you're rich, aren't you?

ANDREW. (*with a quick glance at* RUTH) Yes, I s'pose so.

ROBERT. I'm glad. You can do to the farm all I've undone. But what did you do down there? Tell me. You went in the grain business with that friend of yours?

ANDREW. Yes. After two years I had a share in it. I sold out last year. (*He is answering* ROBERT'S *questions with great reluctance.*)

ROBERT. And then?

ANDREW. I went in on my own.

ROBERT. Still in grain?

ANDREW. Yes.

ROBERT. What's the matter? You look as if I were accusing you of something.

ANDREW. I'm proud enough of the first four years. It's after that I'm not boasting of. I took to speculating.

ROBERT. In wheat?

ANDREW. Yes.

ROBERT. And you made money—gambling?

ANDREW. Yes.

ROBERT. (*thoughtfully*) I've been wondering what the great change was in you. (*After a pause*) You—a farmer—to gamble in a wheat pit with scraps of paper. There's a spiritual significance in that picture, Andy. (*He smiles bitterly*) I'm a failure, and Ruth's another—but we can both justly lay some of the blame for our stumbling on God. But you're the deepest-dyed failure of the three, Andy. You've spent eight years running away from yourself. Do you see what I mean? You used to be a creator when you loved the farm. You and life were in harmonious partnership. And now—(*He stops as if seeking vainly for words*) My brain is muddled. But part of what I mean is that your gambling with the thing you used to love to create proves how far astray— So you'll be punished. You'll have to suffer to win back— (*His voice grows weaker and he sighs wearily*) It's no use. I can't say it. (*He lies back and closes his eyes, breathing pantingly.*)

ANDREW. (*slowly*) I think I know what you're driving at, Rob—and it's true, I guess. (ROBERT *smiles gratefully and stretches out his hand, which* ANDREW *takes in his.*)

ROBERT. I want you to promise me to do one thing, Andy, after—

ANDREW. I'll promise anything, as God is my Judge!

ROBERT. Remember, Andy, Ruth has suffered double her share. (*His voice faltering with weakness*) Only through contact with suffering, Andy, will you—awaken. Listen. You must marry Ruth—afterwards.

RUTH. (*with a cry*) Rob! (ROBERT *lies back, his eyes closed, gasping heavily for breath.*)

ANDREW. (*making signs to her to humor him—gently*) You're tired out, Rob. You better lie down and rest a while, don't you think? We can talk later on.

ROBERT. (*with a mocking smile*) Later on! You always were an optimist, Andy! (*He sighs with exhaustion*) Yes, I'll go and rest a while. (*As* ANDREW *comes to help him*) It must be near sunrise, isn't it?

ANDREW. It's after six.

ROBERT. (*As* ANDREW *helps him into the bedroom*) Shut the door, Andy. I want to be alone. (ANDREW *reappears and shuts the door softly. He comes and sits down on his chair again, supporting his head on his hands. His face drawn with the intensity of his dry-eyed anguish.*)

RUTH. (*glancing at him—fearfully*) He's out of his mind now, isn't he?

ANDREW. He may be a little delirious. The fever would do that. (*With impotent rage*) God, what a shame! And there's nothing we can do but sit and—wait! (*He springs from his chair and walks to the stove.*)

RUTH. (*dully*) He was talking—wild—like he used to—only this time it sounded—unnatural, don't you think?

ANDREW. I don't know. The things he said to me had truth in them —even if he did talk them way up in the air, like he always sees things. Still— (*He glances down at* RUTH *keenly*) Why do you suppose he wanted us to promise we'd— (*Confusedly*) You know what he said.

RUTH. (*dully*) His mind was wandering, I s'pose.

ANDREW. (*with conviction*) No—there was something back of it.

RUTH. He wanted to make sure I'd be all right—after he'd gone, I expect.

ANDREW. No, it wasn't that. He knows very well I'd naturally look after you without—anything like that.

RUTH. He might be thinking of—something happened five years back, the time you came home from the trip.

ANDREW. What happened? What do you mean?

RUTH. (*dully*) We had a fight.

ANDREW. A fight? What has that to do with me?

RUTH. It was about you—in a way.

ANDREW. (*amazed*) About *me*?

RUTH. Yes, mostly. You see I'd found out I'd made a mistake about Rob soon after we were married—when it was too late.

ANDREW. Mistake? (*Slowly*) You mean—you found out you didn't love Rob?

RUTH. Yes.

ANDREW. Good God!

RUTH. And then I thought that when Mary came it'd be different, and I'd love him; but it didn't happen that way. And I couldn't bear with his blundering and book-reading—and I grew to hate him, almost.

ANDREW. Ruth!

RUTH. I couldn't help it. No woman could. It had to be because I loved someone else, I'd found out. (*She sighs wearily*) It can't do no harm to tell you now—when it's all past and gone—and dead. *You* were the one I really loved—only I didn't come to the knowledge of it 'til too late.

ANDREW. (*stunned*) Ruth! Do you know what you're saying?

RUTH. It was true—then. (*With sudden fierceness*) How could I help it? No woman could.

ANDREW. Then—you loved me—that time I came home?

RUTH. (*doggedly*) I'd known your real reason for leaving home the first time—everybody knew it—and for three years I'd been thinking—

ANDREW. That I loved you?

RUTH. Yes. Then that day on the hill you laughed about what a fool you'd been for loving me once—and I knew it was all over.

ANDREW. Good God, but I never thought— (*He stops, shuddering at his remembrance*) And did Rob—

RUTH. That was what I'd started to tell. We'd had a fight just before you came and I got crazy mad—and I told him all I've told you.

ANDREW. (*gaping at her speechlessly for a moment*) You told Rob—you loved me?

RUTH. Yes.

ANDREW. (*shrinking away from her in horror*) You—you—you mad fool, you! How could you do such a thing?

RUTH. I couldn't help it. I'd got to the end of bearing things—without talking.

ANDREW. Then Rob must have known every moment I stayed here! And yet he never said or showed—God, how he must have suffered! Didn't you know how much he loved you?

RUTH. (*dully*) Yes. I knew he liked me.

ANDREW. Liked you! What kind of a woman are you? Couldn't you have kept silent? Did you have to torture him? No wonder he's dying! And you've lived together for five years with this between you?

RUTH. We've lived in the same house.

ANDREW. Does he still think—

RUTH. I don't know. We've never spoke a word about it since that day. Maybe, from the way he went on, he s'poses I care for you yet.

ANDREW. But you don't. It's outrageous. It's stupid! You don't love me!

RUTH. (*slowly*) I wouldn't know how to feel love, even if I tried, any more.

ANDREW. (*brutally*) And I don't love you, that's sure! (*He sinks into his chair, his head between his hands*) It's damnable such a thing should be between Rob and me. Why, I love Rob better'n anybody in the world and always did. There isn't a thing on God's green earth I wouldn't have done to keep trouble away from him. And I have to be the very one—it's damnable! How am I going to face him again? What can I say to him now? (*He groans with anguished rage. After a pause*) He asked me to promise—what am I going to do?

RUTH. You can promise—so's it'll ease his mind—and not mean anything.

ANDREW. What? Lie to him now—when he's dying? (*Determinedly*) No! It's *you* who'll have to do the lying, since it must be done. You've got a chance now to undo some of all the suffering you've brought on Rob. Go in to him! Tell him you never loved me—it was all a mistake. Tell him you only said so because you were mad and didn't know what you were saying! Tell him something, anything, that'll bring him peace!

RUTH. (*dully*) He wouldn't believe me.

ANDREW. (*furiously*) You've got to make him believe you, do you hear? You've got to—now—hurry—you never know when it may be too late. (*As she hesitates—imploringly*) For God's sake, Ruth! Don't you see you owe it to him? You'll never forgive yourself if you don't.

RUTH. (*dully*) I'll go. (*She gets wearily to her feet and walks slowly*

165

toward the bedroom) But it won't do any good. (ANDREW's *eyes are fixed on her anxiously. She opens the door and steps inside the room. She remains standing there for a minute. Then she calls in a frightened voice*) Rob! Where are you? (*Then she hurries back, trembling with fright*) Andy! Andy! He's gone!

ANDREW. (*misunderstanding her—his face pale with dread*) He's not—

RUTH. (*interrupting him—hysterically*) He's gone! The bed's empty. The window's wide open. He must have crawled out into the yard!

ANDREW. (*springing to his feet. He rushes into the bedroom and returns immediately with an expression of alarmed amazement on his face*) Come! He can't have gone far! (*Grabbing his hat he takes* RUTH's *arm and shoves her toward the door*) Come on! (*Opening the door*) Let's hope to God— (*The door closes behind them, cutting off his words as the curtain falls.*)

ACT THREE—SCENE TWO

S AME as *Act One, Scene One—A section of country highway. The sky to the east is already alight with bright color and a thin, quivering line of flame is spreading slowly along the horizon rim of the dark hills. The roadside, however, is still steeped in the grayness of the dawn, shadowy and vague. The field in the foreground has a wild uncultivated appearance as if it had been allowed to remain fallow the preceding summer. Parts of the snake-fence in the rear have been broken down. The apple tree is leafless and seems dead.*

ROBERT *staggers weakly in from the left. He stumbles into the ditch and lies there for a moment; then crawls with a great effort to the top of the bank where he can see the sun rise, and collapses weakly.* RUTH *and* ANDREW *come hurriedly along the road from the left.*

ANDREW. (*stopping and looking about him*) There he is! I knew it! I knew we'd find him here.

ROBERT. (*trying to raise himself to a sitting position as they hasten to his side—with a wan smile*) I thought I'd given you the slip.

ANDREW. (*with kindly bullying*) Well you didn't, you old scoundrel, and we're going to take you right back where you belong—in bed. (*He makes a motion to lift* ROBERT.)

ROBERT. Don't, Andy. Don't, I tell you!

ANDREW. You're in pain?

ROBERT. (*simply*) No. I'm dying. (*He falls back weakly.* RUTH *sinks down beside him with a sob and pillows his head on her lap.* ANDREW *stands looking down at him helplessly.* ROBERT *moves his head restlessly on* RUTH's *lap*) I couldn't stand it back there in the room. It seemed as if all my life—I'd been cooped in a room. So I thought I'd try to end as I might have—if I'd had the courage—alone—in a ditch by the open road—watching the sun rise.

ANDREW. Rob! Don't talk. You're wasting your strength. Rest a while and then we'll carry you—

ROBERT. Still hoping, Andy? Don't. I know. (*There is a pause during which he breathes heavily, straining his eyes toward the horizon*) The sun comes so slowly. (*With an ironical smile*) The doctor told me to go to the far-off places—and I'd be cured. He was right. That was always the cure for me. It's too late—for this life—but— (*He has a fit of coughing which racks his body*).

ANDREW. (*with a hoarse sob*) Rob! (*He clenches his fists in an impotent rage against Fate*) God! God! (RUTH *sobs brokenly and wipes* ROBERT's *lips with her handkerchief.*)

ROBERT. (*in a voice which is suddenly ringing with the happiness of hope*) You mustn't feel sorry for me. Don't you see I'm happy at last —free—free!—freed from the farm—free to wander on and on— eternally! (*He raises himself on his elbow, his face radiant, and points to the horizon*) Look! Isn't it beautiful beyond the hills? I can hear the old voices calling me to come— (*Exultantly*) And this time I'm going! It isn't the end. It's a free beginning—the start of my voyage! I've won to my trip—the right of release—beyond the horizon! Oh, you ought to be glad—glad—for my sake! (*He collapses weakly*) Andy! (ANDREW *bends down to him*) Remember Ruth—

ANDREW. I'll take care of her, I swear to you, Rob!

ROBERT. Ruth has suffered—remember, Andy—only through sacrifice—the secret beyond there— (*He suddenly raises himself with his last remaining strength and points to the horizon where the edge of the sun's disc is rising from the rim of the hills*) The sun! (*He remains with his eyes fixed on it for a moment. A rattling noise throbs from his throat. He mumbles*) Remember! (*And falls back and is still. RUTH gives a cry of horror and springs to her feet, shuddering, her hands over her eyes.* ANDREW *bends on one knee beside the body, placing a hand over ROBERT's heart, then he kisses his brother reverentially on the forehead and stands up.*)

ANDREW. (*facing* RUTH, *the body between them—in a dead voice*) He's dead. (*With a sudden burst of fury*) God damn you, you never told him!

RUTH. (*piteously*) He was so happy without my lying to him.

ANDREW. (*pointing to the body—trembling with the violence of his rage*) This is your doing, you damn woman, you coward, you murderess!

RUTH. (*sobbing*) Don't, Andy! I couldn't help it—and he knew how I'd suffered, too. He told you—to remember.

ANDREW. (*stares at her for a moment, his rage ebbing away, an expression of deep pity gradually coming over his face. Then he glances down at his brother and speaks brokenly in a compassionate voice*) Forgive me, Ruth—for his sake—and I'll remember— (RUTH *lets her hands fall from her face and looks at him uncomprehendingly. He lifts his eyes to hers and forces out falteringly*) I—you—we've both made a mess of things! We must try to help each other—and—in time —we'll come to know what's right— (*Desperately*) And perhaps we— (*But* RUTH, *if she is aware of his words, gives no sign. She remains silent, gazing at him dully with the sad humility of exhaustion, her mind already sinking back into that spent calm beyond the further troubling of any hope.*)

CURTAIN

THE EMPEROR JONES

CHARACTERS

BRUTUS JONES, *Emperor*

HENRY SMITHERS, *A Cockney Trader*

AN OLD NATIVE WOMAN

LEM, *A Native Chief*

SOLDIERS, *Adherents of Lem*

The Little Formless Fears; Jeff; The Negro Convicts; The Prison Guard; The Planters; The Auctioneer; The Slaves; The Congo Witch Doctor; The Crocodile God.

The action of the play takes place on an island in the West Indies as yet not self-determined by White Marines. The form of native government is, for the time being, an Empire.

SCENES

Scene I: In the palace of the Emperor Jones. Afternoon.

Scene II: The edge of the Great Forest. Dusk.

Scene III: In the Forest. Night.

Scene IV: In the Forest. Night.

Scene V: In the Forest. Night.

Scene VI: In the Forest. Night.

Scene VII: In the Forest. Night.

Scene VIII: Same as Scene Two—the edge of the Great Forest. Dawn.

THE EMPEROR JONES

SCENE ONE

THE *audience chamber in the palace of the Emperor—a spacious, high-ceilinged room with bare, whitewashed walls. The floor is of white tiles. In the rear, to the left of center, a wide archway giving out on a portico with white pillars. The palace is evidently situated on high ground for beyond the portico nothing can be seen but a vista of distant hills, their summits crowned with thick groves of palm trees. In the right wall, center, a smaller arched doorway leading to the living quarters of the palace. The room is bare of furniture with the exception of one huge chair made of uncut wood which stands at center, its back to rear. This is very apparently the Emperor's throne. It is painted a dazzling, eye-smiting scarlet. There is a brilliant orange cushion on the seat and another smaller one is placed on the floor to serve as a footstool. Strips of matting, dyed scarlet, lead from the foot of the throne to the two entrances.*

It is late afternoon but the sunlight still blazes yellowly beyond the portico and there is an oppressive burden of exhausting heat in the air.

As the curtain rises, a native Negro woman sneaks in cautiously from the entrance on the right. She is very old, dressed in cheap calico, bare-footed, a red bandana handkerchief covering all but a few stray wisps of white hair. A bundle bound in colored cloth is carried over her shoulder on the end of a stick. She hesitates beside the doorway, peering back as if in extreme dread of being discovered. Then she begins to glide noiselessly, a step at a time, toward the doorway in the rear. At this moment, SMITHERS *appears beneath the portico.*

SMITHERS *is a tall, stoop-shouldered man about forty. His bald head, perched on a long neck with an enormous Adam's apple, looks like an egg. The tropics have tanned his naturally pasty face with its small, sharp features to a sickly yellow, and native rum has painted his pointed nose to a startling red. His little, washy-blue eyes are red-rimmed and dart about him like a ferret's. His expression is one of unscrupulous meanness, cowardly and dangerous. He is dressed in a worn riding suit of dirty white drill, puttees, spurs, and wears a white cork helmet. A cartridge belt with an automatic revolver is around his waist. He carries a riding whip in his hand. He sees the woman and stops to watch her suspiciously. Then, making up his mind, he steps quickly on tiptoe into the room. The woman, looking back over her shoulder continually, does not see him until it is too late. When she does* SMITHERS *springs forward and grabs her firmly by the shoulder. She struggles to get away, fiercely but silently.*

SMITHERS. (*tightening his grasp—roughly*) Easy! None o' that, me birdie. You can't wiggle out, now I got me 'ooks on yer.

WOMAN. (*seeing the uselessness of struggling, gives way to frantic terror, and sinks to the ground, embracing his knees supplicatingly*) No tell him! No tell him, Mister!

SMITHERS. (*with great curiosity*) Tell 'im? (*Then scornfully*) Oh, you mean 'is bloomin' Majesty. What's the gaime, any'ow? What are you sneakin' away for? Been stealin' a bit, I s'pose. (*He taps her bundle with his riding whip significantly.*)

WOMAN. (*shaking her head vehemently*) No, me no steal.

SMITHERS. Bloody liar! But tell me what's up. There's somethin' funny goin' on. I smelled it in the air first thing I got up this mornin'. You blacks are up to some devilment. This palace of 'is is like a bleedin' tomb. Where's all the 'ands? (*The woman keeps sullenly silent.* SMITHERS *raises his whip threateningly*) Ow, yer won't, won't yer? I'll show yer what's what.

WOMAN. (*coweringly*) I tell, Mister. You no hit. They go—all go. (*She makes a sweeping gesture toward the hills in the distance.*)

SMITHERS. Run away—to the 'ills?

WOMAN. Yes, Mister. Him Emperor—Great Father (*She touches her forehead to the floor with a quick mechanical jerk*) Him sleep after eat. Then they go—all go. Me old woman. Me left only. Now me go too.

SMITHERS. (*his astonishment giving way to an immense, mean satisfaction*) Ow! So that's the ticket! Well, I know bloody well wot's in the air—when they runs orf to the 'ills. The tom-tom 'll be thumping out there bloomin' soon. (*With extreme vindictiveness*) And I'm bloody glad of it, for one! Serve 'im right! Puttin' on airs, the stinkin' nigger! 'Is Majesty! Gawd blimey! I only 'opes I'm there when they takes 'im out to shoot 'im. (*Suddenly*) 'E's still 'ere all right, ain't 'e?

WOMAN. Him sleep.

SMITHERS. 'E's bound to find out soon as 'e wakes up. 'E's cunnin' enough to know when 'is time's come. (*He goes to the doorway on right and whistles shrilly with his fingers in his mouth. The old woman springs to her feet and runs out of the doorway, rear.* SMITHERS *goes after her, reaching for his revolver*) Stop or I'll shoot! (*Then stopping—indifferently*) Pop orf then, if yer like, yer black cow. (*He stands in the doorway, looking after her.*)

(JONES *enters from the right. He is a tall, powerfully-built, full-blooded Negro of middle age. His features are typically negroid, yet there is something decidedly distinctive about his face—an underlying strength of will, a hardy, self-reliant confidence in himself that inspires respect. His eyes are alive with a keen, cunning intelligence. In manner he is shrewd, suspicious, evasive. He wears a light blue uniform coat, sprayed with brass buttons, heavy gold chevrons on his shoulders, gold braid on the collar, cuffs, etc. His pants are bright red with a light blue stripe down the side. Patent leather laced boots with brass spurs, and a belt with a long-barreled, pearl-handled revolver in a holster complete his make up. Yet there is something not altogether ridiculous about his grandeur. He has a way of carrying it off.*)

JONES (*not seeing anyone—greatly irritated and blinking sleepily —shouts*) Who dare whistle dat way in my palace? Who dare wake up de Emperor? I'll git de hide frayled off some o' you niggers sho'!

SMITHERS. (*showing himself—in a manner half-afraid and half-defiant*) It was me whistled to yer. (*As* JONES *frowns angrily*) I got news for yer.

JONES. (*putting on his suavest manner, which fails to cover up his contempt for the white man*) Oh, it's you, Mister Smithers. (*He sits down on his throne with easy dignity*) What news you got to tell me?

SMITHERS. (*coming close to enjoy his discomfiture*) Don't yer notice nothin' funny today?

JONES. (*coldly*) Funny? No. I ain't perceived nothin' of de kind!

SMITHERS. Then yer ain't so foxy as I thought yer was. Where's all your court? (*Sarcastically*) the Generals and the Cabinet Ministers and all?

JONES. (*imperturbably*) Where dey mostly runs to minute I closes my eyes—drinkin' rum and talkin' big down in de town. (*Sarcastically*) How come you don't know dat? Ain't you sousin' with 'em most every day?

SMITHERS. (*stung but pretending indifference—with a wink*) That's part of the day's work. I got ter—ain't I—in my business?

JONES. (*contemptuously*) Yo' business!

SMITHERS. (*imprudently enraged*) Gawd blimey, you was glad enough for me ter take yer in on it when you landed here first. You didn't 'ave no 'igh and mighty airs in them days!

JONES. (*his hand going to his revolver like a flash—menacingly*) Talk polite, white man! Talk polite, you heah me! I'm boss heah now, is you fergettin'? (*The Cockney seems about to challenge this last statement with the facts but something in the other's eyes holds and cows him.*)

SMITHERS. (*in a cowardly whine*) No 'arm meant, old top.

JONES. (*condescendingly*) I accepts yo' apology. (*Lets his hand fall from his revolver*) No use'n you rakin' up ole times. What I was den is one thing. What I is now's another. You didn't let me in on yo' crooked work out o' no kind feelin's dat time. I done de dirty work fo' you—and most o' de brain work, too, fo' dat matter—and I was wu'th money to you, dat's de reason.

SMITHERS. Well, blimey, I give yer a start, didn't I?—when no one else would. I wasn't afraid to 'ire you like the rest was—'count of the story about your breakin' jail back in the States.

JONES. No, you didn't have no s'cuse to look down on me fo' dat. You been in jail you'self more'n once.

SMITHERS. (*furiously*) It's a lie! (*Then trying to pass it off by an attempt at scorn*) Garn! Who told yer that fairy tale?

JONES. Dey's some tings I ain't got to be tole. I kin see 'em in folk's eyes. (*Then after a pause—meditatively*) Yes, you sho' give me a start. And it didn't take long from dat time to git dese fool, woods niggers right where I wanted dem. (*With pride*) From stowaway to Emperor in two years! Dat's goin' some!

SMITHERS. (*with curiosity*) And I bet you got yer pile o' money 'id safe some place.

JONES. (*with satisfaction*) I sho' has! And it's in a foreign bank where no pusson don't ever git it out but me no matter what come. You didn't s'pose I was holdin' down dis Emperor job for de glory in it, did you? Sho'! De fuss and glory part of it, dat's only to turn de heads o' de low-flung, bush niggers dat's here. Dey wants de big circus show for deir money. I gives it to 'em an' I gits de money. (*With a grin*) De long green, dat's me every time! (*Then rebukingly*) But you ain't got no kick agin me, Smithers. I'se paid you back all you done for me many times. Ain't I pertected you and winked at all de crooked tradin' you been doin' right out in de broad day? Sho' I has—and me makin' laws to stop it at de same time! (*He chuckles.*)

SMITHERS. (*grinning*) But, meanin' no 'arm, you been grabbin' right

and left yourself, ain't yer? Look at the taxes you've put on 'em!
Blimey! You've squeezed 'em dry!

JONES. (*chuckling*) No, dey ain't *all* dry yet. I'se still heah, ain't I?

SMITHERS. (*smiling at his secret thought*) They're dry right now,
you'll find out. (*Changing the subject abruptly*) And as for me
breakin' laws, you've broke 'em all yerself just as fast as yer made 'em.

JONES. Ain't I de Emperor? De laws don't go for him. (*Judicially*)
You heah what I tells you, Smithers. Dere's little stealin' like you
does, and dere's big stealin' like I does. For de little stealin' dey gits
you in jail soon or late. For de big stealin' dey makes you Emperor
and puts you in de Hall o' Fame when you croaks. (*Reminiscently*)
If dey's one thing I learns in ten years on de Pullman ca's listenin'
to de white quality talk, it's dat same fact. And when I gits a chance
to use it I winds up Emperor in two years.

SMITHERS. (*unable to repress the genuine admiration of the small
fry for the large*) Yes, yer turned the bleedin' trick, all right. Blimey,
I never seen a bloke 'as 'ad the bloomin' luck you 'as.

JONES. (*severely*) Luck? What you mean—luck?

SMITHERS. I suppose you'll say as that swank about the silver bullet
ain't luck—and that was what first got the fool blacks on yer side the
time of the revolution, wasn't it?

JONES. (*with a laugh*) Oh, dat silver bullet! Sho' was luck. But I
makes dat luck, you heah? I loads de dice! Yessuh! When dat mur-
derin' nigger ole Lem hired to kill me takes aim ten feet away and
his gun misses fire and I shoots him dead, what you heah me say?

SMITHERS. You said yer'd got a charm so's no lead bullet'd kill yer.
You was so strong only a silver bullet could kill yer, you told 'em.
Blimey, wasn't that swank for yer—and plain, fat-'eaded luck?

JONES. (*proudly*) I got brains and I uses 'em quick. Dat ain't luck.

SMITHERS. Yer know they wasn't 'ardly liable to get no silver bullets. And it was luck 'e didn't 'it you that time.

JONES. (*laughing*) And dere all dem fool bush niggers was kneelin'

178

down and bumpin' deir heads on de ground like I was a miracle out o' de Bible. Oh, Lawd, from dat time on I has dem all eatin' out of my hand. I cracks de whip and dey jumps through.

SMITHERS. (*with a sniff*) Yankee bluff done it.

JONES. Ain't a man's talkin' big what makes him big—long as he makes folks believe it? Sho', I talks large when I ain't got nothin' to back it up, but I ain't talkin' wild just de same. I knows I kin fool 'em —I *knows* it—and dat's backin' enough fo' my game. And ain't I got to learn deir lingo and teach some of dem English befo' I kin talk to 'em? Ain't dat wuk? You ain't never learned ary word er it, Smithers, in de ten years you been heah, dough you knows it's money in yo' pocket tradin' wid 'em if you does. But you'se too shiftless to take de trouble.

SMITHERS. (*flushing*) Never mind about me. What's this I've 'eard about yer really 'avin' a silver bullet moulded for yourself?

JONES. It's playin' out my bluff. I has de silver bullet moulded and I tells 'em when de time comes I kills myself wid it. I tells 'em dat's 'cause I'm de on'y man in de world big enuff to git me. No use'n deir tryin'. And dey falls down and bumps deir heads. (*He laughs*) I does dat so's I kin take a walk in peace widout no jealous nigger gunnin' at me from behind de trees.

SMITHERS. (*astonished*) Then you 'ad it made—'onest?

JONES. Sho' did. Heah she be. (*He takes out his revolver, breaks it, and takes the silver bullet out of one chamber*) Five lead an' dis silver baby at de last. Don't she shine pretty? (*He holds it in his hand, looking at it admiringly, as if strangely fascinated.*)

SMITHERS. Let me see. (*Reaches out his hand for it.*)

JONES. (*harshly*) Keep yo' hands whar dey b'long, white man. (*He replaces it in the chamber and puts the revolver back on his hip.*)

SMITHERS. (*snarling*) Gawd blimey! Think I'm a bleedin' thief, you would.

JONES. No, 'tain't dat. I knows you'se scared to steal from me.

On'y I ain't 'lowin' nary body to touch dis baby. She's my rabbit's foot.

SMITHERS. (*sneering*) A bloomin' charm, wot? (*Venomously*) Well, you'll need all the bloody charms you 'as before long, s' 'elp me!

JONES. (*judicially*) Oh, I'se good for six months yit 'fore dey gits sick o' my game. Den, when I sees trouble comin', I makes my getaway.

SMITHERS. Ho! You got it all planned, ain't yer?

JONES. I ain't no fool. I knows dis Emperor's time is sho't. Dat why I make hay when de sun shine. Was you thinkin' I'se aimin' to hold down dis job for life? No, suh! What good is gittin' money if you stays back in dis raggedy country? I wants action when I spends. And when I sees dese niggers gittin' up deir nerve to tu'n me out, and I'se got all de money in sight, I resigns on de spot and beats it quick.

SMITHERS. Where to?

JONES. None o' yo' business.

SMITHERS. Not back to the bloody States, I'll lay my oath.

JONES. (*suspiciously*) Why don't I? (*Then with an easy laugh*) You mean 'count of dat story 'bout me breakin' from jail back dere? Dat's all talk.

SMITHERS. (*skeptically*) Ho, yes!

JONES. (*sharply*) You ain't 'sinuatin' I'se a liar, is you?

SMITHERS. (*hastily*) No, Gawd strike me! I was only thinkin' o' the bloody lies you told the blacks 'ere about killin' white men in the States.

JONES. (*angered*) How come dey're lies?

SMITHERS. You'd 'ave been in jail if you 'ad, wouldn't yer then? (*With venom*) And from what I've 'eard, it ain't 'ealthy for a black to kill a white man in the States. They burns 'em in oil, don't they?

JONES. (*with cool deadliness*) You mean lynchin' 'd scare me? Well, I tells you, Smithers, maybe I does kill one white man back dere. Maybe I does. And maybe I kills another right heah 'fore long if he don't look out.

SMITHERS. (*trying to force a laugh*) I was on'y spoofin' yer. Can't yer take a joke? And you was just sayin' you'd never been in jail.

JONES. (*in the same tone—slightly boastful*) Maybe I goes to jail dere for gettin' in an argument wid razors ovah a crap game. Maybe I gits twenty years when dat colored man die. Maybe I gits in 'nother argument wid de prison guard was overseer ovah us when we're wukin' de road. Maybe he hits me wid a whip and I splits his head wid a shovel and runs away and files de chain off my leg and gits away safe. Maybe I does all dat an' maybe I don't. It's a story I tells you so's you knows I'se de kind of man dat if you evah repeats one word of it, I ends yo' stealin' on dis yearth mighty damn quick!

SMITHERS. (*terrified*) Think I'd peach on yer? Not me! Ain't I always been yer friend?

JONES. (*suddenly relaxing*) Sho' you has—and you better be.

SMITHERS. (*recovering his composure—and with it his malice*) And just to show yer I'm yer friend, I'll tell yer that bit o' news I was goin' to.

JONES. Go ahead! Shoot de piece. Must be bad news from de happy way you look.

SMITHERS. (*warningly*) Maybe it's gettin' time for you to resign— with that bloomin' silver bullet, wot? (*He finishes with a mocking grin.*)

JONES. (*puzzled*) What's dat you say? Talk plain.

SMITHERS. Ain't noticed any of the guards or servants about the place today, I 'aven't.

JONES. (*carelessly*) Dey're all out in de garden sleepin' under de trees. When I sleeps, dey sneaks a sleep, too, and I pretends I never suspicions it. All I got to do is to ring de bell and dey come flyin', makin' a bluff dey was wukin' all de time.

SMITHERS. (*in the same mocking tone*) Ring the bell now an' you'll bloody well see what I means.

JONES. (*startled to alertness, but preserving the same careless tone*) Sho' I rings. (*He reaches below the throne and pulls out a big, common dinner bell which is painted the same vivid scarlet as the throne. He rings this vigorously—then stops to listen. Then he goes to both doors, rings again, and looks out.*)

SMITHERS. (*watching him with malicious satisfaction, after a pause —mockingly*) The bloody ship is sinkin' an' the bleedin' rats 'as slung their 'ooks.

JONES. (*in a sudden fit of anger flings the bell clattering into a corner*) Low-flung, woods niggers! (*Then catching* SMITHERS' *eye on him, he controls himself and suddenly bursts into a low chuckling laugh*) Reckon I overplays my hand dis once! A man can't take de pot on a bob-tailed flush all de time. Was I sayin' I'd sit in six months mo'? Well, I'se changed my mind den. I cashes in and resigns de job of Emperor right dis minute.

SMITHERS. (*with real admiration*) Blimey, but you're a cool bird, and no mistake.

JONES. No use'n fussin'. When I knows de game's up I kisses it good-by widout no long waits. Dey've all run off to de hills, ain't dey?

SMITHERS. Yes—every bleedin' man jack of 'em.

JONES. Den de revolution is at de post. And de Emperor better git his feet smokin' up de trail. (*He starts for the door in rear.*)

SMITHERS. Goin' out to look for your 'orse? Yer won't find any. They steals the 'orses first thing. Mine was gone when I went for 'im this mornin'. That's wot first give me a suspicion of wot was up.

JONES. (*alarmed for a second, scratches his head, then philosophically*) Well, den I hoofs it. Feet, do yo' duty! (*He pulls out a gold watch and looks at it*) Three-thuty. Sundown's at six-thuty or dere-

abouts. (*Puts his watch back—with cool confidence*) I got plenty o'
time to make it easy.

SMITHERS. Don't be so bloomin' sure of it. They'll be after you 'ot
and 'eavy. Ole Lem is at the bottom o' this business an' 'e 'ates you
like 'ell. 'E'd rather do for you than eat 'is dinner, 'e would!

JONES. (*scornfully*) Dat fool no-count nigger! Does you think I'se
scared o' him? I stands him on his thick head more'n once befo' dis,
and I does it again if he comes in my way— (*Fiercely*) And dis time
I leave him a dead nigger fo' sho'!

SMITHERS. You'll 'ave to cut through the big forest—an' these blacks
'ere can sniff and follow a trail in the dark like 'ounds. You'd 'ave to
'ustle to get through that forest in twelve hours even if you knew all
the bloomin' trails like a native.

JONES. (*with indignant scorn*) Look-a-heah, white man! Does you
think I'se a natural bo'n fool? Give me credit fo' havin' some sense,
fo' Lawd's sake! Don't you s'pose I'se looked ahead and made sho'
of all de chances? I'se gone out in dat big forest, pretendin' to hunt,
so many times dat I knows it high an' low like a book. I could go
through on dem trails wid my eyes shut. (*With great contempt*)
Think dese ign'rent bush niggers dat ain't got brains enuff to know
deir own names even can catch Brutus Jones? Huh, I s'pects not!
Not on yo' life! Why, man, de white men went after me wid blood-
hounds where I come from an' I jes' laughs at 'em. It's a shame to
fool dese black trash around heah, dey're so easy. You watch me,
man. I'll make dem look sick, I will. I'll be 'cross de plain to de edge
of de forest by time dark comes. Once in de woods in de night, dey
got a swell chance o' findin' dis baby! Dawn tomorrow I'll be out at
de oder side and on de coast whar dat French gunboat is stayin'. She
picks me up, takes me to Martinique when she go dar, and dere I is
safe wid a mighty big bankroll in my jeans. It's easy as rollin' off a log.

SMITHERS. (*maliciously*) But s'posin' somethin' 'appens wrong an'
they do nab yer?

183

JONES. (*decisively*) Dey don't—dat's de answer.

SMITHERS. But, just for argyment's sake—what'd you do?

JONES. (*frowning*) I'se got five lead bullets in dis gun good enuff fo' common bush niggers—and after dat I got de silver bullet left to cheat 'em out o' gittin' me.

SMITHERS. (*jeeringly*) Ho, I was fergettin' that silver bullet. You'll bump yourself orf in style, won't yer? Blimey!

JONES. (*gloomily*) You kin bet yo' whole roll on one thing, white man. Dis baby plays out his string to de end and when he quits, he quits wid a bang de way he ought. Silver bullet ain't none too good for him when he go, dat's a fac'! (*Then shaking off his nervousness —with a confident laugh*) Sho'! What is I talkin' about? Ain't come to dat yit and I never will—not wid trash niggers like dese yere. (*Boastfully*) Silver bullet bring me luck anyway. I kin outguess, outrun, outfight, an' outplay de whole lot o' dem all ovah de board any time o' de day er night! You watch me! (*From the distant hills comes the faint, steady thump of a tom-tom, low and vibrating. It starts at a rate exactly corresponding to normal pulse beat—72 to the minute—and continues at a gradually accelerating rate from this point uninterruptedly to the very end of the play.*)

(*JONES starts at the sound. A strange look of apprehension creeps into his face for a moment as he listens. Then he asks, with an attempt to regain his most casual manner*) What's dat drum beatin' fo'?

SMITHERS. (*with a mean grin*) For you. That means the bleedin' ceremony 'as started. I've 'eard it before and I knows.

JONES. Cer'mony? What cer'mony?

SMITHERS. The blacks is 'oldin' a bloody meetin', 'avin' a war dance, gettin' their courage worked up b'fore they starts after you.

JONES. Let dem! Dey'll sho' need it!

SMITHERS. And they're there 'oldin their 'eathen religious service —makin' no end of devil spells and charms to 'elp 'em against your silver bullet. (*He guffaws loudly*) Blimey, but they're balmy as 'ell!

JONES. (*a tiny bit awed and shaken in spite of himself*) Huh! Takes more'n dat to scare dis chicken!

SMITHERS. (*scenting the other's feeling—maliciously*) Ternight when it's pitch black in the forest, they'll 'ave their pet devils and ghosts 'oundin' after you. You'll find yer bloody 'air 'll be standin' on end before termorrow mornin'. (*Seriously*) It's a bleedin' queer place, that stinkin' forest, even in daylight. Yer don't know what might 'appen in there, it's that rotten still. Always sends the cold shivers down my back minute I gets in it.

JONES. (*with a contemptuous sniff*) I ain't no chicken-liver like you is. Trees an' me, we'se friends, and dar's a full moon comin' bring me light. And let dem po' niggers make all de fool spells dey'se a min' to. Does yo' s'pect I'se silly enuff to b'lieve in ghosts an' ha'nts an' all dat ole woman's talk? G'long, white man! You ain't talkin' to me. (*With a chuckle*) Doesn't you know dey's got to do wid a man was member in good standin' o' de Baptist Church? Sho' I was dat when I was porter on de Pullmans, befo' I gits into my little trouble. Let dem try deir heathen tricks. De Baptist Church done pertect me and land dem all in hell. (*Then with more confident satisfaction*) And I'se got little silver bullet o' my own, don't forgit!

SMITHERS. Ho! You 'aven't give much 'eed to your Baptist Church since you been down 'ere. I've 'eard myself you 'ad turned yer coat an' was takin' up with their blarsted witch doctors, or whatever the 'ell yer calls the swine.

JONES. (*vehemently*) I pretends to! Sho' I pretends! Dat's part o' my game from de fust. If I finds out dem niggers believes dat black is white, den I yells it out louder 'n deir loudest. It don't git me nothin' to do missionary work for de Baptist Church. I'se after de coin, an' I lays my Jesus on de shelf for de time bein'. (*Stops abruptly to look at his watch—alertly*) But I ain't got de time to waste on no more fool talk wid you. I'se gwine away from heah dis secon'. (*He reaches in under the throne and pulls out an expensive Panama hat with a bright multi-colored band and sets it jauntily on his head*) So long, white man! (*With a grin*) See you in jail sometime, maybe!

SMITHERS. Not me, you won't. Well, I wouldn't be in yer bloody boots for no bloomin' money, but 'ere's wishin' yer luck just the same.

JONES. (*contemptuously*) You're de frightenedest man evah I see! I tells you I'se safe's 'f I was in New York City. It takes dem niggers from now to dark to git up de nerve to start somethin'. By dat time, I'se got a head start dey never kotch up wid.

SMITHERS. (*maliciously*) Give my regards to any ghosts yer meets up with.

JONES. (*grinning*) If dat ghost got money, I'll tell him never ha'nt you less'n he wants to lose it.

SMITHERS. (*flattered*) Garn! (*Then curiously*) Ain't yer takin' no luggage with yer?

JONES. I travels light when I wants to move fast. And I got tinned grub buried on de edge o' de forest. (*Boastfully*) Now say dat I don't look ahead an' use my brains! (*With a wide, liberal gesture*) I will all dat's left in de palace to you—and you better grab all you kin sneak away wid befo' dey gits here.

SMITHERS. (*gratefully*) Righto—and thanks ter yer. (*As* JONES *walks toward the door in rear—cautioningly*) Say! Look 'ere, you ain't goin' out that way, are yer?

JONES. Does you think I'd slink out de back door like a common nigger? I'se Emperor yit, ain't I? And de Emperor Jones leaves de way he comes, and dat black trash don't dare stop him—not yit, leastways. (*He stops for a moment in the doorway, listening to the far-off but insistent beat of the tom-tom*) Listen to dat roll-call, will you? Must be mighty big drum carry dat far. (*Then with a laugh*) Well, if dey ain't no whole brass band to see me off, I sho' got de drum part of it. So long, white man. (*He puts his hands in his pockets and*

*with studied carelessness, whistling a tune, he saunters out of the
doorway and off to the left.)*

SMITHERS. *(looks after him with a puzzled admiration)* 'E's got 'is
bloomin' nerve with 'im, s'elp me! *(Then angrily)* Ho—the bleedin'
nigger—puttin' on 'is bloody airs! I 'opes they nabs 'im an' gives 'im
what's what!

CURTAIN

SCENE TWO

THE *end of the plain where the Great Forest begins. The foreground is sandy, level ground dotted by a few stones and clumps
of stunted bushes cowering close against the earth to escape the buf-
feting of the trade wind. In the rear the forest is a wall of darkness
dividing the world. Only when the eye becomes accustomed to the
gloom can the outlines of separate trunks of the nearest trees be made
out, enormous pillars of deeper blackness. A somber monotone of
wind lost in the leaves moans in the air. Yet this sound serves but to
intensify the impression of the forest's relentless immobility, to form
a background throwing into relief its brooding, implacable silence.*

JONES *enters from the left, walking rapidly. He stops as he nears
the edge of the forest, looks around him quickly, peering into the dark
as if searching for some familiar landmark. Then, apparently satisfied
that he is where he ought to be, he throws himself on the ground, dog-
tired.*

Well, heah I is. In de nick o' time, too! Little mo' an' it'd be
blacker'n de ace of spades heahabouts. *(He pulls a bandana handkerchief from his hip pocket and mops off his perspiring face)* Sho'!
Gimme air! I'se tuckered out sho' 'nuff. Dat soft Emperor job ain't
no trainin' fo' a long hike ovah dat plain in de brilin' sun. *(Then*

with a chuckle) Cheer up, nigger, de worst is yet to come. (*He lifts his head and stares at the forest. His chuckle peters out abruptly. In a tone of awe*) My goodness, look at dem woods, will you? Dat no-count Smithers say dey'd be black an' he sho' called de turn. (*Turning away from them quickly and looking down at his feet, he snatches at a chance to change the subject—solicitously*) Feet, you is holdin' up yo' end fine an' I sutinly hopes you ain't blisterin' none. It's time you git a rest. (*He takes off his shoes, his eyes studiously avoiding the forest. He feels of the soles of his feet gingerly*) You is still in de pink —on'y a little mite feverish. Cool yo'selfs. Remember you done got a long journey yit befo' you. (*He sits in a weary attitude, listening to the rhythmic beating of the tom-tom. He grumbles in a loud tone to cover up a growing uneasiness*) Bush niggers! Wonder dey wouldn't git sick o' beatin' dat drum. Sound louder, seem like. I wonder if dey's startin' after me? (*He scrambles to his feet, looking back across the plain*) Couldn't see dem now, nohow, if dey was hundred feet away. (*Then shaking himself like a wet dog to get rid of these depressing thoughts*) Sho', dey's miles an' miles behind. What you gittin' fidgety about? (*But he sits down and begins to lace up his shoes in great haste, all the time muttering reassuringly*) You know what? Yo' belly is empty, dat's what's de matter wid you. Come time to eat! Wid nothin' but wind on yo' stomach, o' course you feels jiggedy. Well, we eats right heah an' now soon's I gits dese pesky shoes laced up. (*He finishes lacing up his shoes*) Dere! Now le's see! (*Gets on his hands and knees and searches the ground around him with his eyes*) White stone, white stone, where is you? (*He sees the first white stone and crawls to it with satisfaction*) Heah you is! I knowed dis was de right place. Box of grub, come to me. (*He turns over the stone and feels in under it—in a tone of dismay*) Ain't heah! Gorry, is I in de right place or isn't I? Dere's 'nother stone. Guess dat's it. (*He scrambles to the next stone and turns it over*) Ain't heah, neither! Grub, whar is you? Ain't heah. Gorry, has I got to go hungry into dem woods—all de night? (*While he is talking he scrambles from one stone to another, turning them over in frantic haste. Finally, he jumps to his feet excitedly*) Is I lost de place? Must have! But how dat happen when I was followin' de trail across de plain in broad daylight? (*Almost plaintively*) I'se hungry, I is! I gotta git my feed. Whar's my strength gonna come from if I doesn't? Gorry, I gotta find dat grub high an' low somehow! Why it come dark so quick like dat? Can't see nothin'. (*He scratches a match on his trousers and peers about him. The rate of the beat of the far-off tom-tom increases perceptibly as he does so. He mutters in a bewildered voice*) How come all dese white stones come heah when I only remembers one? (*Suddenly, with a frightened gasp, he flings the match on the ground and stamps on it*) Nigger, is you gone crazy mad? Is you lightin' matches to show dem whar you is? Fo' Lawd's sake, use yo' haid. Gorry, I'se got to be careful! (*He stares at the plain behind him apprehensively, his hand on his revolver*) But how come all dese white stones? And whar's dat tin box o' grub I hid all wrapped up in oilcloth?

(*While his back is turned, the* LITTLE FORMLESS FEARS *creep out from the deeper blackness of the forest. They are black, shapeless, only their glittering little eyes can be seen. If they have any describable form at all it is that of a grubworm about the size of a creeping child. They move noiselessly, but with deliberate, painful effort, striving to raise themselves on end, failing and sinking prone again.* JONES *turns about to face the forest. He stares up at the tops of the trees, seeking vainly to discover his whereabouts by their conformation.*)

Can't tell nothin' from dem trees! Gorry, nothin' 'round heah looks like I evah seed it befo'. I'se done lost de place sho' 'nuff! (*With mournful foreboding*) It's mighty queer! It's mighty queer! (*With sudden forced defiance—in an angry tone*) Woods, is you tryin' to put somethin' ovah on me?

(*From the formless creatures on the ground in front of him comes*

189

a tiny gale of low mocking laughter like a rustling of leaves. They squirm upward toward him in twisted attitudes. JONES *looks down, leaps backward with a yell of terror, yanking out his revolver as he does so—in a quavering voice*) What's dat? Who's dar? What is you? Git away from me befo' I shoots you up! You don't?—

(*He fires. There is a flash, a loud report, then silence broken only by the far-off, quickened throb of the tom-tom. The formless creatures have scurried back into the forest.* JONES *remains fixed in his position, listening intently. The sound of the shot, the reassuring feel of the revolver in his hand, have somewhat restored his shaken nerve. He addresses himself with renewed confidence.*)

Dey're gone. Dat shot fix 'em. Dey was only little animals—little wild pigs, I reckon. Dey've maybe rooted out yo' grub an' eat it. Sho', you fool nigger, what you think dey is—ha'nts? (*Excitedly*) Gorry, you give de game away when you fire dat shot. Dem niggers heah dat fo' su'tin'! Time you beat it in de woods widout no long waits. (*He starts for the forest—hesitates before the plunge—then urging himself in with manful resolution*) Git in, nigger! What you skeered at? Ain't nothin' dere but de trees! Git in! (*He plunges boldly into the forest.*)

SCENE THREE

I N THE *forest. The moon has just risen. Its beams, drifting through the canopy of leaves, make a barely perceptible, suffused, eerie glow. A dense low wall of underbrush and creepers is in the nearer foreground, fencing in a small triangular clearing. Beyond this is the massed blackness of the forest like an encompassing barrier. A path is dimly discerned leading down to the clearing from left, rear, and winding away from it again toward the right. As the scene opens nothing can be distinctly made out. Except for the beating of the tom-tom, which is a trifle louder and quicker than at the close of the previous*

*scene, there is silence, broken every few seconds by a queer, clicking
sound. Then gradually the figure of the Negro,* JEFF, *can be discerned
crouching on his haunches at the rear of the triangle. He is middle-
aged, thin, brown in color, is dressed in a Pullman porter's uniform
and cap. He is throwing a pair of dice on the ground before him,
picking them up, shaking them, casting them out with the regular,
rigid, mechanical movements of an automaton. The heavy, plodding
footsteps of someone approaching along the trail from the left are
heard and* JONES' *voice, pitched on a slightly higher key and strained
in a cheery effort to overcome its own tremors.*

De moon's rizen. Does you heah dat, nigger? You gits more light
from dis out. No mo' buttin' yo' fool head agin' de trunks an'
scratchin' de hide off yo' legs in de bushes. Now you sees whar yo'se
gwine. So cheer up! From now on you has a snap. (*He steps just to
the rear of the triangular clearing and mops off his face on his sleeve.
He has lost his Panama hat. His face is scratched, his brilliant uniform
shows several large rents*) What time's it gittin' to be, I wonder? I
dassent light no match to find out. Phoo'. It's wa'm an' dat's a fac'!
(*Wearily*) How long I been makin tracks in dese woods? Must be
hours an' hours. Seems like fo'evah! Yit can't be, when de moon's jes'
riz. Dis am a long night fo' yo', yo' Majesty! (*With a mournful
chuckle*) Majesty! Der ain't much majesty 'bout dis baby now. (*With
attempted cheerfulness*) Never min'. It's all part o' de game. Dis night
come to an end like everything else. And when you gits dar safe and
has dat bankroll in yo' hands you laughs at all dis. (*He starts to whistle
but checks himself abruptly*) What yo' whistlin' for, you po' dope!
Want all de worl' to heah you? (*He stops talking to listen*) Heah dat
ole drum! Sho' gits nearer from de sound. Dey's packin' it along wid
'em. Time fo' me to move. (*He takes a step forward, then stops—
worriedly*) What's dat odder queer clickety sound I heah? Dere it is!
Sound close! Sound like—sound like— Fo' God sake, sound like some
nigger was shootin' crap! (*Frightenedly*) I better beat it quick when

I gits dem notions. (*He walks quickly into the clear space—then stands transfixed as he sees* JEFF—*in a terrified gasp*) Who dar? Who dat? Is dat you, Jeff? (*Starting toward the other, forgetful for a moment of his surroundings and really believing it is a living man that he sees—in a tone of happy relief*) Jeff! I'se sho' mighty glad to see you! Dey tol' me you done died from dat razor cut I gives you. (*Stopping suddenly, bewilderedly*) But how you come to be heah, nigger? (*He stares fascinatedly at the other who continues his mechanical play with the dice.* JONES' *eyes begin to roll wildly. He stutters*) Ain't you gwine—look up—can't you speak to me? Is you—is you—a ha'nt? (*He jerks out his revolver in a frenzy of terrified rage*) Nigger, I kills you dead once. Has I got to kill you ag'in? You take it den. (*He fires. When the smoke clears away* JEFF *has disappeared.* JONES *stands trembling—then with a certain reassurance*) He's gone, anyway. Ha'nt or not ha'nt, dat shot fix him. (*The beat of the far-off tom-tom is perceptibly louder and more rapid.* JONES *becomes conscious of it—with a start, looking back over his shoulder*) Dey's gittin' near! Dey's comin' fast! And heah I is shootin' shots to let 'em know jes' whar I is! Oh, Gorry, I'se got to run. (*Forgetting the path he plunges wildly into the underbrush in the rear and disappears in the shadow.*)

SCENE FOUR

IN THE forest. *A wide dirt road runs diagonally from right, front, to left, rear. Rising sheer on both sides the forest walls it in. The moon is now up. Under its light the road glimmers ghastly and unreal. It is as if the forest had stood aside momentarily to let the road pass through and accomplish its veiled purpose. This done, the forest will fold in upon itself again and the road will be no more.* JONES *stumbles in from the forest on the right. His uniform is ragged and torn. He looks about him with numbed surprise when he sees the road, his eyes blinking in the bright moonlight. He flops down exhaustedly and pants heavily for a while. Then with sudden anger.*

I'm meltin' wid heat! Runnin' an' runnin' an' runnin'! Damn dis heah coat! Like a straitjacket! (*He tears off his coat and flings it away from him, revealing himself stripped to the waist*) Dere! Dat's better! Now I kin breathe! (*Looking down at his feet, the spurs catch his eye*) And to hell wid dese high-fangled spurs. Dey're what's been a-trippin' me up an' breakin' my neck. (*He unstraps them and flings them away disgustedly*) Dere! I gits rid o' dem frippety Emperor trappin's an' I travels lighter. Lawd! I'se tired! (*After a pause, listening to the insistent beat of the tom-tom in the distance*) I must 'a' put some distance between myself an' dem—runnin' like dat—and yit—dat damn drum sounds jes' de same—nearer, even. Well, I guess I a'most holds my lead anyhow. Dey won't never catch up. (*With a sigh*) If on'y my fool legs stands up. Oh, I'se sorry I evah went in for dis. Dat Emperor job is sho' hard to shake. (*He looks around him suspiciously*) How'd dis road evah git heah? Good level road, too. I never remembers seein' it befo'. (*Shaking his head apprehensively*) Dese woods is sho' full o' de queerest things at night. (*With a sudden terror*) Lawd God, don't let me see no more o' dem ha'nts! Dey gits my goat! (*Then trying to talk himself into confidence*) Ha'nts! You fool nigger, dey ain't no such things! Don't de Baptist parson tell you dat many time? Is you civilized, or is you like dese ign'rent black niggers heah? Sho'! Dat was all in yo' own head. Wasn't nothin' dere. Wasn't no Jeff! Know what? You jus' get seein' dem things 'cause yo' belly's empty and you's sick wid hunger inside. Hunger 'fects yo' head and yo' eyes. Any fool know dat. (*Then pleading fervently*) But bless God, I don't come across no more o' dem, whatever dey is! (*Then cautiously*) Rest! Don't talk! Rest! You needs it. Den you gits on yo' way again. (*Looking at the moon*) Night's half gone a'most. You hits de coast in de mawning! Den you's all safe.

(*From the right forward a small gang of Negroes enter. They are dressed in striped convict suits, their heads are shaven, one leg drags limpingly, shackled to a heavy ball and chain. Some carry picks, the others shovels. They are followed by a white man dressed in the uniform of a prison guard. A Winchester rifle is slung across his shoulders and he carries a heavy whip. At a signal from the* GUARD *they stop on the road opposite where* JONES *is sitting.* JONES, *who has been staring up at the sky, unmindful of their noiseless approach, suddenly looks down and sees them. His eyes pop out, he tries to get to his feet and fly, but sinks back, too numbed by fright to move. His voice catches in a choking prayer.*)

Lawd Jesus!

(*The* PRISON GUARD *cracks his whip—noiselessly—and at that signal all the convicts start to work on the road. They swing their picks, they shovel, but not a sound comes from their labor. Their movements, like those of* JEFF *in the preceding scene, are those of automatons,— rigid, slow, and mechanical. The* PRISON GUARD *points sternly at* JONES *with his whip, motions him to take his place among the other shovelers.* JONES *gets to his feet in a hypnotized stupor. He mumbles subserviently.*)

Yes, suh! Yes, suh! I'se comin'.

(*As he shuffles, dragging one foot, over to his place, he curses under his breath with rage and hatred.*)

God damn yo' soul, I gits even wid you yit, sometime.

(*As if there were a shovel in his hands he goes through weary, mechanical gestures of digging up dirt, and throwing it to the roadside. Suddenly the* GUARD *approaches him angrily, threateningly. He raises his whip and lashes* JONES *viciously across the shoulders with it.* JONES *winces with pain and cowers abjectly. The* GUARD *turns his back on him and walks away contemptuously. Instantly* JONES *straightens up. With arms upraised as if his shovel were a club in his hands he springs murderously at the unsuspecting* GUARD. *In the act of crashing down his shovel on the white man's skull,* JONES *suddenly becomes aware that his hands are empty. He cries despairingly).*

Whar's my shovel? Gimme my shovel 'til I splits his damn head! *(Appealing to his fellow convicts)* Gimme a shovel, one o' you, fo' God's sake!

(They stand fixed in motionless attitudes, their eyes on the ground. The GUARD *seems to wait expectantly, his back turned to the attacker.* JONES *bellows with baffled, terrified rage, tugging frantically at his revolver).*

I kills you, you white debil, if it's de last thing I evah does! Ghost or debil, I kill you agin!

(He frees the revolver and fires point blank at the GUARD's *back. Instantly the walls of the forest close in from both sides, the road and the figures of the convict gang are blotted out in an enshrouding darkness. The only sounds are a crashing in the underbrush as* JONES *leaps away in mad flight and the throbbing of the tom-tom, still far distant, but increased in volume of sound and rapidity of beat.)*

SCENE FIVE

A LARGE *circular clearing, enclosed by the serried ranks of gigantic trunks of tall trees whose tops are lost to view. In the center is a big dead stump worn by time into a curious resemblance to an auction block. The moon floods the clearing with a clear light.* JONES *forces his way in through the forest on the left. He looks wildly about the clearing with hunted, fearful glances. His pants are in tatters, his shoes cut and misshapen, flapping about his feet. He slinks cautiously to the stump in the center and sits down in a tense position, ready for instant flight. Then he holds his head in his hands and rocks back and forth, moaning to himself miserably.*

Oh, Lawd, Lawd! Oh, Lawd, Lawd! (*Suddenly he throws himself on his knees and raises his clasped hands to the sky—in a voice of agonized pleading*) Lawd Jesus, heah my prayer! I'se a po' sinner, a po' sinner! I knows I done wrong, I knows it! When I cotches Jeff cheatin' wid loaded dice my anger overcomes me and I kills him dead! Lawd, I done wrong! When dat guard hits me wid de whip, my anger overcomes me, and I kills him dead. Lawd, I done wrong! And down heah whar dese fool bush niggers raises me up to the seat o' de mighty, I steals all I could grab. Lawd, I done wrong! I knows it! I'se sorry! Forgive me, Lawd! Forgive dis po' sinner! (*Then beseeching terrifiedly*) And keep dem away, Lawd! Keep dem away from me! And stop dat drum soundin' in my ears! Dat begin to sound ha'nted, too. (*He gets to his feet, evidently slightly reassured by his prayer—with attempted confidence*) De Lawd'll preserve me from dem ha'nts after dis. (*Sits down on the stump again*) I ain't skeered o' real men. Let dem come. But dem odders— (*He shudders—then looks down at his feet, working his toes inside the shoes—with a groan*) Oh, my po' feet! Dem shoes ain't no use no more 'ceptin' to hurt. I'se better off widout dem. (*He unlaces them and pulls them off—holds the wrecks of the shoes in his hands and regards them mournfully*) You was real, A-one patin' leather, too. Look at you now. Emperor, you'se gittin' mighty low!

(*He sighs dejectedly and remains with bowed shoulders, staring down at the shoes in his hands as if reluctant to throw them away. While his attention is thus occupied, a crowd of figures silently enter the clearing from all sides. All are dressed in Southern costumes of the period of the fifties of the last century. There are middle-aged men who are evidently well-to-do planters. There is one spruce, authoritative individual—the* AUCTIONEER. *There is a crowd of curious spectators, chiefly young belles and dandies who have come to the slave-market for diversion. All exchange courtly greetings in dumb show and chat silently together. There is something stiff, rigid, unreal, marionettish about their movements. They group themselves about the stump. Finally a batch of slaves is led in from the left by an attendant—three men of different ages, two women, one with a baby in her arms, nursing. They are placed to the left of the stump, beside* JONES.

The white planters look them over appraisingly as if they were cattle, and exchange judgments on each. The dandies point with their fingers and make witty remarks. The belles titter bewitchingly. All this in silence save for the ominous throb of the tom-tom. The AUC-TIONEER *holds up his hand, taking his place at the stump. The groups strain forward attentively. He touches* JONES *on the shoulder peremptorily, motioning for him to stand on the stump—the auction block.*

JONES *looks up, sees the figures on all sides, looks wildly for some opening to escape, sees none, screams and leaps madly to the top of the stump to get as far away from them as possible. He stands there, cowering, paralyzed with horror. The* AUCTIONEER *begins his silent spiel. He points to* JONES, *appeals to the planters to see for themselves. Here is a good field hand, sound in wind and limb as they can see. Very strong still in spite of his being middle-aged. Look at that back. Look at those shoulders. Look at the muscles in his arms and his sturdy legs. Capable of any amount of hard labor. Moreover, of a good disposition, intelligent and tractable. Will any gentleman start the bidding? The* PLANTERS *raise their fingers, make their bids. They are apparently all eager to possess* JONES. *The bidding is lively, the crowd interested. While this has been going on,* JONES *has been seized by the courage of desperation. He dares to look down and around him. Over his face abject terror gives way to mystification, to gradual realization —stutteringly.)*

What you all doin', white folks? What's all dis? What you all lookin' at me fo'? What you doin' wid me, anyhow? (*Suddenly convulsed with raging hatred and fear*) Is dis a auction? Is you sellin' me like dey uster befo' de war? (*Jerking out his revolver just as the* AUCTIONEER *knocks him down to one of the planters—glaring from him to the purchaser*) And *you* sells me? And *you* buys me? I shows you I'se a free nigger, damn yo' souls! (*He fires at the* AUCTIONEER *and at the* PLANTER *with such rapidity that the two shots are almost simultaneous. As if this were a signal the walls of the forest fold in. Only blackness remains and silence broken by* JONES *as he rushes off, crying with fear—and by the quickened, ever louder beat of the tom-tom.*)

SCENE SIX

A CLEARED *space in the forest. The limbs of the trees meet over it forming a low ceiling about five feet from the ground. The interlocked ropes of creepers reaching upward to entwine the tree trunks give an arched appearance to the sides. The space thus enclosed is like the dark, noisome hold of some ancient vessel. The moonlight is almost completely shut out and only a vague wan light filters through. There is the noise of someone approaching from the left, stumbling and crawling through the undergrowth.* JONES' *voice is heard between chattering moans.*

Oh, Lawd, what I gwine do now? Ain't got no bullet left on'y de silver one. If mo' o' dem ha'nts come after me, how I gwine skeer dem away? Oh, Lawd, on'y de silver one left—an' I gotta save dat fo' luck. If I shoots dat one I'm a goner sho'! Lawd, it's black heah! Whar's de moon? Oh, Lawd, don't dis night evah come to an end! (*By the sounds, he is feeling his way cautiously forward*) Dere! Dis feels like a clear space. I gotta lie down an' rest. I don't care if dem niggers does cotch me. I gotta rest.

(*He is well forward now where his figure can be dimly made out. His pants have been so torn away that what is left of them is no better than a breech cloth. He flings himself full length, face downward on the ground, panting with exhaustion. Gradually it seems to grow lighter in the enclosed space and two rows of seated figures can be seen behind* JONES. *They are sitting in crumpled, despairing attitudes, hunched, facing one another with their backs touching the forest walls as if they were shackled to them. All are Negroes, naked save for loin cloths. At first they are silent and motionless. Then they begin to sway slowly forward toward each other and back again in unison, as if they were laxly letting themselves follow the long roll of a ship at sea. At the same time, a low, melancholy murmur rises among them, increasing gradually by rhythmic degrees which seem to be directed and controlled by the throb of the tom-tom in the distance, to a long, tremulous wail of despair that reaches a certain pitch, unbearably acute, then falls by slow gradations of tone into silence and is taken up again.* JONES *starts, looks up, sees the figures, and throws himself down again to shut out the sight. A shudder of terror shakes his whole body as the wail rises up about him again. But the next time, his voice, as if under some uncanny compulsion, starts with the others. As their chorus lifts he rises to a sitting posture similar to the others, swaying back and forth. His voice reaches the highest pitch of sorrow, of desolation. The light fades out, the other voices cease, and only darkness is left.* JONES *can be heard scrambling to his feet and running off, his voice sinking down the scale and receding as he moves farther and farther away in the forest. The tom-tom beats louder, quicker, with a more insistent, triumphant pulsation.*)

SCENE SEVEN

T HE *foot of a gigantic tree by the edge of a great river. A rough structure of boulders, like an altar, is by the tree. The raised river bank is in the nearer background. Beyond this the surface of the river spreads out, brilliant and unruffled in the moonlight, blotted out and merged into a veil of bluish mist in the distance.* JONES' *voice is heard from the left rising and falling in the long, despairing wail of the chained slaves, to the rhythmic beat of the tom-tom. As his voice sinks into silence, he enters the open space. The expression of his face is fixed and stony, his eyes have an obsessed glare, he moves with a strange deliberation like a sleep-walker or one in a trance. He looks around at the tree, the rough stone altar, the moonlit surface of the river beyond, and passes his hand over his head with a vague gesture of puzzled bewilderment. Then, as if in obedience to some obscure impulse, he sinks into a kneeling, devotional posture before the altar. Then he seems to come to himself partly, to have an uncertain realization of what he is doing, for he straightens up and stares about him horrifiedly—in an incoherent mumble.*

What—what is I doin'? What is—dis place? Seems like I know dat tree—an' dem stones—an' de river. I remember—seems like I been heah befo'. (*Tremblingly*) Oh, Gorry, I'se skeered in dis place! I'se skeered. Oh, Lawd, pertect dis sinner!

(*Crawling away from the altar, he cowers close to the ground, his face hidden, his shoulders heaving with sobs of hysterical fright. From behind the trunk of the tree, as if he had sprung out of it, the figure of the* CONGO WITCH DOCTOR *appears. He is wizened and old, naked except for the fur of some small animal tied about his waist, its bushy tail hanging down in front. His body is stained all over a bright red. Antelope horns are on each side of his head, branching upward. In one hand he carries a bone rattle, in the other a charm stick with a bunch of white cockatoo feathers tied to the end. A great number of glass beads and bone ornaments are about his neck, ears, wrists, and ankles. He struts noiselessly with a queer prancing step to a position in the clear ground between* JONES *and the altar. Then with a preliminary, summoning stamp of his foot on the earth, he begins to dance and to chant. As if in response to his summons the beating of the tom-tom grows to a fierce, exultant boom whose throbs seem to fill the air with vibrating rhythm.* JONES *looks up, starts to spring to his feet, reaches a half-kneeling, half-squatting position and remains rigidly fixed there, paralyzed with awed fascination by this new apparition. The* WITCH DOCTOR *sways, stamping with his foot, his bone rattle clicking the time. His voice rises and falls in a weird, monotonous croon, without articulate word divisions. Gradually his dance becomes clearly one of a narrative in pantomime, his croon is an incantation, a charm to allay the fierceness of some implacable deity demanding sacrifice. He flees, he is pursued by devils, he hides, he flees again. Ever wilder and wilder becomes his flight, nearer and nearer draws the pursuing evil, more and more the spirit of terror gains possession of him. His croon, rising to intensity, is punctuated by shrill cries.* JONES *has become completely hypnotized. His voice joins in the incantation, in the cries, he beats time with his hands and sways his body to and fro from the waist. The whole spirit and meaning of the dance has entered into him, has become his spirit. Finally the theme of the pantomime halts on a howl of despair, and is taken up again in a note of savage hope. There is a salvation. The forces of evil demand sacrifice. They must be appeased. The* WITCH DOCTOR *points with his wand to the sacred tree, to the river beyond, to the altar, and finally to* JONES *with a ferocious command.* JONES *seems to sense the meaning of this. It is he who must offer himself for sacrifice. He beats his forehead abjectly to the ground, moaning hysterically.)*

Mercy, Oh, Lawd! Mercy! Mercy on dis po' sinner.

(The WITCH DOCTOR *springs to the river bank. He stretches out his arms and calls to some God within its depths. Then he starts backward slowly, his arms remaining out. A huge head of a crocodile appears over the bank and its eyes, glittering greenly, fasten upon* JONES. *He stares into them fascinatedly. The* WITCH DOCTOR *prances up to him, touches him with his wand, motions with hideous command toward the waiting monster.* JONES *squirms on his belly nearer and nearer, moaning continually.)*

Mercy, Lawd! Mercy!

(The crocodile heaves more of his enormous hulk onto the land. JONES *squirms toward him. The* WITCH DOCTOR'S *voice shrills out in*

furious exultation, the tom-tom beats madly. JONES *cries out in a fierce, exhausted spasm of anguished pleading.*)

Lawd, save me! Lawd Jesus, heah my prayer!

(*Immediately, in answer to his prayer, comes the thought of the one bullet left him. He snatches at his hip, shouting defiantly.*)

De silver bullet! You don't git me yit!

(*He fires at the green eyes in front of him. The head of the crocodile sinks back behind the river bank, the* WITCH DOCTOR *springs behind the sacred tree and disappears.* JONES *lies with his face to the ground, his arms outstretched, whimpering with fear as the throb of the tom-tom fills the silence about him with a somber pulsation, a baffled but revengeful power.*)

SCENE EIGHT

D AWN. *Same as Scene Two, the dividing line of forest and plain. The nearest tree trunks are dimly revealed but the forest behind them is still a mass of glooming shadow. The tom-tom seems on the very spot, so loud and continuously vibrating are its beats.* LEM *enters from the left, followed by a small squad of his soldiers, and by the Cockney trader,* SMITHERS. LEM *is a heavy-set, ape-faced old savage of the extreme African type, dressed only in a loin cloth. A revolver and cartridge belt are about his waist. His soldiers are in different degrees of rag-concealed nakedness. All wear broad palm-leaf hats. Each one carries a rifle.* SMITHERS *is the same as in Scene One. One of the soldiers, evidently a tracker, is peering about keenly on the ground. He points to the spot where* JONES *entered the forest.* LEM *and* SMITHERS *come to look.*

SMITHERS. (*after a glance, turns away in disgust*) That's where 'e went in right enough. Much good it'll do yer. 'E's miles orf by this

202

an' safe to the Coast, damn 's 'ide! I tole yer yer'd lose 'im, didn't I?—
wastin' the 'ole bloomin' night beatin' yer bloody drum and castin'
yer silly spells! Gawd blimey, wot a pack!

LEM. (*gutturally*) We cotch him. (*He makes a motion to his soldiers
who squat down on their haunches in a semi-circle.*)

SMITHERS. (*exasperatedly*) Well, ain't yer goin' in an' 'unt 'im in the
woods? What the 'ell's the good of waitin'?

LEM. (*imperturbably—squatting down himself*) We cotch him.

SMITHERS. (*turning away from him contemptuously*) Aw! Garn!
'E's a better man than the lot o' you put together. I 'ates the sight o'
'im but I'll say that for 'im. (*A sound comes from the forest. The
soldiers jump to their feet, cocking their rifles alertly.* LEM *remains
sitting with an imperturbable expression, but listening intently. He
makes a quick signal with his hand. His followers creep quickly into
the forest, scattering so that each enters at a different spot.*)

SMITHERS. You ain't thinkin' that would be 'im, I 'ope?

LEM. (*calmly*) We cotch him.

SMITHERS. Blarsted fat 'eads! (*Then after a second's thought—wonderingly*) Still an' all, it might 'appen. If 'e lost 'is bloody way in these
stinkin' woods 'e'd likely turn in a circle without 'is knowin' it.

LEM. (*peremptorily*) Ssshh! (*The reports of several rifles sound
from the forest, followed a second later by savage, exultant yells. The
beating of the tom-tom abruptly ceases.* LEM *looks up at the white
man with a grin of satisfaction*) We cotch him. Him dead.

SMITHERS. (*with a snarl*) 'Ow d'yer know it's 'im an' 'ow d'yer
know 'e's dead?

LEM. My mens dey got um silver bullets. Lead bullet no kill him.
He got um strong charm. I cook um money, make um silver bullet,
make um strong charm, too.

SMITHERS. (*astonished*) So that's wot you was up to all night, wot?
You was scared to put after 'im till you'd moulded silver bullets, eh?

LEM. (*simply stating a fact*) Yes. Him got strong charm. Lead no
good.

SMITHERS. (*slapping his thigh and guffawing*) Haw-haw! If yer don t beat all 'ell! (*Then recovering himself—scornfully*) I'll bet yer it ain't 'im they shot at all, yer bleedin' looney!

LEM. (*calmly*) Dey come bring him now. (*The soldiers come out of the forest, carrying* JONES' *limp body. He is dead. They carry him to* LEM, *who examines his body with great satisfaction.* SMITHERS *leans over his shoulder—in a tone of frightened awe*) Well, they did for yer right enough, Jonesey, me lad! Dead as a 'erring! (*Mockingly*) Where's yer 'igh an' mighty airs now, yer bloomin' Majesty? (*Then with a grin*) Silver bullets! Gawd blimey, but yer died in the 'eight o' style, any'ow!

CURTAIN

THE HAIRY APE

**A COMEDY OF ANCIENT AND MODERN LIFE
IN EIGHT SCENES**

CHARACTERS

ROBERT SMITH, "YANK"

PADDY

LONG

MILDRED DOUGLAS

HER AUNT

SECOND ENGINEER

A GUARD

A SECRETARY OF AN ORGANIZATION

Stokers, Ladies, Gentlemen, etc.

SCENES

THE HAIRY APE

SCENE ONE

THE *firemen's forecastle of a transatlantic liner an hour after sailing from New York for the voyage across. Tiers of narrow, steel bunks, three deep, on all sides. An entrance in rear. Benches on the floor before the bunks. The room is crowded with men, shouting, cursing, laughing, singing—a confused, inchoate uproar swelling into a sort of unity, a meaning—the bewildered, furious, baffled defiance of a beast in a cage. Nearly all the men are drunk. Many bottles are passed from hand to hand. All are dressed in dungaree pants, heavy ugly shoes. Some wear singlets, but the majority are stripped to the waist.*

The treatment of this scene, or of any other scene in the play, should by no means be naturalistic. The effect sought after is a cramped space in the bowels of a ship, imprisoned by white steel. The lines of bunks, the uprights supporting them, cross each other like the steel framework of a cage. The ceiling crushes down upon the men's heads. They cannot stand upright. This accentuates the natural stooping posture which shoveling coal and the resultant over-development of back and shoulder muscles have given them. The men themselves should resemble those pictures in which the appearance of Neanderthal Man is guessed at. All are hairy-chested, with long arms of tremendous power, and low, receding brows above their small, fierce, resentful eyes. All the civilized white races are represented, but except for the slight differentiation in color of hair, skin, eyes, all these men are alike.

The curtain rises on a tumult of sound. YANK *is seated in the fore-*

THE HAIRY APE

ground. He seems broader, fiercer, more truculent, more powerful, more sure of himself than the rest. They respect his superior strength —the grudging respect of fear. Then, too, he represents to them a self-expression, the very last word in what they are, their most highly developed individual.

VOICES. Gif me trink dere, you!
    'Ave a wet!
    Salute!
    Gesundheit!
    Skoal!
    Drunk as a lord, God stiffen you!
    Here's how!
    Luck!
    Pass back that bottle, damn you!
    Pourin' it down his neck!
    Ho, Froggy! Where the devil have you been?
    La Touraine.
    I hit him smash in yaw, py Gott!
    Jenkins—the First—he's a rotten swine—
    And the coppers nabbed him—and I run—
    I like peer better. It don't pig head gif you.
    A slut, I'm saying'! She robbed me aslape—
    To hell with 'em all!
    You're a bloody liar!
    Say dot again! (*Commotion. Two men about to fight are pulled apart.*)
    No scrappin' now!
    Tonight—
    See who's the best man!
    Bloody Dutchman!
    Tonight on the for'ard square.
    I'll bet on Dutchy.

He packa da wallop, I tella you!

Shut up, Wop!

No fightin', maties. We're all chums, ain't we?

(*A voice starts bawling a song.*)

"*Beer, beer, glorious beer!*

Fill yourselves right up to here."

YANK. (*for the first time seeming to take notice of the uproar about him, turns around threateningly—in a tone of contemptuous authority*) Choke off dat noise! Where d'yuh get dat beer stuff? Beer, hell! Beer's for goils—and Dutchmen. Me for somep'n wit a kick to it! Gimme a drink, one of youse guys. (*Several bottles are eagerly offered. He takes a tremendous gulp at one of them; then, keeping the bottle in his hand, glares belligerently at the owner, who hastens to acquiesce in this robbery by saying*) All righto, Yank. Keep it and have another. (YANK *contemptuously turns his back on the crowd again. For a second there is an embarrassed silence. Then—*)

VOICES. We must be passing the Hook.

She's beginning to roll to it.

Six days in hell—and then Southampton.

Py Yesus, I vish somepody take my first vatch for me!

Gittin' seasick, Square-head?

Drink up and forget it!

What's in your bottle?

Gin.

Dot's nigger trink.

Absinthe? It's doped. You'll go off your chump, Froggy!

Cochon!

Whisky, that's the ticket!

Where's Paddy?

Going asleep.

Sing us that whisky song, Paddy. (*They all turn to an old, wizened Irishman who is dozing, very drunk, on the benches forward.*

209

*His face is extremely monkey-like with all the sad, patient pathos of
that animal in his small eyes.)*
  Singa da song, Caruso Pat!
  He's gettin' old. The drink is too much for him.
  He's too drunk.

PADDY. *(blinking about him, starts to his feet resentfully, swaying,
holding on to the edge of a bunk)* I'm never too drunk to sing. 'Tis
only when I'm dead to the world I'd be wishful to sing at all. *(With
a sort of sad contempt)* "Whisky Johnny," ye want? A chanty, ye
want? Now that's a queer wish from the ugly like of you, God help
you. But no matther. *(He starts to sing in a thin, nasal, doleful tone:)*

  "Oh, whisky is the life of man!
    Whisky! O Johnny! (They all join in on this.)
  Oh, whisky is the life of man!
    Whisky for my Johnny! (Again chorus.)

  "Oh, whisky drove my old man mad!
    Whisky! O Johnny!
  Oh, whisky drove my old man mad!
    Whisky for my Johnny!"

YANK. *(again turning around scornfully)* Aw hell! Nix on dat old
sailing ship stuff! All dat bull's dead, see? And you're dead, too, yuh
damned old Harp, on'y yuh don't know it. Take it easy, see. Give us
a rest. Nix on de loud noise. *(With a cynical grin)* Can't youse see
I'm tryin' to t'ink?

ALL. *(repeating the word after him as one with the same cynical
amused mockery)* Think! *(The chorused word has a brazen metallic
quality as if their throats were phonograph horns. It is followed by a
general uproar of hard, barking laughter.)*

VOICES. Don't be cracking your head wit ut, Yank.
  You gat headache, py yingo!
  One thing about it—it rhymes with drink!

Ha, ha, ha!

Drink, don't think!

Drink, don't think!

Drink, don't think! (*A whole chorus of voices has taken up this refrain, stamping on the floor, pounding on the benches with fists.*)

YANK. (*taking a gulp from his bottle—good-naturedly*) Aw right. Can de noise. I got yuh de foist time. (*The uproar subsides. A very drunken sentimental tenor begins to sing*):

> "*Far away in Canada,*
> *Far across the sea,*
> *There's a lass who fondly waits*
> *Making a home for me—*"

YANK. (*fiercely contemptuous*) Shut up, yuh lousy boob! Where d'yuh get dat tripe? Home? Home, hell! I'll make a home for yuh! I'll knock yuh dead. Home! T'hell wit home! Where d'yu get dat tripe? Dis is home, see? What d'yuh want wit home? (*Proudly*) I runned away from mine when I was a kid. On'y too glad to beat it, dat was me. Home was lickings for me, dat's all. But yuh can bet your shoit no one ain't never licked me since! Wanter try it, any of youse? Huh! I guess not. (*In a more placated but still contemptuous tone*) Goils waitin' for yuh, huh? Aw, hell! Dat's all tripe. Dey don't wait for no one. Dey'd double-cross yuh for a nickel. Dey're all tarts, get me? Treat 'em rough, dat's me. To hell wit 'em. Tarts, dat's what, de whole bunch of 'em.

LONG. (*very drunk, jumps on a bench excitedly, gesticulating with a bottle in his hand*) Listen 'ere, Comrades! Yank 'ere is right. 'E says this 'ere stinkin' ship is our 'ome. And 'e says as 'ome is 'ell. And 'e's right! This is 'ell. We lives in 'ell, Comrades—and right enough we'll die in it. (*Raging*) And who's ter blame, I arsks yer? We ain't. We wasn't born this rotten way. All men is born free and ekal. That's in the bleedin' Bible, maties. But what d'they care for the Bible—

them lazy, bloated swine what travels first cabin? Them's the ones.
They dragged us down 'til we're on'y wage slaves in the bowels of a
bloody ship, sweatin', burnin' up, eatin' coal dust! Hit's them's ter
blame—the damned Capitalist clarss! (*There had been a gradual
murmur of contemptuous resentment rising among the men until now
he is interrupted by a storm of catcalls, hisses, boos, hard laughter.*)

VOICES. Turn it off!
  Shut up!
  Sit down!
  Closa da face!
  Tamn fool! (*Etc.*).

YANK. (*standing up and glaring at* LONG) Sit down before I knock
yuh down! (LONG *makes haste to efface himself.* YANK *goes on contemptuously*) De Bible, huh? De Cap'tlist class, huh? Aw nix on
dat Salvation Army-Socialist bull. Git a soapbox! Hire a hall! Come
and be saved, huh? Jerk us to Jesus, huh? Aw g'wan! I've listened
to lots of guys like you, see. Yuh're all wrong. Wanter know what
I t'ink? Yuh ain't no good for no one. Yuh're de bunk. Yuh ain't
got no noive, get me? Yuh're yellow, dat's what. Yellow, dat's you.
Say! What's dem slobs in de foist cabin got to do wit us? We're
better men dan dey are, ain't we? Sure! One of us guys could clean
up de whole mob wit one mit. Put one of 'em down here for one
watch in de stokehole, what'd happen? Dey'd carry him off on a
stretcher. Dem boids don't amount to nothin'. Dey're just baggage.
Who makes dis old tub run? Ain't it us guys? Well den, we belong,
don't we? We belong and dey don't. Dat's all. (*A loud chorus of
approval.* YANK *goes on*) As for dis bein' hell—aw, nuts! Yuh lost
your noive, dat's what. Dis is a man's job, get me? It belongs. It runs
dis tub. No stiffs need apply. But yuh're a stiff, see? Yuh're yellow,
dat's you.

VOICES. (*with a great hard pride in them*)
  Righto!
  A man's job!

Talk is cheap, Long.
He never could hold up his end.
Divil take him!
Yank's right. We make it go.
Py Gott, Yank say right ting!
We don't need no one cryin' over us.
Makin' speeches.
Throw him out!
Yellow!
Chuck him overboard!
I'll break his jaw for him!
(*They crowd around* LONG *threateningly.*)

YANK. (*half good-natured again—contemptuously*) Aw, take it easy.
Leave him alone. He ain't woith a punch. Drink up. Here's how,
whoever owns dis. (*He takes a long swallow from his bottle. All drink
with him. In a flash all is hilarious amiability again, back-slapping,
loud talk, etc.*)

PADDY. (*who has been sitting in a blinking, melancholy daze—suddenly cries out in a voice full of old sorrow*) We belong to this, you're
saying? We make the ship to go, you're saying? Yerra then, that Almighty God have pity on us! (*His voice runs into the wail of a keen,
he rocks back and forth on his bench. The men stare at him, startled
and impressed in spite of themselves*) Oh, to be back in the fine days
of my youth, ochone! Oh, there was fine beautiful ships them days
—clippers wid tall masts touching the sky—fine strong men in them
—men that was sons of the sea as if 'twas the mother that bore them.
Oh, the clean skins of them, and the clear eyes, the straight backs and
full chests of them! Brave men they was, and bold men surely! We'd
be sailing out, bound down round the Horn maybe. We'd be making
sail in the dawn, with a fair breeze, singing a chanty song wid no
care to it. And astern the land would be sinking low and dying out,
but we'd give it no heed but a laugh, and never a look behind. For the
day that was, was enough, for we was free men—and I'm thinking 'tis

only slaves do be giving heed to the day that's gone or the day to come
—until they're old like me. (*With a sort of religious exaltation*) Oh,
to be scudding south again wid the power of the Trade Wind driving her on steady through the nights and the days! Full sail on her!
Nights and days! Nights when the foam of the wake would be flaming wid fire, when the sky'd be blazing and winking wid stars. Or the
full of the moon maybe. Then you'd see her driving through the gray
night, her sails stretching aloft all silver and white, not a sound on the
deck, the lot of us dreaming dreams, till you'd believe 'twas no real
ship at all you was on but a ghost ship like the *Flying Dutchman* they
say does be roaming the seas forevermore widout touching a port.
And there was the days, too. A warm sun on the clean decks. Sun
warming the blood of you, and wind over the miles of shiny green
ocean like strong drink to your lungs. Work—aye, hard work—but
who'd mind that at all? Sure, you worked under the sky and 'twas
work wid skill and daring to it. And wid the day done, in the dog
watch, smoking me pipe at ease, the lookout would be raising land
maybe, and we'd see the mountains of South Americy wid the red
fire of the setting sun painting their white tops and the clouds floating
by them! (*His tone of exaltation ceases. He goes on mournfully*)
Yerra, what's the use of talking? 'Tis a dead man's whisper. (*To*
YANK *resentfully*) 'Twas them days men belonged to ships, not now.
'Twas them days a ship was part of the sea, and a man was part of a
ship, and the sea joined all together and made it one. (*Scornfully*)
Is it one wid this you'd be, Yank—black smoke from the funnels
smudging the sea, smudging the decks—the bloody engines pounding
and throbbing and shaking—wid divil a sight of sun or a breath of
clean air—choking our lungs wid coal dust—breaking our backs and
hearts in the hell of the stokehole—feeding the bloody furnace—
feeding our lives along wid the coal, I'm thinking—caged in by steel
from a sight of the sky like bloody apes in the Zoo! (*With a harsh
laugh*) Ho-ho, divil mend you! Is it to belong to that you're wishing?
Is it a flesh and blood wheel of the engines you'd be?

214

YANK. (*who has been listening with a contemptuous sneer, barks out the answer*) Sure ting! Dat's me. What about it?

PADDY. (*as if to himself—with great sorrow*) Me time is past due. That a great wave wid sun in the heart of it may sweep me over the side sometime I'd be dreaming of the days that's gone!

YANK. Aw, yuh crazy Mick! (*He springs to his feet and advances on* PADDY *threateningly—then stops, fighting some queer struggle within himself—lets his hands fall to his sides—contemptuously*) Aw, take it easy. Yuh're aw right, at dat. Yuh're bugs, dat's all—nutty as a cuckoo. All dat tripe yuh been pullin'— Aw, dat's all right. On'y it's dead, get me? Yuh don't belong no more, see. Yuh don't get de stuff. Yuh're too old. (*Disgustedly*) But aw say, come up for air onct in a while, can't yuh? See what's happened since yuh croaked. (*He suddenly bursts forth vehemently, growing more and more excited*) Say! Sure! Sure I meant it! What de hell— Say, lemme talk! Hey! Hey, you old Harp! Hey, youse guys! Say, listen to me—wait a moment—I gotter talk, see. I belong and he don't. He's dead but I'm livin'. Listen to me! Sure I'm part of de engines! Why de hell not! Dey move, don't dey? Dey're speed, ain't dey? Dey smash trou, don't dey? Twenty-five knots a hour! Dat's goin' some! Dat's new stuff! Dat belongs! But him, he's too old. He gets dizzy. Say, listen. All dat crazy tripe about nights and days; all dat crazy tripe about stars and moons; all dat crazy tripe about suns and winds, fresh air and de rest of it—Aw hell, dat's all a dope dream! Hittin' de pipe of de past, dat's what he's doin'. He's old and don't belong no more. But me, I'm young! I'm in de pink! I move wit it. It, get me! I mean de ting dat's de guts of all dis. It ploughs trou all de tripe he's been sayin'. It blows dat up! It knocks dat dead! It slams dat offen de face of de oith! It, get me! De engines and de coal and de smoke and all de rest of it! He can't breathe and swallow coal dust, but I kin, see? Dat's fresh air for me! Dat's food for me! I'm new, get me? Hell in de stokehole? Sure! It takes a man to work in hell. Hell, sure, dat's my fav'rite climate. I eat it up! I git fat on it! It's me makes it hot! It's

215

me makes it roar! It's me makes it move! Sure, on'y for me everyting stops. It all goes dead, get me? De noise and smoke and all de engines movin' de woild, dey stop. Dere ain't nothin' no more! Dat's what I'm sayin'. Everyting else dat makes de woild move, somep'n makes it move. It can't move witout somep'n else, see? Den yuh get down to me. I'm at de bottom, get me! Dere ain't nothin' foither. I'm de end! I'm de start! I start somep'n and de woild moves! It—dat's me!—de new dat's moiderin' de old! I'm de ting in coal dat makes it boin; I'm steam and oil for de engines; I'm de ting in noise dat makes yuh hear it; I'm smoke and express trains and steamers and factory whistles; I'm de ting in gold dat makes it money! And I'm what makes iron into steel! Steel, dat stands for de whole ting! And I'm steel—steel—steel! I'm de muscles in steel, de punch behind it! (*As he says this he pounds with his fist against the steel bunks. All the men, roused to a pitch of frenzied self-glorification by his speech, do likewise. There is a deafening metallic roar, through which* YANK's *voice can be heard bellowing*) Slaves, hell! We run de whole woiks. All de rich guys dat tink dey're somep'n, dey ain't nothin'! Dey don't belong. But us guys, we're in de move, we're at de bottom, de whole ting is us! (PADDY *from the start of* YANK's *speech has been taking one gulp after another from his bottle, at first frightenedly, as if he were afraid to listen, then desperately, as if to drown his senses, but finally has achieved complete indifferent, even amused, drunkenness.* YANK *sees his lips moving. He quells the uproar with a shout*) Hey, youse guys, take it easy! Wait a moment! De nutty Harp is sayin' somep'n.

PADDY. (*is heard now—throws his head back with a mocking burst of laughter*) Ho-ho-ho-ho-ho—

YANK. (*drawing back his fist, with a snarl*) Aw! Look out who yuh're givin' the bark!

PADDY. (*begins to sing the "Miller of Dee" with enormous good nature*)

> "I care for nobody, no, not I,
> And nobody cares for me."

YANK. (*good-natured himself in a flash, interrupts* PADDY *with a slap on the bare back like a report*) Dat's de stuff! Now yuh're gettin' wise to somep'n. Care for nobody, dat's de dope! To hell with 'em all! And nix on nobody else carin'. I kin care for myself, get me! (*Eight bells sound, muffled, vibrating through the steel walls as if some enormous brazen gong were imbedded in the heart of the ship. All the men jump up mechanically, file through the door silently close upon each other's heels in what is very like a prisoner's lockstep.* YANK *slaps* PADDY *on the back*) Our watch, yuh old Harp! (*Mockingly*) Come on down in hell. Eat up de coal dust. Drink in de heat. It's it, see! Act like yuh liked it, yuh better—or croak yuhself.

PADDY. (*with jovial defiance*) To the divil wid it! I'll not report this watch. Let them log me and be damned. I'm no slave the like of you. I'll be sittin' here at me ease, and drinking, and thinking, and dreaming dreams.

YANK. (*contemptuously*) Tinkin' and dreamin', what'll that get yuh? What's tinkin' got to do wit it? We move, don't we? Speed, ain't it? Fog, dat's all you stand for. But we drive trou dat, don't we? We split dat up and smash trou—twenty-five knots a hour! (*Turns his back on* PADDY *scornfully*) Aw, yuh make me sick! Yuh don't belong! (*He strides out the door in rear.* PADDY *hums to himself, blinking drowsily.*)

CURTAIN

SCENE TWO

Two *days out. A section of the promenade deck.* MILDRED DOUGLAS *and her aunt are discovered reclining in deck chairs. The former is a girl of twenty, slender, delicate, with a pale, pretty face marred by a self-conscious expression of disdainful superiority. She looks fretful, nervous and discontented, bored by her own anemia. Her aunt is a pompous and proud—and fat—old lady. She is a type even to the point of a double chin and lorgnettes. She is dressed pretentiously, as if afraid her face alone would never indicate her position in life.* MIL-DRED *is dressed all in white.*

The impression to be conveyed by this scene is one of the beautiful, vivid life of the sea all about—sunshine on the deck in a great flood, the fresh sea wind blowing across it. In the midst of this, these two incongruous, artificial figures, inert and disharmonious, the elder like a gray lump of dough touched up with rouge, the younger looking as if the vitality of her stock had been sapped before she was conceived, so that she is the expression not of its life energy but merely of the artificialities that energy had won for itself in the spending.

MILDRED. (*looking up with affected dreaminess*) How the black smoke swirls back against the sky! Is it not beautiful?

AUNT. (*without looking up*) I dislike smoke of any kind.

MILDRED. My great-grandmother smoked a pipe—a clay pipe.

AUNT. (*ruffling*) Vulgar!

MILDRED. She was too distant a relative to be vulgar. Time mellows pipes.

AUNT. (*pretending boredom but irritated*) Did the sociology you took up at college teach you that—to play the ghoul on every possible occasion, excavating old bones? Why not let your great-grandmother rest in her grave?

MILDRED. (*dreamily*) With her pipe beside her—puffing in Paradise.

AUNT. (*with spite*) Yes, you are a natural born ghoul. You are even getting to look like one, my dear.

MILDRED. (*in a passionless tone*) I detest you, Aunt. (*Looking at her critically*) Do you know what you remind me of? Of a cold pork pudding against a background of linoleum tablecloth in the kitchen of a—but the possibilities are wearisome. (*She closes her eyes.*)

AUNT. (*with a bitter laugh*) Merci for your candor. But since I am and must be your chaperon—in appearance, at least—let us patch up some sort of armed truce. For my part you are quite free to indulge any pose of eccentricity that beguiles you—as long as you observe the amenities—

MILDRED. (*drawling*) The inanities?

AUNT. (*going on as if she hadn't heard*) After exhausting the morbid thrills of social service work on New York's East Side—how they must have hated you, by the way, the poor that you made so much poorer in their own eyes!—you are now bent on making your slumming international. Well, I hope Whitechapel will provide the needed nerve tonic. Do not ask me to chaperon you there, however. I told your father I would not. I loathe deformity. We will hire an army of detectives and you may investigate everything—they allow you to see.

MILDRED. (*protesting with a trace of genuine earnestness*) Please do not mock my attempts to discover how the other half lives. Give me credit for some sort of groping sincerity in that at least. I would like to help them. I would like to be some use in the world. Is it my fault I don't know how? I would like to be sincere, to touch life somewhere. (*With weary bitterness*) But I'm afraid I have neither the vitality nor integrity. All that was burnt out in our stock before I was born. Grandfather's blast furnaces, flaming to the sky, melting steel, making millions—then father keeping those home fires burning, making more millions—and little me at the tail-end of it all. I'm a waste product in the Bessemer process—like the millions. Or rather, I inherit the acquired trait of the by-product, wealth, but none of the energy, none of the strength of the steel that made it. I am sired by gold and damned by it, as they say at the race track—damned in more ways than one. (*She laughs mirthlessly.*)

AUNT. (*unimpressed—superciliously*) You seem to be going in for sincerity today. It isn't becoming to you, really—except as an obvious pose. Be as artificial as you are, I advise. There's a sort of sincerity in that, you know. And, after all, you must confess you like that better.

MILDRED. (*again affected and bored*) Yes, I suppose I do. Pardon me for my outburst. When a leopard complains of its spots, it must sound rather grotesque. (*In a mocking tone*) Purr, little leopard. Purr, scratch, tear, kill, gorge yourself and be happy—only stay in the jungle where your spots are camouflage. In a cage they make you conspicuous.

AUNT. I don't know what you are talking about.

MILDRED. It would be rude to talk about anything to you. Let's just talk. (*She looks at her wrist watch*) Well, thank goodness, it's about time for them to come for me. That ought to give me a new thrill, Aunt.

AUNT. (*affectedly troubled*) You don't mean to say you're really going? The dirt—the heat must be frightful—

MILDRED. Grandfather started as a puddler. I should have inherited an immunity to heat that would make a salamander shiver. It will be fun to put it to the test.

AUNT. But don't you have to have the captain's—or someone's—permission to visit the stokehole?

MILDRED. (*with a triumphant smile*) I have it—both his and the chief engineer's. Oh, they didn't want to at first, in spite of my social service credentials. They didn't seem a bit anxious that I should investigate how the other half lives and works on a ship. So I had to tell them that my father, the president of Nazareth Steel, chairman of the board of directors of this line, had told me it would be all right.

AUNT. He didn't.

MILDRED. How naïve age makes one! But I said he did, Aunt. I even said he had given me a letter to them—which I had lost. And they were afraid to take the chance that I might be lying. (*Excitedly*) So it's ho! for the stokehole. The second engineer is to escort me. (*Looking at her watch again*) It's time. And here he comes, I think. (*The* SECOND ENGINEER *enters. He is a husky, fine-looking man of thirty-five or so. He stops before the two and tips his cap, visibly embarrassed and ill-at-ease.*)

SECOND ENGINEER. Miss Douglas?

MILDRED. Yes. (*Throwing off her rugs and getting to her feet*) Are we all ready to start?

SECOND ENGINEER. In just a second, ma'am. I'm waiting for the Fourth. He's coming along.

MILDRED. (*with a scornful smile*) You don't care to shoulder this responsibility alone, is that it?

SECOND ENGINEER. (*forcing a smile*) Two are better than one. (*Disturbed by her eyes, glances out to sea—blurts out*) A fine day we're having.

MILDRED. Is it?

SECOND ENGINEER. A nice warm breeze—

MILDRED. It feels cold to me.

SECOND ENGINEER. But it's hot enough in the sun—

MILDRED. Not hot enough for me. I don't like Nature. I was never athletic.

SECOND ENGINEER. (*forcing a smile*) Well, you'll find it hot enough where you're going.

MILDRED. Do you mean hell?

SECOND ENGINEER. (*flabbergasted, decides to laugh*) Ho-ho! No, I mean the stokehole.

MILDRED. My grandfather was a puddler. He played with boiling steel.

SECOND ENGINEER. (*all at sea—uneasily*) Is that so? Hum, you'll excuse me, ma'am, but are you intending to wear that dress?

MILDRED. Why not?

SECOND ENGINEER. You'll likely rub against oil and dirt. It can't be helped.

MILDRED. It doesn't matter. I have lots of white dresses.

SECOND ENGINEER. I have an old coat you might throw over—

MILDRED. I have fifty dresses like this. I will throw this one into the sea when I come back. That ought to wash it clean, don't you think?

SECOND ENGINEER. (*doggedly*) There's ladders to climb down that are none too clean—and dark alleyways—

MILDRED. I will wear this very dress and none other.

SECOND ENGINEER. No offense meant. It's none of my business. I was only warning you—

MILDRED. Warning? That sounds thrilling.

SECOND ENGINEER. (*looking down the deck—with a sigh of relief*) There's the Fourth now. He's waiting for us. If you'll come—

MILDRED. Go on. I'll follow you. (*He goes.* MILDRED *turns a mocking smile on her aunt*) An oaf—but a handsome, virile oaf.

AUNT. (*scornfully*) Poser!

MILDRED. Take care. He said there were dark alleyways—

AUNT. (*in the same tone*) Poser!

MILDRED. (*biting her lips angrily*) You are right. But would that my millions were not so anemically chaste!

AUNT. Yes, for a fresh pose I have no doubt you would drag the name of Douglas in the gutter!

MILDRED. From which it sprang. Good-by, Aunt. Don't pray too hard that I may fall into the fiery furnace.

AUNT. Poser!

MILDRED. (*viciously*) Old hag! (*She slaps her aunt insultingly across the face and walks off, laughing gaily.*)

AUNT. (*screams after her*) I said poser!

CURTAIN

SCENE THREE

THE *stokehole. In the rear, the dimly-outlined bulks of the furnaces and boilers. High overhead one hanging electric bulb sheds just enough light through the murky air laden with coal dust to pile up masses of shadows everywhere. A line of men, stripped to the waist, is before the furnace doors. They bend over, looking neither to right*

*nor left, handling their shovels as if they were part of their bodies,
with a strange, awkward, swinging rhythm. They use the shovels to
throw open the furnace doors. Then from these fiery round holes in
the black a flood of terrific light and heat pours full upon the men
who are outlined in silhouette in the crouching, inhuman attitudes of
chained gorillas. The men shovel with a rhythmic motion, swinging
as on a pivot from the coal which lies in heaps on the floor behind to
hurl it into the flaming mouths before them. There is a tumult of
noise—the brazen clang of the furnace doors as they are flung open
or slammed shut, the grating, teeth-gritting grind of steel against steel,
of crunching coal. This clash of sounds stuns one's ears with its rend-
ing dissonance. But there is order in it, rhythm, a mechanical regulated
recurrence, a tempo. And rising above all, making the air hum with
the quiver of liberated energy, the roar of leaping flames in the furnaces, the monotonous throbbing beat of the engines.*

*As the curtain rises, the furnace doors are shut. The men are taking
a breathing spell. One or two are arranging the coal behind them,
pulling it into more accessible heaps. The others can be dimly made
out leaning on their shovels in relaxed attitudes of exhaustion.*

PADDY. (*from somewhere in the line—plaintively*) Yerra, will this
divil's own watch nivir end? Me back is broke. I'm destroyed entirely.

YANK. (*from the center of the line—with exuberant scorn*) Aw, yuh
make me sick! Lie down and croak, why don't yuh? Always beefin',
dat's you! Say, dis is a cinch! Dis was made for me! It's my meat, get
me! (*A whistle is blown—a thin, shrill note from somewhere overhead in the darkness.* YANK *curses without resentment*) Dere's de
damn engineer crackin' de whip. He tinks we're loafin'.

PADDY. (*vindictively*) God stiffen him!

YANK. (*in an exultant tone of command*) Come on, youse guys! Git
into de game! She's gittin' hungry! Pile some grub in her. Trow it
into her belly! Come on now, all of youse! Open her up! (*At this last
all the men, who have followed his movements of getting into position,*

throw open their furnace doors with a deafening clang. The fiery light floods over their shoulders as they bend round for the coal. Rivulets of sooty sweat have traced maps on their backs. The enlarged muscles form bunches of high light and shadow.)

YANK. (*chanting a count as he shovels without seeming effort*) One —two—tree— (*His voice rising exultantly in the joy of battle*) Dat's de stuff! Let her have it! All togedder now! Sling it into her! Let her ride! Shoot de piece now! Call de toin on her! Drive her into it! Feel her move! Watch her smoke! Speed, dat's her middle name! Give her coal, youse guys! Coal, dat's her booze! Drink it up, baby! Let's see yuh sprint! Dig in and gain a lap! Dere she go-o-es. (*This last in the chanting formula of the gallery gods at the six-day bike race. He slams his furnace door shut. The others do likewise with as much unison as their wearied bodies will permit. The effect is of one fiery eye after another being blotted out with a series of accompanying bangs.*)

PADDY. (*groaning*) Me back is broke. I'm bate out—bate— (*There is a pause. Then the inexorable whistle sounds again from the dim regions above the electric light. There is a growl of cursing rage from all sides.*)

YANK. (*shaking his fist upward—contemptuously*) Take it easy dere, you! Who d'yuh tink's runnin' dis game, me or you? When I git ready, we move. Not before! When I git ready, get me!

VOICES. (*approvingly*) That's the stuff!
Yank tal him, py golly!
Yank ain't affeerd.
Goot poy, Yank!
Give him hell!
Tell 'im 'e's a bloody swine!
Bloody slave-driver!

YANK. (*contemptuously*) He ain't got no noive. He's yellow, get me? All de engineers is yellow. Dey got streaks a mile wide. Aw, to hell wit him! Let's move, youse guys. We had a rest. Come on, she needs it! Give her pep! It ain't for him. Him and his whistle, dey don't belong. But we belong, see! We gotter feed de baby! Come on! (*He turns and flings his furnace door open. They all follow his lead. At this instant the* SECOND *and* FOURTH ENGINEERS *enter from the darkness on the left with* MILDRED *between them. She starts, turns paler, her pose is crumbling, she shivers with fright in spite of the blazing heat, but forces herself to leave the* ENGINEERS *and take a few steps nearer the men. She is right behind* YANK. *All this happens quickly while the men have their backs turned.*)

YANK. Come on, youse guys! (*He is turning to get coal when the whistle sounds again in a peremptory, irritating note. This drives* YANK *into a sudden fury. While the other men have turned full around and stopped dumfounded by the spectacle of* MILDRED *standing there in her white dress,* YANK *does not turn far enough to see her. Besides, his head is thrown back, he blinks upward through the murk trying to find the owner of the whistle, he brandishes his shovel murderously over his head in one hand, pounding on his chest, gorilla-like, with the other, shouting*) Toin off dat whistle! Come down outa dere, yuh yellow, brass-buttoned, Belfast bum, yuh! Come down and I'll knock yer brains out! Yuh lousy, stinkin', yellow mut of a Catholic-moiderin' bastard! Come down and I'll moider yuh! Pullin' dat whistle on me, huh? I'll show yuh! I'll crash yer skull in! I'll drive yer teet' down yer troat! I'll slam yer nose trou de back of yer head! I'll cut yer guts out for a nickel, yuh lousy boob, yuh dirty, crummy, muck-eatin' son of a— (*Suddenly he becomes conscious of all the other men staring at something directly behind his back. He whirls defensively with a snarling, murderous growl, crouching to spring, his lips drawn back over his teeth, his small eyes gleaming ferociously. He sees* MILDRED, *like a white apparition in the full light from the open furnace doors. He glares into her eyes, turned to stone. As for her, during his speech she has listened, paralyzed with horror, terror, her whole personality crushed, beaten in, collapsed, by the terrific impact of this unknown, abysmal brutality, naked and shameless. As she looks at his gorilla face, as his eyes bore into hers, she*

225

utters a low, choking cry and shrinks away from him, putting both hands up before her eyes to shut out the sight of his face, to protect her own. This startles YANK *to a reaction. His mouth falls open, his eyes grow bewildered.*)

MILDRED. (*about to faint—to the* ENGINEERS, *who now have her one by each arm—whimperingly*) Take me away! Oh, the filthy beast! (*She faints. They carry her quickly back, disappearing in the darkness at the left, rear. An iron door clangs shut. Rage and bewildered fury rush back on* YANK. *He feels himself insulted in some unknown fashion in the very heart of his pride. He roars* "God damn yuh!" *and hurls his shovel after them at the door which has just closed. It hits the steel bulkhead with a clang and falls clattering on the steel floor. From overhead the whistle sounds again in a long, angry, insistent command.*)

CURTAIN

SCENE FOUR

THE *firemen's forecastle.* YANK'S *watch has just come off duty and had dinner. Their faces and bodies shine from a soap-and-water scrubbing but around their eyes, where a hasty dousing does not touch, the coal dust sticks like black make-up, giving them a queer, sinister expression.* YANK *has not washed either face or body. He stands out in contrast to them, a blackened, brooding figure. He is seated forward on a bench in the exact attitude of Rodin's "The Thinker." The others, most of them smoking pipes, are staring at* YANK *half-apprehensively, as if fearing an outburst; half-amusedly, as if they saw a joke somewhere that tickled them.*

VOICES. He ain't ate nothin'.
Py golly, a fallar gat to gat grub in him.

Divil a lie.

Yank feeda da fire, no feeda da face.

Ha-ha.

He ain't even washed hisself.

He's forgot.

Hey, Yank, you forgot to wash.

YANK. (*sullenly*) Forgot nothin'! To hell wit washin'.

VOICES. It'll stick to you.

It'll get under your skin.

Give yer the bleedin' itch, that's wot.

It makes spots on you—like a leopard.

Like a piebald nigger, you mean.

Better wash up, Yank.

You sleep better.

Wash up, Yank!

Wash up! Wash up!

YANK. (*resentfully*) Aw say, youse guys. Lemme alone. Can't youse see I'm tryin' to tink?

ALL. (*repeating the word after him as one with cynical mockery*) Think! (*The word has a brazen, metallic quality as if their throats were phonograph horns. It is followed by a chorus of hard, barking laughter.*)

YANK. (*springing to his feet and glaring at them belligerently*) Yes, tink! Tink, dat's what I said! What about it? (*They are silent, puzzled by his sudden resentment at what used to be one of his jokes.* YANK *sits down again in the same attitude of "The Thinker."*)

VOICES. Leave him alone.

He's got a grouch on.

Why wouldn't he?

PADDY. (*with a wink at the others*) Sure I know what's the matther. 'Tis aisy to see. He's fallen in love, I'm telling you.

ALL. (*repeating the word after him as one with cynical mockery*) Love! (*The word has a brazen, metallic quality as if their throats were phonograph horns. It is followed by a chorus of hard, barking laughter.*)

YANK. (*with a contemptuous snort*) Love, Hell! Hate, dat's what. I've fallen in hate, get me?

PADDY. (*philosophically*) 'Twould take a wise man to tell one from the other. (*With a bitter, ironical scorn, increasing as he goes on*) But I'm telling you it's love that's in it. Sure what else but love for us poor bastes in the stokehole would be bringing a fine lady, dressed like a white quane, down a mile of ladders and steps to be havin' a look at us? (*A growl of anger goes up from all sides.*)

LONG. (*jumping on a bench—hectically*) Hinsultin' us! Hinsultin' us, the bloody cow! And them bloody engineers! What right 'as they got to be exhibitin' us 's if we was bleedin' monkeys in a menagerie? Did we sign for hinsults to our dignity as 'onest workers? Is that in the ship's articles? You kin bloody well bet it ain't! But I knows why they done it. I arsked a deck steward 'o she was and 'e told me. 'Er old man's a bleedin' millionaire, a bloody Capitalist! 'E's got enuf bloody gold to sink this bleedin' ship! 'E makes arf the bloody steel in the world! 'E owns this bloody boat! And you and me, Comrades, we're 'is slaves! And the skipper and mates and engineers, they're 'is slaves! And she's 'is bloody daughter and we're all 'er slaves, too! And she gives 'er orders as 'ow she wants to see the bloody animals below decks and down they takes 'er! (*There is a roar of rage from all sides.*)

YANK. (*blinking at him bewilderedly*) Say! Wait a moment! Is all dat straight goods?

LONG. Straight as string! The bleedin' steward as waits on 'em, 'e told me about 'er. And what're we goin' ter do, I arsks yer? 'Ave we got ter swaller 'er hinsults like dogs? It ain't in the ship's articles. I tell yer we got a case. We kin go to law—

YANK. (*with abysmal contempt*) Hell! Law!

ALL. (*repeating the word after him as one with cynical mockery*) Law! (*The word has a brazen metallic quality as if their throats were phonograph horns. It is followed by a chorus of hard, barking laugh-ter.*)

LONG. (*feeling the ground slipping from under his feet—desperately*) As voters and citizens we kin force the bloody governments—

YANK. (*with abysmal contempt*) Hell! Governments!

ALL. (*repeating the word after him as one with cynical mockery*) Governments! (*The word has a brazen metallic quality as if their throats were phonograph horns. It is followed by a chorus of hard, barking laughter.*)

LONG. (*hysterically*) We're free and equal in the sight of God—

YANK. (*with abysmal contempt*) Hell! God!

ALL. (*repeating the word after him as one with cynical mockery*) God! (*The word has a brazen metallic quality as if their throats were phonograph horns. It is followed by a chorus of hard, barking laughter.*)

YANK. (*witheringly*) Aw, join de Salvation Army!

ALL. Sit down! Shut up! Damn fool! Sea-lawyer! (LONG *slinks back out of sight.*)

PADDY. (*continuing the trend of his thoughts as if he had never been interrupted—bitterly*) And there she was standing behind us, and the Second pointing at us like a man you'd hear in a circus would be saying: In this cage is a queerer kind of baboon than ever you'd find in darkest Africy. We roast them in their own sweat—and be damned if you won't hear some of thim saying they like it! (*He glances scornfully at* YANK.)

YANK. (*with a bewildered uncertain growl*) Aw!

PADDY. And there was Yank roarin' curses and turning round wid his shovel to brain her—and she looked at him, and him at her—

YANK. (*slowly*) She was all white. I tought she was a ghost. Sure.

PADDY. (*with heavy, biting sarcasm*) 'Twas love at first sight, divil a doubt of it! If you'd seen the endearin' look on her pale mug when she shriveled away with her hands over her eyes to shut out the sight of him! Sure, 'twas as if she'd seen a great hairy ape escaped from the Zoo!

YANK. (*stung—with a growl of rage*) Aw!

PADDY. And the loving way Yank heaved his shovel at the skull of her, only she was out the door! (*A grin breaking over his face*) 'Twas touching, I'm telling you! It put the touch of home, swate home in the stokehole. (*There is a roar of laughter from all.*)

YANK. (*glaring at* PADDY *menacingly*) Aw, choke dat off, see!

PADDY. (*not heeding him—to the others*) And her grabbin' at the Second's arm for protection. (*With a grotesque imitation of a woman's voice*) Kiss me, Engineer dear, for it's dark down here and me old man's in Wall Street making money! Hug me tight, darlin', for I'm afeerd in the dark and me mother's on deck makin' eyes at the skipper! (*Another roar of laughter.*)

YANK. (*threateningly*) Say! What yuh tryin' to do, kid me, yuh old Harp?

PADDY. Divil a bit! Ain't I wishin' myself you'd brained her?

YANK. (*fiercely*) I'll brain her! I'll brain her yet, wait 'n' see! (*Coming over to* PADDY—*slowly*) Say, is dat what she called me—a hairy ape?

PADDY. She looked it at you if she didn't say the word itself.

YANK. (*grinning horribly*) Hairy ape, huh? Sure! Dat's de way she looked at me, aw right. Hairy ape! So dat's me, huh? (*Bursting into rage—as if she were still in front of him*) Yuh skinny tart! Yuh white-faced bum, yuh! I'll show yuh who's a ape! (*Turning to the others, bewilderment seizing him again*) Say, youse guys. I was bawlin' him out for pullin' de whistle on us. You heard me. And den I seen youse lookin' at somep'n and I tought he'd sneaked down to come up in back of me, and I hopped round to knock him dead wit de shovel. And dere she was wit de light on her! Christ, yuh coulda pushed me over with a finger! I was scared, get me? Sure! I tought she was a ghost, see? She was all in white like dey wrap around stiffs. You seen her. Kin yuh blame me? She didn't belong, dat's what. And den when I come to and seen it was a real skoit and seen de way she was lookin' at me—like Paddy said—Christ, I was sore, get me? I don't stand for dat stuff from nobody. And I flung de shovel—on'y she'd beat it. (*Furiously*) I wished it'd banged her! I wished it'd knocked her block off!

LONG. And be 'anged for murder or 'lectrocuted? She ain't bleedin' well worth it.

YANK. I don't give a damn what! I'd be square wit her, wouldn't I? Tink I wanter let her put somep'n over on me? Tink I'm goin' to let her git away wit dat stuff? Yuh don't know me! No one ain't never put nothin' over on me and got away wit it, see!—not dat kind of stuff—no guy and no skoit neither! I'll fix her! Maybe she'll come down again—

VOICE. No chance, Yank. You scared her out of a year's growth.

YANK. I scared her? Why de hell should I scare her? Who de hell is she? Ain't she de same as me? Hairy ape, huh? (*With his old confident bravado*) I'll show her I'm better'n her, if she on'y knew it. I belong and she don't, see! I move and she's dead! Twenty-five knots a hour, dat's me! Dat carries her but I make dat. She's on'y baggage. Sure! (*Again bewilderedly*) But, Christ, she was funny lookin'! Did yuh pipe her hands? White and skinny. Yuh could see de bones through 'em. And her mush, dat was dead white, too. And her eyes, dey was like dey'd seen a ghost. Me, dat was! Sure! Hairy ape! Ghost, huh? Look at dat arm! (*He extends his right arm, swelling out of the great muscles*) I coulda took her wit dat, wit just my little finger even, and broke her in two. (*Again bewilderedly*) Say, who is dat skoit, huh? What is she? What's she come from? Who made her? Who give her de noive to look at me like dat? Dis ting's got my goat right. I don't get her. She's new to me. What does a skoit like her mean, huh? She don't belong, get me! I can't see her. (*With growing anger*) But one ting I'm wise to, aw right, aw right! Youse all kin bet your shoits I'll git even wit her. I'll show her if she tinks she— She grinds de organ and I'm on de string, huh? I'll fix her!

Let her come down again and I'll fling her in de furnace! She'll move den! She won't shiver at nothin', den! Speed, dat'll be her! She'll belong den! (*He grins horribly.*)

PADDY. She'll never come. She's had her belly-full, I'm telling you. She'll be in bed now, I'm thinking, wid ten doctors and nurses feedin' her salts to clean the fear out of her.

YANK. (*enraged*) Yuh tink I made her sick, too, do yuh? Just lookin' at me, huh? Hairy ape, huh? (*In a frenzy of rage*) I'll fix her! I'll tell her where to git off! She'll git down on her knees and take it back or I'll bust de face offen her! (*Shaking one fist upward and beating on his chest with the other*) I'll find yuh! I'm comin', d'yuh hear? I'll fix yuh, God damn yuh! (*He makes a rush for the door.*)

VOICES. Stop him!
He'll get shot!
He'll murder her!
Trip him up!
Hold him!
He's gone crazy!
Gott, he's strong!
Hold him down!
Look out for a kick!
Pin his arms!

(*They have all piled on him and, after a fierce struggle, by sheer weight of numbers have borne him to the floor just inside the door.*)

PADDY. (*who has remained detached*) Kape him down till he's cooled off. (*Scornfully*) Yerra, Yank, you're a great fool. Is it payin' attention at all you are to the like of that skinny sow widout one drop of rale blood in her?

YANK. (*frenziedly, from the bottom of the heap*) She done me doit! She done me doit, didn't she? I'll git square wit her! I'll get her some way! Git offen me, youse guys! Lemme up! I'll show her who's a ape!

CURTAIN

SCENE FIVE

THREE *weeks later. A corner of Fifth Avenue in the Fifties on a fine Sunday morning. A general atmosphere of clean, well-tidied, wide street; a flood of mellow, tempered sunshine; gentle, genteel breezes. In the rear, the show windows of two shops, a jewelry establishment on the corner, a furrier's next to it. Here the adornments of extreme wealth are tantalizingly displayed. The jeweler's window is gaudy with glittering diamonds, emeralds, rubies, pearls, etc., fashioned in ornate tiaras, crowns, necklaces, collars, etc. From each piece hangs an enormous tag from which a dollar sign and numerals in intermittent electric lights wink out the incredible prices. The same in the furrier's. Rich furs of all varieties hang there bathed in a downpour of artificial light. The general effect is of a background of magnificence cheapened and made grotesque by commercialism, a background in tawdry disharmony with the clear light and sunshine on the street itself.*

Up the side street YANK *and* LONG *come swaggering.* LONG *is dressed in shore clothes, wears a black Windsor tie, cloth cap.* YANK *is in his dirty dungarees. A fireman's cap with black peak is cocked defiantly on the side of his head. He has not shaved for days and around his fierce, resentful eyes—as around those of* LONG *to a lesser degree—the black smudge of coal dust still sticks like make-up. They hesitate and stand together at the corner, swaggering, looking about them with a forced, defiant contempt.*

LONG. (*indicating it all with an oratorical gesture*) Well, 'ere we are. Fif' Avenoo. This 'ere's their bleedin' private lane, as yer might say. (*Bitterly*) We're trespassers 'ere. Proletarians keep orf the grass!
YANK. (*dully*) I don't see no grass, yuh boob. (*Staring at the side-*

233

walk) Clean, ain't it? Yuh could eat a fried egg offen it. The white wings got some job sweepin' dis up. (*Looking up and down the avenue—surlily*) Where's all de white-collar stiffs yuh said was here —and de skoits—*her* kind?

LONG. In church, blarst 'em! Arskin' Jesus to give 'em more money.

YANK. Choich, huh? I useter go to choich onct—sure—when I was a kid. Me old man and woman, dey made me. Dey never went dem-selves, dough. Always got too big a head on Sunday mornin', dat was dem. (*With a grin*) Dey was scrappers for fair, bot' of dem. On Satiday nights when dey bot' got a skinful dey could put up a bout oughter been staged at de Garden. When dey got trough dere wasn't a chair or table wit a leg under it. Or else dey bot' jumped on me for somep'n. Dat was where I loined to take punishment. (*With a grin and a swagger*) I'm a chip offen de old block, get me?

LONG. Did yer old man follow the sea?

YANK. Naw. Worked along shore. I runned away when me old lady croaked wit de tremens. I helped at truckin' and in de market. Den I shipped in de stokehole. Sure. Dat belongs. De rest was nothin'. (*Looking around him*) I ain't never seen dis before. De Brooklyn waterfront, dat was where I was dragged up. (*Taking a deep breath*) Dis ain't so bad at dat, huh?

LONG. Not bad? Well, we pays for it wiv our bloody sweat, if yer wants to know!

YANK. (*with sudden angry disgust*) Aw, hell! I don't see no one, see—like her. All dis gives me a pain. It don't belong. Say, ain't dere a back room around dis dump? Let's go shoot a ball. All dis is too clean and quiet and dolled-up, get me! It gives me a pain.

LONG. Wait and yer'll bloody well see—

YANK. I don't wait for no one. I keep on de move. Say, what yuh drag me up here for, anyway? Tryin' to kid me, yuh simp, yuh?

LONG. Yer wants to get back at 'er, don't yer? That's what yer been sayin' every bloomin' hour since she hinsulted yer.

YANK. (*vehemently*) Sure ting I do! Didn't I try to get even wit her in Southampton? Didn't I sneak on de dock and wait for her by de gangplank? I was goin' to spit in her pale mug, see! Sure, right in her pop-eyes! Dat woulda made me even, see? But no chanct. Dere was a whole army of plainclothes bulls around. Dey spotted me and gimme de bum's rush. I never seen her. But I'll git square wit her yet, you watch. (*Furiously*) De lousy tart! She tinks she kin get away wit moider—but not wit me! I'll fix her! I'll tink of a way!

LONG. (*as disgusted as he dares to be*) Ain't that why I brought yer up 'ere—to show yer? Yer been lookin' at this 'ere 'ole affair wrong. Yer been actin' an' talkin' 's if it was all a bleedin' personal matter between yer and that bloody cow. I wants to convince yer she was on'y a representative of 'er clarss. I wants to awaken yer bloody clarss consciousness. Then yer'll see it's 'er clarss yer've got to fight, not 'er alone. There's a 'ole mob of 'em like 'er, Gawd blind 'em!

YANK. (*spitting on his hands—belligerently*) De more de merrier when I gits started. Bring on de gang!

LONG. Yer'll see 'em in arf a mo', when that church lets out. (*He turns and sees the window display in the two stores for the first time*) Blimey! Look at that, will yer? (*They both walk back and stand looking in the jeweler's.* LONG *flies into a fury*) Just look at this 'ere bloomin' mess! Just look at it! Look at the bleedin' prices on 'em—more'n our 'ole bloody stokehole makes in ten voyages sweatin' in 'ell! And they—'er and 'er bloody clarss—buys 'em for toys to dangle on 'em! One of these 'ere would buy scoff for a starvin' family for a year!

YANK. Aw, cut de sob stuff! T' hell wit de starvin' family! Yuh'll be passin' de hat to me next. (*With naïve admiration*) Say, dem tings is pretty, huh? Bet yuh dey'd hock for a piece of change aw right. (*Then turning away, bored*) But, aw hell, what good are dey? Let her have 'em. Dey don't belong no more'n she does. (*With a gesture of sweeping the jewelers into oblivion*) All dat don't count, get me?

LONG. (*who has moved to the furrier's—indignantly*) And I s'pose

235

this 'ere don't count neither—skins of poor, 'armless animals slaughtered so as 'er and 'ers can keep their bleedin' noses warm!

YANK. (*who has been staring at something inside—with queer excitement*) Take a slant at dat! Give it de once-over! Monkey fur —two t'ousand bucks! (*Bewilderedly*) Is dat straight goods—monkey fur? What de hell—?

LONG. (*bitterly*) It's straight enuf. (*With grim humor*) They wouldn't bloody well pay that for a 'airy ape's skin—no, nor for the 'ole livin' ape with all 'is 'ead, and a body, and soul thrown in!

YANK. (*clenching his fists, his face growing pale with rage as if the skin in the window were a personal insult*) Trowin' it up in my face! Christ! I'll fix her!

LONG. (*excitedly*) Church is out. 'Ere they come, the bleedin' swine. (*After a glance at* YANK's *lowering face—uneasily*) Easy goes, Comrade. Keep yer bloomin' temper. Remember force defeats itself. It ain't our weapon. We must impress our demands through peaceful means—the votes of the on-marching proletarians of the bloody world!

YANK. (*with abysmal contempt*) Votes, hell! Votes is a joke, see. Votes for women! Let dem do it!

LONG. (*still more uneasily*) Calm, now. Treat 'em wiv the proper contempt. Observe the bleedin' parasites but 'old yer 'orses.

YANK. (*angrily*) Git away from me! Yuh're yellow, dat's what. Force, dat's me! De punch, dat's me every time, see! (*The crowd from church enter from the right, sauntering slowly and affectedly, their heads held stiffly up, looking neither to right nor left, talking in toneless, simpering voices. The women are rouged, calcimined, dyed, overdressed to the nth degree. The men are in Prince Alberts, high hats, spats, canes, etc. A procession of gaudy marionettes, yet with something of the relentless horror of Frankensteins in their detached, mechanical unawareness.*)

VOICES. Dear Doctor Caiphas! He is so sincere!
What was the sermon? I dozed off.

About the radicals, my dear—and the false doctrines that
are being preached.

We must organize a hundred per cent American bazaar.

And let everyone contribute one one-hundredth per cent of
their income tax.

What an original idea!

We can devote the proceeds to rehabilitating the veil of the
temple.

But that has been done so many times.

YANK. (*glaring from one to the other of them—with an insulting
snort of scorn*) Huh! Huh! (*Without seeming to see him, they make
wide detours to avoid the spot where he stands in the middle of the
sidewalk.*)

LONG. (*frightenedly*) Keep yer bloomin' mouth shut, I tells yer.

YANK. (*viciously*) G'wan! Tell it to Sweeney! (*He swaggers away
and deliberately lurches into a top-hatted gentleman, then glares at
him pugnaciously*) Say, who d'yuh tink yuh're bumpin'? Tink yuh
own de oith?

GENTLEMAN. (*coldly and affectedly*) I beg your pardon. (*He has not
looked at* YANK *and passes on without a glance, leaving him bewildered.*)

LONG. (*rushing up and grabbing* YANK's *arm*) 'Ere! Come away!
This wasn't what I meant. Yer'll 'ave the bloody coppers down on us.

YANK. (*savagely—giving him a push that sends him sprawling*)
G'wan!

LONG. (*picks himself up—hysterically*) I'll pop orf then. This ain't
what I meant. And whatever 'appens, yer can't blame me. (*He slinks
off left.*)

YANK. T' hell wit youse! (*He approaches a lady—with a vicious
grin and a smirking wink*) Hello, Kiddo. How's every little ting?
Got anyting on for tonight? I know an old boiler down to de docks
we kin crawl into. (*The lady stalks by without a look, without a
change of pace.* YANK *turns to others—insultingly*) Holy smokes,

what a mug! Go hide yuhself before de horses shy at yuh. Gee, pipe de heine on dat one! Say, youse, yuh look like de stoin of a ferryboat. Paint and powder! All dolled up to kill! Yuh look like stiffs laid out for de boneyard! Aw, g'wan, de lot of youse! Yuh give me de eye-ache. Yuh don't belong, get me! Look at me, why don't youse dare? I belong, dat's me! (*Pointing to a skyscraper across the street which is in process of construction—with bravado*) See dat building goin' up dere? See de steel work? Steel, dat's me! Youse guys live on it and tink yuh're somep'n. But I'm *in* it, see! I'm de hoistin' engine dat makes it go up! I'm it—de inside and bottom of it! Sure! I'm steel and steam and smoke and de rest of it! It moves—speed—twenty-five stories up—and me at de top and bottom—movin'! Youse simps don't move. Yuh're on'y dolls I winds up to see 'm spin. Yuh're de garbage, get me—de leavin's—de ashes we dump over de side! Now, what 'a' yuh gotta say? (*But as they seem neither to see nor hear him, he flies into a fury*) Bums! Pigs! Tarts! Bitches! (*He turns in a rage on the men, bumping viciously into them but not jarring them the least bit. Rather it is he who recoils after each collision. He keeps growling*) Git off de oith! G'wan, yuh bum! Look where yuh're goin', can't yuh? Git outa here! Fight, why don't yuh? Put up yer mits! Don't be a dog! Fight or I'll knock yuh dead! (*But, without seeming to see him, they all answer with mechanical affected polite-ness* "I beg your pardon." *Then at a cry from one of the women, they all scurry to the furrier's window.*)

THE WOMAN. (*ecstatically, with a gasp of delight*) Monkey fur! (*The whole crowd of men and women chorus after her in the same tone of affected delight* "Monkey fur!")

YANK. (*with a jerk of his head back on his shoulders, as if he had received a punch full in the face—raging*) I see yuh, all in white! I see yuh, yuh white-faced tart, yuh! Hairy ape, huh? I'll hairy ape yuh! (*He bends down and grips at the street curbing as if to pluck it out and hurl it. Foiled in this, snarling with passion, he leaps to the lamp-*

*post on the corner and tries to pull it up for a club. Just at that moment
a bus is heard rumbling up. A fat, high-hatted, spatted gentleman
runs out from the side street. He calls out plaintively* "Bus! Bus!
Stop there!" *and runs full tilt into the bending, straining* YANK, *who
is bowled off his balance.*)

YANK. (*seeing a fight—with a roar of joy as he springs to his feet*)
At last! Bus, huh? I'll bust yuh! (*He lets drive a terrific swing, his
fist landing full on the fat gentleman's face. But the gentleman stands
unmoved as if nothing had happened.*)

GENTLEMAN. I beg your pardon. (*Then irritably*) You have made
me lose my bus. (*He claps his hands and begins to scream*) Officer!
Officer! (*Many police whistles shrill out on the instant and a whole
platoon of policemen rush in on* YANK *from all sides. He tries to fight
but is clubbed to the pavement and fallen upon. The crowd at the
window have not moved or noticed this disturbance. The clanging
gong of the patrol wagon approaches with a clamoring din.*)

CURTAIN

SCENE SIX

Night *of the following day. A row of cells in the prison on Black-
wells Island. The cells extend back diagonally from right front
to left rear. They do not stop, but disappear in the dark background as
if they ran on, numberless, into infinity. One electric bulb from the
low ceiling of the narrow corridor sheds its light through the heavy
steel bars of the cell at the extreme front and reveals part of the interior.* YANK *can be seen within, crouched on the edge of his cot in the
attitude of Rodin's "The Thinker." His face is spotted with black
and blue bruises. A blood-stained bandage is wrapped around his head.*

YANK. (*suddenly starting as if awakening from a dream, reaches out and shakes the bars—aloud to himself, wonderingly*) Steel. Dis is de Zoo, huh? (*A burst of hard, barking laughter comes from the unseen occupants of the cells, runs back down the tier, and abruptly ceases.*)

VOICES. (*mockingly*) The Zoo? That's a new name for this coop— a damn good name!

Steel, eh? You said a mouthful. This is the old iron house.

Who is that boob talkin'?

He's the bloke they brung in out of his head. The bulls had beat him up fierce.

YANK. (*dully*) I musta been dreamin'. I tought I was in a cage at de Zoo—but de apes don't talk, do dey?

VOICES. (*with mocking laughter*) You're in a cage aw right.

A coop!

A pen!

A sty!

A kennel! (*Hard laughter—a pause.*)

Say, guy! Who are you? No, never mind lying. What are you?

Yes, tell us your sad story. What's your game?

What did they jug yuh for?

YANK. (*dully*) I was a fireman—stokin' on de liners. (*Then with sudden rage, rattling his cell bars*) I'm a hairy ape, get me? And I'll bust youse all in de jaw if yuh don't lay off kiddin' me.

VOICES. Huh! You're a hard boiled duck, ain't you!

When you spit, it bounces! (*Laughter.*)

Aw, can it. He's a regular guy. Ain't you?

What did he say he was—a ape?

YANK. (*defiantly*) Sure ting! Ain't dat what youse all are—apes? (*A silence. Then a furious rattling of bars from down the corridor.*)

A VOICE. (*thick with rage*) I'll show yuh who's a ape, yuh bum!

240

VOICES. Ssshh! Nix!

Can de noise!

Piano!

You'll have the guard down on us!

YANK. (*scornfully*) De guard? Yuh mean de keeper, don't yuh?
(*Angry exclamations from all the cells.*)

VOICE. (*placatingly*) Aw, don't pay no attention to him. He's off his
nut from the beatin'-up he got. Say, you guy! We're waitin' to hear
what they landed you for—or ain't yuh tellin'?

YANK. Sure, I'll tell youse. Sure! Why de hell not? On'y—youse
won't get me. Nobody gets me but me, see? I started to tell de Judge
and all he says was: "Toity days to tink it over."—Tink it over! Christ,
dat's all I been doin' for weeks! (*After a pause*) I was tryin' to git
even wit someone, see?—someone dat done me doit.

VOICES. (*cynically*) De old stuff, I bet. Your goil, huh?

Give yuh the double-cross, huh?

That's them every time!

Did yuh beat up de odder guy?

YANK. (*disgustedly*) Aw, yuh're all wrong! Sure dere was a skoit
in it—but not what youse mean, not dat old tripe. Dis was a new kind
of skoit. She was dolled up all in white—in de stokehole. I tought she
was a ghost. Sure. (*A pause.*)

VOICES. (*whispering*) Gee, he's still nutty.

Let him rave. It's fun listenin'.

YANK. (*unheeding—groping in his thoughts*) Her hands—dey was
skinny and white like dey wasn't real but painted on somep'n. Dere
was a million miles from me to her—twenty-five knots a hour. She
was like some dead ting de cat brung in. Sure, dat's what. She didn't
belong. She belonged in de window of a toy store, or on de top of a
garbage can, see! Sure! (*He breaks out angrily*) But would yuh believe it, she had de noive to do me doit. She lamped me like she was
seein' somep'n broke loose from de menagerie. Christ, yuh'd oughter
seen her eyes! (*He rattles the bars of his cell furiously*) But I'll get

241

back at her yet, you watch! And if I can't find her I'll take it out on de gang she runs wit. I'm wise to where dey hangs out now. I'll show her who belongs! I'll show her who's in de move and who ain't. You watch my smoke!

VOICES. (*serious and joking*) Dat's de talkin'!

Take her for all she's got!

What was this dame, anyway? Who was she, eh?

YANK. I dunno. First cabin stiff. Her old man's a millionaire, dey says—name of Douglas.

VOICES. Douglas? That's the president of the Steel Trust, I bet.

Sure. I seen his mug in de papers.

He's filthy with dough.

VOICE. Hey, feller, take a tip from me. If you want to get back at that dame, you better join the Wobblies. You'll get some action then.

YANK. Wobblies? What de hell's dat?

VOICE. Ain't you ever heard of the I. W. W.?

YANK. Naw. What is it?

VOICE. A gang of blokes—a tough gang. I been readin' about 'em today in the paper. The guard give me the *Sunday Times*. There's a long spiel about 'em. It's from a speech made in the Senate by a guy named Senator Queen. (*He is in the cell next to* YANK's. *There is a rustling of paper*) Wait'll I see if I got light enough and I'll read you. Listen. (*He reads*) "There is a menace existing in this country today which threatens the vitals of our fair Republic—as foul a menace against the very life-blood of the American Eagle as was the foul conspiracy of Catiline against the eagles of ancient Rome!"

VOICE. (*disgustedly*) Aw, hell! Tell him to salt de tail of dat eagle!

VOICE. (*reading*) "I refer to that devil's brew of rascals, jailbirds, murderers and cutthroats who libel all honest working men by calling themselves the Industrial Workers of the World; but in the light of their nefarious plots, I call them the Industrious *Wreckers* of the World!"

YANK. (*with vengeful satisfaction*) Wreckers, dat's de right dope! Dat belongs! Me for dem!

VOICE. Ssshh! (*Reading*) "This fiendish organization is a foul ulcer on the fair body of our Democracy—"

VOICE. Democracy, hell! Give him the boid, fellers—the raspberry! (*They do.*)

VOICE. Ssshh! (*Reading*) "Like Cato I say to this Senate, the I. W. W. must be destroyed! For they represent an ever-present dagger pointed at the heart of the greatest nation the world has ever known, where all men are born free and equal, with equal opportunities to all, where the Founding Fathers have guaranteed to each one happiness, where Truth, Honor, Liberty, Justice, and the Brotherhood of Man are a religion absorbed with one's mother's milk, taught at our father's knee, sealed, signed, and stamped upon in the glorious Constitution of these United States!" (*A perfect storm of hisses, catcalls, boos, and hard laughter.*)

VOICES. (*scornfully*) Hurrah for de Fort' of July!

Pass de hat!

Liberty!

Justice!

Honor!

Opportunity!

Brotherhood!

ALL. (*with abysmal scorn*) Aw, hell!

VOICE. Give that Queen Senator guy the bark! All togedder now—one—two—tree—(*A terrific chorus of barking and yapping.*)

GUARD. (*from a distance*) Quiet there, youse—or I'll git the hose. (*The noise subsides.*)

YANK. (*with growling rage*) I'd like to catch dat senator guy alone for a second. I'd loin him some trute!

VOICE. Ssshh! Here's where he gits down to cases on the Wobblies. (*Reads*) "They plot with fire in one hand and dynamite in the other. They stop not before murder to gain their ends, nor at the outraging

243

of defenseless womanhood. They would tear down society, put the lowest scum in the seats of the mighty, turn Almighty God's revealed plan for the world topsy-turvy, and make of our sweet and lovely civilization a shambles, a desolation where man, God's masterpiece, would soon degenerate back to the ape!"

VOICE. (*to* YANK) Hey, you guy. There's your ape stuff again.

YANK. (*with a growl of fury*) I got him. So dey blow up tings, do dey? Dey turn tings round, do dey? Hey, lend me dat paper, will yuh?

VOICE. Sure. Give it to him. On'y keep it to yourself, see. We don't wanter listen to no more of that slop.

VOICE. Here you are. Hide it under your mattress.

YANK. (*reaching out*) Tanks. I can't read much but I kin manage. (*He sits, the paper in the hand at his side, in the attitude of Rodin's "The Thinker." A pause. Several snores from down the corridor. Suddenly* YANK *jumps to his feet with a furious groan as if some appalling thought had crashed on him—bewilderedly*) Sure—her old man—president of de Steel Trust—makes half de steel in de world— steel—where I tought I belonged—drivin' trou—movin'—in dat—to make* her*—and cage me in for her to spit on! Christ! (*He shakes the bars of his cell door till the whole tier trembles. Irritated, protesting exclamations from those awakened or trying to get to sleep*) He made dis—dis cage! Steel!* It *don't belong, dat's what! Cages, cells, locks, bolts, bars—dat's what it means!—holdin' me down wit him at de top! But I'll drive trou! Fire, dat melts it! I'll be fire—under de heap—fire dat never goes out—hot as hell—breakin' out in de night—(*While he has been saying this last he has shaken his cell door to a clanging accompaniment. As he comes to the "breakin' out" he seizes one bar with both hands and, putting his two feet up against the others so that his position is parallel to the floor like a monkey's, he gives a great wrench backwards. The bar bends like a licorice stick under his tremendous strength. Just at this moment the* PRISON GUARD *rushes in, dragging a hose behind him.*)

GUARD. (*angrily*) I'll loin youse bums to wake me up! (*Sees* YANK)
Hello, it's you, huh? Got the D. T.'s, hey? Well, I'll cure 'em. I'll
drown your snakes for yuh! (*Noticing the bar*) Hell, look at dat bar
bended! On'y a bug is strong enough for dat!

YANK. (*glaring at him*) Or a hairy ape, yuh big yellow bum! Look
out! Here I come! (*He grabs another bar.*)

GUARD. (*scared now—yelling off left*) Toin de hose on, Ben!—full
pressure! And call de others—and a straitjacket! (*The curtain is falling. As it hides* YANK *from view, there is a splattering smash as the
stream of water hits the steel of* YANK's *cell.*)

CURTAIN

SCENE SEVEN

NEARLY *a month later. An I. W. W. local near the waterfront,
showing the interior of a front room on the ground floor, and
the street outside. Moonlight on the narrow street, buildings massed
in black shadow. The interior of the room, which is general assembly
room, office, and reading room, resembles some dingy settlement boys'
club. A desk and high stool are in one corner. A table with papers,
stacks of pamphlets, chairs about it, is at center. The whole is decidedly cheap, banal, commonplace and unmysterious as a room could
well be. The* SECRETARY *is perched on the stool making entries in a
large ledger. An eye shade casts his face into shadows. Eight or ten
men, longshoremen, iron workers, and the like, are grouped about the
table. Two are playing checkers. One is writing a letter. Most of them
are smoking pipes. A big signboard is on the wall at the rear, "Industrial Workers of the World—Local No. 57."*

YANK *comes down the street outside. He is dressed as in Scene
Five. He moves cautiously, mysteriously. He comes to a point opposite
the door; tiptoes softly up to it, listens, is impressed by the silence*

245

within, knocks carefully, as if he were guessing at the password to some secret rite. Listens. No answer. Knocks again a bit louder. No answer. Knocks impatiently, much louder.

SECRETARY. (*turning around on his stool*) What the hell is that—someone knocking? (*Shouts*) Come in, why don't you? (*All the men in the room look up.* YANK *opens the door slowly, gingerly, as if afraid of an ambush. He looks around for secret doors, mystery, is taken aback by the commonplaceness of the room and the men in it, thinks he may have gotten in the wrong place, then sees the signboard on the wall and is reassured.*)

YANK. (*blurts out*) Hello.

MEN. (*reservedly*) Hello.

YANK. (*more easily*) I tought I'd bumped into de wrong dump.

SECRETARY. (*scrutinizing him carefully*) Maybe you have. Are you a member?

YANK. Naw, not yet. Dat's what I come for—to join.

SECRETARY. That's easy. What's your job—longshore?

YANK. Naw. Fireman—stoker on de liners.

SECRETARY. (*with satisfaction*) Welcome to our city. Glad to know you people are waking up at last. We haven't got many members in your line.

YANK. Naw. Dey're all dead to de woild.

SECRETARY. Well, you can help to wake 'em. What's your name? I'll make out your card.

YANK. (*confused*) Name? Lemme tink.

SECRETARY. (*sharply*) Don't you know your own name?

YANK. Sure; but I been just Yank for so long—Bob, dat's it—Bob Smith.

SECRETARY. (*writing*) Robert Smith. (*Fills out the rest of the card*) Here you are. Cost you half a dollar.

YANK. Is dat all—four bits? Dat's easy. (*Gives the* SECRETARY *the money.*)

SECRETARY. (*throwing it in drawer*) Thanks. Well, make yourself at home. No introductions needed. There's literature on the table. Take some of those pamphlets with you to distribute aboard ship. They may bring results. Sow the seed, only go about it right. Don't get caught and fired. We got plenty out of work. What we need is men who can hold their jobs—and work for us at the same time.

YANK. Sure. (*But he still stands, embarrassed and uneasy.*)

SECRETARY. (*looking at him—curiously*) What did you knock for? Think we had a coon in uniform to open doors?

YANK. Naw. I tought it was locked—and dat yuh'd wanter give me the once-over trou a peep-hole or somep'n to see if I was right.

SECRETARY. (*alert and suspicious but with an easy laugh*) Think we were running a crap game? That door is never locked. What put that in your nut?

YANK. (*with a knowing grin, convinced that this is all camouflage, a part of the secrecy*) Dis burg is full of bulls, ain't it?

SECRETARY. (*sharply*) What have the cops got to do with us? We're breaking no laws.

YANK. (*with a knowing wink*) Sure. Youse wouldn't for woilds. Sure. I'm wise to dat.

SECRETARY. You seem to be wise to a lot of stuff none of us knows about.

YANK. (*with another wink*) Aw, dat's aw right, see. (*Then made a bit resentful by the suspicious glances from all sides*) Aw, can it! Youse needn't put me trou de toid degree. Can't youse see I belong? Sure! I'm reg'lar. I'll stick, get me? I'll shoot de woiks for youse. Dat's why I wanted to join in.

SECRETARY. (*breezily, feeling him out*) That's the right spirit. Only are you sure you understand what you've joined? It's all plain and above board; still, some guys get a wrong slant on us. (*Sharply*) What's your notion of the purpose of the I. W. W.?

YANK. Aw, I know all about it.

YANK. (*sarcastically*) Well, give us some of your valuable information.

YANK. (*cunningly*) I know enough not to speak outa my toin. (*Then resentfully again*) Aw, say! I'm reg'lar. I'm wise to de game. I know yuh got to watch your step wit a stranger. For all youse know, I might be a plain-clothes dick, or somep'n, dat's what yuh're tinkin', huh? Aw, forget it! I belong, see? Ask any guy down to de docks if I don't.

SECRETARY. Who said you didn't?

YANK. After I'm 'nitiated, I'll show yuh.

SECRETARY. (*astounded*) Initiated? There's no initiation.

YANK. (*disappointed*) Ain't there no password—no grip nor nothin'?

SECRETARY. What'd you think this is—the Elks—or the Black Hand?

YANK. De Elks, hell! De Black Hand, dey're a lot of yellow backstickin' Ginees. Naw. Dis is a man's gang, ain't it?

SECRETARY. You said it! That's why we stand on our two feet in the open. We got no secrets.

YANK. (*surprised but admiringly*) Yuh mean to say yuh always run wide open—like dis?

SECRETARY. Exactly.

YANK. Den yuh sure got your noive wit youse!

SECRETARY. (*sharply*) Just what was it made you want to join us? Come out with that straight.

YANK. Yuh call me? Well, I got noive, too! Here's my hand. Yuh wanter blow tings up, don't yuh? Well, dat's me! I belong!

SECRETARY. (*with pretended carelessness*) You mean change the unequal conditions of society by legitimate direct action—or with dynamite?

YANK. Dynamite! Blow it offen de oith—steel—all de cages—all de factories, steamers, buildings, jails—de Steel Trust and all dat makes it go.

SECRETARY. So—that's your idea, eh? And did you have any special job in that line you wanted to propose to us? (*He makes a sign to the men, who get up cautiously one by one and group behind* YANK.)

YANK. (*boldly*) Sure, I'll come out wit it. I'll show youse I'm one of de gang. Dere's dat millionaire guy, Douglas—

SECRETARY. President of the Steel Trust, you mean? Do you want to assassinate him?

YANK. Naw, dat don't get yuh nothin'. I mean blow up de factory, de woiks, where he makes de steel. Dat's what I'm after—to blow up de steel, knock all de steel in de woild up to de moon. Dat'll fix tings! (*Eagerly, with a touch of bravado*) I'll do it by me lonesome! I'll show yuh! Tell me where his woiks is, how to git there, all de dope. Gimme de stuff, de old butter—and watch me do de rest! Watch de smoke and see it move! I don't give a damn if dey nab me—long as it's done! I'll soive life for it—and give 'em de laugh! (*Half to himself*) And I'll write her a letter and tell her de hairy ape done it. Dat'll square tings.

SECRETARY. (*stepping away from* YANK) Very interesting. (*He gives a signal. The men, huskies all, throw themselves on* YANK *and before he knows it they have his legs and arms pinioned. But he is too flabbergasted to make a struggle, anyway. They feel him over for weapons.*)

MAN. No gat, no knife. Shall we give him what's what and put the boots to him?

SECRETARY. No. He isn't worth the trouble we'd get into. He's too stupid. (*He comes closer and laughs mockingly in* YANK'S *face*) Ho-ho! By God, this is the biggest joke they've put up on us yet. Hey, you Joke! Who sent you—Burns or Pinkerton? No, by God, you're such a bonehead I'll bet you're in the Secret Service! Well, you dirty spy, you rotten agent provocateur, you can go back and tell whatever skunk is paying you blood-money for betraying your brothers that he's wasting his coin. You couldn't catch a cold. And tell him that all he'll ever get on us, or ever has got, is just his own sneaking plots that he's framed up to put us in jail. We are what our manifesto says we are, neither more nor less—and we'll give him a copy of that any time he calls. And as for you— (*He glares scornfully at* YANK, *who is sunk in an oblivious stupor*) Oh, hell, what's the use of talking? You're a brainless ape.

YANK. (*aroused by the word to fierce but futile struggles*) What's dat, you Sheeny bum, yuh!

SECRETARY. Throw him out, boys. (*In spite of his struggles, this is done with gusto and éclat. Propelled by several parting kicks,* YANK *lands sprawling in the middle of the narrow cobbled street. With a growl he starts to get up and storm the closed door, but stops bewildered by the confusion in his brain, pathetically impotent. He sits there, brooding, in as near to the attitude of Rodin's "The Thinker" as he can get in his position.*)

YANK. (*bitterly*) So dem boids don't tink I belong, neider. Aw, to hell wit 'em! Dey're in de wrong pew—de same old bull—soap-boxes and Salvation Army—no guts! Cut out an hour offen de job a day and make me happy! Gimme a dollar more a day and make me happy! Tree square a day, and cauliflowers in de front yard—ekal rights—a woman and kids—a lousy vote—and I'm all fixed for Jesus, huh? Aw, hell! What does dat get yuh? Dis ting's in your inside, but it ain't your belly. Feedin' your face—sinkers and coffee—dat don't touch it. It's way down—at de bottom. Yuh can't grab it, and yuh can't stop it. It moves, and everything moves. It stops and de whole woild stops. Dat's me now—I don't tick, see?—I'm a busted Ingersoll, dat's what. Steel was me, and I owned de woild. Now I ain't steel, and de woild owns me. Aw, hell! I can't see—it's all dark, get me? It's all wrong! (*He turns a bitter mocking face up like an ape gibbering at the moon*) Say, youse up dere, Man in de Moon, yuh look so wise, gimme de answer, huh? Slip me de inside dope, de information right from de stable—where do I get off at, huh?

A POLICEMAN. (*who has come up the street in time to hear this last —with grim humor*) You'll get off at the station, you boob, if you don't get up out of that and keep movin'.

YANK. (*looking up at him—with a hard, bitter laugh*) Sure! Lock

250

me up! Put me in a cage! Dat's de on'y answer yuh know. G'wan, lock me up!

POLICEMAN. What you been doin'?

YANK. Enuf to gimme life for! I was born, see? Sure, dat's de charge. Write it in de blotter. I was born, get me!

POLICEMAN. (*jocosely*) God pity your old woman! (*Then matter-of-factly*) But I've no time for kidding. You're soused. I'd run you in but it's too long a walk to the station. Come on now, get up, or I'll fan your ears with this club. Beat it now! (*He hauls* YANK *to his feet.*)

YANK. (*in a vague mocking tone*) Say, where do I go from here?

POLICEMAN. (*giving him a push—with a grin, indifferently*) Go to hell.

CURTAIN

SCENE EIGHT

T WILIGHT *of the next day. The monkey house at the Zoo. One spot of clear gray light falls on the front of one cage so that the interior can be seen. The other cages are vague, shrouded in shadow from which chatterings pitched in a conversational tone can be heard. On the one cage a sign from which the word "gorilla" stands out. The gigantic animal himself is seen squatting on his haunches on a bench in much the same attitude as Rodin's "The Thinker."* YANK *enters from the left. Immediately a chorus of angry chattering and screeching breaks out. The gorilla turns his eyes but makes no sound or move.*

YANK. (*with a hard, bitter laugh*) Welcome to your city, huh? Hail, hail, de gang's all here! (*At the sound of his voice the chattering dies away into an attentive silence.* YANK *walks up to the gorilla's*

251

cage and, leaning over the railing, stares in at its occupant, who stares back at him, silent and motionless. There is a pause of dead stillness. Then YANK *begins to talk in a friendly confidential tone, half mockingly, but with a deep undercurrent of sympathy*) Say, yuh're some hard-lookin' guy, ain't yuh? I seen lots of tough nuts dat de gang called gorillas, but yuh're de foist real one I ever seen. Some chest yuh got, and shoulders, and dem arms and mits! I bet yuh got a punch in eider fist dat'd knock 'em all silly! (*This with genuine admiration. The gorilla, as if he understood, stands upright, swelling out his chest and pounding on it with his fist.* YANK *grins sympathetically*) Sure, I get yuh. Yuh challenge de whole woild, huh? Yuh got what I was sayin' even if yuh muffed de woids. (*Then bitterness creeping in*) And why wouldn't yuh get me? Ain't we both members of de same club—de Hairy Apes? (*They stare at each other—a pause—then* YANK *goes on slowly and bitterly*) So yuh're what she seen when she looked at me, de white-faced tart! I was you to her, get me? On'y outa de cage—broke out—free to moider her, see? Sure! Dat's what she tought. She wasn't wise dat I was in a cage, too—worser'n yours—sure—a damn sight—'cause you got some chanct to bust loose—but me— (*He grows confused*) Aw, hell! It's all wrong, ain't it? (*A pause*) I s'pose yuh wanter know what I'm doin' here, huh? I been warmin' a bench down to de Battery—ever since last night. Sure. I seen de sun come up. Dat was pretty, too—all red and pink and green. I was lookin' at de sky-scrapers—steel—and all de ships comin' in, sailin' out, all over de oith—and dey was steel, too. De sun was warm, dey wasn't no clouds, and dere was a breeze blowin'. Sure, it was great stuff. I got it aw right—what Paddy said about dat bein' de right dope—on'y I couldn't get *in* it, see? I couldn't belong in dat. It was over my head. And I kept tinkin'—and den I beat it up here to see what youse was like. And I waited till dey was all gone to git yuh alone. Say, how d'yuh feel sittin' in dat pen all de time, havin' to stand for 'em comin' and starin' at yuh —de white-faced, skinny tarts and de boobs what marry 'em—makin'

fun of yuh, laughin' at yuh, gittin' scared of yuh—damn 'em! (*He
pounds on the rail with his fist. The gorilla rattles the bars of his cage
and snarls. All the other monkeys set up an angry chattering in the
darkness.* YANK *goes on excitedly*) Sure! Dat's de way it hits me,
too. On'y yuh're lucky, see? Yuh don't belong wit 'em and yuh know
it. But me, I belong wit 'em—but I don't, see? Dey don't belong
wit me, dat's what. Get me? Tinkin' is hard— (*He passes one hand
across his forehead with a painful gesture. The gorilla growls impatiently.* YANK *goes on gropingly*) It's dis way, what I'm drivin' at.
Youse can sit and dope dream in de past, green woods, de jungle and
de rest of it. Den yuh belong and dey don't. Den yuh kin laugh at
'em, see? Yuh're de champ of de world. But me—I ain't got no past
to tink in, nor nothin' dat's comin', on'y what's now—and dat don't
belong. Sure, you're de best off! You can't tink, can yuh? Yuh can't
talk neider. But I kin make a bluff at talkin' and tinkin'—a'most git
away wit it—a'most!—and dat's where de joker comes in. (*He laughs*)
I ain't on oith and I ain't in heaven, get me? I'm in de middle tryin'
to separate 'em, takin' all de woist punches from bot' of 'em. Maybe
dat's what dey call hell, huh? But you, yuh're at de bottom. You belong! Sure! Yuh're de on'y one in de woild dat does, yuh lucky stiff!
(*The gorilla growls proudly*) And dat's why dey gotter put yuh in a
cage, see? (*The gorilla roars angrily*) Sure! Yuh get me. It beats it
when you try to tink it or talk it—it's way down—deep—behind—you
'n' me we feel it. Sure! Bot' members of dis club! (*He laughs—then in
a savage tone*) What de hell! T' hell wit it! A little action, dat's our
meat! Dat belongs! Knock 'em down and keep bustin' 'em till dey
croaks yuh wit a gat—wit steel! Sure! Are yuh game? Dey've looked at
youse, ain't dey—in a cage? Wanter git even? Wanter wind up like a
sport 'stead of croakin' slow in dere? (*The gorilla roars an emphatic
affirmative.* YANK *goes on with a sort of furious exaltation*) Sure!
Yuh're reg'lar! Yuh'll stick to de finish! Me 'n' you, huh?—bot' members of dis club! We'll put up one last star bout dat'll knock 'em offen
deir seats! Dey'll have to make de cages stronger after we're trou!

(*The gorilla is straining at his bars, growling, hopping from one foot to the other.* YANK *takes a jimmy from under his coat and forces the lock on the cage door. He throws this open*) Pardon from de governor! Step out and shake hands. I'll take yuh for a walk down Fif' Avenoo. We'll knock 'em offen de oith and croak wit de band playin'. Come on, Brother. (*The gorilla scrambles gingerly out of his cage. Goes to* YANK *and stands looking at him.* YANK *keeps his mocking tone—holds out his hand*) Shake—de secret grip of our order. (*Something, the tone of mockery, perhaps, suddenly enrages the animal. With a spring he wraps his huge arms around* YANK *in a murderous hug. There is a crackling snap of crushed ribs—a gasping cry, still mocking, from* YANK) Hey, I didn't say kiss me! (*The gorilla lets the crushed body slip to the floor; stands over it uncertainly, considering; then picks it up, throws it in the cage, shuts the door, and shuffles off menacingly into the darkness at left. A great uproar of frightened chattering and whimpering comes from the other cages. Then* YANK *moves, groaning, opening his eyes, and there is silence. He mutters painfully*) Say—dey oughter match him—with Zybszko. He got me, aw right. I'm trou. Even him didn't tink I belonged. (*Then, with sudden passionate despair*) Christ, where do I get off at? Where do I fit in? (*Checking himself as suddenly*) Aw, what de hell! No squawkin', see! No quittin', get me! Croak wit your boots on! (*He grabs hold of the bars of the cage and hauls himself painfully to his feet—looks around him bewilderedly—forces a mocking laugh*) In de cage, huh? (*In the strident tones of a circus barker*) Ladies and gents, step forward and take a slant at de one and only— (*His voice weakening*) one and original—Hairy Ape from de wilds of— (*He slips in a heap on the floor and dies. The monkeys set up a chattering, whimpering wail. And, perhaps, the Hairy Ape at last belongs.*)

CURTAIN

254

THE GREAT GOD BROWN

CHARACTERS

WILLIAM A. BROWN

HIS FATHER, *A Contractor*

HIS MOTHER

DION ANTHONY

HIS FATHER, *A Builder*

HIS MOTHER

MARGARET

HER THREE SONS

CYBEL

TWO DRAFTSMEN ⎫
A STENOGRAPHER ⎬ *in Brown's Office*
⎭

SCENES

Prologue: The Pier of the Casino. Moonlight in middle June.

ACT ONE

Scene I: Sitting room, Margaret Anthony's apartment. Afternoon, seven years later.

Scene II: Billy Brown's office. The same afternoon.

Scene III: Cybel's parlor. That night.

ACT TWO

Scene I: Cybel's parlor. Seven years later. Dusk.

Scene II: Drafting room, William A. Brown's office. That evening.

Scene III: Library, William A. Brown's home. That night.

ACT THREE

Scene I: Brown's office, a month later. Morning.

Scene II: Library, Brown's home. That evening.

Scene III: Sitting room, Margaret's home. That night.

ACT FOUR

Scene I: Brown's office, weeks later. Late afternoon.

Scene II: Library, Brown's house, hours later. The same night.

Epilogue: The Pier of the Casino. Four years later.

THE GREAT GOD BROWN

PROLOGUE

S cene—*A cross section of the pier of the Casino. In the rear, built out beyond the edge, is a rectangular space with benches on the three sides. A rail encloses the entire wharf at the back.*

It is a moonlight night in mid-June. From the Casino comes the sound of the school quartet rendering "Sweet Adeline" with many ultra-sentimental barber-shop quavers. There is a faint echo of the ensuing hand-clapping—then nothing but the lapping of ripples against the piles and their swishing on the beach—then footsteps on the boards and BILLY BROWN *walks along from right with his* MOTHER *and* FATHER. *The* MOTHER *is a dumpy woman of forty-five, overdressed in black lace and spangles. The* FATHER *is fifty or more, the type of bustling, genial, successful, provincial business man, stout and hearty in his evening dress.*

BILLY BROWN *is a handsome, tall and athletic boy of nearly eighteen. He is blond and blue-eyed, with a likeable smile and a frank good-humored face, its expression already indicating a disciplined restraint. His manner has the easy self-assurance of a normal intelligence. He is in evening dress.*

They walk arm in arm, the MOTHER *between.*

MOTHER. (*always addressing the* FATHER) This Commencement dance is badly managed. Such singing! Such poor voices! Why doesn't Billy sing?

BILLY. (*to her*) Mine is a regular fog horn! (*He laughs.*)

MOTHER. (*to the air*) I had a pretty voice, when I was a girl. (*Then,*

257

to the FATHER, *caustically*) Did you see young Anthony strutting around the ballroom in dirty flannel pants?

FATHER. He's just showing off.

MOTHER. Such impudence! He's as ignorant as his father.

FATHER. The old man's all right. My only kick against him is he's been too damned conservative to let me branch out.

MOTHER. (*bitterly*) He has kept you down to his level—out of pure jealousy.

FATHER. But he took me into partnership, don't forget—

MOTHER. (*sharply*) Because you were the brains! Because he was afraid of losing you! (*A pause.*)

BILLY. (*admiringly*) Dion came in his old clothes on a bet with me. He's a real sport. He wouldn't have been afraid to appear in his pajamas! (*He grins with appreciation.*)

MOTHER. Isn't the moonlight clear! (*She goes and sits on the center bench.* BILLY *stands at the left corner, forward, his hand on the rail, like a prisoner at the bar, facing the judge. His* FATHER *stands in front of the bench on right. The* MOTHER *announces, with finality*) After he's through college, Billy must study for a profession of some sort, I'm determined on that! (*She turns to her husband, defiantly, as if expecting opposition.*)

FATHER. (*eagerly and placatingly*) Just what I've been thinking, my dear. Architecture! How's that? Billy a first-rate, number-one architect! That's my proposition! What I've always wished I could have been myself! Only I never had the opportunity. But Billy—we'll make him a partner in the firm after. Anthony, Brown *and Son,* architects and builders—instead of *contractors* and builders!

MOTHER. (*yearning for the realization of a dream*) And we won't lay sidewalks—or dig sewers—ever again?

FATHER. (*a bit ruffled*) I and Anthony can build anything your pet can draw—even if it's a church! (*Then, selling his idea*) It's a great chance for him! He'll design—expand us—make the firm famous.

MOTHER. (*to the air—musingly*) When you proposed, I thought

your future promised success—my future—(*With a sigh*) Well, I
suppose we've been comfortable. Now, it's his future. How would
Billy like to be an architect? (*She does not look at him.*)

BILLY. (*to her*) All right, Mother. (*Then sheepishly*) I guess I've
never bothered much about what I'd like to do after college—but
architecture sounds all right to me, I guess.

MOTHER. (*to the air—proudly*) Billy used to draw houses when he
was little.

FATHER. (*jubilantly*) Billy's got the stuff in him to win, if he'll only
work hard enough.

BILLY. (*dutifully*) I'll work hard, Dad.

MOTHER. Billy can do anything!

BILLY. (*embarrassed*) I'll try, Mother. (*There is a pause.*)

MOTHER. (*with a sudden shiver*) The nights are so much colder
than they used to be! Think of it, I once went moonlight bathing
in June when I was a girl—but the moonlight was so warm and
beautiful in those days, do you remember, Father?

FATHER. (*puts his arm around her affectionately*) You bet I do,
Mother. (*He kisses her. The orchestra at the Casino strikes up a
waltz*) There's the music. Let's go back and watch the young folks
dance. (*They start off, leaving* BILLY *standing there.*)

MOTHER. (*suddenly calls back over her shoulder*) I want to watch
Billy dance.

BILLY. (*dutifully*) Yes, Mother! (*He follows them. For a moment
the faint sound of the music and the lapping of waves is heard. Then
footsteps again and the three* ANTHONYS *come in. First come the* FATHER
and MOTHER, *who are not masked. The* FATHER *is a tall lean man of
fifty-five or sixty with a grim, defensive face, obstinate to the point
of stupid weakness. The* MOTHER *is a thin frail faded woman, her
manner perpetually nervous and distraught, but with a sweet and
gentle face that had once been beautiful. The* FATHER *wears an ill-
fitting black suit, like a mourner. The* MOTHER *wears a cheap, plain,
black dress. Following them, as if he were a stranger, walking alone,*

259

is their son, DION. *He is about the same height as young* BROWN *but lean and wiry, without repose, continually in restless nervous movement. His face is masked. The mask is a fixed forcing of his own face —dark, spiritual, poetic, passionately supersensitive, helplessly unprotected in its childlike, religious faith in life—into the expression of a mocking, reckless, defiant, gayly scoffing and sensual young Pan. He is dressed in a gray flannel shirt, open at the neck, sneakers over bare feet, and soiled white flannel trousers. The* FATHER *strides to the center bench and sits down. The* MOTHER, *who has been holding to his arm, lets go and stands by the bench at the right. They both stare at* DION, *who, with a studied carelessness, takes his place at the rail, where young* BROWN *had stood. They watch him, with queer, puzzled eyes.*)

MOTHER. (*suddenly—pleading*) You simply must send him to college!

FATHER. I won't. I don't believe in it. Colleges turn out lazy loafers to sponge on their poor old fathers! Let him slave like I had to! That'll teach him the value of a dollar! College'll only make him a bigger fool than he is already! I never got above grammar school but I've made money and established a sound business. Let him make a man out of himself like I made of myself!

DION. (*mockingly—to the air*) This Mr. Anthony is my father, but he only imagines he is God the Father. (*They both stare at him.*)

FATHER. (*with angry bewilderment*) What—what—what's that?

MOTHER. (*gently remonstrating to her son*) Dion, dear! (*Then to her husband—tauntingly*) Brown takes all the credit! He tells everyone the success is all due to his energy—that you're only an old stick-in-the-mud!

FATHER. (*stung, harshly*) The damn fool! He knows better'n anyone if I hadn't held him down to common sense, with his crazy wild-cat notions, he'd have had us ruined long ago!

MOTHER. He's sending Billy to college—Mrs. Brown just told me—going to have him study architecture afterwards, too, so's he can help expand your firm!

FATHER. (*angrily*) What's that? (*Suddenly turns on* DION *furiously*) Then you can make up your mind to go, too! And you'll learn to be a better architect than Brown's boy or I'll turn you out in the gutter without a penny! You hear?

DION. (*mockingly—to the air*) It's difficult to choose—but architecture sounds less laborious.

MOTHER. (*fondly*) You ought to make a wonderful architect, Dion. You've always painted pictures so well—

DION. (*with a start—resentfully*) Why must she lie? Is it my fault? She knows I only try to paint. (*Passionately*) But I will, some day! (*Then quickly, mocking again*) On to college! Well, it won't be home, anyway, will it? (*He laughs queerly and approaches them. His* FATHER *gets up defensively.* DION *bows to him*) I thank Mr. Anthony for this splendid opportunity to create myself—(*He kisses his mother, who bows with a strange humility as if she were a servant being saluted by the young master—then adds lightly*)—in my mother's image, so she may feel her life comfortably concluded. (*He sits in his* FATHER'S *place at center and his mask stares with a frozen mockery before him. They stand on each side, looking dumbly at him.*)

MOTHER. (*at last, with a shiver*) It's cold. June didn't use to be cold. I remember the June when I was carrying you, Dion—three months before you were born. (*She stares up at the sky*) The moonlight was warm, then. I could feel the night wrapped around me like a gray velvet gown lined with warm sky and trimmed with silver leaves!

FATHER. (*gruffly—but with a certain awe*) My mother used to believe the full of the moon was the time to sow. She was terrible old-fashioned. (*With a grunt*) I can feel it's bringing on my rheumatism. Let's go back indoors.

DION. (*with intense bitterness*) Hide! Be ashamed! (*They both start and stare at him.*)

FATHER. (*with bitter hopelessness—to his wife—indicating their son*) Who is he? You bore him!

MOTHER. (*proudly*) He's my boy! He's Dion!

DION. (*bitterly resentful*) What else, indeed! The identical son! (*Then mockingly*) Are Mr. Anthony and his wife going in to dance? The nights grow cold! The days are dimmer than they used to be! Let's play hide-and-seek! Seek the monkey in the moon! (*He suddenly cuts a grotesque caper, like a harlequin and darts off, laughing with forced abandon. They stare after him—then slowly follow. Again there is silence except for the sound of the lapping waves. Then* MARGARET *comes in, followed by the humble worshiping* BILLY BROWN. *She is almost seventeen, pretty and vivacious, blonde, with big romantic eyes, her figure lithe and strong, her facial expression intelligent but youthfully dreamy, especially now in the moonlight. She is in a simple white dress. On her entrance, her face is masked with an exact, almost transparent reproduction of her own features, but giving her the abstract quality of a Girl instead of the individual,* MARGARET.)

MARGARET. (*looking upward at the moon and singing in low tone as they enter*) "Ah, moon of my delight that knowest no wane!"

BILLY. (*eagerly*) I've got that record—John McCormack. It's a peach! Sing some more. (*She looks upward in silence. He keeps standing respectfully in back of her, glancing embarrassedly toward her averted face. He tries to make conversation*) I think the "Rubáiyát's" great stuff, don't you? I never could memorize poetry worth a darn. Dion can recite lots of Shelley's poems by heart.

MARGARET. (*slowly takes off her mask—to the moon*) Dion! (*A pause.*)

BILLY. (*fidgeting*) Margaret!

MARGARET. (*to the moon*) Dion is so wonderful!

BILLY. (*blunderingly*) I asked you to come out here because I wanted to tell you something.

MARGARET. (*to the moon*) Why did Dion look at me like that? It made me feel so crazy!

BILLY. I wanted to ask you something, too.

MARGARET. That one time he kissed me—I can't forget it! He was only joking—but I felt—and he saw and just laughed!

BILLY. Because that's the uncertain part. My end of it is a sure thing, and has been for a long time, and I guess everybody in town knows it—they're always kidding me—so it's a cinch you must know—how I feel about you.

MARGARET. Dion's so different from all the others. He can paint beautifully and write poetry and he plays and sings and dances so marvelously. But he's sad and shy, too, just like a baby sometimes, and he understands what I'm really like inside—and—and I'd love to run my fingers through his hair—and I love him! Yes, I love him! (*She stretches out her arms to the moon*) Oh, Dion, I love you!

BILLY. I love you, Margaret.

MARGARET. I wonder if Dion— I saw him looking at me again tonight— Oh, I wonder . . . !

BILLY. (*takes her hand and blurts out*) Can't you love me? Won't you marry me—after college—

MARGARET. Where is Dion now, I wonder?

BILLY. (*shaking her hand in an agony of uncertainty*) Margaret! Please answer me!

MARGARET. (*her dream broken, puts on her mask and turns to him —matter-of-factly*) It's getting chilly. Let's go back and dance, Billy.

BILLY. (*desperately*) I love you! (*He tries clumsily to kiss her.*)

MARGARET. (*with an amused laugh*) Like a brother! You can kiss me if you like. (*She kisses him*) A big-brother kiss. It doesn't count. (*He steps back crushed, with head bowed. She turns away and takes off her mask—to the moon*) I wish Dion would kiss me again!

BILLY. (*painfully*) I'm a poor boob. I ought to know better. I'll bet I know. You're in love with Dion. I've seen you look at him. Isn't that it?

MARGARET. Dion! I love the sound of it!

BILLY. (*huskily*) Well—he's always been my best friend—I'm glad it's him—and I guess I know how to lose— (*He takes her hand and shakes it*) So here's wishing you all the success and happiness in the world, Margaret—and remember I'll always be your best friend! (*He gives her hand a final shake—swallows hard—then manfully*) Let's go back in!

MARGARET. (*to the moon—faintly annoyed*) What is Billy Brown doing here? I'll go down to the end of the dock and wait. Dion is the moon and I'm the sea. I want to feel the moon kissing the sea. I want Dion to leave the sky to me. I want the tides of my blood to leave my heart and follow him! (*She whispers like a little girl*) Dion! Margaret! Peggy! Peggy is Dion's girl—Peggy is Dion's little girl— (*She sings laughingly, elfishly*) Dion is my Daddy-O! (*She is walking toward the end of the dock, off left.*)

BILLY. (*who has turned away*) I'm going. I'll tell Dion you're here.

MARGARET. (*more and more strongly and assertively, until at the end she is a wife and a mother*) And I'll be Mrs. Dion—Dion's wife —and he'll be my Dion—my own Dion—my little boy—my baby! The moon is drowned in the tides of my heart, and peace sinks deep through the sea! (*She disappears off left, her upturned unmasked face like that of a rapturous visionary. There is silence again, in which the dance music is heard. Then this stops and* DION *comes in. He walks quickly to the bench at center and throws himself on it, hiding his masked face in his hands. After a moment, he lifts his head, peers about, listens huntedly, then slowly takes off his mask. His real face is revealed in the bright moonlight, shrinking, shy and gentle, full of a deep sadness.*)

DION. (*with a suffering bewilderment*) Why am I afraid to dance, I who love music and rhythm and grace and song and laughter? Why am I afraid to live, I who love life and the beauty of flesh and the living colors of earth and sky and sea? Why am I afraid of love, I who love love? Why am I afraid, I who am not afraid? Why must I pretend to scorn in order to pity? Why must I hide myself in self-contempt in order to understand? Why must I be so ashamed of my strength, so proud of my weakness? Why must I live in a cage like a criminal, defying and hating, I who love peace and friendship? (*Clasping his hands above in supplication*) Why was I born without a skin, O God, that I must wear armor in order to touch or to be touched? (*A second's pause of waiting silence—then he suddenly claps his mask over his face again with a gesture of despair and his voice becomes bitter and sardonic*) Or, rather, Old Graybeard, why the devil was I ever born at all? (*Steps are heard from the right.* DION *stiffens and his mask stares straight ahead.* BILLY *comes in from the right. He is shuffling along disconsolately. When he sees* DION, *he stops abruptly and glowers resentfully—but at once the "good loser" in him conquers this.*)

BILLY. (*embarrassedly*) Hello, Dion. I've been looking all over for you. (*He sits down on the bench at right, forcing a joking tone*) What are you sitting here for, you nut—trying to get more moon-struck? (*A pause—awkwardly*) I just left Margaret—

DION. (*gives a start—immediately defensively mocking*) Bless you, my children!

BILLY. (*gruffly and slangily*) I'm out of it—she gave me the gate. You're the original white-haired boy. Go on in and win! We've been chums ever since we were kids, haven't we?—and—I'm glad it's you, Dion. (*This huskily—he fumbles for* DION's *hand and gives it a shake.*)

DION. (*letting his hand fall back—bitterly*) Chums? Oh, no, Billy Brown would despise me!

BILLY. She's waiting for you now, down at the end of the dock.

DION. For me? Which? Who? Oh, no, girls only allow themselves to look at what is seen!

BILLY. She's in love with you.

DION. (*moved—a pause—stammers*) Miracle? I'm afraid! (*He chants flippantly*) I love, thou lovest, he loves, she loves! She loves, she loves—what?

BILLY. And I know damn well, underneath your nuttiness, you're gone on her.

DION. (*moved*) Underneath? I love love! I'd love to be loved! But I'm afraid! (*Then aggressively*) Was afraid! Not now! Now I can make love—to anyone! Yes, I love Peggy! Why not? Who is she?

Who am I? We love, you love, they love, one loves! No one loves! All the world loves a lover, God loves us all and we love Him! Love is a word—a shameless ragged ghost of a word—begging at all doors for life at any price!

BILLY. (*always as if he hadn't listened to what the other said*) Say, let's you and me room together at college—

DION. Billy wants to remain by her side!

BILLY. It's a bet, then! (*Forcing a grin*) You can tell her I'll see that you behave! (*Turns away*) So long. Remember she's waiting. (*He goes.*)

DION. (*dazedly, to himself*) Waiting—waiting for me! (*He slowly removes his mask. His face is torn and transfigured by joy. He stares at the sky raptly*) O God in the moon, did you hear? She loves me! I am not afraid! I am strong! I can love! She protects me! Her arms are softly around me! She is warmly around me! She is my skin! She is my armor! Now I am born—I—the I!—one and indivisible—I who love Margaret! (*He glances at his mask triumphantly—in tones of deliverance*) You are outgrown! I am beyond you! (*He stretches out his arms to the sky*) O God, now I believe! (*From the end of the wharf, her voice is heard.*)

MARGARET. Dion!

DION. (*raptly*) Margaret!

MARGARET. (*nearer*) Dion!

DION. Margaret!

MARGARET. Dion! (*She comes running in, her mask in her hands. He springs toward her with outstretched arms but she shrinks away with a frightened shriek and hastily puts on her mask.* DION *starts back. She speaks coldly and angrily*) Who are you! Why are you calling me? I don't know you!

DION. (*heart-brokenly*) I love you!

MARGARET (*freezingly*) Is this a joke—or are you drunk?

DION. (*with a final pleading whisper*) Margaret! (*But she only glares at him contemptuously. Then with a sudden gesture he claps his mask on and laughs wildly and bitterly*) Ha-ha-ha! That's one on you, Peg!

MARGARET. (*with delight, pulling off her mask*) Dion! How did you ever— Why, I never knew you!

DION. (*puts his arm around her boldly*) How? It's the moon—the crazy moon—the monkey in the moon—playing jokes on us! (*He kisses her with his masked face with a romantic actor's passion again and again*) You love me! You know you do! Say it! Tell me! I want to hear! I want to feel! I want to know! I want to want! To want you as you want me!

MARGARET. (*in ecstasy*) Oh, Dion, I do! I do love you!

DION. (*with ironic mastery—rhetorically*) And I love you! Oh, madly! Oh, forever and ever, amen! You are my evening star and all my Pleiades! Your eyes are blue pools in which gold dreams glide, your body is a young white birch leaning backward beneath the lips of spring. So! (*He has bent her back, his arms supporting her, his face above hers*) So! (*He kisses her.*)

MARGARET. (*with overpowering passionate languor*) Oh, Dion! Dion! I love you!

DION. (*with more and more mastery in his tone*) I love, you love, we love! Come! Rest! Relax! Let go your clutch on the world! Dim and dimmer! Fading out in the past behind! Gone! Death! Now! Be born! Awake! Live! Dissolve into dew—into silence—into night— into earth—into space—into peace—into meaning—into joy—into God—into the Great God Pan! (*While he has been speaking, the moon has passed gradually behind a black cloud, its light fading out. There is a moment of intense blackness and silence. Then the light gradually comes on again. Dion's voice, at first in a whisper, then increasing in volume with the light, is heard*) Wake up! Time to get up! Time to exist! Time for school! Time to learn! Learn to pretend! Cover your nakedness! Learn to lie! Learn to keep step! Join the procession! Great Pan is dead! Be ashamed!

MARGARET. (*with a sob*) Oh, Dion, I am ashamed!

DION. (*mockingly*) Sssshh! Watch the monkey in the moon! See him dance! His tail is a piece of string that was left when he broke loose from Jehovah and ran away to join Charley Darwin's circus!

MARGARET. I know you must hate me now! (*She throws her arms around him and hides her head on his shoulder.*)

DION. (*deeply moved*) Don't cry! Don't—! (*He suddenly tears off his mask—in a passionate agony*) Hate you? I love you with all my soul! Love me! Why can't you love me, Margaret? (*He tries to kiss her but she jumps to her feet with a frightened cry holding up her mask before her face protectingly.*)

MARGARET. Don't! Please! I don't know you! You frighten me!

DION. (*puts on his mask again—quietly and bitterly*) All's well. I'll never let you see again. (*He puts his arm around her—gently mocking*) By proxy, I love you. There! Don't cry! Don't be afraid! Dion Anthony will marry you some day. (*He kisses her*) "I take this woman—" (*Tenderly joking*) Hello, woman! Do you feel older by æons? Mrs. Dion Anthony, shall we go in and may I have the next dance?

MARGARET. (*tenderly*) You crazy child! (*Then, laughing with joy*) Mrs. Dion Anthony! It sounds wonderful, doesn't it? (*They go out as the curtain falls.*)

ACT ONE—SCENE ONE

SCENE—*Seven years later. The sitting room of* MRS. DION ANTHONY'S *half of a two-family house in the homes section of the town—one of those one-design districts that daze the eye with multiplied ugliness. The four pieces of furniture shown are in keeping—an armchair at left, a table with a chair in back of it at center, a sofa at right. The same courtroom effect of the arrangement of benches in Act One is held to here. The background is a backdrop on which the rear wall is painted with the intolerable lifeless realistic detail of the stereotyped paintings which usually adorn the sitting rooms of such houses. It is late afternoon of a gray day in winter.*

DION *is sitting behind the table, staring before him. The mask hangs on his breast below his neck, giving the effect of two faces. His real face has aged greatly, grown more strained and tortured, but at the same time, in some queer way, more selfless and ascetic, more fixed in its resolute withdrawal from life. The mask, too, has changed. It is older, more defiant and mocking, its sneer more forced and bitter, its Pan quality becoming Mephistophelean. It has already begun to show the ravages of dissipation.*

DION. (*suddenly reaches out and takes up a copy of the New Testament which is on the table and, putting a finger in at random, opens and reads aloud the text at which it points*) "Come unto me all ye who are heavy laden and I will give you rest." (*He stares before him in a sort of trance, his face lighted up from within but painfully confused—in an uncertain whisper*) I will come—but where are you, Savior? (*The noise of the outer door shutting is heard.* DION *starts and claps the mocking mask on his face again. He tosses the Testament aside contemptuously*) Blah! Fixation on old Mama Christianity! You infant blubbering in the dark, you! (*He laughs, with a bitter self-contempt. Footsteps approach. He picks up a newspaper and hides behind it hurriedly.* MARGARET *enters. She is dressed in stylish, expensive clothes and a fur coat, which look as if they had been re-modeled and seen service. She has grown mature and maternal, in spite of her youth. Her pretty face is still fresh and healthy but there is the beginning of a permanently worried, apprehensive expression about the nose and mouth—an uncomprehending hurt in her eyes.* DION *pretends to be engrossed in his paper. She bends down and kisses him.*)

MARGARET. (*with a forced gaiety*) Good morning—at four in the afternoon! You were snoring when I left!

DION. (*puts his arms around her with a negligent, accustomed ges-ture—mockingly*) The Ideal Husband!

MARGARET. (*already preoccupied with another thought—comes and sits in chair on left*) I was afraid the children would disturb you, so I took them over to Mrs. Young's to play. (*A pause. He picks up the paper again. She asks anxiously*) I suppose they'll be all right over there, don't you? (*He doesn't answer. She is more hurt than offended*) I wish you'd try to take more interest in the children, Dion.

DION. (*mockingly*) Become a father—before breakfast? I'm in too delicate a condition. (*She turns away, hurt. Penitently he pats her hand—vaguely*) All right. I'll try.

MARGARET. (*squeezing his hand—with possessive tenderness*) Play with them. You're a bigger kid than they are—underneath.

DION. (*self-mockingly—flipping the Bible*) Underneath—I'm be-coming downright infantile! "Suffer these little ones!"

MARGARET. (*keeping to her certainty*) You're my oldest.

DION. (*with mocking appreciation*) She puts the Kingdom of Heaven in its place!

MARGARET. (*withdrawing her hand*) I was serious.

DION. So was I—about something or other. (*He laughs*) This domestic diplomacy! We communicate in code—when neither has the other's key!

270

MARGARET. (*frowns confusedly—then forcing a playful tone*) I want to have a serious talk with you, young man! In spite of your promises, you've kept up the hard drinking and gambling you started the last year abroad.

DION. From the time I realized it wasn't in me to be an artist—except in living—and not even in that! (*He laughs bitterly.*)

MARGARET. (*with conviction*) But you *can* paint, Dion—beautifully!

DION. (*with deep pain*) No! (*He suddenly takes her hand and kisses it gratefully*) I love Margaret! Her blindness surpasseth all understanding! (*Then bitterly*)—or is it pity?

MARGARET. We've only got about one hundred dollars left in the bank.

DION. (*with dazed surprise*) What! Is all the money from the sale of the house gone?

MARGARET. (*wearily*) Every day or so you've been cashing checks. You've been drinking—you haven't counted—

DION. (*irritably*) I know! (*A pause—soberly*) No more estate to fall back on, eh? Well, for five years it kept us living abroad in peace. It bought us a little happiness—of a kind—didn't it?—living and loving and having children—(*A slight pause—bitterly*)—thinking one was creating before one discovered one couldn't!

MARGARET. (*this time with forced conviction*) But you *can* paint—beautifully!

DION. (*angrily*) Shut up! (*A pause—then jeeringly*) So my wife thinks it behooves me to settle down and support my family in the meager style to which they'll have to become accustomed?

MARGARET. (*shamefacedly*) I didn't say—still—something's got to be done.

DION. (*harshly*) Will Mrs. Anthony helpfully suggest what?

MARGARET. I met Billy Brown on the street. He said you'd have made a good architect, if you'd stuck to it.

DION. Flatterer! Instead of leaving college when my Old Man died? Instead of marrying Peggy and going abroad and being happy?

271

MARGARET. (*as if she hadn't heard*) He spoke of how well you used to draw.

DION. Billy was in love with Margaret at one time.

MARGARET. He wanted to know why you've never been in to see him.

DION. He's bound heaven-bent for success. It's the will of Mammon! Anthony and Brown, contractors and builders—death subtracts Anthony and I sell out—Billy graduates—Brown and Son, architects and builders—old man Brown perishes of paternal pride—and now we have William A. Brown, architect! Why his career itself already has an architectural design! One of God's mud pies!

MARGARET. He particularly told me to ask you to drop in.

DION. (*springs to his feet—assertively*) No! Pride! I have been alive!

MARGARET. Why don't you have a talk with him?

DION. Pride in my failure!

MARGARET. You were always such close friends.

DION. (*more and more desperately*) The pride which came after man's fall—by which he laughs as a creator at his self-defeats!

MARGARET. Not for my sake—but for your own—and, above all, for the children's!

DION. (*with terrible despair*) Pride! Pride without which the Gods are worms!

MARGARET. (*after a pause, meekly and humbly*) You don't want to? It would hurt you? All right, dear. Never mind. We'll manage somehow—you mustn't worry—you must start your beautiful painting again—and I can get that position in the library—it would be such fun for me working there! . . . (*She reaches out and takes his hand—tenderly*) I love you, dear. I understand.

DION. (*slumps down into his chair, crushed, his face averted from hers, as hers is from him, although their hands are still clasped—in a trembling, expiring voice*) Pride is dying! (*As if he were suffocating, he pulls the mask from his resigned, pale, suffering face. He prays like a Saint in the desert, exorcizing a demon*) Pride is dead! Blessed are the meek! Blessed are the poor in spirit!

MARGARET. (*without looking at him—in a comforting, motherly tone*) My poor boy!

DION. (*resentfully—clapping on his mask again and springing to his feet—derisively*) Blessed are the meek for they shall inherit graves! Blessed are the poor in spirit for they are blind! (*Then with tortured bitterness*) All right! Then I ask my wife to go and ask Billy Brown—that's more deadly than if I went myself! (*With wild mockery*) Ask him if he can't find an opening for a talented young man who is only honest when he isn't sober—implore him, beg him in the name of old love, old friendship—to be a generous hero and save the woman and her children! (*He laughs with a sort of diabolical, ironical glee now, and starts to go out.*)

MARGARET. (*meekly*) Are you going up street, Dion?

DION. Yes.

MARGARET. Will you stop at the butchers' and have them send two pounds of pork chops?

DION. Yes.

MARGARET. And stop at Mrs. Young's and ask the children to hurry right home?

DION. Yes.

MARGARET. Will you be back for dinner, Dion?

DION. No. (*He goes, the outer door slams.* MARGARET *sighs with a tired incomprehension and goes to the window and stares out.*)

MARGARET. (*worriedly*) I hope they'll watch out, crossing the street.

CURTAIN

ACT ONE—SCENE TWO

SCENE—BILLY BROWN's *Office, at five in the afternoon. At center, a fine mahogany desk with a swivel chair in back of it. To the left of desk, an office armchair. To the right of desk, an office lounge. The background is a backdrop of an office wall, treated similarly to that of Scene One in its over-meticulous representation of detail.*

BILLY BROWN *is seated at the desk looking over a blueprint by the light of a desk lamp. He has grown into a fine-looking, well-dressed, capable, college-bred American business man, boyish still and with the same engaging personality.*

The telephone rings.

BROWN. (*answering it*) Yes? Who? (*This in surprise—then with eager pleasure*) Let her come right in. (*He gets up and goes to the door, expectant and curious. MARGARET enters. Her face is concealed behind the mask of the pretty young matron, still hardly a woman, who cultivates a naïvely innocent and bravely hopeful attitude toward things and acknowledges no wound to the world. She is dressed as in Scene One but with an added touch of effective primping here and there.*)

MARGARET. (*very gaily*) Hello, Billy Brown!

BROWN. (*awkward in her presence, shakes her hand*) Come in. Sit down. This is a pleasant surprise, Margaret. (*She sits down on the lounge. He sits in his chair behind the desk, as before.*)

MARGARET. (*looking around*) What lovely offices! My, but Billy Brown is getting grand!

BROWN. (*pleased*) I've just moved in. The old place was too stuffy.

MARGARET. It looks so prosperous—but then, Billy is doing so wonderfully well, everyone says.

274

BROWN. (*modestly*) Well, to be frank, it's been mostly luck. Things have come my way without my doing much about it. (*Then, with an abashed pride*) Still—I have done a little something myself. (*He picks the plan from the desk*) See this? It's my design for the new Municipal Building. It's just been accepted—provisionally—by the Committee.

MARGARET. (*taking it—vaguely*) Oh? (*She looks at it abstractedly. There is a pause. Suddenly*) You mentioned the other day how well Dion used to draw—

BROWN. (*a bit stiffly*) Yes, he certainly did. (*He takes the drawing from her and at once becomes interested and squints at it frowningly*) Did you notice that anything seemed lacking in this?

MARGARET. (*indifferently*) Not at all.

BROWN. (*with a cheerful grin*) The Committee want it made a little more American. It's too much of a conventional Greco-Roman tomb, they say. (*Laughs*) They want an original touch of modern novelty stuck in to liven it up and make it look different from other town halls. (*Putting the drawing back on his desk*) And I've been figuring out how to give it to them but my mind doesn't seem to run that way. Have you any suggestion?

MARGARET. (*as if she hadn't heard*) Dion certainly draws well, Billy Brown was saying?

BROWN. (*trying not to show his annoyance*) Why, yes—he did— and still can, I expect. (*A pause. He masters what he feels to be an unworthy pique and turns to her generously*) Dion would have made a cracking good architect.

MARGARET. (*proudly*) I know. He could be anything he wanted to.

BROWN. (*a pause—embarrassedly*) Is he working at anything these days?

MARGARET. (*defensively*) Oh, yes! He's painting wonderfully! But he's just like a child, he's so impractical. He doesn't try to have an exhibition anywhere, or anything.

BROWN. (*surprised*) The one time I ran into him, I thought he told me he'd destroyed all his pictures—that he'd gotten sick of painting and completely given it up.

MARGARET. (*quickly*) He always tells people that. He doesn't want anyone even to look at his things, imagine! He keeps saying they're rotten—when they're really too beautiful! He's too modest for his own good, don't you think? But it is true he hasn't done so much lately since we've been back. You see the children take up such a lot of his time. He just worships them! I'm afraid he's becoming a hopeless family man, just the opposite of what anyone would expect who knew him in the old days.

BROWN. (*painfully embarrassed by her loyalty and his knowledge of the facts*) Yes, I know. (*He coughs self-consciously.*)

MARGARET. (*aroused by something in his manner*) But I suppose the gossips are telling the same silly stories about him they always did. (*She forces a laugh*) Poor Dion! Give a dog a bad name! (*Her voice breaks a little in spite of herself.*)

BROWN. (*hastily*) I haven't heard any stories—(*He stops uncertainly, then decides to plunge in*)—except about money matters.

MARGARET. (*forcing a laugh*) Oh, perhaps they're true enough. Dion is such a generous fool with his money, like all artists.

BROWN. (*with a certain doggedness*) There's a rumor that you've applied for a position at the Library.

MARGARET. (*forcing a gay tone*) Yes, indeed! Won't it be fun! Maybe it'll improve my mind! And one of us has got to be practical, so why not me? (*She forces a gay, girlish laugh.*)

BROWN. (*impulsively reaches out and takes her hand—awkwardly*) Listen, Margaret. Let's be perfectly frank, will you? I'm such an old friend, and I want like the deuce to. . . . You know darn well I'd do anything in the world to help you—or Dion.

MARGARET. (*withdrawing her hand, coldly*) I'm afraid I—don't understand, Billy Brown.

BROWN. (*acutely embarrassed*) Well, I—I just meant—you know, if you needed— (*A pause. He looks questioningly at her averted face*

276

—then ventures on another tack, matter-of-factly) I've got a proposition to make to Dion—if I could ever get hold of him. It's this way: business has been piling up on me—a run of luck—but I'm short-handed I need a crack chief draftsman darn badly—or I'm liable to lose out. Do you think Dion would consider it—as a temporary stop-gap—until he felt in the painting mood again?

MARGARET. (*striving to conceal her eagerness and relief—judicially*) Yes—I really do. He's such a good sport and Billy and he were such pals once. I know he'd be only too tickled to help him out.

BROWN. (*diffidently*) I thought he might be sensitive about work-ing for—I mean, with me—when, if he hadn't sold out to Dad he'd be my partner now— (*Earnestly*) and, by jingo, I wish he was! (*Then, abruptly*) Let's try to nail him down right away, Margaret. Is he home now? (*He reaches for the phone.*)

MARGARET. (*hurriedly*) No, he—he went out for a long walk.

BROWN. Perhaps I can locate him later around town somewhere.

MARGARET. (*with a note of pleading*) Please don't trouble. It isn't necessary. I'm sure when I talk to him—he's coming home to dinner— (*Getting up*) Then it's all settled, isn't it? Dion will be so glad to be able to help an old friend—he's so terribly loyal, and he's always liked Billy Brown so much! (*Holding out her hand*) I really must go now!

BROWN. (*shakes her hand*) Good-by, Margaret. I hope you'll be dropping in on us a lot when Dion gets here.

MARGARET. Yes. (*She goes.*)

BROWN. (*sits at his desk again, looking ahead in a not unsatisfying melancholy reverie. He mutters admiringly but pityingly*) Poor Margaret! She's a game sport, but it's pretty damn tough on her! (*Indignantly*) By God, I'm going to give Dion a good talking-to one of these days!

CURTAIN

ACT ONE—SCENE THREE

Scene—CYBEL's *parlor. An automatic, nickel-in-the-slot player-piano is at center, rear. On its right is a dirty gilt second-hand sofa. At the left is a bald-spotted crimson plush chair. The backdrop for the rear wall is cheap wallpaper of a dull yellow-brown, resembling a blurred impression of a fallow field in early spring. There is a cheap alarm clock on top of the piano. Beside it her mask is lying.*

DION *is sprawled on his back, fast asleep on the sofa. His mask has fallen down on his chest. His pale face is singularly pure, spiritual and sad.*

The player-piano is groggily banging out a sentimental medley of "Mother—Mammy" *tunes.*

CYBEL *is seated on the stool in front of the piano. She is a strong, calm, sensual blonde girl of twenty or so, her complexion fresh and healthy, her figure full-breasted and wide-hipped, her movements slow and solidly languorous like an animal's, her large eyes dreamy with the reflected stirring of profound instincts. She chews gum like a sacred cow forgetting time with an eternal end. Her eyes are fixed, incuriously, on* DION's *pale face.*

CYBEL. (*as the tune runs out, glances at the clock, which indicates midnight, then goes slowly over to* DION *and puts her hand gently on his forehead*) Wake up!

DION. (*stirs, sighs and murmurs dreamily*) "And He laid his hands on them and healed them." (*Then with a start he opens his eyes and, half sitting up, stares at her bewilderedly*) What—where—who are you? (*He reaches for his mask and claps it on defensively.*)

CYBEL. (*placidly*) Only another female. You was camping on my steps, sound asleep. I didn't want to run any risk getting into more trouble with the cops pinching you there and blaming me, so I took you in to sleep it off.

DION. (*mockingly*) Blessed are the pitiful, Sister! I'm broke—but you will be rewarded in Heaven!

CYBEL. (*calmly*) I wasn't wasting my pity. Why should I? You were happy, weren't you?

DION. (*approvingly*) Excellent! You're not a moralist, I see.

CYBEL. (*going on*) And you look like a good boy, too—when you're asleep. Say, you better beat it home to bed or you'll be locked out.

DION. (*mockingly*) Now you're becoming maternal, Miss Earth. Is that the only answer—to pin my soul into every vacant diaper? (*She stares down at his mask, her face growing hard. He laughs*) But please don't stop stroking my aching brow. Your hand is a cool mud poultice on the sting of thought!

CYBEL. (*calmly*) Stop acting. I hate ham fats. (*She looks at him as if waiting for him to remove his mask—then turns her back indifferently and goes to the piano*) Well, if you simply got to be a regular devil like all the other visiting sports, I s'pose I got to play with you. (*She takes her mask and puts it on—then turns. The mask is the rouged and eye-blackened countenance of the hardened prostitute. In a coarse, harsh voice*) Kindly state your dishonorable intentions, if any! I can't sit up all night keeping company! Let's have some music! (*She puts a plug in the machine. The same sentimental medley begins to play. The two masks stare at each other. She laughs*) Shoot! I'm all set! It's your play, Kid Lucifer!

DION. (*slowly removes his mask. She stops the music with a jerk. His face is gentle and sad—humbly*) I'm sorry. It has always been such agony for me to be touched!

CYBEL. (*taking off her mask—sympathetically as she comes back and sits down on her stool*) Poor kid! I've never had one, but I can guess. They hug and kiss you and take you on their laps and pinch you and want to see you getting dressed and undressed—as if they owned you—I bet you I'd never let them treat one of mine that way!

279

DION. (*turning to her*) You're lost in blind alleys, too. (*Suddenly holding out his hand to her*) But you're strong. Let's be friends.

CYBEL. (*with a strange sternness, searches his face*) And never nothing more?

DION. (*with a strange smile*) Let's say, never anything less! (*She takes his hand. There is a ring at the outside-door bell. They stare at each other. There is another ring.*)

CYBEL. (*puts on her mask,* DION *does likewise. Mockingly*) When you got to love to live it's hard to love living. I better join the A. F. of L. and soap-box for the eight-hour night! Got a nickel, baby? Play a tune. (*She goes out.* DION *puts a nickel in. The same sentimental tune starts.* CYBEL *returns, followed by* BILLY BROWN. *His face is rigidly composed, but his superior disgust for* DION *can be seen.* DION *jerks off the music and he and* BILLY *look at each other for a moment,* CYBEL *watching them both—then, bored, she yawns*) He's hunting for you. Put out the lights when you go. I'm going to sleep. (*She starts to go—then, as if reminded of something—to* DION) Life's all right, if you let it alone. (*Then mechanically flashing a trade smile at* BILLY) Now you know the way, Handsome, call again! (*She goes.*)

BROWN. (*after an awkward pause*) Hello, Dion! I've been looking all over town for you. This place was the very last chance. . . . (*Another pause—embarrassedly*) Let's take a walk.

DION. (*mockingly*) I've given up exercise. They claim it lengthens your life.

BROWN. (*persuasively*) Come on, Dion, be a good fellow. You're certainly not staying here—

DION. Billy would like to think me taken in *flagrante delicto*, eh?

BROWN. Don't be a damn fool! Listen to me! I've been looking you up for purely selfish reasons. I need your help.

DION. (*astonished*) What?

BROWN. I've a proposition to make that I hope you'll consider favorably out of old friendship. To be frank, Dion, I need you to lend me a hand down at the office.

DION. (*with a harsh laugh*) So it's the job, is it? Then my poor wife did a-begging go!

BROWN. (*repelled—sharply*) On the contrary, I had to beg her to beg you to take it! (*More angrily*) Look here, Dion! I won't listen to you talk that way about Margaret! And you wouldn't if you weren't drunk! (*Suddenly shaking him*) What in hell has come over you, anyway! You didn't use to be like this! What the devil are you going to do with yourself—sink into the gutter and drag Margaret with you? If you'd heard her defend you, lie about you, tell me how hard you were working, what beautiful things you were painting, how you stayed at home and idolized the children!—when everyone knows you've been out every night sousing and gambling away the last of your estate. . . . (*He stops, ashamed, controlling himself.*)

DION. (*wearily*) She was lying about her husband, not me, you fool! But it's no use explaining. (*Then, in a sudden, excitable passion*) What do you want? I agree to anything—except the humiliation of yelling secrets at the deaf!

BROWN. (*trying a bullying tone—roughly*) Bunk! Don't try to crawl out! There's no excuse and you know it. (*Then as DION doesn't reply—penitently*) But I know I shouldn't talk this way, old man! It's only because we're such old pals—and I hate to see you wasting yourself—you who had more brains than any of us! But, damn it, I suppose you're too much of a rotten cynic to believe I mean what I've just said!

DION. (*touched*) I know Billy was always Dion Anthony's friend.

BROWN. You're damn right I am—and I'd have proved it long ago if you'd only given me half a chance! After all, I couldn't keep chasing after you and be snubbed every time. A man has some pride!

DION. (*bitterly mocking*) Dead wrong! Never more! None whatever! It's unmoral! Blessed are the poor in spirit, Brother! When shall I report?

BROWN. (*eagerly*) Then you'll take the—you'll help me?

DION. (*wearily bitter*) I'll take the job. One must do something to pass away the time, while one is waiting—for one's next incarnation.

BROWN. (*jokingly*) I'd say it was a bit early to be worrying about that. (*Trying to get* DION *started*) Come along, now. It's pretty late.

DION. (*shakes his hand off his shoulder and walks away from him —after a pause*) Is my father's chair still there?

BROWN. (*turns away—embarrassed*) I—I don't really remember, Dion—I'll look it up.

DION. (*taking off his mask—slowly*) I'd like to sit where he spun what I have spent. What aliens we were to each other! When he lay dead, his face looked so familiar that I wondered where I had met that man before. Only at the second of my conception. After that, we grew hostile with concealed shame. And my mother? I remember a sweet, strange girl, with affectionate, bewildered eyes as if God had locked her in a dark closet without any explanation. I was the sole doll our ogre, her husband, allowed her and she played mother and child with me for many years in that house until at last through two tears I watched her die with the shy pride of one who has lengthened her dress and put up her hair. And I felt like a forsaken toy and cried to be buried with her, because her hands alone had caressed without clawing. She lived long and aged greatly in the two days before they closed her coffin. The last time I looked, her purity had forgotten me, she was stainless and imperishable, and I knew my sobs were ugly and meaningless to her virginity; so I shrank away, back into life, with naked nerves jumping like fleas, and in due course of nature another girl called me her boy in the moon and married me and became three mothers in one person, while I got paint on my paws in an endeavor to see God! (*He laughs wildly—claps on his mask*) But that Ancient Humorist had given me weak eyes, so now I'll have to foreswear my quest for Him and go in for the Omnipresent Successful Serious One, the Great God Mr. Brown, instead! (*He makes him a sweeping, mocking bow.*)

BROWN. (*repelled but cajoling*) Shut up, you nut! You're still drunk.

Come on! Let's start! (*He grabs* DION *by the arm and switches off the light.*)

DION. (*from the darkness—mockingly*) I am thy shorn, bald, nude sheep! Lead on, Almighty Brown, thou Kindly Light!

CURTAIN

ACT TWO—SCENE ONE

SCENE—CYBEL'S *parlor—about sunset in spring seven years later. The arrangement of furniture is the same but the chair and sofa are new, bright-colored, costly pieces. The old automatic piano at center looks exactly the same. The cheap alarm clock is still on top of it. On either side of the clock, the masks of* DION *and* CYBEL *are lying. The background backdrop is brilliant, stunning wallpaper, on which crimson and purple flowers and fruits tumble over one another in a riotously profane lack of any apparent design.*

DION *sits in the chair on left,* CYBEL *on the sofa. A cardtable is between them. Both are playing solitaire.* DION *is now prematurely gray. His face is that of an ascetic, a martyr, furrowed by pain and self-torture, yet lighted from within by a spiritual calm and human kindliness.*

CYBEL *has grown stouter and more voluptuous, but her face is still unmarked and fresh, her calm more profound. She is like an unmoved idol of Mother Earth.*

The piano is whining out its same old sentimental medley. They play their cards intently and contentedly. The music stops.

CYBEL. (*musingly*) I love those rotten old sob tunes. They make me wise to people. That's what's inside them—what makes them love and murder their neighbor—crying jags set to music!

DION. (*compassionately*) Every song is a hymn. They keep trying to find the Word in the Beginning.

CYBEL. They try to know too much. It makes them weak. I never puzzled them with myself. I gave them a Tart. They understood her and knew their parts and acted naturally. And on both sides we were able to keep our real virtue, if you get me. (*She plays her last card—indifferently*) I've made it again.

DION. (*smiling*) Your luck is uncanny. It never comes out for me.

CYBEL. You keep getting closer, but it knows you still want to win —a little bit—and it's wise all I care about is playing. (*She lays out another game*) Speaking of my canned music, our Mr. Brown hates that old box. (*At the mention of* BROWN, DION *trembles as if suddenly possessed, has a terrible struggle with himself, then while she continues to speak, gets up like an automaton and puts on his mask. The mask is now terribly ravaged. All of its Pan quality has changed into a diabolical Mephistophelean cruelty and irony*) He doesn't mind the music inside. That gets him somehow. But he thinks the case looks shabby and he wants it junked. But I told him that just because he's been keeping me so long, he needn't start bossing like a husband or I'll— (*She looks up and sees the masked* DION *standing by the piano—calmly*) Hello! Getting jealous again?

DION. (*jeeringly*) Are you falling in love with your keeper, old Sacred Cow?

CYBEL. (*without taking offense*) Cut it! You've been asking me that for years. Be yourself! He's healthy and handsome—but he's too guilty. What makes you pretend you think love is so important, anyway? It's just one of a lot of things you do to keep life living.

DION. (*in same tone*) Then you've lied when you've said you loved me, have you, Old Filth?

CYBEL. (*affectionately*) You'll never grow up! We've been friends haven't we, for seven years? I've never let myself want you nor you me. Yes, I love you. It takes all kinds of love to make a world! Ours is the living cream, I say, living rich and high! (*A pause. Coaxingly*) Stop hiding. I know you.

DION. (*taking off his mask, wearily comes and sits down at her feet and lays his head in her lap—with a grateful smile*) You're strong. You always give. You've given my weakness strength to live.

CYBEL. (*tenderly, stroking his hair maternally*) You're not weak. You were born with ghosts in your eyes and you were brave enough to go looking into your own dark—and you got afraid. (*After a pause*) I don't blame your being jealous of Mr. Brown sometimes. I'm jealous of your wife, even though I know you do love her.

DION. (*slowly*) I love Margaret. I don't know who my wife is.

CYBEL. (*after a pause—with a queer broken laugh*) Oh, God, sometimes the truth hits me such a sock between the eyes I can see the stars!—and then I'm so damn sorry for the lot of you, every damn mother's son-of-a-gun of you, that I'd like to run out naked into the street and love the whole mob to death like I was bringing you all a new brand of dope that'd make you forget everything that ever was for good! (*Then, with a twisted smile*) But they wouldn't see me, any more than they see each other. And they keep right on moving along and dying without my help anyway.

DION. (*sadly*) You've given me strength to die.

CYBEL. You may be important but your life's not. There's millions of it born every second. Life can cost too much even for a sucker to afford it—like everything else. And it's not sacred—only the you inside is. The rest is earth.

DION. (*gets to his knees and with clasped hands looks up raptly and prays with an ascetic fervor*) "Into thy hands, O Lord," . . . (*Then suddenly, with a look of horror*) Nothing! To feel one's life blown out like the flame of a cheap match . . . ! (*He claps on his mask and laughs harshly*) To fall asleep and know you'll never, never be called to get on the job of existence again! "Swift be thine approaching flight! Come soon—soon!" (*He quotes this last with a mocking longing.*)

CYBEL. (*pats his head maternally*) There, don't be scared. It's born in the blood. When the time comes, you'll find it's easy.

DION. (*jumps to his feet and walks about excitedly*) It won't be long. My wife dragged in a doctor the day before yesterday. He says my heart is gone—booze— He warned me, never another drop or— (*Mockingly*) What say? Shall we have a drink?

CYBEL. (*like an idol*) Suit yourself. It's in the pantry. (*Then, as he hesitates*) What set you off on this bat? You were raving on about some cathedral plans. . . .

DION. (*wildly mocking*) They've been accepted—Mr. Brown's designs! My designs really! You don't need to be told that. He hands me one mathematically correct barn after another and I doctor them up with cute allurements so that fools will desire to buy, sell, breed, sleep, love, hate, curse and pray in them! I do this with devilish cleverness to their entire delight! Once I dreamed of painting wind on the sea and the skimming flight of cloud shadows over the tops of trees! Now . . . (*He laughs*) But pride is a sin—even in a memory of the long deceased! Blessed are the poor in spirit! (*He subsides weakly on his chair, his hand pressed to his heart.*)

CYBEL. (*like an idol*) Go home and sleep. Your wife'll be worried.

DION. She knows—but she'll never admit to herself that her husband ever entered your door. (*Mocking*) Aren't women loyal—to their vanity and their other things!

CYBEL. Brown is coming soon, don't forget.

DION. He knows too and can't admit. Perhaps he needs me here—unknown. What first aroused his passion to possess you exclusively, do you think? Because he knew you loved me and he felt himself cheated. He wanted what he thought was my love of the flesh! He feels I have no right to love. He'd like to steal it as he steals my ideas—complacently—righteously. Oh, the good Brown!

CYBEL. But you like him, too! You're brothers, I guess, somehow. Well, remember he's paying, he'll pay—in some way or other.

DION. (*raises his head as if starting to remove the mask*) I know. Poor Billy! God forgive me the evil I've done him!

CYBEL. (*reaches out and takes his hand*) Poor boy!

DION. (*presses her convulsively—then with forced harshness*) Well, homeward Christian Soldier! I'm off! Bye-bye, Mother Earth! (*He starts to go off right. She seems about to let him go.*)

CYBEL. (*suddenly starts and calls with deep grief*) Dion! (*He looks at her. A pause. He comes slowly back. She speaks strangely in a deep, far-off voice—and yet like a mother talking to her little son)* You mustn't forget to kiss me before you go, Dion. (*She removes his mask)* Haven't I told you to take off your mask in the house? Look at me, Dion. I've—just—seen—something. I'm afraid you're going away a long, long ways. I'm afraid I won't see you again for a long, long time. So it's good-by, dear. (*She kisses him gently. He begins to sob. She hands him back his mask)* Here you are. Don't get hurt. Remember, it's all a game, and after you're asleep I'll tuck you in.

DION. (*in a choking, heart-broken cry)* Mother! (*Then he claps on his mask with a terrible effort of will—mockingly)* Go to the devil, you sentimental old pig! See you tomorrow! (*He goes, whistling, slamming the door.)*

CYBEL. (*like an idol again)* What's the good of bearing children? What's the use of giving birth to death? (*She sighs wearily, turns, puts a plug in the piano, which starts up its old sentimental tune. At the same moment* BROWN *enters quietly from the left. He is the ideal of the still-youthful, good-looking, well-groomed, successful provincial American of forty. Just now, he is plainly perturbed. He is not able to see either* CYBEL's *face or her mask.)*

BROWN. Cybel! (*She starts, jams off the music and reaches for her mask but has no time to put it on)* Wasn't that Dion I just saw going out—after all your promises never to see him! (*She turns like an idol, holding the mask behind her. He stares, bewildered—stammers)* I— I beg your pardon—I thought—

CYBEL. (*in her strange voice)* Cybel's gone out to dig in the earth and pray.

BROWN. (*with more assurance)* But—aren't those her clothes?

CYBEL. Cybel doesn't want people to see me naked. I'm her sister. Dion came to see me.

BROWN. (*relieved)* So that's what he's up to, is it? (*Then with a pitying sigh)* Poor Margaret! (*Then with playful reproof)* You really shouldn't encourage him. He's married and got three big sons.

CYBEL. And you haven't.

BROWN. (*stung*) No. I'm not married.

CYBEL. He and I were friends.

BROWN. (*with a playful wink*) Yes, I can imagine how the platonic must appeal to Dion's pure, innocent type! It's no good your kidding me about Dion. We've been friends since we were kids. I know him in and out. I've always stood up for him whatever he's done—so you can be perfectly frank. I only spoke as I did on account of Margaret—his wife—it's pretty tough on her.

CYBEL. You love his wife.

BROWN. (*scandalized*) What? What are you talking about? (*Then uncertainly*) Don't be a fool! (*A pause—then as if impelled by an intense curiosity*) So Dion is your lover, eh? That's very interesting. (*He pulls his chair closer to hers*) Sit down. Let's talk. (*She continues to stand, the mask held behind her*) Tell me—I've always been curious—what is it that makes Dion so attractive to women—especially certain types of women, if you'll pardon me? He always has been and yet I never could see exactly what they saw in him. Is it his looks—or because he's such a violent sensualist—or because he poses as artistic and temperamental—or because he's so wild—or just what is it?

CYBEL. He's alive!

BROWN. (*suddenly takes one of her hands and kisses it—insinuatingly*) Well, don't you think I'm alive, too? (*Eagerly*) Listen. Would you consider giving up Dion—and letting me take care of you under a similar arrangement to the one I've made with Cybel? I like you, you can see that. I won't bother you much—I'm much too busy—you can do what you like—lead your own life—except for seeing him. (*He stops. A pause. She stares ahead unmoved as if she hadn't heard. He pleads*) Well—what do you say? Please do!

CYBEL. (*her voice very weary*) Cybel said to tell you she'd be back next week, Mr. Brown.

BROWN. (*with queer agony*) You mean you won't? Don't be so cruel!

I love you! (*She walks away. He clutches at her pleadingly*) At least
—I'll give you anything you ask!—please promise me you won't see
Dion Anthony again!

CYBEL. (*with deep grief*) He will never see me again, I promise
you. Good-by!

BROWN. (*jubilantly, kissing her hand—politely*) Thank you! Thank
you! I'm exceedingly grateful. (*Tactfully*) I won't disturb you any
further. Please forgive my intrusion, and remember me to Cybel when
you write. (*He bows, turns, and goes off left.*)

CURTAIN

ACT TWO—SCENE TWO

Scene—*The drafting room in* BROWN's *office.* DION's *drafting table
with a high stool in front is at center. Another stool is to the left of
it. At the right is a bench. It is in the evening of the same day. The
black wall drop has windows painted on it with a dim, street-lighted
view of black houses across the way.*

DION *is sitting on the stool in back of the table, reading aloud from
the "Imitation of Christ" by Thomas à Kempis to his mask, which
is on the table before him. His own face is gentler, more spiritual,
more saintlike and ascetic than ever before.*

DION. (*like a priest, offering up prayers for the dying*) "Quickly
must thou be gone from hence, see then how matters stand with
thee. Ah, fool—learn now to die to the world that thou mayst begin
to live with Christ! Do now, beloved, do now all thou canst because
thou knowst not when thou shalt die; nor dost thou know what shall
befall thee after death. Keep thyself as a pilgrim, and a stranger upon
earth, to whom the affairs of this world do not—belong! Keep thy

heart free and raised upwards to God because thou hast not here a lasting abode. 'Because at what hour you know not the Son of Man will come!' " Amen. (*He raises his hand over the mask as if he were blessing it, closes the book and puts it back in his pocket. He raises the mask in his hands and stares at it with a pitying tenderness*) Peace, poor tortured one, brave pitiful pride of man, the hour of our deliverance comes. Tomorrow we may be with Him in Paradise! (*He kisses it on the lips and sets it down again. There is the noise of footsteps climbing the stairs in the hallway. He grabs up the mask in a sudden panic and, as a knock comes on the door, he claps it on and calls mockingly*) Come in, Mrs. Anthony, come in! (MARGARET *enters. In one hand behind her, hidden from him, is the mask of the brave face she puts on before the world to hide her suffering and disillusionment, and which she has just taken off. Her own face is still sweet and pretty but lined, drawn and careworn for its years, sad, resigned, but a bit querulous.*)

MARGARET. (*wearily reproving*) Thank goodness I've found you! Why haven't you been home the last two days? It's bad enough your drinking again without your staying away and worrying us to death!

DION. (*bitterly*) My ears knew her footsteps. One gets to recognize everything—and to see nothing!

MARGARET. I finally sent the boys out looking for you and came myself. (*With tired solicitude*) I suppose you haven't eaten a thing, as usual. Won't you come home and let me fry you a chop?

DION. (*wonderingly*) Can Margaret still love Dion Anthony? Is it possible she does?

MARGARET. (*forcing a tired smile*) I suppose so, Dion. I certainly oughtn't to, had I?

DION. (*in same tone*) And I love Margaret! What haunted, haunting ghosts we are! We dimly remember so much it will take us so many million years to forget! (*He comes forward, putting one arm around her bowed shoulders, and they kiss.*)

MARGARET. (*patting his hand affectionately*) No, you certainly don't deserve it. When I stop to think of all you've made me go through in the years since we settled down here . . . ! I really don't believe I could ever have stood it if it weren't for the boys! (*Forcing a smile*) But perhaps I would, I've always been such a big fool about you.

DION. (*a bit mockingly*) The boys! Three strong sons! Margaret can afford to be magnanimous!

MARGARET. If they didn't find you, they were coming to meet me here.

DION. (*with sudden wildness—torturedly, sinking on his knees beside her*) Margaret! Margaret! I'm lonely! I'm frightened! I'm going away! I've got to say good-by!

MARGARET. (*patting his hair*) Poor boy! Poor Dion! Come home and sleep.

DION. (*springs up frantically*) No! I'm a man! I'm a lonely man! I can't go back! I have conceived myself! (*Then with desperate mockery*) Look at me, Mrs. Anthony! It's the last chance! Tomorrow I'll have moved on to the next hell! Behold your man—the sniveling, cringing, life-denying Christian slave you have so nobly ignored in the father of your sons! Look! (*He tears the mask from his face, which is radiant with a great pure love for her and a great sympathy and tenderness*) O woman—my love—that I have sinned against in my sick pride and cruelty—forgive my sins—forgive my solitude—forgive my sickness—forgive me! (*He kneels and kisses the hem of her dress.*)

MARGARET. (*who has been staring at him with terror, raising her mask to ward off his face*) Dion! Don't! I can't bear it! You're like a ghost! You're dead! Oh, my God! Help! Help! (*She falls back fainting on the bench. He looks at her—then takes her hand which holds her mask and looks at that face—gently,* "And now I am permitted to understand and love you, too!" *He kisses the mask first— then kisses her face, murmuring,* "And you, sweetheart! Blessed, thrice blessed are the meek!" *There is a sound of heavy, hurrying footsteps on the stairs. He puts on his mask in haste. The* THREE SONS *rush into the room. The Eldest is about fourteen, the two others thir-teen and twelve. They look healthy, normal, likeable boys, with much the same quality as* BILLY BROWN's *in Act One, Scene One. They stop short and stiffen all in a row, staring from the woman on the bench to their father, accusingly.)*

ELDEST. We heard someone yell. It sounded like Mother.

DION. *(defensively)* No. It was this lady—my wife.

ELDEST. But hasn't Mother come yet?

DION. *(going to* MARGARET*)* Yes. Your Mother is here. *(He stands between them and puts her mask over* MARGARET's *face—then steps back)* She has fainted. You'd better bring her to.

BOYS. Mother! *(They run to her side, kneel and rub her wrists. The* ELDEST *smooths back her hair.)*

DION. *(watching them)* At least I am leaving her well provided for. *(He addresses them directly)* Tell your mother she'll get word from Mr. Brown's house. I must pay him a farewell call. I am going. Good-by. *(They stop, staring at him fixedly, with eyes a mixture of bewilderment, distrust and hurt.)*

ELDEST. *(awkwardly and shamefacedly)* Honest, I think you ought to have . . .

SECOND. Yes, honest, you ought . . .

YOUNGEST. Yes, honest . . .

DION. *(in a friendly tone)* I know. But I couldn't. That's for you who can. You must inherit the earth for her. Don't forget now, boys. Good-by.

BOYS. *(in the same awkward, self-conscious tone, one after another)* Good-by—good-by—good-by. *(*DION *goes.)*

CURTAIN

ACT TWO—SCENE THREE

SCENE—*The library of* WILLIAM BROWN's *home—night of the same day. A backdrop of carefully painted, prosperous, bourgeois culture, bookcases filled with sets, etc. The heavy table at center is expensive. The leather armchair at left of it and the couch at right are opulently comfortable. The reading lamp on the table is the only light.*

BROWN *sits in the chair at left reading an architectural periodical. His expression is composed and gravely receptive. In outline, his face suggests a Roman consul on an old coin. There is an incongruous distinction about it, the quality of unquestioning faith in the finality of its achievement.*

There is a sudden loud thumping on the front door and the ringing of the bell. BROWN *frowns and listens as a servant answers.* DION's *voice can be heard, raised mockingly.*

DION. Tell him it's the devil come to conclude a bargain.

BROWN. (*suppressing annoyance, calls out with forced good nature*) Come on in, Dion. (DION *enters. He is in a wild state. His clothes are disheveled, his masked face has a terrible deathlike intensity, its mocking irony becomes so cruelly malignant as to give him the appearance of a real demon, tortured into torturing others*) Sit down.

DION. (*stands and sings*) William Brown's soul lies moldering in the crib but his body goes marching on!

BROWN. (*maintaining the same indulgent, big-brotherly tone, which he tries to hold throughout the scene*) Not so loud, for Pete's sake! I don't mind—but I've got neighbors.

DION. Hate them! Fear thy neighbor as thyself! That's the leaden rule for the safe and sane. (*Then advancing to the table with a sort of deadly calm*) Listen! One day when I was four years old, a boy sneaked up behind when I was drawing a picture in the sand he couldn't draw and hit me on the head with a stick ànd kicked out my picture and laughed when I cried. It wasn't what he'd done that made me cry, but him! I had loved and trusted him and suddenly the good God was disproved in his person and the evil and injustice of Man was born! Everyone called me cry-baby, so I became silent for life and designed a mask of the Bad Boy Pan in which to live and rebel against that other boy's God and protect myself from His cruelty. And that other boy, secretly he felt ashamed but he couldn't acknowledge it; so from that day he instinctively developed into the good boy, the good friend, the good man, William Brown!

BROWN. (*shamefacedly*) I remember now. It was a dirty trick. (*Then with a trace of resentment*) Sit down. You know where the booze is. Have a drink, if you like. But I guess you've had enough already.

DION. (*looks at him fixedly for a moment—then strangely*) Thanks be to Brown for reminding me. I must drink. (*He goes and gets a bottle of whisky and a glass.*)

BROWN. (*with a good-humored shrug*) All right. It's your funeral.

DION. (*returning and pouring out a big drink in the tumbler*) And William Brown's! When I die, he goes to hell! Skoal! (*He drinks and stares malevolently. In spite of himself, BROWN is uneasy. A pause.*)

BROWN. (*with forced casualness*) You've been on this toot for a week now.

DION. (*tauntingly*) I've been celebrating the acceptance of *my* design for the cathedral.

BROWN. (*humorously*) You certainly helped me a lot on it.

DION. (*with a harsh laugh*) O perfect Brown! Never mind! I'll make him look in my mirror yet—and drown in it! (*He pours out another big drink.*)

295

BROWN. (*rather tauntingly*) Go easy. I don't want your corpse on my hands.

DION. But I do. (*He drinks*) Brown will still need me—to reassure him he's alive! I've loved, lusted, won and lost, sang and wept! I've been life's lover! I've fulfilled her will and if she's through with me now it's only because I was too weak to dominate her in turn. It isn't enough to be her creature, you've got to create her or she requests you to destroy yourself.

BROWN. (*good-naturedly*) Nonsense. Go home and get some sleep.

DION. (*as if he hadn't heard—bitingly*) But to be neither creature nor creator! To exist only in her indifference! To be unloved by life! (BROWN *stirs uneasily*) To be merely a successful freak, the result of some snide neutralizing of life forces—a spineless cactus—a wild boar of the mountains altered into a packer's hog eating to become food—a Don Juan inspired to romance by a monkey's glands —and to have Life not even think you funny enough to see!

BROWN. (*stung—angrily*) Bosh!

DION. Consider Mr. Brown. His parents bore him on earth as if they were thereby entering him in a baby parade with prizes for the fattest—and he's still being wheeled along in the procession, too fat now to learn to walk, let alone to dance or run, and he'll never live until his liberated dust quickens into earth!

BROWN. (*gruffly*) Rave on! (*Then with forced good-nature*) Well, Dion, at any rate, I'm satisfied.

DION. (*quickly and malevolently*) No! Brown isn't satisfied! He's piled on layers of protective fat, but vaguely, deeply he feels at his heart the knawing of a doubt! And I'm interested in that germ which wriggles like a question mark of insecurity in his blood, because it's part of the creative life Brown's stolen from me!

BROWN. (*forcing a sour grin*) Steal germs? I thought you caught them.

DION. (*as if he hadn't heard*) It's mine—and I'm interested in seeing it thrive and breed and become multitudes and eat until Brown is consumed!

BROWN. (*cannot restrain a shudder*) Sometimes when you're drunk you're positively evil, do you know it?

DION. ·(*somberly*) When Pan was forbidden the light and warmth of the sun he grew sensitive and self-conscious and proud and revengeful—and became Prince of Darkness.

BROWN. (*jocularly*) You don't fit the rôle of Pan, Dion. It sounds to me like Bacchus, alias the Demon Rum, doing the talking. (*DION recovers from his spasm with a start and stares at BROWN with terrible hatred. There is a pause. In spite of himself, BROWN squirms and adopts a placating tone*) Go home. Be a good scout. It's all well enough celebrating our design being accepted but—

DION. (*in a steely voice*) I've been the brains! I've been the design! I've designed even his success—drunk and laughing at him—laughing at his career! Not proud! Sick! Sick of myself and him! Designing and getting drunk! Saving my woman and children! (*He laughs*) Ha! And this cathedral is my masterpiece! It will make Brown the most eminent architect in this state of God's country. I put a lot into it—what was left of my life! It's one vivid blasphemy from sidewalk to the tips of its spires!—but so concealed that the fools will never know. They'll kneel and worship the ironic Silenus who tells them the best good is never to be born! (*He laughs triumphantly*) Well, blasphemy is faith, isn't it? In self-preservation the devil must believe! But Mr. Brown, the Great Brown, has no faith! He couldn't design a cathedral without it looking like the First Supernatural Bank! He only believes in the immortality of the moral belly! (*He laughs wildly—then sinks down in his chair, gasping, his hands pressed to his heart. Then suddenly becomes deadly calm and pronounces like a cruel malignant condemnation*) From now on, Brown will never design anything. He will devote his life to renovating the house of my Cybel into a home for my Margaret!

BROWN. (*springing to his feet, his face convulsed with strange agony*) I've stood enough! How dare you . . . !

DION. (*his voice like a probe*) Why has no woman ever loved him? Why has he always been the Big Brother, the Friend? Isn't their trust—a contempt?

BROWN. You lie!

DION. Why has he never been able to love—since my Margaret? Why has he never married? Why has he tried to steal Cybel, as he once tried to steal Margaret? Isn't it out of revenge—and envy?

BROWN. (*violently*) Rot! I wanted Cybel, and I bought her!

DION. Brown bought her for me! She has loved me more than he will ever know!

BROWN. You lie! (*Then furiously*) I'll throw her back on the street!

DION. To me! To her fellow creature! Why hasn't Brown had children—he who loves children—he who loves *my* children—he who envies me *my* children?

BROWN. (*brokenly*) I'm not ashamed to envy you them!

DION. They like Brown, too—as a friend—as an equal—as Margaret has always liked him—

BROWN. (*brokenly*) And as I've liked her!

DION. How many million times Brown has thought how much better for her it would have been if she'd chosen him instead!

BROWN. (*torturedly*) You lie! (*Then with sudden frenzied defiance*) All right. If you force me to say it, I do love Margaret! I always have loved her and you've always known I did!

DION. (*with a terrible composure*) No! That is merely the appearance, not the truth! Brown loves me! He loves me because I have always possessed the power he needed for love, because I am love!

BROWN. (*frenziedly*) You drunken bum! (*He leaps on* DION *and grabs him by the throat.*)

DION. (*triumphantly, staring into his eyes*) Ah! Now he looks into the mirror! Now he sees his face! (BROWN *lets go of him and staggers back to his chair, pale and trembling.*)

298

BROWN. (*humbly*) Stop, for God's sake! You're mad!

DION. (*sinking in his chair, more and more weakly*) I'm done. My heart, not Brown— (*Mockingly*) My last will and testament! I leave Dion Anthony to William Brown—for him to love and obey—for him to become me—then my Margaret will love me—my children will love me—Mr. and Mrs. Brown and sons, happily ever after! (*Staggering to his full height and looking upward defiantly*) Nothing more—but Man's last gesture—by which he conquers—to laugh! Ha— (*He begins, stops as if paralyzed, and drops on his knees by* BROWN's *chair, his mask falling off, his Christian Martyr's face at the point of death*) Forgive me, Billy. Bury me, hide me, forget me for your own happiness! May Margaret love you! May you design the Temple of Man's Soul! Blessed are the meek and the poor in spirit! (*He kisses* BROWN's *feet—then more and more weakly and childishly*) What was the prayer, Billy? I'm getting so sleepy. . . .

BROWN. (*in a trancelike tone*) "Our Father who art in Heaven."

DION. (*drowsily*) "Our Father." . . . (*He dies. A pause.* BROWN *remains in a stupor for a moment—then stirs himself, puts his hand on* DION's *breast.*)

BROWN. (*dully*) He's dead—at last. (*He says this mechanically but the last two words awaken him—wonderingly*) At last? (*Then with triumph*) At last! (*He stares at* DION's *real face contemptuously*) So that's the poor weakling you really were! No wonder you hid! And I've always been afraid of you—yes, I'll confess it now, in awe of you! Paugh! (*He picks up the mask from the floor*) No, not of you! Of this! Say what you like, it's strong if it is bad! And this is what Margaret loved, not you! Not you! This man!—this man who willed himself to me! (*Struck by an idea, he jumps to his feet*) By God! (*He slowly starts to put the mask on. A knocking comes on the street door. He starts guiltily, laying the mask on the table. Then he picks it up again quickly, takes the dead body and carries it off left. He reappears immediately and goes to the front door as the knocking recommences—gruffly*) Hello! Who's there?

MARGARET. It's Margaret, Billy. I'm looking for Dion.

BROWN. (*uncertainly*) Oh—all right— (*Unfastening door*) Come in. Hello, Margaret. Hello, boys! He's here. He's asleep. I—I was just dozing off too. (MARGARET *enters. She is wearing her mask. The* THREE SONS *are with her.*)

MARGARET. (*seeing the bottle, forcing a laugh*) Has he been celebrating?

BROWN. (*with strange glibness now*) No. I was. He wasn't. He said he'd sworn off tonight—forever—for your sake—and the kids!

MARGARET. (*with amazed joy*) Dion said that? (*Then hastily defensive*) But of course he never does drink much. Where is he?

BROWN. Upstairs. I'll wake him. He felt bad. He took off his clothes to take a bath before he lay down. You just wait here. (*She sits in the chair where* DION *had sat and stares straight before her. The* SONS *group around her, as if for a family photo.* BROWN *hurries out left.*)

MARGARET. It's late to keep you boys up. Aren't you sleepy?

BOYS. No, Mother.

MARGARET. (*proudly*) I'm glad to have three such strong boys to protect me.

ELDEST. (*boastingly*) We'd kill anyone that touched you, wouldn't we?

NEXT. You bet! We'd make him wish he hadn't!

YOUNGEST. You bet!

MARGARET. You're Mother's brave boys! (*She laughs fondly—then curiously*) Do you like Mr. Brown?

ELDEST. Sure thing! He's a regular fellow.

NEXT. He's all right!

YOUNGEST. Sure thing!

MARGARET. (*half to herself*) Your father claims he steals his ideas.

ELDEST. (*with a sheepish grin*) I'll bet father said that when he was —just talking.

NEXT. Mr. Brown doesn't have to steal, does he?

YOUNGEST. I should say not! He's awful rich.

MARGARET. Do you love your father?

ELDEST. (*scuffling—embarrassed*) Why—of course—

NEXT. (*ditto*) Sure thing!

YOUNGEST. Sure I do.

MARGARET. (*with a sigh*) I think you'd better start on before—right now—before your father comes— He'll be very sick and nervous and he'll want to be quiet. So run along!

BOYS. All right. (*They file out and close the front door as* BROWN, *dressed in* DION's *clothes and wearing his mask, appears at left.*)

MARGARET. (*taking off her mask, gladly*) Dion! (*She stares wonderingly at him and he at her; goes to him and puts an arm around him*) Poor dear, do you feel sick? (*He nods*) But you look—(*Squeezing his arms*)—why, you actually feel stronger and better already! Is it true what Billy told me—about your swearing off forever? (*He nods. She exclaims intensely*) Oh, if you'll only—and get well—we can still be so happy! Give Mother a kiss. (*They kiss. A shudder passes through both of them. She breaks away laughing with aroused desire*) Why, Dion? Aren't you ashamed? You haven't kissed me like that in ages!

BROWN. (*his voice imitating* DION's *and muffled by the mask*) I've wanted to, Margaret!

MARGARET. (*gaily and coquettishly now*) Were you afraid I'd spurn you? Why, Dion, something has happened. It's like a miracle! Even your voice is changed! It actually sounds younger, do you know it? (*Then, solicitously*) But you must be worn out. Let's go home. (*With an impulsive movement she flings her arms wide open, throwing her mask away from her as if suddenly no longer needing it*) Oh, I'm beginning to feel so happy, Dion—so happy!

BROWN. (*stifledly*) Let's go home. (*She puts her arm around him. They walk to the door.*)

CURTAIN

ACT THREE—SCENE ONE

SCENE—*The drafting room and private office of* BROWN *are both shown. The former is at left, the latter at right of a dividing wall at center. The arrangement of furniture in each room is the same as in previous scenes. It is ten in the morning of a day about a month later. The backdrop for both rooms is of plain wall with a few tacked-up designs and blueprints painted on it.*

TWO DRAFTSMEN, *a middle-aged and a young man, both stoop-shouldered, are sitting on stools behind what was formerly* DION'S *table. They are tracing plans. They talk as they work.*

OLDER DRAFTSMAN. W. B. is late again.

YOUNGER DRAFTSMAN. Wonder what's got into him the last month? (*A pause. They work silently.*)

OLDER DRAFTSMAN. Yes, ever since he fired Dion. . . .

YOUNGER DRAFTSMAN. Funny his firing him all of a sudden like that. (*A pause. They work.*)

OLDER DRAFTSMAN. I haven't seen Dion around town since then. Have you?

YOUNGER DRAFTSMAN. No, not since Brown told us he'd canned him. I suppose he's off drowning his sorrow!

OLDER DRAFTSMAN. I heard someone had seen him at home and he was sober and looking fine. (*A pause. They work.*)

YOUNGER DRAFTSMAN. What got into Brown? They say he fired all his old servants that same day and only uses his house to sleep in.

OLDER DRAFTSMAN. (*with a sneer*) Artistic temperament, maybe— the real name of which is swelled head! (*There is a noise of footsteps from the hall. Warningly*) Ssstt! (*They bend over their table.* MARGARET *enters. She does not need to wear a mask now. Her face has regained the self-confident spirit of its youth, her eyes shine with happiness.*)

MARGARET. (*heartily*) Good morning! What a lovely day!

BOTH. (*perfunctorily*) Good morning, Mrs. Anthony.

MARGARET. (*looking around*) You've been changing around in here, haven't you? Where is Dion? (*They stare at her*) I forgot to tell him something important this morning and our phone's out of order. So if you'll tell him I'm here— (*They don't move. A pause.* MARGARET *says stiffly*) Oh, I realize Mr. Brown has given strict orders Dion is not to be disturbed, but surely. . . . (*Sharply*) Where is my husband, please?

OLDER DRAFTSMAN. We don't know.

MARGARET. You don't know?

YOUNGER DRAFTSMAN. We haven't seen him.

MARGARET. Why, he left home at eight-thirty!

OLDER DRAFTSMAN. To come here?

YOUNGER DRAFTSMAN. This morning?

MARGARET. (*provoked*) Why, of course, to come here—as he does every day! (*They stare at her. A pause.*)

OLDER DRAFTSMAN. (*evasively*) We haven't seen him.

MARGARET. (*with asperity*) Where is Mr. Brown?

YOUNGER DRAFTSMAN. (*at a noise of footsteps from the hall—sulkily*) Coming now. (BROWN *enters. He is now wearing a mask which is an exact likeness of his face as it was in the last scene—the self-assured success. When he sees* MARGARET, *he starts back apprehensively.*)

BROWN. (*immediately controlling himself—breezily*) Hello, Margaret! This is a pleasant surprise! (*He holds out his hand.*)

MARGARET. (*hardly taking it—reservedly*) Good morning.

BROWN. (*turning quickly to the* DRAFTSMEN) I hope you explained to Mrs. Anthony how busy Dion . . .

MARGARET. (*interrupting him—stiffly*) I certainly can't understand—

BROWN. (*hastily*) I'll explain. Come in here and be comfortable. (*He throws open the door and ushers her into his private office.*)

OLDER DRAFTSMAN. Dion must be putting over some bluff on her.

YOUNGER DRAFTSMAN. Pretending he's still here—and Brown's helping him. . . .

OLDER DRAFTSMAN. But why should Brown, after he . . . ?

YOUNGER DRAFTSMAN. Well, I suppose— Search me. (*They work.*)

BROWN. Have a chair, Margaret. (*She sits on the chair stiffly. He sits behind the desk.*)

MARGARET. (*coldly*) I'd like some explanation. . . .

BROWN. (*coaxingly*) Now, don't get angry, Margaret! Dion is hard at work on his design for the new State Capitol, and I don't want him disturbed, not even by you! So be a good sport! It's for his own good, remember! I asked him to explain to you.

MARGARET. (*relenting*) He told me you'd agreed to ask me and the boys not to come here—but then, we hardly ever did.

BROWN. But you might! (*Then with confidential friendliness*) This is for his sake, Margaret. I know Dion. He's got to be able to work without distractions. He's not the ordinary man, you appreciate that. And this design means his whole future! He's to get full credit for it, and as soon as it's accepted, I take him into partnership. It's all agreed. And after that I'm going to take a long vacation—go to Europe for a couple of years—and leave everything here in Dion's hands! Hasn't he told you all this?

MARGARET. (*jubilant now*) Yes—but I could hardly believe . . . (*Proudly*) I'm sure he can do it. He's been like a new man lately, so full of ambition and energy! It's made me so happy! (*She stops in confusion.*)

BROWN. (*deeply moved, takes her hand impulsively*) And it has made me happy, too!

MARGARET. (*confused—with an amused laugh*) Why, Billy Brown! For a moment, I thought it was Dion, your voice sounded so much . . . !

BROWN. (*with sudden desperation*) Margaret, I've got to tell you!

304

I can't go on like this any longer! I've got to confess . . . ! There's something . . . !

MARGARET. (*alarmed*) Not—not about Dion?

BROWN. (*harshly*) To hell with Dion! To hell with Billy Brown! (*He tears off his mask and reveals a suffering face that is ravaged and haggard, his own face tortured and distorted by the demon of Dion's mask*) Think of me! I love you, Margaret! Leave him! I've always loved you! Come away with me! I'll sell out here! We'll go abroad and be happy!

MARGARET. (*amazed*) Billy Brown, do you realize what you're saying? (*With a shudder*) Are you crazy? Your face—is terrible. You're sick! Shall I phone for a doctor?

BROWN. (*turning away slowly and putting on his mask—dully*) No. I've been on the verge—of a breakdown—for some time. I get spells. . . . I'm better now. (*He turns back to her*) Forgive me! Forget what I said! But, for all our sakes, don't come here again.

MARGARET. (*coldly*) After this—I assure you . . . ! (*Then looking at him with pained incredulity*) Why, Billy—I simply won't believe— after all these years . . . !

BROWN. It will never happen again. Good-by.

MARGARET. Good-by. (*Then, wishing to leave on a pleasant change of subject—forcing a smile*) Don't work Dion to death! He's never home for dinner any more. (*She goes out past the* DRAFTSMAN *and off right, rear.* BROWN *sits down at his desk, taking off the mask again. He stares at it with bitter, cynical amusement.*)

BROWN. You're dead, William Brown, dead beyond hope of resurrection! It's the Dion you buried in your garden who killed you, not you him! It's Margaret's husband who . . . (*He laughs harshly*) Paradise by proxy! Love by mistaken identity! God! (*This is almost a prayer—then fiercely defiant*) But it *is* paradise! I *do* love! (*As he is speaking, a well-dressed, important, stout man enters the drafting room. He is carrying a rolled-up plan in his hand. He nods condescendingly and goes directly to* BROWN's *door, on which he raps sharply, and, without waiting for an answer, turns the knob.* BROWN *has just time to turn his head and get his mask on.*)

MAN. (*briskly*) Ah, good morning! I came right in. Hope I didn't disturb . . . ?

BROWN. (*the successful architect now—urbanely*) Not at all, sir. How are you? (*They shake hands*) Sit down. Have a cigar. And now what can I do for you this morning?

MAN. (*unrolling his plan*) It's your plan. My wife and I have been going over it again. We like it—and we don't—and when a man plans to lay out half a million, why he wants everything exactly right, eh? (BROWN *nods*) It's too cold, too spare, too like a tomb, if you'll pardon me, for a liveable home. Can't you liven it up, put in some decorations, make it fancier and warmer—you know what I mean. (*Looks at him a bit doubtfully*) People tell me you had an assistant, Anthony, who was a real shark on these details but that you've fired him—

BROWN. (*suavely*) Gossip! He's still with me but, for reasons of his own, doesn't wish it known. Yes, I trained him and he's very ingenious. I'll turn this right over to him and instruct him to carry out your wishes. . . .

CURTAIN

ACT THREE—SCENE TWO

SCENE—*The same as Act Two, Scene Three—the library of* BROWN's *home about eight the same night. He can be heard feeling his way in through the dark. He switches on the reading lamp on the table. Directly under it on a sort of stand is the mask of* DION, *its empty eyes staring front.*

BROWN *takes off his own mask and lays it on the table before* DION's.

He flings himself down in the chair and stares without moving into the eyes of DION's *mask. Finally, he begins to talk to it in a bitter, mocking tone.*

BROWN. Listen! Today was a narrow escape—for us! We can't avoid discovery much longer. We must get our plot to working! We've already made William Brown's will, leaving you his money and business. We must hustle off to Europe now—and murder him there! (*A bit tauntingly*) Then you—the I in you—*I* will live with Margaret happily ever after. (*More tauntingly*) She will have children by me! (*He seems to hear some mocking denial from the mask. He bends toward it*) What? (*Then with a sneer*) Anyway, that doesn't matter! Your children already love me more than they ever loved you! And Margaret loves me more! You think you've won, do you— that I've got to vanish into you in order to live? Not yet, my friend! Never! Wait! Gradually Margaret will love what is beneath—me! Little by little I'll teach her to know me, and then finally I'll reveal myself to her, and confess that I stole your place out of love for her, and she'll understand and forgive and love me! And you'll be for- gotten! Ha! (*Again he bends down to the mask as if listening— torturedly*) What's that? She'll never believe? She'll never see? She'll never understand? You lie, devil! (*He reaches out his hands as if to take the mask by the throat, then shrinks back with a shudder of hope- less despair*) God have mercy! Let me believe! Blessed are the merci- ful! Let me obtain mercy! (*He waits, his face upturned—pleadingly*) Not yet? (*Despairingly*) Never? (*A pause. Then, in a sudden panic of dread, he reaches out for the mask of* DION *like a dope fiend after a drug. As soon as he holds it, he seems to gain strength and is able to force a sad laugh*) Now I am drinking your strength, Dion—strength to love in this world and die and sleep and become fertile earth, as you are becoming now in my garden—your weakness the strength of my flowers, your failure as an artist painting their petals with life! (*Then, with bravado*) Come with me while Margaret's bridegroom

307

dresses in your clothes, Mr. Anthony! I need the devil when I'm in the dark! (*He goes off left, but can be heard talking*) Your clothes begin to fit me better than my own! Hurry, Brother! It's time we were home. Our wife is waiting! (*He reappears, having changed his coat and trousers*) Come with me and tell her again I love her! Come and hear her tell me how she loves you! (*He suddenly cannot help kissing the mask*) I love you because she loves you! My kisses on your lips are for her! (*He puts the mask over his face and stands for a moment, seeming to grow tall and proud—then with a laugh of bold self-assurance*) Out by the back way! I mustn't forget I'm a desperate criminal, pursued by God, and by myself! (*He goes out right, laughing with amused satisfaction.*)

CURTAIN

ACT THREE—SCENE THREE

Scene—*The same as Scene One of Act One—the sitting-room of* MARGARET'S *home. It is about half an hour after the last scene.* MARGARET *sits on the sofa, waiting with the anxious, impatient expectancy of one deeply in love. She is dressed with a careful, subtle extra touch to attract the eye. She looks young and happy. She is trying to read a book. The front door is heard opening and closing. She leaps up and runs back to throw her arms around* BROWN *as he enters from right, rear. She kisses him passionately.*

MARGARET. (*as he recoils with a sort of guilt—laughingly*) Why, you hateful old thing, you! I really believe you were trying to avoid kissing me! Well, just for that, I'll never . . .

BROWN. (*with fierce, defiant passion, kisses her again and again*) Margaret!

308

MARGARET. Call me Peggy again. You used to when you really loved me. (*Softly*) Remember the school commencement dance—you and I on the dock in the moonlight?

BROWN. (*with pain*) No. (*He takes his arms from around her.*)

MARGARET. (*still holding him—with a laugh*) Well, I like that! You old bear, you! Why not?

BROWN. (*sadly*) It was so long ago.

MARGARET. (*a bit melancholy*) You mean you don't want to be reminded that we're getting old?

BROWN. Yes. (*He kisses her gently*) I'm tired. Let's sit down. (*They sit on the sofa, his arm about her, her head on his shoulder.*)

MARGARET. (*with a happy sigh*) I don't mind remembering—now I'm happy. It's only when I'm unhappy that it hurts—and I've been so happy lately, dear—and so grateful to you! (*He stirs uneasily. She goes on joyfully*) Everything's changed! I'd gotten pretty resigned to —and sad and hopeless, too—and then all at once you turn right around and everything is the same as when we were first married— much better even, for I was never sure of you then. You were always so strange and aloof and alone, it seemed I was never really touching you. But now I feel you've become quite human—like me—and I'm so happy, dear! (*She kisses him.*)

BROWN. (*his voice trembling*) Then I have made you happy— happier than ever before—no matter what happens? (*She nods*) Then —that justifies everything! (*He forces a laugh.*)

MARGARET. Of course it does! I've always known that. But you— you wouldn't be—or you couldn't be—and I could never help you— and all the time I knew you were so lonely! I could always hear you calling to me that you were lost, but I couldn't find the path to you because I was lost, too! That's an awful way for a wife to feel! (*She laughs—joyfully*) But now you're here! You're mine! You're my long-lost lover, and my husband, and my big boy, too!

BROWN. (*with a trace of jealousy*) Where are your other big boys tonight?

MARGARET. Out to a dance. They've all acquired girls, I'll have you know.

BROWN. (*mockingly*) Aren't you jealous?

MARGARET. (*gaily*) Of course! Terribly! But I'm diplomatic. I don't let them see. (*Changing the subject*) Believe me, they've noticed the change in you! The eldest was saying to me today: "It's great not to have Father so nervous, any more. Why, he's a regular sport when he gets started!" And the other two said very solemnly: "You bet!" (*She laughs.*)

BROWN. (*brokenly*) I—I'm glad.

MARGARET. Dion! You're crying!

BROWN. (*stung by the name, gets up—harshly*) Nonsense! Did you ever know Dion to cry about anyone?

MARGARET. (*sadly*) You couldn't—then. You were too lonely. You had no one to cry to.

BROWN. (*goes and takes a rolled-up plan from the table drawer—dully*) I've got to do some work.

MARGARET. (*disappointedly*) What, has that old Billy Brown got you to work at home again, too?

BROWN. (*ironically*) It's for Dion's good, you know—and yours.

MARGARET. (*making the best of it—cheerfully*) All right. I won't be selfish. It really makes me proud to have you so ambitious. Let me help. (*She brings his drawing-board, which he puts on the table and pins his plan upon. She sits on sofa and picks up her book.*)

BROWN. (*carefully casual*) I hear you were in to see me today?

MARGARET. Yes, and Billy wouldn't hear of it! I was quite furious until he convinced me it was all for the best. When is he going to take you into partnership?

BROWN. Very soon now.

MARGARET. And will he really give you full charge when he goes abroad?

BROWN. Yes.

MARGARET. (*practically*) I'd pin him down if I could. Promises are all right, but— (*She hesitates*) I don't trust him.

BROWN. (*with a start, sharply*) What makes you say that?

MARGARET. Oh, something that happened today.

BROWN. What?

MARGARET. I don't mean I blame him, but—to be frank, I think the Great God Brown, as you call him, is getting a bit queer and it's time he took a vacation. Don't you?

BROWN. (*his voice a bit excited—but guardedly*) But why? What did he do?

MARGARET. (*hesitatingly*) Well—it's really too silly—he suddenly got awfully strange. His face scared me. It was like a corpse. Then he raved on some nonsense about he'd always loved me. He went on like a perfect fool! (*She looks at* BROWN, *who is staring at her. She becomes uneasy*) Maybe I shouldn't tell you this. He simply wasn't responsible. Then he came to himself and was all right and begged my pardon and seemed dreadfully sorry, and I felt sorry for him. (*Then with a shudder*) But honestly, Dion, it was just too disgusting for words to hear him! (*With kind, devastating contempt*) Poor Billy!

BROWN. (*with a show of tortured derision*) Poor Billy! Poor Billy the Goat! (*With mocking frenzy*) I'll kill him for you! I'll serve you his heart for breakfast!

MARGARET. (*jumping up—frightenedly*) Dion!

BROWN. (*waving his pencil knife with grotesque flourishes*) I tell you I'll murder this God-damned disgusting Great God Brown who stands like a fatted calf in the way of our health and wealth and happiness!

MARGARET. (*bewilderedly, not knowing how much is pretending, puts an arm about him*) Don't, dear! You're being horrid and strange again. It makes me afraid you haven't really changed, after all.

BROWN. (*unheeding*) And then my wife can be happy! Ha! (*He laughs. She begins to cry. He controls himself—pats her head—gently*) All right, dear. Mr. Brown is now safely in hell. Forget him!

MARGARET. (*stops crying—but still worriedly*) I should never have told you—but I never imagined you'd take it seriously. I've never thought of Billy Brown except as a friend, and lately not even that! He's just a stupid old fool!

BROWN. Ha-ha! Didn't I say he was in hell? They're torturing him! (*Then controlling himself again—exhaustedly*) Please leave me alone now. I've got to work.

MARGARET. All right, dear. I'll go into the next room and anything you want, just call. (*She pats his face—cajolingly*) Is it all forgotten?

BROWN. Will you be happy?

MARGARET. Yes.

BROWN. Then it's dead, I promise! (*She kisses him and goes out. He stares ahead, then shakes off his thoughts and concentrates on his work—mockingly*) Our beautiful new Capitol calls you, Mr. Dion! To work! We'll adroitly hide old Silenus on the cupola! Let him dance over their law-making with his eternal leer! (*He bends over his work.*)

CURTAIN

ACT FOUR—SCENE ONE

SCENE—*Same as Scene One of Act Three—the drafting room and* BROWN's *office. It is dusk of a day about a month later. The* TWO DRAFTSMEN *are bent over their table, working.*

BROWN, *at his desk, is working feverishly over a plan. He is wearing the mask of* DION. *The mask of* WILLIAM BROWN *rests on the desk beside him. As he works, he chuckles with malicious glee—finally flings down his pencil with a flourish.*

BROWN. Done! In the name of the Almighty Brown, amen, amen! Here's a wondrous fair Capitol! The design would do just as well for a Home for Criminal Imbeciles! Yet to them, such is my art, it will appear to possess a pure common-sense, a fat-bellied finality, as dignified as the suspenders of an assemblyman! Only to me will that pompous façade reveal itself as the wearily ironic grin of Pan as, his ears drowsy with the crumbling hum of past and future civilizations, he half listens to the laws passed by his fleas to enslave him! Ha-ha-ha! (*He leaps grotesquely from behind his desk and cuts a few goatish capers, laughing with lustful merriment*) Long live Chief of Police Brown! District Attorney Brown! Alderman Brown! Assemblyman Brown! Mayor Brown! Congressman Brown! Governor Brown! Senator Brown! President Brown! (*He chants*) Oh, how many persons in one God make up the good God Brown? Hahahaha! (*The* TWO DRAFTSMEN *in the next room have stopped work and are listening.*)

YOUNGER DRAFTSMAN. Drunk as a fool!

OLDER DRAFTSMAN. At least Dion used to have the decency to stay away from the office—

YOUNGER DRAFTSMAN. Funny how it's got hold of Brown so quick!

OLDER DRAFTSMAN. He was probably hitting it up on the Q.T. all the time.

BROWN. (*has come back to his desk, laughing to himself and out of breath*) Time to become respectable again! (*He takes off the* DION *mask and reaches out for the* WILLIAM BROWN *one—then stops, with a hand on each, staring down on the plan with fascinated loathing. His real face is now sick, ghastly, tortured, hollow-cheeked and feverish-eyed*) Ugly! Hideous! Despicable! Why must the demon in me pander to cheapness—then punish me with self-loathing and life-hatred? Why am I not strong enough to perish—or blind enough to be content? (*To heaven, bitterly but pleadingly*) Give me the strength to destroy this!—and myself!—and him!—and I will believe in Thee! (*While he has been speaking there has been a noise from the stairs. The* TWO DRAFTSMEN *have bent over their work.* MARGARET *enters, closing the door behind her. At this sound,* BROWN *starts. He immediately senses who it is—with alarm*) Margaret! (*He grabs up both masks and goes into room off right.*)

MARGARET. (*she looks healthy and happy, but her face wears a worried, solicitous expression—pleasantly to the staring* DRAFTSMEN) Good morning. Oh, you needn't look worried, it's Mr. Brown I want to see, not my husband.

YOUNGER D. (*hesitatingly*) He's locked himself in—but maybe if you'll knock—

MARGARET. (*knocks—somewhat embarrassedly*) Mr. Brown! (BROWN *enters his office, wearing the* WILLIAM BROWN *mask. He comes quickly to the other door and unlocks it.*)

BROWN. (*with a hectic cordiality*) Come on, Margaret! Enter! This is delightful! Sit down! What can I do for you?

MARGARET. (*taken aback—a bit stiffly*) Nothing much.

BROWN. Something about Dion, of course. Well, your darling pet is all right—never better!

MARGARET. (*coldly*) That's a matter of opinion. I think you're working him to death.

BROWN. Oh, no, not him. It's Brown who is to die. We've agreed on that.

MARGARET. (*giving him a queer look*) I'm serious.

BROWN. So am I. Deadly serious! Hahaha!

MARGARET. (*checking her indignation*) That's what I came to see you about. Really, Dion has acted so hectic and on edge lately I'm sure he's on the verge of a breakdown.

BROWN. Well, it certainly isn't drink. He hasn't had a drop. He doesn't need it! Haha! And I haven't either, although the gossips are beginning to say I'm soused all the time! It's because I've started to laugh! Hahaha! They can't believe in joy in this town except by the bottle! What funny little people! Hahaha! When you're the Great God Brown, eh, Margaret? Hahaha!

MARGARET. (*getting up—uneasily*) I'm afraid I—

BROWN. Don't be afraid, my dear! I won't make love to you again! Honor bright! I'm too near the grave for such folly! But it must have been funny for you when you came here the last time—watching a disgusting old fool like me, eh?—too funny for words! Hahaha! (*Then with a sudden movement he flourishes the design before her*) Look! We've finished it! Dion has finished it! His fame is made!

MARGARET. (*tartly*) Really, Billy, I believe you are drunk!

BROWN. Nobody kisses me—so you can all believe the worst! Hahaha!

MARGARET. (*chillingly*) Then if Dion is through, why can't I see him?

BROWN. (*crazily*) See Dion? See Dion? Well, why not? It's an age of miracles. The streets are full of Lazaruses. Pray! I mean—wait a moment, if you please.

(BROWN *disappears into the room off right. A moment later he reappears in the mask of* DION. *He holds out his arms and* MARGARET *rushes into them. They kiss passionately. Finally he sits with her on the lounge.*)

MARGARET. So you finished it.

BROWN. Yes. The Committee is coming to see it soon. I've made all the changes they'll like, the fools!

MARGARET. (*lovingly*) And can we go on that second honeymoon, right away now?

BROWN. In a week or so, I hope—as soon as I've gotten Brown off to Europe.

MARGARET. Tell me—isn't he drinking hard?

BROWN. (*laughing as* BROWN *did*) Haha! Soused to the ears all the time! Soused on life! He can't stand it! It's burning his insides out!

MARGARET. (*alarmed*) Dear! I'm worried about you. You sound as crazy as he did—when you laugh! You must rest!

BROWN. (*controlling himself*) I'll rest in peace—when he's gone!

MARGARET. (*with a queer look*) Why, Dion, that isn't your suit. It's just like—

BROWN. It's his! We're getting to be like twins. I'm inheriting his clothes already! (*Then calming himself as he sees how frightened she is*) Don't be worried, dear. I'm just a trifle elated, now the job's done. I guess I'm a bit soused on life, too! (*The* COMMITTEE, *three important-looking, average personages, come into the drafting-room.*)

MARGARET. (*forcing a smile*) Well, don't let it burn *your* insides out!

BROWN. No danger! Mine were tempered in hell! Hahaha!

MARGARET. (*kissing him, coaxingly*) Come home, dear—please!

OLDER DRAFTSMAN. (*knocks on the door*) The Committee is here, Mr. Brown.

BROWN. (*hurriedly to* MARGARET) You receive them. Hand them the design. I'll get Brown. (*He raises his voice*) Come right in, gentlemen. (*He goes off right, as the* COMMITTEE *enter the office. When they see* MARGARET, *they stop in surprise.*)

MARGARET. (*embarrassedly*) Good afternoon. Mr. Brown will be right with you. (*They bow.* MARGARET *holds out the design to them*) This is my husband's design. He finished it today.

COMMITTEE. Ah! (*They crowd around to look at it—with enthu-*

siasm) Perfect! Splendid! Couldn't be better! Exactly what we suggested!

MARGARET. (*joyfully*) Then you accept it? Mr. Anthony will be so pleased!

MEMBER. Mr. Anthony?

ANOTHER. Is he working here again?

THIRD. Did I understand you to say this was your husband's design?

MARGARET. (*excitedly*) Yes! Entirely his! He's worked like a dog— (*Appalled*) You don't mean to say—Mr. Brown never told you? (*They shake their heads in solemn surprise*) Oh, the contemptible cad! I hate him!

BROWN. (*appearing at right—mockingly*) Hate me, Margaret? Hate Brown? How superfluous! (*Oratorically*) Gentlemen, I have been keeping a secret from you in order that you might be the more impressed when I revealed it. That design is entirely the inspiration of Mr. Dion Anthony's genius. I had nothing to do with it.

MARGARET. (*contritely*) Oh, Billy! I'm sorry! Forgive me!

BROWN. (*ignoring her, takes the plan from the* COMMITTEE *and begins unpinning it from the board—mockingly*) I can see by your faces you have approved this. You are delighted, aren't you? And why not, my dear sirs? Look at it, and look at you! Hahaha! It'll immortalize you, my good men! You'll be as death-defying a joke as any in Joe Miller! (*Then with a sudden complete change of tone— angrily*) You damn fools! Can't you see this is an insult—a terrible, blasphemous insult!—that this embittered failure Anthony is hurling in the teeth of our success—an insult to you, to me, to you, Margaret— and to Almighty God! (*In a frenzy of fury*) And if you are weak and cowardly enough to stand for it, I'm not! (*He tears the plan into four pieces. The* COMMITTEE *stands aghast.* MARGARET *runs forward.*)

MARGARET. (*in a scream*) You coward! Dion! Dion! (*She picks up the plan and hugs it to her bosom.*)

BROWN. (*with a sudden goatish caper*) I'll tell him you're here. (*He disappears, but reappears almost immediately in the mask of* DION.

He is imposing a terrible discipline on himself to avoid dancing and laughing. He speaks suavely) Everything is all right—all for the best —you mustn't get excited! A little paste, Margaret! A little paste, gentlemen! And all will be well! Life is imperfect, Brothers! Men have their faults, Sister! But with a few drops of glue much may be done! A little dab of pasty resignation here and there—and even broken hearts may be repaired to do yeoman service! (*He has edged toward the door. They are all staring at him with petrified bewilderment. He puts his fingers to his lips*) Ssssh! This is Daddy's bedtime secret for today: Man is born broken. He lives by mending. The grace of God is glue! (*With a quick prancing movement, he has opened the door, gone through, and closed it after him silently, shaking with suppressed laughter. He springs lightly to the side of the petrified* DRAFTS-MEN—*in a whisper*) They will find him in the little room. Mr. William Brown is dead! (*With light leaps he vanishes, his head thrown back, shaking with silent laughter. The sound of his feet leaping down the stairs, five at a time, can be heard. Then a pause of silence. The people in the two rooms stare. The* YOUNGER DRAFTSMAN *is the first to recover.*)

YOUNGER DRAFTSMAN. (*rushing into the next room, shouts in terrified tones*) Mr. Brown is dead!

COMMITTEE. He murdered him. (*They all run into the little room off right.* MARGARET *remains, stunned with horror. They return in a moment, carrying the mask of* WILLIAM BROWN, *two on each side, as if they were carrying a body by the legs and shoulders. They solemnly lay him down on the couch and stand looking down at him.*)

FIRST COMMITTEEMAN. (*with a frightened awe*) I can't believe he's gone.

SECOND COMMITTEEMAN. (*in same tone*) I can almost hear him talking. (*As if impelled, he clears his throat and addresses the mask importantly*) Mr. Brown— (*Then stops short.*)

THIRD COMMITTEEMAN. (*shrinking back*) No. Dead, all right! (*Then*

suddenly, hysterically angry and terrified) We must take steps at once
to run Anthony to earth!

MARGARET. (*with a heartbroken cry*) Dion's innocent!

YOUNGER DRAFTSMAN. I'll phone for the police, sir! (*He rushes to
the phone.*)

CURTAIN

ACT FOUR—SCENE TWO

SCENE—*The same as Scene Two of Act Three—the library of WIL-
LIAM BROWN's home. The mask of DION stands on the table beneath
the light, facing front. On his knees beside the table, facing front,
stripped naked except for a white cloth around his loins, is BROWN.
The clothes he has torn off in his agony are scattered on the floor.
His eyes, his arms, his whole body strain upward, his muscles writhe
with his lips as they pray silently in their agonized supplication.
Finally a voice seems torn out of him.*

BROWN. Mercy, Compassionate Savior of Man! Out of my depths
I cry to you! Mercy on thy poor clod, thy clod of unhallowed earth,
thy clay, the Great God Brown! Mercy, Savior! (*He seems to wait
for an answer—then leaping to his feet he puts out one hand to touch
the mask like a frightened child reaching out for its nurse's hand—
then with immediate mocking despair*) Bah! I am sorry, little children, but your kingdom is empty. God has become disgusted and
moved away to some far ecstatic star where life is a dancing flame!
We must die without him. (*Then—addressing the mask—harshly*)
Together, my friend! You, too! Let Margaret suffer! Let the whole
world suffer as I am suffering! (*There is a sound of a door being
pushed violently open, padding feet in slippers, and CYBEL, wearing*

319

her mask, runs into the room. She stops short on seeing BROWN *and the mask, and stares from one to the other for a second in confusion. She is dressed in a black kimono robe and wears slippers over her bare feet. Her yellow hair hangs down in a great mane over her shoulders. She has grown stouter, has more of the deep objective calm of an idol.*)

BROWN. (*staring at her—fascinated—with great peace as if her presence comforted him*) Cybel! I was coming to you! How did you know?

CYBEL. (*takes off her mask and looks from* BROWN *to the* DION *mask, now with a great understanding*) So that's why you never came to me again! You are Dion Brown!

BROWN. (*bitterly*) I am the remains of William Brown! (*He points to the mask of* DION) I am his murderer and his murdered!

CYBEL. (*with a laugh of exasperated pity*) Oh, why can't you ever learn to leave yourselves alone and leave me alone!

BROWN. (*boyishly and naively*) I am Billy.

CYBEL. (*immediately, with a motherly solicitude*) Then run, Billy, run! They are hunting for someone! They came to my place, hunting for a murderer, Dion! They must find a victim! They've got to quiet their fears, to cast out their devils, or they'll never sleep soundly again! They've got to absolve themselves by finding a guilty one! They've got to kill someone now, to live! You're naked! You must be Satan! Run, Billy, run! They'll come here! I ran here to warn—someone! So run away if you want to live!

BROWN. (*like a sulky child*) I'm too tired. I don't want to.

CYBEL. (*with motherly calm*) All right, you needn't, Billy. Don't sulk. (*As a noise comes from outside*) Anyway, it's too late. I hear them in the garden now.

BROWN. (*listening, puts out his hand and takes the mask of* DION— *as he gains strength, mockingly*) Thanks for this one last favor, Dion! Listen! Your avengers! Standing on your grave in the garden! Hahaha! (*He puts on the mask and springs to the left and makes a gesture as if flinging French windows open. Gayly mocking*) Welcome, dumb worshippers! I am your Great God Brown! I have been advised to run from you but it is my almighty whim to dance into escape over your prostrate souls! (*Shouts from the garden and a volley of shots.* BROWN *staggers back and falls on the floor by the couch, mortally wounded.*)

CYBEL. (*runs to his side, lifts him on to the couch and takes off the mask of* DION) You can't take this to bed with you. You've got to go to sleep alone. (*She places the mask of* DION *back on its stand under the light and puts on her own, just as, after a banging of doors, crashing of glass, trampling of feet, a Squad of Police with drawn revolvers, led by a grizzly, brutal-faced Captain, run into the room. They are followed by* MARGARET, *still distractedly clutching the pieces of the plan to her breast.*)

CAPTAIN. (*pointing to the mask of* DION—*triumphantly*) Got him! He's dead!

MARGARET. (*throws herself on her knees, takes the mask and kisses it—heartbrokenly*) Dion! Dion! (*Her face hidden in her arms, the mask in her hands above her bowed head, she remains, sobbing with deep, silent grief.*)

CAPTAIN. (*noticing* CYBEL *and* BROWN—*startled*) Hey! Look at this! What're you doin' here? Who's he?

CYBEL. You ought to know. You croaked him!

CAPTAIN. (*with a defensive snarl—hastily*) It was Anthony! I saw his mug! This feller's an accomplice, I bet yuh! Serves him right! Who is he? Friend o' yours! Crook! What's his name? Tell me or I'll fix yuh!

CYBEL. Billy.

CAPTAIN. Billy what?

CYBEL. I don't know. He's dying. (*Then suddenly*) Leave me alone with him and maybe I'll get him to squeal it.

CAPTAIN. Yuh better! I got to have a clean report. I'll give yuh a couple o' minutes. (*He motions to the Policemen, who follow him off left.* CYBEL *takes off her mask and sits down by* BROWN's *head. He makes an effort to raise himself toward her and she helps him, throwing her kimono over his bare body, drawing his head on to her shoulder.*)

BROWN. (*snuggling against her—gratefully*) The earth is warm.

CYBEL. (*soothingly, looking before her like an idol*) Ssshh! Go to sleep, Billy.

BROWN. Yes, Mother. (*Then explainingly*) It was dark and I couldn't see where I was going and they all picked on me.

CYBEL. I know. You're tired.

BROWN. And when I wake up . . . ?

CYBEL. The sun will be rising again.

BROWN. To judge the living and the dead! (*Frightenedly*) I don't want justice. I want love.

CYBEL. There is only love.

BROWN. Thank you, Mother. (*Then feebly*) I'm getting sleepy. What's the prayer you taught me— Our Father—?

CYBEL. (*with calm exultance*) Our Father Who Art!

BROWN. (*taking her tone—exultantly*) Who art! Who art! (*Suddenly—with ecstasy*) I know! I have found Him! I hear Him speak! "Blessed are they that weep, for they shall laugh!" Only he that has wept can laugh! The laughter of Heaven sows earth with a rain of tears, and out of earth's transfigured birth-pain the laughter of Man returns to bless and play again in innumerable dancing gales of flame upon the knees of God! (*He dies.*)

CYBEL. (*gets up and fixes his body on the couch. She bends down and kisses him gently—she straightens up and looks into space—with a profound pain*) Always spring comes again bearing life! Always again! Always, always forever again!— Spring again!—life again! summer and fall and death and peace again!—(*With agonized sorrow*)—but always, always, love and conception and birth and pain again—spring bearing the intolerable chalice of life gain!—(*Then with agonized exultance*)—bearing the glorious, blazing crown of

322

life again! (*She stands like an idol of Earth, her eyes staring out over the world.*)

MARGARET. (*lifting her head adoringly to the mask—triumphant tenderness mingled with her grief*) My lover! My husband! My boy! (*She kisses the mask*) Good-by. Thank you for happiness! And you're not dead, sweetheart! You can never die till my heart dies! You will live forever! You will sleep under my heart! I will feel you stirring in your sleep, forever under my heart! (*She kisses the mask again. There is a pause.*)

CAPTAIN. (*comes just into sight at left and speaks front without looking at them—gruffly*) Well, what's his name?

CYBEL. Man!

CAPTAIN. (*taking a grimy notebook and an inch-long pencil from his pocket*) How d'yuh spell it?

CURTAIN

EPILOGUE

Scene—*Four years later. The same spot on the same dock as in Prologue on another moonlight night in June. The sound of the waves and of distant dance music.*

MARGARET *and her* THREE SONS *appear from the right. The eldest is now eighteen. All are dressed in the height of correct Prep-school elegance. They are all tall, athletic, strong and handsome-looking. They loom up around the slight figure of their mother like protecting giants, giving her a strange aspect of lonely, detached, small femininity. She wears her mask of the proud, indulgent Mother. She has grown appreciably older. Her hair is now a beautiful gray. There is about her manner and voice the sad but contented feeling of one who knows her life purpose well accomplished but is at the same time a bit empty and comfortless with the finality of it. She is wrapped in a gray cloak.*

ELDEST. Doesn't Bee look beautiful tonight, Mother?

NEXT. Don't you think Mabel's the best dancer in there, Mother?

YOUNGEST. Aw, Alice has them both beat, hasn't she, Mother?

MARGARET. (*with a sad little laugh*) Each of you is right. (*Then, with strange finality*) Good-by, boys.

BOYS. (*surprised*) Good-by.

MARGARET. It was here on a night just like this your father first— proposed to me. Did you ever know that?

BOYS. (*embarrassedly*) No.

MARGARET. (*yearningly*) But the nights now are so much colder than they used to be. Think of it, I went in moonlight bathing in June when I was a girl. It was so warm and beautiful in those days. I remember the Junes when I was carrying you boys— (*A pause.*

324

They fidget uneasily. She asks pleadingly) Promise me faithfully never to forget your father!

BOYS. (*uncomfortably*) Yes, Mother.

MARGARET. (*forcing a joking tone*) But you mustn't waste June on an old woman like me! Go in and dance. (*As they hesitate dutifully*) Go on. I really want to be alone—with my Junes.

BOYS. (*unable to conceal their eagerness*) Yes, Mother. (*They go away.*)

MARGARET. (*slowly removes her mask, laying it on the bench, and stares up at the moon with a wistful, resigned sweetness*) So long ago! And yet I'm still the same Margaret. It's only our lives that grow old. We *are* where centuries only count as seconds and after a thousand lives our eyes begin to open—(*She looks around her with a rapt smile*)—and the moon rests in the sea! I want to feel the moon at peace in the sea! I want Dion to leave the sky for me! I want him to sleep in the tides of my heart! (*She slowly takes from under her cloak, from her bosom, as if from her heart, the mask of* DION *as it was at the last and holds it before her face*) My lover! My husband! My boy! You can never die till my heart dies! You will live forever. You are sleeping under my heart! I feel you stirring in your sleep, forever under my heart. (*She kisses him on the lips with a timeless kiss.*)

CURTAIN

THE STRAW

A Play in Three Acts

CHARACTERS

BILL CARMODY

MARY ⎤
NORA ⎟
TOM ⎬ *his children*
BILLY ⎦

DOCTOR GAYNOR

FRED NICHOLLS

EILEEN CARMODY, *Bill's eldest child*

STEPHEN MURRAY

MISS HOWARD, *a nurse in training*

MISS GILPIN, *superintendent of the Infirmary*

DOCTOR STANTON, *of the Hill Farm Sanatorium*

DOCTOR SIMMS, *his assistant*

MR. SLOAN

PETERS, *a patient*

MRS. TURNER, *matron of the Sanatorium*

MISS BAILEY ⎤
MRS. ABNER ⎬ *Patients*
FLYNN ⎦

OTHER PATIENTS OF THE SANATORIUM

MRS. BRENNAN

SCENES

ACT ONE

Scene I: The Kitchen of the Carmody Home—Evening.

Scene II: The Reception Room of the Infirmary, Hill Farm Sanatorium—An Evening a Week Later.

ACT TWO

Scene I: Assembly Room of the Main Building at the Sanatorium—A Morning Four Months Later.

Scene II: A Crossroads Near the Sanatorium—Midnight of the Same Day.

ACT THREE

An Isolation Room and Porch at the Sanatorium—An Afternoon Four Months Later.

THE STRAW

ACT ONE—SCENE ONE

THE *kitchen of the Carmody home on the outskirts of a manufactur-ing town in Connecticut. On the left, forward, the sink. Farther back, two windows looking out on the yard. In the left corner, rear, the icebox. Immediately to the right of it, in the rear wall, a window opening on the side porch. To the right of this, a dish closet, and a door leading into the hall where the main front entrance to the house and the stairs to the floor above are situated. On the right, to the rear, a door opening on the dining room. Farther forward, the kitchen range with scuttle, wood box, etc. In the center of the room, a table with a red and white cover. Four cane-bottomed chairs are pushed under the table. In front of the stove, two battered, wicker rocking chairs. The floor is partly covered by linoleum strips. The walls are papered a light cheerful color. Several old framed picture-supple-ment prints hang from nails. Everything has a clean, neatly-kept appearance. The supper dishes are piled in the sink ready for wash-ing. A dish pan of water simmers on the stove.*

It is about eight o'clock in the evening of a bitter cold day in late February.

As the curtain rises, BILL CARMODY *is discovered sitting in a rocker by the stove, reading a newspaper and smoking a blackened clay pipe. He is a man of fifty, heavy-set and round-shouldered, with long muscular arms and swollen-veined, hairy hands. His face is bony and ponderous; his nose, short and squat; his mouth large, thick-lipped and harsh; his complexion mottled—red, purple-streaked, and freckled; his hair, short and stubby with a bald spot on the crown.*

The expression of his small, blue eyes is one of selfish cunning. His voice is loud and hoarse. He wears a flannel shirt, open at the neck, criss-crossed by red suspenders; black, baggy trousers gray with dust; muddy brogans.

His youngest daughter, MARY, *is sitting on a chair by the table, front, turning over the pages of a picture book. She is a delicate, dark-haired, blue-eyed, quiet little girl about eight years old.*

CARMODY. (*after watching the child's preoccupation for a moment, in a tone of half-exasperated amusement*) Well, but you're the quiet one, surely! It's the dead spit and image of your sister, Eileen, you are, with your nose always in a book; and you're like your mother, too, God rest her soul. (*He crosses himself with pious unction and* MARY *also does so*) It's Nora and Tom has the high spirits in them like their father; and Billy, too,—if he is a lazy shiftless divil—has the fightin' Carmody blood like me. You're a Cullen like your mother's people. They always was dreamin' their lives out. (*He lights his pipe and shakes his head with ponderous gravity*) It's out rompin' and playin' you ought to be at your age, not carin' a fig for books. (*With a glance at the clock*) Is that auld fool of a doctor stayin' the night? Run out in the hall, Mary, and see if you hear him.

MARY. (*goes out into the hall, rear, and comes back*) He's upstairs. I heard him talking to Eileen.

CARMODY. Close the door, ye little divil! There's a freezin' draught comin' in. (*She does so and comes back to her chair.* CARMODY *continues with a sneer*) I've no use for their drugs at all. They only keep you sick to pay more visits. I'd not have sent for this bucko if Eileen didn't scare me by faintin'.

MARY. (*anxiously*) Is Eileen very sick, Papa?

CARMODY. (*spitting—roughly*) If she is, it's her own fault entirely—weakenin' her health by readin' here in the house. (*Irritably*) Put down that book on the table and leave it be. I'll have no more readin' or I'll take the strap to you!

MARY. (*laying the book on the table*) It's only pictures.

CARMODY. No back talk! Pictures or not, it's all the same mopin' and lazin' in it. (*After a pause—morosely*) Who's to do the work and look after Nora and Tom and yourself, if Eileen is bad took and has to stay in her bed? All that I've saved from slavin' and sweatin' in the sun with a gang of lazy Dagoes'll be up the spout in no time. (*Bitterly*) What a fool a man is to be raisin' a raft of children and him not a millionaire! (*With lugubrious self-pity*) Mary, dear, it's a black curse God put on me when he took your mother just when I needed her most. (MARY *commences to sob.* CARMODY *starts and looks at her angrily*) What are you snifflin' at?

MARY. (*tearfully*) I was thinking—of Mama.

CARMODY. (*scornfully*) It's late you are with your tears, and her cold in her grave for a year. Stop it, I'm tellin' you! (MARY *gulps back her sobs.*)

(*There is a noise of childish laughter and screams from the street in front. The outside door is opened and slammed, footsteps pound along the hall. The door in the rear is shoved open, and* NORA *and* TOM *rush in breathlessly.* NORA *is a bright, vivacious, red-haired girl of eleven—pretty after an elfish, mischievous fashion—light-hearted and robust.*)

(TOM *resembles* NORA *in disposition and appearance. A healthy, good-humored youngster with a shock of sandy hair. He is a year younger than* NORA. *They are followed into the room, a moment later, by their brother,* BILLY, *who is evidently loftily disgusted with their antics.* BILLY *is a fourteen-year-old replica of his father, whom he imitates even to the hoarse, domineering tone of voice.*)

CARMODY. (*grumpily*) Ah, here you are, the lot of you. Shut that door after you! What's the use in me spendin' money for coal if all you do is to let the cold night in the room itself?

NORA. (*hopping over to him—teasingly*) Me and Tom had a race, Papa. I beat him. (*She sticks her tongue out at her younger brother*) Slow poke!

TOM. You didn't beat me, neither!

NORA. I did, too!

TOM. You tripped me comin' up the steps. Brick-top! Cheater!

NORA. (*flaring up*) You're a liar! I beat you fair. Didn't I, Papa?

CARMODY. (*with a grin*) You did, darlin'. (TOM *slinks back to the chair in the rear of the table, sulking.* CARMODY *pats* NORA's *red hair with delighted pride*) Sure it's you can beat the divil himself!

NORA. (*sticks out her tongue again at* TOM) See? Liar! (*She goes and perches on the table near* MARY *who is staring sadly in front of her.*)

CARMODY. (*to* BILLY—*irritably*) Did you get the plug I told you?

BILLY. Sure. (*He takes a plug of tobacco from his pocket and hands it to his father.* NORA *slides down off her perch and disappears, unnoticed, under the table.*)

CARMODY. It's a great wonder you didn't forget it—and me without a chew. (*He bites off a piece and tucks it into his cheek.*)

TOM. (*suddenly clutching at his leg with a yell*) Ouch! Darn you! (*He kicks frantically at something under the table, but* NORA *scrambles out at the other end, grinning.*)

CARMODY. (*angrily*) Shut your big mouth!

TOM. (*indignantly*) She pinched me—hard as she could, too—and look at her laughin'!

NORA. (*hopping on the table again*) Cry-baby!

TOM. I'll tell Eileen, wait 'n' see!

NORA. Tattle-tale! Eileen's sick.

TOM. That's why you dast do it. You dasn't if she was up.

CARMODY. (*exasperated*) Go up to bed, the two of you, and no more talk, and you go with them, Mary.

NORA. (*giving a quick tug at* MARY's *hair*) Come on, Mary.

MARY. Ow! (*She begins to cry.*)

CARMODY. (*raising his voice furiously*) Hush your noise! It's nothin' but blubberin' you do be doin' all the time. (*He stands up threaten-*

ingly) I'll have a moment's peace, I will! Go on, now! (*They scurry out of the rear door.*)

NORA. (*sticks her head back in the door*) Can I say good-night to Eileen, papa?

CARMODY. No. The doctor's with her yet. (*Then he adds hastily*) Yes, go in to her, Nora. It'll drive himself out of the house maybe, bad cess to him, and him stayin' half the night. (NORA *waits to hear no more but darts back, shutting the door behind her.* BILLY *takes the chair in front of the table.* CARMODY *sits down again with a groan*) The rheumatics are in my leg again. (*Shakes his head*) If Eileen's in bed long those brats'll have the house down. Arra, well, it's God's will, I suppose, but where the money'll come from, I dunno. (*With a disparaging glance at his son*) They'll not be raisin' your wages soon, I'll be bound.

BILLY. (*surlily*) Naw.

CARMODY. (*still scanning him with contempt*) A divil of a lot of good it was for me to go against Eileen's wish and let you leave off your schoolin' this year thinkin' the money you'd earn would help with the house.

BILLY. Aw, goin' to school didn't do me no good. The teachers was all down on me. I couldn't learn nothin' there.

CARMODY. (*disgustedly*) Nor any other place, I'm thinkin', you're that thick. (*There is a noise from the stairs in the hall*) Wisht! It's the doctor comin' down from Eileen. (*The door in the rear is opened and Doctor Gaynor enters. He is a stout, bald, middle-aged man, forceful of speech, who in the case of patients of the* CARMODYS' *class dictates rather than advises.* CARMODY *adopts a whining tone*) Aw, Doctor, and how's Eileen now?

GAYNOR. (*does not answer this but comes forward into the room holding out two slips of paper—dictatorially*) Here are two prescriptions that'll have to be filled immediately.

CARMODY. (*frowning*) You take them, Billy, and run round to the drug store. (GAYNOR *hands them to* BILLY.)

BILLY. Give me the money, then.

CARMODY. (*reaches down into his pants pocket with a sigh*) How much will they come to, Doctor?

GAYNOR. About a dollar, I guess.

CARMODY. (*protestingly*) A dollar! Sure it's expensive medicines you're givin' her for a bit of a cold. (*He meets the doctor's cold glance of contempt and he wilts—grumblingly, as he peels a dollar bill off a small roll and gives it to* BILLY) Bring back the change—if there is any. And none of your tricks!

BILLY. Aw, what do you think I am? (*He takes the money and goes out.*)

CARMODY. (*grudgingly*) Take a chair, Doctor, and tell me what's wrong with Eileen.

GAYNOR. (*seating himself by the table—gravely*) Your daughter is very seriously ill.

CARMODY. (*irritably*) Aw, Doctor, didn't I know you'd be sayin' that, anyway!

GAYNOR. (*ignoring this remark—coldly*) She has tuberculosis of the lungs.

CARMODY. (*with puzzled awe*) Too-ber-c'losis?

GAYNOR. Consumption, if that makes it plainer to you.

CARMODY. (*with dazed terror—after a pause*) Consumption? Eileen? (*With sudden anger*) What lie is it you're tellin' me?

GAYNOR. (*icily*) Look here, Carmody!

CARMODY. (*bewilderedly*) Don't be angry, now. Sure I'm out of my wits entirely. Ah, Doctor, sure you must be mistaken!

GAYNOR. There's no chance for a mistake, I'm sorry to say. Her right lung is badly affected.

CARMODY. (*desperately*) It's a cold only, maybe.

GAYNOR. (*curtly*) Don't talk nonsense. (CARMODY *groans.* GAYNOR *continues authoritatively*) She'll have to go to a sanatorium at once. She ought to have been sent to one months ago. (*Casts a look of indignant scorn at* CARMODY *who is sitting staring at the floor with an expression of angry stupor on his face*) It's a wonder to me you didn't see the condition she was in and force her to take care of herself.

CARMODY. (*with vague fury*) God blast it!

GAYNOR. She kept on doing her work, I suppose—taking care of her brothers and sisters, washing, cooking, sweeping, looking after your comfort—worn out—when she should have been in bed—and— (*He gets to his feet with a harsh laugh*) But what's the use of talking? The damage is done. We've got to set to work to repair it at once. I'll write tonight to Dr. Stanton of the Hill Farm Sanatorium and find out if he has a vacancy.

CARMODY. (*his face growing red with rage*) Is it sendin' Eileen away to a hospital you'd be? (*Exploding*) Then you'll not! You'll get that notion out of your head damn quick. It's all nonsense you're stuffin' me with, and lies, makin' things out to be the worst in the world. She'll not move a step out of here, and I say so, and I'm her father!

GAYNOR. (*who has been staring at him with contempt—coldly angry*) You refuse to let her go to a sanatorium?

CARMODY. I do.

GAYNOR. (*threateningly*) Then I'll have to report her case to the Society for the Prevention of Tuberculosis of this county and tell them of your refusal to help her.

CARMODY. (*wavering a bit*) Report all you like, and be damned to you!

GAYNOR. (*ignoring the interruption—impressively*) A majority of the most influential men of this city are back of the Society. (*Grimly*) We'll find a way to move you, Carmody, if you try to be stubborn.

CARMODY. (*thoroughly frightened but still protesting*) Arra, Doctor, you don't see the way of it at all. If Eileen goes to the hospital, who's to be takin' care of the others, and mindin' the house when I'm off to work?

GAYNOR. You can easily hire some woman.

CARMODY. (*at once furious again*) Hire? D'you think I'm a million-aire itself?

GAYNOR. (*contemptuously*) That's where the shoe pinches, eh? (*In a rage*) I'm not going to waste any more words on you, Carmody, but I'm damn well going to see this thing through! You might as well give in first as last.

CARMODY. (*wailing*) But where's the money comin' from?

GAYNOR. The weekly fee at the Hill Farm is only seven dollars. You can easily afford that—the price of a few rounds of drinks.

CARMODY. Seven dollars! And I'll have to pay a woman to come in—and the four of the children eatin' their heads off! Glory be to God, I'll not have a penny saved for me old age—and then it's the poor house!

GAYNOR. Well, perhaps I can get the Society to pay half for your daughter—if you're really as hard up as you pretend.

CARMODY. (*brightening*) Ah, Doctor, thank you.

GAYNOR. (*abruptly*) Then it's all settled?

CARMODY. (*grudgingly—trying to make the best of it*) I'll do my best for Eileen, if it's needful—and you'll not be tellin' them people about it at all, Doctor?

GAYNOR. Not unless you force me to.

CARMODY. And they'll pay the half, surely?

GAYNOR. I'll see what I can do.

CARMODY. God bless you, Doctor! (*Grumblingly*) It's the whole of it they ought to be payin', I'm thinkin', and them with sloos of money. 'Tis them builds the hospitals and why should they be wantin' the poor like me to support them?

GAYNOR. (*disgustedly*) Bah! (*Abruptly*) I'll telephone to Doctor Stanton tomorrow morning. Then I'll know something definite when I come to see your daughter in the afternoon.

CARMODY. (*darkly*) You'll be comin' again tomorrow? (*Half to himself*) Leave it to the likes of you to be drainin' a man dry. (GAYNOR *has gone out to the hall in rear and does not hear this last remark.*

*There is a loud knock from the outside door. The Doctor comes back
into the room carrying his hat and overcoat.)*

GAYNOR. There's someone knocking.

CARMODY. Who'll it be? Ah, it's Fred Nicholls, maybe. (*In a low
voice to* GAYNOR *who has started to put on his overcoat*) Eileen's
young man, Doctor, that she's engaged to marry, as you might say.

GAYNOR. (*thoughtfully*) Hmm—yes—she spoke of him. (*As another knock sounds* CARMODY *hurries to the rear.* GAYNOR, *after a
moment's indecision, takes off his overcoat again and sits down. A
moment later* CARMODY *re-enters followed by* FRED NICHOLLS, *who has
left his overcoat and hat in the hallway.* NICHOLLS *is a young fellow
of twenty-three, stockily built, fair-haired, handsome in a commonplace, conventional mold. His manner is obviously an attempt at
suave gentility; he has an easy, taking smile and a ready laugh, but
there is a petty, calculating expression in his small, observing, blue
eyes. His well-fitting, readymade clothes are carefully pressed. His
whole get-up suggests an attitude of man-about-small-town com-
placency.*)

CARMODY. (*as they enter*) I had a mind to phone to your house but
I wasn't wishful to disturb you, knowin' you'd be comin' to call
tonight.

NICHOLLS. (*with disappointed concern*) It's nothing serious, I hope.

CARMODY. (*grumblingly*) Ah, who knows? Here's the doctor.
You've not met him?

NICHOLLS. (*politely, looking at* GAYNOR *who inclines his head stiffly*)
I haven't had the pleasure. Of course I've heard—

CARMODY. It's Doctor Gaynor. This is Fred Nicholls, Doctor. (*The
two men shake hands with conventional pleased-to-meet yous*) Sit
down, Fred, that's a good lad, and be talkin' to the Doctor a moment
while I go upstairs and see how is Eileen.

NICHOLLS. Certainly, Mr. Carmody—and tell her how sorry I am
to learn she's under the weather.

CARMODY. I will so. (*He goes out.*)

339

GAYNOR. (*after a pause in which he is studying* NICHOLLS) Do you happen to be any relative to Albert Nicholls over at the Downs Manufacturing Company?

NICHOLLS. (*smiling*) He's sort of a near relative—my father.

GAYNOR. Ah, yes?

NICHOLLS. (*with satisfaction*) I work for the Downs Company myself—bookkeeper.

GAYNOR. Miss Carmody had a position there also, didn't she, before her mother died?

NICHOLLS. Yes. She had a job as stenographer for a time. When she graduated from the business college—I was already working at the Downs—and through my father's influence—you understand. (GAYNOR *nods curtly*) She was getting on finely, too, and liked the work. It's too bad—her mother's death, I mean—forcing her to give it up and come home to take care of those kids.

GAYNOR. It's a damn shame. That's the main cause of her breakdown.

NICHOLLS. (*frowning*) I've noticed she's been looking badly lately. Well, it's all her father's fault—and her own, too, because whenever I raised a kick about his making a slave of her, she always defended him. (*With a quick glance at the Doctor—in a confidential tone*) Between us, Carmody's as selfish as they make 'em, if you want my opinion.

GAYNOR. (*with a growl*) He's a hog on two legs.

NICHOLLS. (*with a gratified smile*) You bet! (*With a patronizing air*) I hope to get Eileen away from all this as soon as—things pick up a little. (*Making haste to explain his connection with the dubious household*) Eileen and I have gone around together for years—went to Grammar and High School together—in different classes, of course. She's really a corker—very different from the rest of the family you've seen—like her mother. My folks like her awfully well. Of course, they'd never stand for him.

GAYNOR. You'll excuse my curiosity, but you and Miss Carmody are engaged, aren't you? Carmody said you were.

NICHOLLS. (*embarrassed*) Why, yes, in a way—but nothing definite—no official announcement or anything of that kind. (*With a sentimental smile*) It's always been sort of understood between us. (*He laughs awkwardly.*)

GAYNOR. (*gravely*) Then I can be frank with you. I'd like to be because I may need your help. Besides, you're bound to know anyway. She'd tell you.

NICHOLLS. (*a look of apprehension coming over his face*) Is it—about her sickness?

GAYNOR. Yes.

NICHOLLS. Then—it's serious?

GAYNOR. It's pulmonary tuberculosis—consumption.

NICHOLLS. (*stunned*) Consumption? Good heavens! (*After a dazed pause—lamely*) Are you sure, Doctor?

GAYNOR. Positive. (NICHOLLS *stares at him with vaguely frightened eyes*) It's had a good start—thanks to her father's blind selfishness—but let's hope that can be overcome. The important thing is to ship her off to a sanatorium immediately. That's where you can be of help. It's up to you to help me convince Carmody that it's imperative she be sent away at once—for the safety of those around her as well as her own.

NICHOLLS. (*confusedly*) I'll do my best, Doctor. (*As if he couldn't yet believe his ears—shuddering*) Good heavens! She never said a word about—being so ill. She's had a cold. But Doctor,—do you think this sanatorium will—?

GAYNOR. (*with hearty hopefulness*) She has every chance. The Hill Farm has a really surprising record of arrested cases. Of course, she'll never be able to live as carelessly as before, even after the most favorable results. (*Apologetically*) I'm telling you all this as being the one most intimately concerned. You're the one who'll have to assume responsibility when she returns to everyday life.

NICHOLLS. (*answering as if he were merely talking to screen the thoughts in his mind*) Yes—certainly—. Where is this sanatorium, Doctor?

GAYNOR. Half an hour by train to the town. The sanatorium is two miles out on the hills. You'll be able to see her whenever you've a day off.

NICHOLLS. (*a look of horrified realization has been creeping into his eyes*) You said—Eileen ought to be sent away—for the sake of those around her—?

GAYNOR. T. B. is extremely contagious, you must know that. Yet I'll bet she's been fondling and kissing those brothers and sisters of hers regardless. (NICHOLLS *fidgets uneasily on his chair.*)

NICHOLLS. (*his eyes shiftily avoiding the doctor's face*) Then the kids might have gotten it—by kissing Eileen?

GAYNOR. It stands to reason that's a common means of communication.

NICHOLLS. (*very much shaken*) Yes. I suppose it must be. But that's terrible, isn't it? (*With sudden volubility, evidently extremely anxious to wind up this conversation and conceal his thoughts from* GAYNOR) I'll promise you, Doctor, I'll tell Carmody straight what's what. He'll pay attention to me or I'll know the reason why.

GAYNOR. (*getting to his feet and picking up his overcoat*) Good boy! Tell him I'll be back tomorrow with definite information about the sanatorium.

NICHOLLS. (*helping him on with his overcoat, anxious to have him go*) All right, Doctor.

GAYNOR. (*puts on his hat*) And do your best to cheer the patient up. Give her confidence in her ability to get well. That's half the battle.

NICHOLLS. (*hastily*) I'll do all I can.

GAYNOR. (*turns to the door and shakes* NICHOLLS' *hand sympathetically*) And don't take it to heart too much yourself. In six months she'll come back to you her old self again.

342

NICHOLLS. (*nervously*) It's hard on a fellow—so suddenly, but I'll remember—and—(*Abruptly*) Good-night, Doctor.

GAYNOR. Good-night. (*He goes out. The outer door is heard shutting behind him.* NICHOLLS *closes the door, rear, and comes back and sits in the chair in front of table. He rests his chin on his hands and stares before him, a look of desperate, frightened calculation coming into his eyes.* CARMODY *is heard clumping heavily down the stairs. A moment later he enters. His expression is glum and irritated.*)

CARMODY. (*coming forward to his chair by the stove*) Has he gone away?

NICHOLLS. (*turning on him with a look of repulsion*) Yes. He said to tell you he'd be back tomorrow with definite information—about the sanatorium business.

CARMODY. (*darkly*) Oho, he did, did he? Maybe I'll surprise him. I'm thinkin' it's lyin' he is about Eileen's sickness, and her lookin' as fresh as a daisy with the high color in her cheeks when I saw her now.

NICHOLLS. (*impatiently*) Gaynor knows his business. (*After a moment's hesitation*) He told me all about Eileen's sickness.

CARMODY. (*resentfully*) Small thanks to him to be tellin' our secrets to the town.

NICHOLLS. (*exasperated*) He only told me because you'd said I and Eileen were engaged. You're the one who was telling—secrets.

CARMODY. (*irritated*) Arra, don't be talkin'! That's no secret at all with the whole town watchin' Eileen and you spoonin' together from the time you was kids.

NICHOLLS. (*vindictively*) Well, the whole town is liable to find out— (*He checks himself.*)

CARMODY. (*too absorbed in his own troubles to notice this threat*) So he told you he'd send Eileen away to the hospital? I've half a mind not to let him—and let him try to make me! (*With a frown*) But Eileen herself says she's wantin' to go, now. (*Angrily*) It's all that divil's notion he put in her head that the children'd be catchin' her sickness that makes her willin' to go.

343

NICHOLLS. (*with a superior air*) From what he told me, I should say it's the only thing for Eileen to do if she wants to get well quickly. (*Spitefully*) And I'd certainly not go against Gaynor, if I was you.

CARMODY. (*worriedly*) But what can he do—him and his Sasiety? I'm her father.

NICHOLLS. (*seeing* CARMODY'S *uneasiness with revengeful satisfaction*) You'll make a mistake if you think he's bluffing. It'd probably get in all the papers about you refusing. Everyone would be down on you. (*As a last jab—spitefully*) You might even lose your job over it, people would be so sore.

CARMODY. (*jumping to his feet*) Ah, divil take him! Let him send her where he wants, then.

NICHOLLS. (*as an afterthought*) And, honestly, Mr. Carmody, I don't see how you can object for a second. (*Seeing* CARMODY'S *shaken condition, he finishes boldly*) You've some feeling for your own daughter, haven't you?

CARMODY. (*apprehensively*) Whisht! She might hear you. Let her do what she's wishful.

NICHOLLS. (*complacently—feeling his duty in the matter well done*) That's the right spirit. And you and I'll do all we can to help her. (*He gets to his feet*) Well, I guess I'll have to go. Tell Eileen—

CARMODY. You're not goin'? Sure, Eileen is puttin' on her clothes to come down and have a look at you.

NICHOLLS. (*suddenly panic-stricken by the prospect of facing her*) No—no—I can't stay—I only came for a moment—I've got an appointment—honestly. Besides, it isn't right for her to be up. You should have told her. (*The door in the rear is opened and* EILEEN *enters. She is just over eighteen. Her wavy mass of dark hair is parted in the middle and combed low on her forehead, covering her ears, to a knot at the back of her head. The oval of her face is spoiled by a long, rather heavy, Irish jaw contrasting with the delicacy of her other features. Her eyes are large and blue, confident in their compelling candor and sweetness; her lips, full and red, half-open, over strong even teeth, droop at the corners into an expression of wistful sadness; her clear complexion is unnaturally striking in its contrasting colors, rose and white; her figure is slight and undeveloped. She wears a plain black dress with a bit of white at the neck and wrists. She stands looking appealingly at* NICHOLLS *who avoids her glance. Her eyes have a startled, stunned expression as if the doctor's verdict were still in her ears.*)

EILEEN. (*faintly—forcing a smile*) Good evening, Fred. (*Her eyes search his face anxiously.*)

NICHOLLS. (*confusedly*) Hello, Eileen. I'm so sorry to—. (*Clumsily trying to cover up his confusion, he goes over and leads her to a chair*) You sit down. You've got to take care of yourself. You never ought to have gotten up tonight.

EILEEN. (*sits down*) I wanted to talk to you. (*She raises her face with a pitiful smile.* NICHOLLS *hurriedly moves back to his own chair.*)

NICHOLLS. (*almost brusquely*) I could have talked to you from the hall. You're silly to take chances just now. (EILEEN's *eyes show her hurt at his tone.*)

CARMODY. (*seeing his chance—hastily*) You'll be stayin' a while now, Fred? I'll take a walk down the road. I'm needin' a drink to clear my wits. (*He goes to the door in rear.*)

EILEEN. (*reproachfully*) You won't be long, Father? And please don't—you know.

CARMODY. (*exasperated*) Sure who wouldn't get drunk with all the sorrows of the world piled on him? (*He stamps out. A moment later the outside door bangs behind him.* EILEEN *sighs.* NICHOLLS *walks up and down with his eyes on the floor.*)

NICHOLLS. (*furious at* CARMODY *for having left him in this situation*) Honestly, Eileen, your father is the limit. I don't see how you stand for him. He's the most selfish—

EILEEN. (*gently*) Sssh! You mustn't, Fred. He just doesn't understand. (NICHOLLS *snorts disdainfully*) Don't! Let's not talk about him

345

now. We won't have many more evenings together for a long, long time. Did Father or the doctor tell you— (*She falters.*)

NICHOLLS. (*not looking at her—glumly*) Everything there was to tell, I guess.

EILEEN. (*hastening to comfort him*) You mustn't worry, Fred. Please don't! It'd make it so much worse for me if I thought you did. I'll be all right. I'll do exactly what they tell me, and in a few months I'll be back so fat and healthy you won't know me.

NICHOLLS. (*lamely*) Oh, there's no doubt of that. No one's worrying about your not getting well quick.

EILEEN. It won't be long. We can write often, and it isn't far away. You can come out and see me every Sunday—if you want to.

NICHOLLS. (*hastily*) Of course I will!

EILEEN. (*looking at his face searchingly*) Why do you act so funny? Why don't you sit down—here, by me? Don't you want to?

NICHOLLS. (*drawing up a chair by hers—flushing guiltily*) I—I'm all bawled up, Eileen. I don't know what I'm doing.

EILEEN. (*putting her hand on his knee*) Poor Fred! I'm so sorry I have to go. I didn't want to at first. I knew how hard it would be on Father and the kids—especially little Mary. (*Her voice trembles a bit*) And then the doctor said if I stayed I'd be putting them all in danger. He even ordered me not to kiss them any more. (*She bites her lips to restrain a sob—then coughs, a soft, husky cough.* NICHOLLS *shrinks away from her to the edge of his chair, his eyes shifting nervously with fright.* EILEEN *continues gently*) So I've got to go and get well, don't you see?

NICHOLLS. (*wetting his dry lips*) Yes—it's better.

EILEEN. (*sadly*) I'll miss the kids so much. Taking care of them has meant so much to me since Mother died. (*With a half-sob she suddenly throws her arms about his neck and hides her face on his shoulder. He shudders and fights against an impulse to push her away*) But I'll miss you most of all, Fred. (*She lifts her lips towards his, expecting a kiss. He seems about to kiss her—then averts his face with a shrinking movement, pretending he hasn't seen.* EILEEN's *eyes grow wide with horror. She throws herself back into her own chair, staring accusingly at* NICHOLLS. *She speaks chokingly*) Fred! Why—why didn't you kiss—what is it? Are you—afraid? (*With a moaning sound*) Oooh!

NICHOLLS. (*goaded by this accusation into a display of manhood, seizes her fiercely by the arms*) No! What—what d'you mean? (*He tries to kiss her but she hides her face.*)

EILEEN. (*in a muffled voice of hysterical self-accusation, pushing his head away*) No, no, you mustn't! The doctor told you not to, didn't he? Please don't, Fred! It would be awful if anything happened to you—through me. (NICHOLLS *gives up his attempts, recalled to caution by her words. She raises her face and tries to force a smile through her tears*) But you can kiss me on the forehead, Fred. That can't do any harm. (*His face crimson, he does so. She laughs hysterically*) It seems so silly—being kissed that way—by you. (*She gulps back a sob and continues to attempt to joke*) I'll have to get used to it, won't I?

CURTAIN

ACT ONE—SCENE TWO

THE *reception room of the Infirmary, a large, high-ceilinged room painted white, with oiled, hardwood floor. In the left wall, forward, a row of four windows. Farther back, the main entrance from the driveway, and another window. In the rear wall left, a glass partition looking out on the sleeping porch. A row of white beds, with the faces of patients barely peeping out from under piles of heavy bedclothes, can be seen. To the right of this partition, a bookcase, and a door leading to the hall past the patients' rooms. Farther right, another*

*door opening on the examining room. In the right wall, rear, a door
to the office. Farther forward, a row of windows. In front of the windows, a long dining table with chairs. On the left of the table, toward
the center of the room, a chimney with two open fireplaces, facing left
and right. Several wicker armchairs are placed around the fireplace
on the left in which a cheerful wood fire is crackling. To the left of
center, a round reading and writing table with a green-shaded electric
lamp. Other electric lights are in brackets around the walls. Easy
chairs stand near the table which is stacked with magazines. Rocking
chairs are placed here and there about the room, near the windows,
etc. A Victrola stands near the left wall, forward.*

It is nearing eight o'clock of a cold evening about a week later.

At the rise of the curtain STEPHEN MURRAY *is discovered sitting in a
chair in front of the fireplace, left.* MURRAY *is thirty years old—a tall,
slender, rather unusual-looking fellow with a pale face, sunken under
high cheek bones, lined about the eyes and mouth, jaded and worn
for one still so young. His intelligent, large hazel eyes have a tired,
dispirited expression in repose, but can quicken instantly with a con-
cealment mechanism of mocking, careless humor whenever his inner
privacy is threatened. His large mouth aids this process of protection
by a quick change from its set apathy to a cheerful grin of cynical good
nature. He gives off the impression of being somehow dissatisfied with
himself but not yet embittered enough by it to take it out on others.
His manner, as revealed by his speech—nervous, inquisitive, alert—
seems more an acquired quality than any part of his real nature. He
stoops a trifle, giving him a slightly round-shouldered appearance. He
is dressed in a shabby dark suit, baggy at the knees. He is staring into
the fire, dreaming, an open book lying unheeded on the arm of his
chair. The Victrola is whining out the last strains of Dvorak's Humor-
esque. In the doorway to the office,* MISS GILPIN *stands talking to* MISS
HOWARD. *The former is a slight, middle-aged woman with black hair,
and a strong, intelligent face, its expression of resolute efficiency
softened and made kindly by her warm, sympathetic gray eyes.* MISS

HOWARD *is tall, slender and blonde—decidedly pretty and provokingly conscious of it, yet with a certain air of seriousness underlying her apparent frivolity. She is twenty years old. The elder woman is dressed in the all white of a full-fledged nurse.* MISS HOWARD *wears the gray-blue uniform of one still in training. The record peters out.* MURRAY *sighs with relief but makes no move to get up and stop the grinding needle.* MISS HOWARD *hurries across to the machine.* MISS GILPIN *goes back into the office.*

MISS HOWARD. (*takes off the record, glancing at* MURRAY *with amused vexation*) It's a wonder you wouldn't stop this machine grinding itself to bits, Mr. Murray.

MURRAY. (*with a smile*) I was hoping the darn thing would bust. (MISS HOWARD *sniffs.* MURRAY *grins at her teasingly*) It keeps you from talking to me. That's the real music.

MISS HOWARD. (*comes over to his chair laughing*) I think you're a natural born kidder. All newspaper reporters are like that, I've heard.

MURRAY. You wrong me terribly. (*Then frowning*) And it isn't charitable to remind me of my job.

MISS HOWARD. (*surprised*) I think it's great to be able to write. You ought to be proud of it.

MURRAY. (*glumly*) I'm not. You can't call it writing—not what I did—small town stuff. (*Changing the subject*) Do you know when I'm to be moved to the shacks?

MISS HOWARD. In a few days, I guess. (MURRAY *grunts and moves nervously on his chair*) What's the matter? Don't you like us here at the Infirmary?

MURRAY. (*smiling*) Oh—you—yes! (*Then seriously*) I don't care for the atmosphere, though. (*He waves his hand toward the partition looking out on the porch*) All those people in bed out there on the porch seem so sick. It's depressing.

MISS HOWARD. All the patients have to come here first until Doctor

349

Stanton finds out whether they're well enough to be sent out to the shacks and cottages. And remember you're a patient.

MURRAY. I know it. But I don't feel as if I were—really sick like them.

MISS HOWARD. (*wisely*) None of them do, either.

MURRAY. (*after a moment's reflection—cynically*) Yes, I suppose it's that pipe dream keeps us all going, eh?

MISS HOWARD. Well, you ought to be thankful. (*Lowering her voice*) Shall I tell you a secret? I've seen your chart and *you've* no cause to worry. Doctor Stanton joked about it. He said you were too uninteresting—there was so little the matter with you.

MURRAY. (*pleased but pretending indifference*) Humph! He's original in that opinion.

MISS HOWARD. I know it's hard your being the only one up the week you've been here; but there's another patient due today. Maybe she'll be well enough to be around with you. (*With a quick glance at her wrist watch*) She can't be coming unless she got in on the last train.

MURRAY. (*interestedly*) It's a she, eh?

MISS HOWARD. Yes.

MURRAY. (*grinning provokingly*) Young?

MISS HOWARD. Eighteen, I believe. (*Seeing his grin—with feigned pique*) I suppose you'll be asking if she's pretty next! Her name is Carmody, that's the only other thing I know. So there!

MISS GILPIN. (*appearing in the office doorway*) Miss Howard.

MISS HOWARD. Yes, Miss Gilpin. (*In an aside to* MURRAY *as she leaves him*) It's time for those horrid diets. (*She hurries back into the office.* MURRAY *stares into the fire.* MISS HOWARD *reappears from the office and goes out by the door to the hall, rear. Carriage wheels are heard from the driveway in front of the house on the left. They stop. After a pause there is a sharp rap on the door and a bell rings insistently. Men's muffled voices are heard in argument.* MURRAY *turns curiously in his chair.* MISS GILPIN *comes from the office and walks quickly to*

350

the door, unlocking and opening it. EILEEN *enters, followed by* NICHOLLS, *who is carrying her suitcase, and by her father.*)

EILEEN. I'm Miss Carmody. I believe Doctor Gaynor wrote—

MISS GILPIN. (*taking her hand—with kind affability*) We've been expecting you all day. How do you do? I'm Miss Gilpin. You came on the last train, didn't you?

EILEEN. (*heartened by the other woman's kindness*) Yes. This is my father, Miss Gilpin—and Mr. Nicholls. (MISS GILPIN *shakes hands cordially with the two men who are staring about the room in embarrassment.* CARMODY *has very evidently been drinking. His voice is thick and his face puffed and stupid.* NICHOLLS' *manner is that of one who is accomplishing a necessary but disagreeable duty with the best grace possible, but is frightfully eager to get it over and done with.* CARMODY'S *condition embarrasses him acutely and when he glances at him it is with hatred and angry disgust.*)

MISS GILPIN. (*indicating the chairs in front of the windows on the left, forward*) Won't you gentlemen sit down? (CARMODY *grunts sullenly and plumps himself into the one nearest the door.* NICHOLLS *hesitates, glancing down at the suitcase he carries.* MISS GILPIN *turns to* EILEEN) And now we'll get you settled immediately. Your room is all ready for you. If you'll follow me— (*She turns toward the door in rear, center.*)

EILEEN. Let me take the suitcase now, Fred.

MISS GILPIN. (*as he is about to hand it to her—decisively*) No, my dear, you mustn't. Put the case right down there, Mr. Nicholls. I'll have it taken to Miss Carmody's room in a moment. (*She shakes her finger at* EILEEN *with kindly admonition*) That's the first rule you'll have to learn. Never exert yourself or tax your strength. You'll find laziness is a virtue instead of a vice with us.

EILEEN. (*confused*) I— I didn't know—

MISS GILPIN. (*smiling*) Of course you didn't. And now if you'll come with me I'll show you your room We'll have a little chat there and I can explain all the other important rules in a second. The gentlemen

351

can make themselves comfortable in the meantime. We won't be gone more than a moment.

NICHOLLS. (*feeling called upon to say something*) Yes—we'll wait—certainly, we're all right. (CARMODY *remains silent, glowering at the fire.* NICHOLLS *sits down beside him.* MISS GILPIN *and* EILEEN *go out.* MURRAY *switches his chair so he can observe the two men out of the corner of his eye while pretending to be absorbed in his book.*)

CARMODY. (*looking about shiftily and reaching for the inside pocket of his overcoat*) I'll be havin' a nip now we're alone, and that cacklin' hen gone. (*He pulls out a pint flask, half full.*)

NICHOLLS. (*excitedly*) Put that bottle away! (*In a whisper*) Don't you see that fellow in the chair there?

CARMODY. (*taking a big drink*) Ah, I'm not mindin' a man at all. Sure I'll bet it's himself would be likin' a taste of the same. (*He appears about to get up and invite* MURRAY *to join him but* NICHOLLS *grabs his arm.*)

NICHOLLS. (*with a frightened look at* MURRAY *who appears buried in his book*) Stop it, you— Don't you know he's probably a patient and they don't allow them—

CARMODY. (*scornfully*) It's queer they'd be allowin' the sick ones to read books when I'll bet it's the same lazy readin' in the house brought the half of them down with the consumption itself. (*Raising his voice*) I'm thinkin' this whole shebang is a big, thievin' fake—and I've always thought so.

NICHOLLS. (*furiously*) Put that bottle away, damn it! And don't shout. You're not in a barrel-house.

CARMODY. (*with provoking calm*) I'll put it back when I'm ready, not before, and no lip from you!

NICHOLLS. (*with fierce disgust*) You're drunk now.

CARMODY. (*raging*) Drunk, am I? Is it the like of a young jackass like you that's still wet behind the ears to be tellin' me I'm drunk?

NICHOLLS. (*half-rising from his chair—pleadingly*) For heaven's

352

sake, Mr. Carmody, remember where we are and don't raise any rumpus. What'll Eileen say?

CARMODY. (*puts the bottle away hastily, mumbling to himself—then glowers about the room scornfully with blinking eyes*) It's a grand hotel this is, I'm thinkin', for the rich to be takin' their ease, and not a hospital for the poor, but the poor has to pay for it.

NICHOLLS. (*fearful of another outbreak*) Sshh!

CARMODY. Don't be shshin' at me? I'd make Eileen come back out of this tonight if that divil of a doctor didn't have me by the throat.

NICHOLLS. (*glancing at him nervously*) I wonder how soon she'll be back? We'll have to hurry to make that last train.

CARMODY. (*angrily*) Is it anxious to get out of her sight you are, and you engaged to marry her? (NICHOLLS *flushes guiltily.* MURRAY *pricks up his ears and stares over at* NICHOLLS. *The latter meets his glance, scowls, and hurriedly averts his eyes.* CARMODY *goes on accusingly*) Sure, it's no heart at all you have—and her your sweetheart for years —and her sick with the consumption—and you wild to run away and leave her alone.

NICHOLLS. (*springing to his feet—furiously*) That's a—! (*He controls himself with an effort. His voice trembles*) You're not responsible for the idiotic things you're saying or I'd— (*He turns away, seeking some escape from the old man's tongue*) I'll see if the man is still there with the rig. (*He goes to the door on left and goes out.*)

CARMODY. (*following him with his eyes*) Go to hell, for all I'm preventin'. You've got no guts of a man in you. (*He addresses* MURRAY *with the good nature inspired by the flight of* NICHOLLS) Is it true you're one of the consumptives, young fellow?

MURRAY. (*delighted by this speech—with a grin*) Yes, I'm one of them.

CARMODY. My name's Carmody. What's yours, then?

MURRAY. Murray.

CARMODY. (*slapping his thigh*) Irish as Paddy's pig! (MURRAY *nods.*

353

CARMODY *brightens and grows confidential*) I'm glad to be knowin' you're one of us. You can keep an eye on Eileen.

MURRAY. I'll be glad to do all I can.

CARMODY. Thanks to you—though it's a grand life she'll be havin' here from the fine look of the place. (*With whining self-pity*) It's me it's hard on, God help me, with four small children and me widowed, and havin' to hire a woman to come in and look after them and the house now that Eileen's sick; and payin' for her curin' in this place, and me with only a bit of money in the bank for my old age. That's hard, now, on a man, and who'll say it isn't?

MURRAY. (*made uncomfortable by this confidence*) Hard luck always comes in bunches. (*To head off* CARMODY *who is about to give vent to more woe—quickly, with a glance toward the door from the hall*) If I'm not mistaken, here comes your daughter now.

CARMODY. (*as* EILEEN *comes into the room*) I'll make you acquainted. Eileen! (*She comes over to them, embarrassed to find her father in his condition so chummy with a stranger.* MURRAY *rises to his feet*) This is Mr. Murray, Eileen. He's Irish and he'll put you on to the ropes of the place. He's got the consumption, too, God pity him.

EILEEN. (*distressed*) Oh, Father, how can you— (*With a look at* MURRAY *which pleads for her father*) I'm glad to meet you, Mr. Murray.

MURRAY. (*with a straight glance at her which is so frankly admiring that she flushes and drops her eyes*) I'm glad to meet you. (*The front door is opened and* NICHOLLS *re-appears, shivering with the cold. He stares over at the others with ill-concealed irritation.*)

CARMODY. (*noticing him—with malicious satisfaction*) Oho, here you are again. (NICHOLLS *scowls and turns away.* CARMODY *addresses his daughter with a sly wink at* MURRAY) I thought Fred was slidin' down hill to the train, and him so desperate hurried to get away from here. Look at the knees on him clappin' together with the great fear he'll be catchin' a sickness in this place! (NICHOLLS, *his guilty conscience stabbed to the quick, turns pale with impotent rage.*)

EILEEN. (*remonstrating pitifully*) Father! Please! (*She hurries over to* NICHOLLS) Oh, please don't mind him, Fred! You know what he is when he's drinking.

NICHOLLS. (*thickly*) That's all right—for you to say. But I won't forget—I'm sick and tired standing for—I'm not used to—such people.

EILEEN. (*shrinking from him*) Fred!

NICHOLLS. (*with a furious glance at* MURRAY) Before that cheap slob, too.

EILEEN. (*faintly*) He seems—very nice.

NICHOLLS. You've got your eyes set on him already, have you?

EILEEN. Fred!

NICHOLLS. Well, go ahead if you want to. I don't care. I'll— (*Startled by the look of anguish which comes over her face, he hastily swallows his words. He takes out watch—fiercely*) We'll miss that train, damn it!

EILEEN. (*in a stricken tone*) Oh, Fred! (*Then forcing back her tears she calls to* CARMODY *in a strained voice*) Father! You'll have to go now.

CARMODY. (*shaking hands with* MURRAY) Keep your eye on her. I'll be out soon to see her and you and me'll have another chin.

MURRAY. Glad to. Good-by for the present. (*He walks to windows on the far right, turning his back considerately on their leave-taking.*)

EILEEN. (*comes to* CARMODY *and hangs on his arm as they proceed to the door*) Be sure and kiss them all for me—and bring them out to see me as soon as you can, Father, please! And don't forget to tell Mrs. Brennan all the directions I gave you coming out on the train. I told her but she mightn't remember—about Mary's bath—and to give Tom his—

CARMODY. (*impatiently*) Hasn't she brought up brats of her own, and doesn't she know the way of it?

EILEEN. (*helplessly*) Never mind telling her, then. I'll write to her.

CARMODY. You'd better not. She'll not wish you mixin' in with her work and tellin' her how to do it.

EILEEN. (*aghast*) *Her* work! (*She seems at the end of her tether—*

355

wrung too dry for any further emotion. She kisses her father at the door with indifference and speaks calmly) Good-by, Father.

CARMODY. (*in a whining tone of injury*) A cold kiss! Is your heart a stone? (*Drunken tears well from his eyes and he blubbers*) And your own father going back to a lone house with a stranger in it!

EILEEN. (*wearily in a dead voice*) You'll miss your train, Father.

CARMODY. (*raging in a second*) I'm off, then! Come on, Fred. It's no welcome we have with her here in this place—and a great curse on this day I brought her to it! (*He stamps out.*)

EILEEN. (*in the same dead tone*) Good-by, Fred.

NICHOLLS. (*repenting his words of a moment ago—confusedly*) I'm sorry, Eileen—for what I said. I didn't mean—you know what your father is—excuse me, won't you?

EILEEN. (*without feeling*) Yes.

NICHOLLS. And I'll be out soon—in a week if I can make it. Well then,—good-by for the present. (*He bends down as if to kiss her but she shrinks back out of his reach.*)

EILEEN. (*a faint trace of mockery in her weary voice*) No, Fred. Remember you mustn't now.

NICHOLLS. (*in an instant huff*) Oh, if that's the way you feel about — (*He strides out and slams the door viciously behind him. EILEEN walks slowly back toward the fireplace, her face fixed in the dead calm of despair. As she sinks into one of the armchairs, the strain becomes too much. She breaks down, hiding her face in her hands, her frail shoulders heaving with the violence of her sobs. At this sound, MURRAY turns from the windows and comes over near her chair.*)

MURRAY. (*after watching her for a moment—in an embarrassed tone of sympathy*) Come on, Miss Carmody, that'll never do. I know it's hard at first—but— It isn't so bad up here—really—once you get used to it! (*The shame she feels at giving way in the presence of a stranger only adds to her loss of control and she sobs heartbrokenly. MURRAY walks up and down nervously, visibly nonplussed and upset.*

Finally he hits upon something) One of the nurses will be in any minute. You don't want them to see you like this.

EILEEN. (*chokes back her sobs and finally raises her face and attempts a smile*) I'm sorry—to make such a sight of myself.

MURRAY. (*jocularly*) Well, they say a cry does you a lot of good.

EILEEN. (*forcing a smile*) I do feel—better.

MURRAY. (*staring at her with a quizzical smile—cynically*) You shouldn't take those lovers' squabbles so seriously. Tomorrow he'll be sorry. He'll write begging forgiveness. Result—all serene again.

EILEEN. (*a shadow of pain on her face—with dignity*) Don't—please.

MURRAY. (*angry at himself—hanging his head contritely*) Pardon me. I'm rude sometimes—before I know it. (*He shakes off his confusion with a renewed attempt at a joking tone*) You can blame your father for any breaks I make. He told me to see that you behaved.

EILEEN. (*with a genuine smile*) Oh, Father! (*Flushing*) You mustn't mind anything he said tonight.

MURRAY. (*thoughtlessly*) Yes, he was well lit up. I envied him. (EILEEN *looks very shamefaced.* MURRAY *sees it and exclaims in exasperation at himself*) Darn! There I go again putting my foot in it! (*With an irrepressible grin*) I ought to have my tongue operated on —that's what's the matter with me. (*He laughs and throws himself in a chair.*)

EILEEN. (*forced in spite of herself to smile with him*) You're candid, at any rate, Mr. Murray.

MURRAY. I said I envied him his jag and that's the truth. The same candor compels me to confess that I was pickled to the gills myself when I arrived here. Fact! I made love to all the nurses and generally disgraced myself—and had a wonderful time.

EILEEN. I suppose it does make you forget your troubles.

MURRAY. (*waving this aside*) I didn't want to forget—not for a second. I wasn't drowning my sorrow. I was hilariously celebrating.

EILEEN. (*astonished—by this time quite interested in this queer fel-*

357

low to the momentary forgetfulness of her own grief) Celebrating—coming here? But—aren't you sick?

MURRAY. Yes, of course. (*Confidentially*) But it's only a matter of time when I'll be all right again. I hope it won't be too soon.

EILEEN. (*with wide eyes*) I wonder if you really mean—

MURRAY. I sure do—every word of it!

EILEEN. (*puzzled*) I can't understand how anyone could— (*With a worried glance over her shoulder*) I think I'd better look for Miss Gilpin, hadn't I? She may wonder— (*She half rises from her chair.*)

MURRAY. (*quickly*) No. Please don't go yet. (*She glances at him irresolutely, then resumes her chair*) I'll see to it that you don't fracture any rules. (*Hitching his chair nearer hers,—impulsively*) In all charity to me you've got to stick awhile. I haven't had a chance to really talk to a soul for a week. You found what I said a while ago hard to believe, didn't you?

EILEEN. (*with a smile*) You said you hoped you wouldn't get well too soon!

MURRAY. And I meant it! This place is honestly like heaven to me —a lonely heaven till your arrival. (EILEEN *looks embarrassed*) And why wouldn't it be? Just let me tell you what I was getting away from — (*With a sudden laugh full of weary bitterness*) Do you know what it means to work from seven at night till three in the morning on a morning newspaper in a town of twenty thousand people—for *ten years?* No. You don't. You can't. But what it did to me—it made me happy—yes, happy!—to get out here!

EILEEN. (*looking at him curiously*) But I always thought being a reporter was so interesting.

MURRAY. (*with a cynical laugh*) On a small town rag? A month of it, perhaps, when you're new to the game. But ten years! With only a raise of a couple of dollars every blue moon or so, and a weekly spree on Saturday night to vary the monotony. (*He laughs again*) Interesting, eh? Getting the dope on the Social of the Queen Esther Circle in the basement of the Methodist Episcopal Church, unable to sleep through a meeting of the Common Council on account of the noisy oratory caused by John Smith's application for a permit to build a house; making a note that a tugboat towed two barges loaded with coal up the river, that Mrs. Perkins spent a week-end with relatives in Hickville, that John Jones— Oh help! Why go on? I'm a broken man. God, how I used to pray that our Congressman would commit suicide, or the Mayor murder his wife—just to be able to write a real story!

EILEEN. (*with a smile*) Is it as bad as that? But weren't there other things that were interesting?

MURRAY. (*decidedly*) Nope. Never anything new—and I knew everyone and everything in town by heart years ago. (*With sudden bitterness*) Oh, it was my own fault. Why didn't I get out of it? Well, I was always going to—tomorrow—and tomorrow never came. I got in a rut—and stayed put. People seem to get that way, somehow—in that town. It took T. B. to blast me loose.

EILEEN. (*wonderingly*) But—your family—

MURRAY. I haven't much of a family left. My mother died when I was a kid. My father—he was a lawyer—died when I was nineteen, just about to go to college. He left nothing, so I went to work instead. I've two sisters, respectably married and living in another part of the state. We don't get along—but they're paying for me here, so I suppose I've no kick. (*Cynically*) A family wouldn't have changed things. From what I've seen that blood-thicker-than-water dope is all wrong. It's thinner than table-d'hôte soup. You may have seen a bit of that truth in your own case already.

EILEEN. (*shocked*) How can you say that? You don't know—

MURRAY. Don't I, though? Wait till you've been here three months or four. You'll see then!

EILEEN. (*angrily, her lips trembling*) You must be crazy to say such things! (*Fighting back her tears*) Oh, I think it's hateful—when you see how badly I feel!

MURRAY. (*in acute confusion—stammering*) Look here, Miss Carmody, I didn't mean to— Listen—don't feel mad at me, please. I was only talking. I'm like that. You mustn't take it seriously.

EILEEN. (*still resentful*) I don't see how you can talk—when you've just said you had no family of your own, really.

MURRAY. (*eager to return to her good graces*) Of course I don't know. I was just talking regardless for the fun of it.

EILEEN. (*after a pause*) Hasn't either of your sisters any children?

MURRAY. One of them has—two squally little brats.

EILEEN. (*disapprovingly*) You don't like babies?

MURRAY. (*bluntly*) No. (*Then with a grin at her shocked face*) I don't get them. They're something I can't seem to get acquainted with.

EILEEN. (*with a smile, indulgently*) You're a funny person. (*Then with a superior motherly air*) No wonder you couldn't understand how badly I feel. (*With a tender smile*) I've four of them—my brothers and sisters—though they're not what you'd call babies, except to me. I've been a mother to them now for a whole year—ever since our mother died. (*Sadly*) And I don't know how they'll ever get along while I'm away.

MURRAY. (*cynically*) Oh, they'll— (*He checks what he was going to say and adds lamely*)—get along somehow.

EILEEN. (*with the same superior tone*) It's easy for you to say that. You don't know how children grow to depend on you for everything. You're not a woman.

MURRAY. (*with a grin*) Are you? (*Then with a chuckle*) You're as old as the pyramids, aren't you? I feel like a little boy. Won't you adopt me, too?

EILEEN. (*flushing, with a shy smile*) Someone ought to. (*Quickly changing the subject*) Do you know, I can't get over what you said about hating your work so? I should think it would be wonderful— to be able to write things.

MURRAY. My job had nothing to do with writing. To write—really write—yes, that's something worth trying for. That's what I've always meant to have a stab at. I've run across ideas enough for stories—that sounded good to me, anyway. (*With a forced laugh*) But—like everything else—I never got down to it. I started one or two—but—either I thought I didn't have the time or— (*He shrugs his shoulders.*)

EILEEN. Well, you've plenty of time now, haven't you?

MURRAY. (*instantly struck by this suggestion*) You mean— I could write up here? (*She nods. His face lights up with enthusiasm*) Say! That is an idea! Thank you! I'd never have had sense enough to have thought of that myself. (EILEEN *flushes with pleasure*) Sure there's time—nothing but time up here—

EILEEN. Then you seriously think you'll try it?

MURRAY. (*determinedly*) Yes. Why not? I've got to try and do something real sometime, haven't I? I've no excuse not to, now. My mind isn't sick.

EILEEN. (*excitedly*) That'll be wonderful!

MURRAY. (*confidently*) Listen. I've had ideas for a series of short stories for the last couple of years—small town experiences, some of them actual. I know that life too darn well. I ought to be able to write about it. And if I can sell one—to the *Post,* say—I'm sure they'd take the others, too. And then— I should worry! It'd be easy sailing. But you must promise to help—play critic for me—read them and tell me where they're rotten.

EILEEN. (*pleased but protesting*) Oh, no, I'd never dare. I don't know anything—

MURRAY. Yes, you do. And you started me off on this thing, so you've got to back me up now. (*Suddenly*) Say, I wonder if they'd let me have a typewriter up here?

EILEEN. It'd be fine if they would. I'd like to have one, too—to practice.

MURRAY. I don't see why they wouldn't allow it. You're not sick enough to be kept in bed, I'm sure of that.

EILEEN. I— I don't know—

MURRAY. Here! None of that! You just think you're not and you won't be. Say, I'm keen on that typewriter idea.

EILEEN. (*eagerly*) And I could type your stories after you've written them! I *could* help that way.

MURRAY. (*smiling*) But I'm quite able— (*Then seeing how interested she is he adds hurriedly*) That'd be great! I've always been a bum at a machine. And I'd be willing to pay whatever— (MISS GILPIN *enters from the rear and walks toward them.*)

EILEEN. (*quickly*) Oh, no! I'd be glad to get the practice. I wouldn't accept— (*She coughs slightly.*)

MURRAY. (*with a laugh*) Maybe, after you've read my stuff, you won't type it at any price.

MISS GILPIN. Miss Carmody, may I speak to you for a moment, please? (*She takes* EILEEN *aside and talks to her in low tones of admonition.* EILEEN's *face falls. She nods a horrified acquiescence.* MISS GILPIN *leaves her and goes into the office, rear.*)

MURRAY. (*as* EILEEN *comes back—noticing her perturbation—kindly*) Well? Now, what's the trouble?

EILEEN. (*her lips trembling*) She told me I mustn't forget to shield my mouth with my handkerchief when I cough.

MURRAY. (*consolingly*) Yes, that's one of the rules, you know.

EILEEN. (*falteringly*) She said they'd give me—a—cup to carry around— (*She stops, shuddering.*)

MURRAY. (*easily*) It's not as bad as it sounds. They're only little paste-board things you carry in your pocket.

EILEEN. (*as if speaking to herself*) It's so horrible. (*She holds out her hand to* MURRAY) I'm to go to my room now. Good-night, Mr. Murray.

MURRAY. (*holding her hand for a moment—earnestly*) Don't mind your first impressions here. You'll look on everything as a matter of course in a few days. I felt your way at first. (*He drops her hand and shakes his finger at her*) Mind your guardian, now! (*She forces a trembling smile*) See you at breakfast. Good-night. (EILEEN *goes out to the hall in rear.* MISS HOWARD *comes in from the door just after her, carrying a glass of milk.*)

MISS HOWARD. Almost bedtime, Mr. Murray. Here's your diet. (*He takes the glass. She smiles at him provokingly*) Well, is it love at first sight?

MURRAY. (*with a grin*) Sure thing! You can consider yourself heartlessly jilted. (*He turns and raises his glass toward the door through which* EILEEN *has just gone, as if toasting her.*)

> "A glass of milk, and thou
>   Coughing beside me in the wilderness—
>   Ah—wilderness were Paradise enow!"

(*He takes a sip of milk.*)

MISS HOWARD. (*peevishly*) That's old stuff, Mr. Murray. A patient at Saranac wrote that parody.

MURRAY. (*maliciously*) Aha, you've discovered it's a parody, have you, you sly minx! (MISS HOWARD *turns from him huffily and walks back towards the office, her chin in the air.*)

CURTAIN

ACT TWO—SCENE ONE

THE *assembly room of the main building of the sanatorium—early in the morning of a fine day in June, four months later. The room is large, light and airy, painted a fresh white. On the left forward, an armchair. Farther back, a door opening on the main hall. To the rear of this door a pianola on a raised platform. In back of the pianola, a door leading into the office. In the rear wall, a long series of French windows looking out on the lawn, with wooded hills in the far background. Shrubs in flower grow immediately outside the windows. Inside, there is a row of potted plants. In the right wall, rear, four windows. Farther forward, a long, well-filled bookcase, and a doorway leading into the dining room. Following the walls, but about five feet out from them a stiff line of chairs placed closely against each other forms a sort of right-angled auditorium of which the large, square table that stands at center, forward, would seem to be the stage.*

From the dining room comes the clatter of dishes, the confused murmur of many voices, male and female—all the mingled sounds of a crowd of people at a meal.

After the curtain rises, DOCTOR STANTON *enters from the hall, followed by a visitor,* MR. SLOAN, *and the assistant physician,* DOCTOR SIMMS. DOCTOR STANTON *is a handsome man of forty-five or so with a grave, care-lined, studious face lightened by a kindly, humorous smile. His gray eyes, saddened by the suffering they have witnessed, have the sympathetic quality of real understanding. The look they give is full of companionship, the courage-renewing, human companionship of a hope which is shared. He speaks with a slight Southern accent, soft and slurring.* DOCTOR SIMMS *is a tall, angular young man with a long, sallow face and a sheepish, self-conscious grin.* MR. SLOAN *is fifty, short and stout, well dressed—one of the successful*

364

business men whose endowments have made the Hill Farm a possibility.

STANTON. (*as they enter*) This is the general assembly room, Mr. Sloan—where the patients of both sexes are allowed to congregate together after meals, for diets, and in the evening.

SLOAN. (*looking around him*) Couldn't be more pleasant, I must say. (*He walks where he can take a peep into the dining room*) Ah, they're all at breakfast, I see.

STANTON. (*smiling*) Yes, and with no lack of appetite, let me tell you. (*With a laugh of proud satisfaction*) They'd sure eat us out of house and home at one sitting, if we'd give them the opportunity.

SLOAN. (*with a smile*) That's fine. (*With a nod toward the dining room*) The ones in there are the sure cures, aren't they?

STANTON. (*a shadow coming over his face*) Strictly speaking, there are no sure cures in this disease, Mr. Sloan. When we permit a patient to return to take up his or her activities in the world, the patient is what we call an arrested case. The disease is overcome, quiescent; the wound is healed over. It's then up to the patient to so take care of himself that this condition remains permanent. It isn't hard for them to do this, usually. Just ordinary, bull-headed common sense— added to what they've learned here—is enough. And the precautions we teach them to take don't diminish their social usefulness in the slightest, either, as I can prove by our statistics of former patients. (*With a smile*) It's rather early in the morning for statistics, though.

MR. SLOAN. (*with a wave of the hand*) Oh, you needn't. Your reputation in that respect, Doctor— (STANTON *inclines his head in acknowledgment.* SLOAN *jerks his thumb toward the dining room*) But the ones in there *are* getting well, aren't they?

STANTON. To all appearances, yes. You don't dare swear to it, though. Sometimes, just when a case looks most favorable, there's a sudden, unforeseen breakdown and they have to be sent back to bed, or, if it's very serious, back to the Infirmary again. These are the exceptions, however, not the rule. You can bank on most of those eaters being out in the world and usefully employed within six months.

SLOAN. You couldn't say more than that. (*Abruptly*) But—the unfortunate ones—do you have many deaths?

STANTON. (*with a frown*) No. We're under a very hard, almost cruel imperative which prevents that. If, at the end of six months, a case shows no response to treatment, continues to go down hill—if, in a word, it seems hopeless—we send them away, to one of the State Farms if they have no private means. (*Apologetically*) You see, this sanatorium is overcrowded and has a long waiting list most of the time of others who demand their chance for life. We have to make places for them. We have no time to waste on incurables. There are other places for them—and sometimes, too, a change is beneficial and they pick up in new surroundings. You never can tell. But we're bound by the rule. It may seem cruel—but it's as near justice to all concerned as we can come.

SLOAN. (*soberly*) I see. (*His eyes fall on the pianola—in surprise*) Ah—a piano.

STANTON. (*replying to the other's thought*) Yes, the patients play and sing. (*With a smile*) If you'd call the noise they make by those terms. They'd dance, too, if we permitted it. There's only one song taboo—Home, Sweet Home—for obvious reasons.

SLOAN. I see. (*With a final look around*) Did I understand you to say this is the only place where the sexes are permitted to mingle?

STANTON. Yes, sir.

SLOAN. (*with a smile*) Not much chance for a love affair, then.

STANTON. (*seriously*) We do our best to prevent them. We even have a strict rule which allows us to step in and put a stop to any intimacy which grows beyond the casual. People up here, Mr. Sloan, are expected to put aside all ideas except the one—getting well.

SLOAN. (*somewhat embarrassed*) A damn good rule, too, under the circumstances.

STANTON. (*with a laugh*) Yes, we're strictly anti-Cupid, sir, from top to bottom. (*Turning to the door to the hall*) And now, if you don't mind, Mr. Sloan, I'm going to turn you footloose to wander about the grounds on an unconducted tour. Today is my busy morning—Saturday. We weigh each patient immediately after breakfast.

SLOAN. Every week?

STANTON. Every Saturday. You see we depend on fluctuations in weight to tell us a lot about the patient's condition. If they gain, or stay at normal, all's usually well. If they lose week after week, we keep careful watch. It's a sign that something's wrong.

SLOAN. (*with a smile*) Well, you just shoo me off wherever you please and go on with the good work. I'll be glad of a ramble in the open.

STANTON. After the weighing is over, sir, I'll be free to— (*His words are lost as the three go out. A moment later,* EILEEN *enters from the dining room. She has grown stouter, her face has more of a healthy, out-of-door color, but there is still about her the suggestion of being worn down by a burden too oppressive for her strength. She is dressed in shirtwaist and dark skirt. She goes to the armchair, left forward, and sinks down on it. She is evidently in a state of nervous depression; she twists her fingers together in her lap; her eyes stare sadly before her; she clenches her upper lip with her teeth to prevent its trembling. She has hardly regained control over herself when* STEPHEN MURRAY *comes in hurriedly from the dining room and, seeing her at his first glance, walks quickly over to her chair. He is the picture of health, his figure has filled out solidly, his tanned face beams with suppressed exultation.*)

MURRAY. (*excitedly*) Eileen! I saw you leave your table. I've something to tell you. I didn't get a chance last night after the mail came. Just listen, Eileen—it's too good to be true—but in that mail—guess what?

EILEEN. (*forgetting her depression—with an excited smile*) I know! You've sold your story!

MURRAY. (*triumphantly*) Go to the head of the class. What d'you

367

know about that for luck! My first, too—and only the third magazine I sent it to! (*He cuts a joyful caper.*)

EILEEN. (*happily*) Isn't that wonderful, Stephen! But I knew all the time you would. The story's so good.

MURRAY. Well, you might have known but I didn't think there was a chance in the world. And as for being good— (*With superior air*) —wait till I turn loose with the real big ones, the kind I'm going to write. Then I'll make them sit up and take notice. They can't stop me now. And I haven't told you the best part. The editor wrote saying how much he liked the yarn and asked me for more of the same kind.

EILEEN. And you've the three others about the same person—just as good, too! (*She claps her hands delightedly.*)

MURRAY. And I can send them out right away. They're all typed, thanks to you. That's what's brought me luck, I know. I never had a bit by myself. (*Then, after a quick glance around to make sure they are alone, he bends down and kisses her*) There! A token of gratitude —even if it is against the rules.

EILEEN. (*flushing—with timid happiness*) Stephen! You mustn't! They'll see.

MURRAY. (*boldly*) Let them!

EILEEN. But you know—they've warned us against being so much together, already.

MURRAY. Let them! We'll be out of this prison soon. (EILEEN *shakes her head sadly but he does not notice*) Oh, I wish you could leave when I do. We'd have some celebration together.

EILEEN. (*her lips trembling*) I was thinking last night—that you'd be going away. You look so well. Do you think—they'll let you go— soon?

MURRAY. You bet I do. I caught Stanton in the hall last night and asked him if I could go.

EILEEN. (*anxiously*) What did he say?

MURRAY. He only smiled and said: "We'll see if you gain weight tomorrow." As if that mattered now! Why, I'm way above normal as it is! But you know Stanton—always putting you off.

EILEEN. (*slowly*) Then—if you gain today—

MURRAY. He'll let me go. I'm going to insist on it.

EILEEN. Then—you'll leave—?

MURRAY. The minute I can get packed.

EILEEN. (*trying to force a smile*) Oh, I'm so glad—for your sake; but—I'm selfish—it'll be so lonely here without you.

MURRAY. (*consolingly*) You'll be going away yourself before long. (EILEEN *shakes her head. He goes on without noticing, wrapped in his own success*) Oh, Eileen, you can't imagine all it opens up for me —selling that story. I can go straight to New York, and live, and meet real people who are doing things. I can take my time, and try and do the work I hope to. (*Feelingly*) You don't know how grateful I am to you, Eileen—how you've helped me. Oh, I don't mean just the typing, I mean your encouragement, your faith! The stories would never have been written if it hadn't been for you.

EILEEN. (*choking back a sob*) I didn't do—anything.

MURRAY. (*staring down at her—with rough kindliness*) Here, here, that'll never do! You're not weeping about it, are you, silly? (*He pats her on the shoulder*) What's the matter, Eileen? You didn't eat a thing this morning. I was watching you. (*With kindly severity*) That's no way to gain weight, you know. You'll have to feed up. Do you hear what your guardian commands, eh?

EILEEN. (*with dull hopelessness*) I know I'll lose again. I've been losing steadily the past three weeks.

MURRAY. Here! Don't you dare talk that way! Why, you've been picking up wonderfully—until just lately. Even the old Doc has told you how much he admired your pluck, and how much better you were getting. You're not going to quit now, are you?

EILEEN. (*despairingly*) Oh, I don't care! I don't care—now.

MURRAY. Now? What do you mean by that? What's happened to make things any different?

369

EILEEN. (*evasively*) Oh—nothing. Don't ask me, Stephen.

MURRAY. (*with sudden anger*) I don't have to ask you. I can guess. Another letter from home—or from that ass, eh?

EILEEN. (*shaking her head*) No, it isn't that. (*She looks at him as if imploring him to comprehend.*)

MURRAY. (*furiously*). Of course, you'd deny it. You always do. But don't you suppose I've got eyes? It's been the same damn thing all the time you've been here. After every nagging letter—thank God they don't write often any more!—you've been all in; and after their Sunday visits—you can thank God they've been few, too—you're utterly knocked out. It's a shame!

EILEEN. Stephen!

MURRAY. (*relentlessly*) They've done nothing but worry and torment you and do their best to keep you from getting well.

EILEEN. (*faintly*) You're not fair, Stephen.

MURRAY. Rot! When it isn't your father grumbling about expense, it's the kids, or that stupid housekeeper, or that slick Aleck, Nicholls, with his cowardly lies. Which is it this time?

EILEEN. (*pitifully*) None of them.

MURRAY. (*explosively*) But him, especially—the dirty cad! Oh, I've got a rich notion to pay a call on that gentleman when I leave and tell him what I think of him.

EILEEN. (*quickly*) No—you mustn't ever! He's not to blame. If you knew— (*She stops, lowering her eyes in confusion.*)

MURRAY. (*roughly*) Knew what? You make me sick, Eileen—always finding excuses for him. I never could understand what a girl like you could see— But what's the use? I've said all this before. You're wasting yourself on a— (*Rudely*) Love must be blind. And yet you say you don't love him, really?

EILEEN. (*shaking her head—helplessly*) But I do—like Fred. We've been good friends so many years. I don't want to hurt him—his pride—

MURRAY. That's the same as answering no to my question. Then, if you don't love him, why don't you write and tell him to go to—break it off? (EILEEN *bows her head but doesn't reply. Irritated,* MURRAY *continues brutally*) Are you afraid it would break his heart? Don't be a fool! The only way you could do that would be to deprive him of his meals.

EILEEN. (*springing to her feet—distractedly*) Please stop, Stephen! You're cruel! And you've been so kind—the only real friend I've had up here. Don't spoil it all now.

MURRAY. (*remorsefully*) I'm sorry, Eileen. I won't say another word. (*Irritably*) Still someone ought to say or do something to put a stop to—

EILEEN. (*with a broken laugh*) Never mind. Everything will stop—soon, now!

MURRAY. (*suspiciously*) What do you mean?

EILEEN. (*with an attempt at a careless tone*) Nothing. If you can't see— (*She turns to him with sudden intensity*) Oh, Stephen, if you only knew how wrong you are about everything you've said. It's all true; but it isn't that—any of it—any more— that's— Oh, I can't tell you!

MURRAY. (*with great interest*) Please do, Eileen!

EILEEN. (*with a helpless laugh*) No.

MURRAY. Please tell me what it is! Let me help you.

EILEEN. No. It wouldn't be any use, Stephen.

MURRAY. (*offended*) Why do you say that? Haven't I helped before?

EILEEN. Yes—but this—

MURRAY. Come now! 'Fess up! What is "this"?

EILEEN. No. I couldn't speak of it here, anyway. They'll all be coming out soon.

MURRAY. (*insistently*) Then when? Where?

EILEEN. Oh, I don't know—perhaps never, nowhere. I don't know — Sometime before you leave, maybe.

MURRAY. But I may go tomorrow morning—if I gain weight and Stanton lets me.

EILEEN. (*sadly*) Yes, I was forgetting—you were going right away. (*Dully*) Then nowhere I suppose—never. (*Glancing toward the dining room*) They're all getting up. Let's not talk about it any more —now.

MURRAY. (*stubbornly*) But you'll tell me later, Eileen? You must.

EILEEN. (*vaguely*) Perhaps. It depends— (*The patients, about forty in number, straggle in from the dining room by twos and threes, chatting in low tones. The men and women with few exceptions separate into two groups, the women congregating in the left right angle of chairs, the men sitting or standing in the right right angle. In appearance, most of the patients are tanned, healthy, and cheerful looking. The great majority are under middle age. Their clothes are of the cheap, readymade variety. They are all distinctly of the wage-earning class. They might well be a crowd of cosmopolitan factory workers gathered together after a summer vacation. A hollow-chestedness and a tendency to round shoulders may be detected as a common characteristic. A general air of tension, marked by frequent bursts of laughter in too high a key, seems to pervade the throng.* MURRAY *and* EILEEN, *as if to avoid contact with the others, come over to the right in front of the dining-room door.*)

MURRAY. (*in a low voice*) Listen to them laugh. Did you ever notice —perhaps it's my imagination—how forced they act on Saturday mornings before they're weighed?

EILEEN. (*dully*) No.

MURRAY. Can't you tell me that secret now? No one'll hear.

EILEEN. (*vehemently*) No, no, how could I? Don't speak of it! (*A sudden silence falls on all the groups at once. Their eyes, by a common impulse, turn quickly toward the door to the hall.*)

A WOMAN. (*nervously—as if this moment's silent pause oppressed her*) Play something, Peters. They ain't coming yet. (PETERS, *a stupid-looking young fellow with a sly, twisted smirk which gives*

*him the appearance of perpetually winking his eye, detaches himself
from a group on the right. All join in with urging exclamations:
"Go on, Peters! Go to it! Pedal up, Pete! Give us a rag! That's the
boy, Peters!" etc.)*

PETERS. Sure, if I got time. (*He goes to the pianola and puts in a
roll. The mingled conversation and laughter bursts forth again as
he sits on the bench and starts pedaling.*)

MURRAY. (*disgustedly*) It's sure good to think I won't have to listen
to that old tin-pan being banged much longer! (*The music interrupts him—a quick rag. The patients brighten, hum, whistle, sway
their heads or tap their feet in time to the tune.* DOCTOR STANTON *and*
DOCTOR SIMMS *appear in the doorway from the hall. All eyes are
turned on them.*)

STANTON. (*raising his voice*) They all seem to be here, Doctor. We
might as well start. (MRS. TURNER, *the matron, comes in behind them—
a stout, motherly, capable-looking woman with gray hair. She hears
*STANTON's *remark.*)

MRS. TURNER. And take temperatures after, Doctor?

STANTON. Yes, Mrs. Turner. I think that's better today.

MRS. TURNER. All right, Doctor. (STANTON *and the assistant go out.*
MRS. TURNER *advances a step or so into the room and looks from one
group of patients to the other, inclining her head and smiling
benevolently. All force smiles and nod in recognition of her greeting.*
PETERS, *at the pianola, lets the music slow down, glancing questioningly at the matron to see if she is going to order it stopped. Then,
encouraged by her smile, his feet pedal harder than ever.*)

MURRAY. Look at old Mrs. Grundy's eyes pinned on us! She'll
accuse us of being too familiar again, the old wench!

EILEEN. Ssshh. You're wrong. She's looking at me, not at us.

MURRAY. At you? Why?

EILEEN. I ran a temperature yesterday. It must have been over a
hundred last night.

MURRAY. (*with consoling scepticism*) You're always suffering for trouble, Eileen. How do you know you ran a temp? You didn't see the stick, I suppose?

EILEEN. No—but—I could tell. I felt feverish and chilly. It must have been way up.

MURRAY. Bosh! If it was you'd have been sent to bed.

EILEEN. That's why she's looking at me. (*Piteously*) Oh, I do hope I won't be sent back to bed! I don't know what I'd do. If I could only gain this morning. If my temp has only gone down! (*Hopelessly*) But I feel— I didn't sleep a wink—thinking—

MURRAY. (*roughly*) You'll persuade yourself you've got leprosy in a second. Don't be a nut! It's all imagination, I tell you. You'll gain. Wait and see if you don't. (EILEEN *shakes her head. A metallic rumble and jangle comes from the hallway. Everyone turns in that direction with nervous expectancy.*)

MRS. TURNER. (*admonishingly*) Mr. Peters!

PETERS. Yes, ma'am. (*He stops playing and rejoins the group of men on the right. In the midst of a silence broken only by hushed murmurs of conversation,* DOCTOR STANTON *appears in the hall doorway. He turns to help his assistant wheel in a Fairbanks scale on casters. They place the scale against the wall immediately to the rear of the doorway.* DOCTOR SIMMS *adjusts it to a perfect balance.*)

DOCTOR STANTON. (*takes a pencil from his pocket and opens the record book he has in his hand*) All ready, Doctor?

DOCTOR SIMMS. Just a second, sir.

MURRAY. (*with a nervous smile*) Well, we're all set. Here's hoping!

EILEEN. You'll gain, I'm sure you will. You look so well.

MURRAY. Oh—I—I wasn't thinking of myself, I'm a sure thing. I was betting on you. I've simply got to gain today, when so much depends on it.

EILEEN. Yes, I hope you— (*She falters brokenly and turns away from him.*)

DOCTOR SIMMS. (*straightening up*) All ready, Doctor.

STANTON. (*nods and glances at his book—without raising his voice—*

374

distinctly) Mrs. Abner. (*A middle-aged woman comes and gets on the scales.* SIMMS *adjusts it to her weight of the previous week which* STANTON *reads to him from the book in a low voice, and weighs her.*)

MURRAY. (*with a relieved sigh*) They're off. (*Noticing* EILEEN's *downcast head and air of dejection*) Here! Buck up, Eileen! Old Lady Grundy's watching you—and it's your turn in a second. (EILEEN *raises her head and forces a frightened smile.* MRS. ABNER *gets down off the scales with a pleased grin. She has evidently gained. She rejoins the group of women, chattering volubly in low tones. Her exultant "gained half a pound" can be heard. The other women smile their perfunctory congratulations, their eyes absent-minded, intent on their own worries.* STANTON *writes down the weight in the book.*)

STANTON. Miss Bailey. (*A young girl goes to the scales.*)

MURRAY. Bailey looks badly, doesn't she?

EILEEN. (*her lips trembling*) She's been losing, too.

MURRAY. Well, *you're* going to gain today. Remember, now!

EILEEN. (*with a feeble smile*) I'll try to obey your orders. (MISS BAILEY *gets down off the scales. Her eyes are full of despondency although she tries to make a brave face of it, forcing a laugh as she joins the women. They stare at her with pitying looks and murmur consoling phrases.*)

EILEEN. She's lost again. Oh, I wish I didn't have to get weighed—

STANTON. Miss Carmody. (EILEEN *starts nervously.*)

MURRAY. (*as she leaves him*) Remember now! Break the scales! (*She walks quickly to the scales, trying to assume an air of defiant indifference. The balance stays down as she steps up.* EILEEN's *face shows her despair at this.* SIMMS *weighs her and gives the poundage in a low voice to* STANTON. EILEEN *steps down mechanically, then hesitates as if not knowing where to turn, her anguished eyes flitting from one group to another.*)

MURRAY. (*savagely*) Damn! (DOCTOR STANTON *writes the figures in his book, glances sharply at* EILEEN, *and then nods significantly to* MRS. TURNER *who is standing beside him.*)

375

STANTON. (*calling the next*) Miss Doeffler. (*Another woman comes to be weighed.*)

MRS. TURNER. Miss Carmody! Will you come here a moment, please?

EILEEN. (*her face growing very pale*) Yes, Mrs. Turner. (*The heads of the different groups bend together. Their eyes follow* EILEEN *as they whisper.* MRS. TURNER *leads her down front, left. Behind them the weighing of the women continues briskly. The great majority have gained. Those who have not have either remained stationary or lost a negligible fraction of a pound. So, as the weighing proceeds, the general air of smiling satisfaction rises among the groups of women. Some of them, their ordeal over, go out through the hall doorway by twos and threes with suppressed laughter and chatter. As they pass behind* EILEEN *they glance at her with pitying curiosity.* DOCTOR STANTON'S *voice is heard at regular intervals calling the names in alphabetical order*: Mrs. Elbing, Miss Finch, Miss Grimes, Miss Haines, Miss Hayes, Miss Jutner, Miss Linowski, Mrs. Marini, Mrs. McCoy, Miss McElroy, Miss Nelson, Mrs. Nott, Mrs. O'Brien, Mrs. Olson, Miss Paul, Miss Petrovski, Mrs. Quinn, Miss Robersi, Mrs. Stattler, Miss Unger.)

MRS. TURNER. (*putting her hand on* EILEEN'S *shoulder—kindly*) You're not looking so well, lately, my dear, do you know it?

EILEEN (*bravely*) I feel—fine. (*Her eyes, as if looking for encouragement, seek* MURRAY *who is staring at her worriedly.*)

MRS. TURNER. (*gently*) You lost weight again, you know.

EILEEN. I know—but—

MRS. TURNER. This is the fourth week.

EILEEN. I— I know it is—

MRS. TURNER. I've been keeping my eye on you. You seem—worried. Are you upset about—something we don't know?

EILEEN. (*quickly*) No, no! I haven't slept much lately. That must be it.

MRS. TURNER. Are you worrying about your condition? Is that what keeps you awake?

376

EILEEN. No.

MRS. TURNER. You're sure it's not that?

EILEEN. Yes, I'm sure it's not, Mrs. Turner.

MRS. TURNER. I was going to tell you if you were: Don't do it! You can't expect it to be all smooth sailing. Even the most favorable cases have to expect these little setbacks. A few days' rest in bed will start you on the right trail again.

EILEEN. (*in anguish, although she has realized this was coming*) Bed? Go back to bed? Oh, Mrs. Turner!

MRS. TURNER. (*gently*) Yes, my dear, Doctor Stanton thinks it best. So when you go back to your cottage—

EILEEN. Oh, please—not today—not right away!

MRS. TURNER. You had a temperature and a high pulse yesterday, didn't you realize it? And this morning you look quite feverish. (*She tries to put her hand on* EILEEN's *forehead but the latter steps away defensively.*)

EILEEN. It's only—not sleeping last night. Oh, I'm sure it'll go away.

MRS. TURNER. (*consolingly*) When you lie still and have perfect rest, of course it will.

EILEEN. (*with a longing look over at* MURRAY) But not today—please, Mrs. Turner.

MRS. TURNER. (*looking at her keenly*) There is something upsetting you. You've something on your mind that you can't tell me, is that it? (EILEEN *maintains a stubborn silence.*) But think—*can't* you tell me? (*With a kindly smile*) I'm used to other people's troubles. I've been playing mother-confessor to the patients for years now, and I think I've usually been able to help them. Can't you confide in me, child? (EILEEN *drops her eyes but remains silent.* MRS. TURNER *glances meaningly over at* MURRAY *who is watching them whenever he thinks the matron is not aware of it—a note of sharp rebuke in her voice*) I think I can guess your secret. You've let other notions become more important to you than the idea of getting well. And you've no excuse for it. After I had to warn you a month ago, I expected *that* silliness to stop instantly.

EILEEN (*her face flushed—protesting*) Nothing like that has anything to do with it.

MRS. TURNER. (*sceptically*) What is it that has, then?

EILEEN. (*lying determinedly*) It's my family. They keep writing—and worrying me—and— That's what it is, Mrs. Turner.

MRS. TURNER (*not exactly knowing whether to believe this or not—probing the girl with her eyes*) Your father?

EILEEN. Yes, all of them. (*Suddenly seeing a way to discredit all of the matron's suspicions—excitedly*) And principally the young man I'm engaged to—the one who came to visit me several times—

MRS. TURNER. (*surprised*) So—you're engaged? (EILEEN *nods.* MRS. TURNER *immediately dismisses her suspicions*) Oh, pardon me. I didn't know that, you see, or I wouldn't—(*She pats* EILEEN *on the shoulder comfortingly*) Never mind. You'll tell me all about it, won't you?

EILEEN. (*desperately*) Yes. (*She seems about to go on but the matron interrupts her.*)

MRS. TURNER. Oh, not here, my dear. Not now. Come to my room—let me see—I'll be busy all morning—sometime this afternoon. Will you do that?

EILEEN. Yes. (*Joyfully*) Then I needn't go to bed right away?

MRS. TURNER. No—on one condition. You mustn't take any exercise. Stay in your recliner all day and rest and remain in bed tomorrow morning.

EILEEN. I promise, Mrs. Turner.

MRS. TURNER. (*smiling in dismissal*) Very well, then. I'll see you this afternoon.

EILEEN. Yes, Mrs. Turner. (*The matron goes to the rear where* MISS BAILEY *is sitting with* MRS. ABNER. *She beckons to* MISS BAILEY *who gets up with a scared look, and they go to the far left corner of the room.* EILEEN *stands for a moment hesitating—then starts to go to* MURRAY,

378

but just at this moment PETERS *comes forward and speaks to* MURRAY.)

PETERS. (*with his sly twisted grin*) Say, Carmody musta lost fierce. Did you see the Old Woman handin' her an earful? Sent her back to bed, I betcha. What d'yuh think?

MURRAY. (*impatiently, showing his dislike*) How the hell do I know?

PETERS. (*sneeringly*) Huh, you don't know nothin' 'bout her, I s'pose? Where d'yuh get that stuff?

MURRAY. (*with cold rage before which the other slinks away*) If it wasn't for other people losing weight you couldn't get any joy out of life, could you? (*Roughly*) Get away from me! (*He makes a threatening gesture.*)

PETERS. (*beating a snarling retreat*) Wait'n' see if yuh don't lose too, yuh stuck-up boob! (*Seeing that* MURRAY *is alone again,* EILEEN *starts toward him but this time she is intercepted by* MRS. ABNER *who stops on her way out. The weighing of the women is now finished, and that of the men, which proceeds much quicker, begins.*)

DOCTOR STANTON. Anderson! (ANDERSON *comes to the scales. The men all move down to the left to wait their turn, with the exception of* MURRAY, *who remains by the dining-room door, fidgeting impatiently anxious for a word with* EILEEN.)

MRS. ABNER. (*taking* EILEEN's *arm*) Coming over to the cottage, dearie?

EILEEN. Not just this minute, Mrs. Abner. I have to wait—

MRS. ABNER. For the Old Woman? You lost today, didn't you? Is she sendin' you to bed, the old devil?

EILEEN. Yes, I'm afraid I'll have to—

MRS. ABNER. She's a mean one, ain't she? I gained this week—half a pound. Lord, I'm gettin' fat! All my clothes are gittin' too small for me. Don't know what I'll do. Did you lose much, dearie?

EILEEN. Three pounds.

MRS. ABNER. Ain't that awful! (*Hastening to make up for this*

379

thoughtless remark) All the same, what's three pounds? You can git them back in a week after you're resting more. You've been runnin' a temp, too, ain't you? (EILEEN *nods*) Don't worry about it, dearie. It'll go down. Worryin's the worst. Me, I don't never worry none. (*She chuckles with satisfaction—then soberly*) I just been talkin' with Bailey. She's got to go to bed, too, I guess. She lost two pounds. She ain't runnin' no temp though.

STANTON. Barnes! (*Another man comes to the scales.*)

MRS. ABNER. (*in a mysterious whisper*) Look at Mr. Murray, dearie. Ain't he nervous today? I don't know as I blame him, either. I heard the doctor said he'd let him go home if he gained today. Is it true, d'you know?

EILEEN. (*dully*) I don't know.

MRS. ABNER. Gosh, I wish it was me! My old man's missin' me like the dickens, he writes. (*She starts to go*) You'll be over to the cottage in a while, won't you? Me'n' you'll have a game of casino, eh?

EILEEN. (*happy at this deliverance*) Yes, I'll be glad to.

STANTON. Cordero! (MRS. ABNER *goes out.* EILEEN *again starts toward* MURRAY *but this time* FLYNN, *a young fellow with a brick-colored, homely, good-natured face, and a shaven-necked haircut, slouches back to* MURRAY. EILEEN *is brought to a halt in front of the table where she stands, her face working with nervous strain, clasping and unclasping her trembling hands.*)

FLYNN. (*curiously*) Say, Steve, what's this bull about the Doc lettin' yuh beat it if yuh gain today? Is it straight goods?

MURRAY. He said he might, that's all. (*Impatiently*) How the devil did that story get traveling around?

FLYNN. (*with a grin*) Wha' d'yuh expect with this gang of skirts chewin' the fat? Well, here's hopin' yuh come home a winner, Steve.

MURRAY. (*gratefully*) Thanks. (*With confidence*) Oh, I'll gain all right; but whether he'll let me go or not— (*He shrugs his shoulders.*)

FLYNN. Make 'em behave. I wisht Stanton'd ask waivers on me.

(*With a laugh*) I oughter gain a ton today. I ate enough spuds for breakfast to plant a farm.

STANTON. Flynn!

FLYNN. Me to the plate! (*He strides to the scales.*)

MURRAY. Good luck! (*He starts to join* EILEEN *but* MISS BAILEY, *who has finished her talk with* MRS. TURNER, *who goes out to the hall, approaches* EILEEN *at just this moment.* MURRAY *stops in his tracks, fuming. He and* EILEEN *exchange a glance of helpless annoyance.*)

MISS BAILEY (*her thin face full of the satisfaction of misery finding company—plucks at* EILEEN's *sleeve*) Say, Carmody, she sent you back to bed, too, didn't she?

EILEEN. (*absentmindedly*) I suppose—

MISS BAILEY. You suppose? Of course she did. I got to go, too. (*Pulling* EILEEN's *sleeve*) Come on. Let's get out of here. I hate this place, don't you?

STANTON. (*calling the next*) Hopper!

FLYNN. (*shouts to* MURRAY *as he is going out to the hall*) I hit 'er for a two-bagger, Steve. Come on now, Bo, and bring me home! 'Atta boy! (*Grinning gleefully, he slouches out.* DOCTOR STANTON *and all the patients laugh.*)

MISS BAILEY (*with irritating persistence*) Come on, Carmody. You've got to go to bed, too.

EILEEN. (*at the end of her patience—releasing her arm from the other's grasp*) Let me alone, will you? I don't have to go to bed now—not till tomorrow morning.

MISS BAILEY (*in a whining rage*) Why not? You've been running a temp, too, and I haven't! You must have a pull, that's what! It isn't fair. I'll bet you lost more than I did, too! What right have you got—Well, I'm not going to bed if you don't. Wait 'n' see!

EILEEN (*turning away revolted*) Go away! Leave me alone, please.

STANTON. Lowenstein!

MISS BAILEY (*turns to the hall door, whining*) All right for you! I'm going to find out. It isn't square. I'll write home. (*She disappears in the hallway.* MURRAY *strides over to* EILEEN *whose strength seems to have left her and who is leaning weakly against the table.*)

MURRAY. Thank God—at last! Isn't it hell—all these fools! I couldn't get to you. What did Old Lady Grundy have to say to you? I saw her giving me a hard look. Was it about us—the old stuff? (EILEEN *nods with downcast eyes*) What did she say? Never mind now. You can tell me in a minute. It's my turn next. (*His eyes glance toward the scales.*)

EILEEN. (*intensely*) Oh, Stephen, I wish you weren't going away!

MURRAY. (*excitedly*). Maybe I'm not. It's like gambling—if I win—

STANTON. Murray!

MURRAY. Wait here, Eileen. (*He goes to the scales.* EILEEN *keeps her back turned. Her body stiffens rigidly in the intensity of her conflicting emotions. She stares straight ahead, her eyes full of anguish.* MURRAY *steps on the scales nervously. The balance rod hits the top smartly. He has gained. His face lights up and he heaves a great sigh of relief.* EILEEN *seems to sense this outcome and her head sinks, her body sags weakly and seems to shrink to a smaller size.* MURRAY *gets off the scales, his face beaming with a triumphant smile.* DOCTOR STANTON *smiles and murmurs something to him in a low voice.* MURRAY *nods brightly; then turns back to* EILEEN.)

STANTON. Nathan! (*Another patient advances to the scales.*)

MURRAY (*trying to appear casual*) Well—three rousing cheers! Stanton told me to come to his office at eleven. That means a final exam—and release!

EILEEN. (*dully*) So you gained?

MURRAY. Three pounds.

EILEEN. Funny—I lost three. (*With a pitiful effort at a smile*) I hope you gained the ones I lost. (*Her lips tremble*) So you're surely going away.

MURRAY. (*his joy fleeing as he is confronted with her sorrow— slowly*) It looks that way, Eileen.

EILEEN. (*in a trembling whisper broken by rising sobs*) Oh—I'm so glad—you gained—the ones I lost, Stephen— So glad! (*She breaks down, covering her face with her hands, stifling her sobs.*)

MURRAY (*alarmed*) Eileen! What's the matter? (*Desperately*) Stop it! Stanton'll see you!

ACT TWO—SCENE TWO

MIDNIGHT *of the same day. A crossroads near the sanatorium. The main road comes down forward from the right. A smaller road, leading down from the left, joins it toward left, center.*

Dense woods rise sheer from the grass and bramble-grown ditches at the road's sides. At the junction of the two roads there is a sign-post, its arms pointing toward the right and the left, rear. A pile of round stones is at the road corner, left forward. A full moon, riding high overhead, throws the roads into white shadowless relief and masses the woods into walls of compact blackness. The trees lean heavily together, their branches motionless, unstirred by any trace of wind.

As the curtain rises, EILEEN *is discovered standing in the middle of the road, front center. Her face shows white and clear in the bright moonlight as she stares with anxious expectancy up the road to the left. Her body is fixed in an attitude of rigid immobility as if she were afraid the slightest movement would break the spell of silence and awaken the unknown. She has shrunk instinctively as far away as she can from the mysterious darkness which rises at the road's sides like an imprisoning wall. A sound of hurried footfalls, muffled by the dust, comes from the road she is watching. She gives a startled gasp. Her eyes strain to identify the oncomer. Uncertain, trembling, with fright, she hesitates a second; then darts to the side of the road and crouches down in the shadow.*

STEPHEN MURRAY *comes down the road from the left. He stops by the signpost and peers about him. He wears a cap, the peak of which casts his face into shadow. Finally he calls in a low voice:*

MURRAY. Eileen!

EILEEN. (*coming out quickly from her hiding place—with a glad little cry*) Stephen! At last! (*She runs to him as if she were going to fling her arms about him but stops abashed. He reaches out and takes her hands.*)

MURRAY. It can't be twelve yet. (*He leads her to the pile of stones to the left*) I haven't heard the village clock.

EILEEN. I must have come early. It seemed as if I'd been waiting for ages.

MURRAY. How your hands tremble! Were you frightened?

EILEEN. (*forcing a smile*) A little. The woods are so black and queer looking. I'm all right now.

MURRAY. Sit down. You must rest. (*In a tone of annoyed reproof*) I am going to read you a lecture, young lady. You shouldn't ever have done this—running a temp and— Good heavens, don't you want to get well?

EILEEN. (*dully*) I don't know—

MURRAY. (*irritably*) You make me ill when you talk that way, Eileen. It doesn't sound like you at all. What's come over you lately? I was—knocked out—when I read the note you slipped me after supper. I didn't get a chance to read it until late, I was so busy packing, and by that time you'd gone to your cottage. If I could have reached you any way I'd have refused to come here, I tell you straight. But I couldn't—and I knew you'd be here waiting—and— still, I feel guilty. Damn it, this isn't the thing for you! You ought to be in bed asleep.

EILEEN. (*humbly*) Please, Stephen, don't scold me.

MURRAY. How the devil did you ever get the idea—meeting me here at this ungodly hour?

EILEEN. You'd told me about your sneaking out to go to the village, and I thought there'd be no harm this one night—the last night.

MURRAY. But I'm well. I've been well. It's different. You— Honest, Eileen, you shouldn't lose sleep and tax your strength.

EILEEN. Don't scold me, please. I'll make up for it. I'll rest all the time—after you're gone. I just had to see you some way. (*A clock in the distant village begins striking*) Ssshh! Listen.

MURRAY. That's twelve now. You see I was early. (*In a pause of silence they wait motionlessly until the last mournful note dies in the hushed woods.*)

EILEEN. (*in a stifled voice*) It isn't tomorrow now, is it? It's today— the day you're going.

MURRAY. (*something in her voice making him avert his face and kick at the heap of stones on which she is sitting—brusquely*) Well, I hope you took precautions so you wouldn't be caught sneaking out.

EILEEN. I did just what you'd told me you did—stuffed the pillows under the clothes so the watchman would think I was there.

MURRAY. None of the patients on your porch saw you leave, did they?

EILEEN. No. They were all asleep.

MURRAY. That's all right, then. I wouldn't trust any of that bunch of women. They'd be only too tickled to squeal on you. (*There is an uncomfortable pause.* MURRAY *seems waiting for her to speak. He looks about him at the trees, up into the moonlit sky, breathing in the fresh night air with a healthy delight.* EILEEN *remains with downcast head, staring at the road*) It's beautiful tonight, isn't it? Worth losing sleep for.

EILEEN. (*dully*) Yes. (*Another pause—finally she murmurs faintly*) Are you leaving early?

MURRAY. The ten-forty. Leave the San at ten, I guess.

EILEEN. You're going home?

MURRAY. Home? No. But I'm going to see my sisters—just to say hello. I've got to, I suppose.

EILEEN. I'm sure—I've often felt—you're unjust to your sisters. (*With conviction*) I'm sure they must both love you.

MURRAY. (*frowning*) Maybe, in their own way. But what's love without a glimmer of understanding—a nuisance! They've never seen the real me and never wanted to.

EILEEN. (*as if to herself*) What is—the real you? (MURRAY *kicks at the stones impatiently without answering.* EILEEN *hastens to change the subject*) And then you'll go to New York?

MURRAY. (*interested at once*) Yes. You bet.

EILEEN. And write more?

MURRAY. Not in New York, no. I'm going there to take a vacation and really enjoy myself for a while. I've enough money for that as it is and if the other stories you typed sell—I'll be as rich as Rockefeller. I might even travel— No, I've got to make good with my best stuff first. I know what I'll do. When I've had enough of New York, I'll rent a place in the country—some old farmhouse—and live alone there and work. (*Lost in his own plans—with pleasure*) That's the right idea, isn't it?

EILEEN. (*trying to appear enthused*) It ought to be fine for your work. (*After a pause*) They're fine, those stories you wrote here. They're—so much like you. I'd know it was you wrote them even if —I didn't know.

MURRAY. (*pleased*) Wait till you read the others I'm going to do! (*After a slight pause—with a good-natured grin*) Here I am talking about myself again! But you don't know how good it is to have your dreams coming true. It'd make an egotist out of anyone.

EILEEN. (*sadly*) No. I don't know. But I love to hear you talk of yours.

MURRAY. (*with an embarrassed laugh*) Thanks. Well, I've certainly told you all of them. You're the only one— (*He stops and abruptly changes the subject*) You said in your note that you had something important to tell me. (*He sits down beside her, crossing his legs*) Is it about your interview with Old Mrs. Grundy this afternoon?

EILEEN. No, that didn't amount to anything. She seemed mad because I told her so little. I think she guessed I only told her what I did so she'd let me stay up, maybe—your last day—and to keep her from thinking what she did—about us.

MURRAY. (*quickly, as if he wishes to avoid this subject*) What is it you wanted to tell me, then?

EILEEN. (*sadly*) It doesn't seem so important now, somehow. I suppose it was silly of me to drag you out here, just for that. It can't mean anything to you—much.

MURRAY. (*encouragingly*) How do you know it can't?

EILEEN. (*slowly*) I only thought—you might like to know.

MURRAY. (*interestedly*) Know what? What is it? If I can help—

EILEEN. No. (*After a moment's hesitation*) I wrote to him this afternoon.

MURRAY. Him?

EILEEN. The letter you've been advising me to write.

MURRAY. (*as if the knowledge of this alarmed him—haltingly*) You mean—Fred Nicholls?

EILEEN. Yes.

MURRAY. (*after a pause—uncomfortably*) You mean—you broke it all off?

EILEEN. Yes—for good. (*She looks up at his averted face. He remains silent. She continues apprehensively*) You don't say anything. I thought—you'd be glad. You've always told me it was the honorable thing to do.

MURRAY. (*gruffly*) I know. I say more than my prayers, damn it! (*With sudden eagerness*) Have you mailed the letter yet?

EILEEN. Yes. Why?

MURRAY. (*shortly*) Humph. Oh—nothing.

EILEEN. (*with pained disappointment*) Oh, Stephen, you don't think I did wrong, do you—now—after all you've said?

MURRAY. (*hurriedly*) Wrong? No, not if you were convinced it was the right thing to do yourself—if you know you don't love him.

But I'd hate to think you did it just on my say-so. I shouldn't— I didn't mean to interfere. I don't know enough about your relations for my opinion to count.

EILEEN. (*hurt*) You know all there is to know.

MURRAY. I know you've been frank. But him—I don't know him. He may be quite different from my idea. That's what I'm getting at. I don't want to be unfair to him.

EILEEN. (*bitterly scornful*) You needn't worry. You weren't unfair. And you needn't be afraid you were responsible for my writing. I'd been going to for a long time before you ever spoke.

MURRAY. (*with a relieved sigh*) I'm glad of that—honestly, Eileen. I felt guilty. I shouldn't have knocked him behind his back without knowing him at all.

EILEEN. You said you could read him like a book from his letters I showed you.

MURRAY. (*apologetically*) I know. I'm a fool.

EILEEN. (*angrily*) What makes you so considerate of Fred Nicholls all of a sudden? What you thought about him was right.

MURRAY. (*vaguely*) I don't know. One makes mistakes.

EILEEN. (*assertively*) Well, I know! You needn't waste pity on him. He'll be only too glad to get my letter. He's been anxious to be free of me ever since I was sent here, only he thought it wouldn't be decent to break it off himself while I was sick. He was afraid of what people would say about him when they found it out. So he's just gradually stopped writing and coming for visits, and waited for me to realize. And if I didn't, I know he'd have broken it off himself the first day I got home. I've kept persuading myself that, in spite of the way he's acted, he did love me as much as he could love anyone, and that it would hurt him if I— But now I know that he never loved me, that he couldn't love anyone but himself. Oh, I don't hate him for it. He can't help being what he is. And all people seem to be—like that, mostly. I'm only going to remember that he and I grew up together, and that he was kind to me then when he thought he liked me—and forget all the rest. (*With agitated impatience*) Oh, Stephen, you know all this I've said about him. Why don't you admit it? You've read his letters.

MURRAY. (*haltingly*) Yes, I'll admit that was my opinion—only I wanted to be sure you'd found out for yourself.

EILEEN. (*defiantly*) Well, I have! You see that now, don't you?

MURRAY. Yes; and I'm glad you're free of him, for your own sake. I knew he wasn't the person. (*With an attempt at a joking tone*) You must get one of the right sort—next time.

EILEEN. (*springing to her feet with a cry of pain*) Stephen! (*He avoids her eyes which search his face pleadingly.*)

MURRAY. (*mumbling*) He wasn't good enough—to lace your shoes —nor anyone else, either.

EILEEN. (*with a nervous laugh*) Don't be silly. (*After a pause during which she waits hungrily for some words from him—with a sigh of despair—faintly*) Well, I've told you—all there is. I might as well go back.

MURRAY. (*not looking at her—indistinctly*) Yes. You mustn't lose too much sleep. I'll come to your cottage in the morning to say good-by. They'll permit that, I guess.

EILEEN. (*stands looking at him, imploringly, her face convulsed with anguish, but he keeps his eyes fixed on the rocks at his feet. Finally she seems to give up and takes a few uncertain steps up the road toward the right—in an exhausted whisper*) Good night, Stephen.

MURRAY. (*his voice choked and husky*) Good night, Eileen.

EILEEN. (*walks weakly up the road but, as she passes the signpost, she suddenly stops and turns to look again at* MURRAY *who has not moved or lifted his eyes. A great shuddering sob shatters her pent-up emotions. She runs back to* MURRAY, *her arms outstretched, with a choking cry*) Stephen!

MURRAY. (*startled, whirls to face her and finds her arms thrown around his neck—in a terrified tone*) Eileen!

389

EILEEN. (*brokenly*) I love you, Stephen—you! That's what I wanted to tell! (*She gazes up into his eyes, her face transfigured by the joy and pain of this abject confession.*)

MURRAY. (*wincing as if this were the thing he had feared to hear*) Eileen!

EILEEN. (*pulling down his head with fierce strength and kissing him passionately on the lips*) I love you! I will say it! There! (*With sudden horror*) Oh, I know I shouldn't kiss you! I mustn't! You're all well—and I—

MURRAY. (*protesting frenziedly*) Eileen! Damn it! Don't say that! What do you think I am! (*He kisses her fiercely two or three times until she forces a hand over her mouth.*)

EILEEN. (*with a hysterically happy laugh*) No! Just hold me in your arms—just a little while—before—

MURRAY. (*his voice trembling*) Eileen! Don't talk that way! You're—it's killing me. I can't stand it!

EILEEN. (*with soothing tenderness*) Listen, dear—listen—and you won't say a word— I've so much to say—till I get through—please, will you promise?

MURRAY. (*between clinched teeth*) Yes—anything, Eileen!

EILEEN. Then I want to say—I know your secret. You don't love me— Isn't that it? (MURRAY groans) Ssshh! It's all right, dear. You can't help what you don't feel. I've guessed you didn't—right along. And I've loved you—such a long time now—always, it seems. And you've sort of guessed—that I did—didn't you? No, don't speak! I am sure you've guessed—only you didn't want to know—that—did you? —when you didn't love me. That's why you were lying—but I saw, I knew! Oh, I'm not blaming you, darling. How could I—never! You mustn't look so—so frightened. I know how you felt, dear. I've—I've watched you. It was just a flirtation for you at first. Wasn't it? Oh, I know. It was just fun, and— Please don't look at me so. I'm not hurting you, am I? I wouldn't for worlds, dear—you know—hurt you! And then afterwards—you found we could be such good friends—

390

helping each other—and you wanted it to stay just like that always, didn't you?—I know—and then I had to spoil it all—and fall in love with you—didn't I? Oh, it was stupid—I shouldn't—I couldn't help it, you were so kind and—and different—and I wanted to share in your work and—and everything. I knew you wouldn't want to know I loved you—when you didn't—and I tried hard to be fair and hide my love so you wouldn't see—and I did, didn't I, dear? You never knew till just lately—maybe not till just today—did you?—when I knew you were going away so soon—and couldn't help showing it. You never knew before, did you? Did you?

MURRAY. (*miserably*) No. Oh, Eileen—Eileen, I'm so sorry!

EILEEN. (*in heartbroken protest*) Sorry? Oh no, Stephen, you mustn't be! It's been beautiful—all of it—for me! That's what makes your going—so hard. I had to see you tonight—I'd have gone—crazy —if I didn't know you knew, if I hadn't made you guess. And I thought—if you knew about my writing to Fred—that—maybe—it'd make some difference. (MURRAY *groans—and she laughs hysterically*) I must have been crazy—to think that—mustn't I? As if that could— when you don't love me. Sshh! Please! Let me finish. You mustn't feel sad—or anything. It's made me happier than I've ever been— loving you—even when I did know—you didn't. Only now—you'll forgive me telling you all this, won't you, dear? Now, it's so terrible to think I won't see you any more. I'll feel so—without anybody.

MURRAY. (*brokenly*) But I'll—come back. And you'll be out soon— and then—

EILEEN. (*brokenly*) Sshh! Let me finish. You don't know how alone I am now. Father—he'll marry that housekeeper—and the children— they've forgotten me. None of them need me any more. They've found out how to get on without me—and I'm a drag—dead to them —no place for me home any more—and they'll be afraid to have me back—afraid of catching—I know she won't want me back. And Fred—he's gone—he never mattered, anyway. Forgive me, dear—

worrying you—only I want you to know how much you've meant to me—so you won't forget—ever—after you've gone.

MURRAY. (*in grief-stricken tones*) Forget? Eileen! I'll do anything in God's world—

EILEEN. I know—you like me a lot even if you can't love me—don't you? (*His arms tighten about her as he bends down and forces a kiss on her lips again*) Oh, Stephen! That was for good-by. You mustn't come tomorrow morning. I couldn't bear having you—with people watching. But you'll write after—often—won't you? (*Heartbrokenly*) Oh, please do that, Stephen!

MURRAY. I will! I swear! And when you get out I'll—we'll—I'll find something— (*He kisses her again.*)

EILEEN. (*breaking away from him with a quick movement and stepping back a few feet*) Good-by, darling. Remember me—and perhaps—you'll find out after a time—I'll pray God to make it so! Oh, what am I saying? Only—I'll hope—I'll hope—till I die!

MURRAY. (*in anguish*) Eileen!

EILEEN. (*her breath coming in tremulous heaves of her bosom*) Remember, Stephen—if ever you want—I'll do anything—anything you want—no matter what—I don't care—there's just you and—don't hate me, dear. I love you—love you—remember! (*She suddenly turns and runs away up the road.*)

MURRAY. Eileen! (*He starts to run after her but stops by the sign-post and stamps on the ground furiously, his fists clenched in impotent rage at himself and at Fate.*) Christ!

CURTAIN

ACT THREE

S cene—*Four months later. An isolation room at the Infirmary with a sleeping porch at the right of it. Late afternoon of a Sunday toward the end of October. The room, extending two-thirds of the distance from left to right, is, for reasons of space economy, scantily furnished with the bare necessities—a bureau with mirror in the left corner, rear—two straight-backed chairs—a table with a glass top in the center. The floor is varnished hardwood. The walls and furniture are painted white. On the left, forward, a door to the hallway. On the right, rear, a double glass door opening on the porch. Farther front two windows. The porch, a screened-in continuation of the room, contains only a single iron bed painted white, and a small table placed beside the bed.*

The woods, the leaves of the trees rich in their autumn coloring, rise close about this side of the Infirmary. Their branches almost touch the porch on the right. In the rear of the porch they have been cleared away from the building for a narrow space, and through this opening the distant hills can be seen with the tree tops glowing in the sunlight.

As the curtain rises, eileen *is discovered lying in the bed on the porch, propped up into a half-sitting position by pillows under her back and head. She seems to have grown much thinner. Her face is pale and drawn with deep hollows under her cheek-bones. Her eyes are dull and lusterless. She gazes straight before her into the wood with the unseeing stare of apathetic indifference. The door from the hall in the room behind her is opened and* miss howard *enters followed by* bill carmody, mrs. brennan, *and* mary. carmody's *manner is unwontedly sober and subdued. This air of respectable sobriety is further enhanced by a black suit, glaringly new and stiffly pressed, a new black derby hat, and shoes polished like a mirror. His expression is full of a bitter, if suppressed, resentment. His gentility is evidently forced upon him in spite of himself and correspondingly irksome.* MRS. BRENNAN *is a tall, stout woman of fifty, lusty and loud-voiced, with a broad, snub-nosed, florid face, a large mouth, the upper lip darkened by a suggestion of mustache, and little round blue eyes, hard and restless with a continual fuming irritation. She is got up regardless in her ridiculous Sunday-best.* MARY *appears tall and skinny-legged in a starched, outgrown frock. The sweetness of her face has disappeared, giving way to a hangdog sullenness, a stubborn silence, with sulky, furtive glances of rebellion directed at her stepmother.*

MISS HOWARD. (*pointing to the porch*) She's out there on the porch.

MRS. BRENNAN. (*with dignity*) Thank you, ma'am.

MISS HOWARD. (*with a searching glance at the visitors as if to appraise their intentions*) Eileen's been very sick lately, you know, so be careful not to worry her about anything. Do your best to cheer her up.

CARMODY. (*mournfully*) We'll try to put life in her spirits, God help her. (*With an uncertain look at* MRS. BRENNAN) Won't we, Maggie?

MRS. BRENNAN. (*turning sharply on* MARY *who has gone over to examine the things on the bureau*) Come away from that, Mary. Curiosity killed a cat. Don't be touchin' her things. Remember what I told you. Or is it admirin' your mug in the mirror you are? (*Turning to* MISS HOWARD *as* MARY *moves away from the bureau, hanging her head—shortly*) Don't you worry, ma'am. We won't trouble Eileen at all.

MISS HOWARD. Another thing. You mustn't say anything to her of what Miss Gilpin just told you about her being sent away to the State Farm in a few days. Eileen isn't to know till the very last minute. It would only disturb her.

CARMODY. (*hastily*) We'll not say a word of it.

MISS HOWARD. (*turning to the hall door*) Thank you. (*She goes out, shutting the door.*)

MRS. BRENNAN. (*angrily*) She has a lot of impudent gab, that one, with her don't do this and don't do that! (*Gazing about the room critically*) Two sticks of chairs and a table! They don't give much for the money.

CARMODY. Catch them! It's a good thing she's clearin' out of this and her worse off after them curin' her eight months than she was when she came. She'll maybe get well in the new place.

MRS. BRENNAN. (*indifferently*) It's God's will, what'll happen. (*Irritably*) And I'm thinkin' it's His punishment she's under now for having no heart in her and never writin' home a word to you or the children in two months or more. If the doctor hadn't wrote us himself to come see her, we'd have been no wiser.

CARMODY. Whisht. Don't be blamin' a sick girl.

MARY. (*who has drifted to one of the windows at right—curiously*) There's somebody in bed out there. Is it Eileen?

MRS. BRENNAN. Don't be goin' out there till I tell you, you imp! (*Coming closer to him and lowering her voice*) Are you going to tell her about it?

CARMODY. (*pretending ignorance*) About what?

MRS. BRENNAN. About what, indeed! About our marryin' two weeks back, of course. What else?

CARMODY. (*uncertainly*) Yes—I disremembered she didn't know. I'll have to tell her, surely.

MRS. BRENNAN. (*flaring up*) You speak like you wouldn't. Are you afraid of a slip of a girl? Well, then, I'm not! I'll tell her to her face soon enough.

CARMODY. (*angry in his turn—assertively*) You'll not, now! Keep your mouth out of this and your rough tongue! I tell you I'll tell her.

MRS. BRENNAN. (*satisfied*) Let's be going out to her, then. (*They move toward the door to the porch*) And keep your eye on your watch. We mustn't miss the train. Come with us, Mary, and remember to keep your mouth shut. (*They go out on the porch and stand just outside the door waiting for* EILEEN *to notice them; but the girl in bed continues to stare into the woods, oblivious to their presence.*)

MRS. BRENNAN. (*nudging* CARMODY *with her elbow—in a harsh whisper*) Glory be, it's bad she's lookin'. The look on her face'd frighten you. Speak to her, you! (EILEEN *stirs uneasily as if this whisper had disturbed her unconsciously.*)

CARMODY. (*wetting his lips and clearing his throat huskily*) Eileen.

EILEEN. (*startled, turns and stares at them with frightened eyes. After a pause she ventures uncertainly as if she were not sure but what these figures might be creatures of her dream*) Father. (*Her eyes shift to* MRS. BRENNAN's *face and she shudders*) Mrs. Brennan.

MRS. BRENNAN. (*quickly—in a voice meant to be kindly*) Here we are, all of us, come to see you. How is it you're feelin' now, Eileen? (*While she is talking she advances to the bedside, followed by* CARMODY, *and takes one of the sick girl's hands in hers.* EILEEN *withdraws it as if stung and holds it out to her father.* MRS. BRENNAN's *face flushes angrily and she draws back from the bedside.*)

CARMODY. (*moved—with rough tenderness patting her hand*) Ah, Eileen, sure it's a sight for sore eyes to see you again! (*He bends down as if to kiss her, but, struck by a sudden fear, hesitates, straightens himself, and shamed by the understanding in* EILEEN's *eyes, grows red and stammers confusedly*) How are you now? Sure it's the picture of health you're lookin'. (EILEEN *sighs and turns her eyes away from his with a resigned sadness.*)

MRS. BRENNAN. What are you standin' there for like a stick, Mary? Haven't you a word to say to your sister?

EILEEN. (*twisting her head around and seeing* MARY *for the first time—with a glad cry*) Mary! I—why I didn't see you before! Come here. (MARY *approaches gingerly with apprehensive side glances at* MRS. BRENNAN *who watches her grimly.* EILEEN's *arms reach out for her hungrily. She grasps her about the waist and seems trying to press the unwilling child to her breast.*)

MARY. (*fidgeting nervously—suddenly in a frightened whine*) Let me go! (EILEEN *releases her, looks at her face dazedly for a second, then falls back limply with a little moan and shuts her eyes.* MARY, *who has stepped back a pace, remains fixed there as if fascinated with fright by her sister's face. She stammers*) Eileen—you look so—so funny.

EILEEN. (*without opening her eyes—in a dead voice*) You, too! I never thought you— Go away, please.

MRS. BRENNAN. (*with satisfaction*) Come here to me, Mary, and don't be botherin' your sister. (MARY *avoids her stepmother but retreats to the far end of the porch where she stands shrunk back against the wall, her eyes fixed on* EILEEN *with the same fascinated horror.*)

CARMODY. (*after an uncomfortable pause, forcing himself to speak*) Is the pain bad, Eileen?

EILEEN. (*dully—without opening her eyes*) There's no pain. (*There is another pause—then she murmurs indifferently*) There are chairs in the room you can bring out if you want to sit down.

MRS. BRENNAN. (*sharply*) We've not time to be sittin'. We've the train back to catch.

EILEEN. (*in the same lifeless voice*) It's a disagreeable trip. I'm sorry you had to come.

CARMODY. (*fighting against an oppression he cannot understand, bursts into a flood of words*) Don't be talking of the trip. Sure we're glad to take it to get a sight of you. It's three months since I've had a look at you and I was anxious. Why haven't you written a line to us? You could do that without trouble, surely. Don't you ever think of us at all any more? (*He waits for an answer but* EILEEN *remains silent with her eyes closed.* CARMODY *starts to walk up and down talking with an air of desperation*) You're not asking a bit of news from home. I'm thinkin' the people out here have taken all the thought of us out of your head. We're all well, thank God. I've another good job on the streets from Murphy and one that'll last a long time, praise be! I'm needin' it surely, with all the expenses—but no matter. Billy had a raise from his old skinflint of a boss a month back. He's gettin' seven a week now and proud as a turkey. He was comin' out with us today

397

but he'd a date with his girl. Sure, he's got a girl now, the young bucko! What d'you think of him? It's old Malloy's girl he's after—the pop-eyed one with glasses, you remember—as ugly as a blind sheep, only he don't think so. He said to give you his love. (EILEEN *stirs and sighs wearily, a frown appearing for an instant on her forehead*) And Tom and Nora was comin' out too, but Father Fitz had some doin's or other up to the school, and he told them to be there, so they wouldn't come with us, but they sent their love to you too. They're growin' so big you'd not know them. Tom's no good at the school. He's like Billy was. I've had to take the strap to him often. He's always playin' hookey and roamin' the streets. And Nora—(*With pride*) There's the divil for you! Up to everything she is and no holdin' her high spirits. As pretty as a picture, and the smartest girl in her school, Father Fitz says. Am I lyin', Maggie?

MRS. BRENNAN. (*grudgingly*) She's smart enough—and too free with her smartness.

CARMODY. (*pleased*) Ah, don't be talkin'! She'll know more than the lot of us before she's grown even. (*He pauses in his walk and stares down at* EILEEN, *frowning*) Are you sick, Eileen, that you're keepin' your eyes shut without a word out of you?

EILEEN. (*wearily*) No. I'm tired, that's all.

CARMODY. (*resuming his walk*) And who else is there, let me think? Oh, Mary—she's the same as ever, you can see for yourself.

EILEEN. (*bitterly*) The same? Oh, no!

CARMODY. She's grown, you mean? I suppose. You'd notice, not seeing her so long? (*He can think of nothing else to say but walks up and down with a restless, uneasy expression.*)

MRS. BRENNAN. (*sharply*) What time is it gettin'?

CARMODY. (*fumbles for his watch*) Half past four, a bit after.

MRS. BRENNAN. We'll have to leave soon. It's a long jaunt down the hill in that buggy. (*She catches his eye and makes violent signs to him to tell* EILEEN *what he has come to tell.*)

CARMODY. (*after an uncertain pause—clenching his fists and clearing his throat*) Eileen.

EILEEN. Yes.

CARMODY. (*irritably*) Can't you open your eyes on me? It's like talkin' to myself I am.

EILEEN. (*looking at him—dully*) What is it?

CARMODY. (*stammering—avoiding her glance*) It's this, Eileen— me and Maggie—Mrs. Brennan, that is—we—

EILEEN. (*without surprise*) You're going to marry her?

CARMODY. (*with an effort*) Not goin' to. It's done.

EILEEN. (*without a trace of feeling*) Oh, so you've been married already? (*Without further comment, she closes her eyes.*)

CARMODY. Two weeks back we were, by Father Fitz. (*He stands staring down at his daughter, irritated, perplexed and confounded by her silence, looking as if he longed to shake her.*)

MRS. BRENNAN. (*angry at the lack of enthusiasm shown by* EILEEN) Let us get out of this, Bill. It's little she's caring about you, and little thanks she has for all you've done for her and the money you've spent.

CARMODY. (*with a note of pleading*) Is that a proper way to be treatin' your father, Eileen, after what I've told you? Is it nothin' to you you've a good, kind woman now for mother?

EILEEN. (*fiercely, her eyes flashing open on him*) No, No! Never!

MRS. BRENNAN. (*plucking at* CARMODY's *elbow. He stands looking at* EILEEN *helplessly, his mouth open, a guilty flush spreading over his face*) Come out of here, you big fool, you! Is it to listen to insults to your livin' wife you're waiting?

CARMODY. (*turning on her threateningly*) Will you shut your gab?

EILEEN. (*with a moan*) Oh, go away. Father! Please! Take her away!

MRS. BRENNAN. (*pulling at his arm*) Take me away this second or I'll never speak again to you till the day I die!

CARMODY. (*pushes her violently away from him—raging, his fist uplifted*) Shut your gab, I'm saying!

MRS. BRENNAN. The devil mend you and yours then! I'm leavin' you. (*She starts for the door.*)

CARMODY. (*hastily*) Wait a bit, Maggie. I'm coming. (*She goes into the room, slamming the door, but once inside she stands still, trying to listen.* CARMODY *glares down at his daughter's pale twitching face with closed eyes. Finally he croaks in a whining tone of fear*) Is your last word a cruel one to me this day, Eileen? (*She remains silent. His face darkens. He turns and strides out of the door.* MARY *darts after him with a frightened cry of "Papa."* EILEEN *covers her face with her hands and a shudder of relief runs over her body.*)

MRS. BRENNAN. (*as* CARMODY *enters the room—in a mollified tone*) So you've come, have you? Let's go, then! (CARMODY *stands looking at her in silence, his expression full of gloomy rage. She bursts out impatiently*) Are you comin' or are you goin' back to her? (*She grabs* MARY's *arm and pushes her toward the door to the hall*) Are you comin' or not, I'm asking?

CARMODY. (*somberly—as if to himself*) There's something wrong in the whole of this—that I can't make out. (*With sudden fury he brandishes his fists as though defying someone and growls threateningly*) And I'll get drunk this night—dead, rotten drunk! (*He seems to detect disapproval in* MRS. BRENNAN's *face for he shakes his fist at her and repeats like a solemn oath*) I'll get drunk if my soul roasts for it—and no one in the whole world is strong enough to stop me! (MRS. BRENNAN *turns from him with a disgusted shrug of her shoulders and hustles* MARY *out of the door.* CARMODY, *after a second's pause, follows them.* EILEEN *lies still, looking out into the woods with empty, desolate eyes.* MISS HOWARD *comes into the room from the hall and goes to the porch, carrying a glass of milk in her hand.*)

MISS HOWARD. Here's your diet, Eileen. I forgot it until just now. Did you have a nice visit with your folks?

EILEEN. (*forcing a smile*) Yes.

MISS HOWARD. I hope they didn't worry you over home affairs?

EILEEN. No. (*She sips her milk and sets it back on the table with a shudder of disgust.*)

MISS HOWARD. (*with a smile*) What a face! You'd think you were taking poison.

EILEEN. (*with deep passion*) I wish it was poison!

MISS HOWARD. (*jokingly*) Oh, come now! That isn't a nice way to feel on the Sabbath. (*With a meaning smile*) I've some news that'll cheer you up, I bet. (*Archly*) Guess who's here on a visit?

EILEEN. (*startled—in a frightened whisper*) Who?

MISS HOWARD. Mr. Murray. (EILEEN *closes her eyes wincingly for a moment and a shadow of pain comes over her face*) He came just about the time your folks did. I saw him for a moment, not to speak to. (*Beaming—with a certain curiosity*) What do you think of that for news?

EILEEN. (*trying to conceal her agitation and assume a casual tone*) He must have come to be examined.

MISS HOWARD. (*with a meaning laugh*) Oh, I'd hardly say that was his main reason. (*In business-like tones*) Well, I've got to get back on the job. (*She turns to the door calling back jokingly*) He'll be in to see you of course, so look your prettiest. (*She goes out and shuts the door to the porch.* EILEEN *gives a frightened gasp and struggles up in bed as if she wanted to call the nurse to return. Then she lies back in a state of great nervous excitement, twisting her head with eager, fearful glances toward the door, listening, clasping and unclasping her thin fingers on the white spread. As* MISS HOWARD *walks across the room to the hall door, it is opened and* STEPHEN MURRAY *enters. A great change is visible in his face. It is much thinner and the former healthy tan has faded to a sallow pallor. Puffy shadows of sleeplessness and dissipation are marked under his heavy-lidded eyes. He is dressed in a well-fitting, expensive, dark suit, a white shirt with a soft collar and bright-colored tie.*)

MISS HOWARD. (*with pleased surprise, holding out her hand*) Hello, Mr. Murray.

MURRAY. (*shaking her hand—with a forced pleasantness*) How are you, Miss Howard?

MISS HOWARD. Fine as ever. It certainly looks natural to see you around here again—not that I hope you're here to stay, though. (*With a smile*) I suppose you're on your way to Eileen now. Well, I won't keep you. I've oodles of work to do. (*She opens the hall door. He starts for the porch*) Oh, I was forgetting— Congratulations! I've read those stories—all of us have. They're great. We're all so proud of you. You're one of our graduates, you know.

MURRAY. (*indifferently*) Oh,—that stuff.

MISS HOWARD. (*gaily*) Don't be so modest. Well, see you later, I hope.

MURRAY. Yes. Doctor Stanton invited me to stay for supper and I may—

MISS HOWARD. Fine! Be sure to! (*She goes out.* MURRAY *walks to porch door and steps out. He finds* EILEEN'S *eyes waiting for him. As their eyes meet she gasps involuntarily and he stops short in his tracks. For a moment they remain looking at each other in silence.*)

EILEEN. (*dropping her eyes—faintly*) Stephen.

MURRAY. (*much moved, strides to her bedside and takes her hands awkwardly*) Eileen. (*Then after a second's pause in which he searches her face and is shocked by the change illness has made—anxiously*) How are you feeling, Eileen? (*He grows confused by her gaze and his eyes shift from hers, which search his face with wild yearning.*)

EILEEN. (*forcing a smile*) Oh, I'm all right. (*Eagerly*) But you, Stephen? How are you? (*Excitedly*) Oh, it's good to see you again! (*Her eyes continue fixed on his face pleadingly, questioningly.*)

MURRAY. (*haltingly*) And it's sure great to see you again, Eileen. (*He releases her hand and turns away*) And I'm fine and dandy. I look a little done up, I guess, but that's only the result of too much New York.

EILEEN. (*sensing from his manner that whatever she has hoped for from his visit is not to be, sinks back on the pillows, shutting her eyes hopelessly, and cannot control a sigh of pain.*)

MURRAY. (*turning to her anxiously*) What's the matter, Eileen? You're not in pain, are you?

EILEEN. (*wearily*) No.

MURRAY. You haven't been feeling badly lately, have you? Your letters suddenly stopped—not a line for the past three weeks—and I—

EILEEN. (*bitterly*) I got tired of writing and never getting any answer, Stephen.

MURRAY. (*shamefaced*) Come, Eileen, it wasn't as bad as that. You'd think I never—and I did write, didn't I?

EILEEN. Right after you left here, you did, Stephen. Lately—

MURRAY. I'm sorry, Eileen. It wasn't that I didn't mean to—but—in New York it's so hard. You start to do one thing and something else interrupts you. You never seem to get any one thing done when it ought to be. You can understand that, can't you, Eileen?

EILEEN. (*sadly*) Yes. I understand everything now.

MURRAY. (*offended*) What do you mean by everything? You said that so strangely. You mean you don't believe— (*But she remains silent with her eyes shut. He frowns and takes to pacing up and down beside the bed*) Why have they got you stuck out here on this isolation porch, Eileen?

EILEEN. (*dully*) There was no room on the main porch, I suppose.

MURRAY. You never mentioned in any of your letters—

EILEEN. It's not very cheerful to get letters full of sickness. I wouldn't like to, I know.

MURRAY. (*hurt*) That isn't fair, Eileen. You know I— How long have you been back in the Infirmary?

EILEEN. About a month.

MURRAY. (*shocked*) A month! But you were up and about—on exercise, weren't you—before that?

EILEEN. No. I had to stay in bed while I was at the cottage.

MURRAY. You mean—ever since that time they sent you back—the day before I left?

EILEEN. Yes.

MURRAY. But I thought from the cheery tone of your letters that you were—

EILEEN. (*uneasily*) Getting better? I am, Stephen. I'm strong enough to be up now but Doctor Stanton wants me to take a good long rest this time so that when I get up again I'll be sure— (*She breaks off impatiently*) But don't let's talk about it. I'm all right. (MURRAY *glances down at her face worriedly. She changes the subject*) You've been over to see Doctor Stanton, haven't you?

MURRAY. Yes.

EILEEN. Did he examine you?

MURRAY. Yes. (*Carelessly*) Oh, he found me O.K.

EILEEN. I'm glad, Stephen. (*After a pause*) Tell about yourself— what you've been doing. You've written a lot lately, haven't you?

MURRAY. (*frowning*) No. I haven't been able to get down to it— somehow. There's so little time to yourself once you get to know people in New York. The sale of the stories you typed put me on easy street as far as money goes, so I've felt no need— (*He laughs weakly*) I guess I'm one of those who have to get down to hard pan before they get the kick to drive them to hard work.

EILEEN. (*surprised*) Was it hard work writing them up here? You used to seem so happy just in doing them.

MURRAY. I was—happier than I've been before or afterward. (*Cynically*) But—I don't know—it was a new game to me then and I was chuck full of illusions about the glory of it. (*He laughs half-heartedly*) Now I'm hardly a bit more enthusiastic over it than I used to be over newspaper work. It's like everything else, I guess. When you've got it, you find you don't want it.

EILEEN. (*looking at him wonderingly—disturbed*) But isn't just the writing itself worth while?

MURRAY. (*as if suddenly ashamed of himself—quickly*) Yes. Of course it is. I'm talking like a fool. I'm sore at everything because I'm dissatisfied with my own cussedness and laziness—and I want to pass the buck. (*With a smile of cheerful confidence*) It's only a fit. I'll come out of it all right and get down to brass tacks again.

EILEEN. (*with an encouraging smile*) That's the way you ought to feel. It'd be wrong—I've read the two stories that have come out so far over and over. They're fine, I think. Every line in them sounds like you, and at the same time sounds natural and like people and things you see every day. Everybody thinks they're fine, Stephen.

MURRAY. (*pleased but pretending cynicism*) Then they must be rotten. (*Then with self-assurance*) Well, I've plenty more of those stories in my head. (*Spiritedly*) And I'll make them so much better than what I've done so far, you won't recognize them. (*Smiling*) Darn it, do you know just talking about it makes me feel as if I could sit right down now and start in on one. Is it the fact I've worked here before—or is it seeing you, Eileen? (*Gratefully*) I really believe it's you. I haven't forgotten how you helped me before.

EILEEN. (*in a tone of pain*) Don't, Stephen. I didn't do anything.

MURRAY. (*eagerly*) Yes, you did. You made it possible. And since I've left the San, I've looked forward to your letters to boost up my spirits. When I felt down in the mouth over my own idiocy, I used to reread them, and they always were good medicine. I can't tell you how grateful I've felt, honestly!

EILEEN. (*faintly*) You're kind to say so, Stephen—but it was nothing, really.

MURRAY. And I can't tell you how I've missed those letters for the past three weeks. They left a big hole in things. I was worried about you—not having heard a word. (*With a smile*) So I came to look you up.

EILEEN. (*faintly—forcing an answering smile*) Well, you see now I'm all right.

MURRAY. (*concealing his doubt*) Yes, of course you are. Only I'd a darn sight rather see you up and about. We could take a walk, then

405

—through the woods. (*A wince of pain shadows* EILEEN s *face. She closes her eyes.* MURRAY *continues softly, after a pause*) You haven't forgotten that last night—out there—Eileen?

EILEEN. (*her lips trembling—trying to force a laugh*) Please, please don't remind me of that, Stephen. I was so silly and so sick, too. My temp was so high it must have made me—completely crazy—or I'd never dreamed of doing such a stupid thing. My head must have been full of wheels because I don't remember anything I did or said, hardly.

MURRAY. (*his pride taken down a peg by this—in a hurt tone*) Oh! Well—I haven't forgotten and I never will, Eileen. (*Then his face clears up as if a weight had been taken off his conscience*) Well—I rather thought you wouldn't take it seriously—afterward. You were all up in the air that night. And you never mentioned it in your letters—

EILEEN. (*pleadingly*) Don't talk about it! Forget it ever happened. It makes me feel— (*With a half-hysterical laugh*) like a fool!

MURRAY. (*worried*) All right, Eileen. I won't. Don't get worked up over nothing. That isn't resting, you know. (*Looking down at her closed eyes—solicitously*) Perhaps all my talking has tired you out? Do you feel done up? Why don't you try and take a nap now?

EILEEN. (*dully*) Yes, I'd like to sleep.

MURRAY. (*clasps her hands gently*) I'll leave you then. I'll drop back to say good-by and stay awhile before I go. I won't leave until the last train. (*As she doesn't answer*) Do you hear, Eileen?

EILEEN. (*weakly*) Yes. You'll come back—to say good-by.

MURRAY. Yes. I'll be back sure. (*He presses her hand and after a kindly glance of sympathy down at her face, tiptoes to the door and goes into the room, shutting the door behind him. When she hears the door shut* EILEEN *struggles up in bed and stretches her arms after him with an agonized sob* "Stephen!" *She hides her face in her hands and sobs brokenly.* MURRAY *walks across to the hall door and is about to go out when the door is opened and* MISS GILPIN *enters.*)

406

MISS GILPIN. (*hurriedly*) How do you do, Mr. Murray. Doctor Stanton just told me you were here.

MURRAY. (*as they shake hands—smiling*) How are you, Miss Gilpin?

MISS GILPIN. He said he'd examined you, and that you were O.K. I'm glad. (*Glancing at him keenly*) You've been talking to Eileen?

MURRAY. Just left her this second. She wanted to sleep for a while.

MISS GILPIN. (*wonderingly*) Sleep? (*Then hurriedly*) It's too bad. I wish I'd known you were here sooner. I wanted very much to talk to you before you saw Eileen. (*With a worried smile*) I still think I ought to have a talk with you.

MURRAY. Certainly, Miss Gilpin.

MISS GILPIN. (*takes a chair and places it near the hall door*) Sit down. She can't hear us here. Goodness knows this is hardly the place for confidences, but there are visitors all over and it'll have to do. Did you close the door tightly? She mustn't hear me above all. (*She goes to the porch door and peeps out for a moment; then comes back to him with flashing eyes*) She's crying! What have you been saying to her? Oh, it's too late, I know! What has happened out there? Tell me!

MURRAY. (*stammering*) Nothing. She's crying? Why, Miss Gilpin— you know I wouldn't hurt her for worlds.

MISS GILPIN. (*more calmly*) Intentionally, I know you wouldn't. But something has happened. (*Then briskly*) Since you don't seem inclined to confide in me, I'll have to in you. You noticed how badly she looks, didn't you?

MURRAY. Yes, I did.

MISS GILPIN. (*gravely*) She's been going down hill steadily— (*Meaningly*) ever since you left. She's in a very serious state, let me impress you with that. Doctor Stanton has given up hope of her improving here, and her father is unwilling to pay for her elsewhere now he knows there's a cheaper place—the State Farm. So she's to be sent there in a day or so.

MURRAY. (*springing to his feet—horrified*) To the State Farm!

MISS GILPIN. Her time here is long past. You know the rule—and she isn't getting better.

MURRAY. (*appalled*) That means—!

MISS GILPIN. (*forcibly*) Death! That's what it means for her!

MURRAY. (*stunned*) Good God, I never dreamed—

MISS GILPIN. In her case, it's certain. She'll die. And it wouldn't do any good to keep her here, either. She'd die here. She'll die anywhere because lately she's given up hope, she hasn't wanted to live any more. She's let herself go—and now it's too late.

MURRAY. Too late? You mean there's no chance—now? (MISS GILPIN *nods.* MURRAY *is overwhelmed—after a pause—stammering*) Isn't there—anything—we can do?

MISS GILPIN. (*sadly*) I don't know. I should have talked to you before. You see, she's seen you now. She knows. (*As he looks mystified she continues slowly*) I suppose you know that Eileen loves you, don't you?

MURRAY. (*as if defending himself against an accusation—with confused alarm*) No—Miss Gilpin. She may have felt something like that —once—but that was long ago before I left the San. She's forgotten all about it since, I know she has. (MISS GILPIN *smiles bitterly*) Why— just now—she said that part of it had all been so silly she felt she'd acted like a fool and didn't ever want to be reminded of it.

MISS GILPIN. She saw that you didn't love her—any more than you did in the days before you left. Oh, I used to watch you then. I sensed what was going on between you. I would have stopped it then out of pity for her, if I could have, if I didn't know that any interference would only make matters worse. (*She sighs—then after a pause*) You'll have to forgive me for speaking to you so boldly on a delicate subject. But, don't you see, it's for her sake. I love Eileen. We all do. (*Averting her eyes from his—in a low voice*) I know how Eileen feels, Mr. Murray. Once—a long time ago—I suffered as she is suffering— from the same mistake. But I had resources to fall back upon that Eileen hasn't got—a family who loved me and understood—friends—

so I pulled through. But it spoiled my life for a long time. (*Looking at him again and forcing a smile*) So I feel that perhaps I have a right to speak for Eileen who has no one else.

MURRAY. (*huskily—much moved*) Say anything you like, Miss Gilpin.

MISS GILPIN. (*after a pause—sadly*) You don't love her—do you?

MURRAY. No—I— I don't believe I've ever thought much of loving anyone—that way.

MISS GILPIN. (*sadly*) Oh, it's too late, I'm afraid. If we had only had this talk before you had seen her! I meant to talk to you frankly and if I found out you didn't love Eileen—there was always the forlorn hope that you might—I was going to tell you not to see her, for her sake—not to let her face the truth. For I'm sure she continued to hope in spite of everything, and always would—to the end—if she didn't see you. I was going to implore you to stay away, to write her letters that would encourage her hope, and in that way she'd never learn the truth. I thought of writing you all this—but—it's so delicate a matter—I didn't have the courage. (*With intense grief*) And now Doctor Stanton's decision to send her away makes everything doubly hard. When she knows *that*—she'll throw everything that holds her to life—out of the window! And think of it—her dying there alone!

MURRAY. (*very pale*) Don't! That shan't happen. I have money enough—I'll make more—to send her any place you think—

MISS GILPIN. That's something—but it doesn't touch the source of her unhappiness. If there were only some way to make her happy in the little time that's left to her! She has suffered so much through you. Oh, Mr. Murray, can't you tell her you love her?

MURRAY. (*after a pause—slowly*) But she'll never believe me, I'm afraid, now.

MISS GILPIN. (*eagerly*) But you must make her believe! And you must ask her to marry you. If you're engaged it will give you the right in her eyes to take her away. You can take her to some private San. There's a small place but a very good one at White Lake. It's

409

not too expensive, and it's a beautiful spot, out of the world, and you can live and work near by. And she'll be happy to the very last. Don't you think that's something you can give in return for her love for you?

MURRAY. (*slowly—deeply moved*) Yes. (*Then determinedly*) But I won't go into this thing by halves. It isn't fair to her. I'm going to marry her—yes, I mean it. I owe her that if it will make her happy.

MISS GILPIN. (*with a sad smile*) She'll never consent—for your sake —until she's well again. And stop and think, Mr. Murray. Even if she did consent to marry you right now the shock—it'd be suicide for her. I'd have to warn her against it myself. I've talked with Dr. Stanton. God knows I'd be the first one to hold out hope if there was any. There isn't. It's merely a case of prolonging the short time left to her and making it happy. You must bear that in mind—as a fact!

MURRAY. (*dully*) All right. I'll remember. But it's hell to realize— (*He turns suddenly toward the porch door*) I'll go out to her now while I feel—that—yes, I know I can make her believe me now.

MISS GILPIN. You'll tell me—later on?

MURRAY. Yes. (*He opens the door to the porch and goes out.* MISS GILPIN *stands for a moment looking after him worriedly. Then she sighs helplessly and goes out to the hall.* MURRAY *steps noiselessly out on the porch.* EILEEN *is lying motionless with her eyes closed.* MURRAY *stands looking at her, his face showing the emotional stress he is under, a great pitying tenderness in his eyes. Then he seems to come to a revealing decision on what is best to do for he tiptoes to the bedside and bending down with a quick movement, takes her in his arms, and kisses her*) Eileen!

EILEEN. (*startled at first, resists automatically for a moment*) Stephen! (*Then she succumbs and lies back in his arms with a happy sigh, putting both hands to the sides of his face and staring up at him adoringly*) Stephen, dear!

MURRAY. (*quickly questioning her before she can question him*)

You were fibbing—about that night—weren't you? You do love me, don't you, Eileen?

EILEEN. (*breathlessly*) Yes—I—but you, Stephen—you don't love me. (*She makes a movement as if to escape from his embrace.*)

MURRAY. (*genuinely moved—with tender reassurance*) Why do you suppose I came away up here if not to tell you I did? But they warned me—Miss Gilpin—that you were still weak and that I mustn't excite you in any way. And I—I didn't want—but I had to come back and tell you.

EILEEN. (*convinced—with a happy laugh*) And is that why you acted so strange—and cold? Aren't they silly to tell you that! As if being happy could hurt me! Why, it's just that, just you I've needed!

MURRAY. (*his voice trembling*) And you'll marry me, Eileen?

EILEEN. (*a shadow of doubt crossing her face momentarily*) Are you sure—you want me, Stephen?

MURRAY. (*a lump in his throat—huskily*) Yes. I do want you, Eileen.

EILEEN. (*happily*) Then I will—after I'm well again, of course. (*She kisses him.*)

MURRAY. (*chokingly*) That won't be long now, Eileen.

EILEEN. (*joyously*) No—not long—now that I'm happy for once in my life. I'll surprise you, Stephen, the way I'll pick up and grow fat and healthy. You won't know me in a month. How can you ever love such a skinny homely thing as I am now! (*With a laugh*) I couldn't if I was a man—love such a fright.

MURRAY. Ssshh!

EILEEN. (*confidently*) But you'll see now. I'll make myself get well. We won't have to wait long, dear. And can't you move up to the town near here where you can see me every day, and you can work and I can help you with your stories just as I used to—and I'll soon be strong enough to do your typing again. (*She laughs*) Listen to me—talking about helping you—as if they weren't all your own work, those blessed stories!—as if I had anything to do with it!

MURRAY. (*hoarsely*) You had! You did! They're yours. (*Trying to calm himself*) But you mustn't stay here, Eileen. You'll let me take you away, won't you?—to a better place—not far away—White Lake, it's called. There's a small private sanatorium there. Doctor Stanton says it's one of the best. And I'll live near by—it's a beautiful spot—and see you every day.

EILEEN. (*in the seventh heaven*) And did you plan out all this for me beforehand, Stephen? (*He nods with averted eyes. She kisses his hair*) You wonderful, kind dear! And it's a small place—this White Lake? Then we won't have so many people around to disturb us, will we? We'll be all to ourselves. And you ought to work so well up there. I know New York wasn't good for you—alone—without me. And I'll get well and strong so quick! And you say it's a beautiful place? (*Intensely*) Oh, Stephen, any place in the world would be beautiful to me—if you were with me! (*His face is hidden in the pillow beside her. She is suddenly startled by a muffled sob—anxiously*) Why—Stephen—you're—you're crying! (*The tears start to her own eyes.*)

MURRAY. (*raising his face which is this time alight with a passionate awakening—a revelation*) Oh, I do love you, Eileen! I do! I love you, love you!

EILEEN. (*thrilled by the depths of his present sincerity—but with a teasing laugh*) Why, you say that as if you'd just made the discovery, Stephen!

MURRAY. Oh, what does it matter, Eileen! Oh, what a blind selfish ass I've been! You are my life—everything! I love you, Eileen! I do! I do! And we'll be married— (*Suddenly his face grows frozen with horror as he remembers the doom. For the first time Death confronts him face to face as a menacing reality.*)

EILEEN. (*terrified by the look in his eyes*) What is it, Stephen? What—?

MURRAY. (*with a groan—protesting half aloud in a strangled voice*) No! No! It can't be—! My God! (*He clutches her hands and hides his face in them.*)

EILEEN. (*with a cry*) Stephen! What is the matter? (*Her face suddenly betrays an awareness, an intuitive sense of the truth*) Oh— Stephen— (*Then with a childish whimper of terror*) Oh, Stephen, I'm going to die! I'm going to die!

MURRAY. (*lifting his tortured face—wildly*) No!

EILEEN. (*her voice sinking to a dead whisper*) I'm going to die.

MURRAY. (*seizing her in his arms in a passionate frenzy and pressing his lips to hers*) No, Eileen, no, my love, no! What are you saying? What could have made you think it? You—die? Why, of course, we're all going to die—but— Good God! What damned nonsense! You're getting well—every day. Everyone—Miss Gilpin—Stanton— everyone told me that. I swear before God, Eileen, they did! You're still weak, that's all. They said—it won't be long. You mustn't think that—not now.

EILEEN. (*miserably—unconvinced*) But why did you look at me— that way—with that awful look in your eyes—? (*While she is speaking* MISS GILPIN *enters the room from the hallway. She appears worried, agitated. She hurries toward the porch but stops inside the doorway, arrested by* MURRAY'S *voice.*)

MURRAY. (*takes* EILEEN *by the shoulders and forces her to look into his eyes*) I wasn't thinking about you then— No, Eileen—not you. I didn't mean you—but me—yes, me! I couldn't tell you before. They'd warned me—not to excite you—and I knew that would—if you loved me.

EILEEN. (*staring at him with frightened amazement*) You mean you—you're sick again?

MURRAY. (*desperately striving to convince her*) Yes. I saw Stanton. I lied to you before—about that. It's come back on me, Eileen—you see how I look—I've let myself go. I don't know how to live without you, don't you see? And you'll—marry me now—without waiting— and help me to get well—you and I together—and not mind their lies—what they say to prevent you? You'll do that, Eileen?

EILEEN. I'll do anything for you— And I'd be so happy— (*She breaks down*) But, Stephen, I'm so afraid. I'm all mixed up. Oh, Stephen, I don't know what to believe!

MISS GILPIN. (*who has been listening thunderstruck to* MURRAY'S *wild pleading, at last summons up the determination to interfere—steps out on the porch—in a tone of severe remonstrance*) Mr. Murray!

MURRAY. (*starts to his feet with wild, bewildered eyes—confusedly*) Oh—you— (MISS GILPIN *cannot restrain an exclamation of dismay as she sees his face wrung by despair.* EILEEN *turns her head away with a little cry as if she would hide her face in the bedclothes. A sudden fierce resolution lights up* MURRAY'S *countenance—hoarsely*) You're just in time, Miss Gilpin! Eileen! Listen! You'll believe Miss Gilpin, won't you? She knows all about it. (EILEEN *turns her eyes questioningly on the bewildered nurse.*)

MISS GILPIN. What—?

MURRAY. (*determinedly*) Doctor Stanton—he must have told you about me. Eileen doesn't believe me—when I tell her I got T. B. again. She thinks—I don't know what. I know you're not supposed to, but—can't you tell her—?

MISS GILPIN. (*stunned by being thus defiantly confronted—stammeringly*) Mr. Murray! I—I—how can you ask—

MURRAY. (*quickly*) She loves me—and I—I—love her! (*He holds her eyes and speaks with a passion of sincerity that compels belief*) I love her, do you hear?

MISS GILPIN. (*falteringly*) You—love—Eileen?

MURRAY. Yes! I do! (*Entreatingly*) So—tell her—won't you?

MISS GILPIN. (*swallowing hard, her eyes full of pity and sorrow fixed on* EILEEN) Yes—Eileen— (*She turns away slowly toward the door.*)

EILEEN. (*with a little cry of alarmed concern, stretches out her hands to* MURRAY *protectingly*) Poor Stephen—dear! (*He grasps her hands and kisses them.*)

MISS GILPIN. (*in a low voice*) Mr. Murray. May I speak to you?

MURRAY. (*with a look of questioning defiance at her*) Certainly.

MISS GILPIN. (*turns to* EILEEN *with a forced smile*) I won't steal him away for more than a moment, Eileen. (EILEEN *smiles happily.*)

MURRAY. (*follows* MISS GILPIN *into the room. She leads him to the far end of the room near the door to the hall, after shutting the porch door carefully behind him. He looks at her defiantly*) Well?

MISS GILPIN. (*in low, agitated tones*) What has happened? I feel as if I may have done a great wrong to myself—to you—to her—by that lie. And yet—something forced me.

MURRAY. (*moved*) It has saved her—us. Oh, how can I explain what happened? I suddenly saw—how beautiful and sweet and good she is—how I couldn't bear the thought of life without her— That's all. (*Determinedly*) She must marry me at once and I'll take her away— the far West—any place Stanton thinks can help. And she can take care of me—as she thinks—and I know she'll grow well as I seem to grow well. Oh Miss Gilpin, don't you see? No half and half measures can help us—help her. (*Fiercely as if defying her*) But we'll win together. We can! We must! There are things doctors can't value—can't know the strength of! (*Exultantly*) You'll see! I'll make Eileen get well, I tell you! Happiness will cure! Love is stronger than— (*He suddenly breaks down before the pitying negation she cannot keep from her eyes. He sinks on a chair, shoulders bowed, face hidden in his hands, with a groan of despair*) Oh, why did you give me a hopeless hope?

MISS GILPIN. (*putting her hand on his shoulder—with tender compassion—sadly*) Isn't all life just that—when you think of it? (*Her face lighting up with a consoling revelation*) But there must be something back of it—some promise of fulfillment—somehow—somewhere—in the spirit of hope itself.

MURRAY. (*dully*) What do words mean to me now? (*Then suddenly starting to his feet and flinging off her hand with disdainful strength—violently and almost insultingly*) What damned rot! I tell you we'll win! We must! All the verdicts of all the doctors—what do they matter? This is—beyond you! And we'll win in spite of you!

(*Scornfully*) How dare you use the word hopeless—as if it were the last! Come now, confess, damn it! There's always hope, isn't there? What do you *know*? Can you say you *know* anything?

MISS GILPIN. (*taken aback by his violence for a moment, finally bursts into a laugh of helplessness which is close to tears*) I? I know nothing—absolutely nothing! God bless you both! (*She raises her handkerchief to her eyes and hurries out to the hallway without turning her head.* MURRAY *stands looking after her for a moment; then strides out to the porch.*)

EILEEN. (*turning and greeting him with a shy smile of happiness as he comes and kneels by her bedside*) Stephen! (*He kisses her. She strokes his hair and continues in a tone of motherly, self-forgetting solicitude*) I'll have to look out for you, Stephen, won't I? From now on? And see that you rest so many hours a day—and drink your milk when I drink mine—and go to bed at nine sharp when I do—and obey everything I tell you—and—

CURTAIN

DYNAMO

CHARACTERS

REVEREND HUTCHINS LIGHT

AMELIA, *his wife*

REUBEN, *their son*

RAMSAY FIFE, *superintendent of a hydro-electric plant*

MAY, *his wife*

ADA, *their daughter*

JENNINGS, *an operator at the plant*

GENERAL SCENE

The exterior of the homes of the Lights and the Fifes in a small town in Connecticut. These houses stand side by side, facing front, on the street. They are separated by narrow strips of lawn, with a lilac hedge at center marking the boundary-line between the two properties, and a row of tall maples in the background behind the yards and the two houses. The Fife house, a small brownish-tinted modern stucco bungalow type, recently built, is at left; the Light home, a little old New England white frame cottage with green shutters, at right. Only the half sections of the two houses are visible which are nearest to each other, the one containing the Fife sitting room, with Ramsay's and May's bedroom directly above it, and the section of the Lights' home in which are their sitting room and Reuben's bedroom on the floor above.

As the separate scenes require, the front walls of these rooms are removed to show the different interiors. All these rooms are small, the ones in the Light home particularly so.

It is the month of May of the present day. The lilacs are in bloom, the grass is a fresh green.

SCENE 1—The Light sitting room and Reuben's bedroom above it.

SCENE 2—The Fife sitting room with Ramsay's and May's bedroom on the floor above.

SCENE 3—The Light and Fife sitting rooms.

SCENE 4—Reuben's bedroom.

ACT TWO

SCENE 1—Same as Act One, Scene One.
The Light sitting room.
Fifteen months later.

SCENE 2—Same as Scene One, except that Reuben's bedroom is revealed.

SCENE 3—Exterior of the Light and Power Company's hydro-electric plant.
A half hour later.

ACT THREE

GENERAL SCENE—The Hydro-Electric Power Plant near the town.
Four months later.

SCENE 1—Exterior of the plant.

SCENE 2—Interiors of the upper and lower switch galleries.

SCENE 3—Interiors of the two switch galleries, the switchboard room, and the dynamo room.

DYNAMO

ACT ONE

Scene one—*It is evening. In the background between the two houses the outlines of the maples are black against a sky pale with the light of a quarter-moon. Now and then there is a faint flash of lightning from far off and a low rumble of thunder.*

The LIGHT *sitting room and* REUBEN'S *bedroom are revealed. Both are sparsely furnished with the bare necessities.* REUBEN'S *bedroom contains an old four-poster bed, front, facing left, a small table on which are stacked his textbooks, and a chair in left corner, front. In the left wall is a window. A washstand with bowl and pitcher is in the left corner, rear, and an old-fashioned bureau in the middle of the rear wall. To the right of this is the door of a clothes closet. The door to the hall and the stairs is at right, rear. There is a lighted kerosene lamp on the table.*

In the sitting room below there is a table at center, front. The minister's armchair is beside this on the left. His wife's rocker is at the right of the table. Farther right is another chair. Three small hooked rugs are on the floor. Several framed prints of scenes from the Bible hang on the walls. The minister's small desk is placed against the left wall beside the window. On the table at center are a cheap oil reading lamp, a Bible, and some magazines. There is a door to the hall in the right wall, rear.

The ceilings of both rooms are low, the wallpaper so faded that the ugliness of its color and design has been toned down into a neutral blur. But everything in this home is spotlessly clean and in order, the old furniture and floors are oiled and polished.

The REVEREND HUTCHINS LIGHT *is seated in his armchair, his wife in her rocker. He is a man in his early sixties, slightly under medium height, ponderously built. His face is square, ribbed with wrinkles, the forehead low, the nose heavy, the eyes small and gray-blue, the reddish hair grizzled and bushy, the stubborn jaw weakened by a big indecisive mouth. His voice is the bullying one of a sermonizer who is the victim of an inner uncertainty that compensates itself by being boomingly overassertive.*

His wife, AMELIA, *is fifteen years his junior and appears even younger. Her stout figure is still firm and active, with large breasts and broad, round hips. She must have been pretty as a girl. Even now her dark-complected face, with its big brown eyes and wavy black hair, retains its attractiveness although it has grown fleshy. Her expression is one of virtuous resignation. Only her mouth is rebellious. It is a thin small mouth, determined and stubborn.*

In the bedroom above, their son, REUBEN, *is sitting in his shirt sleeves on the side of his bed. He is seventeen, tall and thin. His eyes are large, shy and sensitive, of the same gray-blue as his father's. His mouth is like his father's. His jaw is stubborn, his thick hair curly and reddish-blond. He speaks timidly and hesitatingly, as a much younger boy might. His natural voice has an almost feminine gentleness. In intercourse with the world, however, he instinctively imitates his father's tone, booming self-protectively.*

HUTCHINS LIGHT *has a pad on which he has been trying to make notes for his next sermon, but his mind is abstracted. He stares before him with the resentful air of one brooding over a wrong done him and unsuccessfully plotting revenge. His wife is pretending to read, but her thoughts are actively elsewhere, and she glances calculatingly at her husband from under lowered lids.*

In the bedroom above, REUBEN'S *eyes are turned toward the window, his face eager with dreams.*

LIGHT. (*arguing tormentedly within himself*)
What did he mean about Reuben? . . . that foul-mouthed scoundrel! . . . "Better call in your son or some night I might mistake

his odor of sanctity for a skunk's and fill his" . . . filthy word
belching from his grinning mouth! . . . "full of buckshot" . . . I
heard the corner loafers laugh . . . and I had to slink by and pretend not to hear! . . . If it weren't for my cloth I'd have beaten
his face to a bloody pulp! . . . I'd . . .

(*Suddenly horrified at himself*)

A murderer's thoughts! . . . Lord God, forgive me! . . .

MRS. LIGHT. (*glances at him and speaks in a gentle tone that carries
a challenging quality*) Hutchins, do you realize Reuben will grad-
uate from school in less than a month?

LIGHT. (*oblivious*)

But, Lord, Thou knowest what a thorn in the flesh that atheist,
Fife, has been since the devil brought him next door! . . .

(*Protesting petulantly to his God*)

How long, O Lord . . . does not his foul ranting begin to try
Thy patience? . . . is not the time ripe to smite this blasphemer
who defies Thee publicly to strike him dead? . . . Lord God of
Hosts, why dost Thou not strike him? . . . If Thou didst, I would
proclaim the awful warning of it over all America! . . . I would
convert multitudes, as it was once my dream to do! . . .

MRS. LIGHT. Hutchins, please pay attention to what I'm saying.
Don't you think we ought to decide definitely about Reuben's future?

LIGHT. (*turns to her with a frown*) I have decided. He shall follow
in my footsteps—mine and those of my father before me and his father
before him. It is God's manifest will! (*He presses his lips tightly together—an effort to appear implacable that gives his face the expression of a balky animal's.*)

MRS. LIGHT. (*thinks scornfully*)

He is always so sure of what God wills! . . . but Reuben'll never be
a minister if I can prevent it! . . . I'd rather see him dead than go
through the poverty and humiliation I've had to face! . . . Reuben's
got to go to college . . . then into business . . . marry a nice girl
with money . . . he doesn't care anything about girls yet, thank
goodness!

(*She speaks in a meek, persuasive tone*) Each of us must judge about

423

Reuben according to the light vouchsafed by God. He doesn't feel any call to the ministry and I think it would be a great sin if—

LIGHT. (*his voice booming*) And I tell you, Amelia, it is God's will!

REUBEN. (*hearing his father's voice, jumps to his feet and stares down toward the room with an expression of boyish apprehension*) What's he shouting about? . . . has he heard about Ada and me? . . . he'll raise the roof! . . . but Mother'll take my side against him . . . she's always sided with me . . .

(*Then resentfully*)

What do I care about him anyway? . . . he hates Fife because he's scared of him . . . he's scared to take up Fife's challenge to debate about whether there's a God or not . . . when Fife took out his watch and said if there was a God let Him prove it by striking him dead in five minutes, why was it nothing happened? . . . I should think if . . .

(*He looks around uneasily, afraid of where his thoughts are leading him. A faint flash of lightning from the distant storm flickers through his window. He starts guiltily and hastily makes a reassuring declaration of faith*)

Of course there's a God . . . He wouldn't pay any attention to a fool like Fife, that's all . . .

LIGHT. I believe that storm must be coming this way. (*He gets to his feet—a bit shamefacedly*) I think I'll close the shutters.

MRS. LIGHT. But it'll make it so dreadfully close in here! (*Then seeing his ashamed look, she smiles*) Oh, all right, close them if you're getting scared.

LIGHT. (*his dignity ruffled, turns his back on her and goes to the window*) Lightning gets on lots of people's nerves without their being afraid of it.

REUBEN.

Aw, what's the matter with me? . . . that lightning had nothing to do with what I was thinking . . .

(*He goes to the window and looks over toward the* FIFE *home*)

Ada said she'd put a record on the Victrola as soon as she was free . . . then I was to meet her down by the lilacs . . .

(He breathes in the spring)

> Gee, those lilacs smell sweet . . . I wish she'd hurry up . . . I've got to get up my nerve and tell her I love her . . .

LIGHT. *(stands by the window and sniffs the air)* Can you smell the perfume of the lilacs, Amelia? Do you remember our first spring here?

MRS. LIGHT. Of course. *(Then, after a pause, her voice turned bitter)* Twenty-three years! It's a long time to live in this awful little house! Hutchins, are you ever going to insist that they install electric lighting here? It's a shame the way they deny you the ordinary comforts of life!

LIGHT. *(turns away and leans out of the window. staring into the night)*

> Comforts of life . . . she has always desired the comfortable path . . . where the spirit decays in the sinful sloth of the flesh . . .

(From the open, curtained windows of the FIFE *living room a burst of laughter is heard—*FIFE's *voice, sardonic and malicious.* LIGHT *draws back into the room, muttering viciously)* Scum of the earth! *(Then turning on his wife)* Tell me, has Reuben been having anything to do with that cursed pack next door? That scoundrel called something at me on the street today—

MRS. LIGHT. *(impatiently)* Don't you know that man well enough by this time not to pay attention to his trying to rile you?

LIGHT. Then answer me this: why has Reuben taken such a sudden notion to going out in the evening lately?

MRS. LIGHT. Do you expect a boy of his age to stay in like a poor stick-in-the-mud just because he happens to be a minister's son—especially when it's spring?

LIGHT. I remembered that it's spring—and I've just remembered that Fife has a daughter!

MRS. LIGHT. That painted flapper with her skirts hitched up over her knees! Do you think for one moment that Reuben, who never looks at girls anyway—and knowing what her father is— Really,

Hutchins, you're getting just too stupid! (*From the* FIFE *house comes the sound of a Victrola starting a jazz record.*)

REUBEN. (*starts from his dream by the window upstairs*)
That's her signal! . . .
(*He hurriedly puts on his coat*)
I better sneak out the back . . .
(*He blows out the light and makes his way carefully out of the bedroom door in right, rear.*)

LIGHT. (*listening to the Victrola, fixes his eyes on his wife combatively*) You may call me as stupid as you like but I insist there was something back of what Fife said about Reuben. He sneered that we'd better keep him home at night and insinuated he was hanging around their place. The thought of that girl of his never entered my head until a moment ago—but what else could he mean? I'm going to face Reuben with it right now and we'll see what he has to say for himself.

MRS. LIGHT. (*sharply*) Now don't you go preaching at him again. You better let me talk to him first. He's never lied to me. (*She goes toward the door in rear, plainly worried now but trying to make little of it*) You're always so ready to believe the worst of him. I know it's all nonsense. (*She goes out.*)

LIGHT. (*sits thinking gloomily*)
Never lied to her . . . she means he does to me . . . why? . . .
have I been too stern? . . . but even when he was little I sensed in
him his mother's rebellious spirit . . . and now . . . if it is Fife's
daughter . . . what a feather in that blasphemer's cap to corrupt
my son! . . . how the gossips would sneer at me! . . .
(*This thought drives him frantic—he paces up and down trying vainly to calm himself*)
No, no! . . . Reuben could never be guilty of so base a
treachery! . . .
(*He sits down by the table and, picking up his Bible, begins to read in a determined effort to get his mind off the subject.*)

MRS. LIGHT. (*can be dimly made out entering the bedroom above*

426

just as REUBEN, *coming from the back door of the house, slinks stealthily around the rear corner across the patch of moonlit lawn to the shadow of the lilacs. Keeping in this shadow he moves down until he comes to a small gap that is almost at the end of the hedge, front. He stands by this, waiting nervously, peering through the gap at the* FIFE *house.* MRS. LIGHT *thinks worriedly)*

> Gone to bed? . . . so early? . . . was he sick and didn't tell me? . . .

(She has come to the bed—with sudden fear)

> He's not here! . . . he sneaked out! . . . the first time he ever did such a thing! . . . but how do I know it's the first? . . . all the evenings I thought he was here studying . . . it can only mean one thing! . . . a girl! . . . not a good girl! . . . it must be that Fife girl! . . .

(She goes to the window, peering out but keeping her head carefully inside—with fierce jealousy)

> That dirty little . . . I'd like to see her try to catch my Reuben! . . .

(There is a strong flash of distant lightning that suddenly reveals REUBEN *in his hiding place by the hedge. She gives a gasp)*

> Oh! . . . there he is! . . . watching their house! . . . I'll just watch him and make sure. . . . Oh, Reuben, I can't believe it, you've never noticed girls! . . .

There is darkness for a moment—(as if the moon had passed behind a cloud)—to mark the end of Scene One. No time elapses between Scenes One and Two.

ACT ONE—SCENE TWO

W HEN *it grows light again the outer walls of the two rooms in the* LIGHT *home have been replaced, while the interiors of the* FIFE *sitting room and the couple's bedroom above it are now revealed. There is one small window on the top floor front of the*

LIGHT *home, two on the ground floor.* MRS. LIGHT's *head can be seen peering out of the side bedroom window at* REUBEN, *crouched in the shadow of the lilacs. The two rooms in the* FIFE *home, bright with all their electric lights on, are of a glaring newness. There is a table at center, front, in the sitting room, a Victrola in the rear corner, left, near the door in the left wall which leads to the hall. In the right wall are three windows looking out on the lawn toward the lilac hedge and the* LIGHT *home. These windows are repeated in the same series in the bedroom above. The bed is at left, front, its head against the left wall. In the same wall, to the rear of the bed, is the door. There is a dressing table with a big mirror against the rear wall, right, near the windows.*

RAMSAY FIFE *is seated at the left of the table, glancing through the pages of a technical book on Hydro-Electric Engineering. His wife is lying back in a chaise longue that she has pushed close to the windows on the right so she can stare out up at the sky.*

FIFE *is a small wiry man of fifty, of Scotch-Irish origin, with a sharp face and keen black eyes. His thin mouth is full of the malicious humor of the practical joker. He has a biting tongue, but at bottom is a good-natured man except where the religious bigotry of his atheism is concerned. His wife is tall and stout, weighing well over two hundred. Her face must have once been one of those rosy-cheeked pretty doll-like faces and, in spite of its fat, it has kept its girlish naïveté and fresh complexion. Her figure is not formless nor flabby. It suggests, rather, an inert strength. A mass of heavy copper-colored hair is piled without apparent design around her face. Her mouth is small with full lips. Her eyes are round and dark blue. Their expression is blank and dreamy. Her voice is sentimental and wondering. She is about forty years old.*

Their daughter, ADA, *sixteen, who is upstairs in the bedroom putting on a heavy make-up of rouge and mascara, resembles her father more than her mother. She has his alert quality. Her pretty face, with her mother's big blue eyes, is alive and keen, her mouth has a touch of*

*her father's malicious humor. Her brown hair is boyishly bobbed. Her
speech is self-assertive and consciously slangy. Beneath her flip talk,
however, one senses a strong trace of her mother's sentimentality.*

MRS. FIFE. (*dreaming sentimentally*)
  I hear Ada upstairs . . . she's primping up before my mirror . . .
  she's falling in love . . . it's nice to be in love in May . . . I love
  May better than any other month . . . May is when I first met
  Ramsay . . . it's warm tonight . . . I mustn't forget to make
  Ramsay change to his summer underwear this week . . . he always
  wears his heavies too long and gets prickly heat and then he's
  terrible cross . . .

FIFE. (*reading—disgustedly*)
  "Hydro-Electric Engineering" . . . it's studying this stuff gives
  those stuck-up engineers their diplomas . . . "Frequency and number of phases" . . . "Inherent Regulations" . . . "Parallel Working" . . . "Wave Form" . . . diagrams and equations! . . . "The
  kinetic energy of a rotor of diameter D and axial length L, running
  at a speed of rotation n, is theoretically proportional to $D4 Ln2$"
  . . . arrh! . . . the devil take their theories! . . . when anything
  goes wrong at the plant it's me who fixes it without any theory! . . .
(*He tosses the book on the table and speaks to his wife*) I wish Town-
send wouldn't go forcing his books on me, telling me I owe it to myself to pass for engineer's papers. (*With a chuckle*) Him arguing
with me and at the same time admitting "Fife, you know a damn
sight more about this game than I do."

MRS. FIFE. (*mooning at him with adoring eyes*) You know more
than anyone, Ramsay.

FIFE. (*pleased but amused—teasing her as he would a big child*)
Oho, I do, do I? How the hell do you know? (*Then complacently*)
Well, I do know more than most. There isn't a damn job in the game
I haven't had a hand at sometime or another. (*He looks at her and
sees she is not listening any more*)
  Look at her . . . in a dope dream again . . . I might as well
  be married to a cow . . .

(*Then amusedly*)

> Well, she's a damn funny woman . . . I've never seen her equal anywhere . . .

(*He sees the newspaper on the table and reaches for it, glances at the headlines and settles down to reading with a grunt of awakened interest.*)

MRS. FIFE. (*has again fallen to dreaming sentimentally of the past*)

> When I first met Ramsay he was a linesman . . . I loved him at first sight . . . he was so romantic looking with those steel climbing things on his legs . . . and he wore a colored handkerchief round his neck just like a cowboy . . . Pa and Ma warned me linesmen were no good . . . they just ruined you and went their way . . . they were wrong about Ramsay . . . except he did ruin me . . . I said, why is it wrong when I love him? . . . Pa yelled to get out, I'd disgraced the family . . . I never expected Ramsay'd marry me . . . he was the roving kind . . . but as soon as he knew he'd got me into trouble he spoke right up . . . "Oh, hell, then I guess I've got to marry you" . . . and I said yes, and I was awful happy . . . and five months after Ada was born and he was crazy about her from the first . . . and we've all been happy ever since . . .

(*She sighs contentedly.*)

ADA. (*in the bedroom above, finishes making up and inspects herself critically in the mirror—approvingly*)

> I got to hand it to you, baby, you're there! . . . Gosh, how long is it since I put on that record? . . . Rube'll be waiting . . . he's as bashful as a kid . . . but that's what I like about him . . . I'm sick of these fresh guys that think all they have to do is wink and you fall! . . . Rube has got honest-to-God feelings . . . but of course, I'd never love him . . . he's too big a Mama's boy for me . . .

(*She goes to the door and puts her hand on the switch*)

> Well, let's go . . . I'm dying to see if he'll have nerve enough to kiss me . . .

(*She turns out the light.*)

REUBEN. (*crouched by the hedge, gives a start as a flash of lightning flickers over the sky*)

Gosh, I wish Ada'd hurry up . . . this isn't much fun . . . I'm losing all my nerve waiting . . .

MRS. LIGHT. (*bending out of the window in* REUBEN's *bedroom—in suspense between suspicion and hope*)
She doesn't seem to be coming . . . maybe it's only some game he's playing . . . waiting to scare some friend of his . . .

FIFE. (*looking up from his paper with a snort of disgust just as* ADA *enters the room*) The bloody swinepot!

ADA. (*comes and puts an arm around his shoulder—teasingly*) What's the bad news, Pop? Has another Fundamentalist been denying Darwin?

FIFE. (*boiling over with indignation, thrusting the paper on her, his finger pointing out the article*) Read this and you won't joke about it! (*As* ADA *begins to read, he speaks to his wife*) Of all the yellow tricks!

MRS. FIFE. (*coming out of her dream with a start*) What, Ramsay?

FIFE. This story in the paper! There was a man in Ohio many years back killed another fellow in a fight about a girl. He got twenty years for it, but the girl helped him to escape and they both got clean away to the Coast, where he settled down under another name and they were married and had a daughter. He became one of the town's best citizens, and damned if his daughter didn't get engaged to the minister's son! Then, just before the wedding, the old man feels he's honor bound to tell his future son-in-law the secret of his past; so the damned idiot blathers the whole story of his killing the man and breaking jail! And what do you suppose that young skunk does? Breaks off with the girl and goes to the police with the story, saying he's bound by his conscience to squeal on him!

ADA. (*who has finished reading the story*) Phew! Some louse, that boy!

FIFE. Arrh! They're all the same, the Bible-punching breed! (*Then with a touch of severity*) And mind you bear that in mind, young lady, when you're fooling with that young ass next door!

431

ADA. Hey, listen, Pop! Honestly, I think you've got a nerve to—Why, it was you said to start up an acquaintance with him, when I told you I'd caught him staring at me, because you knew how it'd get his old man's goat!

FIFE. (*his sense of humor returning—with a malicious grin*) Aye, it will that! I gave him a strong hint on the street today that upset him. Oh, if you'd only make a prize jackass of that yellow Nancy son of his!

ADA. Say, why have you got it in for Rube so? He's not to blame for his father. (*Then hastily*) Not that it's anything in my young life. I'm simply having fun kidding him along. (*Then defensively again*) But Rube's a good scout—in his way. He isn't yellow.

MRS. FIFE. (*suddenly—with a placid certainty*) You're falling in love, Ada.

ADA. (*confused*) Aw, Mom, where d'you get that stuff?

FIFE. (*has glanced at her with suspicion*) So you don't believe that lad's yellow, don't you? What'll you bet he isn't? (*Then as she doesn't answer*) I dare you to bring him in tonight, and let me talk to him and you listen, and if I don't show him up yellow then I'll buy you the best dress you can find in the town! (*As she hesitates—tauntingly*) Are you afraid to take me up?

ADA. (*with defensive flippancy, turns to go*) I'll think about it. There's a dress in Steele's I've had my eye on. (*She goes out the door at left.*)

FIFE. (*looks after her—frowning*)

She acts queer about him . . . it's time I took a hand in this . . . I've got to fix up a scheme on him quick . . . she'll bring him back if she has to drag him . . .

ADA. (*has come out of the house by the front door, off left, and enters from the left, then hesitates for a moment, debating with herself*)

Shall I make him come in? . . . he'll be scared stiff! . . . but Pop was only bluffing . . . well, I'll just call his bluff! . . . he can't get away with that stuff with me! . . .

(*She walks toward the gap in the hedge.*)

MRS. LIGHT. (*can see her now from the window*)
There she comes . . . the little harlot! . . .

ADA. (*calling*) Rube.

REUBEN. (*comes through the hedge to her—sheepishly*) Hello, Ada.
(*Then, as he stands beside her, looking down into her face, a sudden
thrill of desire almost overcomes his timidity*) Gosh, Ada,—you're
pretty in the moonlight. I—I wish— (*His courage fails him—lamely*)
It's certainly grand tonight, isn't it?

ADA. Yeah. It's great. (*She takes one of his hands*) Come on in my
house and meet Pop. I want you to see he isn't the devil out of hell
your old man makes him out to be.

REUBEN. (*immediately terrified*) I can't, Ada! You know I can't.
Why don't we walk the same as—

ADA. I'm sick of walking. (*As he still holds back—tauntingly*) Are
you scared Pop will eat you? You make me sick, Rube!

REUBEN. It's not because I'm scared of your father; it's because—

ADA. Afraid your Mama would spank you if she found out? (*Then
as he still hesitates*) Oh, very well, you know what you can do, don't
you? (*She turns her back on him and walks away.*)

REUBEN. Ada! Wait a minute! Please don't get sore! I'll come!

ADA. Good boy! (*She suddenly raises herself on tiptoe and kisses
him—with a little laugh*) There! That's to help keep your nerve up!

REUBEN. (*a wave of passion coming over him, grabs her by the shoulders and bends his face close to hers*) Ada!

ADA. Ouch! That hurts, Rube!

REUBEN. I don't care if it does! I love you, Ada! (*He tries to kiss her.*)

ADA. (*struggling away from him*) Hey, cut it out! What do you
think I am? (*Then, as, brought back to himself he releases her in
shamefaced confusion, she adds tartly, her confidence restored and
her temper a bit ruffled*) Listen here, Rube, just because I kissed you
in fun, don't get too fresh!

REUBEN. I—I didn't mean nothing bad—honest I didn't!

433

ADA. All right, only don't get rough again. (*Taking his hand—in a bullying tone*) Come on. Let's go in. (REUBEN *follows her off left mechanically, a look of growing dread on his face.*)

MRS. LIGHT.

She kissed him! . . . the brazen little harlot! . . . where is she taking him? . . . I've got to stop her! . . .

(*She draws back quickly from the window and can be made out going hurriedly from the bedroom.*)

FIFE. (*irritably*)

May the devil kill me if I can think up a good scheme . . .

(*He turns his exasperation on his wife*) How can I think in the same room with you? It's like trying to swim in glue! For God's sake, get out of here!

MRS. FIFE. (*raises herself to her feet placidly, without a trace of resentment*) I'll go upstairs and read the paper.

FIFE. (*starts to thrust the paper on her*) Here you are then! (*But as he does so his eye lights on the same headline that had attracted his attention before and suddenly he has an inspiration and grins elatedly*) By God, I've got it, May! I'll try that on him! All the pious folks in this town think I've a bad record behind me— (*He pushes the paper into her hands*) Get out of here quick! I don't want you around to give her away. (*She goes out. He waits, looking at the door, a grin of malicious expectancy on his face. At this moment* MRS. LIGHT, *who has come out by her kitchen door, appears around the corner of her house and slinks hurriedly across the patch of lawn to the shadow of the lilacs at the extreme edge of the hedge, front.*)

MRS. LIGHT. (*peers stealthily around the corner of the hedge down the street—in an extreme state of agitation*)

I can't see them . . . they're hiding somewheres . . . she'll be kissing him . . . oh, just wait till I tell her what I think of her! . . .

(*She starts out of the shadow of the lilacs as if to go down the street but the brightness of the moonlight frightens her and she moves quickly back into the shadow*)

434

Supposing any one should see me . . . oh, I don't know what to do! . . . that nasty wicked boy! . . . he'll be punished good for this! . . .

There is darkness again for a moment, to mark the end of Scene Two. No time elapses between Scenes Two and Three.

ACT ONE—SCENE THREE

W HEN *the light comes on again, the wall of the* FIFE *bedroom has been replaced. Their sitting room is revealed as before with* FIFE *still sitting looking expectantly at the door. And now the interior of the* LIGHT *sitting room is again shown with* LIGHT *sitting as at the end of Scene One. He holds the open Bible but he is staring moodily over it.* MRS. LIGHT, *as before, is hiding in the shadow of the lilac hedge, peering down the road, ashamed of her position and afraid she will be discovered.*

LIGHT. (*thinking gloomily*)
   I must be honest with myself . . . who am I to cast the first stone at Reuben if he desires a woman? . . . hasn't my love for Amelia been one long desire of the senses? . . . I should understand Reuben's weakness and forgive him . . .
(*Then his resentment smoldering up*)
   But to betray me to Fife! . . . that would go deeper! . . . it would be treachery to God! . . .
MRS. FIFE. (*leans out of the front window of the bedroom upstairs*)
   I don't want to read the paper . . . I'd rather look at the moon . . .
(*Mooning up at the moon*)
   Ada loves that Light boy . . . he must be nice . . . he isn't to blame because his father believes in religion . . . maybe his father is nice too if you got to know him off the job . . . Ramsay is always so cranky when he's at the plant . . . I love the plant . . .

435

I love the dynamos . . . I could sit forever and listen to them sing . . . they're always singing about everything in the world . . . (*She hums to herself for a moment—an imitation of the whirring purr of a dynamo.*)

MRS. LIGHT. (*hearing this noise, looks up around the corner of the hedge and sees her and immediately dissolves into abject shame and fright*)

Oh, my God! . . . did she see me? . . . she'll tell the whole town I was spying! . . . oh, this is terrible! . . . I ought to get Hutchins . . . but I can't move while she's watching . . .

FIFE. (*standing up and looking at the door*)

Ada's a long time bringing him . . . there's a lot of whispering in the hall . . . he's afraid, I'm thinking . . . about to enter the presence of Satan . . . I'll have to start in making him think I'm the devil himself! . . .

(ADA *comes in the doorway of the sitting room, left, followed by* REUBEN.)

FIFE. (*without waiting for an introduction, goes up and shakes* REUBEN'S *hand with an exaggerated cordiality*) So you're young Mr. Light, are you? I'm damned glad to make your acquaintance. Sit down and make yourself at home. (*All the time he is talking, he stares at* REUBEN'S *flustered face, keenly sizing him up. He forces him to sit in the chair across the table from him.* ADA *sits down at right, watching her father with a challenging smile.*)

REUBEN. (*stammers*) Pleased to meet you. Thank you. Thanks.

FIFE. (*with a sudden change to severity*) I want a damned serious talk with you, young man! That's why I had Ada invite you in! (*As* REUBEN *stares at him bewilderedly*) But before we start that, let me ask you, is your reverend father ever going to take up my challenge to debate with me?

REUBEN. (*shamefacedly*) I—I don't think so.

FIFE. (*jeeringly*) He's afraid I'd beat him!

REUBEN. (*defensively*) No, he isn't! He can answer all your arguments easy—with things right out of the Bible! He's only scared that folks'd think he was wrong to argue with you! (*Then raising his voice defiantly*) But I'd argue if I was in his place!

MRS. LIGHT. (*from her hiding place by the hedge has caught* REUBEN's *raised voice—with horrified stupefaction*)

That was Reuben's voice! . . . he's actually in there talking to that atheist! . . . oh, I wish I could get closer to the window! . . . but she'd see me! . . .

(*But she comes around the end of the hedge as far as she can get and strains her ears.*)

FIFE. (*smiling mockingly at* REUBEN) Well, maybe after you're a minister you and me'll argue it out sometime.

REUBEN. (*glad to make a show of his independence before* FIFE) I'm not going to be a minister! Father wants me to but Mother doesn't— and I don't want to be. Besides, I've never felt the call. You have to feel God calling you to His service.

FIFE. (*with a leer*) And how does God call you, tell me? I'm thinkin' He wouldn't use the telegraph or telephone or radio for they're contraptions that belong to His archenemy Lucifer, the God of Electricity. (REUBEN's *face has flushed with mingled indignation and fear. He looks up at the ceiling apprehensively, then opens his mouth to make some retort to* FIFE *when there is a vivid flash of lightning. He gives a start and half rises from his chair, controlling an impulse to run from the room.* FIFE's *keen eyes are watching him and he grins with satisfaction.*)

REUBEN. (*stammers*) You better not—talk like that, or—you better look out!

FIFE. What's the trouble, young fellow? Are you afraid of a bit of lightning? Don't worry about me. The devil looks after his own! But a minister's son has reason to worry, maybe, when he's in a den of atheism, holding intimate converse with a damned man! I'm thinking your Jehovah might aim a thunderbolt at me but Lucifer would deflect it on to you—and he's the better electrical expert of the two, being more modern in his methods than your God!

REUBEN. (*in a turmoil of guilt and fright*)
  I wish I'd never come here! . . . God may strike him! . . . He
  certainly ought to! . . . if I was God, I'd kill him for blaspheming
  like that! . . .

ADA. (*observing* REUBEN—*worriedly*)
  Why did the poor boob let Pop get wise he was scared of lightning? . . .

(*Then indignantly*)
  Pop has no right to pick on religion! . . . that's hitting below the
  belt! . . .

(*Protestingly*) Aw, Pop, lay off religion, can't you!

FIFE. (*glances at her irritably—then with a calculating tone to* REU-
BEN) Ada's right, Mr. Light. I didn't have you in to convert you to
atheism. This is a free country and you're free to believe any God-for-
saken lie you like—even the book of Genesis! (*Then solemnly*) But
here's what I did have you in for, and I'll come right to the point. As
a father I want to know what your intentions are regarding my
daughter! (REUBEN *stares at him in open-mouthed amazement.*)

ADA. (*embarrassed but cannot help a giggle of amusement when she
looks at* REUBEN) Aw, Pop, what—

FIFE. Keep your tongue out of this! (*Sternly to* REUBEN) I trust you
mean honorably by her, young fellow, or it'll be the worse for you!
I'll have no young spark seducing my daughter—getting her with
child, maybe, and then deserting her with no marriage lines to save
her from disgrace! (ADA *begins to see this as a huge joke and she has
to bury her face in her hands to choke back her laughter as she looks
at* REUBEN'S *face on which is at first a shocked look of stupefaction.
But this gives way to a fit of indignation that anyone could think him
so low.*)

REUBEN. What do you think I am? You have no right to say that
about me! I'm not that kind of— (*Then his voice booming like his
father's with moral self-righteousness*) I respect Ada just as much as
I do my mother! I'm going to marry her!

ADA. (*genuinely flustered—trying to laugh it off*) Gee, Rube, did I

438

say you had no nerve? I take it all back! (REUBEN's *nerve immediately deserts him. He hangs his head in acute embarrassment, his eyes on the floor.*)

MRS. LIGHT. (*by the end of the hedge*)

Marry her! . . . I heard it clear as day! . . . respect her like he does me! . . . damn her! . . . Oh, I didn't mean to swear! . . . I don't know what I'm doing! . . .

(*Then weeping hysterically and trying to stifle it*)

Oh, I'll get Hutchins to beat him within an inch of his life! . . .

(*She sinks down on the ground, her hands over her face*)

I've got to stop! . . . she'll hear me up there! . . . she'll tell how I was crying! . . .

MRS. FIFE. (*has noticed the noise of* MRS. LIGHT's *movements and looks down vaguely*)

Some animal's in the garden . . . maybe it's a skunk . . . I'd love to have a skunk-skin coat next winter . . . maybe Ramsay'll give me one for Christmas . . . Ramsay calls the minister a skunk . . . poor Mr. Light! . . . Ramsay says awful mean things sometimes . . . but it's only because he loves to make jokes . . . he's the kindest man in the world . . .

FIFE. (*pretending to be sunk in thought has been staring calculatingly at* REUBEN—*solemnly*) Young man, I'll be honest with you. In view of your honorable intentions I feel bound by my conscience to let you know the secret of the family you're wanting to marry into. But you must give me your word of honor, as man to man—I don't ask you to swear on the Bible—that you'll never repeat what I'm saying to anyone, no matter how dreadful it seems to you! Will you give me your word?

REUBEN. (*made visibly uneasy but forcing a manly tone*) Sure. I wouldn't ever say anything.

ADA. (*leaning forward in her chair and watching her father worriedly*)

What's Pop going to spring? . . . Rube's looking pale behind the gills, poor guy! . . . aw, poor nothing! . . . he ought to have more guts! . . .

439

FIFE. (*with a tragic sigh*) There's not a living soul knows it, barring my wife and Ada. It's like putting my life in your hands. You know, don't you, that no one knows what I done before I came to this town, nor where I came from. I've good reason for keeping it dark. Listen now. Twenty years ago there was a man by the name of Andrew Clark lived in the town of Arming, Ohio. (*He pauses significantly, giving a quick side glance at* ADA *to see if she's caught the joke —then goes on with a guilty furtiveness—lowering his voice*) Now Clark was in love with a girl whose family had got her engaged to another fellow, but she loved Clark and used to meet him in the woods. But this fellow who was engaged to her got suspicious and one night he sneaked up on them lying in each other's arms—in sin, as you'd call it—and he rushed out with a knife at them both, but Clark picked up an ax and split his skull! (*He finishes up with well-feigned savagery*) And serve him right, the bloody sneak!

REUBEN. (*stares at* FIFE *with horror*) You mean—Clark murdered him?

FIFE. (*with a great pretense of guilt-stricken protest*) Oh, don't say that! Not murder! He killed him in self-defense! Wouldn't you do the same if Ada was the girl and you was Clark?

REUBEN.
> What is he asking? . . . Ada? . . . would I? . . .
(*Then his horror turning to a confused rage*)
> I'd kill Ada if I caught her! . . . but it was the other man who caught! . . . and they were engaged, too! . . . she belonged to him! . . .

(*Harshly and condemningly—in his father's tone*) That other fellow should have killed them, that's what I think! That girl was engaged to the other fellow! She had no right to love Clark! That wasn't love, it was lust! She was an adulteress! It would have been only her just punishment if that fellow had killed her! I would have!

FIFE. For the love of God, don't be so hard on me—for what I was coming to tell you was that I was Clark! (*As if to punctuate this dramatic confession, there is a flash of lightning, brighter than any that has gone before.*)

REUBEN. (*clutches the arms of his chair in superstitious terror, all the passion drained out of him instantly, leaving him weak and penitent*)

Oh, God, please forgive me! . . . I didn't mean it! . . . I wouldn't ever kill her! . . .

(*Then glancing at* FIFE *with fear*)

He's a murderer! . . . he said himself he was damned! . . .

FIFE. (*eyeing* REUBEN *keenly*) After I'd killed him I gave myself up. The jury said it was murder in the second degree and gave me twenty years—but I fooled 'em with the help of the girl and escaped and we both ran off to the far west and settled down in Niclum, California, and I married her under the name of Fife and we had a daughter. That's Ada.

REUBEN. (*keeping his eyes averted from* ADA)

Then that's her mother! . . . she's the daughter of an adulteress! . . . and a murderer!. . . how can I ever trust her? . . . she's gone around with lots of fellows . . . how do I know she never—? . . .

(*Then torturedly*)

Oh, God, why did I ever come here tonight? . . .

FIFE. (*with a great pretense of uneasiness*) You don't say a word. Well, maybe I shouldn't have told you, because now I've made you an accessory in the murder for you'll be shielding me unlawfully by keeping silence. And the devil knows what sin you'll think it in the sight of God! (*The clap of thunder from the preceding flash comes with a great rumble.*)

REUBEN.

Accessory! . . . the police can arrest me! . . .

(*Then summoning his manhood*)

But I won't tell them! . . . ever! . . . I gave my word! . . .

(*Then conscience-strickenly*)

But God! . . . I'll be guilty before God! . . . but He knows I gave my word! . . . but does that count with Him? . . . when I didn't swear on the Bible? . . .

(*Then frantically*)

But He knows I love Ada . . . He wouldn't want me to tell on her
father . . .

(*He suddenly jumps up and mumbles to* FIFE) I won't tell the police,
you needn't worry.

ADA. (*with a triumphant glance at her father*) Good for you, Rube!

REUBEN. (*avoiding her eyes*) I've got to go home now.

FIFE. (*searching* REUBEN's *face—insistently*) I'm sorry to put such
a load on your conscience, Mr. Light, but I felt it was only right of me.

REUBEN.

Why does he rub it in? . . . God, I hate him! . . . I wish they'd
hung him! . . .

(*Angrily—his voice booming denouncingly like his father's*) You
needn't be afraid I'll tell—but you ought to go and tell yourself! You
know you're guilty in the sight of God! Do you want to burn forever
in hell?

FIFE. (*jeeringly*) Your hell and God mean no more to me than old
women's nonsense when they're scared of the dark!

REUBEN. Don't you dare talk like that! I won't stand for it—not
now! If you don't stop your blaspheming, I'll—I mean, it'd serve
you right if I— (*Hurrying toward the door as if in flight*) I got to
get home. (*He stops at the door and turns to* ADA, *but keeps his eyes
averted*) Good night, Ada. (*He goes out.*)

ADA.

He was threatening Pop already he'd tell on him! . . . gee, he is
yellow all right! . . .

(*Tears of mortification and genuine hurt come to her eyes—she
brushes them back*)

Aw, what do I care about him? . . .

FIFE. (*with a chuckle*) He'll be blabbin' my dreadful secret to his
old man yet, wait and see!

ADA. (*to his surprise, turns on him angrily*) It wasn't fair! He
never had a chance! (*She flings herself on the chaise longue and begins to cry.*)

442

FIFE. (*stares at her in astonishment*) Are you turning against me—for that lump! (*Then he comes and pats her on the shoulder*) I was only doing it for your sake, Ada. You ought to see him in his true colors so you'd not be thinking too much about him.

ADA. (*forces back her tears and jumps up*) I didn't think anything! Leave me alone about him, can't you? (*With a great pretense of indifference she gets a book from the table and sits down again*) I should worry about that poor fish! I've got to study my algebra. (*Her father stares at her puzzledly. There is a bright flash of lightning and* LIGHT, *sitting as before in the sitting room of the other house reading the Bible, jumps nervously to his feet.*)

LIGHT.

> I ought to conquer that silly fear in myself . . . the lightning is God's will . . . what on earth can Amelia be doing with Reuben all this time? . . .

(*He listens for a moment—uneasily*)

> I'll go upstairs to them . . . she should be more considerate than to leave me alone when . . .

(*He walks toward the door on right.*)

There is a pause of darkness here to mark the end of Scene Three. In this darkness the clap of thunder from the preceding flash comes. No time elapses between Scenes Three and Four.

ACT ONE—SCENE FOUR

WHEN *the light comes on again—but this time very dimly, as if the moon were behind clouds—the walls of the* FIFE *and* LIGHT *sitting rooms have been replaced while the interior of* REUBEN's *bedroom is now revealed.* MRS. FIFE *still leans out of her bedroom window and* MRS. LIGHT *sits crouching by the hedge.*

443

MRS. LIGHT. (*suddenly jumping to her feet and peering up through the leaves at* MRS. FIFE)

Oh, God, isn't she ever going in? . . . I'll scream in a minute! . . .

MRS. FIFE.

I love to watch lightning . . . the thunder clouds are getting nearer the moon . . . I'd like to be a cloud . . . it must be nice to float in the wind . . . but it must be getting bedtime . . .

(*She slowly backs herself into her room.*)

MRS. LIGHT. (*as* MRS. FIFE *disappears*)

Now I can get Hutchins . . .

(*She slinks back along the hedge and then quickly across the lawn around the corner of her house just as* REUBEN *enters from the left by the* FIFE *house.*)

REUBEN. (*stands hesitating—uneasily*)

I thought I'd walk around and think up some lie . . . Mother'll guess something is wrong as soon as she looks at me . . . but I'm not going to stay out in the storm . . .

(*He walks slowly over to where he had stood with* ADA—*dully*)

Here's where she kissed me . . . why couldn't we have gone for a walk? . . . she'd have let me kiss her . . . I'd have had her in my arms . . . like her mother was with Clark? . . . no, I didn't mean that! . . . I didn't mean sin! . . .

(*Then with desperate bravado*)

Aw, what is sin, anyway? . . . maybe that's just old women's nonsense, like Fife says! . . . why should I have a guilty conscience? . . . it's God's fault! . . . why hasn't He done something to Fife? . . . I should think He'd have to punish adultery and murder . . . if there is any God . . .

(*There is a great flash of lightning and he stands paralyzed with superstitious terror*)

It comes every time! . . . when I deny! . . .

(*More and more obsessed by a feeling of guilt, of being a condemned sinner alone in the threatening night*)

Fife's damned me with him! . . there's no use praying! . . . it's getting black! . . . I'm afraid of God! . . .

444

(*There is a crash of thunder. He cowers, trembling—then cries like a frightened little boy*) Mother! Mother! (*He runs off right, forgetting that he has sneaked out by the back, making for the front door. At the same moment* LIGHT *can be dimly made out as he enters* REUBEN's *bedroom, and* FIFE *sticks his head out of his sitting-room window and looks toward the* LIGHT *home.*)

FIFE.
> That was him I heard passing . . . I'll wait here and watch the fun . . .

(*He chuckles to himself.*)

LIGHT. (*pauses just inside* REUBEN's *bedroom door in alarm at finding the room dark and empty—calls uneasily*) Amelia! Reuben! (*He lights a match with trembling fingers and hurries over to the lamp and lights it. His wife's voice comes excitedly from below and then from the stairs in the hallway.*)

MRS. LIGHT. Hutchins! Hutchins! Where are you?

LIGHT. (*hurries to the door calling*) Here—upstairs.

MRS. LIGHT. (*a moment later hurries in excitedly, her words pouring out*) Oh, Hutchins, something awful has happened—that Fife girl—I heard Reuben asking Fife if he could marry her! (LIGHT, *completely stunned, stares at her blankly. There is the noise of the front door being slammed and* REUBEN's *voice calling desperately.*)

REUBEN. Mother! Where are you?

MRS. LIGHT. Sshh! Let him come up here. (*Pushing him toward the closet in rear*) You hide in that closet and listen! I'll make him acknowledge everything! He'd only lie to you! (*Vindictively*) I promise I won't stand between him and punishment this time! (*She gives him a final shove inside the door and closes it.*)

REUBEN. (*his voice comes from the hall as he rushes upstairs*) Mother! (*A second later he runs in and, too distracted to notice her expression, throws his arms around her*) Mother! (*He breaks down and sobs.*)

MRS. LIGHT. (*alarmed by the state he is in, puts her arms around*

445

him, her immediate reaction one of maternal tenderness. She leads him front and sits on the side of the bed) There, there! It's all right, Reuben! Mother's here! *(Then indignantly)* What have those awful people been doing to my boy to get him in such a state? *(As he gives a start—sharply)* Now don't deny you were there! Don't make matters worse by lying! What happened between you and that man? Tell Mother!

REUBEN. *(brokenly)* I can't! I promised him I wouldn't. I can't tell anyone!

MRS. LIGHT. *(changing to a tone of wheedling affection)* Yes you can, Reuben. You can always tell Mother everything. You always have.

REUBEN. *(clinging to her)*

> I love Mother better'n anything in the world . . . she always for-gives me . . . I wish I could tell her . . . she'd know what was right . . .

(There is a bright flash of lightning. He shrinks closer to her and blurts out) I'm scared, Mother! I'm guilty! I'm damned!

MRS. LIGHT. *(startled)*

> Guilty? . . . does he mean he? . . .

(With sudden strong revulsion)

> And to think he's had those same arms hugging that little filthpot this very evening! . . .

(She pushes him away, but, holding his shoulders, stares down into his face) Do you mean to say you refuse to tell your own mother, just because you were forced into promising not to by that atheist? Then all I can say is that my boy I thought I could trust has turned into a liar and a sneak, and I don't wonder you feel guilty in God's sight! *(As she finishes speaking, the roll of the thunder from the preceding flash comes crashing and rumbling.* REUBEN *sinks down on his knees beside her, hiding his face in her lap.)*

REUBEN. *(stammers)* I'll tell you, Mother—if you promise to keep it a secret—just between me and you—and never tell Father.

MRS. LIGHT. All right. I'll promise.

REUBEN. (*made uneasy by something in her tone—insistently*) You'll swear it on the Bible?

MRS. LIGHT. Yes, I'll swear on the Bible I won't tell him.

REUBEN. (*in a passion of eagerness to get the guilty tale off his conscience*) His name isn't even Fife, it's Clark! He changed it because he murdered a man out in Ohio where he used to live. He got twenty years but he escaped and ran away to California! Fife's a murderer, that's what he really is! (*While he has been telling this story, the closet door has opened and LIGHT stands there, listening greedily. In his hand is a belt of REUBEN's.*)

LIGHT. (*thinking with a fierce, revengeful joy*)
Lord God of Righteous Vengeance, I thank Thee! . . . at last Thou strikest! . . .

MRS. LIGHT. (*dumbfounded, not knowing what to make of this strange tale—and disappointed that it is not a confession about Ada*) Wherever did you get hold of this story?

REUBEN. He told me himself.

MRS. LIGHT. Do you expect me to believe Fife's such an idiot as to confess such things to you?

REUBEN. He had a good reason to tell me! I asked him if I could marry Ada and he thought he was honor bound to tell me! He knew it'd be safe with me when I gave him my word— (*Then thinking with guilty shame*)
But I've told! . . . I've just told! . . . why did I? . . . Oh, how Ada would hate me if she knew! . . .
(*Pleadingly*) Remember you swore on the Bible you'd never tell! Remember, Mother!

MRS. LIGHT. (*glaring into his face vindictively*) So you want to marry that little harlot, do you?

REUBEN. (*shakes her hands off his shoulders—shrinking back from her, still on his knees*) Don't you say that, Mother! I love Ada, Mother! I love her with all my heart!

MRS. LIGHT. (*calls over her shoulder*) Do you hear that, Hutchins?

447

LIGHT. (*grimly*) Yes, I hear. (*He takes a threatening step forward.*)

REUBEN. Father! (*Then his eyes turn to his mother's vindictive face and he thinks in a tortured agony of spirit*)

>He was hiding in the closet! . . . she knew it! . . . she cheated me! . . . when I trusted her! . . . when I loved her better than anyone in the world! . . .

(*He cries out in a passion of reproach*) Oh, Mother! Mother!

MRS. LIGHT. (*misunderstanding this as a plea*) No, you needn't think I'm going to get you off this time! You punish him good, Hutchins! The very idea—kissing that dirty little—!

REUBEN. Don't you say that!

LIGHT. (*walks toward him*) Hold your tongue! How dare you address your mother—!

REUBEN. (*his thoughts whirling in his head*)

>Mother's face . . . she looks terrible . . . she wants him to beat me . . . she wants to hear me yell . . .

(*Then with a defiant determination as if some hidden strength in him had suddenly been tapped*)

>But I won't give her the satisfaction! . . . no matter how it hurts! . . .

LIGHT. Let this put back the fear of God into your sinful heart, Reuben! (*He brings the belt down heavily across* REUBEN's *back.* REUBEN *quivers but not a sound comes from his lips. At the same moment there is a glaring flash of lightning and* LIGHT *cringes back with a frightened exclamation.*)

MRS. LIGHT. (*has winced when* REUBEN *was hit—conscience-strickenly*)

>That must have hurt dreadfully! . . . poor Reuben! . . .

(*Then with an exasperated sense of frustration, gazing at* REUBEN's *set face*)

>Why doesn't he cry? . . . if he'd cry I'd stop Hutchins . . . that girl has changed him! . . .

REUBEN. (*expecting the next blow, thinking with a grim elation*)

>Come on! . . . hit again! . . . hit a million times! . . . you can't make me show her you hurt me! . . .

(*Then stealing a glance up at his father's face*)
He looks scared! . . . it was that lightning! . . . I'll never be
scared of lightning again! . . .
(*Then resolutely*)
I'll be damned if I'm going to let him beat me! . . .
(*He jumps to his feet and faces his father defiantly.*)
LIGHT. (*guiltily*)
I can't bear him looking at me like that . . . I really ought to feel
grateful to him . . . his folly has delivered Fife into my hands . . .
(*He throws the belt on the bed—to his wife*) Reuben's punishment
can wait. I have my duty of denouncing that murderer to the proper
authorities. (*Triumphantly*) Haven't I always said, if the truth were
known, that man was a criminal! (*Turning toward the door*) Keep
Reuben here. He might warn Fife. I'll lock this door after me. (*Then
hurriedly, as a crash of thunder comes*) I must hurry. I want to get
to the police station before the rain. (*He shuts the door behind him
and locks it.*)

REUBEN. (*staring after him with the same look of defiance—calls
jeeringly*) Look out for the lightning! (*Then he turns to his mother
with a sneer—contemptuously*) Picture my being scared of that boob
all my life! What did you ever see in him, to marry him? He's
yellow!

MRS. LIGHT. (*frightened by the change in him but attempting a
bullying tone*) How dare you talk so disrespectfully—!

REUBEN. But you're yellow, too. And I'm yellow. How could I
help being? It's in my blood. (*Harshly*) But I'll get him out of my
blood, by God! And I'll get you out, too!

MRS. LIGHT. (*pitiably now*) What have I done, Reuben?

REUBEN. (*bitterly*) You knew he was in that closet! You led me
on to tell! I thought you loved me better'n anyone, and you'd
never squeal on me to him! (*He starts to break down miserably.*)

MRS. LIGHT. (*goes to him as if to take him in her arms*) I do love
you better than anyone, Reuben! I didn't mean—

449

REUBEN. (*steps back from her—accusingly*) And you called Ada a harlot—after I told you I loved her with all my heart! (*Then a note of pleading*) Do you mean you didn't mean that part of it—about her?

MRS. LIGHT. (*immediately furious again*) Yes, I did mean it about her! I meant it and a lot more!

REUBEN. Then I'm through with you! And as for him—! (*He suddenly is reminded of something—thinking wildly*)
He went! . . . police station! . . . that'll finish me with Ada! . . . (*There is the noise of the front door slamming*)
He's leaving! . . .
(*He rushes to the door but finds it locked—pushes and pulls at it, trying to force it open.*)

MRS. LIGHT. I suppose you want to run over and warn your fine friends! Fife'll be in a cell before long, please God, and if there was any real justice his girl'd be put in along with him for she's no better than a street walker!

REUBEN. (*turns and glares at her*) I'm glad you're talking like that! It shows you up and I can hate you now!

MRS. LIGHT. (*breaking down*) Reuben! For God's sake, don't say that—to your mother!

REUBEN. You're not my mother any more! I'll do without a mother rather than have your kind! (*He turns from her to the window and looks out. As he does so, his father appears from right, coming from the front door. He is buttoned up to the neck in an old raincoat and carries an umbrella.*)

FIFE. (*still leaning out of his sitting-room window, catches sight of LIGHT—calls excitedly over his shoulder*) Here's the old man now! Come quick, Ada! (*A moment later, just as LIGHT comes up, she appears at the window next to her father. Her face is set in an ugly, sneering expression. FIFE calls to LIGHT in a mocking tone*) Good evening, Your Holiness.

LIGHT. (*stops short and stares at FIFE with a rage that chokes him so that for a moment his lips move, forming words, but he can't utter them—finally finding his voice, he stammers*) You—you murderer!

FIFE. (*nudging* ADA—*with a great pretense of guilt*) Murderer? In the name of God, has your son?—after he'd sworn his word of honor—!

LIGHT. (*triumphantly*) You thought you had him caught in your snares, did you?—but God was simply using Reuben to bring retribution on your head! (*In a booming triumph*) "Vengeance is mine, saith the Lord!"

REUBEN. (*watching from his window*)
He's talking to Fife! . . . he's telling! . . .
(*Then cursing his father aloud*) God damn him! I'll show him! (*He drives back at the door with the weight of his whole body, and it crashes open and he stumbles over it and disappears in the hall.*)

MRS., LIGHT. (*starts after him, calling frightenedly*) Reuben! Don't! Reuben!

FIFE. (*enjoying himself hugely*) You wouldn't give me up to the police, would you—a kind-hearted Shepherd of the Lord like you?

ADA. (*suddenly flares up into a temper*) Aw, cut it out, Pop! This has gone far enough! (*To* LIGHT *with sneering contempt*) No wonder your son is a sap! Can't you see this is only a joke on you? Why, you poor fish, that murder story is in today's *Star*—the name Clark and everything! Pop simply copied that story—and if you go to the police you'll only be making a boob of yourself—but go ahead if you like! (*As she speaks* REUBEN *runs in from the right. He advances threateningly on his father who is staring at* ADA *stupidly, overwhelmed by the conviction that what she has told him is true.*)

REUBEN. Did you tell—?

ADA. Look who's here! I was just telling your old man it was only a murder story out of the paper Pop told you to prove you were yellow! And you are, all right! Don't you ever dare speak to me again! You're a yellow rat! (*She breaks down, weeping, and rushes back into the room.*)

451

FIFE. (*following her*) Ada! Don't waste crying over—

REUBEN. Ada! Listen! I didn't mean—I didn't know—! (*He takes a few steps toward the window, then stops, thinking bitterly*)
So it was all a lie! . . . a joke she played on me! . . . that's why she made me meet her old man! . . . so she could make a fool of me! . . .
(*He yells at the window*) It's you who're the rat, Ada! You can go to hell!

MRS. LIGHT. (*Hurrying in from the right. She runs to him and tries to put her arms around him*) Reuben!

REUBEN. (*Pushing her away from him—furiously*) Leave me alone! You're to blame for this! You cheated me! I hate you!

MRS. LIGHT. For God's sake, Reuben!

LIGHT. (*comes out of the state of humiliated stupefaction into which the knowledge of the joke has thrown him—bursting into a fatuous rage—to his wife*) As if I have not had enough to bear of humiliation! (*He points a shaking finger at* REUBEN) This dunce—this stupid dolt—now I shall be the butt of all their sneers! And to think I stayed my hand—! But wait! I'll show him what a real whipping is!

REUBEN. (*fiercely*) You'll never dare touch me again, you old fool! I'm not scared of you or your God any more! (*There is a blinding flash of lightning.* LIGHT, *his nerves already at the breaking point, gives a gasp of superstitious fright.*)

LIGHT. God have mercy!

REUBEN. (*with a sneer*) What God? Fife's God? Electricity? Are you praying to It for mercy? It can't hear you! It doesn't give a damn about you! (*There is a tremendous crash of thunder.* REUBEN *looks up and gives a wild laugh as though the thunder elated him. His mother and father shrink back from him as he shouts up at the sky*) Shoot away, Old Bozo! I'm not scared of You!

MRS. LIGHT. Reuben! You don't know what you're saying!

REUBEN. (*with a hard, mocking laugh—to his mother*) What's the matter? Do you still believe in his fool God? I'll show you! (*He jumps to his father's side and grabs his raincoat by the lapel—addressing the sky with insulting insolence*) If there is his God let Him strike me dead this second! I dare Him! (*His father squeals with terror and tries to break away from his hold. His mother screams. He laughs triumphantly*) There! Didn't I tell you! (LIGHT *finally tears his coat from* REUBEN's *grip and runs panic-stricken off right, dragging his moaning wife by the arm.* REUBEN *turns his back on his home determinedly and starts walking off left—with bitter defiance*) There is no God! No God but Electricity! I'll never be scared again! I'm through with the lot of you! (*As he disappears off left, the sound of wind and rain sweeping down on the town from the hills is heard.*)

CURTAIN

ACT TWO—SCENE ONE

THE *same as Act One, Scene One. The interior of the* LIGHT *sitting room is revealed. It is an early morning of a hot day in August. Fifteen months have elapsed.* MRS. FIFE *is leaning out of one of the windows of their sitting room, basking contentedly in the sun. She wears a faded blue wrapper.*

> MRS. FIFE. (*thinking with a sleepy content*)
> The sun is hot . . . I feel so dozy . . . I know why dogs love to lie in the sun . . . and cats and chickens . . . they forget to think they're living . . . they're just alive . . .

(*She looks toward the* LIGHT *house—with drowsy melancholy*)

> Alive . . . poor Mrs. Light is dead . . . what is death like, I wonder? . . . I suppose I'll have to die sometime . . . I don't want to die before Ramsay . . . he wouldn't know how to take care of himself . . .

(*At a noise in the room behind her she half turns her head—then* ADA *leans out of the window next to her mother. Her face has a peaked look. Her manner is touchy and irritable and she has lost her former air of flippancy. There is no rouge on her face and she is dressed as if she had grown indifferent about her personal appearance.*)

ADA. For heaven's sake, what're you dope-dreaming about now, Mom?

MRS. FIFE. I was thinking of poor Mrs. Light—

ADA. Poor nothing! She hated us worse than poison! She'd have sung hymns of joy if any of us had died! And why feel sorry for her, anyway? She's lucky, if you ask me! Life is the bunk!

MRS. FIFE. (*looks at her worriedly—with a sigh*) I wish that Light boy would come back.

ADA. (*immediately flying into a temper*) For God's sake, shut up!

I've told you a million times how dumb that talk is and yet you keep on harping—!

MRS. FIFE. All right, Ada. I won't say anything.

ADA. What do I care about that poor fish! He can be dead for all I care! (*Then, as* FIFE's *voice is heard calling from somewhere in the house*) There's Pop howling his head off about something. You go in and smooth him down, Mom. I'm sick of his grouches.

MRS. FIFE. (*as she turns to go*) I wish you'd make it up with your Pop, Ada. He feels so bad about it. You've kept a grudge against him ever since the night that Light boy—

ADA. There you go again! For Pete's sake, leave me alone! (MRS. FIFE *disappears meekly without another word.* ADA *stares before her, thinking resentfully*)

> I've got a good right to have a grudge against him . . . what he did that night wasn't on the level . . . it isn't a question of Rube . . . I don't give a darn about him . . . then why are you all the time thinking about him? . . . I'm not! . . . I liked him but that was all . . . and he was yellow, wasn't he? . . . well, maybe you'd be worse if everything was framed against you the way Pop got him! . . . poor Rube! . . . what's he been doing all this time, I wonder? . . .

(*With a sad smile of scorn for herself*)

> You poor boob! . . . it must be love! . . .

(*In the sitting room of the* LIGHT *home,* HUTCHINS LIGHT *enters from the rear, right. The grief over his wife's death has made him an old man. His hair has turned almost white, his mouth droops forlornly, his eyes are dull, his whole face is a mask of stricken loneliness. He comes and sits in his old chair and mechanically picks up his Bible from the table but lets it drop again and stares before him.*)

LIGHT. (*thinking dully*)

> Another day . . . empty . . . all days are empty now . . . how long, O Lord? . . .

(*He sighs heavily*)

> No sleep again last night except for a few minutes . . . and then

nightmare . . . I dreamed Amelia was in my arms . . . and Reuben came and beckoned her and she went away with him . . .

(*He shudders, flinging off the memory—then wondering bitterly*)
Does that dream mean Reuben is dead, too? . . . what does it matter? . . . ever since that night he has been dead for me . . . but he never gave Amelia a chance to forget him . . . a postal card every month or so . . . each with the same blasphemy . . . "We have electrocuted your God. Don't be a fool!" . . . her last words! . . . "Don't be a fool," she kept saying to me . . . she couldn't have known what she was saying . . .

(*He breaks down, sobbing, and buries his head in his arms on the table*)

MRS. FIFE. (*reappears in the window beside* ADA. *She is smiling with a doting good nature*) Your Pop told me to get out of the room and stop looking at him or he'd start breaking plates. My, but he's in a breakfast temper, though! The men at the plant'll catch it—but they don't mind him. They know, like I do, that he's really the kindest man in the world.

ADA. (*resentfully*) Oh, is he? I suppose that's why he acted the way he did to Rube!

MRS. FIFE. He couldn't help being mean then. He'd be mean at first to any man he thought you cared for—especially a minister's son. But he'd get over it, you'd see. He'd like to see you happy, before everything. I'm sure he's been wishing for a long time that Light boy'd come home so he could make friends with him.

ADA. Aw, you're crazy, Mom. (*Suddenly she leans over and kisses her mother affectionately*) It's you who are the kindest in the world. (*Then embarrassed—irritably*) Gosh, this sun's hot! I don't see how you stand it. (*She retreats into the house.*)

MRS. FIFE. (*blinking placidly in the sun*)
It was awful nice the way Ada kissed me . . . I wish she'd get to kissing her Pop again that way . . . she does it now as if she wished she was a mosquito with a stinger . . . the screen up in her room has a hole rusted in it . . . I must remember to get it fixed or they'll be flying in keeping her awake. . . .

456

(*A pause—then* REUBEN LIGHT *comes slowly in from the left and stands there, his eyes fixed for a while on his home, taking in every detail. He does not for a moment notice* MRS. FIFE *nor she him. A great change has come over him; he is hardly recognizable as the* REUBEN *of Act One. Nearly nineteen now, his body has filled out, his skin is tanned and weather-beaten. In contrast to his diffident, timid attitude of before, his manner is now consciously hard-boiled. The look on his face emphasizes the change in him. It is much older than his years, and it is apparent that he has not grown its defensive callousness without a desperate struggle to kill the shrinking boy in him. But it is in his eyes that the greatest change has come. Their soft gray-blue has become chilled and frozen, and yet they burn in their depths with a queer devouring intensity. He is dressed roughly in battered shoes, dungaree trousers faded by many washings, a blue flannel shirt open at the neck, with a dirty colored handkerchief knotted about his throat, and wears the coat of his old suit. Under his arm he carries six books, bound together with a strap.*)

REUBEN. (*thinking jeeringly*)
Home, Sweet Home! . . . the prodigal returns! . . . what for?
. . . I felt a sudden hunch I had to come . . . to have a talk with
Mother, anyway . . . well, I'll soon know what it's all about . . .
and won't the old man be glad to see me! . . . yes! . . . he'll
poison the fatted calf! . . .

(*He laughs aloud.* MRS. FIFE *turns and gives a startled exclamation as she recognizes him. He turns and looks at her for a moment—then with a swaggering impudence.*) Fine day, isn't it?

MRS. FIFE. (*her eyes mooning at him, with a simple, pleased smile*)
I'm glad you've come home. Ada'll be glad. (*She stirs as if to go into the house*) I'll tell her you're here.

REUBEN. (*frowning*) No. I've got no time for her now. (*Then with a peculiar air of indifferent curiosity*) Are you sure Ada'll be glad I'm back? I shouldn't think she would after what happened.

MRS. FIFE. That wasn't her doing. She's been sorry about it ever since.

457

REUBEN. (*with the same detached interest*) She called me a yellow rat —and she had the right dope. I sure was dumb when it came to guessing what she really wanted or I would have— (*With a cold smile*) Well, never mind what—but you can tell her I've changed. I've lived a lot and read a lot to find out for myself what's really what—and I've found out all right! You can tell her I've read up on love in biology, and I know what it is now, and I've proved it with more than one female.

MRS. FIFE. (*preoccupied with her own thoughts*) It was just one of Ramsay's jokes.

REUBEN. He's a great little joker! And I certainly fell for it. Well, there's no hard feelings. He did me a favor. He woke me up. (*With a laugh, a queer expression coming into his eyes*) You can tell him I've joined his church. The only God I believe in now is electricity.

MRS. FIFE. (*simply*) Ramsay'll be glad.

REUBEN. (*indicating the books he carries*) I'm studying a lot of science. Sometimes I've gone without eating to buy books—and often I've read all night—books on astronomy and biology and physics and chemistry and evolution. It all comes down to electricity in the end. What the fool preachers call God is in electricity somewhere. (*He breaks off—then strangely*) Did you ever watch dynamos? What I mean is in them—somehow.

MRS. FIFE. (*dreamily*) I love dynamos. I love to hear them sing. They're singing all the time about everything in the world! (*She hums her imitation of a dynamo's whirring purr.*)

REUBEN. (*startled—looks at her with growing interest*)

"Singing all the time about everything in the world" . . . she gets them all right . . . listen to her . . . she's caught the sound . . . (*Abruptly he puts down his books and walks up to MRS. FIFE*) Say, you're all right! (*He takes one of her hands in his clumsily—then lets go of it, grinning awkwardly.*)

MRS. FIFE. (*sentimentally touched—beaming on him*) I always knew you must be a nice boy. (*With a coquettish, incongruously girlish air*)

But you save your holding hands for Ada! (*Then she half turns around at some sound in the room behind her—in a hurried whisper to* REUBEN) She's coming! You hide behind those bushes and we'll surprise her!

(*Mechanically, reacting instinctively for a moment as the timid boy of formerly, he runs to the gap in the lilac bushes and hides in the old place.* ADA *appears in the window beside her mother. Her face wears an expression of eager expectation. Her eyes glance quickly on all sides as if searching for someone.*)

ADA. (*flusteredly*)

I'm sure I heard someone . . . it sounded like . . .

REUBEN. (*almost as soon as he reaches his old hiding place is overcome by shame*)

What'd I do that for? . . . hide! . . . the old stuff! . . .

(*Savagely*)

No, by God! . . . her mother put it in my head . . . but I'll soon show Ada! . . . she'll find out if I'm yellow now! . . .

(*With a swagger and a cold smile on his lips he walks through the gap just as* MRS. FIFE *speaks to* ADA.)

MRS. FIFE. (*with a teasing smile*) Ada, I've got a big surprise for you. Guess— (*But* ADA *has already seen him.*)

ADA. (*with a cry of joy*) Rube!

REUBEN. (*walks toward her, the smile frozen on his lips, his eyes fixed on hers*)

Go right up and kiss her! . . . look at the way she's looking at you! . . . she's easy now! . . .

ADA. (*staring at him, stammers his name again in a tone in which there is now a note of panic*) Rube!

REUBEN. (*pulls her head down and kisses her, keeping his lips on hers while she struggles instinctively for a moment, until she gives up and returns his kiss—then he pushes her a little away from him and laughs quietly, his confidence in himself completely restored*) Well, this prodigal gets the fatted kiss even if "there ain't no calf." Hello, Ada! How's every little thing?

MRS. FIFE. (*sentimentally*) That's right. You two kiss and make up. I'll leave you alone. (*She goes back into the room.*)

ADA. (*is staring at him with eyes that search his face apprehensively*) Rube! You—you've changed. I—I hardly know you! I shouldn't have kissed you—like that. I don't know why I—

REUBEN. Well, I know. (*He takes her face between his hands again and brings his close to it*) Because you love me. Isn't that right? (*As she hesitates—insistently, giving her head a little shake*) Isn't it?

ADA. (*helplessly*) I guess it is, Rube.

REUBEN. Guess, nothing! You loved me before I went away—even when you were bawling me out for a yellow rat. That was what made you so mad, wasn't it? You were ashamed of loving me when I was so dumb and didn't get what you wanted and was so damned scared to touch you. (*He laughs—a self-assured, insinuating laugh that for her has something at once fascinating and frightening about it*) But you needn't worry any more, Ada. I've learned a lot about love since I left—and I get you now, all right! (*Then with a sudden burst of threatening assertiveness*) You're damned right I've changed. I'm not yellow about you or God or anything else! Don't forget that, Ada! (*Then as suddenly changing to a passionate tone of desire*) Gosh, you're pretty! I'd forgotten how pretty you were! You make all the girls I've been playing around with look like mistakes! Your eyes are grand—and your hair—and your mouth—! (*He kisses them hungrily as he speaks—then controls himself and breaks away from her, forcing a laugh*) Continued in our next! Let's take a walk tonight.

ADA. (*staring at him helplessly*) Yes—no—I don't think—

REUBEN. Sure you will. We'll walk out to the top of Long Hill. That's where I was all during the storm that night after I left here. I made myself stand there and watch the lightning. After that storm was over I'd changed, believe me! I knew nothing could ever scare me again—and a whole lot of me was dead and a new lot started living. And that's the right place for us to love—on top of that hill—close to

the sky—driven to love by what makes the earth go round—by what
drives the stars through space! Did you ever think that all life comes
down to electricity in the end, Ada? Did you ever watch dynamos?
(*She stares at him, frightened and fascinated, and shakes her head*)
I've watched them for hours. Sometimes I'd go in a plant and get
talking to the guys just to hang around, and I tried everywhere to get
a job in a plant but never had any luck. But every job I've had—I
never stuck to one long, I wanted to keep moving and see everything
—every job was connected with electricity some way. I've worked for
electricians, I've gone out helping linesmen, I shoveled sand on a big
waterpower job out West. (*Then with sudden eagerness*) Say, Ada,
I've just had a hunch! I know now what drove me back here, all right!
You've got to get your old man to give me a job in his plant—any
job, I don't care what!

ADA. Sure—I'll try, Rube.

REUBEN. (*with a cold assurance*) You've got to, Ada. Because I can't
stay on here without a job. I'm broke and I won't live home—even if
the old gent would let me. And that reminds me, I better go and pay
my little visit. I don't want to see him but I want to have a talk with
Mother. I've got over my hard feelings about her. She was so crazy
jealous of you she didn't care what she did. I can make allowances for
her—now. So I'll be friends again if she wants to—and then you watch
me convert her over from that old God stuff of his! (*He grins with
resentful anticipation.*)

ADA. (*has listened with blank astonishment—pityingly*) Then you
don't—? Why, I thought— Didn't they send for you?

REUBEN. (*unsuspectingly—with a grin*) Send for me to come home
and be good? I never gave them my address, kid. I didn't want them
bothering me. I never wrote, except some postcards to Mother I sent
to get her goat—and his. (*Then picking up his books and turning
toward his home*) Guess I'll go round by the back. I don't want to
run into him unless I have to. So long, Ada. Tell your old man I'd sure

461

like that job! (*He walks to the hedge and then, stealthily, across the lawn and disappears behind the house.*)

ADA. (*looking after him*)

He doesn't know she's dead . . . ought I to have told him? . . . oh, I couldn't! . . . poor Rube! . . .

(*Then admiringly*)

How strong he's gotten! . . . but it makes me afraid, too . . . his eyes seemed to take all the clothes off me . . . and I didn't feel ashamed . . . I felt glad! . . .

(*Defiantly*)

I love him! . . . I want him as much as he wants me! . . . what of it? . . .

(*Then with a shudder she cannot repress*)

But his eyes are so queer . . . like lumps of ice with fire inside them . . . and he never said he loved me . . . aw, of course he does! . . . he was nuts about me before he went away, wasn't he? . . .

(*Determinedly*)

I've got to make Pop give him that job or he might beat it again . . . he owes it to Rube to do something for him . . . I'll talk to him right now . . .

(*She disappears inside the house just as* REUBEN *slowly opens the door of the* LIGHT *sitting room. There is an expression of puzzled uneasiness on his face as he peers around the half-opened door, then slinks in as if he were a burglar.* LIGHT *is still sitting, his face hidden in his arms on the table, in an attitude of exhausted grief.* REUBEN *does not at first see him.*)

REUBEN.

Something's all wrong here . . . where the hell is everyone? . . . where's Mother? . . .

(*He has stepped on tiptoe into the room and now suddenly he sees his father and a sneering smile immediately comes to his lips*)

There he is, anyway . . . praying as usual . . . the poor boob . . . there isn't a damn prayer ever got him a thing . . . Mother used to make him pray for electric lights in the house . .

(*Suddenly with a pleased grin*)

That's a good hunch . . . I'll get them put in the first money I
save . . . it'll be like bringing my gospel to the heathen . . . let
there be electric light! . . .

(*He chuckles, then bends closer to look at his father*)

He must be asleep . . . that's one on him to catch him . . .

(*He speaks with mocking geniality*) Hello! (*His father gives a frightened start, as if dodging a blow, and stares at his son's face with stupefied bewilderment*) Sorry to disturb your little snooze. (*His father
continues to look at him, as if he can't believe his eyes*) Oh, this is me,
all right. (*Then the fact of his father's changed appearance strikes him
for the first time, and he blurts out in a tone that is almost kindly*)
Say, you look all in. What's the trouble? Been sick?

LIGHT. (*thinking gropingly*)

It's Reuben . . . Reuben . . . but he doesn't seem like
Reuben . . .

REUBEN. (*misunderstanding his father's silence as intentional, immediately becomes resentful*) What's the matter? Don't you want to talk
to me? Well, I'm not here to talk to you, either. I was just passing this
way and thought I'd drop in to say hello to Mother. Where is she?

LIGHT. (*thinking more clearly now—an unstrung fury rising within
him*)

Oh, yes, it's Reuben! . . . I recognize him now! . . . the same
as that night! . . . cruel and evil! . . . and now he's asking for
the mother he . . . my poor Amelia! . . . he killed her! . . .

(*He lurches to his feet and leans against the back of his chair weakly,
glaring at his son*) Murderer! You killed her!

REUBEN. (*stares at him with a stunned look*) What the hell do you
mean? (*Then harshly, taking a threatening step forward*) Where's
Mother, I'm asking you!

LIGHT. (*his strength failing him—in a faltering tone hardly above a
whisper*) She's dead—Reuben.

REUBEN. (*terribly shaken*) You're a liar! You're just saying that to
get my goat!

LIGHT. (*going on as if he hadn't heard—in a tone of monotonous *grief*) You can't see her—I can't—never—never see her again! (*He breaks down abjectly, sinking on his chair and sobbing, his face in his hands.*)

REUBEN. (*stands looking at him stupidly, convinced now of the truth and trying to make himself realize it and accept it*)
> Then it's straight goods . . . she is dead . . . gone . . . no use making a fuss . . . let him cry . . . why can't his religion buck him up now? . . . he ought to feel sure he's going to see her again soon . . . in heaven . . . I'd like to see her again . . . tell her I'm sorry for acting so rough to her that night . . .

(*He gulps and his lips twitch*)
> I wish he'd stop crying . . .

(*He goes forward and pats his father on the back gingerly*) Buck up. (*His father doesn't seem to hear him. He turns and slumps into the chair at the far side of the table*)
> Why couldn't I have seen her just once again . . . this is a rotten break . . .

(*He asks mechanically*) How long ago did she die?

LIGHT. (*mechanically in his turn—without lifting his head*) Two weeks ago yesterday.

REUBEN.
> Two weeks . . . it was about then I first felt that hunch to come home and see her . . . that's damn queer . . .

(*He stares at his father—uneasily*)
> He said I killed her . . . what the hell did he mean? . . .

(*Forcing a casual tone*) What did she die of?

LIGHT. (*dully*) Pneumonia.

REUBEN. (*heaving a sigh of relief*)
> Sure . . . I knew he was only saying that to get my goat . . .

(*He speaks to his father in a defensive, accusing tone*) Pneumonia, eh? Well, it's a damn wonder we didn't all die of it years ago, living in this dump! Ever since I can remember the cellar's leaked like a sieve. You never could afford to get it fixed right. Mother was always after you about it. And I can remember the ceiling in my room. Every storm the water'd begin to drip down and Mother'd put the wash basin on the floor to catch it. It was always damp in this house. Mother was always after you to make them put in a decent furnace instead of—

LIGHT. (*has lifted his head and is glaring at his son*) Are you trying to say I killed her? It was you! She'd been pining away for almost a year. Her heart was broken because you'd gone. She hoped for a time you'd come back but finally she gave up hoping—and gave up wanting to live! And your horrible blasphemous postcards kept coming! She blamed herself for your ruin and she wrote long letters begging your forgiveness, and asking you to come home! But you'd never given her an address! She couldn't mail them, she knew you'd never read them, and that broke her heart most of all! You killed her as surely as if you'd given her poison, you unnatural accursed son!

REUBEN. (*deeply disturbed but trying desperately to conceal it*) I never gave her my address because I thought she'd only write bawling me out. (*Then harshly*) Where are those letters she wrote? They're mine!

LIGHT. I destroyed them! I burnt them to the last scrap!

REUBEN. (*starts for his father threateningly, his fists clenched*) You rotten son of a— (*He chokes it back—then helplessly, with a wounded look*) Say, that was a dirty trick! I'd like to have read— (LIGHT *averts his eyes and suddenly hides his face in his hands.*)

LIGHT. (*remorsefully now*)

He's right . . . I had no right . . . no right even to read them . . . how I wish I'd never read them! . . .

(*Lifting his head*) I destroyed them in a fit of anger. When I read them I realized that Amelia had been thinking of you all the time. And I felt betrayed! I hated her and you! I was insane with hatred! God forgive me!

REUBEN. (*after a pause—dully*) Did she ever talk about me?

LIGHT. (*immediately jealous again*) She never mentioned your name! (*Then forcing himself to say it*) I—I had forbidden her to.

REUBEN. (*his face lights up with anger again but he controls it*) Sure,

465

you had to, didn't you?—so what the hell? (*Then insistently*) But—didn't she?—at the last?—when she was dying?—say anything?

LIGHT. (*fighting a furious battle with himself*)
Have I got to tell him? . . . that she'd even forgotten God? . . . that her last words were his words? . . . even her soul lost to me? . . . must I tell this? . . .
(*Savagely*)
No! . . . I don't owe him the truth! . . . I must make him feel he is accursed! . . .

(*He springs from his chair and leaning across the table, points his finger at* REUBEN *denouncingly*) Yes, with her last breath she cursed you for all the ruin and suffering you had brought on her—and on me! (*Then as he sees* REUBEN *shrinking back in his chair, a haunted look of horror on his face, the consciousness of the evil of the lie he is telling overwhelms him with guilty remorse. He stammers*) No!—that's a lie, Reuben!—a terrible lie!—don't listen!—don't believe me! (*He stumbles hastily around the table to the dazed* REUBEN *and with a pitiful gesture puts a trembling hand on his head—pleadingly*) Forgive me, Reuben! You are my son as well as hers, remember. I haven't the strength to resist evil. I wanted to punish you. She didn't curse you. Her last words were the very words you had written her. "Don't be a fool!" she kept saying to me! (*He shudders.*)

REUBEN. (*springs from his chair in extreme agitation and grabbing his father by both shoulders, stares hungrily in his face*) What? What's that? Mother said that?

LIGHT. (*seeming to shrivel up in his son's grip—trying unconvincingly to reassure himself*) She was delirious. She must have been delirious.

REUBEN. (*lets go of his father. The old man turns and stumbles back to his chair.* REUBEN *stares before him, thinking excitedly*)
"We have electrocuted your God. Don't be a fool" . . . that's what I kept writing her . . . her last words! . . . then I'd converted her away from his God! . . . the dying see things beyond . . . she saw I'd found the right path to the truth! . . .

466

(*His eyes shine with a new elation*)

By God, I'll go on now all right! . . .

(*He laughs aloud to himself exultantly.*)

LIGHT. Don't, for the love of God!

REUBEN. (*immediately ashamed of himself*) I wasn't laughing at you, honest. (*Then suddenly*) Say, I think I'll go and visit Mother's grave. There's some things I'd like to get off my chest—even if she can't hear me. (*Turning to the door*) Well, so long.

LIGHT. (*dully*) Shall I have your room put in order for you?

REUBEN. (*frowning*) No. It isn't my room now. That me is dead. (*Then an idea comes to him—thinking*)

But maybe Mother'd want me to? . . . maybe I'd get some message from her if I stayed here? . . .

(*Then casually to his father*) All right. I'll stay for a couple of days. After that I'm going to get a room out near the plant. Say, I might as well break the bad news to you. I'm getting a job in Fife's power house. (*Then quickly*) I suppose you think I'm doing it to spite you, but I'm not.

LIGHT. (*dully*) You sold your soul to Satan, Reuben.

REUBEN. (*immediately resentful—with his cold smile*) your Satan is dead. We electrocuted him along with your God. Electricity is God now. And we've got to learn to know God, haven't we? Well, that's what I'm after! (*In a lighter tone—mockingly*) Did you ever watch dynamos? Come down to the plant and I'll convert you! (*He cannot restrain a parting shot*) I converted Mother, didn't I? Well, so long. (*He goes out and a moment later walks past the front of the house from the right. He is off guard and the callousness has gone from his face, which is now very like that of the boy of Act One*)

I wish she hadn't died . . . but she forgave me . . .

ADA. (*sticks her head out of their sitting-room window as he passes the lilac hedge. Her face is flushed with excitement, happy and pretty now. She calls*) It's all right, Rube. Pop's got a job for you. A floor man is leaving Saturday.

REUBEN. (*startled out of his thoughts, at first frowns, then forces the cold smile to his lips*) That's great.

ADA. (*coquettishly*) Well, don't I get anything?

REUBEN. (*with his cold smile*) Sure! (*He goes to her and reaches up as if to kiss her—then checks himself, thinking remorsefully*) What the hell am I doing? . . . I'm going out to Mother's grave . . . she hated her . . . (*He steps back, frowning*) Wait till later, Ada. Well, so long. See you tonight. (*He turns his back on her abruptly and walks off left. She looks after him, bewildered and hurt.*)

CURTAIN

ACT TWO—SCENE TWO

THE *same except that* REUBEN'S *bedroom is now revealed while the wall of the sitting room has been replaced. It is about half past eleven on the same night—a sultry, hazy sky with few stars visible. There is no light in either house.*

REUBEN *and* ADA *come in from the left. She is hanging on his arm, pressing close to him as if she were afraid of his leaving her, glancing up into his face with a timid look of mingled happiness and apprehension.*

REUBEN'S *face shows that he also is struggling with conflicting emotions. There is a fixed smile of triumph and gratified vanity on his lips, but his eyes are restless and there is a nervous uneasiness apparent in his whole manner.*

ADA. You're sure you don't hate me now—because I let you—maybe I shouldn't have—but oh, Rube, I do love you so much! Say you love me just as much—that you always will!

468

REUBEN. (*preoccupiedly*) Sure I will.

ADA. (*pleadingly*) Put your arms around me tight and kiss me again. Then I won't be scared—or sorry.

REUBEN. (*mechanically puts his arms around her and kisses her at first perfunctorily, then with reawakening passion*) Gee, you're pretty, Ada! You've certainly got me going!

ADA. (*happily now*) Oh, Rube, when you kiss me like that nothing in the world matters but you! Up on the hill when we—oh, I felt I was just you, a part of you and you were part of me! I forgot everything!

REUBEN. (*suddenly moves away from her and stares around him nervously—in a strange voice*) Sure. You forget everything for a minute. You're happy. Then something has to wake you up—and start you thinking again.

ADA. What is it you're thinking about? Tell me and maybe I can help you forget it.

REUBEN. (*shaking his head*) I can't forget. (*Then determinedly*) And I don't want to. I want to face things. I won't ever be satisfied now until I've found the truth about everything.

ADA. (*trying to force a joking tone*) And where do I come in?

REUBEN. (*coldly*) You don't come in.

ADA. Rube! Don't say that—not after— You scare me!

REUBEN. (*irritatedly*) Cut out that talk of being scared! What are you scared about? Scared what we did was a sin? You're the hell of an atheist! (*Then jeeringly*) And you're the one that used to be always kidding me about being a goody boy! There's nothing to be scared about or sorry for. What we did was just plain sex—an act of nature—and that's all there is to it!

ADA. (*pitifully—her voice trembling*) Is that all—it means to you?

REUBEN. That's all it means to any one! What people call love is just sex—and there's no sin about it!

ADA. I wasn't saying there was, was I? I've proved to you I don't—

469

only— (*Then frightenedly*) It's you, Rube. I can't get used to you talking like that. You've changed so.

REUBEN. (*with a coarse grin*) Well, you've got no kick coming. If I'd stayed the same poor boob I used to be you might have died an old maid.

ADA. But—you wanted to marry me then, Rube.

REUBEN. (*roughly*) And a lot that got me, didn't it?

ADA. (*faintly*) Don't you want to—any more?

REUBEN. Don't I what? Talk sense, Ada! We're married by Nature now. We don't need any old fool of a minister saying prayers over us! (*Then after a moment's pause—with a forced laugh*) Say, here's one on me, Ada—speaking of praying. It was out at Mother's grave. Before I thought, I started to do a prayer act—and then suddenly it hit me that there was nothing to pray to. (*He forces another laugh*) It just goes to show you what a hold that bunk gets on you when you've had it crammed down your throat from the time you were born! You can't pray to electricity unless you're foolish in the head, can you? (*Then strangely*) But maybe you could, at that—if you knew how!

ADA. Is that where you went this afternoon—out to her grave?

REUBEN. (*with affected indifference*) Sure. What of it?

ADA. (*pityingly*) Poor Rube!

REUBEN. (*frowning*) Poor nothing! She's dead, and that's all there is about it. You've got to face death as well as life.

ADA. I'm sorry she hated me so. I hope now she forgives us—for loving each other.

REUBEN. (*with his cold smile*) You mean forgives us for what we did to-night? You don't know her! She never would! But what's the use of talking about it? Who gives a damn? Good night, Ada. I'm tired. I'm going to bed. See you to-morrow. (*He turns his back on her abruptly and walks off right toward the front door of his house.*)

ADA. (*stands looking after him with bewildered hurt for a moment, then turns back toward her own front door and begins to cry softly, at the same time trying to reassure herself*)

I mustn't . . . feel bad . . . he doesn't mean to hurt me . . .
he's changed, that's all . . .

(*She disappears off left. A moment later,* REUBEN *appears in his bedroom and lights the lamp. He sits down on the bed and stares before him.*)

REUBEN. (*looking about the room now, thinking bitterly*)
The last time I was here . . . there's the closet where she hid him
. . . here's where she sat lying to me . . . watching him beat
me . . .

(*He springs to his feet—viciously*)
I'm glad she's dead! . . .

(*Then immediately remorseful*)
No . . . I don't mean that, Mother . . . I was thinking of how
you acted that night . . . I wish I could have seen you after you'd
changed . . . after you'd come back to my side . . .

(*He goes to the window on the left and looks out*)
Here's where I was looking out, waiting for Ada to signal on the
Victrola . . . gosh, that seems a million years ago! . . . how
scared I was of even kissing her! . . . and tonight she was dead
easy . . . like rolling off a log! . . .

(*He comes back to the bed and sits down*)
Mother said she was no better than a streetwalker . . . she certainly didn't put up a fight . . . marry her! . . . what does she
think I am, a boob? . . . she put one over on me and now I've
put one over on her! . . . we're square . . . and whatever's going to happen, will happen, but it won't be a wedding! . . .

(*Then with coarse sensuality*)
But it's grand to have her around handy whenever I want . . . the
flesh, as the old man would call it! . . . and she's all right other
ways, too . . . I like her . . . she got me the job . . . she'll be
useful . . . and I'll treat her decent . . . maybe it's love . . .
whatever the hell love is! . . . did Mother really love the old
man? . . . she must have or how could she stand him? . . . and
she made me with him . . . act of Nature . . . like me and
Ada . . .

(*He jumps to his feet distractedly*)

God, that seems lousy somehow! . . . I don't want to think of it! . . .

(*He paces up and down—then pauses and appears to be listening for something*)

There's something queer about this dump now . . . as if no one was living here . . . I suppose that's because Mother's gone . . . I'd like to reach her somehow . . . no one knows what happens after death . . . even science doesn't . . . there may be some kind of hereafter . . . I used to kneel down here and say my prayers . . . she taught them to me . . . then she'd tuck me in, even after I'd grown up . . . and kiss me good night . . .

(*As if automatically he slips to his knees by the bed*)

I'm sorry, Mother . . . sorry you're dead . . . I wish I could talk to you . . .

(*He scrambles to his feet—angry at himself*)

You damn fool! . . . what's come over you, anyway? . . . what are you praying to? . . . when there's nothing . . .

(*Then strangely*)

Funny, that hunch I got when I was talking to Ada . . . about praying to electricity, if you knew how . . . it was like a message . . . Mother believed what I believed when she died . . . maybe it came from her . . .

(*Then suspicious of himself again*)

Aw, that's just superstitious junk . . . but why is it? . . . look at how mysterious all this electrical wave stuff is in radio and everything . . . that's scientific fact . . . and why couldn't something like that that no one understands yet? . . . between the dead and the living? . . .

(*He walks around nervously*)

No use trying to go to sleep . . . and I want to keep on thinking . . . but not in here . . . I'll go for a walk . . . why not go down to the plant? . . . take a look in at the dynamos . . . watching them always helps me somehow . . . sure, that's the stuff! . . .

(*He turns down the light and blows it out and can be seen going through the door in rear.*)

CURTAIN

ACT TWO—SCENE THREE

A HALF *hour later. Exterior of the Light and Power Company's hydro-electric plant about two miles from the town. The plant is comparatively a small one. The building is red brick. The section on the left, the dynamo room, is much wider than the right section but is a story less in height. An immense window and a big sliding door are in the lower part of the dynamo-room wall, and there is a similar window in the upper part of the section on right. Through the window and the open door of the dynamo room, which is brilliantly lighted by a row of powerful bulbs in white globes set in brackets along both walls, there is a clear view of a dynamo, huge and black, with something of a massive female idol about it, the exciter set on the main structure like a head with blank, oblong eyes above a gross, rounded torso.*

Through the upper window of the right section of the building, in the switch galleries, by a dim light, one gets a glimpse of the mathematically ordered web of the disconnecting switches, double busses, and other equipment stretching up through the roof to the outgoing feeders leading to the transmission towers.

The air is full of sound, a soft overtone of rushing water from the dam and the river bed below, penetrated dominatingly by the harsh, throaty, metallic purr of the dynamo.

REUBEN *comes in from the right and approaches until he is opposite the open doorway. He stands there staring at the dynamo and listening to it.*

REUBEN. (*after a pause—fascinatedly*)
It's so mysterious . . . and grand . . . it makes you feel things
. . . you don't need to think . . . you almost get the secret . . .

473

what electricity is . . . what life is . . . what God is . . . it's all the same thing . . .

(*A pause—then he goes on in the same fascinated tone*)

It's like a great dark idol . . . like the old stone statues of gods people prayed to . . . only it's living and they were dead . . . that part on top is like a head . . . with eyes that see you without seeing you . . . and below it is like a body . . . not a man's . . . round like a woman's . . . as if it had breasts . . . but not like a girl . . . not like Ada . . . no, like a woman . . . like her mother . . . or mine . . . a great, dark mother! . . . that's what the dynamo is! . . . that's what life is! . . .

(*He stares at it raptly now*)

Listen to her singing . . . that beats all organs in church . . . it's the hymn of electricity . . . "always singing about everything in the world" . . . if you could only get back into that . . . know what it means . . . then you'd know the real God! . . .

(*Then longingly*)

There must be some way! . . . there must be something in her song that'd tell you if you had ears to hear! . . . some way that she'd teach you to know her . . .

(*He begins to hum, swaying his body—then stops when he can't catch the right tone*)

No, you can't get it! . . . it's as far off as the sky and yet it's all around you! . . . in you! . . .

(*Excitedly*)

I feel like praying now! . . . I feel there is something in her to pray to! . . . something that'll answer me! . . .

(*He looks around him and moves to the right out of the square of light from the open doorway*)

Supposing anyone saw me . . . they'd think I was nutty . . . the old prayer stuff! . . .

(*Then arguing tormentedly with himself*)

But I feel it's right . . . I feel Mother wants me to . . . it's the least I can do for her . . . to say a prayer . . .

(*He gets down on his knees and prays aloud to the dynamo*) Oh, Mother of Life, my mother is dead, she has passed back into you, tell her to forgive me, and to help me find your truth! (*He pauses on his*

474

knees for a moment, then gets slowly to his feet. There is a look of calm and relief on his face now. He thinks reverentially)

    Yes, that did it . . . I feel I'm forgiven . . . Mother will help me . . . I can sleep . . . I'll go home . . .

(He walks slowly off right.)

CURTAIN

ACT THREE—SCENE ONE

SAME *as Act Two, Scene Three—Exterior of the power house four months later. It is a little after sunset and the equipment on the roof is outlined blackly against a darkening crimson sky.*

The door of the dynamo room is shut but the interior is brilliantly lighted and the dynamo can be partly seen through the window. There is a dim light above in the switch galleries as in the previous scene. The overtone of rushing water from the dam sounds louder because of the closed door which muffles the noise of the dynamo to a minor strain.

REUBEN *enters from the left accompanied by* MRS. FIFE. *He has grown very thin, his dungarees sag about his angular frame. His face is gaunt and pale. His eyes are deeply sunken. He is talking with unnatural excitement as they come in.* MRS. FIFE *is unchanged. If anything, her moony dreaminess is more pronounced. She listens to* REUBEN *with a fascinated, far-away look, as if the sound of his voice hypnotized her rather than the meaning of the words.*

REUBEN. (*insistently*) You understood all I explained to you up on the dam, didn't you?—about how life first came out of the sea?

MRS. FIFE. (*nods dreamily*) Yes, Reuben. It sounds like poetry— "life out of the sea."

REUBEN. It is like poetry. Her song in there—Dynamo's—isn't that the greatest poem of all—the poem of eternal life? And listen to the water rushing over the dam! Like music! It's as if that sound was cool water washing over my body!—washing all dirt and sin away! Like some one singing me to sleep—my mother—when I was a kid—calling me back to somewhere far off where I'd been once long ago and known peace! (*He sighs with longing, his body suddenly gone limp and weary.*)

476

MRS. FIFE. (*Dreamily*) That's awful pretty, Reuben. (*She puts her arm around him—sentimentally*) I'll be your mother—yours and Ada's. I've always wanted a boy.

REUBEN. (*Leans against her gratefully, his head almost on her shoulder, his eyes half closed*) Yes. You're like her—Dynamo—the Great Mother—big and warm— (*With a sudden renewal of his unnatural excitement, breaks away from her*) But I've got to finish telling you all I've come to know about her—how all things end up in her! Did I tell you that our blood plasm is the same right now as the sea was when life came out of it? We've got the sea in our blood still! It's what makes our hearts live! And it's the sea rising up in clouds, falling on the earth in rain, made that river that drives the turbines that drive Dynamo! The sea makes her heart beat, too!— but the sea is only hydrogen and oxygen and minerals, and they're only atoms, and atoms are only protons and electrons—even our blood and the sea are only electricity in the end! And think of the stars! Driving through space, round and round, just like the electrons in the atom! But there must be a center around which all this moves, mustn't there? There is in everything else! And that center must be the Great Mother of Eternal Life, Electricity, and Dynamo is her Divine Image on earth! Her power houses are the new churches! She wants us to realize the secret dwells in her! She wants some one man to love her purely and when she finds him worthy she will love him and give him the secret of truth and he will become the new saviour who will bring happiness and peace to men! And I'm going to be that saviour—that's why I asked you to come—I want you to be a witness! I know the miracle will happen to me tonight because I had a message from my mother last night. I woke up and saw her standing beside my bed—just as she used to when she came in to kiss me good night—and she smiled and held out her arms to me. I know she came from the spirit of the Great Mother into which she passed when she died to tell me she had at last found me worthy of her love.

477

MRS. FIFE. (*sentimentally*) Most people don't believe in ghosts. Ramsay don't. But I do. Has she come many times, Reuben?

REUBEN. (*strangely*) Not lately—not since I gave up seeing Ada. Before that she used to come almost every night. to warn me.

MRS. FIFE. Warn you about what, Reuben?

REUBEN. That I was living in sin—that Dynamo would never find me worthy of her secret until I'd given up the flesh and purified myself! (*Then proudly*) And I found the strength to do it. It was hard! I was beginning to really love Ada.

MRS. FIFE. (*simply*) Of course, you love Ada—and you shouldn't act so mean to her, Reuben. You haven't been around in a month or more. She's making herself sick worrying.

REUBEN. (*intensely*) I'd like to see her! I'd love to! But I can't. Don't you understand I can't—that my finding the secret is more important than—? (*Then thinking with sudden fear and doubt*)

> But supposing the miracle doesn't happen tonight? . . . Ada keeps coming in dreams . . . her body . . . I've beaten myself with my belt . . . I can't keep on much longer . . .

(*He sways dizzily on his feet, passing his hand over his eyes—then straightens himself and turns to* MRS. FIFE) I've got to go in. They'll be missing me. And I've got to pray to her. (*He goes to the door*) You wait until your husband's gone home. Then you come in.

MRS. FIFE. All right, Reuben. (REUBEN *slides back the dynamo-room door a few feet and enters, closing it behind him.* MRS. FIFE *stares after him mooningly. A moment later the door from the dynamo room is opened again and* FIFE *comes out, closing it behind him. He hasn't changed since his last appearance. He starts to walk hesitatingly off right—then stops without looking around him and does not notice his wife.*)

FIFE. (*thinking exasperatedly*)

> That damned Rube! . . . there's a queer look in those cold eyes of his lately! . . . by God, I'd fire him to-night if Ada wouldn't make my life a hell for it! . . . but he does his work good . . . too

damned good! . . . he's always pawing around a dynamo when he's no business . . .

MRS. FIFE. Hello, Ramsay. You better get home to supper. I had mine early. I had to go out.

FIFE. (*turns on her witih an irritated start*) Oh, you did, did you? You're always having to go out these days, it seems! I won't have you gallivanting down here at all hours and staring at the dynamos and humming like a half-wit! What the hell's come over you, anyway?

MRS. FIFE. Nothing's come over me, Ramsay. I was talking to Reuben. He took me up on the dam and told me about how we all used to live in the ocean once. (*Then in her tone of childish mooning*) D'you suppose I ever was a fish, Ramsay?

FIFE. Aye, a jellyfish, I'm thinking! You've the brains for that! (*Then angrily*) You do too much gabbing with that Rube! He'll addle the little sense you've left! But if you've got to talk to him, make him talk turkey and say when is he planning to marry Ada! Aren't you her mother, and don't you see she's worrying her heart out? (*Lowering his voice*) D'you think it's happened between them— you know what I mean?

MRS. FIFE. (*with naïve simplicity*) Yes, of course it has, Ramsay. She loves him the same as I did you when we—

FIFE. Don't be comparing him to me! I was more of a decent man than he ever will be! (*In a passion*) I'll have a talk with that lad and if he don't do the decent thing by her, I'll beat decency into him! (*He turns from her in a tantrum*) To hell with you! I'm hungry! I'm going home! (*He goes off right.* MRS. FIFE *looks after him with a placid smile—then she gives the big door a push that slides it open to its full width and steps inside and, as she sees* REUBEN, *stops as she is about to pull the door closed again. He is kneeling just inside the doorway before the dynamo in the foreground, his arms stretched out to it supplicatingly.*)

REUBEN. (*suddenly cries out with a note of despair*) Mother! Don't

479

you hear me? Can't you give me some sign? O Dynamo, who gives life to things, hear my prayer! Grant me the miracle of your love! (*He waits, his body strained with suspense, listening as if he expected the dynamo to answer him.* ADA *comes from around the corner of the building at the left. Her manner is furtive as if she were doing something she is ashamed of. She looks worried and run down, although she has made a defiant effort with rouge and mascara to hide this.*)

ADA.

He must be around some place . . .

(*She moves cautiously to the window and peeks in, but cannot see him*)

I don't want no one to see me . . . I'll knock on the window when I see him and get him to come out . . .

(*Then with bitter self-contempt*)

Here I am chasing after him! . . . but I couldn't stand it any more, waiting . . . oh, what a damn fool I was to give in so easy! . . . no wonder he's sick of me! . . . but he can't throw me over this way! . . .

(*She looks in the window again.*)

REUBEN. (*his tense, supplicating attitude suddenly relaxing dejectedly*)

She won't answer me . . . there must still be something I've got to do . . .

(*Then guiltily*)

Maybe she feels I haven't killed all desire for Ada yet? . . . that I ought to face her and conquer the flesh once for all . . .

(*He jumps to his feet and turns to* MRS. FIFE *pleadingly*) Can't you tell me? You know what she means sometimes. (*He lowers his voice cautiously as if he didn't want the dynamo to overhear*) Do you think it's something I've got to do about Ada?

MRS. FIFE. (*simply*) Yes, you've got to do the right thing by Ada, Reuben.

REUBEN. (*thinking with unnatural excitement*)

Then that is it! . . . I'll have to go and face Ada right now! . . .

(*Turning to* MRS. FIFE) You stay here! I'll be back. (*He comes out, sliding the door closed after him.*)

ADA. (*turns at the noise of the door closing from where she is looking in the window and calls to him*) Rube!

REUBEN. (*whirls around and stands staring at her with strange fixity for a moment, his thoughts seizing on this coincidence*) It's Ada! . . . Dynamo sent her here! . . . she wanted to prove I've conquered the flesh! . . .

ADA. (*frightenedly*) What's the matter? Don't look at me like that, Rube!

REUBEN. (*moved in spite of himself, instinctively takes a step toward her—in a queer, detached tone*) I didn't mean to scare you, Ada. You gave me a start, seeing you all of a sudden.

ADA. (*looking at him hopefully*) You're not sore at me for coming, are you?

REUBEN. No. It's as if you'd been sent. Didn't you feel something driving you to come here right now?

ADA (*quickly*) Yes, I just had to come!

REUBEN. (*strangely*) It was she who made you come.

ADA. She? Who's she?

REUBEN. (*a lightning change comes over his face. He takes a threatening step toward her—denouncingly, his voice booming like his father's*) You blasphemous fool, you! Do you dare to deny her! "The fool saith in his heart—" (*He suddenly checks himself and forces a strange, shamefaced laugh*) Say, did you get me quoting from the Bible, Ada? That's one on me! That comes from arguing with the old man lately. He's got some fool notion that Dynamo is the devil. (*Then his expression abruptly changing again—fiercely*) But I'll make the old fool get down on his knees to her yet before I'm through with him! And I'll make you, too, Ada! (*This puts a sudden idea into his head—thinking excitedly.*)

What made me say that? . . . you, Mother? . . . not only conquer her flesh, but convert her? . . . make her pray to you? . . .

481

Listen to me, Ada! Tonight the miracle will happen!—and then there will be only the kingdom of happiness on earth—my kingdom!—for us, Ada! (*Then suddenly grabbing her by the arm*) Only you've got to help me!

ADA. (*thinking frightenedly*)

For God's sake, what's come over him? . . . the damned dynamo! . . . it's driving him crazy! . . .

(*She puts her arms around him pityingly and tries to hug him to her*) I'll do anything, Rube! Don't you know how much I love you?

REUBEN. (*pushing her away from him—in a stammering panic*) Don't do that! (*Then pleadingly*) Why can't you understand? You've got to believe in Dynamo, and bow down to her will!

ADA. (*soothingly*) All right, Rube.

REUBEN. (*taking her hand—insistently*) Come with me! I want to explain everything to you—to prove everything!—all this plant means about her—you've got to believe in her, Ada! (*She follows him off left, frightened but pitying and resolved to humor him. His voice is heard explaining excitedly as they climb to the dam. It recedes and then grows louder as they cross from the dam to the dynamo-room roof, and a moment later he is seen there. He comes forward until he stands by the coping, front. He still has* ADA *by the hand. She follows him, holding back as much as she dares, a nervous look on her face. His unnatural excitement has increased, he looks around him with the rapt expression of one in a trance*) Oh, Ada, you simply can't help believing in her! You only have to listen to her! Her song is the hymn of eternal generation, the song of eternal life!

ADA. (*uneasily*) Rube! I'm scared up here!

REUBEN. (*Turns and looks at her like a sleepwalker for a second— then with a sudden hungry passion*) You're so damned pretty! God, how I wish the miracle was over and we could—!

ADA. (*persuasively*) I'm scared on this roof, Rube. Let's go down!

REUBEN. (*excitedly*) Yes, down to her! I was forgetting her! She's waiting for me! (*Then as she starts to go back the way they have*

*come, he takes her hand again and pulls her through the door from
the roof to the galleries.*)

ADA. (*frightenedly*) Rube! I don't want to go— (*He slams the door
behind them.*)

*There is a pause of darkness here to indicate the end of Scene One.
No time elapses between Scenes One and Two.*

ACT THREE—SCENE TWO

W HEN *the light comes on again the interiors of the upper and
lower switch galleries are revealed. The lower gallery of the
oil switches is a deep but narrow compartment with red brick walls.
The oil switches, with their spindly steel legs, their square, criss-
crossed steel bodies (the containers inside looking like bellies), their
six cupped arms stretching upward, seem like queer Hindu idols
tortured into scientific supplications. These switches extend in a
straight row backward down the middle of the gallery, but in the dim
light of one bulb in a bracket in the left wall only the front one in the
foreground can be made out. Against the wall on the right is a stairway that extends backward halfway up this wall, then turns and
ascends diagonally toward the left to the upper gallery, and from
thence up to the door from the roof of the dynamo room.*

*The upper gallery contains the disconnecting switches and the
double busses. It is of double width and extends over the switchboard
room also. This second gallery, dimly lighted like the one below, is a
fretwork of wires, steel work, insulators, busses, switches, etc., stretching upward to the roof. Below the disconnecting switches is a raised
platform.*

REUBEN *and* ADA *are discovered by the dim light of this upper gallery
standing just inside the door to the dynamo-room roof at the top of
the stairway.*

ADA. (*looking around her frightenedly at the weird shadows of the equipment writhing upward in the dimly lighted gallery—shrinking close to* REUBEN, *who is staring at all this with a rapt, questioning, listening look*) All this stuff scares me. I've only seen it in daylight before. It looks as if it was alive!

REUBEN. (*strangely*) You're beginning to see, Ada! It is alive! Alive with the mighty spirit of her eternal life! (*Then with a start, he pushes her away from him roughly*) What the hell are you doing? Don't press against me, I tell you! I'm wise to your dirty game—and I won't stand for it! Don't you realize we're in her temple now!

ADA. (*pitifully*) Rube! Please don't talk like that—when you know how I love you!

REUBEN. (*clutching her arm fiercely*) You mustn't say you love me in here, you fool you! Don't you know all this is watching—listening —that she knows everything! Sssh! I want to hear if she's angry at me! (*He stands in a strained attitude of attention, listening to the dynamo's hum sounding from below—then evidently satisfied, turns to* ADA *with a relieved air*) No, she isn't angry on account of you being here because she knows you're beginning to believe in her! It's all right for you to come close to me now, Ada. (*He puts an arm around her and pulls her to him.*)

ADA. (*persuasively*) Please let's go down, Rube.

REUBEN. (*gently*) All right, Ada. (*They go down the first flight of steps. He stops as they get to the bottom and glances up and around him*) You know, Ada, there used to be times when I was scared here too—when all these switches and busses and wires seemed like the arms of a devil fish—stretching out to suck me in— (*He gives a shudder and presses her to him.*)

ADA. (*soothingly*) You mustn't be afraid. I'm here with you.

REUBEN. (*pleadingly—pointing to the platform beneath the disconnecting switches*) Listen, Ada! I want you to pray to her—up there where I pray sometimes—under her arms—with your arms like her arms, stretching out for me! (*He suddenly bends his face to her face, his eyes devouring it desirously*) God, you're pretty! (*He controls himself with a violent effort and pushes her away from him, keeping his face averted from hers—in a voice that is almost supplicating*) You must pray that she may find me worthy. You must pray for me, if you love me!

ADA. (*soothingly—humoring him*) All right, Rube. (*She goes up the stairs to the platform and stands directly under the switches, stretching her arms up in the same position as the switch arms.*)

REUBEN. (*remains standing below—thinking confusedly*)
Mother would warn me if I was doing wrong . . . Dynamo means all this to happen to me . . . it's the great temptation . . . perhaps she wants me even to kiss Ada . . .
(*He ascends to the platform and stands before her.*)

ADA. (*tenderly and soothingly*) Why did you say a minute ago, if I loved you? Don't you know I do? Why have you stayed away from me so long, Rube? I've almost died, longing for you!

REUBEN. (*without looking at her—dully*) You believe in her now, don't you? You wouldn't do anything to make me unworthy in her sight, would you?—when it means happiness for me—and for all mankind? You couldn't, could you?

ADA. (*humoring him—gently*) Of course not.

REUBEN. (*mechanically*) You swear to her?

ADA. (*in the same tone*) Yes, I swear.

REUBEN. (*mechanically*) Then I'm going to kiss you, Ada—just once —only kiss you—she wants me to—as a final test—to prove I'm purified— (*He looks up at her now and lurches forward with a moan of passion and takes her in his arms*) Ada! (*He kisses her frantically, bending her backward and down toward the floor of the platform. She cries out frightenedly.*)

There is a pause of darkness to indicate the end of Scene Two. A short time is supposed to elapse between Scenes Two and Three.

ACT THREE—SCENE THREE

As THE *light slowly comes on again,* REUBEN *is heard sobbing brokenly from the gallery. The interiors of the dynamo and switchboard rooms are now also revealed.*

The dynamo room is high and wide with red brick walls and a row of great windows in the left wall. The floor and an observation balcony which projects into the dynamo room from the switchboard room on the right (one story up) are of concrete. The nearest dynamo, which we have seen previously through the doorway, occupies most of the floor space in the foreground. A steel ladder runs up its side on the right to a platform around the exciter.

The switchboard room is a small compartment to the right of the dynamo room, one story up in the other section of the building. In it are the switchboard and a couple of chairs. It is lighted by a shaded drop light over the desk. JENNINGS, *the operator on duty, a man of thirty or so, is seated at the desk.*

MRS. FIFE *is sitting in the dynamo room just under and to the left of the observation balcony. She is staring dreamily at the front dynamo, humming to herself, her big body relaxed as if she had given herself up completely to the spell of its hypnotic, metallic purr which flows insistently through the ears, numbing the brain, charging the nerves with electricity, making the heart strain with the desire to beat in its rhythm of unbroken, eternal continuity.*

In the gallery, ADA *and* REUBEN *are still on the platform beneath the disconnecting switches.* REUBEN *is on his knees, his back bowed, his face covered by his hands.* ADA *is standing before him, directly beneath the switches as before. She is bending over him in a tender attitude, one hand reaching down, touching his hair.*

486

REUBEN. (*thinking torturedly*)

Mother! . . . I've betrayed you . . . you will never bless me with the miracle now! . . . you have shut me from your heart forever! . . .

(*He groans and beats his head against the floor.*)

ADA. (*pats him on the back consolingly*) Poor Rube! I love you. You'll be all right, dear.

REUBEN. (*shrinking away*) Don't touch me! (*He springs to his feet, and shielding his face with one hand from the sight of her, runs down the stairs to the lower oil switch gallery. He stops there, looking around him distractedly as if he didn't know where to hide, his thoughts hounded by remorse*)

Mother! . . . have mercy on me! . . . I hate her now! . . . as much as you hate her! . . . give me one more chance! . . . what can I do to get you to forgive me? . . . tell me! . . . yes! . . . I hear you, Mother! . . . and then you'll forgive me? . . . and I can come to you? . . .

(*A terrible look of murder comes on his face. He starts for the stairs, his hands outstretched as if he were already strangling her—then stops*)

No . . . not with my hands. . . . Never touch her flesh again . . . how? . . . I see. . . . Switchboard room . . . in the desk. . . .

(*He dashes over into the switchboard room through the door at left of the gallery. He has the startled and terrified* JENNINGS *by the throat before the latter knows it and flings him away from the desk, tears out a drawer and gets the revolver and with it motions him to the door of the office in the rear*) Get in there! Quick! (JENNINGS *obeys hastily.* REUBEN *turns the key in the lock after him. In contrast to his furious haste of a moment before, he now walks deliberately back through the door to the oil switch gallery. His face is as drained of all human feeling as a plaster mask*)

I won't be a murderer . . . I'm your executioner, Mother . . . that's why I'm so calm . . .

(*He glides stealthily across toward the foot of the stairs.*)

ADA. (*worried about him has come down from the platform and is beginning to descend the stairs to the lower switch gallery—she calls uneasily*) Rube! Where are you?

REUBEN

Harlot! . . . that's what Mother called her! . . .

(*He springs up the stairs to her, shouting fiercely*) Harlot!

ADA. (*she sees the revolver aimed at her breast as he stops directly beneath her—in a terrified whisper*) Rube! (REUBEN *fires twice and she jerks back and pitches sideways on the stairs.*)

REUBEN. (*stares down at her body for a moment and lets the gun fall from his hand and begins to tremble all over. He calls pitifully*) Ada! I didn't mean to hurt you! (*Then thinking with an anguished appeal*) Mother! . . . where are you? . . . I did it for your sake! . . . why don't you call to me? . . . don't leave me alone! . . .

(*He turns and runs headlong through the switchboard room, and down the stairs to the dynamo-room floor, where he lunges for the rungs on the dynamo's side and clambers up frenziedly. Up on the platform, he stops for a moment, gasping for breath, stretching out his arms to the exciter-head of his Dynamo-Mother with its whirling metal brain and its blank, oblong eyes.*)

MRS. FIFE. (*dimly aware of him—dreamily*) What was that noise up there, Reuben? It sounded like a shot.

REUBEN. (*pleading to the dynamo like a little boy*) I don't want any miracle, Mother! I don't want to know the truth! I only want you to hide me, Mother! Never let me go from you again! Please, Mother! (*He throws his arms out over the exciter, his hands grasp the carbon brushes. There is a flash of bluish light about him and all the lights in the plant dim down until they are almost out and the noise of the dynamo dies until it is the faintest purring hum. Simultaneously* REUBEN'S *voice rises in a moan that is a mingling of pain and loving consummation, and this cry dies into a sound that is like the crooning of a baby and merges and is lost in the dynamo's hum. Then his body crumples to the steel platform and from there falls heavily to the*

488

floor. There is a startled cry from MRS. FIFE *as she runs to the body. The dynamo's throaty metallic purr rises slowly in volume and the lights begin to come up again in the plant.*)

MRS. FIFE. (*kneeling beside* REUBEN, *one hand on the forehead of his upturned face*) Reuben! Are you hurt bad? (*She turns with childish bewildered resentment and hurt to the dynamo*) What are you singing for? I should think you'd be ashamed! And I thought you was nice and loved us! (*The dynamo's purr has regained its accustomed pitch now. The lights in the plant are again at their full brightness. Everything is as before.* MRS. FIFE *pounds the steel body of the generator in a fit of childish anger*) You hateful old thing, you! (*Then she leaves off, having hurt her hands, and begins to cry softly.*)

CURTAIN

DAYS WITHOUT END

To

CARLOTTA

CHARACTERS

(In the order in which they appear)

JOHN
LOVING
WILLIAM ELIOT
FATHER MATTHEW BAIRD
ELSA, *John Loving's wife*
MARGARET
LUCY HILLMAN
DR. HERBERT STILLWELL
NURSE

SCENES

ACT ONE

PLOT FOR A NOVEL

Scene: John Loving's office in the offices of Eliot and Company, New York City—an afternoon in early Spring, 1932.

ACT TWO

PLOT FOR A NOVEL (CONTINUED)

Scene: Living-room of the Lovings' duplex apartment—later the same afternoon.

ACT THREE

PLOT FOR A NOVEL (CONTINUED)

Scene I: The living-room again—evening of the same day.
Scene II: John Loving's study—later that night.

ACT FOUR

THE END OF THE END

Scene I: The study and Elsa's bedroom—a little before dawn of a day about a week later.
Scene II: The interior of a church—a few minutes later.

DAYS WITHOUT END

ACT ONE

PLOT FOR A NOVEL

SCENE—JOHN LOVING'S *private office in the offices of* ELIOT AND COM-PANY, *New York City. On the left, a window. Before it, a chair, its back to the window, and a table. At rear of table, an armchair, facing front. A third chair is at right of table. In the rear wall, a door leading to the outer offices. At center of the room, toward right, another chair.*

It is afternoon of a cloudy day in Spring, 1932. The light from the window is chill and gray. At the rise of the curtain, this light is concentrated around the two figures seated at the table. As the action goes on, the light imperceptibly spreads until, at the close of the opening scene between JOHN *and* LOVING, *it has penetrated to all parts of the room.*

JOHN *is seated in the chair at left of desk. He is forty, of medium height. His face is handsome, with the rather heavy, conventional American type of good looks—a straight nose and a square jaw, a wide mouth that has an incongruous feminine sensitiveness, a broad forehead, blue eyes. He is dressed in a dark suit, white shirt and collar, a dark tie, black shoes and socks.*

LOVING *sits in the armchair at rear of table. He is the same age, of the same height and figure, is dressed in every detail exactly the same. His hair is the same—dark, streaked with gray. In contrast to this similarity between the two, there is an equally strange dissimilarity. For* LOVING'S *face is a mask whose features reproduce exactly the features of* JOHN'S *face—the death mask of a* JOHN *who has died with a*

493

*sneer of scornful mockery on his lips. And this mocking scorn is re-
peated in the expression of the eyes which stare bleakly from behind
the mask.*

JOHN *nervously writes a few words on a pad—then stops abruptly
and stares before him.* LOVING *watches him.*

LOVING. (*his voice singularly toneless and cold but at the same time
insistent*) Surely, you don't need to make any more notes for the second part—your hero's manhood up to the time he (*A sneer comes into
his voice*) at last finds love. I should think you could remember that—
only too well.

JOHN. (*mechanically*) Yes.

LOVING. (*sneeringly*) As for the third part, I know you have the most
vivid recollection of his terrible sin.

JOHN. Don't mock, damn you!

LOVING. So it's only in the last part that you will have to use your
imagination. How are you going to end this interesting plot of yours?
Given your hero's ridiculous conscience, what happens then?

JOHN. He has the courage to confess—and she forgives.

LOVING. The wish is father to that thought, eh? A pretty, sentimental
ending—but a bit too pointed, don't you think? I'm afraid she might
begin to wonder—

JOHN. (*apprehensively*) Yes. That's true.

LOVING. I advise you to make the last part so obviously fictitious that
it will kill any suspicion which might be aroused by what has gone
before.

JOHN. How can I end it, then?

LOVING. (*after a second's pause—in a voice he tries to make casual
but which is indefinably sinister*) Why not have the wife die?

JOHN. (*starts—with a shudder*) Damn you! What makes you think
of that?

LOVING. Why, nothing—except I thought you'd agreed that the fur-

494

ther removed from present actuality you make your ending, the better it will be.

JOHN. Yes—but—

LOVING. (*mockingly*) I hope you don't suspect some hidden, sinister purpose behind my suggestion.

JOHN. I don't know. I feel— (*Then, as if desperately trying to shake off his thoughts*) No! I won't think of it!

LOVING. And I was thinking, too, that it would be interesting to work out your hero's answer to his problem, if his wife died, and imagine what he would do with his life then.

JOHN. No! Damn you, stop making me think—!

LOVING. Afraid to face your ghosts—even by proxy? Surely, even you can have that much courage!

JOHN. It is dangerous—to call things.

LOVING. Still superstitious? Well, I hope you realize I'm only trying to encourage you to make something of this plot of yours more significant—for your soul, shall I say?—than a cowardly trick!

JOHN. You know it's more than that. You know I'm doing it to try and explain to myself, as well as to her.

LOVING. (*sneeringly*) To excuse yourself to yourself, you mean! To lie and escape admitting the obvious natural reason for—

JOHN. You lie! I want to get at the real truth and understand what was behind—what evil spirit of hate possessed me to make me—

LOVING. (*contemptuously—but as he goes on a strange defiant note of exultance comes into his voice*) So it's come back to that again, eh? Your old familiar nightmare! You poor, damned superstitious fool! I tell you again what I have always told you: There is nothing— nothing to hope for, nothing to fear—neither devils nor gods—nothing at all! (*There is a knock on the door at rear.* JOHN *immediately pretends to be writing. At the same time his features automatically assume the meaninglessly affable expression which is the American business man's welcoming poker face.* LOVING *sits motionlessly regarding him with scornful eyes.*)

495

JOHN. (*without looking up, calls*) Come in. (*The door .n rear is half opened and* WILLIAM ELIOT, JOHN LOVING's *partner, looks in. He is about forty, stout, with a prematurely bald head, a round face, a humorous, good-natured mouth, small eyes behind horn-rimmed spectacles.*)

ELIOT. Hello, John. Busy?

JOHN. Foolish question, Bill.

ELIOT. (*his eyes pass over* LOVING *without seeing him. He does not see him now or later. He sees and hears only* JOHN, *even when* LOVING *speaks. And it will be so with all the characters. They are quite unaware of* LOVING's *existence, although at times one or another may subtly sense his presence.* ELIOT *comes forward. He says jokingly*) You sound downhearted, John. Don't let our little depression get you. There's always the poorhouse. Quite cozy, too, they say. Peace for the weary—

LOVING. (*cuts in—mockingly*) There is much to be said for peace.

ELIOT. (*as if it were* JOHN *who had spoken*) Yes, John, there sure is—these damned days. (*Then giving* JOHN *a glance of concern*) Look here. I think our troubles are getting your nerve. You've seemed worn ragged lately. Why not take a few days in the country?

JOHN. Nonsense! I'm fine. (*Forcing a humorous tone*) What, besides the poorhouse, is on your mind, Bill?

ELIOT. Nothing but lunch. Ate too much again, damn it. What were you doping out when I came in? Got some new scheme for us?

JOHN. No.

LOVING. Merely trying to work out the answer to a puzzle—a human puzzle.

JOHN. (*hurriedly*) That is, I'm playing around with a plot for a novel that's come into my mind lately.

ELIOT. (*with amused surprise*) What? Good God, don't tell me the literary bug is biting you again? I thought you'd got that out of your system long ago when you got engaged to Elsa and decided to come in with me and make some money.

496

JOHN. Well, I thought I might as well do something with all this leisure. Oh, I'll probably never write it, but it's amusing to dope out.

ELIOT. Why shouldn't you write it? You certainly showed you could write in the old days—articles, anyway. (*Then with a grin*) Why, I can remember when I couldn't pick up an advanced-thinker organ without running into a red-hot article of yours denouncing Capitalism or religion or something.

JOHN. (*smiling good-naturedly*) You always did have a mean memory, Bill.

ELIOT. (*laughs*) God, John, how you've changed! What hymns of hate you used to emit against poor old Christianity! Why, I remember one article where you actually tried to prove that no such figure as Christ had ever existed.

LOVING. (*his tone suddenly cold and hostile*) I still feel the same on that subject.

ELIOT. (*gives* JOHN *a surprised glance*) Feel? Can't understand any one having feelings any more on such a dead issue as religion.

JOHN. (*confused*) Well, to tell the truth, I haven't given it a thought in years, but— (*Then hurriedly*) But, for Pete's sake, let's not get started on religion.

ELIOT. (*changes the subject tactfully*) Tell me about this novel of yours, John. What's it all about?

JOHN. Nothing to tell yet. I haven't got it finally worked out.

LOVING. The most important part, that is—the end.

JOHN. (*in a joking tone*) But when I have, Bill, I'll be only too glad to get your esteemed criticism.

ELIOT. That's a promise, remember— (*Then getting up*) Well, I suppose I better get back to my office. (*He starts for the door—then turns back*) Oh, I knew there was something I'd forgotten to tell you. Lucy Hillman called up while you were out.

JOHN. (*carelessly*) Yes? What did she want?

ELIOT. Wanted you. Got my office by mistake. She'll call up later. It was important, she said to tell you.

JOHN. Her idea of important! Probably wants my advice on what to give Walter for a birthday present.

ELIOT. What the devil's got into Walter lately, anyway? Getting drunk as a pastime may have its points, but as an exclusive occupation— Not to mention all his affairs with women. How does Lucy stand it? But I hear she's going to pieces, too.

JOHN. I don't believe it. She isn't the kind to have affairs.

ELIOT. I don't mean that. I mean booze.

JOHN. Oh. Well, if it's true, you can hardly blame her.

ELIOT. There are children, aren't there? Why hasn't she the guts to divorce him?

JOHN. Don't ask me. We haven't seen much of Lucy, either, for a long time. (*He dismisses the subject by looking down at his pad, as if he wanted to start writing.*)

ELIOT. (*taking the hint*) Well, I'll move along.

JOHN. See you later, Bill. (ELIOT *goes out, rear. After the door closes behind him* JOHN *speaks tensely*) Why did she phone? Important, she said. What can have happened?

LOVING. (*coldly*) Who knows? But you know very well she can't be trusted. You'd better be prepared for any stupid folly. And better get the end of your novel decided upon, so you can tell your plot—before it's too late.

JOHN. (*tensely*) Yes.

LOVING. (*the hidden sinister note again creeping into his coldly casual tone*) There can be only one sensible, logical end for your hero, after he has lost his wife forever—that is, provided he loves her as much as he boasts to himself he does—and if he has any honor or courage left!

JOHN. (*gives a start—then bitterly*) Ah! I see now what you're driving at! And you talk of courage and honor! (*Defiantly*) No! He must go on! He must find a faith—somewhere!

LOVING. (*an undercurrent of anger in his sneering*) Somewhere, eh? Now I wonder what hides behind that somewhere? Is it your old secret weakness—the cowardly yearning to go back—?

JOHN. (*defensively*) I don't know what you're thinking about.

LOVING. You lie! I know you! And I'll make you face it in the end of your story—face it and kill it, finally and forever! (*There is again a knock on the door and* JOHN's *eyes go to his pad. This time* ELIOT *comes in immediately, without waiting for an answer.*)

JOHN. Hello, Bill. What's up now?

ELIOT. (*comes forward, a twinkle in his eye*) John, there's a mysterious visitor outside demanding to see you.

JOHN. You mean—Lucy?

ELIOT. Lucy? No. This is a man. He ran into me before he got to Miss Sims and asked you. (*Grinning*) And as it's liable to be a bitter blow, I thought I better break the news in person.

JOHN. What's the joke? Who is it?

ELIOT. It's a priest.

JOHN. A priest?

LOVING. (*harshly*) I don't know any priests! Tell him to get out!

ELIOT. Now don't be disrespectful. He claims he's your uncle.

JOHN. My uncle? Did he give his name?

ELIOT. Yes. Father Baird. Said he'd just got in from the West.

JOHN. (*dumbfounded—forcing a smile*) Well, I'll be damned.

ELIOT. (*laughs*) My God, think of you having a priest for an uncle! That's too rich!

JOHN. I haven't seen him since I was a boy.

ELIOT. Why so scared? Afraid he's come to lecture you on your sins?

LOVING. (*angrily*) He may be a joke to you. He's not to me, damn him!

ELIOT. (*gives* JOHN *a surprised, disapproving glance*) Oh, come, John. Not as bad as that, is it? He struck me as a nice old guy.

JOHN. (*hurriedly*) He is. I didn't mean that. I always liked him. He was very kind to me when I was a kid. He acted as my guardian for a while. But I wish he'd given me warning. (*Then picking up the telephone*) Well, it's rotten to keep him cooling his heels. Hello. Send Father Baird in.

ELIOT. (*turning to the door*) I'll get out.

JOHN. No, as a favor, stay around until the ice is broken. (*He has gotten up and is going toward the door.* LOVING *remains in his chair, his eyes fixed before him in a hostile stare, his body tensed defensively.*)

ELIOT. Sure. (*A knock comes on the door.* JOHN *opens it and* FATHER MATTHEW BAIRD *enters. He is seventy, about* JOHN *and* LOVING's *height, erect, robust, with thick white hair, ruddy complexion. There is a clear resemblance to* JOHN *and* LOVING *in the general cast of his features and the color of his eyes. His appearance and personality radiate health and observant kindliness—also the confident authority of one who is accustomed to obedience and deference—and one gets immediately from him the sense of an unshakable inner calm and certainty, the peace of one whose goal in life is fixed by an end beyond life.*)

JOHN. (*constrained and at the same time affectionate*) Hello, Uncle! What in the world brings you—

FATHER BAIRD. (*clasping* JOHN's *hand in a strong grip*) Jack! (*His manner is very much what it must have been when* JOHN *was a boy and he was the guardian. Deeply moved, he puts his arm around* JOHN *and gives him an affectionate hug*) My dear Jack! This is— (*He sees* ELIOT *and stops, a bit embarrassed.*)

JOHN. (*moved and embarrassed, getting away from his arm*) I want you to meet my partner—Bill Eliot—my uncle, Father Baird.

ELIOT. It's a great pleasure, Father.

FATHER BAIRD. (*shakes his hand—a formal, old-fashioned courtesy in his manner*) The pleasure is mine, Mr. Eliot. But I feel I've had the privilege of your acquaintance already through Jack's letters.

JOHN. Sit down, Uncle. (*He indicates the chair at right of desk.* FATHER BAIRD *sits down.* JOHN *sits in his chair at left.* ELIOT *stands by the chair at right, center.*)

ELIOT. Well, I'll leave you two alone and pretend to be busy. That's the hardest job we have now, Father—keeping up the pretense of work.

FATHER BAIRD. You have plenty of company, if that's any consolation. I get the same tale of woe from every one in our part of the country.

ELIOT. I'm afraid the company doesn't console a bit. They're all too darned whiney.

FATHER BAIRD. (*a twinkle coming into his eye*) Ah, who can blame you for whining when your omnipotent Golden Calf explodes into sawdust before your adoring eyes right at the height of his deification? It's tragic, no other word—unless the word be comic.

LOVING. (*his voice a mocking sneer*) And what salvation for us are you preaching? The Second Coming?

FATHER BAIRD. (*startled, turns to stare at* JOHN. ELIOT *also looks at him, surprised and disapproving of this taunt.* FATHER BAIRD *says quietly, without any sign of taking offense*) The First Coming is enough, Jack—for those who remember it. (*Then he turns to* ELIOT— *in a joking tone*) If you knew how familiar that note sounds from him, Mr. Eliot. Here I've been feeling strange, looking at him and seeing what a big man of affairs he'd grown, and saying to myself, can this be my old Jack? And then he has to go and give himself away with a strain of his old bold whistling in the dark, and I see he's still only out of short pants a while, as I knew him last! (*He gives a comic sigh of relief*) Thank you, Jack. I feel quite at home with you now.

ELIOT. (*immensely amused, especially at the expression of boyish discomfiture on* JOHN's *face—laughingly*) John, I begin to feel sorry for you. You've picked on someone out of your class.

FATHER BAIRD. (*with a wink at* ELIOT) Did you hear him throw the word preaching in my face, Mr. Eliot—with a dirty sneer in his voice? There's injustice for you. If you knew what a burden he made my life for years with his preaching. Letter upon letter—each with a soap box inclosed, so to speak. The plague began right after I'd had to go West and leave him to his own devices. He was about to pass out of my guardianship and go to college with the bit of money his parents had left for him when he reached eighteen. So I had to let him go his own way. I'd learned it was no use fighting him, anyway. I'd done that and found it was a great satisfaction to him and only made him worse. And I had faith, if let alone, he'd come back to his senses in the end.

LOVING. (*sneeringly*) And how mistaken you were in that faith!

FATHER BAIRD. (*without turning—quietly*) No. The end isn't yet, Jack. (*He goes on to* ELIOT *with a renewal of his humorously complaining tone*) You wouldn't believe what a devil's advocate he was in those days, Mr. Eliot.

ELIOT. You needn't tell me, Father. I was his classmate. He organized an Atheists' Club—or tried to—and almost got fired for it.

FATHER BAIRD. Yes, I remember his writing to boast about that. Well, you can appreciate then what I went through, even if he didn't write you letters.

ELIOT. But he delivered harangues, Father, when he could get anybody to listen!

FATHER BAIRD. (*pityingly*) Ah, that must have been cruel, too! Mr. Eliot, I feel drawn to you. We've been through the same frightful trials.

JOHN. (*with a boyishly discomfited air*) I hope you're having a good time, you two.

FATHER BAIRD. (*ignoring him*) Not a moment's peace did he give me. I was the heathen to him and he was bound he'd convert me to something. First it was Atheism unadorned. Then it was Atheism wedded to Socialism. But Socialism proved too weak-kneed a mate, and the next I heard Atheism was living in free love with Anarchism, with a curse by Nietzsche to bless the union. And then came the Bolshevik dawn, and he greeted that with unholy howls of glee and wrote me he'd found a congenial home at last in the bosom of Karl Marx. He was particularly delighted when he thought they'd abolished love and marriage, and he couldn't contain himself when the news came they'd turned naughty schoolboys and were throwing spitballs at Almighty God and had supplanted Him with the slave-owning State —the most grotesque god that ever came out of Asia!

ELIOT. (*chuckling*) I recognize all this, Father. I used to read his articles, as I was reminding him just before you came.

FATHER BAIRD. Don't I know them! Didn't he send me every one with blue pencil underlinings! But to get back to my story: Thinks I at this juncture, well, he's run away as far as he can get in that direction. Where will he hide himself next?

LOVING. (*stiffening in his chair—with angry resentment*) Run away? You talk as if I were afraid of something. Hide? Hide from what?

FATHER BAIRD. (*without turning—quietly*) Don't you know, Jack? Well, if you don't yet, you will some day. (*Again to* ELIOT) I knew Communism wouldn't hold him long—and it didn't. Soon his letters became full of pessimism, and disgust with all sociological nostrums. Then followed a long silence. And what do you think was his next hiding place? Religion, no less—but as far away as he could run from home—in the defeatist mysticism of the East. First it was China and Lao Tze that fascinated him, but afterwards he ran on to Buddha, and his letters for a time extolled passionless contemplation so passionately that I had a mental view of him regarding his navel frenziedly by the hour and making nothing of it! (ELIOT *laughs and* JOHN *chuckles sheepishly in spite of himself.* LOVING *stares before him with a cold, angry disdain.*)

ELIOT. Gosh, I'm sorry I missed that! When was all this, Father?

FATHER BAIRD. In what I'd call his middle hide-and-go-seek period. But the next I knew, he was through with the East. It was not for the Western soul, he decided, and he was running through Greek philosophy and found a brief shelter in Pythagoras and numerology. Then came a letter which revealed him bogged down in evolutionary scientific truth again—a dyed-in-the-wool mechanist. That was the last I heard of his peregrinations—and, thank heaven, it was long ago. I enjoyed a long interval of peace from his missionary zeal, until finally he wrote me he was married. That letter was full of more ardent hymns of praise for a mere living woman than he'd ever written before about any of his great spiritual discoveries. And ever since then I've heard nothing but the praises of Elsa—in which I know I'll be ready to join after I've met her.

JOHN. (*his face lighting up*) You bet you will! We can agree on that, at least.

FATHER BAIRD. (*with a wink at* ELIOT) He seems to be fixed in his last religion. I hope so. The only constant faith I've found in him before was his proud belief in himself as a bold Antichrist. (*He gives* JOHN *a side glance, half smiling and half reproachful*) Ah well, it's a rocky road, full of twists and blind alleys, isn't it, Jack—this running away from truth in order to find it? I mean, until the road finally turns back toward home.

LOVING. (*with harsh defiance*) You believe I—? (*Then sneeringly*) But, of course, you would read that into it.

JOHN. (*bursts out irritably, as if he couldn't control his nerves*) But don't you think I'm about exhausted as a subject, Uncle? I do. (*He gets up nervously and moves around and stands behind* LOVING's *chair, his hands on the back of the chair, his face directly above* LOVING's *masked one.*)

ELIOT. (*gives the priest an amused smile*) Well, I'll get back to my office. (FATHER BAIRD *gets up and he shakes his hand heartily*) I hope we'll meet again, Father. Are you here for long?

FATHER BAIRD. Only a few days, I'm afraid.

JOHN. (*coming around to them*) I'll fix up something with Elsa for the four of us, Bill—as soon as she's feeling stronger. We won't let him run away in a few days, now we've got him here.

ELIOT. Fine! See you again, then, Father. (*He goes toward the door.*)

FATHER BAIRD. I hope so, Mr. Eliot. Good day to you.

ELIOT. (*with the door open, turns back with a grin*) I feel it my duty, Father, to warn you that John's got writer's itch again. He's

going to give us a novel. (*He laughs and closes the door behind him.*
JOHN *frowns and gives his uncle a quick uneasy glance.*)

JOHN. (*indicating the chair at right, center*) Take that chair, Uncle.
It's more comfortable. (*He sits down in the chair at right of table
where* FATHER BAIRD *had sat, while the priest sits in the one at right,
center.* FATHER BAIRD *gives him a puzzled, concerned look, as if he
were trying to figure something out. Then he speaks casually.*)

FATHER BAIRD. A novel? Is that right, Jack?

JOHN. (*without looking at him*) Thinking of it—to pass the time.

FATHER BAIRD. Then, judging from your letters, it ought to be a love
story.

JOHN. It is—a love story.

LOVING. (*mockingly*) About God's love for us!

FATHER BAIRD. (*quietly rebuking*) Jack! (*A pause of silence.* FATHER
BAIRD *gives* JOHN *a quick glance again—then casually*) If you've any
appointments, don't stand on ceremony; just shoo me out.

JOHN. (*turns to him shamefacedly*) Don't talk that way, Uncle. You
know I wouldn't—(*With a natural, boyishly affectionate smile*) You
know darned well how tickled I am to have you here.

FATHER BAIRD. I hope you're half as glad as I am to see you, Jack. (*He
sighs*) It has been a long time—too long.

JOHN. Yes. (*Smiling*) But I'm still flabbergasted. I never dreamed
you— Why didn't you wire me you were coming?

FATHER BAIRD. Oh, I thought I'd surprise you. (*He smiles*) To tell
you the truth, I confess I had a sneaking Sherlock Holmes desire to
have a good look at you before you were expecting it.

JOHN. (*frowning—uneasily*) Why? Why should you?

FATHER BAIRD. Well, I suppose because, not having seen you, I'm
afraid that to me you were still the boy I'd known, and I was still
your suspicious guardian.

JOHN. (*relieved—with a boyish grin*) Oh! I see.

FATHER BAIRD. And now I have seen you, I still must admit that the gray in your hair is lost on me, and I can't get it out of my head you're the same old Jack.

JOHN. (*grinning with a boyish discomfiture*) Yes, and the devil of it is you make me feel that way, too. It's an unfair advantage, Uncle. (FATHER BAIRD *laughs and* JOHN *joins in.*)

FATHER BAIRD. Well, I never took unfair advantage of you in the old days, did I?

JOHN. You certainly didn't. When I look back, I'm amazed you could have been so fair. (*Quickly—changing the subject*) But you haven't told me yet how you happened to come East.

FATHER BAIRD. (*a bit evasively*) Oh, I decided a vacation was due me. And I've had a great longing for some time to see you again.

JOHN. I only wish I could have you stay with us, but there's no room. But you must have dinner with us to-night, and every night you're here, of course.

FATHER BAIRD. Yes, I'd like to see all of you I can. But there's this, Jack. You spoke to Mr. Eliot as if Elsa were ill.

JOHN. Oh, it's nothing serious. She's just getting over the flu, and still feels a bit low.

FATHER BAIRD. Then I'd better not come to-night.

JOHN. You better had or she'll never forgive you—or me!

FATHER BAIRD. Very well. I'm only too happy. (*A pause. He glances at* JOHN *again with a curious puzzled fixity.* JOHN *catches his eyes, is held by them for a moment, then looks away almost furtively.*)

JOHN. (*forcing a smile*) Is that the suspicious guardian look? I've forgotten.

FATHER BAIRD. (*as if to himself—slowly*) I feel— (*Then suddenly*) There's something I want to tell you, Jack. (*A stern note comes into his voice*) But first give me your word of honor there will be no cheap sneering.

JOHN. (*stares at him, taken aback—then quietly*) There won't be.

FATHER BAIRD. Well, it's often come to me in the past that I shouldn't have let you get so far from me, that I might be in part responsible for your continued estrangement from your Faith.

LOVING. (*with mocking scorn*) My faith?

JOHN. You know that's nonsense, Uncle.

LOVING. You have always nobly done your duty. You've never let a letter pass without some pious reminder of my fall—with the calm assurance that I would again see the light. That never failed to make me laugh—your complacent assumption that like the Prodigal of His fairy tale, I—

FATHER BAIRD. (*sharply*) Jack! You promised!

JOHN. (*confusedly*) I know. I didn't mean— Go on with what you started to tell me.

FATHER BAIRD. First answer me frankly one question. Have you been greatly troubled in spirit by anything lately?

JOHN. (*startled*) I? Why do you ask that? Of course not. (*Then evasively*) Oh, well—yes, maybe, if you mean business worries.

FATHER BAIRD. Nothing else?

JOHN. No. What could there be?

FATHER BAIRD. (*unconvinced—looking away*) The reason I asked— You'll see in what I'm going to tell you. It happened one night while I was praying for you in my church, as I have every day since I left you. A strange feeling of fear took possession of me—a feeling you were unhappy, in some great spiritual danger. I told myself it was foolish. I'd had a letter from you only that day, reiterating how happy you were. I tried to lose my dread in prayer—and my guilt. Yes, I felt stricken with guilt, too—that I was to blame for whatever was happening to you. Then, as I prayed, suddenly as if by some will outside me, my eyes were drawn to the Cross, to the face of Our Blessed Lord. And it was like a miracle! His face seemed alive as a living man's would be, but radiant with eternal life, too, especially the sad, pitying eyes. But there was a sternness in His eyes, too, an accusation against me—a command about you! (*He breaks off and gives* JOHN *a quick glance, as if afraid of finding him sneering. Then, looking away, he*

507

adds simply) That's the real reason I decided to take my vacation in the East, Jack.

JOHN. (*stares at him fascinatedly*) You saw—?

LOVING. (*in a bitter, sneering tone*) It could hardly have been any concern for me you saw in His face—even if He did exist or ever had existed!

FATHER BAIRD. (*sternly*) Jack! (*Then, after a pause, quietly*) Do you know Francis Thompson's poem—The Hound of Heaven?

LOVING. I did once. Why?

FATHER BAIRD. (*quotes in a low voice but with deep feeling*)
>   "*Ah, fondest, blindest, weakest,*
>   *I am He Whom thou seekest!*
>   *Thou dravest love from thee, who dravest Me.*"

LOVING. (*in what is close to a snarl of scorn*) Love!

JOHN. (*defensively*) I have love!

FATHER BAIRD. (*as if he hadn't heard*) Why do you run and hide from Him, as from an enemy? Take care. There comes a time in every man's life when he must have his God for friend, or he has no friend at all, not even himself. Who knows? Perhaps you are on the threshold of that time now.

JOHN. (*uneasily*) What do you mean?

FATHER BAIRD. I don't know. It's for you to know that. You say you have love?

JOHN. You know I have. Or, if you don't, you soon will after you've met Elsa.

FATHER BAIRD. I'm not doubting your love for her nor hers for you. It's exactly because I do not doubt. I am thinking that such love needs the hope and promise of eternity to fulfill itself—above all, to feel itself secure. Beyond the love for each other should be the love of God, in Whose Love yours may find the triumph over death.

LOVING. (*sneeringly*) Old superstition, born of fear! Beyond death there is nothing. That, at least, is certain—a certainty we should be thankful for. One life is boring enough. Do not condemn us to another. Let us rest in 'peace at last!

FATHER BAIRD. (*quietly*) Would you talk that way if Elsa should die?

JOHN. (*with a shudder*) For God's sake, don't speak about—

LOVING. Do you think I haven't imagined her death many times?

JOHN. The dread of it has haunted me ever since we were married.

FATHER BAIRD. Ah.

LOVING. You'll see that I face it—by proxy, at least—in my novel. (*A sneering taunt in his voice*) I think you'll be interested in this novel, Uncle.

FATHER BAIRD. (*staring at* JOHN, *whose face is averted*) It's autobiographical, then?

JOHN. (*hastily*) No. Of course not. I only meant— Don't get that idea in your head, for Pete's sake. As I explained to Elsa, when I told her about the first part, it's really the story of a man I once knew.

LOVING. The first part will particularly interest you, Uncle. I am afraid you will be terribly shocked—especially in the light of your recent mystic vision!

FATHER BAIRD. I'm very curious to hear it, Jack. When will you tell me?

LOVING. (*defiantly*) Now!

JOHN. (*uneasily*) But no. I don't want to bore you.

FATHER BAIRD. You won't bore me.

JOHN. No— I—

LOVING. (*with harsh insistence*) The first part concerns my hero's boyhood here in New York, up to the age of fifteen.

JOHN. (*under* LOVING'S *compulsion, he picks up the thread of the story*) He was an only child. His father was a fine man. The boy adored him. And he adored his mother even more. She was a wonderful woman, a perfect type of our old beautiful ideal of wife and mother.

LOVING. (*sneeringly*) But there was one ridiculous weakness in her character, an absurd obsession with religion. In the father's, too.

509

They were both devout Catholics. (*The priest gives a swift, reproach-ful look at* JOHN, *seems about to protest, thinks better of it, and drops his eyes.*)

JOHN. (*quickly*) But not the ignorant, bigoted sort, please understand. No, their piety had a genuine, gentle, mystic quality to it. Their faith was the great comforting inspiration of their lives. And their God was One of Infinite Love—not a stern, self-righteous Being Who condemned sinners to torment, but a very human, lovable God Who became man for love of men and gave His life that they might be saved from themselves. And the boy had every reason to believe in such a Divinity of Love as the Creator of Life. His home atmosphere was one of love. Life *was* love for him then. And he was happy, happier than he ever afterward— (*He checks himself abruptly.*)

FATHER BAIRD. (*nods his head approvingly*) Yes.

JOHN. Later, at school, he learned of the God of Punishment, and he wondered. He couldn't reconcile Him with his parents' faith. So it didn't make much impression on him.

LOVING. (*bitterly*) Then! But afterward he had good reason to—

JOHN. But then he was too sure in his faith. He grew up as devout as his parents. He even dreamed of becoming a priest. He used to love to kneel in the church before the Cross.

LOVING. Oh, he was a remarkably superstitious young fool! (*his voice suddenly changes to hard bitterness*) And then when he was fifteen, all these pious illusions of his were destroyed forever! Both his parents were killed!

JOHN. (*hurriedly*) That is, they died during a flu epidemic in which they contracted pneumonia—and he was left alone—without love. First, his father died. The boy had prayed with perfect faith that his father's life might be spared.

LOVING. But his father died! And the poor simpleton's naïve faith was a bit shaken, and a sinful doubt concerning the Divine Love assailed him!

JOHN. Then his mother, worn out by nursing his father and by her grief, was taken ill. And the horrible fear came to him that she might die, too.

LOVING. It drove the young idiot into a panic of superstitious remorse. He imagined her sickness was a terrible warning to him, a punishment for the doubt inspired in him by his father's death. (*With harsh bitterness*) His God of Love was beginning to show Himself as a God of Vengeance, you see!

JOHN. But he still trusted in His Love. Surely He would not take his mother from him, too.

LOVING. So the poor fool prayed and prayed and vowed his life to piety and good works! But he began to make a condition now—*if his* mother were spared to him!

JOHN. Finally he knew in his heart she was going to die. But even then he hoped and prayed for a miracle.

LOVING. He abased and humbled himself before the Cross—and, in reward for his sickening humiliation, saw that no miracle would happen.

JOHN. Something snapped in him then.

LOVING. (*his voice suddenly takes on a tone of bitter hatred*) He saw his God as deaf and blind and merciless—a Deity Who returned hate for love and revenged Himself upon those who trusted Him!

JOHN. His mother died. And, in a frenzy of insane grief—

LOVING. No! In his awakened pride he cursed his God and denied Him, and, in revenge, promised his soul to the Devil—on his knees, when every one thought he was praying! (*He laughs with malignant bitterness.*)

JOHN. (*quickly—in a casual tone*) And that's the end of Part One, as I've outlined it.

FATHER BAIRD. (*horrified*) Jack! I can't believe that you—

JOHN. (*defensively*) I? What have I to do with it? You're forgetting I explained to you— Oh, I admit there are certain points of resemblance between some of his boyhood experiences and mine—his parents' death, for example. But that's only coincidence.

FATHER BAIRD. (*recovered now—staring at him—quietly*) I see.

JOHN. (*forcing a smile*) And please don't bring up those coincidences before Elsa, Uncle. She didn't notice them because I've never bored her with boyhood reminiscences. And I don't want her to get the wrong angle on my plot.

FATHER BAIRD. I'll remember, Jack. When will you tell me the rest of it?

JOHN. Oh, some time while you're here, maybe.

FATHER BAIRD. Why not to-night at your home?

JOHN. Well, I might—

LOVING. That is, if I can decide on my end before then!

JOHN. It would give me a chance to get your and Elsa's criticisms at the same time. She's been wanting to hear the rest of it, too.

FATHER BAIRD. (*regarding him—quietly*) Then, by all means. (*Abruptly changing to a brisk casualness*) Well, I'll leave you and attend to some errands I have to do. (*He gets to his feet. He takes* JOHN's *hand.*)

JOHN. Dinner is at seven-thirty. But come as long before that as you like. I'll be home early. (*Then with a genuine boyish affection*) I want to tell you again, Uncle, how grand it is to have you here— in spite of our arguments.

FATHER BAIRD. I'm not worried by our arguments. But I am about something about you that admits of no argument—to me.

JOHN. (*forcing a smile*) You're wasting worry. But what is it?

FATHER BAIRD. You've written me you were happy, and I believed you. But, now I see you, I don't believe you. You're not happy. Why? Perhaps if you had it out with me—

LOVING. (*mockingly*) Confess, eh?

JOHN. Don't be foolish, Uncle. I am happy, happier than I ever dreamed I could be. And, for heaven's sake, don't go telling Elsa I'm unhappy.

FATHER BAIRD. (*quietly*) Very well. We'll say no more about it. And now I'll be off. Good-bye until this evening, Jack.

JOHN. So long, Uncle. (FATHER BAIRD *goes out.* JOHN *stands by the door, looking after him—then he comes slowly back and sits down in his chair and stares before him.* LOVING's *eyes are fastened on him with a cold contempt.*)

LOVING. Damned old fool with his bedtime tales for second childhood about the love of God! And you—you're worse—with your hypocritical lies about your great happiness!

(*The telephone on the table rings.* JOHN *jumps nervously—then answers it in an apprehensive voice.*)

JOHN. Hello. Who? Tell her I'm out.

LOVING. You'd better find out what she wants.

JOHN. No, wait. I'll take it. (*Then, his voice becoming guarded and pleasantly casual*) Hello, Lucy. Bill told me you'd called. What—? (*He listens—then anxiety creeping into his tone*) She phoned again? What about? Oh. I'm glad you called me. Yes, she has been wondering why she hasn't heard from you in so long. Yes, by all means, go. Yes, she's sure to be in this afternoon. Good-bye. (*He hangs up mechanically.*)

LOVING. (*sneeringly*) Your terrible sin begins to close in on you, eh? But then, it wasn't you, was it? It was some evil spirit that possessed you! (*He gives a mocking laugh—then stops abruptly and continues in his tone of cold, sinister insistence*) But enough of that nonsense. Let's return to your plot. The wife dies—of influenza that turns into pneumonia, let's say.

JOHN. (*starts violently—stammers*) What—God damn you—what makes you choose that?

CURTAIN

ACT TWO

PLOT FOR A NOVEL

(Continued)

S CENE—*The living room of the* LOVINGS' *duplex apartment. Venetian blinds soften the light from a big window at right. In front of this window is a table with a lamp. At left, front, an upholstered chair. At right of chair, a small table with a lamp. At right of table, in the center of the room, a sofa. In front of sofa, a low stand with cigarette box and ash trays. Toward right, another chair. In the left wall is a door leading to the dining-room. At rear of door, a writing desk. In the middle of the rear wall is a doorway leading to the hall.*

It is later the same afternoon.

ELSA *enters from the hall at rear. She is thirty-five but looks much younger. She is beautiful with that Indian Summer renewal of physical charm which comes to a woman who loves and is loved, particularly to one who has not found that love until comparatively late in life. This beauty is a trifle dimmed now by traces of recent illness. Her face is drawn and she fights against a depressing lassitude. She wears a simple negligée.*

As she comes in, she presses a button by the door and a buzzer is heard in the pantry. She comes forward and sits on the sofa. A moment later MARGARET, *the maid, appears from the dining-room at left. She is a middle-aged Irishwoman with a kindly face.*

MARGARET. Yes, Madame?

ELSA. Hasn't the afternoon paper come yet, Margaret?

MARGARET. No, Madame, not yet. (*Then with kindly reproof*) Didn't you take a nap like you promised you would?

ELSA. I couldn't get to sleep. But I do feel rested, so don't begin to scold me. (*She smiles and* MARGARET *smiles back, a look of devoted affection lighting up her face.*)

MARGARET. You have to take care. The flu's a bad thing the way it leaves you weak after. And you're only out of your bed two days.

ELSA. Oh, I'm really quite well again. And I was too excited to sleep. I kept thinking of Mr. Loving's uncle. (*The telephone in the hall rings and* MARGARET *goes toward the door in rear to answer it.*) Heavens, I hope that isn't he now. Mr. Loving phoned me he told him to come early. But surely he wouldn't this early!

MARGARET. (*disappears in the hall. Her voices comes*) Just a moment and I'll see if she's in. (*She appears again in the doorway*) It's Mrs. Hillman calling to see you, Madame.

ELSA. Oh, I'm glad. Tell her to come right up. (MARGARET *disappears and is heard relaying this instruction. Then she appears in the hall outside the doorway, waiting to answer the door.* ELSA *speaks to her*) I wish I didn't look so like a sick cat. Why is it every one decides to turn up when you look your worst?

MARGARET. Ah, you needn't worry, Madame. You look fine.

ELSA. Well, anyway, I don't mind Lucy. (*Nevertheless, she goes to the desk at left, rear, takes out a vanity case, powders her nose, etc. While she is doing this,* MARGARET *moves to the entrance door in the hall and is heard admitting* MRS. HILLMAN *and exchanging greetings with her, as she helps her off with her things.* ELSA *calls*) Hello, Stranger.

LUCY. (*calls back in a voice whose breeziness rings a bit strained*) That's right, sit on me the minute I set foot in your house! Well, I know I deserve it. (ELSA *goes to the doorway and meets her as she comes in, kissing her affectionately.* LUCY HILLMAN *is about the same age as* ELSA. *She is still an extremely attractive woman but, in contrast to* ELSA, *her age shows, in spite of a heavy make-up. There are wrinkles about her eyes, and her small, full, rather weak mouth is drawn down by sharp lines at the corners. She is dressed expensively in clothes a bit*

515

too youthful and extreme in style. She responds to ELSA's *greeting with a nervous constraint*) Hello, Elsa.

ELSA. You're a nice one! How long has it been—months!—not since before I went to Boston in February. (*She sits on the sofa and draws* LUCY *down beside her.*)

LUCY. I know. I'm in the dust at your feet.

ELSA. I've phoned you a dozen times, but you were always out. Or did you just tell them to say that? I've completely lost faith in you.

LUCY. But I was out, Elsa. How can you think—

ELSA. (*laughing—gives her a hug*) You're not taking me seriously, are you? I know you'd hardly do that with me, after all these years.

LUCY. Of course, I wouldn't.

ELSA. But I did wonder a little at your sudden complete ignoring of our existence. So did John.

LUCY. (*hurriedly*) If you knew all the stupid engagements that pile up—and all the idiotic parties Walter lets me in for. (*Then changing the subject abruptly*) May I have a cigarette? (*She takes one from the box on the stand and lights it*) Aren't you having one?

ELSA. Not now. (*She gives* LUCY *a puzzled glance.* LUCY *avoids her eyes, nervously flipping her cigarette over the ash tray.* ELSA *asks*) How are the kids?

LUCY. Oh, fine, thanks. At least, I think so, from the little I get to see of them nowadays. (*Bitterness has crept into this last. She again hurriedly changes the subject*) But tell me all your news. What have you been doing with yourself?

ELSA. Oh, the same peaceful routine—going to a concert now and then, reading a lot, keeping house, taking care of John.

LUCY. The old perfect marriage that's been the wonder of us all, eh? (*Again changing the subject*) What time does John usually get home? I don't want to run into him.

ELSA. Oh, not for an hour or so yet. (*Smiling*) But why? What have you got against John?

LUCY. (*smiling with a strange wryness*) Nothing—except myself.

(*Then hurriedly*) I mean, look at me, I look like hell. I've had the damndest insomnia lately. And I'm vain enough not to crave any male viewing the wreckage until I've spruced up on a bath and cocktails.

ELSA. But that's silly. You look wonderful.

LUCY. (*dryly*) Thanks, liar! (*With a side glance of frank envy— unable to keep resentment out of her voice*) I especially don't care to be up for inspection beside you. The contrast is too glaring.

ELSA. But it's I who look like the devil, not you. I'm just getting over flu.

LUCY. Flu makes no never mind. It doesn't affect—what I mean. (*Then with a hard flippant air*) Pardon me if I seem to indulge in the melancholy jitters. I'm becoming the damndest whiner and self-pitier. It's really too boring. (*She lights another cigarette. Her hands have a nervous tremor.* ELSA *watches her with a worried, affectionately pitying look.*)

ELSA. What is it, Lucy? Tell me.

LUCY. (*stiffening defensively*) What is what?

ELSA. I want to know what's troubling you. Now, there's no use denying it. I've known you too long. I felt it the moment you came in, that you were upset about something and trying to hide it.

LUCY. I don't know where you got that idea. (*Defensively flippant*) Oh, really now, Elsa. Don't you go psychic on us!

ELSA. All right, then. Forgive me trying to pump you. But you got me into the bad habit yourself, you know, by always coming to me with your troubles. I only thought I might be able to help.

LUCY. You! (*She gives a hard little laugh.*)

ELSA. (*hurt*) You used to think I could.

LUCY. "Once, long ago—" (*Then, suddenly with repentant shame-facedness*) Forgive me, Elsa. I'm rotten to be flip about that. You've been the most wonderful friend. And I'm such an ungrateful little slut!

ELSA. Lucy! You mustn't say that.

LUCY. (*hurries on with a simulation of frankness*) But honestly, you're mistaken this time. There's nothing wrong, except what seems to be wrong with every one, the stupid lives we lead—and, of course, the usual financial worries. So please don't bother your head about my troubles.

ELSA. All right, dear. (*Then, after a slight pause—casually*) How is Walter these days?

LUCY. (*with a twisted smile*) I thought we weren't going to talk about my troubles! Oh, Walter is—Walter. You know him, Elsa. Why ask? But do you know any one, I wonder? Darned if I think you ever see what people really are. You somehow manage to live in some lost world where human beings are still decent and honorable. I don't see how you do it. If you'd always been a little innocent, protected from all ugly contacts— But, my God, your first marriage must have slapped your face with about every filthy thing a man can be—and that's plenty! Yet you sit here, calm and beautiful and unscarred—!

ELSA. (*quietly*) I have my share of scars. But the wounds are all healed—completely healed. John's love has done that for me.

LUCY. Yes—of course. (*Then, as if she couldn't control herself, she bursts out*) Oh, you and your John! You bring him up as the answer to everything.

ELSA. (*smiling*) Well, he is for me.

LUCY. Do you mean to tell me you're as much in love with him now as when you married him?

ELSA. Oh, much more so, for he's become my child and father now, as well as being a husband and—

LUCY. Lover. Say it. How incredibly Mid-Victorian you can be! Don't you know that's all we married ladies discuss nowadays? But you're lucky. Usually the men discussed aren't our husbands, and aren't even good lovers. But never say die. We keep on hoping and experimenting!

ELSA. (*repelled*) Don't talk in that disgusting way. I know you don't mean a word of it.

LUCY. (*stares at her resentfully for a second, then turns away, reaching for another cigarette—dryly*) Oh, you're quite sure of that, are you?

ELSA. (*gently*) Lucy, what is it has made you so bitter? I've noticed it growing on you for the past few years, but now it's completely got you. I—honestly, I hardly know you this time, you've changed so.

LUCY. (*hurriedly*) Oh, it's nothing that happened lately. You mustn't get that idea. (*Then letting herself go—with increasing bitterness*) It's simply that I've grown sick of my life, sick of all the lying and faking of it, sick of marriage and motherhood, sick of myself! Particularly sick of myself because I endure the humiliation of Walter's open affairs with every damned floosie he meets! And I'm tired of pretending I don't mind, tired of really minding underneath, tired of pretending to myself I have to go on for the children's sakes, and that they make up to me for everything, which they don't at all!

ELSA. (*indignantly*) How can Walter be such a beast!

LUCY. (*with a look at* ELSA *that is almost vindictive*) Oh, he's no worse than a lot of others. At least, he doesn't lie about it.

ELSA. But, for heaven's sake, why do you stand it? Why don't you leave him?

LUCY. Oh, don't be so superior and scornful, Elsa. I'll bet you wouldn't— (*She checks herself abruptly.*)

ELSA. What do you mean? You know very well I left my first husband the minute I found out—

LUCY. (*hurriedly*) I know. I didn't— Why don't I leave Walter? I guess because I'm too worn out to have the guts. And then I did try it once. The first time I knew he'd been unfaithful I did the correct thing and went home. I intended to tell Father I was through as Walter's wife. Only Father was away. Mother was there, and I broke down and told her. She took it quite philosophically—said I was a fool to expect too much, men were like that, even my father had— (*She gives a little shiver of aversion*) That sort of squelched me. So I went back to Walter and he doesn't know to this day I ever left him.

ELSA. I'm so sorry, Lucy.

LUCY. (*returning to her air of hard cynicism*) No pity, please. After all, the situation has its compensations. He has tried nobly to be fair. He said I could have equal liberty to indulge any of my sexual whims.

ELSA. What a stupid fool!

LUCY. (*bitterly*) Oh, he didn't really mean it, you know. His vanity couldn't admit I'd ever feel the slightest desire outside of him. It was only a silly gesture he felt safe in making because he was so damned sure of me—because he knows, damn him, that in spite of all he's done to kill it there's still a cowardly slavish something in me, dating back to the happiness of our first married days, which still—loves him! (*She starts to break down, but fights this back and bursts out vindictively, a look of ugly satisfaction coming into her face*) But I warned him he'd humiliate me once too often—and he did!

ELSA. (*shocked*) You mean you—

LUCY. (*with a return of her flippant tone*) Yes, I went in for a little fleeting adultery. And I must say, as a love substitute or even a pleasurable diversion, it's greatly overrated. (*She gives a hard little laugh*) How horribly shocked you look! Are you going to order me from your virtuous home?

ELSA. Lucy! Don't talk like that! It's only that I can't believe—none of this is really you. That's what makes it so— But please don't think I'm condemning you. You know how I love you, don't you?

LUCY. (*stares at her with a strange panic*) Don't, for God's sake! I don't want you to love me! I'd rather you hated me! (*But ELSA pulls her to her and she breaks down finally, sobbing, her face buried against ELSA's shoulder.*)

ELSA. There, there. You mustn't, dear. (*Then as LUCY grows calmer —quietly*) Don't think I don't understand, because I do. I felt exactly the same when I found out about Ned Howell. Even though I'd stopped caring for him and our marriage had always been unhappy,

my pride was so hurt I wanted to revenge myself and take the first
man I met for a lover.

LUCY. (*looks up in amazement*) You went through that? I never
dreamed—

ELSA. All that saved me from doing something stupid was the faith
I had that somewhere the man was waiting whom I could really
love. I felt I owed it to him and to my own self-respect not to deliberately disfigure myself out of wounded pride and spite.

LUCY. (*with sad bitterness*) You hit it when you say disfigure. That's
how I've felt ever since. Cheap! Ugly! As if *I'd* deliberately disfigured
myself. And not only myself—the man—and others I wouldn't hurt
for anything in the world—if I was in my right mind. But I wasn't!
You realize I wasn't, don't you, Elsa? You must! You above every
one!

ELSA. I do, dear. Of course I do.

LUCY. I've got to tell you just how it came to happen—so you'll see.
It was one of Walter's parties. You know the would-be Bohemian
gang he likes to have. They were there in all their vulgarity, their
poisonous, envious tongues wise-cracking at everything with any
decent human dignity and worth. Oh, there were a few others there,
too—our own people—this man was one of them. Walter was drunk,
pawing over his latest female, and she got him to go home with her.
Everybody watched to see how I'd take it. I wanted to kill him and
her, but I only laughed and had some more to drink. But I was in
hell, I can tell you, and inside I kept swearing to myself that I'd show
Walter— And I picked out this man—yes, deliberately! It was all deliberate and crazy! And I had to do all the seducing—because he's quite
happy. I knew that, but I was crazy. His happiness filled me with
rage—the thought that he made others happy. I wanted to take his
happiness from him and kill it as mine had been killed!

ELSA. Lucy!

LUCY. (*with a hard laugh*) I told you I was in hell, didn't I? You
can't live there without becoming like the rest of the crowd! (*Hurry-*

ing on with her story) I got him in my bedroom on some excuse. But he pushed me away, as if he were disgusted with himself and me. But I wouldn't let him go. And then came the strange part of it. Suddenly, I don't know how to explain it, you'll think I'm crazy, or being funny, but it was as if he were no longer there. It was another man, a stranger whose eyes were hateful and frightening. He seemed to look through me at some one else, and I seemed for a moment to be watching some hidden place in his mind where there was something as evil and revengeful as I was. It frightened and fascinated me—and called to me too; that's the hell of it! (*She forces a laugh*) I suppose all this sounds too preposterous. Well, maybe it was the booze working. I'd had a lot. (*She reaches for a cigarette—returning to her hard flippancy*) And then followed my little dip into adultery.

ELSA. (*with a little shiver of repulsion*) Oh!

LUCY. But what a hideous bore this must be to you. Why did I have to tell you, I wonder? It was the last thing I ever wanted— (*Turns on her in a flash of resentful vindictiveness*) It makes me out worse than you expected, eh? But suppose John were unfaithful to you—

ELSA. (*startled—frightenedly*) Don't! (*Then indignantly*) Lucy! I won't have you say that, not even—

LUCY. I'm only asking you to suppose.

ELSA. I can't! I won't! And I won't let you! It's too—! (*Then controlling herself—forcing a smile*) But I'm a bigger fool than you are to get angry. You simply don't know John, that's all. You don't know what an old-fashioned romantic idealist he is at heart about love and marriage. And I thank God he is! You'll laugh at me but I know he never had a single affair in his life before he met me.

LUCY. Oh, come on, Elsa. That's too much!

ELSA. Oh, please don't think I'm a naïve fool. I was as cynical about men in those days as you are now. I wouldn't have believed it of another man in the world, but with John I felt it was absolutely true to what I knew he was like inside him.

LUCY. You loved him and you wanted to believe.

ELSA. No. Even before I loved him, I felt that. It was what made me love him, more than anything else—the feeling that he would be mine, only mine, that I wouldn't have to share him even with the past. If you only could realize how much that meant to me—especially at that time, when I was still full of the disgust and hurt of my first marriage.

LUCY. Well, that's all very fine, but it's not proving to me how you can be so certain that never since then—

ELSA. (*proudly*) I know he loves me. I know he knows how much I love him. He knows what that would do to me. It would kill forever all my faith in life—all truth, all beauty, all love! I wouldn't want to live!

LUCY. You shouldn't let yourself be so completely at the mercy of any man—not even John.

ELSA. I'm not afraid. (*She smiles*) The trouble with you is, you old cynic, you can't admit that our marriage is a real ideal marriage. But it is—and that's entirely John's work, not mine.

LUCY. His work?

ELSA. Yes. When I first met him I thought I was through with marriage for good. Even after I fell in love with him, I didn't want to marry. I was afraid of marriage. I proposed quite frankly that we should simply live together and each keep entire freedom of action. (*She laughs*) Oh, I was quite ultra-modern about it! And it shocked John terribly, poor dear—in spite of all his old radical ideas. I'm sure it almost disillusioned him with me for life! He sternly scorned my offer. He argued with me. How he argued—like a missionary converting a heathen! He said he loathed the ordinary marriage as much as I did, but that the ideal in back of marriage was a beautiful one, and he knew we could realize that ideal.

LUCY. Ah, yes, the ideal! I heard a little talk about that once, too!

ELSA. He said no matter if every other marriage on earth were rotten and a lie, our love could make ours into a true sacrament—sacrament was the word he used—a sacrament of faith in which each of

523

us would find the completest self-expression in making our union a beautiful thing. (*She smiles lovingly*) You see, all this was what I had longed to hear the man I loved say about the spiritual depth of his love for me—what every woman dreams of hearing her lover say, I think.

LUCY. (*stirring uneasily—mechanically*) Yes. I know.

ELSA. And, of course, it blew my petty modern selfishness right out the window. I couldn't believe he meant it at first, but when I saw he did, that finished me. (*She smiles—then with quiet pride*) And I think we've lived up to that ideal ever since. I hope I have. I know he has. It was his creation, you see.

LUCY. Of course he has. Of course.

ELSA. And our marriage has meant for us, not slavery or boredom but freedom and harmony within ourselves—and happiness. So we must have both lived true to it. Happiness is proof, isn't it?

LUCY. (*deeply moved—without looking at* ELSA, *takes her hand and squeezes it—huskily*) Of course it is. Please forget the stupid rot I've said. I was only trying to get a rise out of you. We all know how wonderfully happy you and John are. Only remember, the world is full of spiteful liars who would do anything to wreck your happiness and drag you down to their level—what I was doing. So never listen— But of course you won't, will you? You have faith. (*She turns and kisses her impulsively*) God bless you—and preserve your happiness!

ELSA. Thank you, Lucy. That's dear of you. (*Then puzzledly*) But why should you be afraid that anyone—

LUCY. (*jumps to her feet nervously*) Only my morbidness. I've been accused of so many rotten things I never did that I suppose I'm hipped on the subject. (*Then abruptly*) Got to run now, Elsa—go home and get on my armor for another of Walter's parties. It's a gay life. The only hope is he'll be so broke before long no one will call on us but our forgotten friends. (*She gives a bitter little laugh and starts to go around the left of sofa—then, at a noise of a door opening in the hall —nervously*) Isn't that some one—?

524

ELSA. It must be John. (*She hurries around the right of sofa and back toward the doorway.*)

JOHN. (*calls from the hall*) Hello.

ELSA. (*going out, meets him as he appears in the hall just beyond the doorway—kissing him*) Hello, darling. You're early. I'm so glad.

JOHN. I thought, as I'd told Uncle to come early, I better— (*He kisses her*) How do you feel, dear? You look much better.

ELSA. Oh, I'm fine, John. (LUCY *has remained standing by the left corner of the sofa, in a stiff, strained attitude, the expression on her face that of one caught in a corner, steeling herself for an ordeal.* ELSA *and* JOHN *come in, their arms around each other. As they do so,* LUCY *recovers her poise and calls to him.*)

LUCY. Hello, John.

JOHN. (*coming to her, his face wearing its most cordial, poker-faced smile*) Why, hello, Lucy. I thought I heard a familiar voice when I came in. (*They shake hands*) A pleasant surprise. Been a long time since we've had this pleasure. (ELSA *has come forward behind him. The figure of the masked* LOVING *appears in the doorway. During the next few speeches he moves silently to the corner of the long table before the window, right front, and stands there, without looking at them, facing front, his eyes fixed in the same cold stare, the expression of his masked face seeming to be more than ever sneering and sinister.*)

LUCY. Now, don't you begin on that! Elsa has already given me hell.

ELSA. (*laughing*) And she's repented and been forgiven.

JOHN. Oh, that's all right, then.

LUCY. (*nervously*) I was just leaving. Sorry I've got to run, John.

ELSA. Oh, you can't, now. John will think he's driven you out.

LUCY. No, really, Elsa, I—

ELSA. You simply must keep John company for a few minutes. Because I've got to go to the kitchen. I trust Emmy on ordinary occasions, but when a long-lost uncle is coming to dinner, a little personal supervision is in order. (*She moves toward the dining room at left.*)

525

LUCY. (*with a note of desperation*) Well—but I can't stay more than a second.

ELSA. I'll be back right away. (*She disappears through the dining-room door. The moment she is gone,* JOHN's *cordial smile vanishes and his face takes on a tense, harried look. He is now standing behind the right end of sofa,* LUCY *behind the left end. In the pause while they wait for* ELSA *to get out of earshot,* LOVING *moves silently over until he is standing just behind* JOHN *but a step toward rear from him, facing half toward him, half toward front.*)

JOHN. (*lowering his voice—hurriedly*) I hope you've been careful and not said anything that—

LUCY. Might give you away? Of course, I didn't. And even if I were rotten enough to come right out and tell her, she'd never believe me, she has such a touching faith in you.

JOHN. (*wincing*) Don't!

LUCY. No. You're perfectly safe. There's only one thing I've got to warn you about. It's nothing, really, but—

JOHN. What?

LUCY. Walter has been telling people. He has to, you see, to keep up his pose of friendly understanding—

JOHN. But how does Walter know?

LUCY. Don't look so dismayed! He doesn't know—who it was. And you'd be the last one he'd ever suspect.

JOHN. How is it he knows about you?

LUCY. (*hesitates—then defiantly*) I told him.

JOHN. You told him? In God's name, why? But I know. You couldn't resist—watching him squirm!

LUCY. (*stung*) Exactly, John. Why do you suppose I ever did it, except for his benefit—if you want the truth?

JOHN. Good God, don't you think I know that? Do you imagine I ever thought it was anything but revenge on your part?

LUCY. And whom were you revenging yourself on, John?—now we're being frank.

LOVING. (*with sinister mockery*) Who knows? Perhaps on love. Perhaps, in my soul, I hate love!

LUCY. (*stares at* JOHN *with frightened bewilderment*) John! Now you're like—that night!

JOHN. (*confusedly*) I? It wasn't I. (*Angrily*) What do you mean by saying I was revenging myself? Why should I revenge myself on her?

LUCY. I don't know, John. That's a matter for your conscience. I've got enough on my own, thank you. I must say I resent your attitude, John. (*With a flippant sneer*) Hardly the lover-like tone, is it?

JOHN. (*with disgust*) Lover!

LUCY. Oh, I know. I feel the same way. But why hate me? Why not hate yourself?

JOHN. As if I didn't! Good God, if you knew! (*Then bitterly*) And how long do you think you'll be able to resist telling Walter it was I, his old friend—so you can watch him squirm some more!

LUCY. John!

JOHN. And Walter will have to tell that to every one, too—to live up to his pose! And then—

LUCY. John! You know I wouldn't, even if I hated you as you seem to hate me. I wouldn't for Elsa's sake. Oh, I know you think I'm a rotten liar, but I love Elsa! (*Then brokenly*) Oh, it's such a vile mess! What fools we were!

JOHN. (*dully*) Yes. (*Bitterly again*) I'm sorry I can't trust you, Lucy. I can when you're yourself. But full of booze— I see what it will come to. I'll have to tell her myself to save her the humiliation of hearing it through dirty gossip!

LUCY. John! Oh, please don't be such a fool! Please!

JOHN. You think she couldn't forgive?

LUCY. I'm thinking of what it would do to her. Can't you see—?

JOHN. (*warningly, as he hears the pantry door opening*) Ssshh! (*Quickly, raising his voice to a conversational tone*) Uncle is a grand old fellow. You'll have to meet him some time. You'd like him.

LUCY. I'm sure I would. (*Then, as* ELSA *comes in from the dining*

527

room) Ah, here you are. Well, I've got to fly. (*She holds out her hand to* JOHN) Good-bye, John. Take care of Elsa.

JOHN. Good-bye, Lucy. (ELSA *puts an arm around her waist and they go back to the hall doorway.*)

ELSA. I'll get your things. (*They disappear in the hall. As soon as they have gone,* JOHN *turns and, coming around the sofa, sits down on it and stares before him with hunted eyes.* LOVING *moves until he is standing directly behind him. He bends over and whispers mockingly.*)

LOVING. I warned you it was closing in! You had better make up your mind now to tell the rest of your novel tonight—while there is still time!

JOHN. (*tensely*) Yes. I must.

LOVING. But, first, it still remains to decide what is to be your hero's end. (*He gives a little jeering laugh*) Strange, isn't it, what difficult problems your little dabble in fiction has brought up which demand a final answer! (*He laughs again—then turns to face the doorway as* ELSA *re-enters the room. His eyes remain fixed on her as she comes forward. She comes quietly to the right end of the sofa.* JOHN *does not notice her coming.* LOVING *remains standing at right, rear, of* JOHN.)

ELSA. A penny for your thoughts, John. (*He starts. She sits down beside him—with a smile*) Did I scare you?

JOHN. (*forcing a smile*) Don't know what's the matter with me. I seem to have the nervous jumps lately. (*Then carelessly*) Glad to see Lucy again, were you?

ELSA. Yes—of course. Only she's changed so. Poor Lucy.

JOHN. Why poor? Oh, you mean on account of Walter's antics?

ELSA. Then you know?

JOHN. Who doesn't? He's been making as public an ass of himself as possible. But let's not talk about Walter. What did you think of the big event to-day: Uncle dropping out of the blue?

ELSA. It must have been a surprise for you. I'm dying to meet him. I'm so glad he could come to-night.

JOHN. Yes. So am I. (*As if his conversation had run dry, he falls into an uneasy silence.* ELSA *looks at him worriedly. Then she nestles up close to him.*)

ELSA. (*tenderly*) Still love me, do you?

JOHN. (*takes her in his arms and kisses her—with intense feeling*) You know I do! There's nothing in life I give a damn about except your love! You know that, don't you?

ELSA. Yes, dear.

JOHN. (*avoiding her eyes now*) And you'll always love me—no matter what an unworthy fool I am?

ELSA. Ssshh! You mustn't say things like that. It's not true. (*Then smiling teasingly*) Well, if you love me so much, prove it by telling me.

JOHN. (*controlling a start*) Telling you what?

ELSA. Now, don't pretend. I know there's something that's been troubling you for weeks—ever since I came back from Boston.

JOHN. No, honestly, Elsa.

ELSA. Something you're keeping back because you're afraid of worrying me. So you might as well confess.

JOHN. (*forcing a smile*) Confess? And will you promise—to forgive?

ELSA. Forgive you for not wanting to worry me? Foolish one!

JOHN. (*hurriedly*) No, I was only joking. There's nothing.

ELSA. Now! But I think I can guess. It's about business, isn't it?

JOHN. (*grasps at this*) Well—yes, if you must know.

ELSA. And you were afraid that would upset me? Oh, John, you're such a child at times you ought to be spanked. You must think I've become a poor, helpless doll!

JOHN. No, but—

ELSA. Just because you've pampered me so terribly the past few years! But remember, we had barely enough to get along on when we were married—and I didn't appear so terribly unhappy then, did

529

I? And no matter how poor we become, do you think it would ever really matter one bit to me as long as I had you?

JOHN. (*stammers miserably*) Sweetheart! You make me feel—so damned ashamed! God, I can't tell you!

ELSA. (*kissing him*) But, darling, it's nothing! And now promise me you'll forget it and not worry any more?

JOHN. Yes.

ELSA. Good! Let's talk of something else. Tell me, have you been doing anything more on the rest of your idea for a novel?

JOHN. Yes, I— I've got most of it thought out.

ELSA. (*encouragingly*) That's splendid. You just put your mind on that and forget your silly worries. But when am I going to hear it?

JOHN. Well, I told Uncle the first part and he was curious, too. So I threatened him I might give you both an outline of the rest tonight.

ELSA. Oh, that's fine. (*Then she laughs*) And I'll confess it will be a great aid to me as a hostess. I'll probably feel a bit self-conscious, entertaining a strange priest-uncle for the first time.

JOHN. Oh, you won't be with him a minute before you'll feel he's an old friend.

ELSA. Well, that sounds encouraging. But you tell your story just the same. (*She gets up*) It must be getting on. I'd better go up and start getting dressed. (*She goes around the left end of the sofa and back toward the hall door*) Are you going up to your study for a while?

JOHN. Yes, in a minute. I want to do a little more work on my plot. The end isn't clearly worked out yet.

LOVING. That is, my hero's end!

ELSA. (*smiling at* JOHN *encouragingly*) Then you get busy, by all means, so you'll have no excuse! (*She goes out. As soon as she is gone,* JOHN's *expression changes and becomes tense and hunted again.* LOVING *remains standing behind him, staring down at him with cold, scornful eyes. There is a pause of silence.*)

JOHN. (*suddenly—his face full of the bitterest, tortured self-loathing —aloud to himself*) You God-damned rotten swine!

LOVING. (*mockingly*) Yes, unfit to live. Quite unfit for life, I think. But there is always death to wash one's sins away—sleep, untroubled by Love's betraying dream! (*He gives a low, sinister laugh*) Merely a consoling reminder—in case you've forgotten! (JOHN *listens fascinatedly, as if to an inner voice. Then a look of terror comes into his face and he shudders.*)

JOHN. (*torturedly*) For God's sake! Leave me alone!

CURTAIN

ACT THREE—SCENE ONE

PLOT FOR A NOVEL

(Continued)

Scene—*The living room again. It is immediately after dinner.*
Father Baird is sitting in the chair at left, front, Elsa on the sofa,
John beside her on her left, the masked Loving at right, rear, of John,
in the chair by the end of the table before the window. John and
Loving are in dinner clothes of identical cut. Elsa wears a white
evening gown of extremely simple lines. Father Baird is the same as
in Act One.

   Margaret *is serving them the after-dinner coffee. She goes out*
through the dining-room door.

   JOHN. (*puts an arm around* ELSA's *waist playfully*) Well, now you've
got to know her, what do you think of her, Uncle? Weren't my letters
right?

   FATHER BAIRD. (*gallantly*) They were much too feeble. You didn't
do her justice by half!

   ELSA. Thank you, Father. It's so kind of you to say that.

   JOHN. Ah! I told you that was one subject we'd agree on! (*Then
to* ELSA *in a tenderly chiding tone*) But I've got a bone to pick with
you, my lady. You ate hardly any dinner, do you know it?

   ELSA. Oh, but I did, dear.

   JOHN. No, you only went through the motions. I was watching you.
That's no way to get back your strength.

   FATHER BAIRD. Yes, you need all the nourishment you can take when
you're getting over the flu.

JOHN. (*worriedly—grasping her hand*) Sure you're warm enough? Want me to get you something to put over your shoulders?

ELSA. No, dear, thank you.

JOHN. Remember it's a rotten, chilly, rainy day out and even indoors you can't be too careful.

ELSA. Oh, but I'm quite all right now, John. Please don't worry about me.

JOHN. Well, don't let yourself get tired now, you hear? If you find yourself feeling at all worn-out, you just send Uncle and me off to my study. He'll understand. Won't you, Uncle?

FATHER BAIRD. Of course. I hope Elsa will feel I'm one of the family and treat me without ceremony.

ELSA. I do feel that, Father. (*Then teasingly*) But do you know what I think is behind all this solicitude of John's? He's simply looking for an excuse to get out of telling us the rest of his novel. But we won't let him back out, will we?

FATHER BAIRD. Indeed we won't.

ELSA. The first part is so unusual and interesting. Don't you think so, Father?

FATHER BAIRD. (*quietly*) Yes. Tragic and revealing to me.

ELSA. You see, John, it's no use. We're simply going to insist.

LOVING. (*coldly mocking*) You're sure—you insist?

ELSA. Of course I do. So come on.

JOHN. (*nervously*) Well— (*He hesitates—gulps down the rest of his coffee.*)

ELSA. (*smiling*) I never saw you so flustered before, John. You'd think you were going to address an audience of literary critics.

JOHN. (*begins jerkily*) Well— But before I start, there's one thing I want to impress on you both again. My plot, up to the last part, which is wholly imaginary, is taken from life. It's the story of a man I once knew.

LOVING. (*mockingly*) Or thought I knew.

ELSA. May I be inquisitive? Did I ever know the man?

533

LOVING. (*a hostile, repellent note in his voice*) No. I can swear to that. You have never known him.

ELSA. (*taken aback, gives* JOHN *a wondering look—then apologetically*) I'm sorry I butted in with a silly question. Go on, dear.

JOHN. (*nervously—forcing a laugh*) I— It's hard getting started. (*He turns and reaches for his coffee, forgetting he has drunk it— sets the cup down again abruptly and goes on hurriedly*) Well, you will remember my first part ended when the boy's parents had died.

LOVING. And he had denied all his old superstitions!

JOHN. Well, as you can imagine, for a long while after their deaths, he went through a terrific inner conflict. He was seized by fits of terror, in which he felt he really had given his soul to some evil power. He would feel a tortured longing to pray and beg for forgiveness. It seemed to him that he had forsworn all love forever—and was cursed. At these times he wanted only to die. Once he even took his father's revolver—

LOVING. (*sneeringly*) But he was afraid to face death. He was still too religious-minded, you see, to accept the one beautiful, comforting truth of life: that death is final release, the warm, dark peace of annihilation.

FATHER BAIRD. (*quietly*) I cannot see the beauty and comfort.

LOVING. He often regretted afterwards he had not had the courage to die then. It would have saved him so much silly romantic pursuit of meaningless illusions.

ELSA. (*uneasily*) Oh, you mustn't talk that way, John. It sounds so bitter—and false—coming from you.

JOHN. (*confusedly*) I— I didn't— You forget I'm simply following what this man told me. (*Hurrying on*) Well, finally, he came out of this period of black despair. He taught himself to take a rationalistic attitude. He read all sorts of scientific books. He ended up by becoming an atheist. But his experience had left an indelible scar on his spirit. There always remained something in him that felt itself damned by life, damned with distrust, cursed with the inability ever to reach a

534

lasting belief in any faith, damned by a fear of the lie hiding behind the mask of truth.

FATHER BAIRD. Ah!

LOVING. (*sneeringly*) So romantic, you see—to think of himself as possessed by a damned soul!

JOHN. And in after years, even at the height of his rationalism, he never could explain away a horror of death—and a strange fascination it had for him. And coupled with this was a dread of life—as if he constantly sensed a malignant Spirit hiding behind life, waiting to catch men at its mercy, in their hour of secure happiness— Something that hated life!— Something that laughed with mocking scorn! (*He stares before him with a fascinated dread, as if he saw this Something before him. Then, suddenly, as if in reply,* LOVING *gives a little mocking laugh, barely audible.* JOHN *shudders.* ELSA *and* FATHER BAIRD *start and stare at* JOHN *uneasily, but he is looking straight ahead and they turn away again.*)

LOVING. A credulous, religious-minded fool, as I've pointed out! And he carried his credulity into the next period of his life, where he believed in one social or philosophical Ism after another, always on the trail of Truth! He was never courageous enough to face what he really knew was true, that there is no truth for men, that human life is unimportant and meaningless. No. He was always grasping at some absurd new faith to find an excuse for going on!

JOHN. (*proudly*) And he did go on! And he found his truth at last—in love, where he least expected he ever would find it. For he had always been afraid of love. And when he met the woman who afterwards became his wife and realized he was in love with her, it threw him into a panic of fear. He wanted to run away from her— but found he couldn't.

LOVING. (*scornfully*) So he weakly surrendered—and immediately began building a new superstition of love around her.

JOHN. He was happy again for the first time since his parents' death—to his bewildered joy.

LOVING. (*mockingly*) And secret fear!

ELSA. (*gives* JOHN *a curious, uneasy glance*) Secret fear?

JOHN. Yes, he—he came to be afraid of his happiness. His love made him feel at the mercy of that mocking Something he dreaded. And the more peace and security he found in his wife's love, the more he was haunted by fits of horrible foreboding—the recurrent dread that she might die and he would be left alone again, without love. So great was the force of this obsession at times that he felt caught in a trap, desperate—

LOVING. And he often found himself regretting—

JOHN. (*hastily*) Against his will—

LOVING. (*inexorably*) That he had again let love put him at the mercy of life!

JOHN. (*hurriedly*) But, of course, he realized this was all morbid and ridiculous—for wasn't he happier than he had ever dreamed he could be again?

LOVING. (*with gloating mockery*) And so he deliberately destroyed that happiness!

ELSA. (*startledly*) Destroyed his happiness? How, John?

JOHN. (*turns to her, forcing a smile*) I'm afraid you will find this part of his story hard to believe, Elsa. This damned fool, who loved his wife more than anything else in life, was unfaithful to her. (FATHER BAIRD *starts and stares at him with a shocked expression.*)

ELSA. (*frightenedly*) It is—hard to believe. But this part is all the story of the man you knew, isn't it?

JOHN. Yes, of course, and you mustn't condemn him entirely until you've heard how it came to happen. (*He turns away from her again —jerkily*) His wife had gone away. It was the first time. He felt lost without her—fearful, disintegrated. His familiar dread seized him. He began imagining all sorts of catastrophes. Horrible pictures formed in his mind. She was run over by a car. Or she had caught pneumonia and lay dying. Every day these evil visions possessed him. He tried to escape them in work. He couldn't. (*He pauses for a second, nerving himself to go on. Then starts again*) Then one night an old friend called—to drag him off to a party. He loathed such affairs usually, but this time he thought it would help him to escape himself for a while. So he went. He observed with disgust how his friend, who was drunk, was pawing over some woman right under the nose of his wife. He knew that this friend was continually having affairs of this sort and that his wife was aware of it. He had often wondered if she cared, and he was curious now to watch her reactions. And very soon he had an example of what her pride had to endure, for the husband went off openly with his lady. The man felt a great sympathy for her—and, as if she guessed his thought, she came to him, and he overdid himself in being kind. (*He gives a short bitter laugh*) A great mistake! For she reacted to it in a way that at first shocked him but ended up in arousing his curiosity. He had known her for years. It wasn't like her. It fascinated him, in a way, that she should have become so corrupted. He became interested to see how far she would go with it—purely as an observer, he thought—the poor idiot! (*He laughs again.* FATHER BAIRD *has remained motionless, his eyes on the floor.* ELSA's *face is pale and set, her eyes have a bewildered, stricken look.* JOHN *goes on*) Remember, all this time he saw through her; he laughed to himself at her crude vamping; he felt he was only playing a game. Just as he knew she was playing a game; that it was no desire for him but hatred for her husband that inspired her. (*He gives a short contemptuous laugh again*) Oh, he had it all analyzed quite correctly, considering the known elements. It was the unknown—

FATHER BAIRD. (*without raising his head*) Yes. (*He casts a quick glance at* ELSA, *then looks as quickly away. Her eyes are fastened on the floor now. Her face has frozen into a mask with the tense effort she is making not to give herself away.*)

JOHN. He had not the slightest desire for this woman. When she threw herself into his arms, he was repelled. He determined to end the game. He thought of his wife— (*He forces a laugh*) But, as I've said, there was the unknown to reckon with. At the thought of his wife, suddenly it was as if something outside him, a hidden spirit of evil, took possession of him.

LOVING. (*coldly vindictive now*) That is, he saw clearly that this situation was the climax of a long death struggle between his wife and him. The woman with him counted only as a means. He saw that underneath all his hypocritical pretense he really hated love. He wanted to deliver himself from its power and be free again. He wanted to kill it!

ELSA. (*with horrified pain*) Oh! (*Trying to control herself*) I —I don't understand. He hated love? He wanted to kill it? But that's —too horrible!

JOHN. (*stammers confusedly*) No—I— Don't you see it wasn't he?

LOVING. But, I'm afraid, Elsa, that my hero's silly idea that he was possessed by a demon must strike you as an incredible superstitious excuse to lie out of his responsibility.

FATHER BAIRD. (*without lifting his eyes—quietly*) Quite credible to me, Jack. One may not give one's soul to a devil of hate—and remain forever scatheless.

LOVING. (*sneeringly*) As for the adultery itself, the truth is that this poor fool was making a great fuss about nothing—an act as meaningless as that of one fly with another, of equal importance to life!

ELSA. (*stares at* JOHN *as if he had become a stranger—a look of sick repulsion coming over her face*) John! You're disgusting! (*She shrinks away from him to the end of the sofa near* FATHER BAIRD.)

JOHN. (*stammers confusedly*) But I—I didn't mean—forgive me. I only said that—as a joke—to get a rise out of Uncle.

FATHER BAIRD. (*gives a quick anxious look at* ELSA—*then quietly, an undercurrent of sternness in his voice*) I don't think it's a joke. But go on with your story, Jack.

JOHN. (*forcing himself to go on*) Well I—I know you can imagine the hell he went through from the moment he came to himself and realized the vileness he had been guilty of. He couldn't forgive himself—and that's what his whole being now cried out for—forgiveness.

FATHER BAIRD. (*quietly*) I can well believe that, Jack.

JOHN. He wanted to tell his wife and beg for forgiveness—but he was afraid of losing her love. (*He gives a quick glance at* ELSA, *as if to catch her reaction to this, but she is staring straight before her with a still, set face. He forces a smile and adopts a joking tone*) And here's where I'd like to have your opinion, Elsa. The question doesn't come up in my story, as you'll see, but— Could his wife have forgiven him, do you think?

ELSA. (*starts—then tensely*) You want me to put myself in the wife's place?

JOHN. Yes. I want to see whether the man was a fool or not—in his fear.

ELSA. (*after a second's pause—tensely*) No. She could never forgive him.

JOHN. (*desperately*) But it wasn't he! Can't you see—

ELSA. No. I'm afraid—I can't see.

JOHN. (*dully now*) Yes. That's what I thought you'd say.

ELSA. But what does it matter what I think? You said the question of her forgiving doesn't come up in your novel.

LOVING. (*coldly*) Not while the wife is alive.

JOHN. (*dully*) He never tells her.

LOVING. She becomes seriously ill.

ELSA. (*with a start*) Oh.

LOVING. (*in a cold voice, as if he were pronouncing a death sentence*) Flu, which turns into pneumonia. And she dies.

ELSA. (*frightenedly now*) Dies?

LOVING. Yes. I need her death for my end. (*Then in a sinister, jeering tone*) That is, to make my romantic hero come finally to a rational conclusion about his life!

ELSA. (*stares before her, not seeming to have heard this last—her*

539

eyes full of a strange, horrified fascination—as if she were talking aloud to herself) So she dies.

FATHER BAIRD. (*after a worried glance at her—an undercurrent of warning in his quiet tone*) I think you've tired Elsa out with your sensational imaginings, Jack. I'd spare her, for the present, at least, he fog of gloom your novel is plunging into.

ELSA. (*grasps at this—tensely*) Yes, I'm afraid it has been too exciting— I really don't feel up to— During dinner I began to get a headache and it's splitting now.

JOHN. (*gets up—worriedly*) But why didn't you tell me? If I'd known that, I'd never have bored you with my damned plot.

ELSA. I—I think I'll lie down here on the sofa—and take some aspirin—and rest for a while. You can go with your uncle up to your study—and tell him the rest of your story there.

FATHER BAIRD. (*gets up*) An excellent idea. Come on, Jack, and give your poor wife a respite from the horrors of authorship. (*He goes to the doorway in rear.*)

JOHN. (*comes to* ELSA. *As he does so,* LOVING *comes and stands behind her, at rear of sofa*) I'm so darned sorry, Elsa, if I've—

ELSA. Oh, please! It's only a headache.

JOHN. You—you don't feel really sick, do you, dearest? (*He puts a hand to her forehead timidly.*)

ELSA. (*shrinks from his touch*) No, no, it's nothing.

LOVING. (*slowly, in his cold tone with its undercurrent of sinister hidden meaning*) You must be very careful, Elsa. Remember it's cold and raining out.

ELSA. (*staring before her strangely—repeats fascinatedly*) It's raining?

LOVING. Yes.

*JOHN. (*stammers confusedly*) Yes, you—you must be careful, dearest.

FATHER BAIRD. (*from the doorway in rear—sharply*) Come along, Jack! (JOHN *goes back to him and* LOVING *follows* JOHN. FATHER BAIRD

goes into the hall, turning left to go upstairs to the study. JOHN *stops
in the doorway and looks back for a moment at* ELSA *frightenedly.*
LOVING *comes to his side and also stops and looks at her, his eyes cold
and remorseless in his mask of sinister mockery. They stand there
for a moment side by side. Then* JOHN *turns and disappears in the
hall toward left, following* FATHER BAIRD. LOVING *remains, his gaze
concentrated on the back of* ELSA's *head with a cruel, implacable
intensity. She is still staring before her with the same strange fascinated dread. Then, as if in obedience to his will, she rises slowly to
her feet and walks slowly and woodenly back past him and disappears in the hall, turning right toward the entrance door to the
apartment. For a second* LOVING *remains looking after her. Then he
turns and disappears in the hall toward left, following* FATHER BAIRD
and JOHN *to the study.*)

CURTAIN

ACT THREE—SCENE TWO

S CENE—JOHN LOVING's *study on the upper floor of the apartment. At
left front is a door leading into* ELSA's *bedroom. Bookcases extend along the rear and right walls. There is a door to the upper
hall at rear, right. A long table with a lamp is at center, front. At
left of table is a chair. In front of table a similar chair. At right, front,
is a chaise-longue, facing left.*

FATHER BAIRD, JOHN *and* LOVING *are discovered. The priest is sitting
on the chaise-longue,* JOHN *in the chair at front of table,* LOVING *in
the chair at left of table.* FATHER BAIRD *sits in the same attitude as he
had in the previous scene, his eyes on the floor, his expression sad
and a bit stern.* LOVING's *masked face stares at* JOHN, *his eyes cold and
still.* JOHN *is talking in a strained tone, monotonously, insistently.
It is as if he were determinedly talking to keep himself from thinking.*

JOHN. I listen to people talking about this universal breakdown we are in and I marvel at their stupid cowardice. It is so obvious that they deliberately cheat themselves because their fear of change won't let them face the truth. They don't want to understand what has happened to them. All they want is to start the merry-go-round of blind greed all over again. They no longer know what they want this country to be, what they want it to become, where they want it to go. It has lost all meaning for them except as a pig-wallow. And so their lives as citizens have no beginnings, no ends. They have lost the ideal of the Land of the Free. Freedom demands initiative, courage, the need to decide what life must mean to oneself. To them, that is terror. They explain away their spiritual cowardice by whining that the time for individualism is past, when it is their courage to possess their own souls which is dead—and stinking! No, they don't want to be free. Slavery means security—of a kind, the only kind they have courage for. It means they need not think. They have only to obey orders from owners who are, in turn, their slaves!

LOVING. (*breaks in—with bored scorn*) But I'm denouncing from my old soap box again. It's all silly twaddle, of course. Freedom was merely our romantic delusion. We know better now. We know we are all the slaves of meaningless chance—electricity or something, which whirls us—on to Hercules!

JOHN. (*with a proud assertiveness*) But, in spite of that, I say: Very well! On to Hercules! Let us face that! Once we have accepted it without evasion, we can begin to create new goals for ourselves, ends for our days! A new discipline for life will spring into being, a new will and power to live, a new ideal to measure the value of our lives by!

LOVING. (*mockingly*) What? Am I drooling on about my old social ideals again? Sorry to bore you, Uncle.

FATHER BAIRD. (*quietly, without looking up*) You are not boring me, Jack.

JOHN. (*an idealistic exaltation coming into his voice*) We need a

542

new leader who will teach us that ideal, who by his life will ex-
emplify it and make it a living truth for us—a man who will prove
that man's fleeting life in time and space can be noble. We need,
above all, to learn again to believe in the possibility of nobility of
spirit in ourselves! A new savior must be born who will reveal to us
how we can be saved from ourselves, so that we can be free of the
past and inherit the future and not perish by it!

LOVING. (*mockingly*) Must sound like my old letters to you, Uncle.
It's more nonsense, of course. But there are times of stress and flight
when one hides in any old empty barrel!

FATHER BAIRD. (*ignoring this—quietly*) You are forgetting that men
have such a Savior, Jack. All they need is to remember Him.

JOHN. (*slowly*) Yes, perhaps if we could again have faith in—

LOVING. (*harshly*) No! We have passed beyond gods! There can
be no going back!

FATHER BAIRD. Jack! Take care!

LOVING. (*mockingly again*) But, on the other hand, I'll grant you
the pseudo-Nietzschean savior I just evoked out of my past is an
equally futile ghost. Even if he came, we'd only send him to the
insane asylum for teaching that we should have a nobler aim for
our lives than getting all four feet in a trough of swill! (*He laughs
sardonically*) How could we consider such an unpatriotic idea as
anything but insane, eh? (*There is a pause. FATHER BAIRD looks up
and studies JOHN's face searchingly, hopefully.*)

FATHER BAIRD. (*finally speaks quietly*) Jack, ever since we came
upstairs, I've listened patiently while you've discussed every subject
under the sun except the one I know is really on your mind.

JOHN. I don't know what you mean.

FATHER BAIRD. The end of your story.

JOHN. Oh, forget that. I'm sick of the damned thing—now, at any
rate.

FATHER BAIRD. Sick of the damned thing, yes. That's why I feel it's
important you tell it—now. This man's wife dies, you said. (*He

543

stares fixedly at JOHN *now and adds slowly*) Of influenza which turns into pneumonia.

JOHN. (*uneasily*) Why do you stare like that?

FATHER BAIRD. (*dropping his eyes—quietly*) Go on with your story.

JOHN. (*hesitantly*) Well—I— You can imagine the anguish he feels after his wife's death—the guilt which tortures him a thousand-fold now she is dead.

FATHER BAIRD. I can well imagine it, Jack.

LOVING. (*sneeringly*) And under the influence of his ridiculous guilty conscience, all the superstitions of his childhood, which he had prided himself his reason had killed, return to plague him. He feels at times an absurd impulse to pray. He fights this nonsense back. He analyzes it rationally. He sees it clearly as a throwback to boyhood experiences. But, in spite of himself, that cowardly something in him he despises as superstition seduces his reason with the old pathetic lie of survival after death. He begins to believe his wife is alive in some mythical hereafter!

JOHN. (*strangely*) He knows she knows of his sin now. He can hear her promising to forgive if he can only believe again in his old God of Love, and seek her through Him. She will be beside him in spirit in this life, and at his death she will be waiting. Death will not be an end but a new beginning, a reunion with her in which their love will go on forever within the eternal peace and love of God! (*His voice has taken on a note of intense longing.*)

FATHER BAIRD. Ah, then you do see, Jack! Thank God!

JOHN. (*as if he hadn't heard*) One night when he is hounded beyond endurance he rushes out—in the hope that if he walks himself into exhaustion he may be able to sleep for a while and forget. (*Strangely, staring before him, as if he were visualizing the scene he is describing*) Without his knowing how he got there, he finds he has walked in a circle and is standing before the old church, not far from where he now lives, in which he used to pray as a boy.

LOVING. (*jeeringly*) And now we come to the great temptation scene, in which he finally confronts his ghosts! (*With harsh defiance*) The church challenges him—and he accepts the challenge and goes in!

JOHN. He finds himself kneeling at the foot of the Cross. And he feels he is forgiven, and the old comforting peace and security and joy steal back into his heart. (*He hesitates, as if reluctant to go on, as if this were the end.*)

FATHER BAIRD. (*Deeply moved*) And that is your end? Thank God!

LOVING. (*jeeringly*) I'm afraid your rejoicing is a bit premature— for this cowardly giving in to his weakness is not the end! Even while he is kneeling, there is a mocking rational something in him that laughs with scorn—and at the last moment his will and pride revive in him again! He sees clearly by the light of reason the degradation of his pitiable surrender to old ghostly comforts—and he rejects them! (*His voice with surprising suddenness takes on a savage vindictive quality*) He curses his God again as he had when a boy! He defies Him finally! He—!

FATHER BAIRD. (*sternly*) Jack! Take care!

JOHN. (*protests confusedly*) No—that's not right—I—

LOVING. (*strangely confused in his turn—hurriedly*) Pardon me, Uncle. Of course, that's wrong—afraid for a moment I let an author's craving for a dramatic moment run away with my sane judgment. Naturally, he could never be so stupid as to curse what he knew didn't exist!

JOHN. (*despondently*) No. He realizes he can never believe in his lost faith again. He walks out of the church—without love forever now—but daring to face his eternal loss and hopelessness, to accept it as his fate and go on with life.

LOVING. (*mockingly*) A very, very heroic end, as you see! But, unfortunately, absolutely meaningless!

FATHER BAIRD. Yes. Meaningless. I'm glad you see that.

JOHN. (*rousing a bit—defensively*) No—I take that back—it isn't meaningless. It is man's duty to life to go on!

LOVING. (*jeeringly*) The romantic idealist again speaks! On to Hercules! What an inspiring slogan! (*Then a sinister note coming into his voice*) But there is still another end to my story—the one sensible happy end!

FATHER BAIRD. (*as if he hadn't heard this last*) Jack! Are you so blind you cannot see what your imagining his finding peace in the church reveals about the longing of your own soul—the salvation from yourself it holds out to you? Why, if you had any honesty with yourself, you would get down on your knees now and—

LOVING. Rot! How can you believe such childish superstition!

FATHER BAIRD. (*angrily*) Jack! I've endured all I can of your blasphemous insults to—

JOHN. (*confusedly—hurriedly*) I—I didn't mean—I'm sorry, Uncle. But it's only a story. Don't take it so seriously.

FATHER BAIRD. (*has immediately controlled himself—quietly*) Only a story, Jack? You're sure you still want me to believe that?

JOHN. (*defensively*) Why, what else could you believe? Do you think I—? (*Then in an abrupt, angry tone*) But that's enough about the damned story. I don't want to talk any more about it! (FATHER BAIRD *stares at him but keeps silent.* JOHN *starts to pace up and down with nervous restlessness—then stops abruptly*) I—if you'll excuse me—I think I'll go down and see how Elsa is. (*He goes back toward the door.* LOVING *follows him*) I'll be right back.

FATHER BAIRD. (*quietly*) Of course, Jack. Don't bother about me. I'll take a look at your library. (*He gets up.* JOHN *goes out.* LOVING *turns for a moment to* FATHER BAIRD, *his eyes full of a mocking derision. Then he turns and follows* JOHN. FATHER BAIRD *goes to the bookcase at right and runs his eyes over the titles of books. But he only does this mechanically. His mind is preoccupied, his expression sad and troubled.* JOHN's *voice can be heard from below calling* "Elsa." FATHER BAIRD *starts and listens. Then from* ELSA's *bedroom* JOHN's *voice is heard, as he looks for her there. He calls anxiously* "Elsa"—*then evidently hurries out again, closing the door behind him.* FATHER BAIRD'S *face grows more worried. He goes to the doorway in rear and stands listening to a brief conversation from below. A moment later* JOHN *comes in from rear. He is making a great effort to conceal a feeling of dread. He comes forward.* LOVING *follows silently but stops and remains standing by the bookcase at left of doorway.*)

JOHN. She's—gone out.

FATHER BAIRD. Gone out? But it's still raining, isn't it?

JOHN. Pouring. I—I can't understand. It's a crazy thing for her to do when she's just getting over—

FATHER BAIRD. (*with an involuntary start*) Ah!

JOHN. What?

FATHER BAIRD. Nothing.

JOHN. (*frightenedly*) I can't imagine—

FATHER BAIRD. How long has she been gone?

JOHN. I don't know. Margaret says she heard some one go out right after we came upstairs.

FATHER BAIRD. (*with lowered voice to himself*) My fault, God forgive me. I had a feeling then I shouldn't leave her.

JOHN. (*sinks down in the chair by the table and waits tensely—then suddenly he bursts out*) I never should have told her the story! I'm a God-damned fool.

FATHER BAIRD. (*sternly*) You would be more honest with yourself if you said a self-damned fool! (*Hearing a sound from below*) There. Isn't that someone now? (JOHN *stops for a second to listen, then hurries to the door in rear.* LOVING *remains where he is, standing motionlessly by the bookcase.*)

JOHN. (*calls*) Is that you, Elsa?

ELSA. (*from downstairs—hurriedly*) Yes. Don't come down. I'm coming up. (*A moment later she appears in the hallway.*)

JOHN. Darling! I've been so damned worried. (*He starts to take her in his arms.*)

ELSA. Please! (*She wards him off and steps past him into the study.*

547

She has taken off her coat and hat downstairs, but the lower part of her skirt and her stockings and shoes are soaking wet. Her face is pinched and drawn and pale, with flushed spots over the cheek bones, and her eyes are bright and hard. FATHER BAIRD *stares at her searchingly, his face sad and pitying.*)

FATHER BAIRD. (*forcing a light tone—as she comes forward*) Well! You have given us a scare, my lady.

ELSA. (*tensely*) I'm sorry, Father.

FATHER BAIRD. Your husband was half out of his mind worrying about what had happened to you. (*She sits in the chair in front of table.* JOHN *stands at right of her.* LOVING *has come up and stands by the right end of table, at right, rear, of* JOHN. *His eyes are fixed on* ELSA's *face with an eager, sinister intentness.*)

JOHN. (*with increasing uneasiness*) Elsa! You look sick. Do you feel—?

FATHER BAIRD. I'll get her some whisky. And you make her go to bed at once. (*He goes out the door in rear.*)

JOHN. (*grabbing her hands*) Your hands are like ice!

ELSA. (*Pulls them away from him—coldly, without looking at him*) It's chilly out.

JOHN. Look at your shoes! They're soaked!

ELSA. It doesn't matter, does it? (*A chill runs through her body.*)

JOHN. You've taken a chill. (*Then forcing a tenderly bullying tone*) You'll go right to bed, that's what. And no nonsense about it, you hear!

ELSA. Are you trying the bossy tender husband on me, John? I'm afraid that's no longer effective.

JOHN. (*guiltily*) Why do you say that?

ELSA. Are you determined to act out this farce to the end?

JOHN. I—I don't know what you mean. What makes you look at me—as if you hated me?

ELSA. (*bitterly*) Hate you? No, I only hate myself for having been such a fool! (*Then with a hard, mocking tone*) Shall I tell you where

I went, and why? But perhaps I'd better put it in the form of a novel plot!

JOHN. I—I don't know what you're driving at.

ELSA. I went out because I thought I'd like to drop in on one of Lucy's parties. But it wasn't exciting—hardly any adultery going on— I had no opportunity—even if I'd been seized by any peculiar impulse of hatred and revenge on you. So I came home. (*She forces a hard, bitter laugh*) There! Are you satisfied? It's all a lie, of course. I simply went for a walk. But so is your story about the novel a lie.

JOHN. (*stunned—stammers*) Elsa, I—

ELSA. For God's sake, John, don't lie to me any more or I—I know, I tell you! Lucy told me all about it this afternoon.

JOHN. She told you? The damned—

ELSA. Oh, she didn't tell me it was you. But she gave me all the sordid details and they were the same as those in your story. So it was you who told on yourself. Rather a joke on you, isn't it? (*She laughs bitterly.*)

JOHN. I— (*He blurts out miserably*) Yes—it's true.

ELSA. And it was a fine joke on me, her coming here. You would appreciate it, if you had seen how I sympathized with her, how I excused her to myself and pitied her. And all the while, she was pitying me! She was gloating! She's always envied us our happiness. Our happiness!

JOHN. (*writhing*) Don't!

ELSA. She must have been laughing at me for a fool, sneering to herself about my stupid faith in you. And you gave her that chance— you! You made our love a smutty joke for her and every one like her—you whom I loved so! And all the time I was loving you, you were only waiting for this chance to kill that love, you were hating me underneath, hating our happiness, hating the ideal of our marriage you had given me, which had become all the beauty and truth of life to me! (*She springs to her feet—distractedly*) Oh, I can't— I can't! (*She starts as if to run from the room.*)

JOHN. (*grabbing her—imploringly*) Elsa! For God's sake! Didn't my story explain? Can't you believe—it wasn't I? Can't you forgive?

ELSA. No! I can't forgive! How can I forgive—when all that time I loved you so, you were wishing in your heart that I would die!

JOHN. (*frantically*) Don't say that! It's mad! Elsa! Good God, how can you think—

ELSA. What else can I think? (*Then wildly*) Oh, John, stop talking! What's the good of talk? I only know I hate life! It's dirty and insulting—and evil! I want my dream back—or I want to be dead with it! (*She is shaken again by a wave of uncontrollable chill, her teeth chatter—pitiably*) Oh, John, leave me alone! I'm cold, I'm sick. I feel crazy!

FATHER BAIRD. (*comes in through the doorway at rear—sharply*) Jack! Why haven't you got her to bed? Can't you see she's ill? Phone for your doctor. (JOHN *goes out.* LOVING, *his eyes remaining fixed on* ELSA *with the same strange look, backs out of the doorway after him.*)

FATHER BAIRD. (*coming to* ELSA—*with great compassion*) My dear child, I can't tell you how deeply—

ELSA. (*tensely*) Don't! I can't bear— (*She is shaken again by a chill.*)

FATHER BAIRD. (*worriedly, but trying to pretend to treat it lightly, reassuringly*) You've taken a bad chill. You were very foolhardy to— But a day or two in bed and you'll be fine again.

ELSA. (*strangely serious and bitterly mocking at the same time*) But that would spoil John's story, don't you think? That would be very inconsiderate after he's worked out such a convenient end for me.

FATHER BAIRD. Elsa! For the love of God, don't tell me you took his morbid nonsense seriously! Is that why you—?

ELSA. (*as if she hadn't heard him*) And when he reminded me it was raining, it all seemed to fit in so perfectly—like the will of God! (*She laughs with hysterical mockery, her eyes shining feverishly.*)

FATHER BAIRD. (*sternly—more to break her mood than because he takes her impiety seriously*) Elsa! Stop that mockery! It has no part in you!

ELSA. (*confusedly*) I'm sorry. I forgot that you were— (*Then suddenly hectic again*) But I've never had any God, you see—until I met John. (*She laughs hysterically—then suddenly forces control on herself and gets shakily to her feet*) I'm sorry. I seem to be talking nonsense. My head has gone woolly. I— (JOHN *enters from the hall at rear. As he comes forward,* LOVING *appears in the doorway behind him.*)

JOHN. (*coming to* ELSA) Stillwell says for you to—

ELSA. (*distractedly*) No! (*Then dully*) I'll go—to my room. (*She sways weakly.* JOHN *starts toward her.*)

JOHN. Elsa! Sweetheart!

ELSA. No! (*By an effort of will, she overcomes her weakness and walks woodenly into her bedroom and closes the door behind her.* JOHN *makes a movement as if to follow her.*)

FATHER BAIRD. (*sharply*) Leave her alone, Jack. (JOHN *sinks down hopelessly on the chaise-longue.* LOVING *stands behind him, his cold eyes fixed with a sinister intensity on the door through which* ELSA *has just disappeared.* FATHER BAIRD *makes a movement as if he were going to follow* ELSA *into her room. Then he stops. There is an expression of sorrowful foreboding on his face. He bows his head with a simple dignity and begins to pray silently.*)

LOVING. (*his eyes now on* JOHN—*with a gloating mockery*) She seems to have taken her end in your story very seriously. Let's hope she doesn't carry that too far! You have enough on your conscience already—without murder! You couldn't live, I know, if—

JOHN. (*shuddering—clutches his head in both hands as if to crush out his thoughts*) For God's sake! (*His eyes turn to the priest. Then their gaze travels to a point in front of* FATHER BAIRD, *and slowly his expression changes to one of fearful, fascinated awe, as if he suddenly sensed a Presence there the priest is praying to. His lips part and words come haltingly, as if they were forced out of him, full of*

551

imploring fear) Thou wilt not—do that to me again—wilt Thou? Thou wilt not—take love from me again?

LOVING. (*jeeringly*) Is it your old demon you are praying to for mercy? Then I hope you hear his laughter! (*Then breaking into a cold, vicious rage*) You cowardly fool! I tell you there is nothing—nothing!

JOHN. (*starts back to himself—stammers with a confused air of relief*) Yes—of course—what's the matter with me? There's nothing —nothing to fear!

CURTAIN

ACT FOUR—SCENE ONE

THE END OF THE END

S CENE—*The study is shown as in preceding scene, but this scene
also reveals the interior of* ELSA'S *bedroom at left of study.*

*At right of bedroom, front, is the door between the two rooms.
At rear of this door, in the middle of the wall, is a dressing table,
mirror and chair. In the left wall, rear, is the door to the bathroom.
Before this door is a screen. At left, front, is the bed, its head against
the left wall. By the head of the bed is a small stand on which is a
reading lamp with a piece of cloth thrown over it to dim its light.
An upholstered chair is beside the foot of the bed. Another chair is
by the head of the bed at rear. A chaise-longue is at right, front, of
the room.*

It is nearing daybreak of a day about a week later.

In the bedroom, ELSA *lies in the bed, her eyes closed, her face pallid
and wasted.* JOHN *sits in the chair toward the foot of the bed, front.
He looks on the verge of complete mental and physical collapse.
His unshaven cheeks are sunken and sallow. His eyes, bloodshot
from sleeplessness, stare from black hollows with a frozen anguish at*
ELSA'S *face.*

LOVING *stands by the back of his chair, facing front. The sinister,
mocking character of his mask is accentuated now, evilly intensified.*

FATHER BAIRD *is standing by the middle of the bed, at rear. His face
also bears obvious traces of sleepless strain. He is conferring in whispers with* DOCTOR STILLWELL, *who is standing at his right. Both are
watching* ELSA *with anxious eyes. At rear of* STILLWELL *on his right,
a trained nurse is standing.*

STILLWELL *is in his early fifties, tall, with a sharp, angular face and
gray hair. The* NURSE *is a plump woman in her late thirties.*

553

For a moment after the curtain rises the whispered pantomime between STILLWELL *and the priest continues, the* NURSE *watching and listening. Then* ELSA *stirs restlessly and moans. She speaks without opening her eyes, hardly above a whisper, in a tone of despairing bitterness.*

ELSA. John! How could you? Our dream! (*She moans.*)

JOHN. (*in anguish*) Elsa! Forgive!

LOVING. (*in a cold, inexorable tone*) She will never forgive.

STILLWELL. (*frowning, makes a motion to* JOHN *to be silent*) Ssshh! (*He whispers to* FATHER BAIRD, *his eyes on* JOHN. *The priest nods and comes around the corner of the bed toward* JOHN. STILLWELL *sits in the chair by the head of the bed, rear, and feels* ELSA's *pulse. The* NURSE *moves close behind him.*)

FATHER BAIRD. (*bends over* JOHN's *chair and speaks in a low cautioning voice*) Jack. You must be quiet.

JOHN. (*his eyes are on* STILLWELL's *face, desperately trying to read some answer there. He calls to him frightenedly*) Doctor! What is it? Is she—?

STILLWELL. Ssshh! (*He gives* JOHN *a furious look and motions* FATHER BAIRD *to keep him quiet.*)

FATHER BAIRD. Jack! Don't you realize you're only harming her?

JOHN. (*Confusedly repentant—in a low voice*) I'm sorry. I try not to, but— I know it's crazy, but I can't help being afraid—

LOVING. That my prophecy is coming true—her end in my story.

JOHN. (*with anguished appeal*) No! Elsa! Don't believe that! (ELSA *moans.*)

FATHER BAIRD. You see! You've disturbed her again! (STILLWELL *gets up and, after exchanging a whispered word with the* NURSE, *who nods and takes his place by the bedside, comes quickly around the end of the bed to* JOHN.)

STILLWELL. What the devil is the matter with you? I thought you promised me if I let you stay in here you'd keep quiet.

JOHN. (*dazedly now—suddenly overcome by a wave of drowsiness he tries in vain to fight back*) I won't again. (*His head nods.*)

STILLWELL. (*gives him a searching look—to* FATHER BAIRD) We've got to get him out of here.

JOHN. (*rousing himself—desperately fighting back his drowsiness*) I won't sleep! God, how can I sleep when—!

STILLWELL. (*taking one arm and signaling* FATHER BAIRD *to take the other—sharply but in a voice just above a whisper*) Loving, come into your study. I want to talk with you about your wife's condition.

JOHN. (*terrified*) Why? What do you mean? She isn't—?

STILLWELL. (*hastily, in a forced tone of reassurance*) No, no, no! What put that nonsense in your head? (*He flashes a signal to the priest and they both lift* JOHN *to his feet*) Come along, that's a good fellow. (*They lead* JOHN *to the door to the study at right.* LOVING *follows them silently, moving backward, his eyes fixed with sinister gloating intentness on* ELSA's *face.* FATHER BAIRD *opens the door and they pass through,* LOVING *slipping after them.* FATHER BAIRD *closes the door. They lead* JOHN *to the chaise-longue at right, front, of study, passing in front of the table.* LOVING *keeps pace with them, passing to rear of table.*)

JOHN. (*starts to resist feebly*) Let me go! I mustn't leave her! I'm afraid! (*They get him seated on the chaise-longue,* LOVING *taking up a position directly behind him on the other side of the chaise-longue*) I feel there's something—

LOVING. (*with a gloating mockery*) A demon who laughs, hiding behind the end of my story! (*He gives a sinister laugh.* FATHER BAIRD *and even* STILLWELL, *in spite of himself, are appalled by this laughter.*)

JOHN. (*starts to his feet—in anguish*) No!

FATHER BAIRD. Jack!

STILLWELL. (*recovering, angry at himself and furious with* JOHN—*seizes him by the arm and forces him down on the chaise-longue again*) Stop your damned nonsense! Get a grip on yourself! I've warned you you'd go to pieces like this if you kept on refusing to

555

rest or take nourishment. But that's got to stop, do you hear me? You've got to get some sleep!

FATHER BAIRD. Yes, Jack. You must!

STILLWELL. You've been a disturbing factor from the first and I've been a fool to stand— But I've had enough! You'll stay out of her room—

JOHN. No!

STILLWELL. Don't you want her to get well? By God, from the way you've been acting—

JOHN. (*wildly*) For God's sake, don't say that!

STILLWELL. Can't you see you're no help to her in this condition? While if you'll sleep for a while—

JOHN. No! (*Imploringly*) She's much better, isn't she? For God's sake, tell me you know she isn't going to— Tell me that and I'll do anything you ask!

LOVING. And don't lie, please! I want the truth!

STILLWELL. (*forcing an easy tone*) What's all this talk? She's resting quietly. There's no question of— (*Then quickly*) And now I've satisfied you on that, lie down as you promised. (JOHN *stares at him uncertainly for a moment—then obediently lies down*) Close your eyes now. (JOHN *closes his eyes.* LOVING *stands by his head, staring down at his face.* JOHN *almost immediately drops off into a drugged half-sleep, his breathing becomes heavy and exhausted.* STILLWELL *nods to* FATHER BAIRD *with satisfaction—then moves quietly to the other side of the room, by the door to* ELSA's *bedroom, beckoning* FATHER BAIRD *to follow him. He speaks to him in a low voice*) We'll have to keep an eye on him. He's headed straight for a complete collapse. But I think he'll sleep now, for a while anyway. (*He opens the door to the bedroom, looks in and catches the eye of the* NURSE, *who is still sitting in the chair by the head of the bed, watching* ELSA. *The* NURSE *shakes her head, answering his question. He softly closes the door again.*)

FATHER BAIRD. No change, Doctor?

STILLWELL. No. But I'm not giving up hope! She still has a fighting chance! (*Then in a tone of exasperated dejection*) If she'd only fight!

FATHER BAIRD. (*nods with sad understanding*) Yes. That's it.

STILLWELL. Damn it, she seems to want to die. (*Then angrily*) And, by God, in spite of his apparent grief, I've suspected at times that underneath he wants—

LOVING. (*His eyes fixed on* JOHN's *face, speaks in a cold implacable tone*) She is going to die.

JOHN. (*starts half-awake—mutters*) No! Elsa! Forgive! (*He sinks into drugged sleep again.*)

STILLWELL. You see. He keeps insisting to himself—

FATHER BAIRD. (*defensively*) That's a horrible charge for you to make, Doctor. Why, any one can see the poor boy is crazed with fear and grief.

STILLWELL. (*a bit ashamed*) Sorry. But there have been times when I've had the strongest sense of—well, as he said, Something— (*Then curtly, feeling this makes him appear silly*) Afraid I've allowed this case to get on my nerves. Don't usually go in for psychic nonsense.

FATHER BAIRD. Your feeling isn't nonsense, Doctor.

STILLWELL. She won't forgive him. That's her trouble as well as his. (*He sighs, giving way for a moment to his own physical weariness*) A strange case. Too many undercurrents. The pneumonia has been more a means than a cause. (*With a trace of condescension*) More in your line. A little casting out of devils would have been of benefit— might still be.

FATHER BAIRD. Might still be. Yes.

STILLWELL. (*exasperatedly*) Damn it. I've seen many worse cases where the patient pulled through. If I could only get her will to live functioning again! If she'd forgive him and get that off her mind, I know she'd fight. (*He abruptly gets to his feet—curtly*) Well, talk won't help her, that's sure. I'll get back. (*He goes into the bedroom and closes the door silently behind him.* FATHER BAIRD *remains for a moment staring sadly at the floor. In the bedroom,* STILLWELL *goes*

557

to the bedside. The NURSE *gets up and he speaks to her in a whisper, hears what she has to report, gives her some quick instructions. She goes to the bathroom. He sits in the chair by the bed and feels* ELSA'S *pulse. The* NURSE *comes back and hands him a hypodermic needle. He injects this into* ELSA's *arm. She moans and her body twitches for a second. He sits, watching her face worriedly, his fingers on her wrist. In the study,* FATHER BAIRD *starts to pace back and forth, frowning, his face tense, feeling desperately that he is facing inevitable tragedy, that he must do something to thwart it at once. He stops at the foot of the chaise-longue and stares down at the sleeping* JOHN. *Then he prays.*)

FATHER BAIRD. Dear Jesus, grant me the grace to bring Jack back to Thee. Make him see that Thou, alone, hast the words of Eternal Life, the power still to save—

LOVING. (*his eyes fixed on* JOHN's *face in the same stare—speaks as if in answer to* FATHER BAIRD's *prayer*) Nothing can save her.

JOHN. (*shuddering in his sleep*) No!

LOVING. Her end in your story is coming true. It was a cunning method of murder!

FATHER BAIRD. (*horrified*) Jack!

JOHN. (*with a tortured cry that starts him awake*) No! It's a lie! (*He stares around him at the air, as if he were trying to see some presence he feels there*) Liar! Murderer! (*Suddenly he seems to see* FATHER BAIRD *for the first time—with a cry of appeal—brokenly*) Uncle! For God's sake, help me! I—I feel I'm going mad!

FATHER BAIRD. (*eagerly*) If you would only let me help you, Jack! If you would only be honest with yourself and admit the truth in your own soul now, for Elsa's sake—while there is still time.

JOHN. (*frightenedly*) Still time? What do you mean? Is she— worse?

FATHER BAIRD. No. You've only been sleeping a few minutes. There has been no change.

JOHN. Then why did you say—?

558

FATHER BAIRD. Because I have decided you must be told the truth now, the truth you already know in your heart.

JOHN. What—truth?

FATHER BAIRD. It is the crisis. Human science has done all it can to save her. Her life is in the hands of God now.

LOVING. There is no God!

FATHER BAIRD. (*sternly*) Do you dare say that—now?

JOHN. (*frightenedly*) No—I—I don't know what I'm saying— It isn't I—

FATHER BAIRD. (*recovering himself—quietly*) No. I know you couldn't blaspheme at such a time—not your true self.

LOVING. (*angrily*) It is my true self—my only self! And I see through your stupid trick—to use the fear of death to—

FATHER BAIRD. It's the hatred you once gave your soul to which speaks, not you. (*Pleadingly*) I implore you to cast that evil from your soul! If you would only pray!

LOVING. (*fiercely*) No!

JOHN. (*stammers torturedly*) I—I don't know— I can't think!

FATHER BAIRD. (*intensely*) Pray with me, Jack. (*He sinks to his knees*) Pray that Elsa's life may be spared to you! It is only God Who can open her heart to forgiveness and give her back the will to live! Pray for His forgiveness, and He will have compassion on you! Pray to Him Who is Love. Who is Infinite Tenderness and Pity!

JOHN. (*half-slipping to his knees—longingly*) Who is Love? If I could only believe again!

FATHER BAIRD. Pray for your lost faith and it will be given you!

LOVING. (*sneeringly*) You forget I once prayed to your God and His answer was hatred and death—and a mocking laughter!

JOHN. (*starts up from his half-kneeling position, under the influence of this memory*) Yes, I prayed then. No. It's no good, Uncle. I can't believe. (*Then suddenly—with eagerness*) Let Him prove to me His Love exists! Then I will believe in Him again!

FATHER BAIRD. You may not bargain with your God, Jack. (*He gets*

559

wearily to his feet, his shoulders bowed, looking tragically old and beaten—then with a last appeal) But I beseech you still! I warn you!—before it's too late!—look into your soul and force yourself to admit the truth you find there—the truth you have yourself revealed in your story where the man, who is you, goes to the church and, at the foot of the Cross is granted the grace of faith again!

LOVING. In a moment of stupid madness! But remember that is not the end!

FATHER BAIRD. (*ignoring this*) There is a fate in that story, Jack— the fate of the will of God made manifest to you through the secret longing of your own heart for faith! Take care! It has come true so far, and I am afraid if you persist in your mad denial of Him and your own soul, you will have willed for yourself the accursed end of that man—and for Elsa, death!

JOHN. (*terrified*) Stop! Stop talking damned nonsense! (*Distractedly*) Leave me alone! I'm sick of your damned croaking! You're lying! Stillwell said there was no danger! She's asleep! She's getting better! (*Then terrified again*) What made you say, a fate in my story—the will of God? Good God, that's—that's nonsense! I— (*He starts for the bedroom door*) I'm going back to her. There's Something—

FATHER BAIRD. (*tries to hold him back*) You can't go there now, Jack.

JOHN. (*pushing him roughly away*) Leave me alone! (*He opens the bedroom door and lurches in. LOVING has come around behind the table and slips in after him. FATHER BAIRD, recovering from the push which has sent him back against the table, front, comes quickly to the doorway. As JOHN comes in, STILLWELL turns from where he sits beside the bedside, a look of intense anger and exasperation on his face. JOHN, as soon as he enters, falls under the atmosphere of the sick-room, his wildness drops from him and he looks at STILLWELL with pleading eyes.*)

STILLWELL. (*giving up getting him out again as hopeless, makes a gesture for him to be silent*) Ssshh! (*The NURSE looks at JOHN with shocked rebuke.* STILLWELL *motions* JOHN *to sit down. He does so meekly, sinking into the chair at right, center.* LOVING *stands behind the chair.* FATHER BAIRD, *after a look into the room to see if his help is needed, exchanges a helpless glance with* STILLWELL, *and then, turning back into the study but leaving the communicating door ajar, goes back as far as the table. There, after a moment's pause, he bows his head and begins praying silently to himself. In the bedroom,* STILLWELL *turns back to his patient. There is a pause of silent immobility in the room.* JOHN's *eyes are fixed on* ELSA's *face with a growing terror.* LOVING *stares over his head with cold, still eyes.*)

JOHN. (*in a low, tense voice—as if he were thinking aloud*) A fate in my story—the will of God! Something— (*He shudders.*)

LOVING. (*in the same low tone, but with a cold, driving intensity*) She will soon be dead.

JOHN. No!

LOVING. What will you do then? Love will be lost to you forever. You will be alone again. There will remain only the anguish of endless memories, endless regrets—a torturing remorse for murdered happiness!

JOHN. I know! For God's sake, don't make me think—

LOVING. (*coldly remorseless—sneeringly*) Do you think you can choose your stupid end in your story now, when you have to live it? —on to Hercules? But if you love her, how can you desire to go on— with all that was Elsa rotting in her grave behind you!

JOHN. (*torturedly*) No! I can't! I'll kill myself!

ELSA. (*suddenly moans frightenedly*) No, John! No!

LOVING. (*triumphantly*) Ah! At last you accept the true end! At last you see the empty posing of your old ideal about man's duty to go on for Life's sake, your meaningless gesture of braving fate—a childish nose-thumbing at Nothingness at which Something laughs with a weary scorn! (*He gives a low, scornful laugh*) Shorn of your boastful words, all it means is to go on like an animal in dumb obedience to the law of the blind stupidity of life that it must live at all costs! But where will you go—except to death? And why should you wait for an end you know when it is in your power to grasp that end—now!

ELSA. (*again moans frightenedly*) No, John—no!—please, John!

LOVING. Surely you cannot be afraid of death. Death is not the dying. Dying is life, its last revenge upon itself. But death is what the dead know, the warm, dark womb of Nothingness—the Dream in which you and Elsa may sleep as one forever, beyond fear of separation!

JOHN. (*longingly*) Elsa and I—forever beyond fear!

LOVING. Dust within dust to sleep!

JOHN. (*mechanically*) Dust within dust. (*Then frightenedly questioning*) Dust? (*A shudder runs over him and he starts as if awakening from sleep*) Fool! Can the dust love the dust? No! (*Desperately*) O God, have pity! Show me the way!

LOVING. (*furiously—as if he felt himself temporarily beaten*) Coward!

JOHN. If I could only pray! If I could only believe again!

LOVING. You cannot!

JOHN. A fate in my story, Uncle said—the will of God!—I went to the church—a fate in the church— (*He suddenly gets to his feet as if impelled by some force outside him. He stares before him with obsessed eyes*) Where I used to believe, where I used to pray!

LOVING. You insane fool! I tell you that's ended!

JOHN. If I could see the Cross again—

LOVING. (*with a shudder*) No! I don't want to see! I remember too well!—when Father and Mother—!

JOHN. Why are you so afraid of Him, if—

LOVING. (*shaken—then with fierce defiance*) Afraid? I who once cursed Him, who would again if— (*Then hurriedly catching himself*) But what superstitious nonsense you make me remember. He doesn't exist!

JOHN. (*takes a step toward the door*) I am going!

LOVING. (*tries to bar his path*) No!

JOHN. (*without touching him, makes a motion of pushing him aside*) I am going. (*He goes through the door to the study, moving like one in a trance, his eyes fixed straight before him.* LOVING *continues to try to bar his path, always without touching him.* FATHER BAIRD *looks up as they pass the table.*)

LOVING. (*in impotent rage*) No! You coward! (JOHN *goes out the door in rear of study and* LOVING *is forced out before him.*)

FATHER BAIRD. (*starting after him*) Jack! (*But he turns back in alarm as, in the bedroom,* ELSA *suddenly comes out of the half-coma she is in with a cry of terror and, in spite of* STILLWELL, *springs up to a half-sitting position in bed, her staring eyes on the doorway to the study.*)

ELSA. John! (*Then to* STILLWELL) Oh, please! Look after him! He might— John! Come back! I'll forgive!

STILLWELL. (*soothingly*) There, don't be frightened. He's only gone to lie down for a while. He's very tired. (FATHER BAIRD *has come in from the study and is approaching the bed.* STILLWELL, *with a significant look, calls on him for confirmation*) Isn't that right, Father?

FATHER BAIRD. Yes, Elsa.

ELSA. (*relieved*) Oh. (*She smiles faintly*) Poor John. I'm so sorry. Tell him he mustn't worry. I understand now. I love—I forgive. (*She sinks back and closes her eyes.* STILLWELL *reaches for her wrist in alarm, but as he feels her pulse his expression changes to one of excited surprise.*)

FATHER BAIRD. (*misreading his look—in a frightened whisper*) Merciful God! She isn't—?

STILLWELL. No. She's asleep. (*Then with suppressed excitement*) That's done it! She'll want to live now!

FATHER BAIRD. God be praised! (STILLWELL, *his air curtly professional again turns and whispers some orders to the* NURSE.)

CURTAIN

563

ACT FOUR—SCENE TWO

SCENE—*A section of the interior of an old church. A side wall runs diagonally back from left, front, two-thirds of the width of the stage, where it meets an end wall that extends back from right, front. The walls are old gray stone. In the middle of the side wall is a great Cross, its base about five feet from the floor, with a life-size figure of Christ, an exceptionally fine piece of wood carving. In the middle of the end wall is an arched doorway. On either side of this door, but high up in the wall, their bases above the level of the top of the doorway, are two narrow, stained-glass windows.*

It is a few minutes after the close of the preceding scene. The church is dim and empty and still. The only light is the reflection of the dawn, which, stained by the color in the windows, falls on the wall on and around the Cross.

The outer doors beyond the arched doorway are suddenly pushed open with a crash and JOHN *and* LOVING *appear in the doorway.* LOVING *comes first, retreating backward before* JOHN *whom he desperately, but always without touching him, endeavors to keep from entering the church. But* JOHN *is the stronger now and, the same look of obsessed resolution in his eyes, he forces* LOVING *back.*

LOVING. (*as they enter—desperately, as if he were becoming exhausted by the struggle*) You fool! There is nothing here but hatred!

JOHN. No! There was love! (*His eyes fasten themselves on the Cross and he gives a cry of hope*) The Cross!

LOVING. The symbol of hate and derision!

JOHN. No! Of love! (LOVING *is forced back until the back of his head is against the foot of the Cross.* JOHN *throws himself on his knees before it and raises his hands up to the figure of Christ in supplication*) Mercy! Forgive!

564

LOVING. (*raging*) Fool! Grovel on your knees! It is useless! To pray, one must believe!

JOHN. I have come back to Thee!

LOVING. Words! There is nothing!

JOHN. Let me believe in Thy love again!

LOVING. You cannot believe!

JOHN. (*imploringly*) O God of Love, hear my prayer!

LOVING. There is no God! There is only death!

JOHN. (*more weakly now*) Have pity on me! Let Elsa live!

LOVING. There is no pity! There is only scorn!

JOHN. Hear me while there is still time! (*He waits, staring at the Cross with anguished eyes, his arms outstretched. There is a pause of silence.*)

LOVING. (*with triumphant mockery*) Silence! But behind it I hear mocking laughter!

JOHN. (*agonized*) No! (*He gives way, his head bowed, and sobs heartbrokenly—then stops suddenly, and looking up at the Cross again, speaks sobbingly in a strange humble tone of broken reproach*) O Son of Man, I am Thou and Thou art I! Why hast Thou forsaken me? O Brother Who lived and loved and suffered and died with us, Who knoweth the tortured hearts of men, canst Thou not forgive—now—when I surrender all to Thee—when I have forgiven Thee—the love that Thou once took from me!

LOVING. (*with a cry of hatred*) No! Liar! I will never forgive!

JOHN. (*his eyes fixed on the face of the Crucified suddenly lighting up as if he now saw there the answer to his prayer—in a voice trembling with awakening hope and joy*) Ah! Thou hast heard me at last! Thou hast not forsaken me! Thou hast always loved me! I am forgiven! I can forgive myself—through Thee! I can believe!

LOVING. (*stumbles weakly from beneath the Cross*) No! I deny! (*He turns to face the Cross with a last defiance*) I defy Thee! Thou canst not conquer me! I hate Thee! I curse Thee!

JOHN. No! I bless! I love!

LOVING. (*as if this were a mortal blow, seems to sag and collapse—with a choking cry*) No!

JOHN. (*with a laugh that is half sob*) Yes! I see now! At last I see! I have always loved! O Lord of Love, forgive Thy poor blind fool!

LOVING. No! (*His legs crumple under him, he slumps to his knees beside* JOHN, *as if some invisible force crushed him down.*)

JOHN. (*his voice rising exultantly, his eyes on the face of the Crucified*) Thou art the Way—the Truth—the Resurrection and the Life, and he that believeth in Thy Love, his love shall never die!

LOVING. (*faintly, at last surrendering, addressing the Cross not without a final touch of pride in his humility*) Thou hast conquered, Lord. Thou art—the End. Forgive—the damned soul—of John Loving! (*He slumps forward to the floor and rolls over on his back, dead, his head beneath the foot of the Cross, his arms outflung so that his body forms another cross.* JOHN *rises from his knees and stands with arms stretched up and out, so that he, too, is like a cross. While this is happening the light of the dawn on the stained-glass windows swiftly rises to a brilliant intensity of crimson and green and gold, as if the sun had risen. The gray walls of the church, particularly the wall where the Cross is, and the face of the Christ shine with this radiance.*)

(JOHN LOVING—*he, who had been only* JOHN—*remains standing with his arms stretched up to the Cross, an expression of mystic exaltation on his face. The corpse of* LOVING *lies at the foot of the Cross, like a cured cripple's testimonial offering in a shrine.*)

(FATHER BAIRD *comes in hurriedly through the arched doorway. He stops on seeing* JOHN LOVING, *then comes quietly up beside him and stares searchingly into his face. At what he sees there he bows his head and his lips move in grateful prayer.* JOHN LOVING *is oblivious to his presence.*)

FATHER BAIRD. (*finally taps him gently on the shoulder*) Jack.

JOHN LOVING. (*still in his ecstatic mystic vision—strangely*) I am John Loving.

566

FATHER BAIRD. (*stares at him—gently*) It's all right now, Jack. Elsa will live.

JOHN LOVING. (*exaltedly*) I know! Love lives forever! Death is dead! Ssshh! Listen! Do you hear?

FATHER BAIRD. Hear what, Jack?

JOHN LOVING. Life laughs with God's love again! Life laughs with love!

CURTAIN

THE ICEMAN COMETH
(1939)

CHARACTERS

HARRY HOPE, *proprietor of a saloon and rooming house**

ED MOSHER, *Hope's brother-in-law, one-time circus man**

PAT MCGLOIN, *one-time Police Lieutenant**

WILLIE OBAN, *a Harvard Law School alumnus**

JOE MOTT, *one-time proprietor of a Negro gambling house**

PIET WETJOEN ("THE GENERAL"), *one-time leader of a Boer commando**

CECIL LEWIS ("THE CAPTAIN"), *one-time Captain of British infantry**

JAMES CAMERON ("JIMMY TOMORROW"), *one-time Boer war correspondent**

HUGO KALMAR, *one-time editor of Anarchist periodicals*

LARRY SLADE, *one-time Syndicalist-Anarchist**

ROCKY PIOGGI, *night bartender**

DON PARRITT*

PEARL*

MARGIE* } *street walkers*

CORA

CHUCK MORELLO, *day bartender**

THEODORE HICKMAN (HICKEY), *a hardware salesman*

MORAN

LIEB

* Roomers at Harry Hope's

SCENES

Harry Hope's is a Raines-Law hotel of the period, a cheap ginmill of the five-cent whiskey, last-resort variety situated on the downtown West Side of New York. The building, owned by Hope, is a narrow five-story structure of the tenement type, the second floor a flat occupied by the proprietor. The renting of rooms on the upper floors, under the Raines-Law loopholes, makes the establishment legally a hotel and gives it the privilege of serving liquor in the back room of the bar after closing hours and on Sundays, provided a meal is served with the booze, thus making a back room legally a hotel restaurant. This food provision was generally circumvented by putting a property sandwich in the middle of each table, an old desiccated ruin of dust-laden bread and mummified ham or cheese which only the drunkest yokel from the sticks ever regarded as anything but a noisome table decoration. But at Harry Hope's, Hope being a former minor Tammanyite and still possessing friends, this food technicality is ignored as irrelevant, except during the fleeting alarms of reform agitation. Even Hope's back room is not a separate room, but simply the rear of the barroom divided from the bar by drawing a dirty black curtain across the room.

THE ICEMAN COMETH

ACT ONE

Scene—*The back room and a section of the bar of* HARRY HOPE'S *saloon on an early morning in summer, 1912. the right wall of the back room is a dirty black curtain which separates it from the bar. At rear, this curtain is drawn back from the wall so the bartender can get in and out. The back room is crammed with round tables and chairs placed so close together that it is a difficult squeeze to pass between them. In the middle of the rear wall is a door opening on a hallway. In the left corner, built out into the room, is the toilet with a sign "This is it" on the door. Against the middle of the left wall is a nickel-in-the-slot phonograph. Two windows, so glazed with grime one cannot see through them, are in the left wall, looking out on a backyard. The walls and ceiling once were white, but it was a long time ago, and they are now so splotched, peeled, stained and dusty that their color can best be described as dirty. The floor, with iron spittoons placed here and there, is covered with sawdust. Lighting comes from single wall brackets, two at left and two at rear.*

There are three rows of tables, from front to back. Three are in the front line. The one at left-front has four chairs; the one at center-front, four; the one at right-front, five. At rear of, and half between, front tables one and two is a table of the second row with five chairs. A table, similarly placed at rear of front tables two and three, also has five chairs. The third row of tables, four chairs to one and six to the other, is against the rear wall on either side of the door.

At right of this dividing curtain is a section of the barroom, with the end of the bar seen at rear, a door to the hall at left of it. At front is a

573

table with four chairs. Light comes from the street windows off right, the gray subdued light of early morning in a narrow street. In the back room, LARRY SLADE and HUGO KALMAR are at the table at left-front, HUGO in a chair facing right, LARRY at rear of table facing front, with an empty chair between them. A fourth chair is at right of table, facing left. HUGO is a small man in his late fifties. He has a head much too big for his body, a high forehead, crinkly long black hair streaked with gray, a square face with a pug nose, a walrus mustache, black eyes which peer near-sightedly from behind thick-lensed spectacles, tiny hands and feet. He is dressed in threadbare black clothes and his white shirt is frayed at collar and cuffs, but everything about him is fastidiously clean. Even his flowing Windsor tie is neatly tied. There is a foreign atmosphere about him, the stamp of an alien radical, a strong resemblance to the type Anarchist as portrayed, bomb in hand, in newspaper cartoons. He is asleep now, bent forward in his chair, his arms folded on the table, his head resting sideways on his arms.

LARRY SLADE is sixty. He is tall, raw-boned, with coarse straight white hair, worn long and raggedly cut. He has a gaunt Irish face with a big nose, high cheekbones, a lantern jaw with a week's stubble of beard, a mystic's meditative pale-blue eyes with a gleam of sharp sardonic humor in them. As slovenly as HUGO is neat, his clothes are dirty and much slept in. His gray flannel shirt, open at the neck, has the appearance of having never been washed. From the way he methodically scratches himself with his long-fingered, hairy hands, he is lousy and reconciled to being so. He is the only occupant of the room who is not asleep. He stares in front of him, an expression of tired tolerance giving his face the quality of a pitying but weary old priest's.

All four chairs at the middle table, front, are occupied. JOE MOTT *sits at left-front of the table, facing front. Behind him, facing right-front, is* PIET WETJOEN *("The General"). At center of the table, rear,* JAMES CAMERON *("Jimmy Tomorrow") sits facing front. At right of table, opposite* JOE, *is* CECIL LEWIS *("The Captain").*

JOE MOTT *is a Negro, about fifty years old, brown-skinned, stocky, wearing a light suit that had once been flashily sporty but is now about to fall apart. His pointed tan buttoned shoes, faded pink shirt and bright tie belong to the same vintage. Still, he manages to preserve an atmosphere of nattiness and there is nothing dirty about his appearance. His face is only mildly negroid in type. The nose is thin and his lips are not noticeably thick. His hair is crinkly and he is beginning to get bald. A scar from a knife slash runs from his left cheek-bone to jaw. His face would be hard and tough if it were not for its good nature and lazy humor. He is asleep, his nodding head supported by his left hand.*

PIET WETJOEN, *the Boer, is in his fifties, a huge man with a bald head and a long grizzled beard. He is slovenly dressed in a dirty shapeless patched suit, spotted by food. A Dutch farmer type, his once great muscular strength has been debauched into flaccid tallow. But despite his blubbery mouth and sodden bloodshot blue eyes, there is still a suggestion of old authority lurking in him like a memory of the drowned. He is hunched forward, both elbows on the table, his hand on each side of his head for support.*

JAMES CAMERON *("Jimmy Tomorrow") is about the same size and age as* HUGO, *a small man. Like* HUGO, *he wears threadbare black, and everything about him is clean. But the resemblance ceases there.* JIMMY *has a face like an old well-bred, gentle bloodhound's, with folds of flesh hanging from each side of his mouth, and big brown friendly guileless eyes, more bloodshot than any bloodhound's ever were. He has mouse-colored thinning hair, a little bulbous nose, buck teeth in a small rabbit mouth. But his forehead is fine, his eyes are intelligent and there once was a competent ability in him. His speech is educated, with the ghost of a Scotch rhythm in it. His manners are those of a gentleman. There is a quality about him of a prim, Victorian old maid, and at the same time of a likable, affectionate boy who has never grown up. He sleeps, chin on chest, hands folded in his lap.*

CECIL LEWIS *("The Captain") is as obviously English as Yorkshire pudding and just as obviously the former army officer. He is going on sixty. His hair and military mustache are white, his eyes bright blue, his complexion that of a turkey. His lean figure is still erect and square-shouldered. He is stripped to the waist, his coat, shirt, undershirt, collar and tie crushed up into a pillow on the table in front of him, his head sideways on this pillow, facing front, his arms dangling toward the floor. On his lower left shoulder is the big ragged scar of an old wound.*

At the table at right, front, HARRY HOPE, *the proprietor, sits in the middle, facing front, with* PAT MCGLOIN *on his right and* ED MOSHER *on his left, the other two chairs being unoccupied.*

Both MCGLOIN *and* MOSHER *are big paunchy men.* MCGLOIN *has his old occupation of policeman stamped all over him. He is in his fifties, sandy-haired, bullet-headed, jowly, with protruding ears and little round eyes. His face must once have been brutal and greedy, but time and whiskey have melted it down into a good-humored, parasite's characterlessness. He wears old clothes and is slovenly. He is slumped sideways on his chair, his head drooping jerkily toward one shoulder.*

ED MOSHER *is going on sixty. He has a round kewpie's face—a kewpie who is an unshaven habitual drunkard. He looks like an enlarged, elderly, bald edition of the village fat boy—a sly fat boy, congenitally indolent, a practical joker, a born grafter and con merchant. But amusing and essentially harmless, even in his most enterprising days, because always too lazy to carry crookedness beyond petty swindling. The influence of his old circus career is apparent in his get-up. His worn clothes are flashy; he wears phony rings and a heavy brass watch-chain (not connected to a watch). Like* MCGLOIN, *he is slovenly. His head is thrown back, his big mouth open.*

HARRY HOPE *is sixty, white-haired, so thin the description "bag of bones" was made for him. He has the face of an old family horse, prone to tantrums, with balkiness always smoldering in its wall eyes, waiting for any excuse to shy and pretend to take the bit in its teeth.* HOPE *is one of those men whom everyone likes on sight, a softhearted slob, without malice, feeling superior to no one, a sinner among sinners, a born easy mark for every appeal. He attempts to hide his defenselessness behind a testy truculent manner, but this has never fooled anyone. He*

*is a little deaf, but not half as deaf as he sometimes pretends. His sight
is failing but is not as bad as he complains it is. He wears five-and-ten-
cent-store spectacles which are so out of alignment that one eye at times
peers half over one glass while the other eye looks half under the other.
He has badly fitting store teeth, which click like castanets when he begins to fume. He is dressed in an old coat from one suit and pants from
another.*

*In a chair facing right at the table in the second line, between the
first two tables, front, sits* WILLIE OBAN, *his head on his left arm outstretched along the table edge. He is in his late thirties, of average
height, thin. His haggard, dissipated face has a small nose, a pointed
chin, blue eyes with colorless lashes and brows. His blond hair, badly in
need of a cut, clings in a limp part to his skull. His eyelids flutter continually as if any light were too strong for his eyes. The clothes he wears
belong on a scarecrow. They seem constructed of an inferior grade of
dirty blotting paper. His shoes are even more disreputable, wrecks of
imitation leather, one laced with twine, the other with a bit of wire.
He has no socks, and his bare feet show through holes in the soles, with
his big toes sticking out of the uppers. He keeps muttering and twitching
in his sleep.*

As the curtain rises, ROCKY, *the night bartender, comes from the bar
through the curtain and stands looking over the back room. He is a
Neapolitan-American in his late twenties, squat and muscular, with a
flat, swarthy face and beady eyes. The sleeves of his collarless shirt are
rolled up on his thick, powerful arms and he wears a soiled apron. A
tough guy but sentimental, in his way, and good-natured. He signals
to* LARRY *with a cautious "Sstt" and motions him to see if* HOPE *is asleep.*
LARRY *rises from his chair to look at* HOPE *and nods to* ROCKY. ROCKY
*goes back in the bar but immediately returns with a bottle of bar whis-
key and a glass. He squeezes between the tables to* LARRY.

ROCKY. (*in a low voice out of the side of his mouth*) Make it fast.
(LARRY *pours a drink and gulps it down.* ROCKY *takes the bottle and puts*

577

it on the table where WILLIE OBAN *is*) Don't want de Boss to get wise when he's got one of his tightwad buns on. (*He chuckles with an amused glance at* HOPE) Jees, ain't de old bastard a riot when he starts dat bull about turnin' over a new leaf? "Not a damned drink on de house," he tells me, "and all dese bums got to pay up deir room rent. Beginnin' tomorrow," he says. Jees, yuh'd tink he meant it! (*He sits down in the chair at* LARRY's *left.*)

LARRY. (*grinning*) I'll be glad to pay up—tomorrow. And I know my fellow inmates will promise the same. They've all a touching credulity concerning tomorrows. (*A half-drunken mockery in his eyes*) It'll be a great day for them, tomorrow—the Feast of All Fools, with brass bands playing! Their ships will come in, loaded to the gunwales with cancelled regrets and promises fulfilled and clean slates and new leases!

ROCKY. (*cynically*) Yeah, and a ton of hop!

LARRY. (*leans toward him, a comical intensity in his low voice*) Don't mock the faith! Have you no respect for religion, you unregenerate Wop? What's it matter if the truth is that their favoring breeze has the stink of nickel whiskey on its breath, and their sea is a growler of lager and ale, and their ships are long since looted and scuttled and sunk on the bottom? To hell with the truth! As the history of the world proves, the truth has no bearing on anything. It's irrelevant and immaterial, as the lawyers say. The lie of a pipe dream is what gives life to the whole misbegotten mad lot of us, drunk or sober. And that's enough philosophic wisdom to give you for one drink of rot-gut.

ROCKY. (*grins kiddingly*) De old Foolosopher, like Hickey calls yuh, ain't yuh? I s'pose you don't fall for no pipe dream?

LARRY. (*a bit stiffly*) I don't, no. Mine are all dead and buried behind me. What's before me is the comforting fact that death is a fine long sleep, and I'm damned tired, and it can't come too soon for me.

ROCKY. Yeah, just hangin' around hopin' you'll croak, ain't yuh? Well, I'm bettin' you'll have a good long wait. Jees, somebody'll have to take an axe to croak you!

578

LARRY. (*grins*) Yes, it's my bad luck to be cursed with an iron constitution that even Harry's booze can't corrode.

ROCKY. De old anarchist wise guy dat knows all de answers! Dat's you, huh?

LARRY. (*frowns*) Forget the anarchist part of it. I'm through with the Movement long since. I saw men didn't want to be saved from themselves, for that would mean they'd have to give up greed, and they'll never pay that price for liberty. So I said to the world, God bless all here, and may the best man win and die of gluttony! And I took a seat in the grandstand of philosophical detachment to fall asleep observing the cannibals do their death dance. (*He chuckles at his own fancy— reaches over and shakes* HUGO's *shoulder*) Ain't I telling him the truth, Comrade Hugo?

ROCKY. Aw, fer Chris' sake, don't get dat bughouse bum started!

HUGO. (*raises his head and peers at* ROCKY *blearily through his thick spectacles—in a guttural declamatory tone*) Capitalist swine! Bourgeois stool pigeons! Have the slaves no right to sleep even? (*Then he grins at* ROCKY *and his manner changes to a giggling, wheedling playfulness, as though he were talking to a child*) Hello, leedle Rocky! Leedle monkey-face! Vere is your leedle slave girls? (*With an abrupt change to a bullying tone*) Don't be a fool! Loan me a dollar! Damned bourgeois Wop! The great Malatesta is my good friend! Buy me a trink! (*He seems to run down, and is overcome by drowsiness. His head sinks to the table again and he is at once fast asleep.*)

ROCKY. He's out again. (*More exasperated than angry*) He's lucky no one don't take his cracks serious or he'd wake up every mornin' in a hospital.

LARRY. (*regarding* HUGO *with pity*) No. No one takes him seriously. That's his epitaph. Not even the comrades any more. If I've been through with the Movement long since, it's been through with him, and, thanks to whiskey, he's the only one doesn't know it.

ROCKY. I've let him get by wid too much. He's goin' to pull dat slave-girl stuff on me once too often. (*His manner changes to defensive argu-*

ment) Hell, yuh'd tink I wuz a pimp or somethin'. Everybody knows me knows I ain't. A pimp don't hold no job. I'm a bartender. Dem tarts, Margie and Poil, dey're just a side line to pick up some extra dough. Strictly business, like dey was fighters and I was deir manager, see? I fix the cops fer dem so's dey can hustle widout gettin' pinched. Hell, dey'd be on de Island most of de time if it wasn't fer me. And I don't beat dem up like a pimp would. I treat dem fine. Dey like me. We're pals, see? What if I do take deir dough? Dey'd on'y trow it away. Tarts can't hang on to dough. But I'm a bartender and I work hard for my livin' in dis dump. You know dat, Larry.

LARRY. (*with inner sardonic amusement—flatteringly*) A shrewd business man, who doesn't miss any opportunity to get on in the world. That's what I'd call you.

ROCKY. (*pleased*) Sure ting. Dat's me. Grab another ball, Larry. (LARRY *pours a drink from the bottle on* WILLIE's *table and gulps it down.* ROCKY *glances around the room*) Yuh'd never tink all dese bums had a good bed upstairs to go to. Scared if dey hit the hay dey wouldn't be here when Hickey showed up, and dey'd miss a coupla drinks. Dat's what kept you up too, ain't it?

LARRY. It is. But not so much the hope of booze, if you can believe that. I've got the blues and Hickey's a great one to make a joke of everything and cheer you up.

ROCKY. Yeah, some kidder! Remember how he woiks up dat gag about his wife, when he's cockeyed, cryin' over her picture and den springin' it on yuh all of a sudden dat he left her in de hay wid de iceman? (*He laughs*) I wonder what's happened to him. Yuh could set your watch by his periodicals before dis. Always got here a coupla days before Harry's birthday party, and now he's on'y got till tonight to make it. I hope he shows soon. Dis dump is like de morgue wid all dese bums passed out. (WILLIE OBAN *jerks and twitches in his sleep and begins to mumble. They watch him.*)

WILLIE. (*blurts from his dream*) It's a lie! (*Miserably*) Papa! Papa!

580

LARRY. Poor devil. (*Then angry with himself*) But to hell with pity! It does no good. I'm through with it!

ROCKY. Dreamin' about his old man. From what de old-timers say, de old gent sure made a pile of dough in de bucket-shop game before de cops got him. (*He considers* WILLIE *frowningly*) Jees, I've seen him bad before but never dis bad. Look at dat get-up. Been playin' de old reliever game. Sold his suit and shoes at Solly's two days ago. Solly give him two bucks and a bum outfit. Yesterday he sells de bum one back to Solly for four bits and gets dese rags to put on. Now he's through. Dat's Solly's final edition he wouldn't take back for nuttin'. Willie sure is on de bottom. I ain't never seen no one so bad, except Hickey on de end of a coupla his bats.

LARRY. (*sardonically*) It's a great game, the pursuit of happiness.

ROCKY. Harry don't know what to do about him. He called up his old lady's lawyer like he always does when Willie gets licked. Yuh remember dey used to send down a private dick to give him the rush to a cure, but de lawyer tells Harry nix, de old lady's off of Willie for keeps dis time and he can go to hell.

LARRY. (*watches* WILLIE, *who is shaking in his sleep like an old dog*) There's the consolation that he hasn't far to go! (*As if replying to this,* WILLIE *comes to a crisis of jerks and moans.* LARRY *adds in a comically intense, crazy whisper*) Be God, he's knocking on the door right now!

WILLIE. (*suddenly yells in his nightmare*) It's a God-damned lie! (*He begins to sob*) Oh, Papa! Jesus! (*All the occupants of the room stir on their chairs but none of them wakes up except* HOPE.)

ROCKY. (*grabs his shoulder and shakes him*) Hey, you! Nix! Cut out de noise! (WILLIE *opens his eyes to stare around him with a bewildered horror.*)

HOPE. (*opens one eye to peer over his spectacles—drowsily*) Who's that yelling?

ROCKY. Willie, Boss. De Brooklyn boys is after him.

HOPE. (*querulously*) Well, why don't you give the poor feller a drink and keep him quiet? Bejees, can't I get a wink of sleep in my own back room?

ROCKY. (*indignantly to* LARRY) Listen to that blind-eyed deef old bastard, will yuh? He give me strict orders not to let Willie hang up no more drinks, no matter—

HOPE. (*mechancally puts a hand to his ear in the gesture of deafness*) What's that? I can't hear you (*Then drowsily irascible*) You're a cock-eyed liar. Never refused a drink to anyone needed it bad in my life! Told you to use your judgment. Ought to know better. You're too busy thinking up ways to cheat me. Oh, I ain't as blind as you think. I can still see a cash register, bejees!

ROCKY. (*grins at him affectionately now—flatteringly*) Sure, Boss. Swell chance of foolin' you!

HOPE. I'm wise to you and your sidekick, Chuck. Bejees, you're burg-lars, not barkeeps! Blind-eyed, deef old bastard, am I? Oh, I heard you! Heard you often when you didn't think. You and Chuck laughing be-hind my back, telling people you throw the money up in the air and whatever sticks to the ceiling is my share! A fine couple of crooks! You'd steal the pennies off your dead mother's eyes!

ROCKY. (*winks at* LARRY) Aw, Harry, me and Chuck was on'y kiddin'.

HOPE. (*more drowsily*) I'll fire both of you. Bejees, if you think you can play me for an easy mark, you've come to the wrong house. No one every played Harry Hope for a sucker!

ROCKY. (*to* LARRY) No one but everybody.

HOPE. (*his eyes shut again—mutters*) Least you could do—keep things quiet—(*He falls asleep.*)

WILLIE. (*pleadingly*) Give me a drink, Rocky. Harry said it was all right. God, I need a drink.

ROCKY. Den grab it. It's right under your nose.

WILLIE. (*avidly*) Thanks. (*He takes the bottle with both twitching hands and tilts it to his lips and gulps down the whiskey in big swallows.*)

ROCKY. (*sharply*) When! When! (*He grabs the bottle*) I didn't say, take a bath! (*Showing the bottle to* LARRY—*indignantly*) Jees, look! He's killed a half pint or more! (*He turns on* WILLIE *angrily, but* WILLIE *has closed his eyes and is sitting quietly, shuddering, waiting for the effect.*)

LARRY. (*with a pitying glance*) Leave him be, the poor devil. A half pint of that dynamite in one swig will fix him for a while—if it doesn't kill him.

ROCKY. (*shrugs his shoulders and sits down again*) Aw right by me. It ain't my booze. (*Behind him, in the chair at left of the middle table,* JOE MOTT, *the Negro, has been waking up.*)

JOE. (*his eyes blinking sleepily*) Whose booze? Gimme some. I don't care whose. Where's Hickey? Ain't he come yet? What time's it, Rocky?

ROCKY. Gettin' near time to open up. Time you begun to sweep up in de bar.

JOE. (*lazily*) Never mind de time. If Hickey ain't come, it's time Joe goes to sleep again. I was dreamin' Hickey come in de door, crackin' one of dem drummer's jokes, wavin' a big bankroll and we was all goin' be drunk for two weeks. Wake up and no luck. (*Suddenly his eyes open wide*) Wait a minute, dough. I got idea. Say, Larry, how 'bout dat young guy, Parritt, came to look you up last night and rented a room? Where's he at?

LARRY. Up in his room, asleep. No hope in him, anyway, Joe. He's broke.

JOE. Dat what he told you? Me and Rocky knows different. Had a roll when he paid you his room rent, didn't he, Rocky? I seen it.

ROCKY. Yeah. He flashed it like he forgot and den tried to hide it quick.

LARRY. (*surprised and resentful*) He did, did he?

ROCKY. Yeah, I figgered he don't belong, but he said he was a friend of yours.

LARRY. He's a liar. I wouldn't know him if he hadn't told me who he was. His mother and I were friends years ago on the Coast. (*He hesitates —then lowering his voice*) You've read in the papers about that bombing on the Coast when several people got killed? Well, the one

583

woman they pinched, Rosa Parritt, is his mother. They'll be coming up for trial soon, and there's no chance for them. She'll get life, I think. I'm telling you this so you'll know why if Don acts a bit queer, and not jump on him. He must be hard hit. He's her only kid.

ROCKY. (*nods—then thoughtfully*) Why ain't he out dere stickin' by her?

LARRY. (*frowns*) Don't ask questions. Maybe there's a good reason.

ROCKY. (*stares at him—understandingly*) Sure. I get it. (*Then wonderingly*) But den what kind of a sap is he to hang on to his right name?

LARRY. (*irritably*) I'm telling you I don't know anything and I don't want to know. To hell with the Movement and all connected with it! I'm out of it, and everything else, and damned glad to be.

ROCKY. (*shrugs his shoulders—indifferently*) Well, don't tink I'm interested in dis Parritt guy. He's nuttin' to me.

JOE. Me neider. If dere's one ting mor'n anudder I cares nuttin' about, it's de sucker game you and Hugo call de Movement. (*He chuckles—reminiscently*) Reminds me of damn fool argument me and Mose Porter has de udder night. He's drunk and I'm drunker. He says, "Socialist and Anarchist, we ought to shoot dem dead. Dey's all no-good sons of bitches." I says, "Hold on, you talk 's if Anarchists and Socialists was de same." "Dey is," he says. "Dey's both no-good bastards." "No, dey ain't," I says. "I'll explain the difference. De Anarchist he never works. He drinks but he never buys, and if he do ever get a nickel, he blows it in on bombs, and he wouldn't give you nothin'. So go ahead and shoot him. But de Socialist, sometimes, he's got a job, and if he gets ten bucks, he's bound by his religion to split fifty-fifty wid you. You say—how about my cut, Comrade? And you gets de five. So you don't shoot no Socialists while I'm around. Dat is, not if dey got anything. Of course, if dey's broke, den dey's no-good bastards, too." (*He laughs, immensely tickled.*)

LARRY. (*grins with sardonic appreciation*) Be God, Joe, you're got all the beauty of human nature and the practical wisdom of the world in that little parable.

ROCKY. (*winks at* JOE) Sure, Larry ain't de on'y wise guy in dis dump, hey, Joe? (*At a sound from the hall he turns as* DON PARRITT *appears in the doorway.* ROCKY *speaks to* LARRY *out of the side of his mouth*) Here's your guy. (PARRITT *comes forward. He is eighteen, tall and broad-shouldered but thin, gangling and awkward. His face is good-looking, with blond curly hair and large regular features, but his personality is unpleasant. There is a shifting defiance and ingratiation in his light-blue eyes and an irritating aggressiveness in his manner. His clothes and shoes are new, comparatively expensive, sporty in style. He looks as though he belonged in a pool room patronized by would-be sports. He glances around defensively, sees* LARRY *and comes forward.*)

PARRITT. Hello, Larry. (*He nods to* ROCKY *and* JOE) Hello. (*They nod and size him up with expressionless eyes.*)

LARRY. (*without cordiality*) What's up? I thought you'd be asleep.

PARRITT. Couldn't make it. I got sick of lying awake. Thought I might as well see if you were around.

LARRY. (*indicates the chair on the right of table*) Sit down and join the bums then. (PARRITT *sits down.* LARRY *adds meaningfully*) The rules of the house are that drinks may be served at all hours.

PARRITT. (*forcing a smile*) I get you. But, hell, I'm just about broke. (*He catches* ROCKY's *and* JOE's *contemptuous glances—quickly*) Oh, I know you guys saw— You think I've got a roll. Well, you're all wrong. I'll show you. (*He takes a small wad of dollar bills from his pocket*) It's all ones. And I've got to live on it till I get a job. (*Then with defensive truculence*) You think I fixed up a phony, don't you? Why the hell would I? Where would I get a real roll? You don't get rich doing what I've been doing. Ask LARRY. You're lucky in the Movement if you have enough to eat. (LARRY *regards him puzzledly.*)

ROCKY. (*coldly*) What's de song and dance about? We ain't said nuttin'.

PARRITT. (*lamely—placating them now*) Why, I was just putting you right. But I don't want you to think I'm a tightwad. I'll buy a drink if you want one.

JOE. (*cheering up*) If? Man, when I don't want a drink, you call de morgue, tell dem come take Joe's body away, 'cause he's sure enuf dead. Gimme de bottle quick, Rocky, before he changes his mind! (ROCKY *passes him the bottle and glass. He pours a brimful drink and tosses it down his throat, and hands the bottle and glass to* LARRY.)

ROCKY. I'll take a cigar when I go in de bar. What're you havin'?

PARRITT. Nothing. I'm on the wagon. What's the damage? (*He holds out a dollar bill.*)

ROCKY. Fifteen cents. (*He makes change from his pocket.*)

PARRITT. Must be some booze!

LARRY. It's cyanide cut with carbolic acid to give it a mellow flavor. Here's luck! (*He drinks.*)

ROCKY. Guess I'll get back in de bar and catch a coupla winks before opening-up time. (*He squeezes through the tables and disappears, right-rear, behind the curtain. In the section of bar at right, he comes forward and sits at the table and slumps back, closing his eyes and yawning.*)

JOE. (*stares calculatingly at* PARRITT *and then looks away—aloud to himself, philosophically*) One-drink guy. Dat well done run dry. No hope till Harry's birthday party. 'Less Hickey shows up. (*He turns to* LARRY) If Hickey comes, Larry, you wake me up if you has to bat me wid a chair. (*He settles himself and immediately falls asleep.*)

PARRITT. Who's Hickey?

LARRY. A hardware drummer. An old friend of Harry Hope's and all the gang. He's a grand guy. He comes here twice a year regularly on a periodical drunk and blows in all his money.

PARRITT. (*with a disparaging glance around*) Must be hard up for a place to hang out.

LARRY. It has its points for him. He never runs into anyone he knows in his business here.

PARRITT. (*lowering his voice*) Yes, that's what I want, too. I've got to stay under cover, Larry, like I told you last night.

586

LARRY. You did a lot of hinting. You didn't tell me anything.

PARRITT. You can guess, can't you? (*He changes the subject abruptly*) I've been in some dumps on the Coast, but this is the limit. What kind of joint is it, anyway?

LARRY. (*with a sardonic grin*) What is it? It's the No Chance Saloon. It's Bedrock Bar, The End of the Line Café, The Bottom of the Sea Rathskeller! Don't you notice the beautiful calm in the atmosphere? That's because it's the last harbor. No one here has to worry about where they're going next, because there is no farther they can go. It's a great comfort to them. Although even here they keep up the appearances of life with a few harmless pipe dreams about their yesterdays and tomorrows, as you'll see for yourself if you're here long.

PARRITT. (*stares at him curiously*) What's your pipe dream, Larry?

LARRY. (*hiding resentment*) Oh, I'm the exception. I haven't any left, thank God. (*Shortly*) Don't complain about this place. You couldn't find a better for lying low.

PARRITT. I'm glad of that, Larry. I don't feel any too damned good. I was knocked off my base by that business on the Coast, and since then it's been no fun dodging around the country, thinking every guy you see might be a dick.

LARRY. (*sympathetically now*) No, it wouldn't be. But you're safe here. The cops ignore this dump. They think it's as harmless as a graveyard. (*He grins sardonically*) And, be God, they're right.

PARRITT. It's been lonely as hell. (*Impulsively*) Christ, Larry, I was glad to find you. I kept saying to myself, "If I can only find Larry. He's the one guy in the world who can understand—" (*He hesitates, staring at* LARRY *with a strange appeal.*)

LARRY. (*watching him puzzledly*) Understand what?

PARRITT. (*hastily*) Why, all I've been through. (*Looking away*) Oh, I know you're thinking, This guy has a hell of a nerve. I haven't seen him since he was a kid. I'd forgotten he was alive. But I've never forgotten you, Larry. You were the only friend of Mother's who ever paid attention to me, or knew I was alive. All the others were too busy with the Movement. Even Mother. And I had no Old Man. You used to take me on your knee and tell me stories and crack jokes and make me laugh. You'd ask me questions and take what I said seriously. I guess I got to feel in the years you lived with us that you'd taken the place of my Old Man. (*Embarrassedly*) But, hell, that sounds like a lot of mush. I suppose you don't remember a damned thing about it.

LARRY. (*moved in spite of himself*) I remember well. You were a serious lonely little shaver. (*Then resenting being moved, changes the subject*) How is it they didn't pick you up when they got your mother and the rest?

PARRITT. (*in a lowered voice but eagerly, as if he wanted this chance to tell about it*) I wasn't around, and as soon as I heard the news I went under cover. You've noticed my glad rags. I was staked to them—as a disguise, sort of. I hung around pool rooms and gambling joints and hooker shops, where they'd never look for a Wobbly, pretending I was a sport. Anyway, they'd grabbed everyone important, so I suppose they didn't think of me until afterward.

LARRY. The papers say the cops got them all dead to rights, that the Burns dicks knew every move before it was made, and someone inside the Movement must have sold out and tipped them off.

PARRITT. (*turns to look* LARRY *in the eyes—slowly*) Yes, I guess that must be true, Larry. It hasn't come out who it was. It may never come out. I suppose whoever it was made a bargain with the Burns men to keep him out of it. They won't need his evidence.

LARRY. (*tensely*) By God, I hate to believe it of any of the crowd, if I am through long since with any connection with them. I know they're damned fools, most of them, as stupidly greedy for power as the worst capitalist they attack, but I'd swear there couldn't be a yellow stool pigeon among them.

PARRITT. Sure. I'd have sworn that, too, Larry.

LARRY. I hope his soul rots in hell, whoever it is!

PARRITT. Yes, so do I.

LARRY. (*after a pause—shortly*) How did you locate me? I hoped I'd found a place of retirement here where no one in the Movement would ever come to disturb my peace.

PARRITT. I found out through Mother.

LARRY. I asked her not to tell anyone.

PARRITT. She didn't tell me, but she'd kept all your letters and I found where she'd hidden them in the flat. I sneaked up there one night after she was arrested.

LARRY. I'd never have thought she was a woman who'd keep letters.

PARRITT. No, I wouldn't, either. There's nothing soft or sentimental about Mother.

LARRY. I never answered her last letters. I haven't written her in a couple of years—or anyone else. I've gotten beyond the desire to communicate with the world—or, what's more to the point, let it bother me any more with its greedy madness.

PARRITT. It's funny Mother kept in touch with you so long. When she's finished with anyone, she's finished. She's always been proud of that. And you know how she feels about the Movement. Like a revivalist preacher about religion. Anyone who loses faith in it is more than dead to her; he's a Judas who ought to be boiled in oil. Yet she seemed to forgive you.

LARRY. (sardonically) She didn't, don't worry. She wrote to denounce me and try to bring the sinner to repentance and a belief in the One True Faith again.

PARRITT. What made you leave the Movement, Larry? Was it on account of Mother?

LARRY. (starts) Don't be a damned fool! What the hell put that in your head?

PARRITT. Why, nothing—except I remember what a fight you had with her before you left.

LARRY. (resentfully) Well, if you do, I don't. That was eleven years ago. You were only seven. If we did quarrel, it was because I told her I'd become convinced the Movement was only a beautiful pipe dream.

PARRITT. (with a strange smile) I don't remember it that way.

LARRY. Then you can blame your imagination—and forget it. (*He changes the subject abruptly*) You asked me why I quit the Movement. I had a lot of good reasons. One was myself, and another was my comrades, and the last was the breed of swine called men in general. For myself, I was forced to admit, at the end of thirty years' devotion to the Cause, that I was never made for it. I was born condemned to be one of those who has to see all sides of a question. When you're damned like that, the questions multiply for you until in the end it's all question and no answer. As history proves, to be a worldly success at anything, especially revolution, you have to wear blinders like a horse and see only straight in front of you. You have to see, too, that this is all black, and that is all white. As for my comrades in the Great Cause, I felt as Horace Walpole did about England, that he could love it if it weren't for the people in it. The material the ideal free society must be constructed from is men themselves and you can't build a marble temple out of a mixture of mud and manure. When man's soul isn't a sow's ear, it will be time enough to dream of silk purses. (*He chuckles sardonically—then irritably as if suddenly provoked at himself for talking so much*) Well, that's why I quit the Movement, if it leaves you any wiser. At any rate, you see it had nothing to do with your mother.

PARRITT. (*smiles almost mockingly*) Oh, sure, I see. But I'll bet Mother has always thought it was on her account. You know her, Larry. To hear her go on sometimes, you'd think she was the Movement.

LARRY. (*stares at him, puzzled and repelled—sharply*) That's a hell of a way for you to talk, after what happened to her!

PARRITT. (*at once confused and guilty*) Don't get me wrong. I wasn't sneering, Larry. Only kidding. I've said the same thing to her lots of times to kid her. But you're right. I know I shouldn't now. I keep forgetting she's in jail. It doesn't seem real. I can't believe it about her. She's always been so free. I— But I don't want to think of it. (LARRY *is moved to a puzzled pity in spite of himself.* PARRITT *changes the subject*) What have you been doing all the years since you left—the Coast, Larry?

LARRY. (*sardonically*) Nothing I could help doing. If I don't believe in the Movement, I don't believe in anything else either, especially not the State. I've refused to become a useful member of its society. I've been a philosophical drunken bum, and proud of it. (*Abruptly his tone sharpens with resentful warning*) Listen to me. I hope you've deduced that I've my own reason for answering the impertinent questions of a stranger, for that's all you are to me. I have a strong hunch you've come here expecting something of me. I'm warning you, at the start, so there'll be no misunderstanding, that I've nothing left to give, and I want to be left alone, and I'll thank you to keep your life to yourself. I feel you're looking for some answer to something. I have no answer to give anyone, not even myself. Unless you can call what Heine wrote in his poem to morphine an answer. (*He quotes a translation of the closing couplet sardonically*)

"Lo, sleep is good; better is death; in sooth,
The best of all were never to be born."

PARRITT. (*shrinks a bit frightenedly*) That's the hell of an anwser. (*Then with a forced grin of bravado*) Still, you never know when it might come in handy. (*He looks away.* LARRY *stares at him puzzledly, interested in spite of himself and at the same time vaguely uneasy.*)

LARRY. (*forcing a casual tone*) I don't suppose you've had much chance to hear news of your mother since she's been in jail?

PARRITT. No. No chance. (*He hestitates—then blurts out*) Anyway, I don't think she wants to hear from me. We had a fight just before that business happened. She bawled me out because I was going around with tarts. That got my goat, coming from her. I told her, "You've always acted the free woman, you've never let anything stop you from—" (*He checks himself—goes on hurriedly*) That made her sore. She said she wouldn't give a damn what I did except she'd begun to suspect I was too interested in outside things and losing interest in the Movement.

LARRY. (*stares at him*) And were you?

PARRITT. (*hesitates—then with intensity*) Sure I was! I'm no damned fool! I couldn't go on believing forever that gang was going to change the world by shooting off their loud traps on soapboxes and sneaking around blowing up a lousy building or a bridge! I got wise it was all a crazy pipe dream! (*Appealingly*) The same as you did, Larry. That's why I came to you. I knew you'd understand. What finished me was this last business of someone selling out. How can you believe anything after a thing like that happens? It knocks you cold! You don't know what the hell is what! You're through! (*Appealingly*) You know how I feel, don't you, Larry? (LARRY *stares at him, moved by sympathy and pity in spite of himself, disturbed, and resentful at being disturbed, and puzzled by something he feels about* PARRITT *that isn't right. But before he can reply,* HUGO *suddenly raises his head from his arms in a half-awake alcoholic daze and speaks.*)

HUGO. (*quotes aloud to himself in a guttural declamatory style*) "The days grow hot, O Babylon! 'Tis cool beneath thy villow trees!" (PARRITT *turns startledly as* HUGO *peers muzzily without recognition at him.* HUGO *exclaims automatically in his tone of denunciation*) Gottammed stool pigeon!

PARRITT. (*shrinks away—stammers*) What? Who do you mean? (*Then furiously*) You lousy bum, you can't call me that! (*He draws back his fist.*)

HUGO. (*ignores this—recognizing him now, bursts into his childish teasing giggle*) Hello, leedle Don! Leedle monkey-face. I did not recognize you. You have grown big boy. How is your mother? Where you come from? (*He breaks into his wheedling, bullying tone*) Don't be a fool! Loan me a dollar! Buy me a trink! (*As if this exhausted him, he abruptly forgets it and plumps his head down on his arms again and is asleep.*)

PARRITT. (*with eager relief*) Sure, I'll buy you a drink, Hugo. I'm broke, but I can afford one for you. I'm sorry I got sore. I ought to have remembered when you're soused you call everyone a stool pigeon. But it's no damned joke right at this time. (*He turns to* LARRY, *who is regarding him now fixedly with an uneasy expression as if he suddenly were afraid of his own thoughts—forcing a smile*) Gee, he's passed out again. (*He stiffens defensively*) What are you giving me the hard look for? Oh, I know. You thought I was going to hit him? What do you think I am? I've always had a lot of respect for Hugo. I've always stood up for him when people in the Movement panned him for an old drunken has-been. He had the guts to serve ten years in the can in his own country and get his eyes ruined in solitary. I'd like to see some of them here stick that. Well, they'll get a chance now to show— (*Hastily*) I don't mean— But let's forget that. Tell me some more about this dump. Who are all these tanks? Who's that guy trying to catch pneumonia? (*He indicates* LEWIS.)

LARRY. (*stares at him almost frightenedly—then looks away and grasps eagerly this chance to change the subject. He begins to describe the sleepers with sardonic relish but at the same time showing his affection for them*) That's Captain Lewis, a one-time hero of the British Army. He strips to display that scar on his back he got from a native spear whenever he's completely plastered. The bewhiskered bloke opposite' him is General Wetjoen, who led a commando in the War. The two of them met when they came here to work in the Boer War spectacle at the St. Louis Fair and they've been bosom pals ever since. They dream the hours away in happy dispute over the brave days in South Africa when they tried to murder each other. The little guy between them was in it, too, as correspondent for some English paper. His nickname here is Jimmy Tomorrow. He's the leader of our Tomorrow Movement.

PARRITT. What do they do for a living?

LARRY. As little as possible. Once in a while one of them makes a successful touch somewhere, and some of them get a few dollars a month from connections at home who pay it on condition they never come back. For the rest, they live on free lunch and their old friend, Harry

593

Hope, who doesn't give a damn what anyone does or doesn't do, as long as he likes you.

PARRITT. It must be a tough life.

LARRY. It's not. Don't waste your pity. They wouldn't thank you for it. They manage to get drunk, by hook or crook, and keep their pipe dreams, and that's all they ask of life. I've never known more contented men. It isn't often that men attain the true goal of their heart's desire. The same applies to Harry himself and his two cronies at the far table. He's so satisfied with life he's never set foot out of this place since his wife died twenty years ago. He has no need of the outside world at all. This place has a fine trade from the Market people across the street and the waterfront workers, so in spite of Harry's thirst and his generous heart, he comes out even. He never worries in hard times because there's always old friends from the days when he was a jitney Tammany politician, and a friendly brewery to tide him over. Don't ask me what his two pals work at because they don't. Except at being his lifetime guests. The one facing this way is his brother-in-law, Ed Mosher, who once worked for a circus in the ticket wagon. Pat McGloin, the other one, was a police lieutenant back in the flush times of graft when everything went. But he got too greedy and when the usual reform investigation came he was caught red-handed and thrown off the Force. (*He nods at* JOE) Joe here has a yesterday in the same flush period. He ran a colored gambling house then and was a hell of a sport, so they say. Well, that's our whole family circle of inmates, except the two barkeeps and their girls, three ladies of the pavement that room on the third floor.

PARRITT. (*bitterly*) To hell with them! I never want to see a whore again! (*As* LARRY *flashes him a puzzled glance, he adds confusedly*) I mean, they always get you in dutch. (*While he is speaking* WILLIE OBAN *has opened his eyes. He leans toward them, drunk now from the effect of the huge drink he took, and speaks with a mocking suavity.*)

WILLIE. Why omit me from your Who's Who in Dypsomania, Larry? An unpardonable slight, especially as I am the only inmate of royal blood. (*To* PARRITT—*ramblingly*) Educated at Harvard, too. You must

have noticed the atmosphere of culture here. My humble contribution.
Yes, Generous Stranger—I trust you're generous—I was born in the
purple, the son, but unfortunately not the heir, of the late world-famous
Bill Oban, King of the Bucket Shops. A revolution deposed him, con-
ducted by the District Attorney. He was sent into exile. In fact, not to
mince matters, they locked him in the can and threw away the key.
Alas, his was an adventurous spirit that pined in confinement. And so he
died. Forgive these reminiscences. Undoubtedly all this is well known to
you. Everyone in the world knows.

PARRITT. (*uncomfortably*) Tough luck. No, I never heard of him.

WILLIE. (*blinks at him incredulously*) Never heard? I thought everyone in the world— Why, even at Harvard I discovered my father was
well known by reputation, although that was some time before the District Attorney gave him so much unwelcome publicity. Yes, even as a
freshman I was notorious. I was accepted socially with all the warm
cordiality that Henry Wadsworth Longfellow would have shown a
drunken Negress dancing the can can at high noon on Brattle Street.
Harvard was my father's idea. He was an ambitious man. Dictatorial,
too. Always knowing what was best for me. But I did make myself a
brilliant student. A dirty trick on my classmates, inspired by revenge, I
fear. (*He quotes*) "Dear college days, with pleasure rife! The grandest
gladdest days of life!" But, of course, that is a Yale hymn, and they're
given to rah-rah exaggeration at New Haven. I was a brilliant student at
Law School, too. My father wanted a lawyer in the family. He was a
calculating man. A thorough knowledge of the law close at hand in the
house to help him find fresh ways to evade it. But I discovered the
loophole of whiskey and escaped his jurisdiction. (*Abruptly to* PARRITT)
Speaking of whiskey, sir, reminds me—and, I hope, reminds you—
that when meeting a Prince the customary salutation is "What'll you
have?"

PARRITT. (*with defensive resentment*) Nix! All you guys seem to
think I'm made of dough. Where would I get the coin to blow everyone?

WILLIE. (*sceptically*) Broke? You haven't the thirsty look of the impecunious. I'd judge you to be a plutocrat, your pockets stuffed with ill-gotten gains. Two or three dollars, at least. And don't think we will question how you got it. As Vespasian remarked, the smell of all whiskey is sweet.

PARRITT. What do you mean, how I got it? (*To* LARRY, *forcing a laugh*) It's a laugh, calling me a plutocrat, isn't it, Larry, when I've been in the Movement all my life. (LARRY *gives him an uneasy suspicious glance, then looks away, as if avoiding something he does not wish to see.*)

WILLIE. (*disgustedly*) Ah, one of those, eh? I believe you now, all right! Go away and blow yourself up, that's a good lad. Hugo is the only licensed preacher of that gospel here. A dangerous terrorist, Hugo! He would as soon blow the collar off a schooner of beer as look at you! (*To* LARRY) Let us ignore this useless youth, Larry. Let us join in prayer that Hickey, the Great Salesman, will soon arrive bringing the blessed bourgeois long green! Would that Hickey or Death would come! Meanwhile, I will sing a song. A beautiful Old New England folk ballad which I picked up at Harvard amid the debris of education. (*He sings in a boisterous baritone, rapping on the table with his knuckles at the indicated spots in the song:*)

> "Jack, oh, Jack, was a sailor lad
> And he came to a tavern for gin.
> He rapped and he rapped with a (*Rap, rap, rap*)
> But never a soul seemed in."

(*The drunks at the tables stir.* ROCKY *gets up from his chair in the bar and starts back for the entrance to the back room.* HOPE *cocks one irritable eye over his specs.* JOE MOTT *opens both of his and grins.* WILLIE *interposes some drunken whimsical exposition to* LARRY) The origin of this beautiful ditty is veiled in mystery, Larry. There was a legend bruited about in Cambridge lavatories that Waldo Emerson composed it during his uninformative period as a minister, while he was trying to write a sermon. But my own opinion is, it goes back much further, and Jonathan Edwards was the author of both words and music. (*He sings:*)

> "He rapped and rapped, and tapped and tapped
> Enough to wake the dead
> Till he heard a damsel (*Rap, rap, rap*)
> On a window right over his head."

(*The drunks are blinking their eyes now, grumbling and cursing.* ROCKY *appears from the bar at rear, right, yawning.*)

HOPE. (*with fuming irritation*) Rocky! Bejees, can't you keep that crazy bastard quiet? (ROCKY *starts for* WILLIE.)

WILLIE. And now the influence of a good woman enters our mariner's life. Well, perhaps "good" isn't the word. But very, very kind. (*He sings:*)

> "Oh, come up," she cried, "my sailor lad,
> And you and I'll agree,
> And I'll show you the prettiest (*Rap, rap, rap*)
> That ever you did see."

(*He speaks*) You see, Larry? The lewd Puritan touch, obviously, and it grows more marked as we go on. (*He sings:*)

> "Oh, he put his arm around her waist,
> He gazed in her bright blue eyes
> And then he—"

(*But here* ROCKY *shakes him roughly by the shoulder.*)

ROCKY. Piano! What d'yuh tink dis dump is, a dump?

HOPE. Give him the bum's rush upstairs! Lock him in his room!

ROCKY. (*yanks* WILLIE *by the arm*) Come on, Bum.

WILLIE. (*dissolves into pitiable terror*) No! Please, Rocky! I'll go crazy

597

up in that room alone! It's haunted! I— (*He calls to* HOPE) Please, Harry! Let me stay here! I'll be quiet!

HOPE. (*immediately relents—indignantly*) What the hell you doing to him, Rocky? I didn't tell you to beat up the poor guy. Leave him alone, long as he's quiet. (ROCKY *lets go of* WILLIE *disgustedly and goes back to his chair in the bar.*)

WILLIE. (*huskily*) Thanks, Harry. You're a good scout. (*He closes his eyes and sinks back in his chair exhaustedly, twitching and quivering again.*)

HOPE. (*addressing* MCGLOIN *and* MOSHER, *who are sleepily awake— accusingly*) Always the way. Can't trust nobody. Leave it to that Dago to keep order and it's like bedlam in a cathouse, singing and everything. And you two big barflies are a hell of a help to me, ain't you? Eat and sleep and get drunk! All you're good for, bejees! Well, you can take that "I'll-have-the-same" look off your maps! There ain't going to be no more drinks on the house till hell freezes over! (*Neither of the two is impressed either by his insults or his threats. They grin hangover grins of tolerant affection at him and wink at each other.* HARRY *fumes*) Yeah, grin! Wink, bejees! Fine pair of sons of bitches to have glued on me for life! (*But he can't get a rise out of them and he subsides into a fuming mumble. Meanwhile, at the middle table,* CAPTAIN LEWIS *and* GENERAL WETJOEN *are as wide awake as heavy hangovers permit.* JIMMY TO-MORROW *nods, his eyes blinking.* LEWIS *is gazing across the table at* JOE MOTT, *who is still chuckling to himself over* WILLIE's *song. The expression on* LEWIS's *face is that of one who can't believe his eyes.*)

LEWIS. (*aloud to himself, with a muzzy wonder*) Good God! Have I been drinking at the same table with a bloody Kaffir?

JOE. (*grinning*) Hello, Captain. You comin' up for air? Kaffir? Who's he?

WETJOEN. (*blurrily*) Kaffir, dot's a nigger, Joe. (JOE *stiffens and his eyes narrow.* WETJOEN *goes on with heavy jocosity*) Dot's joke on him, Joe. He don't know you. He's still plind drunk, the ploody Limey chentleman! A great mistake I missed him at the pattle of Modder

River. Vit mine rifle I shoot damn fool Limey officers py the dozen, but him I miss. De pity of it! (*He chuckles and slaps* LEWIS *on his bare shoulder*) Hey, wake up, Cecil, you ploody fool! Don't you know your old friend, Joe? He's no damned Kaffir! He's white, Joe is!

LEWIS. (*light dawning—contritely*) My profound apologies, Joseph, old chum. Eyesight a trifle blurry, I'm afraid. Whitest colored man I ever knew. Proud to call you my friend. No hard feelings, what? (*He holds out his hand.*)

JOE. (*at once grins good-naturedly and shakes his hand*) No, Captain, I know it's mistake. Youse regular, if you is a Limey. (*Then his face hardening*) But I don't stand for "nigger" from nobody. Never did. In de old days, people calls me "nigger" wakes up in de hospital. I was de leader ob de Dirty Half-Dozen Gang. All six of us colored boys, we was tough and I was de toughest.

WETJOEN. (*inspired to boastful reminiscence*) Me, in old days in Transvaal, I vas so tough and strong I grab axle of ox wagon mit full load and lift like feather.

LEWIS. (*smiling amiably*) As for you, my balmy Boer that walks like a man, I say again it was a grave error in our foreign policy ever to set you free, once we nabbed you and your commando with Cronje. We should have taken you to the London zoo and incarcerated you in the baboons' cage. With a sign: "Spectators may distinguish the true baboon by his blue behind."

WETJOEN. (*grins*) Gott! To dink, ten better Limey officers, at least, I shoot clean in the mittle of forehead at Spion Kopje, and you I miss! I neffer forgive myself! (JIMMY TOMORROW *blinks benignantly from one to the other with a gentle drunken smile.*)

JIMMY. (*sentimentally*) Now, come, Cecil, Piet! We must forget the War. Boer and Briton, each fought fairly and played the game till the better man won and then we shook hands. We are all brothers within the Empire united beneath the flag on which the sun never sets. (*Tears come to his eyes. He quotes with great sentiment, if with slight application*) "Ship me somewhere east of Suez—"

LARRY. (*breaks in sardonically*) Be God, you're there already, Jimmy. Worst is best here, and East is West, and tomorrow is yesterday. What more do you want?

JIMMY. (*with bleery benevolence, shaking his head in mild rebuke*) No, Larry, old friend, you can't deceive me. You pretend a bitter, cynic philosophy, but in your heart you are the kindest man among us.

LARRY. (*disconcerted—irritably*) The hell you say!

PARRITT. (*leans toward him—confidentially*) What a bunch of cuckoos!

JIMMY. (*as if reminded of something—with a pathetic attempt at a brisk, no-more-nonsense air*) Tomorrow, yes. It's high time I straightened out and got down to business again. (*He brushes his sleeve fastidiously*) I must have this suit cleaned and pressed. I can't look like a tramp when I—

JOE. (*who has been brooding—interrupts*) Yes, suh, white folks always said I was white. In de days when I was flush, Joe Mott's de only colored man dey allows in de white gamblin' houses. "You're all right, Joe, you're white," dey says. (*He chuckles*) Wouldn't let me play craps, dough. Dey know I could make dem dice behave. "Any odder game and any limit you like, Joe," dey says. Man, de money I lost! (*He chuckles—then with an underlying defensiveness*) Look at de Big Chief in dem days. He knew I was white. I'd saved my dough so I could start my own gamblin' house. Folks in de know tells me, see de man at de top, den you never has trouble. You git Harry Hope give you a letter to de Chief. And Harry does. Don't you, Harry?

HOPE. (*preoccupied with his own thoughts*) Eh? Sure. Big Bill was a good friend of mine. I had plenty of friends high up in those days. Still could have if I wanted to go out and see them. Sure, I gave you a letter. I said you was white. What the hell of it?

JOE. (*to CAPTAIN LEWIS who has relapsed into a sleepy daze and is listening to him with an absurd strained attention without comprehending a word*) Dere. You see, Captain. I went to see de Chief, shakin' in my boots, and dere he is sittin' behind a big desk, lookin' as big as a freight train. He don't look up. He keeps me waitin' and waitin', and after 'bout an hour, seems like to me, he says slow and quiet like dere wasn't no harm in him, "You want to open a gamblin' joint, does you, Joe?" But he don't give me no time to answer. He jumps up, lookin' as big as two freight trains, and he pounds his fist like a ham on de desk, and he shouts, "You black son of a bitch, Harry says you're white and you better be white or dere's a little iron room up de river waitin' for you!" Den he sits down and says quiet again, "All right. You can open. Git de hell outa here!" So I opens, and he finds out I'se white, sure 'nuff, 'cause I run wide open for years and pays my sugar on de dot, and de cops and I is friends. (*He chuckles with pride*) Dem old days! Many's de night I come in here. Dis was a first-class hangout for sports in dem days. Good whiskey, fifteen cents, two for two bits. I t'rows down a fifty-dollar bill like it was trash paper and says, "Drink it up, boys, I don't want no change." Ain't dat right, Harry?

HOPE. (*caustically*) Yes, and bejees, if I ever seen you throw fifty cents on the bar now, I'd know I had delirium tremens! You've told that story ten million times and if I have to hear it again, that'll give me D.T.s anyway!

JOE. (*chuckling*) Gittin' drunk every day for twenty years ain't give you de Brooklyn boys. You needn't be scared of me!

LEWIS. (*suddenly turns and beams on* HOPE) Thank you, Harry, old chum. I will have a drink, now you mention it, seeing it's so near your birthday. (*The others laugh.*)

HOPE. (*puts his hand to his ear—angrily*) What's that? I can't hear you.

LEWIS. (*sadly*) No, I fancied you wouldn't.

HOPE. I don't have to hear, bejees! Booze is the only thing you ever talk about!

LEWIS. (*sadly*) True. Yet there was a time when my conversation was more comprehensive. But as I became burdened with years, it seemed rather pointless to discuss my other subject.

HOPE. You can't joke with me! How much room rent do you owe me, tell me that?

LEWIS. Sorry. Adding has always baffled me. Subtraction is my forte.

HOPE. (*snarling*) Arrh! Think you're funny! Captain, bejees! Showing off your wounds! Put on your clothes, for Christ's sake! This ain't no Turkish bath! Lousy Limey army! Took 'em years to lick a gang of Dutch hayseeds!

WETJOEN. Dot's right, Harry. Gif him hell!

HOPE. No lip out of you, neither, you Dutch spinach! General, hell! Salvation Army, that's what you'd ought t'been General in! Bragging what a shot you were, and, bejees, you missed him! And he missed you, that's just as bad! And now the two of you bum on me! (*Threateningly*) But you've broke the camel's back this time, bejees! You pay up tomorrow or out you go!

LEWIS. (*earnestly*) My dear fellow, I give you my word of honor as an officer and a gentleman, you shall be paid tomorrow.

WETJOEN. Ve swear it, Harry! Tomorrow vidout fail!

MCGLOIN. (*a twinkle in his eye*) There you are, Harry. Sure, what could be fairer?

MOSHER. (*with a wink at* MCGLOIN) Yes, you can't ask more than that, Harry. A promise is a promise—as I've often discovered.

HOPE. (*turns on them*) I mean the both of you, too! An old grafting flatfoot and a circus bunco steerer! Fine company for me, bejees! Couple of con men living in my flat since Christ knows when! Getting fat as hogs, too! And you ain't even got the decency to get me upstairs where I got a good bed! Let me sleep on a chair like a bum! Kept me down here waitin' for Hickey to show up, hoping I'd blow you to more drinks!

MCGLOIN. Ed and I did our damnedest to get you up, didn't we, Ed?

MOSHER. We did, But you said you couldn't bear the flat because it was one of those nights when memory brought poor old Bessie back to you.

HOPE. (*his face instantly becoming long and sad and sentimental— mournfully*) Yes, that's right, boys. I remember now. I could almost see her in every room just as she used to be—and it's twenty years since she— (*His throat and eyes fill up. A suitable sentimental hush falls on the room.*)

LARRY. (*in a sardonic whisper to* PARRITT) Isn't a pipe dream of yesterday a touching thing? By all accounts, Bessie nagged the hell out of him.

JIMMY. (*who has been dreaming, a look of prim resolution on his face, speaks aloud to himself*) No more of this sitting around and loafing. Time I took hold of myself. I must have my shoes soled and heeled and shined first thing tomorrow morning. A general spruce-up. I want to have a well-groomed appearance when I— (*His voice fades out as he stares in front of him. No one pays any attention to him except* LARRY *and* PARRITT.)

LARRY. (*as before, in a sardonic aside to* PARRITT) The tomorrow movement is a sad and beautiful thing, too!

MCGLOIN. (*with a huge sentimental sigh—and a calculating look at* HOPE) Poor old Bessie! You don't find her like in these days. A sweeter woman never drew breath.

MOSIIER. (*in a similar calculating mood*) Good old Bess. A man couldn't want a better sister than she was to me.

HOPE. (*mournfully*) Twenty years, and I've never set foot out of this house since the day I buried her. Didn't have the heart. Once she'd gone, I didn't give a damn for anything. I lost all my ambition. Without her, nothing seemed worth the trouble. You remember, Ed, you, too, Mac—the boys was going to nominate me for Alderman. It was all fixed. Bessie wanted it and she was so proud. But when she was taken, I told them, "No, boys, I can't do it. I simply haven't the heart. I'm through." I would have won the election easy, too. (*He says this a bit defiantly*) Oh, I know there was jealous wise guys said the boys was giving me the nomination because they knew they couldn't win that year in this ward. But that's a damned lie! I knew every man, woman and child in the ward, almost. Bessie made me make friends with everyone, helped me remember all their names. I'd have been elected easy.

MCGLOIN. You would, Harry. It was a sure thing.

MOSHER. A dead cinch, Harry. Everyone knows that.

HOPE. Sure they do. But after Bessie died, I didn't have the heart. Still, I know while she'd appreciate my grief, she wouldn't want it to keep me cooped up in here all my life. So I've made up my mind I'll go out soon. Take a walk around the ward, see all the friends I used to know, get together with the boys and maybe tell 'em I'll let 'em deal me a hand in their game again. Yes, bejees, I'll do it. My birthday, to-morrow, that'd be the right time to turn over a new leaf. Sixty. That ain't too old.

MCGLOIN. (*flatteringly*) It's the prime of life, Harry.

MOSHER. Wonderful thing about you, Harry, you keep young as you ever was.

JIMMY. (*dreaming aloud again*) Get my things from the laundry. They must still have them. Clean collar and shirt. If I wash the ones I've got on any more, they'll fall apart. Socks, too. I want to make a good appearance. I met Dick Trumbull on the street a year or two ago. He said, "Jimmy, the publicity department's never been the same since you got—resigned. It's dead as hell." I said, "I know. I've heard rumors the management were at their wits' end and would be only too glad to have me run it for them again. I think all I'd have to do would be go and see them and they'd offer me the position. Don't you think so, Dick?" He said, "Sure, they would, Jimmy. Only take my advice and wait a while until business conditions are better. Then you can strike them for a bigger salary than you got before, do you see?" I said, "Yes, I do see, Dick, and many thanks for the tip." Well, conditions must be better by this time. All I have to do is get fixed up with a decent front tomorrow, and it's as good as done.

HOPE. (*glances at* JIMMY *with a condescending affectionate pity—in a hushed voice*) Poor Jimmy's off on his pipe dream again. Bejees, he takes the cake! (*This is too much for* LARRY. *He cannot restrain a sardonic guffaw. But no one pays any attention to him.*)

LEWIS. (*opens his eyes, which are drowsing again—dreamily to* WET-

JOEN) I'm sorry we had to postpone our trip again this April, Piet. I hoped the blasted old estate would be settled up by then. The damned lawyers can't hold up the settlement much longer. We'll make it next year, even if we have to work and earn our passage money, eh? You'll stay with me at the old place as long as you like, then you can take the *Union Castle* from Southampton to Cape Town. (*Sentimentally, with real yearning*) England in April. I want you to see that, Piet. The old veldt has its points, I'll admit, but it isn't home—especially home in April.

WETJOEN. (*blinks drowsily at him—dreamily*) Ja, Cecil, I know how beautiful it must be, from all you tell me many times. I vill enjoy it. But I shall enjoy more ven I am home, too. The veldt, ja! You could put England on it, and it would look like a farmer's small garden. Py Gott, there is space to be free, the air like vine is, you don't need booze to be drunk! My relations vill so surprised be. They vill not know me, it is so many years. Dey vill be so glad I haf come home at last.

JOE. (*dreamily*) I'll make my stake and get my new gamblin' house open before you boys leave. You got to come to de openin'. I'll treat you white. If you're broke, I'll stake you to buck any game you chooses. If you wins, dat's velvet for you. If you loses, it don't count. Can't treat you no whiter dan dat, can I?

HOPE. (*again with condescending pity*) Bejees, Jimmy's started them off smoking the same hop. (*But the three are finished, their eyes closed again in sleep or a drowse.*)

LARRY. (*aloud to himself—in his comically tense, crazy whisper*) Be God, this bughouse will drive me stark, raving loony yet!

HOPE. (*turns on him with fuming suspicion*) What? What d'you say?

LARRY. (*placatingly*) Nothing, Harry. I had a crazy thought in my head.

HOPE. (*irascibly*) Crazy is right! Yah! The old wise guy! Wise, hell! A damned old fool Anarchist I-Won't-Worker! I'm sick of you and Hugo, too. Bejees, you'll pay up tomorrow, or I'll start a Harry Hope

Revolution! I'll tie a dispossess bomb to your tails that'll blow you out in the street! Bejees, I'll make your Movement move! (*The witticism delights him and he bursts into a shrill cackle. At once* MCGLOIN *and* MOSHER *guffaw enthusiastically.*)

MOSHER. (*flatteringly*) Harry, you sure say the funniest things! (*He reaches on the table as if he expected a glass to be there—then starts with well-acted surprise*) Hell, where's my drink? That Rocky is too damned fast cleaning tables. Why, I'd only taken one sip of it.

HOPE. (*his smiling face congealing*) No, you don't! (*Acidly*) Any time you only take one sip of a drink, you'll have lockjaw and paralysis! Think you can kid me with those old circus con games?—me, that's known you since you was knee-high, and, bejees, you was a crook even then!

MCGLOIN. (*grinning*) It's not like you to be so hard-hearted, Harry. Sure, it's hot, parching work laughing at your jokes so early in the morning on an empty stomach!

HOPE. Yah! You, Mac! Another crook! Who asked you to laugh? We was talking about poor old Bessie, and you and her no-good brother start to laugh! A hell of a thing! Talking mush about her, too! "Good old Bess." Bejees, she'd never forgive me if she knew I had you two bums living in her flat, throwing ashes and cigar butts on her carpet. You know her opinion of you, Mac. "That Pat McGloin is the biggest drunken grafter that ever disgraced the police force," she used to say to me. "I hope they send him to Sing Sing for life."

MCGLOIN. (*unperturbed*) She didn't mean it. She was angry at me because you used to get me drunk. But Bess had a heart of gold underneath her sharpness. She knew I was innocent of all the charges.

WILLIE. (*jumps to his feet drunkenly and points a finger at* MCGLOIN *—imitating the manner of a cross-examiner—coldly*) One moment, please. Lieutenant McGloin! Are you aware you are under oath? Do you realize what the penalty for perjury is? (*Purringly*) Come now, Lieutenant, isn't it a fact that you're as guilty as hell? No, don't say, "How about your old man?" I am asking the questions. The fact that he was a crooked old bucket-shop bastard has no bearing on your case. (*With a change to maudlin joviality*) Gentlemen of the Jury, court will now recess while the D.A. sings out a little ditty he learned at Harvard. It was composed in a wanton moment by the Dean of the Divinity School on a moonlight night in July, 1776, while sobering up in a Turkish bath. (*He sings:*)

"Oh, come up," she cried, "my sailor lad,
And you and I'll agree.
And I'll show you the prettiest (*Rap, rap, rap on table*)
That ever you did see."

(*Suddenly he catches* HOPE's *eyes fixed on him condemningly, and sees* ROCKY *appearing from the bar. He collapses back on his chair, pleading miserably*) Please, Harry! I'll be quiet! Don't make Rocky bounce me upstairs! I'll go crazy alone! (*To* MCGLOIN) I apologize, Mac. Don't get sore. I was only kidding you. (ROCKY, *at a relenting glance from* HOPE, *returns to the bar.*)

MCGLOIN (*good-naturedly*) Sure, kid all you like, Willie. I'm hardened to it. (*He pauses—seriously*) But I'm telling you some day before long I'm going to make them reopen my case. Everyone knows there was no real evidence against me, and I took the fall for the ones higher up. I'll be found innocent this time and reinstated. (*Wistfully*) I'd like to have my old job on the Force back. The boys tell me there's fine pickings these days, and I'm not getting rich here, sitting with a parched throat waiting for Harry Hope to buy a drink. (*He glances reproachfully at* HOPE.)

WILLIE. Of course, you'll be reinstated, Mac. All you need is a brilliant young attorney to handle your case. I'll be straightened out and on the wagon in a day or two. I've never practiced but I was one of the most brilliant students in Law School, and your case is just the opportunity I need to start. (*Darkly*) Don't worry about my not forcing the D.A. to reopen your case. I went through my father's papers before the

607

cops destroyed them, and I remember a lot of people, even if I can't prove— (*Coaxingly*) You will let me take your case, won't you, Mac?

MCGLOIN. (*soothingly*) Sure I will and it'll make your reputation, Willie. (MOSHER *winks at* HOPE, *shaking his head, and* HOPE *answers with identical pantomime, as though to say, "Poor dopes, they're off again!"*)

LARRY. (*aloud to himself more than to* PARRITT—*with irritable wonder*) Ah, be damned! Haven't I heard their visions a thousand times? Why should they get under my skin now? I've got the blues, I guess. I wish to hell Hickey'd turn up.

MOSHER. (*calculatingly solicitous—whispering to* HOPE) Poor Willie needs a drink bad, Harry—and I think if we all joined him it'd make him feel he was among friends and cheer him up.

HOPE. More circus con tricks! (*Scathingly*) You talking of your dear sister! Bessie had you sized up. She used to tell me, "I don't know what you can see in that worthless, drunken, petty-larceny brother of mine. If I had my way," she'd say, "he'd get booted out in the gutter on his fat behind." Sometimes she didn't say behind, either.

MOSHER. (*grins genially*) Yes, dear old Bess had a qiuck temper, but there was no real harm in her. (*He chuckles reminiscently*) Remember the time she sent me down to the bar to change a ten-dollar bill for her?

HOPE. (*has to grin himself*) Bejees, do I! She coulda bit a piece out of a stove lid, after she found it out. (*He cackles appreciatively.*)

MOSHER. I was sure surprised when she gave me the ten spot. Bess usually had better sense, but she was in a hurry to go to church. I didn't really mean to do it, but you know how habit gets you. Besides, I still worked then, and the circus season was going to begin soon, and I needed a little practice to keep my hand in. Or, you never can tell, the first rube that came to my wagon for a ticket might have left with the right change and I'd be disgraced. (*He chuckles*) I said, "I'm sorry, Bess, but I had to take it all in dimes. Here, hold out your hands and I'll count it out for you, so you won't kick afterwards I short-changed you." (*He begins a count which grows more rapid as he goes on*) Ten, twenty, thirty, forty, fifty, sixty, seventy, eighty, ninety, a dollar. Ten, twenty, thirty, forty, fifty, sixty— You're counting with me, Bess, aren't you?—eighty, ninety, two dollars. Ten, twenty— Those are pretty shoes you got on, Bess—forty, fifty, seventy, eighty, ninety, three dollars. Ten, twenty, thirty— What's on at the church tonight, Bess?—fifty, sixty, seventy, ninety, four dollars. Ten, twenty, thirty, fifty, seventy, eighty, ninety— That's a swell new hat, Bess, looks very becoming— six dollars. (*He chuckles*) And so on. I'm bum at it now for lack of prac- tice, but in those days I could have short-changed the Keeper of the Mint.

HOPE. (*grinning*) Stung her for two dollars and a half, wasn't it, Ed?

MOSHER. Yes. A fine percentage, if I do say so, when you're dealing to someone who's sober and can count. I'm sorry to say she discovered my mistakes in arithmetic just after I beat it around the corner. She counted it over herself. Bess somehow never had the confidence in me a sister should. (*He sighs tenderly*) Dear old Bess.

HOPE. (*Indignant now*) You're a fine guy bragging how you short- changed yur own sister! Bejees, if there was a war and you was in it, they'd have to padlock the pockets of the dead!

MOSHER. (*a bit hurt at this*) That's going pretty strong, Harry. I always gave a sucker some chance. There wouldn't be no fun robbing the dead. (*He becomes reminiscently melancholy*) Gosh, thinking of the old ticket wagon brings those days back. The greatest life on earth with the greatest show on earth! The grandest crowd of regular guys ever gathered under one tent! I'd sure like to shake their hands again!

HOPE. (*acidly*) They'd have guns in theirs. They'd shoot you on sight. You've touched every damned one of them. Bejees, you've even bor- rowed fish from the trained seals and peanuts from every elephant that remembered you! (*This fancy tickles him and he gives a cackling laugh.*)

MOSHER. (*overlooking this—dreamily*) You know, Harry, I've made up my mind I'll see the boss in a couple of days and ask for my old job. I can get back my magic touch with change easy, and I can throw him a line of bull that'll kid him I won't be so unreasonable about sharing the profits next time. (*With insinuating complaint*) There's no percentage in hanging around this dive, taking care of you and shooting away your snakes, when I don't even get an eye-opener for my trouble.

HOPE. (*implacably*) No! (MOSHER *sighs and gives up and closes his eyes. The others, except* LARRY *and* PARRITT, *are all dozing again now.* HOPE *goes on grumbling*) Go to hell or the circus, for all I care. Good riddance, bejees! I'm sick of you! (*Then worriedly*) Say, Ed, what the hell you think's happened to Hickey? I hope he'll turn up. Always got a million funny stories. You and the other bums have begun to give me the graveyard fantods. I'd like a good laugh with old Hickey. (*He chuckles at a memory*) Remember that gag he always pulls about his wife and the iceman? He'd make a cat laugh! (ROCKY *appears from the bar. He comes front, behind* MOSHER's *chair, and begins pushing the black curtain along the rod to the rear wall.*)

ROCKY. Openin' time, Boss. (*He presses a button at rear which switches off the lights. The back room becomes drabber and dingier than ever in the gray daylight that comes from the street windows, off right, and what light can penetrate the grime of the two backyard windows at left.* ROCKY *turns back to* HOPE—*grumpily*) Why don't you go up to bed, Boss? Hickey'd never turn up dis time of de mornin'!

HOPE. (*starts and listens*) Someone's coming now.

ROCKY. (*listens*) Aw, dat's on'y my two pigs. It's about time dey showed. (*He goes back toward the door at left of the bar.*)

HOPE. (*sourly disappointed*) You keep them dumb broads quiet. I don't want to go to bed. I'm going to catch a couple more winks here and I don't want no damn-fool laughing and screeching. (*He settles himself in his chair, grumbling*) Never thought I'd see the day when Harry Hope's would have tarts rooming in it. What'd Bessie think? But I don't let 'em use my rooms for business. And they're good kids. Good as anyone else. They got to make a living. Pay their rent, too, which is more than I can say for—(*He cocks an eye over his specs at* MOSHER *and grins with satisfaction*) Bejees, Ed, I'll bet Bessie is doing somersaults in her grave! (*He chuckles. But* MOSHER's *eyes are closed, his head nodding, and he doesn't reply, so* HOPE *closes his eyes.* ROCKY *has opened the barroom door at rear and is standing in the hall beyond it, facing right. A girl's laugh is heard.*)

ROCKY. (*warningly*) Nix! Piano! (*He comes in, beckoning them to follow. He goes behind the bar and gets a whiskey bottle and glasses and chairs.* MARGIE *and* PEARL *follow him, casting a glance around. Everyone except* LARRY *and* PARRITT *is asleep or dozing. Even* PARRITT *has his eyes closed. The two girls, neither much over twenty, are typical dollar street walkers, dressed in the usual tawdry get-up.* PEARL *is obviously Italian with black hair and eyes.* MARGIE *has brown hair and hazel eyes, a slum New Yorker of mixed blood. Both are plump and have a certain prettiness that shows even through their blobby make-up. Each retains a vestige of youthful freshness, although the game is beginning to get them and give them hard, worn expressions. Both are sentimental, feather-brained, giggly, lazy, good-natured and reasonably contented with life. Their attitude toward* ROCKY *is much that of two maternal, affectionate sisters toward a bullying brother whom they like to tease and spoil. His attitude toward them is that of the owner of two performing pets he has trained to do a profitable act under his management. He feels a proud proprietor's affection for them, and is tolerantly lax in his discipline.*)

MARGIE. (*glancing around*) Jees, Poil, it's de Morgue wid all de stiffs on deck. (*She catches* LARRY'S *eye and smiles affectionately*) Hello, Old Wise Guy, ain't you died yet?

LARRY. (*grinning*) Not yet, Margie. But I'm waiting impatiently for the end. (PARRITT *opens his eyes to look at the two girls, but as soon as they glance at him he closes them again and turns his head away.*)

MARGIE. (*as she and* PEARL *come to the table at right, front, followed by* ROCKY) Who's de new guy? Friend of yours, Larry? (*Automatically she smiles seductively at* PARRITT *and addresses him in a professional chant*) Wanta have a good time, kid?

PEARL. Aw, he's passed out. Hell wid him!

HOPE. (*cocks an eye over his specs at them—with drowsy irritation*) You dumb broads cut the loud talk. (*He shuts his eye again.*)

ROCKY. (*admonishing them good-naturedly*) Sit down before I knock yuh down. (MARGIE *and* PEARL *sit at left, and rear, of table,* ROCKY *at right of it. The girls pour drinks.* ROCKY *begins in a brisk, business-like manner but in a lowered voice with an eye on* HOPE) Well, how'd you tramps do?

MARGIE. Pretty good. Didn't we, Poil?

PEARL. Sure. We nailed a coupla all-night guys.

MARGIE. On Sixth Avenoo. Boobs from de sticks.

PEARL. Stinko, de bot' of 'em.

MARGIE. We thought we was in luck. We steered dem to a real hotel. We figgered dey was too stinko to bother us much and we could cop a good sleep in beds that ain't got cobble stones in de mattress like de ones in dis dump.

PEARL. But we was outa luck. Dey didn't bother us much dat way, but dey wouldn't go to sleep either, see? Jees, I never hoid such gabby guys.

MARGIE. Dey got onta politics, drinkin' outa de bottle. Dey forgot we was around. "De Bull Moosers is de on'y reg'lar guys," one guy says. And de other guy says, "You're a God-damned liar! And I'm a Republican!" Den dey'd laugh.

PEARL. Den dey'd get mad and make a bluff dey was goin' to scrap, and den dey'd make up and cry and sing "School Days." Jees, imagine tryin' to sleep wid dat on de phonograph!

MARGIE. Maybe you tink we wasn't glad when de house dick come up and told us all to git dressed and take de air!

PEARL. We told de guys we'd wait for dem 'round de corner.

MARGIE. So here we are.

ROCKY. (*sententiously*) Yeah. I see you. But I don't see no dough yet.

PEARL. (*with a wink at* MARGIE—*teasingly*) Right on de job, ain't he, Margie?

MARGIE. Yeah, our little business man! Dat's him!

ROCKY. Come on! Dig! (*They both pull up their skirts to get the money from their stockings.* ROCKY *watches this move carefully.*)

PEARL. (*amused*) Pipe him keepin' cases, Margie.

MARGIE. (*amused*) Scared we're holdin' out on him.

PEARL. Way he grabs, yuh'd tink it was him done de woik. (*She holds out a little roll of bills to* ROCKY) Here y'are, Grafter!

MARGIE. (*holding hers out*) We hope it chokes yuh. (ROCKY *counts the money quickly and shoves it in his pocket.*)

ROCKY. (*genially*) You dumb baby dolls gimme a pain. What would you do wid money if I wasn't around? Give it all to some pimp.

PEARL. (*teasingly*) Jees, what's the difference—? (*Hastily*) Aw, I don't mean dat, Rocky.

ROCKY. (*his eyes growing hard—slowly*) A lotta difference, get me?

PEARL. Don't get sore. Jees, can't yuh take a little kiddin'?

MARGIE. Sure, Rocky, Poil was on'y kiddin'. (*Soothingly*) We know yuh got a reg'lar job. Dat's why we like yuh, see? Yuh don't live offa us. Yuh're a bartender.

ROCKY. (*genially again*) Sure, I'm a bartender. Everyone knows me knows dat. And I treat you goils right, don't I? Jees, I'm wise yuh hold out on me, but I know it ain't much, so what the hell, I let yuh get away wid it. I tink yuh're a coupla good kids. Yuh're aces wid me, see?

PEARL. You're aces wid us, too. Ain't he, Margie?

MARGIE. Sure, he's aces. (ROCKY *beams complacently and takes the glasses back to the bar.* MARGIE *whispers*) Yuh sap, don't yuh know enough not to kid him on dat? Serve yuh right if he beat yuh up!

PEARL. (*admiringly*) Jees, I'll bet he'd give yuh an awful beatin', too, once he started. Ginnies got awful tempers.

MARGIE. Anyway, we wouldn't keep no pimp, like we was reg'lar old whores. We ain't dat bad.

PEARL. No. We're tarts, but dat's all.

ROCKY. (*rinsing glasses behind the bar*) Cora got back around three o'clock. She woke up Chuck and dragged him outa de hay to go to a chop suey joint. (*Disgustedly*) Imagine him standin' for dat stuff!

MARGIE. (*disgustedly*) I'll bet dey been sittin' around kiddin' demselves wid dat old pipe dream about gettin' married and settlin' down on a farm. Jees, when Chuck's on de wagon, dey never lay off dat dope! Dey give yuh an earful every time yuh talk to 'em!

PEARL. Yeah. Chuck wid a silly grin on his ugly map, de big boob, and Cora gigglin' like she was in grammar school and some tough guy'd just told her babies wasn't brung down de chimney by a boid!

MARGIE. And her on de turf long before me and you was! And bot' of 'em arguin' all de time, Cora sayin' she's scared to marry him because he'll go on drunks again. Just as dough any drunk could scare Cora!

PEARL. And him swearin', de big liar, he'll never go on no more periodicals! An' den her pretendin'— But it gives me a pain to talk about it. We ought to phone de booby hatch to send round de wagon for 'em.

ROCKY. (*comes back to the table—disgustedly*) Yeah, of all de pipe dreams in dis dump, dey got de nuttiest! And nuttin' stops dem. Dey been dreamin' it for years, every time Chuck goes on de wagon. I never could figger it. What would gettin' married get dem? But de farm stuff is de sappiest part. When bot' of 'em was dragged up in dis ward and ain't never been nearer a farm dan Coney Island! Jees, dey'd tink dey'd gone deaf if dey didn't hear de El rattle! Dey'd get D.T.s if dey ever hoid a cricket choip! I hoid crickets once on my cousin's place in Joisey. I couldn't sleep a wink. Dey give me de heebie-jeebies. (*With deeper disgust*) Jees, can yuh picture a good barkeep like Chuck diggin' spuds? And imagine a whore hustlin' de cows home! For Christ sake! Ain't dat a sweet picture!

MARGIE. (*rebukingly*) Yuh oughtn't to call Cora dat, Rocky. She's a good kid. She may be a tart, but—

ROCKY. (*considerately*) Sure, dat's all I meant, a tart.

PEARL. (*giggling*) But he's right about de damned cows, Margie. Jees, I bet Cora don't know which end of de cow has de horns! I'm goin' to ask her. (*There is the noise of a door opening in the hall and the sound of a man's and woman's arguing voices.*)

ROCKY. Here's your chance. Dat's dem two nuts now. (CORA *and* CHUCK *look in from the hallway and then come in.* CORA *is a thin peroxide blonde, a few years older than* PEARL *and* MARGIE, *dressed in similar style, her round face showing more of the wear and tear of her trade than theirs, but still with traces of a doll-like prettiness.* CHUCK *is a tough, thick-necked, barrel-chested Italian-American, with a fat, amiable, swarthy face. He has on a straw hat with a vivid band, a loud suit, tie and shirt, and yellow shoes. His eyes are clear and he looks healthy and strong as an ox.*)

CORA. (*gaily*) Hello, bums. (*She looks around*) Jees, de Morgue on a rainy Sunday night! (*She waves to* LARRY—*affectionately*) Hello, Old Wise Guy! Ain't you croaked yet?

LARRY. (*grins*) Not yet, Cora. It's damned tiring, this waiting for the end.

CORA. Aw, gwan, you'll never die! Yuh'll have to hire someone to croak yuh wid an axe.

HOPE. (*cocks one sleepy eye at her—irritably*) You dumb hookers, cut the loud noise! This ain't a cat-house!

CORA. (*teasingly*) My, Harry! Such language!

HOPE. (*closes his eyes—to himself with a gratified chuckle*) Bejees, I'll bet Bessie's turning over in her grave! (CORA *sits down between* MARGIE *and* PEARL. CHUCK *takes an empty chair from* HOPE's *table and puts it by hers and sits down. At* LARRY's *table,* PARRITT *is glaring resentfully toward the girls.*)

PARRITT. If I'd known this dump was a hooker hangout, I'd never have come here.

LARRY. (*watching him*) You seem down on the ladies.

PARRITT. (*vindictively*) I hate every bitch that ever lived! They're all alike! (*Catching himself guiltily*) You can understand how I feel, can't you, when it was getting mixed up with a tart that made me have that fight with Mother? (*Then with a resentful sneer*) But what the hell does it matter to you? You're in the grandstand. You're through with life.

LARRY. (*sharply*) I'm glad you remember it. I don't want to know a damned thing about your business. (*He closes his eyes and settles on his chair as if preparing for sleep.* PARRITT *stares at him sneeringly. Then he looks away and his expression becomes furtive and frightened.*)

CORA. Who's de guy wid Larry?

ROCKY. A tightwad. To hell wid him.

PEARL. Say, Cora, wise me up. Which end of a cow is de horns on?

CORA. (*embarrassed*) Aw, don't bring dat up. I'm sick of hearin' about dat farm.

ROCKY. You got nuttin' on us!

CORA. (*ignoring this*) Me and dis overgrown tramp has been scrappin' about it. He says Joisey's de best place, and I says Long Island because we'll be near Coney. And I tells him, How do I know yuh're off of periodicals for life? I don't give a damn how drunk yuh get, the way we are, but I don't wanta be married to no soak.

CHUCK. And I tells her I'm off de stuff for life. Den she beefs we won't be married a month before I'll trow it in her face she was a tart. "Jees, Baby," I tells her. "Why should I? What de hell yuh tink I tink I'm marryin', a voigin? Why should I kick as long as yuh lay off it and don't do no cheatin' wid de iceman or nobody?" (*He gives her a rough hug*) Dat's on de level, Baby. (*He kisses her.*)

CORA. (*kissing him*) Aw, yuh big tramp!

ROCKY. (*shakes his head with profound disgust*) Can yuh tie it? I'll buy a drink. I'll do anything. (*He gets up.*)

CORA. No, dis round's on me. I run into luck. Dat's why I dragged Chuck outa bed to celebrate. It was a sailor. I rolled him. (*She giggles*) Listen, it was a scream. I've run into some nutty souses, but dis guy was de nuttiest. De booze dey dish out around de Brooklyn Navy Yard must be as turrible bugjuice as Harry's. My dogs was givin' out when I seen dis guy holdin' up a lamppost, so I hurried to get him before a cop did. I says, "Hello, Handsome, wanta have a good time?" Jees, he was paralyzed! One of dem polite jags. He tries to bow to me, imagine, and I had to prop him up or he'd fell on his nose. And what d'yuh tink

616

he said? "Lady," he says, "can yuh kindly tell me de nearest way to de Museum of Natural History?" (*They all laugh*) Can yuh imagine! At two A.M. As if I'd know where de dump was anyway. But I says, "Sure ting, Honey Boy, I'll be only too glad." So I steered him into a side street where it was dark and propped him against a wall and gave him a frisk. (*She giggles*) And what d'yuh tink he does? Jees, I ain't lyin', he begins to laugh, de big sap! He says, "Quit ticklin' me." While I was friskin' him for his roll! I near died! Den I toined him 'round and give him a push to start him. "Just keep goin'," I told him. "It's a big white building on your right. You can't miss it." He must be swimmin' in de North River yet! (*They all laugh.*)

CHUCK. Ain't Uncle Sam de sap to trust guys like dat wid dough!

CORA. (*with a business-like air*) I picked twelve bucks offa him. Come on, Rocky. Set 'em up. (ROCKY *goes back to the bar.* CORA *looks around the room*) Say, Chuck's kiddin' about de iceman a minute ago reminds me. Where de hell's Hickey?

ROCKY. Dat's what we're all wonderin'.

CORA. He oughta be here. Me and Chuck seen him.

ROCKY. (*excited, comes back from the bar, forgetting the drinks*) You seen Hickey? (*He nudges* HOPE) Hey, Boss, come to! Cora's seen Hickey. (HOPE *is instantly wide awake and everyone in the place, except* HUGO *and* PARRITT, *begins to rouse up hopefully, as if a mysterious wireless message had gone round.*)

HOPE. Where'd you see him, Cora?

CORA. Right on de next corner. He was standin' dere. We said, "Welcome to our city. De gang is expectin' yuh wid deir tongues hangin' out a yard long." And I kidded him, "How's de iceman, Hickey? How's he doin' at your house?" He laughs and says, "Fine." And he says, "Tell de gang I'll be along in a minute. I'm just finishin' figurin' out de best way to save dem and bring dem peace."

HOPE. (*chuckles*) Bejees, he's thought up a new gag! It's a wonder he didn't borry a Salvation Army uniform and show up in that! Go out and get him, Rocky. Tell him we're waitin' to be saved! (ROCKY *goes out, grinning.*)

CORA. Yeah, Harry, he was only kiddin'. But he was funny, too, somehow. He was different, or somethin'.

CHUCK. Sure, he was sober, Baby. Dat's what made him different. We ain't never seen him when he wasn't on a drunk, or had de willies gettin' over it.

CORA. Sure! Gee, ain't I dumb?

HOPE. (*with conviction*) The dumbest broad I ever seen! (*Then puzzledly*) Sober? That's funny. He's always lapped up a good starter on his way here. Well, bejees, he won't be sober long! He'll be good and ripe for my birthday party tonight at twelve. (*He chuckles with excited anticipation—addressing all of them*) Listen! He's fixed some new gag to pull on us. We'll pretend to let him kid us, see? And we'll kid the pants off him. (*They all say laughingly, "Sure, Harry," "Righto," "That's the stuff," "We'll fix him," etc., etc., their faces excited with the same eager anticipation.* ROCKY *appears in the doorway at the end of the bar with* HICKEY, *his arm around* HICKEY's *shoulders.*)

ROCKY. (*with an affectionate grin*) Here's the old son of a bitch! (*They all stand up and greet him with affectionate acclaim, "Hello, Hickey!" etc. Even* HUGO *comes out of his coma to raise his head and blink through his thick spectacles with a welcoming giggle.*)

HICKEY. (*jovially*) Hello, Gang! (*He stands a moment, beaming around at all of them affectionately. He is about fifty, a little under medium height, with a stout, roly-poly figure. His face is round and smooth and big-boyish with bright blue eyes, a button nose, a small, pursed mouth. His head is bald except for a fringe of hair around his temples and the back of his head. His expression is fixed in a salesman's winning smile of self-confident affability and a hearty good fellowship. His eyes have the twinkle of a humor which delights in kidding others but can also enjoy equally a joke on himself. He exudes a friendly, generous personality that makes everyone like him on sight. You get the impression, too, that he must have real ability in his line. There is an efficient, business-like approach in his manner, and his eyes can take you in shrewdly at a glance. He has the salesman's mannerisms of speech, an easy flow of glib, persuasive convincingness. His clothes are those of a successful drummer whose territory consists of minor cities and small towns—not flashy but conspicuously spic and span. He immediately puts on an entrance act, places a hand affectedly on his chest, throws back his head, and sings in a falsetto tenor)* "It's always fair weather, when good fellows get together!" *(Changing to a comic bass and another tune)* "And another little drink won't do us any harm!" *(They all roar with laughter at this burlesque which his personality makes really funny. He waves his hand in a lordly manner to* ROCKY*)* Do your duty, Brother Rocky. Bring on the rat poison! *(*ROCKY *grins and goes behind the bar to get drinks amid an approving cheer from the crowd.* HICKEY *comes forward to shake hands with* HOPE*—with affectionate heartiness)* How goes it, Governor?

HOPE. *(enthusiastically)* Bejees, Hickey, you old bastard, it's good to see you! *(*HICKEY *shakes hands with* MOSHER *and* MCGLOIN*; leans right to shake hands with* MARCIE *and* PEARL*; moves to the middle table to shake hands with* LEWIS, JOE MOTT, WETJOEN *and* JIMMY*; waves to* WILLIE, LARRY *and* HUGO. *He greets each by name with the same affectionate heartiness and there is an interchange of* "How's the kid?" "How's the old scout?" "How's the boy?' "How's everything?" *etc., etc.* ROCKY *begins setting out drinks, whiskey glasses with chasers, and a bottle for each table, starting with* LARRY*'s table.* HOPE *says:)* Sit down, Hickey. Sit down. *(*HICKEY *takes the chair, facing front, at the front of the table in the second row which is half between* HOPE*'s table and the one where* JIMMY TOMORROW *is.* HOPE *goes on with excited pleasure)* Bejees, Hickey, it seems natural to see your ugly, grinning map. *(With a scornful nod to* CORA*)* This dumb broad was tryin' to tell us you'd changed, but you ain't a damned bit. Tell us about yourself. How've you been doin'? Bejees, you look like a million dollars.

ROCKY. *(coming to* HICKEY*'s table, puts a bottle of whiskey, a glass and* *a chaser on it—then hands* HICKEY *a key*) Here's your key, Hickey. Same old room.

HICKEY. (*shoves the key in his pocket*) Thanks, Rocky. I'm going up in a little while and grab a snooze. Haven't been able to sleep lately and I'm tired as hell. A couple of hours good kip will fix me.

HOPE. (*as* ROCKY *puts drink on his table*) First time I ever heard you worry about sleep. Bejees, you never would go to bed. (*He raises his glass, and all the others except* PARRITT *do likewise*) Get a few slugs under your belt and you'll forget sleeping. Here's mud in your eye, Hickey. (*They all join in with the usual humorous toasts.*)

HICKEY. (*heartily*) Drink hearty, boys and girls! (*They all drink, but* HICKEY *drinks only his chaser.*)

HOPE. Bejees, is that a new stunt, drinking your chaser first?

HICKEY. No, I forgot to tell Rocky— You'll have to excuse me, boys and girls, but I'm off the stuff. For keeps. (*They stare at him in amazed incredulity.*)

HOPE. What the hell— (*Then with a wink at the others, kiddingly*) Sure! Joined the Salvation Army, ain't you? Been elected President of the W.C.T.U.? Take that bottle away from him, Rocky. We don't want to tempt him into sin. (*He chuckles and the others laugh.*)

HICKEY. (*earnestly*) No, honest, Harry. I know it's hard to believe but— (*He pauses—then adds simply*) Cora was right, Harry. I have changed. I mean, about booze. I don't need it any more. (*They all stare, hoping it's a gag, but impressed and disappointed and made vaguely uneasy by the change they now sense in him.*)

HOPE. (*his kidding a bit forced*) Yeah, go ahead, kid the pants off us! Bejees, Cora said you was coming to save us! Well, go on. Get this joke off your chest! Start the service! Sing a God-damned hymn if you like. We'll all join in the chorus. "No drunkard can enter this beautiful home." That's a good one. (*He forces a cackle.*)

HICKEY. (*grinning*) Oh, hell, Governor! You don't think I'd come around here peddling some brand of temperance bunk, do you? You know me better than that! Just because I'm through with the stuff don't mean I'm going Prohibition. Hell, I'm not that ungrateful! It's given me too many good times. I feel exactly the same as I always did. If anyone wants to get drunk, if that's the only way they can be happy, and feel at peace with themselves, why the hell shouldn't they? They have my full and entire sympathy. I know all about that game from soup to nuts. I'm the guy that wrote the book. The only reason I've quit is— Well, I finally had the guts to face myself and throw overboard the damned lying pipe dream that'd been making me miserable, and do what I had to do for the happiness of all concerned—and then all at once I found I was at peace with myself and I didn't need booze any more. That's all there was to it. (*He pauses. They are staring at him, uneasy and beginning to feel defensive.* HICKEY *looks round and grins affectionately—apologetically*) But what the hell! Don't let me be a wet blanket, making fool speeches about myself. Set 'em up again, Rocky. Here. (*He pulls a big roll from his pocket and peels off a ten-dollar bill. The faces of all brighten*) Keep the balls coming until this is killed. Then ask for more.

ROCKY. Jees, a roll dat'd choke a hippopotamus! Fill up, youse guys. (*They all pour out drinks.*)

HOPE. That sounds more like you, Hickey. That water-wagon bull— Cut out the act and have a drink, for Christ's sake.

HICKEY. It's no act, Governor. But don't get me wrong. That don't mean I'm a teetotal grouch and can't be in the party. Hell, why d'you suppose I'm here except to have a party, same as I've always done, and help celebrate your birthday tonight? You've all been good pals to me, the best friends I've ever had. I've been thinking about you ever since I left the house—all the time I was walking over here—

HOPE. Walking? Bejees, do you mean to say you walked?

HICKEY. I sure did. All the way from the wilds of darkest Astoria. Didn't mind it a bit, either. I seemed to get here before I knew it. I'm a bit tired and sleepy but otherwise I feel great. (*Kiddingly*) That ought to encourage you, Governor—show you a little walk around the ward is nothing to be so scared about. (*He winks at the others.* HOPE *stiffens*

621

resentfully for a second. HICKEY *goes on*) I didn't make such bad time either for a fat guy, considering it's a hell of a ways, and I sat in the park for a while thinking. It was going on twelve when I went in the bedroom to tell Evelyn I was leaving. Six hours, say. No, less than that. I'd been standing on the corner some time before Cora and Chuck came along, thinking about all of you. Of course, I was only kidding Cora with that stuff about saving you. (*Then seriously*) No, I wasn't either. But I didn't mean booze. I meant save you from pipe dreams. I know now, from my experience, they're the things that really poison and ruin a guy's life and keep him from finding any peace. If you knew how free and contented I feel now. I'm like a new man. And the cure for them is so damned simple, once you have the nerve. Just the old dope of honesty is the best policy—honesty with yourself, I mean. Just stop lying about yourself and kidding yourself about tomorrows. (*He is staring ahead of him now as if he were talking aloud to himself as much as to them. Their eyes are fixed on him with uneasy resentment. His manner becomes apologetic again*) Hell, this begins to sound like a damned sermon on the way to lead the good life. Forget that part of it. It's in my blood, I guess. My old man used to whale salvation into my heinie with a birch rod. He was a preacher in the sticks of Indiana, like I've told you. I got my knack of sales gab from him, too. He was the boy who could sell those Hoosier hayseeds building lots along the Golden Street! (*Taking on a salesman's persuasiveness*) Now listen, boys and girls, don't look at me as if I was trying to sell you a goldbrick. Nothing up my sleeve, honest. Let's take an example. Any one of you. Take you, Governor. That walk around the ward you never take—

HOPE. (*defensively sharp*) What about it?

HICKEY. (*grinning affectionately*) Why, you know as well as I do, Harry. Everything about it.

HOPE. (*defiantly*) Bejees, I'm going to take it!

HICKEY. Sure, you're going to—this time. Because I'm going to help you. I know it's the thing you've got to do before you'll ever know what real peace means. (*He looks at* JIMMY TOMORROW) Same thing with you, Jimmy. You've got to try and get your old job back. And no tomorrow about it! (*As* JIMMY *stiffens with a pathetic attempt at dignity—placatingly*) No, don't tell me, Jimmy. I know all about tomorrow. I'm the guy that wrote the book.

JIMMY. I don't understand you. I admit I've foolishly delayed, but as it happens, I'd just made up my mind that as soon as I could get straightened out—

HICKEY. Fine! That's the spirit! And I'm going to help you. You've been damned kind to me, Jimmy, and I want to prove how grateful I am. When it's all over and you don't have to nag at yourself any more, you'll be grateful to me, too! (*He looks around at the others*) And all the rest of you, ladies included, are in the same boat, one way or another.

LARRY. (*who has been listening with sardonic appreciation—in his comically intense, crazy whisper*) Be God, you've hit the nail on the head, Hickey! This dump is the Palace of Pipe Dreams!

HICKEY. (*grins at him with affectionate kidding*) Well, well! The Old Grandstand Foolosopher speaks! You think you're the big exception, eh? Life doesn't mean a damn to you any more, does it? You're retired from the circus. You're just waiting impatiently for the end— the good old Long Sleep! (*He chuckles*) Well, I think a lot of you, Larry, you old bastard. I'll try and make an honest man of you, too!

LARRY. (*stung*) What the devil are you hinting at, anyway?

HICKEY. You don't have to ask me, do you, a wise old guy like you? Just ask yourself. I'll bet you know.

PARRITT. (*is watching* LARRY's *face with a curious sneering satisfaction*) He's got your number, all right, Larry! (*He turns to* HICKEY) That's the stuff, Hickey. Show the old faker up! He's got no right to sneak out of everything.

HICKEY. (*regards him with surprise at first, then with a puzzled interest*) Hello. A stranger in our midst. I didn't notice you before, Brother.

PARRITT. (*embarrassed, his eyes shifting away*) My name's Parritt. I'm an old friend of Larry's. (*His eyes come back to* HICKEY *to find him still sizing him up—defensively*) Well? What are you staring at?

HICKEY. (*continuing to stare—puzzledly*) No offense, Brother. I was trying to figure— Haven't we met before some place?

PARRITT. (*reassured*) No. First time I've ever been East.

HICKEY. No, you're right. I know that's not it. In my game, to be a shark at it, you teach yourself never to forget a name or a face. But still I know damned well I recognized something about you. We're members of the same lodge—in some way.

PARRITT. (*uneasy again*) What are you talking about? You're nuts.

HICKEY. (*dryly*) Don't try to kid me, Little Boy. I'm a good salesman —so damned good the firm was glad to take me back after every drunk— and what made me good was I could size up anyone. (*Frowningly puzzled again*) But I don't see— (*Suddenly breezily good-natured*) Never mind. I can tell you're having trouble with yourself and I'll be glad to do anything I can to help a friend of Larry's.

LARRY. Mind your own business, Hickey. He's nothing to you—or to me, either. (HICKEY *gives him a keen inquisitive glance.* LARRY *looks away and goes on sarcastically*) You're keeping us all in suspense. Tell us more about how you're going to save us.

HICKEY. (*good-naturedly but seeming a little hurt*) Hell, don't get sore, Larry. Not at me. We've always been good pals, haven't we? I know I've always liked you a lot.

LARRY. (*a bit shamefaced*) Well, so have I liked you. Forget it, Hickey.

HICKEY. (*beaming*) Fine! That's the spirit! (*Looking around at the others, who have forgotten their drinks*) What's the matter, everybody? What is this, a funeral? Come on and drink up! A little action! (*They all drink*) Have another. Hell, this is a celebration! Forget it, if anything I've said sounds too serious. I don't want to be a pain in the neck. Any time you think I'm talking out of turn, just tell me to go chase myself! (*He yawns with growing drowsiness and his voice grows a bit muffled*) No, boys and girls, I'm not trying to put anything over on you. It's just that I know now from experience what a lying pipe dream can do to you—and how damned relieved and contented with yourself you feel when you're rid of it. (*He yawns again*) God, I'm sleepy all of a sudden. That long walk is beginning to get me. I better go upstairs. Hell of a trick to go dead on you like this. (*He starts to get up but relaxes again. His eyes blink as he tries to keep them open*) No, boys and girls, I've never known what real peace was until now. It's a grand feeling, like when you're sick and suffering like hell and the Doc gives you a shot in the arm, and the pain goes, and you drift off. (*His eyes close*) You can let go of yourself at last. Let yourself sink down to the bottom of the sea. Rest in peace. There's no farther you have to go. Not a single damned hope or dream left to nag you. You'll all know what I mean after you— (*He pauses—mumbles*) Excuse—all in—got to grab forty winks— Drink up, everybody—on me— (*The sleep of complete exhaustion overpowers him. His chin sags to his chest. They stare at him with puzzled uneasy fascination.*)

HOPE. (*forcing a tone of irritation*) Bejees, that's a fine stunt, to go to sleep on us! (*Then fumingly to the crowd*) Well, what the hell's the matter with you bums? Why don't you drink up? You're always crying for booze, and now you've got it under your nose, you sit like dummies! (*They start and gulp down their whiskies and pour another.* HOPE *stares at* HICKEY) Bejees, I can't figure Hickey. I still say he's kidding us. Kid his own grandmother, Hickey would. What d'you think, Jimmy?

JIMMY (*unconvincingly*) It must be another of his jokes, Harry, although— Well, he does appear changed. But he'll probably be his natural self again tomorrow— (*Hastily*) I mean, when he wakes up.

LARRY (*staring at* HICKEY *frowningly—more aloud to himself than to them*) You'll make a mistake if you think he's only kidding.

PARRITT (*in a low confidential voice*) I don't like that guy, Larry. He's too damned nosy. I'm going to steer clear of him. (LARRY *gives him a suspicious glance, then looks hastily away.*)

JIMMY. (*with an attempt at open-minded reasonableness*) Still, Harry,

625

I have to admit there was some sense in his nonsense. It is time I got my job back—although I hardly need him to remind me.

HOPE. (*with an air of frankness*) Yes, and I ought to take a walk around the ward. But I don't need no Hickey to tell me, seeing I got it all set for my birthday tomorrow.

LARRY. (*sardonically*) Ha! (*Then in his comically intense, crazy whisper*) Be God, it looks like he's going to make two sales of his peace at least! But you'd better make sure first it's the real McCoy and not poison.

HOPE. (*disturbed—angrily*) You bughouse I-Won't-Work harp, who asked you to shove in an oar? What the hell d'you mean, poison? Just because he has your number— (*He immediately feels ashamed of this taunt and adds apologetically*) Bejees, Larry, you're always croaking about something to do with death. It gets my nanny. Come on, fellers, let's drink up. (*They drink.* HOPE's *eyes are fixed on* HICKEY *again*) Stone cold sober and dead to the world! Spilling that business about pipe dreams! Bejees, I don't get it. (*He bursts out again in angry complaint*) He ain't like the old Hickey! He'll be a fine wet blanket to have around at my birthday party! I wish to hell he'd never turned up!

MOSHER. (*who has been the least impressed by* HICKEY's *talk and is the first to recover and feel the effect of the drinks on top of his hangover—genially*) Give him time, Harry, and he'll come out of it. I've watched many cases of almost fatal teetotalism, but they all came out of it completely cured and as drunk as ever. My opinion is the poor sap is temporarily bughouse from overwork. (*Musingly*) You can't be too careful about work. It's the deadliest habit known to science, a great physician once told me. He practiced on street corners under a torchlight. He was positively the only doctor in the world who claimed that rattlesnake oil, rubbed on the prat, would cure heart failure in three days. I remember well his saying to me, "You are naturally delicate, Ed, but if you drink a pint of bad whiskey before breakfast every evening, and never work if you can help it, you may live to a ripe old age. It's staying sober and working that cuts men off in their prime." (*While he is talking, they*

turn to him with eager grins. They are longing to laugh, and as he fin-
ishes they roar. Even PARRITT *laughs.* HICKEY *sleeps on like a dead man,*
but HUGO, *who had passed into his customary coma again, head on table,*
looks up through his thick spectacles and giggles foolishly.)

HUGO. (*blinking around at them. As the laughter dies he speaks in his*
giggling, wheedling manner, as if he were playfully teasing children)
Laugh, leedle bourgeois monkey-faces! Laugh like fools, leedle stupid
peoples! (*His tone suddenly changes to one of guttural soapbox denun-*
ciation and he pounds on the table with a small fist) I vill laugh, too!
But I vill laugh last! I vill laugh at you! (*He declaims his favorite quo-*
tation) "The days grow hot, O Babylon! 'Tis cool beneath thy villow
trees!" (*They all hoot him down in a chorus of amused jeering.* HUGO *is*
not offended. This is evidently their customary reaction. He giggles
good-naturedly. HICKEY *sleeps on. They have all forgotten their uneasi-*
ness about him now and ignore him.)

LEWIS. (*tipsily*) Well, now that our little Robespierre has got the daily
bit of guillotining off his chest, tell me more about your doctor friend,
Ed. He strikes me as the only bloody sensible medico I ever heard of.
I think we should appoint him house physician here without a moment's
delay. (*They all laughingly assent.*)

MOSHER. (*warming to his subject, shakes his head sadly*) Too late! The
old Doc has passed on to his Maker. A victim of overwork, too. He
didn't follow his own advice. Kept his nose to the grindstone and sold
one bottle of snake oil too many. Only eighty years old when he was
taken. The saddest part was that he knew he was doomed. The last time
we got paralyzed together he told me: "This game will get me yet, Ed.
You see before you a broken man, a martyr to medical science. If I had
any nerves I'd have a nervous breakdown. You won't believe me, but
this last year there was actually one night I had so many patients, I didn't
even have time to get drunk. The shock to my system brought on a
stroke which, as a doctor, I recognized was the beginning of the end."
Poor old Doc! When he said this he started crying. "I hate to go before
my task is completed, Ed," he sobbed. "I'd hoped I'd live to see the day

when, thanks to my miraculous cure, there wouldn't be a single vacant cemetery lot left in this glorious country." (*There is a roar of laughter. He waits for it to die and then goes on sadly*) I miss Doc. He was a gentleman of the old school. I'll bet he's standing on a street corner in hell right now, making suckers of the damned, telling them there's nothing like snake oil for a bad burn. (*There is another roar of laughter. This time it penetrates* HICKEY's *exhausted slumber. He stirs on his chair, trying to wake up, managing to raise his head a little and force his eyes half open. He speaks with a drowsy, affectionately encouraging smile. At once the laughter stops abruptly and they turn to him startledly.*)

HICKEY. That's the spirit—don't let me be a wet blanket—all I want is to see you happy— (*He slips back into heavy sleep again. They all stare at him, their faces again puzzled, resentful and uneasy.*)

CURTAIN

ACT TWO

Scene—*The back room only. The black curtain dividing it from the bar is the right wall of the scene. It is getting on toward midnight of the same day.*

The back room has been prepared for a festivity. At center, front, four of the circular tables are pushed together to form one long table with an uneven line of chairs behind it, and chairs at each end. This improvised banquet table is covered with old table cloths, borrowed from a neighboring beanery, and is laid with glasses, plates and cutlery before each of the seventeen chairs. Bottles of bar whiskey are placed at intervals within reach of any sitter. An old upright piano and stool have been moved in and stand against the wall at left, front. At right, front, is a table without chairs. The other tables and chairs that had been in the room have been moved out, leaving a clear floor space at rear for dancing. The floor has been swept clean of sawdust and scrubbed. Even the walls show evidence of having been washed, although the result is only to heighten their splotchy leprous look. The electric-light brackets are adorned with festoons of red ribbon. In the middle of the separate table at right, front, is a birthday cake with six candles. Several packages, tied with ribbon, are also on the table. There are two necktie boxes, two cigar boxes, a fifth containing a half dozen handkerchiefs, the sixth is a square jeweler's watch box.

As the curtain rises, CORA, CHUCK, HUGO, LARRY, MARGIE, PEARL *and* ROCKY *are discovered.* CHUCK, ROCKY *and the three girls have dressed up for the occasion.* CORA *is arranging a bouquet of flowers in a vase, the vase being a big schooner glass from the bar, on top of the piano.* CHUCK *sits in a chair at the foot (left) of the banquet table. He has turned it so he can watch her. Near the middle of the row of chairs behind the table,* LARRY *sits, facing front, a drink of whiskey before him. He is staring before him in frowning, disturbed meditation. Next to him, on his left,* HUGO *is in his habitual position, passed out, arms on table, head on arms, a full whiskey glass by his head. By the separate table at right, front,* MARGIE *and* PEARL *are arranging the cake and presents, and* ROCKY *stands by them. All of them, with the exception of* CHUCK *and* ROCKY, *have had plenty to drink and show it, but no one, except* HUGO, *seems to be drunk. They are trying to act up in the spirit of the occasion but there is something forced about their manner, an undercurrent of nervous irritation and preoccupation.*

CORA. (*standing back from the piano to regard the flower effect*) How's dat, Kid?

CHUCK. (*grumpily*) What de hell do I know about flowers?

CORA. Yuh can see dey're pretty, can't yuh, yuh big dummy?

CHUCK. (*mollifyingly*) Yeah, Baby, sure. If yuh like 'em, dey're aw right wid me. (CORA *goes back to give the schooner of flowers a few more touches.*)

MARGIE. (*admiring the cake*) Some cake, huh, Poil? Lookit! Six candles. Each for ten years.

PEARL. When do we light de candles, Rocky?

ROCKY (*grumpily*) Ask dat bughouse Hickey. He's elected himself boss of dis boithday racket. Just before Harry comes down, he says. Den Harry blows dem out wid one breath, for luck. Hickey was goin' to have sixty candles, but I says, Jees, if de old guy took dat big a breath, he'd croak himself.

MARGIE. (*challengingly*) Well, anyways, it's some cake, ain't it?

ROCKY. (*without enthusiasm*) Sure, it's aw right by me. But what de hell is Harry goin' to do wid a cake? If he ever et a hunk, it'd croak him.

PEARL. Jees, yuh're a dope! Ain't he, Margie?

MARGIE. A dope is right!

ROCKY. (*stung*) You broads better watch your step or—

PEARL. (*defiantly*) Or what?

MARGIE. Yeah! Or what! (*They glare at him truculently.*)

ROCKY. Say, what de hell's got into youse? It'll be twelve o'clock and Harry's boithday before long. I ain't lookin' for no trouble.

PEARL. (*ashamed*) Aw, we ain't neider, Rocky. (*For the moment this argument subsides.*)

CORA. (*over her shoulder to* CHUCK—*acidly*) A guy what can't see flowers is pretty must be some dumbbell.

CHUCK. Yeah? Well, if I was as dumb as you— (*Then mollifyingly*) Jees, yuh got your scrappin' pants on, ain't yuh? (*Grins good-naturedly*) Hell, Baby, what's eatin' yuh? All I'm tinkin' is, flowers is dat louse Hickey's stunt. We never had no flowers for Harry's boithday before. What de hell can Harry do wid flowers? He don't know a cauliflower from a geranium.

ROCKY. Yeah, Chuck, it's like I'm tellin' dese broads about de cake. Dat's Hickey's wrinkle, too. (*Bitterly*) Jees, ever since he woke up, yuh can't hold him. He's taken on de party like it was his boithday.

MARGIE. Well, he's payin' for everything, ain't he?

ROCKY. Aw, I don't mind de boithday stuff so much. What gets my goat is de way he's tryin' to run de whole dump and everyone in it.

He's buttin' in all over de place, tellin' everybody where dey get off. On'y he don't really tell yuh. He just keeps hintin' around.

PEARL. Yeah. He was hintin' to me and Margie.

MARGIE. Yeah, de lousy drummer.

ROCKY. He just gives yuh an earful of dat line of bull about yuh got to be honest wid yourself and not kid yourself, and have de guts to be what yuh are. I got sore. I told him dat's aw right for de bums in dis dump. I hope he makes dem wake up. I'm sick of listenin' to dem hop demselves up. But it don't go wid me, see? I don't kid myself wid no pipe dream. (PEARL *and* MARGIE *exchange a derisive look. He catches it and his eyes narrow*) What are yuh grinnin' at?

PEARL. (*her face hard—scornfully*) Nuttin'.

MARGIE. Nuttin'.

ROCKY. It better be nuttin'! Don't let Hickey put no ideas in your nuts if you wanta stay healthy! (*Then angrily*) I wish de louse never showed up! I hope he don't come back from de delicatessen. He's gettin' everyone nuts. He's ridin' someone every minute. He's got Harry and Jimmy Tomorrow run ragged, and de rest is hidin' in deir rooms so dey won't have to listen to him. Dey're all actin' cagey wid de booze, too, like dey was scared if dey get too drunk, dey might spill deir guts, or somethin'. And everybody's gettin' a prize grouch on.

CORA. Yeah, he's been hintin' round to me and Chuck, too. Yuh'd tink he suspected me and Chuck hadn't no real intentions of gettin' married. Yuh'd tink he suspected Chuck wasn't goin' to lay off periodicals—or maybe even didn't want to.

CHUCK. He didn't say it right out or I'da socked him one. I told him, "I'm on de wagon for keeps and Cora knows it."

CORA. I told him, "Sure, I know it. And Chuck ain't never goin' to trow it in my face dat I was a tart, neider. And if yuh tink we're just kiddin' ourselves, we'll show yuh!"

CHUCK. We're goin' to show him!

CORA. We got it all fixed. We've decided Joisey is where we want de

631

farm, and we'll get married dere, too, because yuh don't need no license. We're goin' to get married tomorrow. Ain't we, Honey?

CHUCK. You bet, Baby.

ROCKY. (*disgusted*) Christ, Chuck, are yuh lettin' dat bughouse louse Hickey kid yuh into—

CORA. (*turns on him angrily*) Nobody's kiddin' him into it, nor me neider! And Hickey's right. If dis big tramp's goin' to marry me, he ought to do it, and not just shoot off his old bazoo about it.

ROCKY. (*ignoring her*) Yuh can't be dat dumb, Chuck.

CORA. You keep outa dis! And don't start beefin' about crickets on de farm drivin' us nuts. You and your crickets! Yuh'd tink dey was elephants!

MARGIE. (*coming to* ROCKY's *defense—sneeringly*) Don't notice dat broad, Rocky. Yuh heard her say "tomorrow," didn't yuh? It's de same old crap.

CORA. (*glares at her*) Is dat so?

PEARL. (*lines up with* MARGIE—*sneeringly*) Imagine Cora a bride! Dat's a hot one! Jees, Cora, if all de guys you've stayed wid was side by side, yuh could walk on 'em from here to Texas!

CORA. (*starts moving toward her threateningly*) Yuh can't talk like dat to me, yuh fat Dago hooker! I may be a tart, but I ain't a cheap old whore like you!

PEARL. (*furiously*) I'll show yuh who's a whore! (*They start to fly at each other, but* CHUCK *and* ROCKY *grab them from behind.*)

CHUCK. (*forcing* CORA *onto a chair*) Sit down and cool off, Baby.

ROCKY. (*doing the same to* PEARL) Nix on de rough stuff, Poil.

MARGIE. (*glaring at* CORA) Why don't you leave Poil alone, Rocky? She'll fix dat blonde's clock! Or if she don't, I will!

ROCKY. Shut up, you! (*Disgustedly*) Jees, what dames! D'yuh wanta gum Harry's party?

PEARL. (*a bit shamefaced—sulkily*) Who wants to? But nobody can't call me a —.

ROCKY. (*exasperatedly*) Aw, bury it! What are you, a voigin? (PEARL *stares at him, her face growing hard and bitter. So does* MARGIE.)

PEARL. Yuh mean you tink I'm a whore, too, huh?

MARGIE. Yeah, and me?

ROCKY. Now don't start nuttin'!

PEARL. I suppose it'd tickle you if me and Margie did what dat louse, Hickey, was hintin' and come right out and admitted we was whores.

ROCKY. Aw right! What of it? It's de truth, ain't it?

CORA. (*lining up with* PEARL *and* MARGIE—*indignantly*) Jees, Rocky, dat's a fine hell of a ting to say to two goils dat's been as good to yuh as Poil and Margie! (*To* PEARL) I didn't mean to call yuh dat, Poil. I was on'y mad.

PEARL. (*accepts the apology gratefully*) Sure, I was mad, too, Cora. No hard feelin's.

ROCKY. (*relieved*) Dere. Dat fixes everyting, don't it?

PEARL. (*turns on him—hard and bitter*) Aw right, Rocky. We're whores. You know what dat makes you, don't you?

ROCKY. (*angrily*) Look out, now!

MARGIE. A lousy little pimp, dat's what!

ROCKY. I'll loin yuh! (*He gives her a slap on the side of the face.*)

PEARL. A dirty little Ginny pimp, dat's what!

ROCKY. (*gives her a slap, too*) And dat'll loin you! (*But they only stare at him with hard sneering eyes.*)

MARGIE. He's provin' it to us, Poil.

PEARL. Yeah! Hickey's convoited him. He's give up his pipe dream!

ROCKY. (*furious and at the same time bewildered by their defiance*) Lay off me or I'll beat de hell—

CHUCK. (*growls*) Aw, lay off dem. Harry's party ain't no time to beat up your stable.

ROCKY. (*turns to him*) Whose stable? Who d'yuh tink yuh're talkin' to? I ain't never beat dem up! What d'yuh tink I am? I just give dem a slap, like any guy would his wife, if she got too gabby. Why don't yuh

633

THE ICEMAN COMETH

tell dem to lay off me? I don't want no trouble on Harry's boithday party.

MARGIE. (*a victorious gleam in her eye—tauntingly*) Aw right, den, yuh poor little Ginny. I'll lay off yuh till de party's over if Poil will.

PEARL. (*tauntingly*) Sure, I will. For Harry's sake, not yours, yuh little Wop!

ROCKY. (*stung*) Say, listen, youse! Don't get no wrong idea— (*But an interruption comes from* LARRY *who bursts into a sardonic laugh. They all jump startledly and look at him with unanimous hostility.* ROCKY *transfers his anger to him*) Who de hell yuh laughin' at, yuh half-dead old stew bum?

CORA. (*sneeringly*) At himself, he ought to be! Jees, Hickey's sure got his number!

LARRY. (*Ignoring them, turns to* HUGO *and shakes him by the shoulder—in his comically intense, crazy whisper*) Wake up, Comrade! Here's the Revolution starting on all sides of you and you're sleeping through it! Be God, it's not to Bakunin's ghost you ought to pray in your dreams, but to the great Nihilist, Hickey! He's started a movement that'll blow up the world!

HUGO. (*blinks at him through his thick spectacles—with guttural denunciation*) You, Larry! Renegade! Traitor! I vill have you shot! (*He giggles*) Don't be a fool! Buy me a trink! (*He sees the drink in front of him, and gulps it down. He begins to sing the Carmagnole in a guttural basso, pounding on the table with his glass*) "Dansons la Carmagnole! Vive le son! Vive le son! Dansons la Carmagnole! Vive le son des canons!"

ROCKY. Can dat noise!

HUGO. (*ignores this—to* LARRY, *in a low tone of hatred*) That bourgeois svine, Hickey! He laughs like good fellow, he makes jokes, he dares make hints to me so I see what he dares to think. He thinks I am finish, it is too late, and so I do not vish the Day come because it vill not be my Day. Oh, I see what he thinks! He thinks lies even vorse, dat I— (*He stops abruptly with a guilty look, as if afraid he was letting*

634

something slip—then revengefully) I vill have him hanged the first one of all on de first lamppost! (*He changes his mood abruptly and peers around at* ROCKY *and the others—giggling again*) Vhy you so serious, leedle monkey-faces? It's all great joke, no? So ve get drunk, and ve laugh like hell, and den ve die, and de pipe dream vanish! (*A bitter mocking contempt creeps into his tone*) But be of good cheer, leedle stupid peoples! "The days grow hot, O Babylon!" Soon, leedle prole-tarians, ve vill have free picnic in the cool shade, ve vill eat hot dogs and trink free beer beneath the villow trees! Like hogs, yes! Like beautiful leedle hogs! (*He stops startledly, as if confused and amazed at what he has heard himself say. He mutters with hatred*) Dot Got-tamned liar, Hickey. It is he who makes me sneer. I want to sleep. (*He lets his head fall forward on his folded arms again and closes his eyes.* LARRY *gives him a pitying look, then quickly drinks his drink.*)

CORA. (*uneasily*) Hickey ain't overlookin' no bets, is he? He's even give Hugo de woiks.

LARRY. I warned you this morning he wasn't kidding.

MARGIE. (*sneering*) De old wise guy!

PEARL. Yeah, still pretendin' he's de one exception, like Hickey told him. He don't do no pipe dreamin'! Oh, no!

LARRY (*sharply resentful*) I—! (*Then abruptly he is drunkenly good-natured, and you feel this drunken manner is an evasive exaggeration*) All right, take it out on me, if it makes you more content. Sure, I love every hair of your heads, my great big beautiful baby dolls, and there's nothing I wouldn't do for you!

PEARL. (*stiffly*) De old Irish bunk, huh? We ain't big. And we ain't your baby dolls! (*Suddenly she is mollified and smiles*) But we admit we're beautiful. Huh, Margie?

MARGIE. (*smiling*) Sure ting! But what would he do wid beautiful dolls, even if he had de price, de old goat? (*She laughs teasingly—then pats* LARRY *on the shoulder affectionately*) Aw, yuh're aw right at dat, Larry, if yuh are full of bull!

PEARL. Sure. Yuh're aces wid us. We're noivous, dat's all. Dat lousy drummer—why can't he be like he's always been? I never seen a guy change so. You pretend to be such a fox, Larry. What d'yuh tink's happened to him?

LARRY. I don't know. With all his gab I notice he's kept that to himself so far. Maybe he's saving the great revelation for Harry's party. (*Then irritably*) To hell with him! I don't want to know. Let him mind his own business and I'll mind mine.

CHUCK. Yeah, dat's what I say.

CORA. Say, Larry, where's dat young friend of yours disappeared to?

LARRY. I don't care where he is, except I wish it was a thousand miles away! (*Then, as he sees they are surprised at his vehemence, he adds hastily*) He's a pest.

ROCKY. (*breaks in with his own preoccupation*) I don't give a damn what happened to Hickey, but I know what's gonna happen if he don't watch his step. I told him, "I'll take a lot from you, Hickey, like everyone else in dis dump, because yuh've always been a grand guy. But dere's tings I don't take from you nor nobody, see? Remember dat, or you'll wake up in a hospital—or maybe worse, wid your wife and de iceman walkin' slow behind yuh."

CORA. Aw, yuh shouldn't make dat iceman crack, Rocky. It's aw right for him to kid about it but—I notice Hickey ain't pulled dat old iceman gag dis time. (*Excitedly*) D'yuh suppose dat he did catch his wife cheatin'? I don't mean wid no iceman, but wid some guy.

ROCKY. Aw, dat's de bunk. He ain't pulled dat gag or showed her photo around because he ain't drunk. And if he'd caught her cheatin' he'd be drunk, wouldn't he? He'd have beat her up and den gone on de woist drunk he'd ever staged. Like any other guy'd do. (*The girls nod, convinced by this reasoning.*)

CHUCK. Sure! Rocky's got de right dope, Baby. He'd be paralyzed. (*While he is speaking, the Negro, JOE, comes in from the hallway. There is a noticeable change in him. He walks with a tough, truculent swagger and his good-natured face is set in sullen suspicion.*)

JOE. (*to* ROCKY—*defiantly*) I's stood tellin' people dis dump is closed for de night all I's goin' to. Let Harry hire a doorman, pay him wages, if he wants one.

ROCKY. (*scowling*) Yeah? Harry's pretty damned good to you.

JOE. (*shamefaced*) Sure he is. I don't mean dat. Anyways, it's all right. I told Schwartz, de cop, we's closed for de party. He'll keep folks away. (*Aggressively again*) I want a big drink, dat's what!

CHUCK. Who's stoppin' yuh? Yuh can have all yuh want on Hickey.

JOE. (*has taken a glass from the table and has his hand on a bottle when* HICKEY's *name is mentioned. He draws his hand back as if he were going to refuse—then grabs it defiantly and pours a big drink*) All right, I's earned all de drinks on him I could drink in a year for listenin' to his crazy bull. And here's hopin' he gets de lockjaw! (*He drinks and pours out another*) I drinks on him but I don't drink wid him. No, suh, never no more!

ROCKY. Aw, bull! Hickey's aw right. What's he done to you?

JOE. (*sullenly*) Dat's my business. I ain't buttin' in yours, is I? (*Bitterly*) Sure, you think he's all right. He's a white man, ain't he? (*His tone becomes aggressive*) Listen to me, you white boys! Don't you get it in your heads I's pretendin' to be what I ain't, or dat I ain't proud to be what I is, get me? Or you and me's goin' to have trouble! (*He picks up his drink and walks left as far away from them as he can get and slumps down on the piano stool.*)

MARGIE. (*in a low angry tone*) What a noive! Just because we act nice to him, he gets a swelled nut! If dat ain't a coon all over!

CHUCK. Talkin' fight, huh? I'll moider de nigger! (*He takes a threatening step toward* JOE, *who is staring before him guiltily now.*)

JOE. (*speaks up shamefacedly*) Listen, boys, I's sorry. I didn't mean dat. You been good friends to me. I's nuts, I guess. Dat Hickey, he gets my head all mixed up wit' craziness. (*Their faces at once clear of resentment against him.*)

CORA. Aw, dat's aw right, Joe. De boys wasn't takin' yuh serious. (*Then to the others, forcing a laugh*) Jees, what'd I say, Hickey ain't overlookin' no bets. Even Joe. (*She pauses—then adds puzzledly*) De

637

funny ting is, yuh can't stay sore at de bum when he's around. When he forgets de bughouse preachin', and quits tellin' yuh where yuh get off, he's de same old Hickey. Yuh can't help likin' de louse. And yuh got to admit he's got de right dope— (*She adds hastily*) I mean, on some of de bums here.

MARGIE. (*with a sneering look at* ROCKY) Yeah, he's coitinly got one guy I know sized up right! Huh, Poil?

PEARL. He coitinly has!

ROCKY. Cut it out, I told yuh!

LARRY. (*is staring before him broodingly. He speaks more aloud to himself than to them*) It's nothing to me what happened to him. But I have a feeling he's dying to tell us, inside him, and yet he's afraid. He's like that damned kid. It's strange the queer way he seemed to recognize him. If he's afraid, it explains why he's off booze. Like that damned kid again. Afraid if he got drunk, he'd tell— (*While he is speaking,* HICKEY *comes in the doorway at rear. He looks the same as in the previous act, except that now his face beams with the excited expectation of a boy going to a party. His arms are piled with packages.*)

HICKEY. (*booms in imitation of a familiar Polo Grounds bleacherite cry—with rising volume*) Well! Well!! Well!!! (*They all jump startledly. He comes forward, grinning*) Here I am in the nick of time. Give me a hand with these bundles, somebody. (*MARGIE and* PEARL *start taking them from his arms and putting them on the table. Now that he is present, all their attitudes show the reaction* CORA *has expressed. They can't help liking him and forgiving him.*)

MARGIE. Jees, Hickey, yuh scared me outa a year's growth, sneakin' in like dat.

HICKEY. Sneaking? Why, me and the taxi man made enough noise getting my big surprise in the hall to wake the dead. You were all so busy drinking in words of wisdom from the Old Wise Guy here, you couldn't hear anything else. (*He grins at* LARRY) From what I heard, Larry, you're not so good when you start playing Sherlock Holmes. You've got me all wrong. I'm not afraid of anything now—not even myself.

You better stick to the part of Old Cemetery, the Barker for the Big Sleep—that is, if you can still let yourself get away with it! (*He chuckles and gives* LARRY *a friendly slap on the back.* LARRY *gives him a bitter angry look.*)

CORA. (*giggles*) Old Cemetery! That's him, Hickey. We'll have to call him dat.

HICKEY. (*watching* LARRY *quizzically*) Beginning to do a lot of puzzling about me, aren't you, Larry? But that won't help you. You've got to think of yourself. I couldn't give you my peace. You've got to find your own. All I can do is help you, and the rest of the gang, by showing you the way to find it. (*He has said this with a simple persuasive earnestness. He pauses, and for a second they stare at him with fascinated resentful uneasiness.*)

ROCKY. (*breaks the spell*) Aw, hire a church!

HICKEY. (*placatingly*) All right! All right! Don't get sore, boys and girls. I guess that did sound too much like a lousy preacher. Let's forget it and get busy on the party. (*They look relieved.*)

CHUCK. Is dose bundles grub, Hickey? You bought enough already to feed an army.

HICKEY. (*with boyish excitement again*) Can't be too much! I want this to be the biggest birthday Harry's ever had. You and Rocky go in the hall and get the big surprise. My arms are busted lugging it. (*They catch his excitement.* CHUCK *and* ROCKY *go out, grinning expectantly. The three girls gather around* HICKEY, *full of thrilled curiosity.*)

PEARL. Jees, yuh got us all het up! What is it, Hickey?

HICKEY. Wait and see. I got it as a treat for the three of you more than anyone. I thought to myself, I'll bet this is what will please those whores more than anything. (*They wince as if he had slapped them, but before they have a chance to be angry, he goes on affectionately*) I said to myself, I don't care how much it costs, they're worth it. They're the best little scouts in the world, and they've been damned kind to me when I was down and out! Nothing is too good for them. (*Earnestly*) I mean every word of that, too—and then some! (*Then, as if he noticed*

639

the expression on their faces for the first time) What's the matter? You look sore. What—? (*Then he chuckles*) Oh, I see. But you know how I feel about that. You know I didn't say it to offend you. So don't be silly now.

MARGIE. (*lets out a tense breath*) Aw right, Hickey. Let it slide.

HICKEY. (*jubilantly, as* CHUCK *and* ROCKY *enter carrying a big wicker basket*) Look! There it comes! Unveil it, boys. (*They pull off a covering burlap bag. The basket is piled with quarts of champagne.*)

PEARL. (*with childish excitement*) It's champagne! Jees, Hickey, if you ain't a sport! (*She gives him a hug, forgetting all animosity, as do the other girls.*)

MARGIE. I never been soused on champagne. Let's get stinko, Poil.

PEARL. You betcha my life! De bot' of us! (*A holiday spirit of gay festivity has seized them all. Even* JOE MOTT *is standing up to look at the wine with an admiring grin, and* HUGO *raises his head to blink at it.*)

JOE. You sure is hittin' de high spots, Hickey. (*Boastfully*) Man, when I runs my gamblin' house, I drinks dat old bubbly water in steins! (*He stops guiltily and gives* HICKEY *a look of defiance*) I's goin' to drink it dat way again, too, soon's I make my stake! And dat ain't no pipe dream, neider! (*He sits down where he was, his back turned to them.*)

ROCKY. What'll we drink it outa, Hickey? Dere ain't no wine glasses.

HICKEY. (*enthusiastically*) Joe has the right idea! Schooners! That's the spirit for Harry's birthday! (*ROCKY and CHUCK carry the basket of wine into the bar. The three girls go back and stand around the entrance to the bar, chatting excitedly among themselves and to CHUCK and ROCKY in the bar.*)

HUGO. (*with his silly giggle*) Ve vill trink vine beneath the villow trees!

HICKEY. (*grins at him*) That's the spirit, Brother—and let the lousy slaves drink vinegar! (*HUGO blinks at him startledly, then looks away.*)

HUGO. (*mutters*) Gottamned liar! (*He puts his head back on his arms and closes his eyes, but this time his habitual pass-out has a quality of hiding.*)

LARRY. (*gives* HUGO *a pitying glance—in a low tone of anger*) Leave Hugo be! He rotted ten years in prison for his faith! He's earned his dream! Have you no decency or pity?

HICKEY. (*quizzically*) Hello, what's this? I thought you were in the grandstand. (*Then with a simple earnestness, taking a chair by* LARRY, *and putting a hand on his shoulder*) Listen, Larry, you're getting me all wrong. Hell, you ought to know me better. I've always been the best-natured slob in the world. Of course, I have pity. But now I've seen the light, it isn't my old kind of pity—the kind yours is. It isn't the kind that lets itself off easy by encouraging some poor guy to go on kidding himself with a lie—the kind that leaves the poor slob worse off because it makes him feel guiltier than ever—the kind that makes his lying hopes nag at him and reproach him until he's a rotten skunk in his own eyes. I know all about that kind of pity. I've had a bellyful of it in my time, and it's all wrong! (*With a salesman's persuasiveness*) No, sir. The kind of pity I feel now is after final results that will really save the poor guy, and make him contented with what he is, and quit battling himself, and find peace for the rest of his life. Oh, I know how you resent the way I have to show you up to yourself. I don't blame you. I know from my own experience it's bitter medicine, facing yourself in the mirror with the old false whiskers off. But you forget that, once you're cured. You'll be grateful to me when all at once you find you're able to admit, without feeling ashamed, that all the grandstand foolosopher bunk and the waiting for the Big Sleep stuff is a pipe dream. You'll say to yourself, I'm just an old man who is scared of life, but even more scared of dying. So I'm keeping drunk and hanging on to life at any price, and what of it? Then you'll know what real peace means, Larry, because you won't be scared of either life or death any more. You simply won't give a damn! Any more than I do!

LARRY. (*has been staring into his eyes with a fascinated wondering dread*) Be God, if I'm not beginning to think you've gone mad! (*With a rush of anger*) You're a liar!

HICKEY. (*injuredly*) Now, listen, that's no way to talk to an old pal who's trying to help you. Hell, if you really wanted to die, you'd just take a hop off your fire escape, wouldn't you? And if you really were in the grandstand, you wouldn't be pitying everyone. Oh, I know the truth is tough at first. It was for me. All I ask is for you to suspend judgment and give it a chance. I'll absolutely guarantee— Hell, Larry, I'm no fool. Do you suppose I'd deliberately set out to get under everyone's skin and put myself in dutch with all my old pals, if I wasn't certain, from my own experience, that it means contentment in the end for all of you? (LARRY *again is staring at him fascinatedly.* HICKEY *grins*) As for my being bughouse, you can't crawl out of it that way. Hell, I'm too damned sane. I can size up guys, and turn 'em inside out, better than I ever could. Even where they're strangers like that Parritt kid. He's licked, Larry. I think there is only one possible way out you can help him to take. That is, if you have the right kind of pity for him.

LARRY. (*uneasily*) What do you mean? (*Attempting indifference*) I'm not advising him, except to leave me out of his troubles. He's nothing to me.

HICKEY. (*shakes his head*) You'll find he won't agree to that. He'll keep after you until he makes you help him. Because he has to be punished, so he can forgive himself. He's lost all his guts. He can't manage it alone, and you're the only one he can turn to.

LARRY. For the love of God, mind your own business! (*With forced scorn*) A lot you know about him! He's hardly spoken to you!

HICKEY. No, that's right. But I do know a lot about him just the same. I've had hell inside me. I can spot it in others. (*Frowning*) Maybe that's what gives me the feeling there's something familiar about him, something between us. (*He shakes his head*) No, it's more than that. I can't figure it. Tell me about him. For instance, I don't imagine he's married, is he?

LARRY. No.

HICKEY. Hasn't he been mixed up with some woman? I don't mean trollops. I mean the old real love stuff that crucifies you.

LARRY. (*with a calculating relieved look at him—encouraging him along this line*) Maybe you're right. I wouldn't be surprised.

HICKEY. (*grins at him quizzically*) I see. You think I'm on the wrong track and you're glad I am. Because then I won't suspect whatever he did about the Great Cause. That's another lie you tell yourself, Larry, that the good old Cause means nothing to you any more. (LARRY *is about to burst out in denial but* HICKEY *goes on*) But you're all wrong about Parritt. That isn't what's got him stopped. It's what's behind that. And it's a woman. I recognize the symptoms.

LARRY. (*sneeringly*) And you're the boy who's never wrong! Don't be a damned fool. His trouble is he was brought up a devout believer in the Movement and now he's lost his faith. It's a shock, but he's young and he'll soon find another dream just as good. (*He adds sardonically*) Or as bad.

HICKEY. All right. I'll let it go at that, Larry. He's nothing to me except I'm glad he's here because he'll help me make you wake up to yourself. I don't even like the guy, or the feeling there's anything between us. But you'll find I'm right just the same, when you get to the final showdown with him.

LARRY. There'll be no showdown! I don't give a tinker's damn—

HICKEY. Sticking to the old grandstand, eh? Well, I knew you'd be the toughest to convince of all the gang, Larry. And, along with Harry and Jimmy Tomorrow, you're the one I want most to help. (*He puts an arm around* LARRY's *shoulder and gives him an affectionate hug*) I've always liked you a lot, you old bastard! (*He gets up and his manner changes to his bustling party excitement—glancing at his watch*) Well, well, not much time before twelve. Let's get busy, boys and girls. (*He looks over the table where the cake is*) Cake all set. Good. And my presents, and yours, girls, and Chuck's, and Rocky's. Fine. Harry'll certainly be touched by your thought of him. (*He goes back to the girls*) You go in the bar, Pearl and Margie, and get the grub ready so it can be brought right in. There'll be some drinking and toasts first, of course. My idea is to use the wine for that, so get it all set. I'll go upstairs now and root everyone out. Harry the last. I'll come back with him. Somebody light the candles on the cake when you hear us coming, and you start playing Harry's favorite tune, Cora. Hustle now, everybody. We want this to come off in style. (*He bustles into the hall.* MARGIE *and* PEARL *disappear in the bar.* CORA *goes to the piano.* JOE *gets off the stool sullenly to let her sit down.*)

CORA. I got to practice. I ain't laid my mits on a box in Gawd knows when. (*With the soft pedal down, she begins gropingly to pick out "The Sunshine of Paradise Alley"*) Is dat right, Joe? I've forgotten dat has-been tune. (*She picks out a few more notes*) Come on, Joe, hum de tune so I can follow. (JOE *begins to hum and sing in a low voice and correct her. He forgets his sullenness and becomes his old self again.*)

LARRY. (*suddenly gives a laugh—in his comically intense, crazy tone*) Be God, it's a second feast of Belshazzar, with Hickey to do the writing on the wall!

CORA. Aw, shut up, Old Cemetery! Always beefin'! (WILLIE *comes in from the hall. He is in a pitiable state, his face pasty, haggard with sleeplessness and nerves, his eyes sick and haunted. He is sober.* CORA *greets him over her shoulder kiddingly*) If it ain't Prince Willie! (*Then kindly*) Gee, kid, yuh look sick. Git a coupla shots in yuh.

WILLIE. (*tensely*) No, thanks. Not now. I'm tapering off. (*He sits down weakly on* LARRY's *right.*)

CORA. (*astonished*) What d'yuh know? He means it!

WILLIE. (*leaning toward* LARRY *confidentially—in a low shaken voice*) It's been hell up in that damned room, Larry! The things I've imagined! (*He shudders*) I thought I'd go crazy. (*With pathetic boastful pride*) But I've got it beat now. By tomorrow morning I'll be on the wagon. I'll get back my clothes the first thing. Hickey's loaning me the money. I'm going to do what I've always said—go to the D.A.'s office. He was a good friend of my Old Man's. He was only assistant, then. He was in on the graft, but my Old Man never squealed on him. So he certainly owes it to me to give me a chance. And he knows that I really was a brilliant law student. (*Self-reassuringly*) Oh, I know I can make good, now I'm getting off the booze forever. (*Moved*) I owe a lot to Hickey. He's made me wake up to myself—see what a fool— It wasn't nice to face but— (*With bitter resentment*) It isn't what he says. It's what you feel behind—what he hints— Christ, you'd think all I really wanted to do with my life was sit here and stay drunk. (*With hatred*) I'll show him!

LARRY. (*masking pity behind a sardonic tone*) If you want my advice, you'll put the nearest bottle to your mouth until you don't give a damn for Hickey!

WILLIE. (*stares at a bottle greedily, tempted for a moment—then bitterly*) That's fine advice! I thought you were my friend! (*He gets up with a hurt glance at* LARRY, *and moves away to take a chair in back of the left end of the table, where he sits in dejected, shaking misery, his chin on his chest.*)

JOE. (*to* CORA) No, like dis. (*He beats time with his finger and sings in a low voice*) "She is the sunshine of Paradise Alley." (*She plays*) Dat's more like it. Try it again. (*She begins to play through the chorus again.* DON PARRITT *enters from the hall. There is a frightened look on his face. He slinks in furtively, as if he were escaping from someone. He looks relieved when he sees* LARRY *and comes and slips into the chair on his right.* LARRY *pretends not to notice his coming, but he instinctively shrinks with repulsion.* PARRITT *leans toward him and speaks ingratiatingly in a low secretive tone.*)

PARRITT. Gee, I'm glad you're here, Larry. That damned fool, Hickey, knocked on my door. I opened up because I thought it must be you, and he came busting in and made me come downstairs. I don't know what for. I don't belong in this birthday celebration. I don't know this gang and I don't want to be mixed up with them. All I came here for was to find you.

LARRY. (*tensely*) I've warned you—

PARRITT. (*goes on as if he hadn't heard*) Can't you make Hickey mind his own business? I don't like that guy, Larry. The way he acts, you'd think he had something on me. Why, just now he pats me on the shoulder, like he was sympathizing with me, and says, "I know how it is, Son, but you can't hide from yourself, not even here on the bottom of the sea. You've got to face the truth and then do what must be done for your own peace and the happiness of all concerned." What did he mean by that, Larry?

LARRY. How the hell would I know?

PARRITT. Then he grins and says, "Never mind, Larry's getting wise to himself. I think you can rely on his help in the end. He'll have to choose between living and dying, and he'll never choose to die while there is a breath left in the old bastard!" And then he laughs like it was a joke on you. (*He pauses.* LARRY *is rigid on his chair, staring before him.* PARRITT *asks him with a sudden taunt in his voice*) Well, what do you say to that, Larry?

LARRY. I've nothing to say. Except you're a bigger fool than he is to listen to him.

PARRITT. (*with a sneer*) Is that so? He's no fool where you're concerned. He's got your number, all right! (LARRY's *face tightens but he keeps silent.* PARRITT *changes to a contrite, appealing air*) I don't mean that. But you keep acting as if you were sore at me, and that gets my goat. You know what I want most is to be friends with you, Larry. I haven't a single friend left in the world. I hoped you— (*Bitterly*) And you could be, too, without it hurting you. You ought to, for Mother's sake. She really loved you. You loved her, too, didn't you?

LARRY. (*tensely*) Leave what's dead in its grave.

PARRITT. I suppose, because I was only a kid, you didn't think I was wise about you and her. Well, I was. I've been wise, ever since I can remember, to all the guys she's had, although she'd tried to kid me along it wasn't so. That was a silly stunt for a free Anarchist woman, wasn't it, being ashamed of being free?

LARRY. Shut your damned trap!

PARRITT. (*guiltily but with a strange undertone of satisfaction*) Yes, I know I shouldn't say that now. I keep forgetting she isn't free any more. (*He pauses*) Do you know, Larry, you're the one of them all she cared

646

most about? Anyone else who left the Movement would have been dead to her, but she couldn't forget you. She'd always make excuses for you. I used to try and get her goat about you. I'd say, "Larry's got brains and yet he thinks the Movement is just a crazy pipe dream." She'd blame it on booze getting you. She'd kid herself that you'd give up booze and come back to the Movement—tomorrow! She'd say, "Larry can't kill in himself a faith he's given his life to, not without killing himself." (*He grins sneeringly*) How about it, Larry? Was she right? (LARRY *remains silent. He goes on insistently*) I suppose what she really meant was, come back to her. She was always getting the Movement mixed up with herself. But I'm sure she really must have loved you, Larry. As much as she could love anyone besides herself. But she wasn't faithful to you, even at that, was she? That's why you finally walked out on her, isn't it? I remember that last fight you had with her. I was listening. I was on your side, even if she was my mother, because I liked you so much; you'd been so good to me—like a father. I remember her putting on her high-and-mighty free-woman stuff, saying you were still a slave to bourgeois morality and jealousy and you thought a woman you loved was a piece of private property you owned. I remember that you got mad and you told her, "I don't like living with a whore, if that's what you mean!"

LARRY. (*bursts out*) You lie! I never called her that!

PARRITT. (*goes on as if* LARRY *hadn't spoken*) I think that's why she still respects you, because it was you who left her. You were the only one to beat her to it. She got sick of the others before they did of her. I don't think she ever cared much about them, anyway. She just had to keep on having lovers to prove to herself how free she was (*He pauses— then with a bitter repulsion*) It made home a lousy place. I felt like you did about it. I'd get feeling it was like living in a whorehouse—only worse, because she didn't have to make her living—

LARRY. You bastard! She's your mother! Have you no shame?

PARRITT. (*bitterly*) No! She brought me up to believe that family-respect stuff is all bourgeois, property-owning crap. Why should I be ashamed?

LARRY. (*making a move to get up*) I've had enough!

PARRITT. (*catches his arm—pleadingly*) No! Don't leave me! Please! I promise I won't mention her again! (LARRY *sinks back in his chair*) I only did it to make you understand better. I know this isn't the place to— Why didn't you come up to my room, like I asked you? I kept waiting. We could talk everything over there.

LARRY. There's nothing to talk over!

PARRITT. But I've got to talk to you. Or I'll talk to Hickey. He won't let me alone! I feel he knows, anyway! And I know he'd understand, all right—in his way. But I hate his guts! I don't want anything to do with him! I'm scared of him, honest. There's something not human behind his damned grinning and kidding.

LARRY. (*starts*) Ah! You feel that, too?

PARRITT. (*pleadingly*) But I can't go on like this. I've got to decide what I've got to do. I've got to tell you, Larry!

LARRY. (*again starts up*) I won't listen!

PARRITT. (*again holds him by the arm*) All right! I won't. Don't go! (LARRY *lets himself be pulled down on his chair.* PARRITT *examines his face and becomes insultingly scornful*) Who do you think you're kidding? I know damned well you've guessed—

LARRY. I've guessed nothing!

PARRITT. But I want you to guess now! I'm glad you have! I know now, since Hickey's been after me, that I meant you to guess right from the start. That's why I came to you. (*Hurrying on with an attempt at a plausible frank air that makes what he says seem doubly false*) I want you to understand the reason. You see, I began studying American history. I got admiring Washington and Jefferson and Jackson and Lincoln. I began to feel patriotic and love this country. I saw it was the best government in the world, where everybody was equal and had a chance. I saw that all the ideas behind the Movement came from a lot of Russians like Bakunin and Kropotkin and were meant for Europe, but we didn't need them here in a democracy where we were free already. I didn't want this country to be destroyed for a damned foreign pipe dream. After all, I'm from old American pioneer stock. I began to feel I was a traitor for helping a lot of cranks and bums and free women plot to overthrow our government. And then I saw it was my duty to my country—

LARRY. (*nauseated—turns on him*) You stinking rotten liar! Do you think you can fool me with such hypocrite's cant! (*Then turning away*) I don't give a damn what you did! It's on your head—whatever it was! I don't want to know—and I won't know!

PARRITT. (*as if LARRY had never spoken—falteringly*) But I never thought Mother would be caught. Please believe that, Larry. You know I never would have—

LARRY. (*his face haggard, drawing a deep breath and closing his eyes— as if he were trying to hammer something into his own brain*) All I know is I'm sick of life! I'm through! I've forgotten myself! I'm drowned and contented on the bottom of a bottle. Honor or dishonor, faith or treachery are nothing to me but the opposites of the same stupidity which is ruler and king of life, and in the end they rot into dust in the same grave. All things are the same meaningless joke to me, for they grin at me from the one skull of death. So go away. You're wasting breath. I've forgotten your mother.

PARRITT. (*jeers angrily*) The old foolosopher, eh? (*He spits out contemptuously*) You lousy old faker!

LARRY. (*so distracted he pleads weakly*) For the love of God, leave me in peace the little time that's left to me!

PARRITT. Aw, don't pull that pitiful old-man junk on me! You old bastard, you'll never die as long as there's a free drink of whiskey left!

LARRY. (*stung—furiously*) Look out how you try to taunt me back into life, I warn you! I might remember the thing they call justice there, and the punishment for— (*He checks himself with an effort—then with a real indifference that comes from exhaustion*) I'm old and tired.

649

To hell with you! You're as mad as Hickey, and as big a liar. I'd never let myself believe a word you told me.

PARRITT. (*threateningly*) The hell you won't! Wait till Hickey gets through with you! (PEARL *and* MARGIE *come in from the bar. At the sight of them,* PARRITT *instantly subsides and becomes self-conscious and defensive, scowling at them and then quickly looking away.*)

MARGIE. (*eyes him jeeringly*) Why, hello, Tightwad Kid. Come to join de party? Gee, don't he act bashful, Poil?

PEARL. Yeah. Especially wid his dough. (PARRITT *slinks to a chair at the left end of the table, pretending he hasn't heard them. Suddenly there is a noise of angry, cursing voices and a scuffle from the hall.* PEARL *yells*) Hey, Rocky! Fight in de hall! (ROCKY *and* CHUCK *run from behind the bar curtain and rush into the hall.* ROCKY'S *voice is heard in irritated astonishment, "What de hell?" and then the scuffle stops and* ROCKY *appears holding* CAPTAIN LEWIS *by the arm, followed by* CHUCK *with a similar hold on* GENERAL WETJOEN. *Although these two have been drinking they are both sober, for them. Their faces are sullenly angry, their clothes disarranged from the tussle.*)

ROCKY. (*leading* LEWIS *forward—astonished, amused and irritated*) Can yuh beat it? I've heard youse two call each odder every name yuh could think of but I never seen you— (*Indignantly*) A swell time to stage your first bout, on Harry's boithday party! What started de scrap?

LEWIS. (*forcing a casual tone*) Nothing, old chap. Our business, you know. That bloody ass, Hickey, made some insinuation about me, and the boorish Boer had the impertinence to agree with him.

WETJOEN. Dot's a lie! Hickey made joke about me, and this Limey said yes, it was true!

ROCKY. Well, sit down, de bot' of yuh, and cut out de rough stuff. (*He and* CHUCK *dump them down in adjoining chairs toward the left end of the table, where, like two sulky boys, they turn their backs on each other as far as possible in chairs which both face front.*)

MARGIE. (*laughs*) Jees, lookit de two bums! Like a coupla kids! Kiss and make up, for Gawd's sakes!

650

ROCKY. Yeah. Harry's party begins in a minute and we don't want no soreheads around.

LEWIS. (*stiffly*) Very well. In deference to the occasion, I apologize, General Wetjoen—provided that you do also.

WETJOEN. (*sulkily*) I apologize, Captain Lewis—because Harry is my goot friend.

ROCKY. Aw, hell! If yuh can't do better'n dat—! (MOSHER *and* MCGLOIN *enter together from the hall. Both have been drinking but are not drunk.*)

PEARL. Here's de star boarders. (*They advance, their heads together, so interested in a discussion they are oblivious to everyone.*)

MCGLOIN. I'm telling you, Ed, it's serious this time. That bastard, Hickey, has got Harry on the hip. (*As he talks,* MARGIE, PEARL, ROCKY *and* CHUCK *prick up their ears and gather round.* CORA, *at the piano, keeps running through the tune, with soft pedal, and singing the chorus half under her breath, with* JOE *still correcting her mistakes. At the table,* LARRY, PARRITT, WILLIE, WETJOEN *and* LEWIS *sit motionless, staring in front of them.* HUGO *seems asleep in his habitual position*) And you know it isn't going to do us no good if he gets him to take that walk tomorrow.

MOSHER. You're damned right. Harry'll mosey around the ward, dropping in on everyone who knew him when. (*Indignantly*) And they'll all give him a phony glad hand and a ton of good advice about what a sucker he is to stand for us.

MCGLOIN. He's sure to call on Bessie's relations to do a little cryin' over dear Bessie. And you know what that bitch and all her family thought of me.

MOSHER. (*with a flash of his usual humor—rebukingly*) Remember, Lieutenant, you are speaking of my sister! Dear Bessie wasn't a bitch. She was a God-damned bitch! But if you think my loving relatives will have time to discuss you, you don't know them. They'll be too busy telling Harry what a drunken crook I am and saying he ought to have me put in Sing Sing!

MCGLOIN. (*dejectedly*) Yes, once Bessie's relations get their hooks in him, it'll be as tough for us as if she wasn't gone.

MOSHER. (*dejectedly*) Yes, Harry has always been weak and easily influenced, and now he's getting old he'll be an easy mark for those grafters. (*Then with forced reassurance*) Oh, hell, Mac, we're saps to worry. We've heard Harry pull that bluff about taking a walk every birthday he's had for twenty years.

MCGLOIN. (*doubtfully*) But Hickey wasn't sicking him on those times. Just the opposite. He was asking Harry what he wanted to go out for when there was plenty of whiskey here.

MOSHER. (*with a change to forced carelessness*) Well, after all, I don't care whether he goes out or not. I'm clearing out tomorrow morning anyway. I'm just sorry for you, Mac.

MCGLOIN. (*resentfully*) You needn't be, then. Ain't I going myself? I was only feeling sorry for you.

MOSHER. Yes, my mind is made up. Hickey may be a lousy, interfering pest, now he's gone teetotal on us, but there's a lot of truth in some of his bull. Hanging around here getting plastered with you, Mac, is pleasant, I won't deny, but the old booze gets you in the end, if you keep lapping it up. It's time I quit for a while. (*With forced enthusiasm*) Besides, I feel the call of the old carefree circus life in my blood again. I'll see the boss tomorrow. It's late in the season but he'll be glad to take me on. And won't all the old gang be tickled to death when I show up on the lot!

MCGLOIN. Maybe—if they've got a rope handy!

MOSHER. (*turns on him—angrily*) Listen! I'm damned sick of that kidding!

MCGLOIN. You are, are you? Well, I'm sicker of your kidding me about getting reinstated on the Force. And whatever you'd like, I can't spend my life sitting here with you, ruining my stomach with rotgut. I'm tapering off, and in the morning I'll be fresh as a daisy. I'll go and have a private chin with the Commissioner. (*With forced enthusiasm*)

Man alive, from what the boys tell me, there's sugar galore these days, and I'll soon be ridin' around in a big red automobile—

MOSHER. (*derisively—beckoning an imaginary Chinese*) Here, One Lung Hop! Put fresh peanut oil in the lamp and cook the Lieutenant another dozen pills! It's his gowed-up night!

MCGLOIN. (*stung—pulls back a fist threateningly*) One more crack like that and I'll—!

MOSHER. (*putting up his fists*) Yes? Just start—! (CHUCK *and* ROCKY *jump between them.*)

ROCKY. Hey! Are you guys nuts? Jees, it's Harry's boithday party! (*They both look guilty*) Sit down and behave.

MOSHER. (*grumpily*) All right. Only tell him to lay off me. (*He lets* ROCKY *push him in a chair, at the right end of the table, rear.*)

MCGLOIN. (*grumpily*) Tell him to lay off me. (*He lets* CHUCK *push him into the chair on* MOSHER's *left. At this moment* HICKEY *bursts in from the hall, bustling and excited.*)

HICKEY. Everything all set? Fine! (*He glances at his watch*) Half a minute to go. Harry's starting down with Jimmy. I had a hard time getting them to move! They'd rather stay hiding up there, kidding each other along. (*He chuckles*) Harry don't even want to remember it's his birthday now! (*He hears a noise from the stairs*) Here they come! (*Urgently*) Light the candles! Get ready to play, Cora! Stand up, everybody! Get that wine ready, Chuck and Rocky! (MARGIE *and* PEARL *light the candles on the cake.* CORA *gets her hands set over the piano keys, watching over her shoulder.* ROCKY *and* CHUCK *go in the bar. Everybody at the table stands up mechanically.* HUGO *is the last, suddenly coming to and scrambling to his feet.* HARRY HOPE *and* JIMMY TOMORROW *appear in the hall outside the door.* HICKEY *looks up from his watch*) On the dot! It's twelve! (*Like a cheer leader*) Come on now, everybody, with a Happy Birthday, Harry! (*With his voice leading they all shout* "Happy Birthday, Harry!" *in a spiritless chorus.* HICKEY *signals to* CORA, *who starts playing and singing in a whiskey soprano "She's the Sunshine of Paradise Alley."* HOPE *and* JIMMY *stand in the doorway. Both*

653

have been drinking heavily. In HOPE *the effect is apparent only in a bristling, touchy, pugnacious attitude. It is entirely different from the usual irascible beefing he delights in and which no one takes seriously. Now he really has a chip on his shoulder.* JIMMY, *on the other hand, is plainly drunk, but it has not had the desired effect, for beneath a pathetic assumption of gentlemanly poise, he is obviously frightened and shrinking back within himself.* HICKEY *grabs* HOPE's *hand and pumps it up and down. For a moment* HOPE *appears unconscious of this handshake. Then he jerks his hand away angrily.*)

HOPE. Cut out the glad hand, Hickey. D'you think I'm a sucker? I know you, bejees, you sneaking, lying drummer! (*With rising anger, to the others*) And all you bums! What the hell you trying to do, yelling and raising the roof? Want the cops to close the joint and get my license taken away? (*He yells at* CORA *who has stopped singing but continues to play mechanically with many mistakes*) Hey, you dumb tart, quit banging that box! Bejees, the least you could do is learn the tune!

CORA. (*stops—deeply hurt*) Aw, Harry! Jees, ain't I— (*Her eyes begin to fill.*)

HOPE. (*glaring at the other girls*) And you two hookers, screaming at the top of your lungs! What d'you think this is, a dollar cathouse? Bejees, that's where you belong!

PEARL. (*miserably*) Aw, Harry— (*She begins to cry.*)

MARGIE. Jees, Harry, I never thought you'd say that—like yuh meant it. (*She puts her arm around* PEARL—*on the verge of tears herself*) Aw, don't bawl, Poil. He don't mean it.

HICKEY. (*reproachfully*) Now, Harry! Don't take it out on the gang because you're upset about yourself. Anyway, I've promised you you'll come through all right, haven't I? So quit worrying! (*He slaps* HOPE *on the back encouragingly.* HOPE *flashes him a glance of hate*) Be yourself, Governor. You don't want to bawl out the old gang just when they're congratulating you on your birthday, do you? Hell, that's no way!

HOPE. (*looking guilty and shamefaced now—forcing an unconvincing attempt at his natural tone*) Bejees, they ain't as dumb as you. They know I was only kidding them. They know I appreciate their congratulations. Don't you, fellers? (*There is a listless chorus of* "*Sure, Harry,*" "*Yes,*" "*Of course we do,*" *etc. He comes forward to the two girls, with* JIMMY *and* HICKEY *following him, and pats them clumsily*) Bejees, I like you broads. You know I was only kidding. (*Instantly they forgive him and smile affectionately.*)

MARGIE. Sure we know, Harry.

PEARL. Sure.

HICKEY. (*grinning*) Sure. Harry's the greatest kidder in this dump and that's saying something! Look how he's kidded himself for twenty years! (*As* HOPE *gives him a bitter, angry glance, he digs him in the ribs with his elbow playfully*) Unless I'm wrong, Governor, and I'm betting I'm not. We'll soon know, eh? Tomorrow morning. No, by God, it's *this* morning now!

JIMMY. (*with a dazed dread*) This morning?

HICKEY. Yes, it's today at last, Jimmy. (*He pats him on the back*) Don't be so scared! I've promised I'll help you.

JIMMY. (*trying to hide his dread behind an offended, drunken dignity*) I don't understand you. Kindly remember I'm fully capable of settling my own affairs!

HICKEY. (*earnestly*) Well, isn't that exactly what I want you to do, settle with yourself once and for all? (*He speaks in his ear in confidential warning*) Only watch out on the booze, Jimmy. You know, not too much from now on. You've had a lot already, and you don't want to let yourself duck out of it by being too drunk to move—not this time! (*JIMMY gives him a guilty, stricken look and turns away and slumps into the chair on* MOSHER's *right.*)

HOPE. (*to* MARGIE—*still guiltily*) Bejees, Margie, you know I didn't mean it. It's that lousy drummer riding me that's got my goat.

MARGIE. I know. (*She puts a protecting arm around* HOPE *and turns him to face the table with the cake and presents*) Come on. You ain't noticed your cake yet. Ain't it grand?

HOPE. (*trying to brighten up*) Say, that's pretty. Ain't ever had a cake since Bessie— Six candles. Each for ten years, eh? Bejees, that's thoughtful of you.

PEARL. It was Hickey got it.

HOPE. (*his tone forced*) Well, it was thoughtful of him. He means well, I guess. (*His eyes, fixed on the cake, harden angrily*) To hell with his cake. (*He starts to turn away.* PEARL *grabs his arm.*)

PEARL. Wait, Harry. Yuh ain't seen de presents from Margie and me and Cora and Chuck and Rocky. And dere's a watch all engraved wid your name and de date from Hickey.

HOPE. To hell with it! Bejees, he can keep it. (*This time he does turn away.*)

PEARL. Jees, he ain't even goin' to look at our presents.

MARGIE. (*bitterly*) Dis is all wrong. We gotta put some life in dis party or I'll go nuts! Hey, Cora, what's de matter wid dat box? Can't yuh play for Harry? Yuh don't have to stop just because he kidded yuh!

HOPE. (*rouses himself—with forced heartiness*) Yes, come on, Cora. You was playing it fine. (CORA *begins to play half-heartedly.* HOPE *suddenly becomes almost tearfully sentimental*) It was Bessie's favorite tune. She was always singing it. It brings her back. I wish— (*He chokes up.*)

HICKEY. (*grins at him—amusedly*) Yes, we've all heard you tell us you thought the world of her, Governor.

HOPE. (*looks at him with frightened suspicion*) Well, so I did, bejees! Everyone knows I did! (*Threateningly*) Bejees, if you say I didn't—

HICKEY. (*soothingly*) Now, Governor. I didn't say anything. You're the only one knows the truth about that. (HOPE *stares at him confusedly.* CORA *continues to play. For a moment there is a pause, broken by* JIMMY TOMORROW *who speaks with muzzy, self-pitying melancholy out of a sentimental dream.*)

JIMMY. Marjorie's favorite song was "Loch Lomond." She was beautiful and she played the piano beautifully and she had a beautiful voice. (*With gentle sorrow*) You were lucky, Harry. Bessie died. But there are more bitter sorrows than losing the woman one loves by the hand of death—

HICKEY. (*with an amused wink at* HOPE) Now, listen, Jimmy, you needn't go on. We've all heard that story about how you came back to Cape Town and found her in the hay with a staff officer. We know you like to believe that was what started you on the booze and ruined your life.

JIMMY. (*stammers*) I—I'm talking to Harry. Will you kindly keep out of— (*With a pitiful defiance*) My life is not ruined!

HICKEY. (*ignoring this—with a kidding grin*) But I'll bet when you admit the truth to yourself, you'll confess you were pretty sick of her hating you for getting drunk. I'll bet you were really damned relieved when she gave you such a good excuse. (JIMMY *stares at him strickenly.* HICKEY *pats him on the back again—with sincere sympathy*) I know how it is, Jimmy. I— (*He stops abruptly and for a second he seems to lose his self-assurance and become confused.*)

LARRY. (*seizing on this with vindictive relish*) Ha! So that's what happened to you, is it? Your iceman joke finally came home to roost, did it? (*He grins tauntingly*) You should have remembered there's truth in the old superstition that you'd better look out what you call because in the end it comes to you!

HICKEY. (*himself again—grins to* LARRY *kiddingly*) Is that a fact, Larry? Well, well! Then you'd better watch out how you keep calling for that old Big Sleep! (LARRY *starts and for a second looks superstitiously frightened. Abruptly* HICKEY *changes to his jovial, bustling, master-of-ceremonies manner*) But what are we waiting for, boys and girls? Let's start the party rolling! (*He shouts to the bar*) Hey, Chuck and Rocky! Bring on the big surprise! Governor, you sit at the head of the table here. (*He makes* HARRY *sit down on the chair at the end of the table, right. To* MARGIE *and* PEARL) Come on, girls, sit down. (*They sit side by side on* JIMMY'S *right.* HICKEY *bustles down to the left end of table*) I'll sit here at the foot. (*He sits, with* CORA *on his left and* JOE *on her left.* ROCKY *and* CHUCK *appear from the bar, each bearing a big tray laden with schooners of champagne which they start shoving in front of each member of the party.*)

ROCKY. (*with forced cheeriness*) Real champagne, bums! Cheer up! What is dis, a funeral? Jees, mixin' champagne wid Harry's redeye will knock yuh paralyzed! Ain't yuh never satisfied? (*He and* CHUCK *finish serving out the schooners, grab the last two themselves and sit down in the two vacant chairs remaining near the middle of the table. As they do so,* HICKEY *rises, a schooner in his hand.*)

HICKEY. (*rapping on the table for order when there is nothing but a dead silence*) Order! Order, Ladies and Gents! (*He catches* LARRY'S *eyes on the glass in his hand*) Yes, Larry, I'm going to drink with you this time. To prove I'm not teetotal because I'm afraid booze would make me spill my secrets, as you think. (LARRY *looks sheepish.* HICKEY *chuckles and goes on*) No, I gave you the simple truth about that. I don't need booze or anything else any more. But I want to be sociable and propose a toast in honor of our old friend, Harry, and drink it with you. (*His eyes fix on* HUGO, *who is out again, his head on his plate— To* CHUCK, *who is on* HUGO's *left*) Wake up our demon bomb-tosser, Chuck. We don't want corpses at this feast.

CHUCK. (*gives* HUGO *a shake*) Hey, Hugo, come up for air! Don't yuh see de champagne? (HUGO *blinks around and giggles foolishly*)

HUGO. Ve vill eat birthday cake and trink champagne beneath the villow tree! (*He grabs his schooner and takes a greedy gulp—then sets it back on the table with a grimace of distaste—in a strange, arrogantly disdainful tone, as if he were rebuking a butler*) Dis vine is unfit to trink. It has not properly been iced.

HICKEY. (*amusedly*) Always a high-toned swell at heart, eh, Hugo? God help us poor bums if you'd ever get to telling us where to get off! You'd have been drinking our blood beneath those willow trees! (*He chuckles.* HUGO *shrinks back in his chair, blinking at him, but* HICKEY *is now looking up the table at* HOPE. *He starts his toast, and as he goes on he becomes more moved and obviously sincere*) Here's the toast, Ladies and Gents! Here's to Harry Hope, who's been a friend in need to every one of us! Here's to the old Governor, the best sport and the kindest, biggest-hearted guy in the world! Here's wishing you all the luck there is, Harry, and long life and happiness! Come on, everybody! To Harry! Bottoms up! (*They have all caught his sincerity with eager relief. They raise their schooners with an enthusiastic chorus of "Here's how, Harry!" "Here's luck, Harry!" etc., and gulp half the wine down,* HICKEY *leading them in this.*)

HOPE. (*deeply moved—his voice husky*) Bejees, thanks, all of you. Bejees, Hickey you old son of a bitch, that's white of you! Bejees, I know you meant it, too.

HICKEY. (*moved*) Of course I meant it, Harry, old friend! And I mean it when I say I hope today will be the biggest day in your life, and in the lives of everyone here, the beginning of a new life of peace and contentment where no pipe dreams can ever nag at you again. Here's to that, Harry! (*He drains the remainder of his drink, but this time he drinks alone. In an instant the attitude of everyone has reverted to uneasy, suspicious defensiveness.*)

ROCKY. (*growls*) Aw, forget dat bughouse line of bull for a minute, can't yuh?

HICKEY. (*sitting down—good-naturedly*) You're right, Rocky, I'm talking too much. It's Harry we want to hear from. Come on, Harry! (*He pounds his schooner on the table*) Speech! Speech! (*They try to recapture their momentary enthusiasm, rap their schooners on the table, call "Speech," but there is a hollow ring in it.* HOPE *gets to his feet reluctantly, with a forced smile, a smoldering resentment beginning to show in his manner.*)

HOPE. (*lamely*) Bejees, I'm no good at speeches. All I can say is thanks to everybody again for remembering me on my birthday. (*Bitterness coming out*) Only don't think because I'm sixty I'll be a bigger damned fool easy mark than ever! No, bejees! Like Hickey says, it's going to be a new day! This dump has got to be run like other dumps, so I can make some money and not just split even. People has got to pay what they owe me! I'm not running a damned orphan asylum for bums and crooks! Nor a God-damned hooker shanty, either! Nor an Old Men's Home for lousy Anarchist tramps that ought to be in jail! I'm sick of being played for a sucker! (*They stare at him with stunned, bewildered hurt. He goes on in a sort of furious desperation, as if he hated himself for every word he said, and yet couldn't stop*) And don't think you're kidding me right now, either! I know damned well you're giving me the laugh behind my back, thinking to yourselves, The old, lying, pipe-dreaming faker, we've heard his bull about taking a walk around the ward for years, he'll never make it! He's yellow, he ain't got the guts, he's scared he'll find out— (*He glares around at them almost with hatred*) But I'll show you, bejees! (*He glares at* HICKEY) I'll show you, too, you son of a bitch of a frying-pan-peddling bastard!

HICKEY. (*heartily encouraging*) That's the stuff, Harry! Of course you'll try to show me! That's what I want you to do! (HARRY *glances at him with helpless dread—then drops his eyes and looks furtively around the table. All at once he becomes miserably contrite.*)

HOPE. (*his voice catching*) Listen, all of you! Bejees, forgive me. I lost my temper! I ain't feeling well! I got a hell of a grouch on! Bejees, you know you're all as welcome here as the flowers in May! (*They look at him with eager forgiveness.* ROCKY *is the first one who can voice it.*)

ROCKY. Aw, sure, Boss, you're always aces wid us, see?

HICKEY. (*rises to his feet again. He addresses them now with the simple, convincing sincerity of one making a confession of which he is genuinely ashamed*) Listen, everybody! I know you are sick of my gabbing, but I think this is the spot where I owe it to you to do a little explaining and apologize for some of the rough stuff I've had to pull on you. I know how it must look to you. As if I was a damned busybody who was not only interfering in your private business, but even sicking some of you on to nag at each other. Well, I have to admit that's true, and I'm damned sorry about it. But it simply had to be done! You must believe that! You know old Hickey. I was never one to start trouble. But this time I had to—for your own good! I had to make you help me with each other. I saw I couldn't do what I was after alone. Not in the time at my disposal. I knew when I came here I wouldn't be able to stay with you long. I'm slated to leave on a trip. I saw I'd have to hustle and use every means I could. (*With a joking boastfulness*) Why, if I had enough time, I'd get a lot of sport out of selling my line of salvation to each of you all by my lonesome. Like it was fun in the old days, when I traveled house to house, to convince some dame, who was sicking her dog on me, her house wouldn't be properly furnished unless she bought another wash boiler. And I could do it with you, all right. I know every one of you, inside and out, by heart. I may have been drunk when I've been here before, but old Hickey could never be so drunk he didn't have to see through people. I mean, everyone except himself. And, finally, he had to see through himself, too. (*He pauses. They stare at him, bitter, uneasy and fascinated. His manner changes to deep earnestness*) But here's the point to get. I swear I'd never act like I have if I wasn't absolutely sure it will be worth it to you in the end, after you're rid of the damned guilt that makes you lie to yourselves you're something you're not, and the remorse that nags at you and makes you hide behind lousy pipe dreams about tomorrow. You'll be in a today where there is no yesterday or tomorrow to worry you. You won't give a damn what you are any more. I wouldn't say this unless I knew, Brothers and Sisters. This peace is real! It's a fact! I know! Because I've got it! Here! Now! Right in front of you! You see the difference in me! You remember how I used to be! Even when I had two quarts of rotgut under my belt and joked and sang "Sweet Adeline," I still felt like a guilty skunk. But you can all see that I don't give a damn about anything now. And I promise you, by the time this day is over, I'll have every one of you feeling the same way! (*He pauses. They stare at him fascinatedly. He adds with a grin*) I guess that'll be about all from me, boys and girls—for the present. So let's get on with the party. (*He starts to sit down.*)

LARRY. (*sharply*) Wait! (*Insistently—with a sneer*) I think it would help us poor pipe-dreaming sinners along the sawdust trail to salvation if you told us now what it was happened to you that converted you to this great peace you've found. (*More and more with a deliberate, provocative taunting*) I notice you didn't deny it when I asked you about the iceman. Did this great revelation of the evil habit of dreaming about tomorrow come to you after you found your wife was sick of you? (*While he is speaking the faces of the gang have lighted up vindictively, as if all at once they saw a chance to revenge themselves. As he finishes, a chorus of sneering taunts begins, punctuated by nasty, jeering laughter.*)

HOPE. Bejees, you've hit it, Larry! I've noticed he hasn't shown her picture around this time!

MOSHER. He hasn't got it! The iceman took it away from him!

MARGIE. Jees, look at him! Who could blame her?

PEARL. She must be hard up to fall for an iceman!

CORA. Imagine a sap like him advisin' me and Chuck to git married!

CHUCK. Yeah! He done so good wid it!

JIMMY. At least I can say Marjorie chose an officer and a gentleman.

LEWIS. Come to look at you, Hickey, old chap, you've sprouted horns like a bloody antelope!

WETJOEN. Pigger, py Gott! Like a water buffalo's!

WILLIE. (*sings to his Sailor Lad tune*)

> "Come up," she cried, "my iceman lad,
> And you and I'll agree—"

(*They all join in a jeering chorus, rapping with knuckles or glasses on the table at the indicated spot in the lyric*)

> "And I'll show you the prettiest (*Rap, rap, rap*)
> That ever you did see!"

(*A roar of derisive, dirty laughter. But* HICKEY *has remained unmoved by all this taunting. He grins good-naturedly, as if he enjoyed the joke at his expense, and joins in the laughter.*)

HICKEY. Well, boys and girls, I'm glad to see you getting in good spirits for Harry's party, even if the joke is on me. I admit I asked for it by always pulling that iceman gag in the old days. So laugh all you like. (*He pauses. They do not laugh now. They are again staring at him with baffled uneasiness. He goes on thoughtfully*) Well, this forces my hand, I guess, your bringing up the subject of Evelyn. I didn't want to tell you yet. It's hardly an appropriate time. I meant to wait until the party was over. But you're getting the wrong idea about poor Evelyn, and I've got to stop that. (*He pauses again. There is a tense stillness in the room. He bows his head a little and says quietly*) I'm sorry to tell you my dearly beloved wife is dead. (*A gasp comes from the stunned company. They look away from him, shocked and miserably ashamed of themselves, except* LARRY *who continues to stare at him.*)

LARRY. (*aloud to himself with a superstitious shrinking*) Be God, I felt he'd brought the touch of death on him! (*Then suddenly he is even more ashamed of himself than the others and stammers*) Forgive me, Hickey! I'd like to cut my dirty tongue out! (*This releases a chorus of shamefaced mumbles from the crowd.* "Sorry, HICKEY," "I'm sorry, HICKEY." "We're sorry, HICKEY.")

HICKEY. (*looking around at them—in a kindly, reassuring tone*) Now look here, everybody. You mustn't let this be a wet blanket on Harry's party. You're still getting me all wrong. There's no reason— You see, I don't feel any grief. (*They gaze at him startledly. He goes on with convincing sincerity*) I've got to feel glad, for her sake. Because she's at peace. She's rid of me at last. Hell, I don't have to tell you—you all know what I was like. You can imagine what she went through, married to a no-good cheater and drunk like I was. And there was no way out of it for her. Because she loved me. But now she is at peace like she always longed to be. So why should I feel sad? She wouldn't want me to feel sad. Why, all that Evelyn ever wanted out of life was to make me happy. (*He stops, looking around at them with a simple, gentle frankness. They stare at him in bewildered, incredulous confusion.*)

CURTAIN

663

ACT THREE

S CENE—*Barroom of* HARRY HOPE'S, *including a part of what had been the back room in Acts One and Two. In the right wall are two big windows, with the swinging doors to the street between them. The bar itself is at rear. Behind it is a mirror, covered with white mosquito netting to keep off the flies, and a shelf on which are barrels of cheap whiskey with spiggots and a small show case of bottled goods. At left of the bar is the doorway to the hall. There is a table at left, front, of barroom proper, with four chairs. At right, front, is a small free-lunch counter, facing left, with a space between it and the window for the dealer to stand when he dishes out soup at the noon hour. Over the mirror behind the bar are framed photographs of Richard Croker and Big Tim Sullivan, flanked by framed lithographs of John L. Sullivan and Gentleman Jim Corbett in ring costume.*

At left, in what had been the back room, with the dividing curtain drawn, the banquet table of Act Two has been broken up, and the tables are again in the crowded arrangemnet of Act One. Of these, we see one in the front row with five chairs at left of the barroom table, another with five chairs at left-rear of it, a third back by the rear wall with five chairs, and finally, at extreme left-front, one with four chairs, partly on and partly off stage, left.

It is around the middle of the morning of HOPE'S *birthday, a hot summer day. There is sunlight in the street outside, but it does not hit the windows and the light in the back-room section is dim.*

JOE MOTT *is moving around, a box of sawdust under his arm, strewing it over the floor. His manner is sullen, his face set in gloom. He ignores everyone. As the scene progresses, he finishes his sawdusting job, goes behind the lunch counter and cuts loaves of bread.* ROCKY *is behind the bar, wiping it, washing glasses, etc. He wears his working*

664

clothes, sleeves rolled up. He looks sleepy, irritable and worried. At the barroom table, front, LARRY *sits in a chair, facing right-front. He has no drink in front of him. He stares ahead, deep in harried thought. On his right, in a chair facing right,* HUGO *sits sprawled forward, arms and head on the table as usual, a whiskey glass beside his limp hand. At rear of the front table at left of them, in a chair facing left,* PARRITT *is sitting. He is staring in front of him in a tense, strained immobility.*

As the curtain rises, ROCKY *finishes his work behind the bar. He comes forward and drops wearily in the chair at right of* LARRY's *table, facing left.*

ROCKY. Nuttin' now till de noon rush from de Market. I'm goin' to rest my fanny. (*Irritably*) If I ain't a sap to let Chuck kid me into workin' his time so's he can take de mornin' off. But I got sick of arguin' wid 'im. I says, "Aw right, git married! What's it to me?" Hickey's got de bot' of dem bugs. (*Bitterly*) Some party last night, huh? Jees, what a funeral! It was jinxed from de start, but his tellin' about his wife croakin' put de K.O. on it.

LARRY. Yes, it turned out it wasn't a birthday feast but a wake!

ROCKY. Him promisin' he'd cut out de bughouse bull about peace— and den he went on talkin' and talkin' like he couldn't stop! And all de gang sneakin' upstairs, leavin' free booze and eats like dey was poison! It didn't do dem no good if dey thought dey'd shake him. He's been hoppin' from room to room all night. Yuh can't stop him. He's got his Reform Wave goin' strong dis mornin'! Did yuh notice him drag Jimmy out de foist ting to get his laundry and his clothes pressed so he wouldn't have no excuse? And he give Willie de dough to buy his stuff back from Solly's. And all de rest been brushin' and shavin' demselves wid de shakes—

LARRY. (*defiantly*) He didn't come to my room! He's afraid I might ask him a few questions.

ROCKY. (*scornfully*) Yeah? It don't look to me he's scared of yuh. I'd say you was scared of him.

665

LARRY. (*stung*) You'd lie, then!

PARRITT. (*jerks round to look at* LARRY—*sneeringly*) Don't let him kid you, Rocky. He had his door locked. I couldn't get in, either.

ROCKY. Yeah, who d'yuh tink yuh're kiddin', Larry? He's showed you up, aw right. Like he says, if yuh was so anxious to croak, why wouldn't yuh hop off your fire escape long ago?

LARRY (*defiantly*) Because it'd be a coward's quitting, that's why!

PARRITT. He's all quitter, Rocky. He's a yellow old faker!

LARRY. (*turns on him*) You lying punk! Remember what I warned you—!

ROCKY. (*scowls at* PARRITT) Yeah, keep outta dis, you! Where d'yuh get a license to butt in? Shall I give him de bum's rush, Larry? If you don't want him around, nobody else don't.

LARRY. (*forcing an indifferent tone*) No. Let him stay. I don't mind him. He's nothing to me. (ROCKY *shrugs his shoulders and yawns sleepily.*)

PARRITT. You're right, I have nowhere to go now. You're the only one in the world I can turn to.

ROCKY. (*drowsily*) Yuh're a soft old sap, Larry. He's a no-good louse like Hickey. He don't belong. (*He yawns*) I'm all in. Not a wink of sleep. Can't keep my peepers open. (*His eyes close and his head nods.* PARRITT *gives him a glance and then gets up and slinks over to slide into the chair on* LARRY's *left, between him and* ROCKY. LARRY *shrinks away, but determinedly ignores him.*)

PARRITT. (*bending toward him—in a low, ingratiating, apologetic voice*) I'm sorry for riding you, Larry, But you get my goat when you act as if you didn't care a damn what happened to me, and keep your door locked so I can't talk to you. (*Then hopefully*) But that was to keep Hickey out, wasn't it? I don't blame you. I'm getting to hate him. I'm getting more and more scared of him. Especially since he told us his wife was dead. It's that queer feeling he gives me that I'm mixed up with him some way. I don't know why, but it started me thinking about Mother—as if she was dead. (*With a strange undercurrent of something like satisfaction in his pitying tone*) I suppose she might as well be. Inside herself, I mean. It must kill her when she thinks of me— I know she doesn't want to, but she can't help it. After all, I'm her only kid. She used to spoil me and made a pet of me. Once in a great while, I mean. When she remembered me. As if she wanted to make up for something. As if she felt guilty. So she must have loved me a little, even if she never let it interfere with her freedom. (*With a strange pathetic wistfulness*) Do you know, Larry, I once had a sneaking suspicion that maybe, if the truth was known, you were my father.

LARRY. (*violently*) You damned fool! Who put that insane idea in your head? You know it's a lie! Anyone in the Coast crowd could tell you I never laid eyes on your mother till after you were born.

PARRITT. Well, I'd hardly ask them, would I? I know you're right, though, because I asked her. She brought me up to be frank and ask her anything, and she'd always tell me the truth. (*Abruptly*) But I was talking about how she must feel now about me. My getting through with the Movement. She'll never forgive that. The Movement is her life. And it must be the final knockout for her if she knows I was the one who sold—

LARRY. Shut up, damn you!

PARRITT. It'll kill her. And I'm sure she knows it must have been me. (*Suddenly with desperate urgency*) But I never thought the cops would get her! You've got to believe that! You've got to see what my only reason was! I'll admit what I told you last night was a lie—that bunk about getting patriotic and my duty to my country. But here's the true reason, Larry—the only reason! It was just for money! I got stuck on a whore and wanted dough to blow in on her and have a good time! That's all I did it for! Just money! Honest! (*He has the terrible grotesque air, in confessing his sordid baseness, of one who gives an excuse which exonerates him from any real guilt.*)

LARRY. (*grabs him by the shoulder and shakes him*) God damn you, shut up! What the hell is it to me? (ROCKY *starts awake.*)

ROCKY. What's comin' off here?

667

LARRY. (*controlling himself*) Nothing. This gabby young punk was talking my ear off, that's all. He's a worse pest than Hickey.

ROCKY. (*drowsily*) Yeah, Hickey— Say, listen, what d'yuh mean about him bein' scared you'd ask him questions? What questions?

LARRY. Well, I feel he's hiding something. You notice he didn't say what his wife died of.

ROCKY. (*rebukingly*) Aw, lay off dat. De poor guy— What are yuh gettin' at, anyway? Yuh don't tink it's just a gag of his?

LARRY. I don't. I'm damned sure he's brought death here with him. I feel the cold touch of it on him.

ROCKY. Aw, bunk! You got croakin' on de brain, Old Cemetery. (*Suddenly* ROCKY's *eyes widen*) Say! D'yuh mean yuh tink she committed suicide, 'count of his cheatin' or something?

LARRY. (*grimly*) It wouldn't surprise me. I'd be the last to blame her.

ROCKY. (*scornfully*) But dat's crazy! Jees, if she'd done dat, he wouldn't tell us he was glad about it, would he? He ain't dat big a bastard.

PARRITT. (*speaks up from his own preoccupation—strangely*) You know better than that, Larry. You know she'd never commit suicide. She's like you. She'll hang on to life even when there's nothing left but—

LARRY. (*stung—turns on him viciously*) And how about you? Be God, if you had any guts or decency—! (*He stops guiltily.*)

PARRITT. (*sneeringly*) I'd take that hop off your fire escape you're too yellow to take, I suppose?

LARRY. (*as if to himself*) No! Who am I to judge? I'm done with judging.

PARRITT. (*tauntingly*) Yes, I suppose you'd like that, wouldn't you?

ROCKY. (*irritably mystified*) What de hell's all dis about? (*To* PARRITT) What d'you know about Hickey's wife? How d'yuh know she didn't—?

LARRY. (*with forced belittling casualness*) He doesn't. Hickey's addled the little brains he's got. Shove him back to his own table, Rocky. I'm sick of him.

668

ROCKY. (*to* PARRITT, *threateningly*) Yuh heard Larry? I'd like an excuse to give yuh a good punch in de snoot. So move quick!

PARRITT. (*gets up—to* LARRY) If you think moving to another table will get rid of me! (*He moves away—then adds with bitter reproach*) Gee, Larry, that's a hell of a way to treat me, when I've trusted you, and I need your help. (*He sits down in his old place and sinks into a wounded, self-pitying brooding.*)

ROCKY. (*going back to his train of thought*) Jees, if she committed suicide, yuh got to feel sorry for Hickey, huh? Yuh can understand how he'd go bughouse and not be responsible for all de crazy stunts he's stagin' here. (*Then puzzledly*) But how can yuh be sorry for him when he says he's glad she croaked, and yuh can tell he means it? (*With weary exasperation*) Aw, nuts! I don't get nowhere tryin' to figger his game. (*His face hardening*) But I know dis. He better lay off me and my stable! (*He pauses—then sighs*) Jees, Larry, what a night dem two pigs give me! When de party went dead, dey pinched a coupla bottles and brung dem up deir room and got stinko. I don't get a wink of sleep, see? Just as I'd drop off on a chair there, dey'd come down lookin' for trouble. Or else dey'd raise hell upstairs, laughin' and singin', so I'd get scared dey'd get de joint pinched and go up to tell dem to can de noise. And every time dey'd crawl my frame wid de same old argument. Dey'd say, "So yuh agree wid Hickey, do yuh, yuh dirty little Ginny? We're whores, are we? Well, we agree wid Hickey about you, see! Yuh're nuttin' but a lousy pimp!" Den I'd slap dem. Not beat 'em up, like a pimp would. Just slap dem. But it don't do no good. Dey'd keep at it over and over. Jees, I get de earache just thinkin' of it! "Listen," dey'd say, "if we're whores we gotta right to have a reg'lar pimp and not stand for no punk imitation! We're sick of wearin' out our dogs poundin' sidewalks for a double-crossin' bartender, when all de thanks we get is he looks down on us. We'll find a guy who really needs us to take care of him and ain't ashamed of it. Don't expect us to work tonight, 'cause we won't, see? Not if de streets was blocked wid sailors! We're goin' on strike and yuh can like it or lump it!" (*He*

669

shakes his head) Whores goin' on strike! Can yuh tie dat? (*Going on with his story*) Dey says, "We're takin' a holiday. We're goin' to beat it down to Coney Island and shoot the chutes and maybe we'll come back and maybe we won't. And you can go to hell!" So dey put on deir lids and beat it, de bot' of dem stinko. (*He sighs dejectedly. He seems grotesquely like a harried family man, henpecked and browbeaten by a nagging wife.* LARRY *is deep in his own bitter preoccupation and hasn't listened to him.* CHUCK *enters from the hall at rear. He has his straw hat with the gaudy band in his hand and wears a Sunday-best blue suit with a high stiff collar. He looks sleepy, hot, uncomfortable and grouchy.*)

CHUCK. (*glumly*) Hey, Rocky. Cora wants a sherry flip. For her noives.

ROCKY. (*turns indignantly*) Sherry flip! Christ, she don't need nuttin' for her noive! What's she tink dis is, de Waldorf?

CHUCK. Yeah, I told her, what would we use for sherry, and dere wasn't no egg unless she laid one. She says, "Is dere a law yuh can't go out and buy de makings, yuh big tramp?" (*Resentfully puts his straw hat on his head at a defiant tilt*) To hell wid her! She'll drink booze or nuttin'! (*He goes behind the bar to draw a glass of whiskey from a barrel.*)

ROCKY. (*sarcastically*) Jees, a guy oughta give his bride anything she wants on de weddin' day, I should tink! (*As* CHUCK *comes from behind the bar,* ROCKY *surveys him derisively*) Pipe de bridegroom, Larry! All dolled up for de killin'! (*LARRY pays no attention.*)

CHUCK. Aw, shut up.

ROCKY. One week on dat farm in Joisey, dat's what I give yuh! Yuh'll come runnin' in here some night yellin' for a shot of booze 'cause de crickets is after yuh! (*Disgustedly*) Jees, Chuck, dat louse Hickey's coitinly made a prize coupla suckers outa youse.

CHUCK. (*unguardedly*) Yeah. I'd like to give him one sock in de puss—just one! (*Then angrily*) Aw, can dat! What's he got to do wid it? Ain't we always said we was goin' to? So we're goin' to, see? And don't give me no argument! (*He stares at* ROCKY *truculently. But* ROCKY *only shrugs his shoulders with weary disgust and* CHUCK *subsides into complaining gloom*) If on'y Cora'd cut out de beefin'. She don't gimme a minute's rest all night. De same old stuff over and over! Do I really want to marry her? I says, "Sure, Baby, why not?" She says, "Yeah, but after a week yuh'll be tinkin' what a sap you was. Yuh'll make dat an excuse to go off on a periodical, and den I'll be tied for life to a no-good soak, and de foist ting I know yuh'll have me out hustlin' again, your own wife!" Den she'd bust out cryin', and I'd get sore. "Yuh're a liar," I'd say. "I ain't never taken your dough 'cept when I was drunk and not workin'!" "Yeah," she'd say, "and how long will yuh stay sober now? Don't tink yuh can kid me wid dat water-wagon bull! I've heard it too often." Dat'd make me sore and I'd say, "Don't call me a liar. But I wish I was drunk right now, because if I was, yuh wouldn't be keepin' me awake all night beefin'. If yuh opened your yap, I'd knock de stuffin' outa yuh!" Den she'd yell, "Dat's a sweet way to talk to de goil yuh're goin' to marry." (*He sighs explosively*) Jees, she's got me hangin' on de ropes! (*He glances with vengeful yearning at the drink of whiskey in his hand*) Jees, would I like to get a quart of dis redeye under my belt!

ROCKY. Well, why the hell don't yuh?

CHUCK. (*instantly suspicious and angry*) Sure! You'd like dat, wouldn't yuh? I'm wise to you! Yuh don't wanta see me get married and settle down like a reg'lar guy! Yuh'd like me to stay paralyzed all de time, so's I'd be like you, a lousy pimp!

ROCKY. (*springs to his feet, his face hardened viciously*) Listen! I don't take dat even from you, see!

CHUCK. (*puts his drink on the bar and clenches his fists*) Yeah? Wanta make sometin' of it? (*Jeeringly*) Don't make me laugh! I can lick ten of youse wid one mit!

ROCKY. (*reaching for his hip pocket*) Not wid lead in your belly, yuh won't!

JOE. (*has stopped cutting when the quarrel started—expostulating*)

Hey, you, Rocky and Chuck! Cut it out! You's ole friends! Don't let dat Hickey make you crazy!

CHUCK. (*turns on him*) Keep outa our business, yuh black bastard!

ROCKY. (*like* CHUCK, *turns on* JOE, *as if their own quarrel was forgotten and they became natural allies against an alien*) Stay where yuh belong, yuh doity nigger!

JOE. (*snarling with rage, springs from behind the lunch counter with the bread knife in his hand*) You white sons of bitches! I'll rip your guts out! (CHUCK *snatches a whiskey bottle from the bar and raises it above his head to hurl at* JOE. ROCKY *jerks a short-barreled, nickel-plated revolver from his hip pocket. At this moment* LARRY *pounds on the table with his fist and bursts into a sardonic laugh.*)

LARRY. That's it! Murder each other, you damned loons, with Hickey's blessing! Didn't I tell you he'd brought death with him? (*His interruption startles them. They pause to stare at him, their fighting fury suddenly dies out and they appear deflated and sheepish.*)

ROCKY. (*to* JOE) Aw right, you. Leggo dat shiv and I'll put dis gat away. (JOE *sullenly goes back behind the counter and slaps the knife on top of it.* ROCKY *slips the revolver back in his pocket.* CHUCK *lowers the bottle to the bar.* HUGO, *who has awakened and raised his head when* LARRY *pounded on the·table, now giggles foolishly.*)

HUGO. Hello, leedle peoples! Neffer mind! Soon you vill eat hot dogs beneath the villow trees and trink free vine— (*Abruptly in a haughty fastidious tone*) The champagne vas not properly iced. (*With guttural anger*) Gottamned liar, Hickey! Does that prove I vant to be aristocrat? I love only the proletariat! I vill lead them! I vill be like a Gott to them! They vill be my slaves! (*He stops in bewildered self-amazement—to* LARRY *appealingly*) I am very trunk, no, Larry? I talk foolishness. I am so trunk, Larry, old friend, am I not, I don't know vhat I say?

LARRY. (*pityingly*) You're raving drunk, Hugo. I've never seen you so paralyzed. Lay your head down now and sleep it off.

HUGO. (*gratefully*) Yes. I should sleep. I am too crazy trunk. (*He puts his head on his arms and closes his eyes.*)

JOE. (*behind the lunch counter—brooding superstitiously*) You's right, Larry. Bad luck come in de door when Hickey come. I's an ole gamblin' man and I knows bad luck when I feels it! (*Then defiantly*) But it's white man's bad luck. He can't jinx me! (*He comes from behind the counter and goes to the bar—addressing* ROCKY *stiffly*) De bread's cut and I's finished my job. Do I get de drink I's earned? (ROCKY *gives him a hostile look but shoves a bottle and glass at him.* JOE *pours a brimful drink—sullenly*) I's finished wid dis dump for keeps. (*He takes a key from his pocket and slaps it on the bar*) Here's de key to my room. I ain't comin' back. I's goin' to my own folks where I belong. I don't stay where I's not wanted. I's sick and tired of messin' round wid white men. (*He gulps down his drink—then looking around defiantly he deliberately throws his whiskey glass on the floor and smashes it.*)

ROCKY. Hey! What de hell—!

JOE. (*with a sneering dignity*) I's on'y savin' you de trouble, White Boy. Now you don't have to break it, soon's my back's turned, so's no white man kick about drinkin' from de same glass. (*He walks stiffly to the street door—then turns for a parting shot—boastfully*) I's tired of loafin' 'round wid a lot of bums. I's a gamblin' man. I's gonna get in a big crap game and win me a big bankroll. Den I'll get de okay to open up my old gamblin' house for colored men. Den maybe I comes back here sometime to see de bums. Maybe I throw a twenty-dollar bill on de bar and say, "Drink it up," and listen when dey all pat me on de back and say, "Joe, you sure is white." But I'll say, "No, I'm black and my dough is black man's dough, and you's proud to drink wid me or you don't get no drink!" Or maybe I just says, "You can all go to hell. I don't lower myself drinkin' wid no white trash!" (*He opens the door to go out—then turns again*) And dat ain't no pipe dream! I'll git de money for my stake today, somehow, somewheres! If I has to borrow a gun and stick up some white man, I gets it! You wait and see! (*He swaggers out through the swinging doors.*)

CHUCK. (*angrily*) Can yuh beat de noive of dat dinge! Jees, if I wasn't dressed up, I'd go out and mop up de street wid him!

ROCKY. Aw, let him go, de poor old dope! Him and his gamblin' house! He'll be back tonight askin' Harry for his room and bummin' me for a ball. (*Vengefully*) Den I'll be de one to smash de glass. I'll loin him his place! (*The swinging doors are pushed open and* WILLIE OBAN *enters from the street. He is shaved and wears an expensive, well-cut suit, good shoes and clean linen. He is absolutely sober, but his face is sick, and his nerves in a shocking state of shakes.*)

CHUCK. Another guy all dolled up! Got your clothes from Solly's, huh, Willie? (*Derisively*) Now yuh can sell dem back to him again to-morrow.

WILLIE. (*stiffly*) No, I—I'm through with that stuff. Never again. (*He comes to the bar.*)

ROCKY. (*sympathetically*) Yuh look sick, Willie. Take a ball to pick yuh up. (*He pushes a bottle toward him.*)

WILLIE. (*eyes the bottle yearningly but shakes his head—determinedly*) No, thanks. The only way to stop is to stop. I'd have no chance if I went to the D.A.'s office smelling of booze.

CHUCK. Yuh're really goin' dere?

WILLIE. (*stiffly*) I said I was, didn't I? I just came back here to rest a few minutes, not because I needed any booze. I'll show that cheap drummer I don't have to have any Dutch courage— (*Guiltily*) But he's been very kind and generous staking me. He can't help his insulting manner, I suppose. (*He turns away from the bar*) My legs are a bit shaky yet. I better sit down a while. (*He goes back and sits at the left of the second table, facing* PARRITT, *who gives him a scowling, suspicious glance and then ignores him.* ROCKY *looks at* CHUCK *and taps his head disgustedly.* CAPTAIN LEWIS *appears in the doorway from the hall.*)

CHUCK. (*mutters*) Here's anudder one. (LEWIS *looks spruce and clean-shaven. His ancient tweed suit has been brushed and his frayed linen is clean. His manner is full of a forced, jaunty self-assurance. But he is sick and beset by katzenjammer.*)

LEWIS. Good morning, gentlemen all. (*He passes along the front of bar to look out in the street*) A jolly fine morning, too. (*He turns back to the bar*) An eye-opener? I think not. Not required, Rocky, old chum. Feel extremely fit, as a matter of fact. Though can't say I slept much, thanks to that interfering ass, Hickey, and that stupid bounder of a Boer. (*His face hardens*) I've had about all I can take from that fellow. It's my own fault, of course, for allowing a brute of a Dutch farmer to become familiar. Well, it's come to a parting of the ways now, and good riddance. Which reminds me, here's my key. (*He puts it on the bar*) I shan't be coming back. Sorry to be leaving good old Harry and the rest of you, of course, but I can't continue to live under the same roof with that fellow. (*He stops, stiffening into hostility as* WETJOEN *enters from the hall, and pointedly turns his back on him.* WETJOEN *glares at him sneeringly. He, too, has made an effort to spruce up his appearance, and his bearing has a forced swagger of conscious physical strength. Behind this, he is sick and feebly holding his booze-sodden body together.*)

ROCKY. (*to* LEWIS—*disgustedly putting the key on the shelf in back of the bar*) So Hickey's kidded the pants offa you, too? Yuh tink yuh're leavin' here, huh?

WETJOEN. (*jeeringly*) Ja! Dot's vhat he kids himself.

LEWIS. (*ignores him—airily*) Yes, I'm leaving, Rocky. But that ass, Hickey, has nothing to do with it. Been thinking things over. Time I turned over a new leaf, and all that.

WETJOEN. He's going to get a job! Dot's what he says!

ROCKY. What at, for Chris' sake?

LEWIS. (*keeping his airy manner*) Oh, anything. I mean, not manual labor, naturally, but anything that calls for a bit of brains and education. However humble. Beggars can't be choosers. I'll see a pal of mine at the Consulate. He promised any time I felt an energetic fit he'd get me a post with the Cunard—clark in the office or something of the kind.

WETJOEN. Ja! At Limey Consulate they promise anything to get rid of him vhen he comes there tronk! They're scared to call the police and have him pinched because it vould scandal in the papers make about a Limey officer and chentleman!

LEWIS. As a matter of fact, Rocky, I only wish a post temporarily.

Means to an end, you know. Save up enough for a first-class passage home, that's the bright idea.

WETJOEN. He's sailing back to home, sveet home! Dot's biggest pipe dream of all. What leetle brain the poor Limey has left, dot isn't in whiskey pickled, Hickey has made crazy! (LEWIS' *fists clench, but he manages to ignore this.*)

CHUCK. (*feels sorry for* LEWIS *and turns on* WETJOEN—*sarcastically*) Hickey ain't made no sucker outa you, huh? You're too foxy, huh? But I'll bet you tink yuh're goin' out and land a job, too.

WETJOEN. (*bristles*) I am, ja. For me, it is easy. Because I put on no airs of chentleman. I am not ashamed to vork vith my hands. I vas a farmer before the war ven ploody Limey thieves steal my country. (*Boastfully*) Anyone I ask for job can see vith one look I have the great strength to do work of ten ordinary mens.

LEWIS. (*sneeringly*) Yes, Chuck, you remember he gave a demonstration of his extraordinary muscles last night when he helped to move the piano.

CHUCK. Yuh couldn't even hold up your corner. It was your fault de damned box almost fell down de satirs.

WETJOEN. My hands vas sweaty! Could I help dot my hands slip? I could de whole veight of it lift! In old days in Transvaal, I lift loaded oxcart by the axle! So vhy shouldn't I get job? Dot longshoreman boss, Dan, he tell me any time I like, he take me on. And Benny from de Market he promise me same.

LEWIS. You remember, Rocky, it was one of those rare occasions when the Boer that walks like a man—spelled with a double o, by the way— was buying drinks and Dan and Benny were stony. They'd bloody well have promised him the moon.

ROCKY. Yeah, yuh big boob, dem boids was on'y kiddin' yuh.

WETJOEN. (*angrily*) Dot's lie! You vill see dis morning I get job! I'll show dot bloody Limey chentleman, and dot liar, Hickey! And I need vork only leetle vhile to save money for my passage home. I need not much money because I am not ashamed to travel steerage. I don't put on

676

first-cabin airs! (*Tauntingly*) Und *I can* go home to my country! Vhen I get there, they vill let *me* come in!

LEWIS. (*grows rigid—his voice trembling with repressed anger*) There was a rumor in South Africa, Rocky, that a certain Boer officer—if you call the leaders of a rabble of farmers officers—kept advising Cronje to retreat and not stand and fight—

WETJOEN. And I vas right! I vas right! He got surrounded at Poardeberg! He had to surrender!

LEWIS. (*ignoring him*) Good strategy, no doubt, but a suspicion grew afterwards into a conviction among the Boers that the officer's caution was prompted by a desire to make his personal escape. His countrymen felt extremely savage about it, and his family disowned him. So I imagine there would be no welcoming committee waiting on the dock, nor delighted relatives making the veldt ring with their happy cries—

WETJOEN. (*with guilty rage*) All lies! You Gottamned Limey— (*Trying to control himself and copy* LEWIS' *manner*) I also haf heard rumors of a Limey officer who, after the war, lost all his money gambling vhen he vas tronk. But they found out it vas regiment money, too, he lost—

LEWIS. (*loses his control and starts for him*) You bloody Dutch scum!

ROCKY. (*leans over the bar and stops* LEWIS *with a straight-arm swipe on the chest*) Cut it out! (*At the same moment* CHUCK *grabs* WETJOEN *and yanks him back.*)

WETJOEN. (*struggling*) Let him come! I saw them come before—at Modder River, Magersfontein, Spion Kopje—waving their silly swords, so afraid they couldn't show off how brave they vas!—and I kill them vith my rifle so easy! (*Vindictively*) Listen to me, you Cecil! Often vhen I am tronk and kidding you I say I am sorry I missed you, but now, py Gott, I am sober, and I don't joke, and I say it!

LARRY. (*gives a sardonic guffaw—with his comically crazy, intense whisper*) Be God, you can't say Hickey hasn't the miraculous touch to raise the dead, when he can start the Boer War raging again! (*This interruption acts like a cold douche on* LEWIS *and* WETJOEN. *They sub-*

side, and ROCKY *and* CHUCK *let go of them.* LEWIS *turns his back on the Boer.*)

LEWIS. (*attempting a return of his jaunty manner, as if nothing had happened*) Well, time I was on my merry way to see my chap at the Consulate. The early bird catches the job, what? Good-bye and good luck, Rocky, and everyone. (*He starts for the street door.*)

WETJOEN. Py Gott, if dot Limey can go, I can go! (*He hurries after* LEWIS. *But* LEWIS, *his hand about to push the swinging doors open, hesitates, as though struck by a sudden paralysis of the will, and* WETJOEN *has to jerk back to avoid bumping into him. For a second they stand there, one behind the other, staring over the swinging doors into the street.*)

ROCKY. Well, why don't yuh beat it?

LEWIS. (*guiltily casual*) Eh? Oh, just happened to think. Hardly the decent thing to pop off without saying good-bye to old Harry. One of the best, Harry. And good old Jimmy, too. They ought to be down any moment. (*He pretends to notice* WETJOEN *for the first time and steps away from the door—apologizing as to a stranger*) Sorry. I seem to be blocking your way out.

WETJOEN. (*stiffly*) No. I vait to say good-bye to Harry and Jimmy, too. (*He goes to right of door behind the lunch counter and looks through the window, his back to the room.* LEWIS *takes up a similar stand at the window on the left of door.*)

CHUCK. Jees, can yuh beat dem simps! (*He picks up* CORA's *drink at the end of the bar*) Hell, I'd forgot Cora. She'll be trowin' a fit. (*He goes into the hall with the drink.*)

ROCKY. (*looks after him disgustedly*) Dat's right, wait on her and spoil her, yuh poor sap! (*He shakes his head and begins to wipe the bar mechanically.*)

WILLIE. (*is regarding* PARRITT *across the table from him with an eager, calculating eye. He leans over and speaks in a low confidential tone*) Look here, Parritt. I'd like to have a talk with you.

PARRITT. (*starts—scowling defensively*) What about?

678

WILLIE. (*his manner becoming his idea of a crafty criminal lawyer's*) About the trouble you're in. Oh, I know. You don't admit it. You're quite right. That's my advice. Deny everything. Keep your mouth shut. Make no statements whatever without first consulting your attorney.

PARRITT. Say! What the hell—?

WILLIE. But you can trust me. I'm a lawyer, and it's just occurred to me you and I ought to co-operate. Of course I'm going to see the D.A. this morning about a job on his staff. But that may take time. There may not be an immediate opening. Meanwhile it would be a good idea for me to take a case or two, on my own, and prove my brilliant record in law school was no flash in the pan. So why not retain me as your attorney?

PARRITT. You're crazy! What do I want with a lawyer?

WILLIE. That's right. Don't admit anything. But you can trust me, so let's not beat about the bush. You got in trouble out on the Coast, eh? And now you're hiding out. Any fool can spot that. (*Lowering his voice still more*) You feel safe here, and maybe you are, for a while. But remember, they get you in the end. I know from my father's experience. No one could have felt safer than he did. When anyone mentioned the law to him, he nearly died laughing. But—

PARRITT. You crazy mutt! (*Turning to* LARRY *with a strained laugh*) Did you get that, Larry? This damned fool thinks cops are after me!

LARRY. (*bursts out with his true reaction before he thinks to ignore him*) I wish to God they were! And so should you, if you had the honor of a louse! (PARRITT *stares into his eyes guiltily for a second. Then he smiles sneeringly.*)

PARRITT. And you're the guy who kids himself he's through with the Movement! You old lying faker, you're still in love with it! (LARRY *ignores him again now.*)

WILLIE. (*disappointedly*) Then you're not in trouble, Parritt? I was hoping— But never mind. No offense meant. Forget it.

PARRITT. (*condescendingly—his eyes on* LARRY) Sure. That's all right, Willie. I'm not sore at you. It's that damned old faker that gets my goat.

(*He slips out of his chair and goes quietly over to sit in the chair beside* LARRY *he had occupied before—in a low, insinuating, intimate tone*) I think I understand, Larry. It's really Mother you still love—isn't it?—in spite of the dirty deal she gave you. But hell, what did you expect? She was never true to anyone but herself and the Movement. But I understand how you can't help still feeling—because I still love her, too. (*Pleading in a strained, desperate tone*) You know I do, don't you? You must! So you see I couldn't have expected they'd catch her! You've got to believe me that I sold them out just to get a few lousy dollars to blow in on a whore. No other reason, honest! There couldn't possibly be any other reason! (*Again he has a strange air of exonerating himself from guilt by this shameless confession.*)

LARRY. (*trying not to listen, has listened with increasing tension*) For the love of Christ, will you leave me in peace! I've told you you can't make me judge you! But if you don't keep still, you'll be saying something soon that will make you vomit your own soul like a drink of nickel rotgut that won't stay down! (*He pushes back his chair and springs to his feet*) To hell with you! (*He goes to the bar.*)

PARRITT. (*jumps up and starts to follow him—desperately*) Don't go, Larry! You've got to help me! (*But* LARRY *is at the bar, back turned, and* ROCKY *is scowling at him. He stops, shrinking back into himself helplessly, and turns away. He goes to the table where he had been before, and this time he takes the chair at rear facing directly front. He puts his elbows on the table, holding his head in his hands as if he had a splitting headache.*)

LARRY. Set 'em up, Rocky. I swore I'd have no more drinks on Hickey, if I died of drought, but I've changed my mind! Be God, he owes it to me, and I'd get blind to the world now if it was the Iceman of Death himself treating! (*He stops, startledly, a superstitious awe coming into his face*) What made me say that, I wonder. (*With a sardonic laugh*) Well, be God, it fits, for Death was the Iceman Hickey called to his home!

ROCKY. Aw, forget dat iceman gag! De poor dame is dead. (*Pushing*

680

a bottle and glass at LARRY) Gwan and get paralyzed! I'll be glad to see one bum in dis dump act natural. (LARRY *downs a drink and pours another.*)

(ED MOSHER *appears in the doorway from the hall. The same change which is apparent in the manner and appearance of the others shows in him. He is sick, his nerves are shattered, his eyes are apprehensive, but he, too, puts on an exaggeratedly self-confident bearing. He saunters to the bar between* LARRY *and the street entrance.*)

MOSHER. Morning, Rocky. Hello, Larry. Glad to see Brother Hickey hasn't corrupted you to temperance. I wouldn't mind a shot myself. (*As* ROCKY *shoves a bottle toward him he shakes his head*) But I remember the only breath-killer in this dump is coffee beans. The boss would never fall for that. No man can run a circus successfully who believes guys chew coffee beans because they like them. (*He pushes the bottle away*) No, much as I need one after the hell of a night I've had—(*He scowls*) That drummer son of a drummer! I had to lock him out. But I could hear him through the wall doing his spiel to someone all night long. Still at it with Jimmy and Harry when I came down just now. But the hardest to take was that flannel-mouth, flatfoot Mick trying to tell me where I got off! I had to lock him out, too. (*As he says this,* MCGLOIN *comes in the doorway from the hall. The change in his appearance and manner is identical with that of* MOSHER *and the others.*)

MCGLOIN. He's a liar, Rocky! It was me who locked him out! (MOSHER *starts to flare up—then ignores him. They turn their backs on each other.* MCGLOIN *starts into the back-room section.*)

WILLIE. Come and sit here, Mac. You're just the man I want to see. If I'm to take your case, we ought to have a talk before we leave.

MCGLOIN. (*contemptuously*) We'll have no talk. You damned fool, do you think I'd have your father's son for my lawyer? They'd take one look at you and bounce us both out on our necks! (WILLIE *winces and shrinks down in his chair.* MCGLOIN *goes to the first table beyond him and sits with his back to the bar*) I don't need a lawyer, anyway. To hell with the law! All I've got to do is see the right ones and get them to pass the word. They will, too. They know I was framed. And once they've passed the word, it's as good as done, law or no law.

MOSHER. God, I'm glad I'm leaving this madhouse! (*He pulls his key from his pocket and slaps it on the bar*) Here's my key, Rocky.

MCGLOIN. (*pulls his from his pocket*) And here's mine. (*He tosses it to* ROCKY) I'd rather sleep in the gutter than pass another night under the same roof with that loon, Hickey, and a lying circus grifter! (*He adds darkly*) And if that hat fits anyone here, let him put it on! (MOSHER *turns around toward him furiously but* ROCKY *leans over the bar and grabs his arm.*)

ROCKY. Nix! Take it easy! (MOSHER *subsides.* ROCKY *tosses the keys on the shelf—disgustedly*) You boids gimme a pain. It'd soive you right if I wouldn't give de keys back to yuh tonight. (*They both turn on him resentfully, but there is an interruption as* CORA *appears in the doorway from the hall with* CHUCK *behind her. She is drunk, dressed in her gaudy best, her face plastered with rouge and mascara, her hair a bit disheveled, her hat on anyhow.*)

CORA. (*comes a few steps inside the bar—with a strained bright giggle*) Hello, everybody! Here we go! Hickey just told us, ain't it time we beat it, if we're really goin'. So we're showin' de bastard, ain't we, Honey? He's comin' right down wid Harry and Jimmy. Jees, dem two look like dey was goin' to de electric chair! (*With frightened anger*) If I had to listen to any more of Hickey's bunk, I'd brain him. (*She puts her hand on* CHUCK's *arm*) Come on, Honey. Let's get started before he comes down.

CHUCK. (*sullenly*) Sure, anyting yuh say, Baby.

CORA. (*turns on him truculently*) Yeah? Well, I say we stop at de foist reg'lar dump and yuh gotta blow me to a sherry flip—or four or five, if I want 'em! —or all bets is off!

CHUCK. Aw, yuh got a fine bun on now!

CORA. Cheap skate! I know what's eatin' you, Tightwad! Well, use my dough, den, if yuh're so stingy. Yuh'll grab it all, anyway, right after de ceremony. I know you! (*She hikes her skirt up and reaches inside the top of her stocking*) Here, yuh big tramp!

CHUCK. (*knocks her hand away—angrily*) Keep your lousy dough! And don't show off your legs to dese bums when yuh're goin' to be married, if yuh don't want a sock in de puss!

CORA. (*pleased—meekly*) Aw right, Honey. (*Looking around with a foolish laugh*) Say, why don't all you barflies come to de weddin'? (*But they are all sunk in their own apprehensions and ignore her. She hesitates, miserably uncertain*) Well, we're goin', guys. (*There is no comment. Her eyes fasten on* ROCKY—*desperately*) Say, Rocky, yuh gone deef? I said me and Chuck was goin' now.

ROCKY. (*wiping the bar—with elaborate indifference*) Well, good-bye. Give my love to Joisey.

CORA. (*tearfully indignant*) Ain't yuh goin' to wish us happiness, yuh doity little Ginny?

ROCKY. Sure. Here's hopin' yuh don't moider each odder before next week.

CHUCK. (*angrily*) Aw, Baby, what d'we care for dat pimp? (ROCKY *turns on him threateningly, but* CHUCK *hears someone upstairs in the hall and grabs* CORA's *arm*) Here's Hickey comin'! Let's get outa here! (*They hurry into the hall. The street door is heard slamming behind them.*)

ROCKY. (*gloomily pronounces an obituary*) One regular guy and one all-right tart gone to hell! (*Fiercely*) Dat louse Hickey oughta be croaked! (*There is a muttered growl of assent from most of the gathering. Then* HARRY HOPE *enters from the hall, followed by* JIMMY TOMORROW, *with* HICKEY *on his heels.* HOPE *and* JIMMY *are both putting up a front of self-assurance, but* CORA's *description of them was apt. There is a desperate bluff in their manner as they walk in, which suggests the last march of the condemned.* HOPE *is dressed in an old black Sunday suit, black tie, shoes, socks, which give him the appearance of being in mourning.* JIMMY's *clothes are pressed, his shoes shined, his white linen immaculate. He has a hangover and his gently appealing dog's eyes have*

683

a boiled look. HICKEY's *face is a bit drawn from lack of sleep and his voice is hoarse from continual talking, but his bustling energy appears nervously intensified, and his beaming expression is one of triumphant accomplishment.*)

HICKEY. Well, here we are! We've got this far, at least! (*He pats* JIMMY *on the back*) Good work, Jimmy. I told you you weren't half as sick as you pretended. No excuse whatever for postponing—

JIMMY. I'll thank you to keep your hands off me! I merely mentioned I would feel more fit tomorrow. But it might as well be today, I suppose.

HICKEY. Finish it now, so it'll be dead forever, and you can be free! (*He passes him to clap* HOPE *encouragingly on the shoulder*) Cheer up, Harry. You found your rheumatism didn't bother you coming downstairs, didn't you? I told you it wouldn't. (*He winks around at the others. With the exception of* HUGO *and* PARRITT, *all their eyes are fixed on him with bitter animosity. He gives* HOPE *a playful nudge in the ribs*) You're the damnedest one for alibis, Governor! As bad as Jimmy!

HOPE. (*putting on his deaf manner*) Eh? I can't hear— (*Defiantly*) You're a liar! I've had rheumatism on and off for twenty years. Ever since Bessie died. Everybody knows that.

HICKEY. Yes, we know it's the kind of rheumatism you turn on and off! We're on to you, you old faker! (*He claps him on the shoulder again, chuckling.*)

HOPE. (*looks humiliated and guilty—by way of escape he glares around at the others*) Bejees, what are all you bums hanging round staring at me for? Think you was watching a circus! Why don't you get the hell out of here and 'tend to your own business, like Hickey's told you? (*They look at him reproachfully, their eyes hurt. They fidget as if trying to move.*)

HICKEY. Yes, Harry, I certainly thought they'd have had the guts to be gone by this time. (*He grins*) Or maybe I did have my doubts. (*Abruptly he becomes sincerely sympathetic and earnest*) Because I know exactly what you're up against, boys. I know how damned yellow a man can be when it comes to making himself face the truth. I've been through the mill, and I had to face a worse bastard in myself than any of you will have to in yourselves. I know you become such a coward you'll grab at any lousy excuse to get out of killing your pipe dreams. And yet, as I've told you over and over, it's exactly those damned tomorrow dreams which keep you from making peace with yourself. So you've got to kill them like I did mine. (*He pauses. They glare at him with fear and hatred. They seem about to curse him, to spring at him. But they remain silent and motionless. His manner changes and he becomes kindly bullying*) Come on, boys! Get moving! Who'll start the ball rolling? You, Captain, and you, General. You're nearest the door. And besides, you're old war heroes! You ought to lead the forlorn hope! Come on, now, show us a little of that good old battle of Modder River spirit we've heard so much about! You can't hang around all day looking as if you were scared the street outside would bite you!

LEWIS. (*turns with humiliated rage—with an attempt at jaunty casualness*) Right you are, Mister Bloody Nosey Parker! Time I pushed off. Was only waiting to say good-bye to you, Harry, old chum.

HOPE. (*dejectedly*) Good-bye, Captain. Hope you have luck.

LEWIS. Oh, I'm bound to, Old Chap, and the same to you. (*He pushes the swinging doors open and makes a brave exit, turning to his right and marching off outside the window at right of door.*)

WETJOEN. Py Gott, if dot Limey can, I can! (*He pushes the door open and lumbers through it like a bull charging an obstacle. He turns left and disappears off rear, outside the farthest window.*)

HICKEY. (*exhortingly*) Next? Come on, Ed. It's a fine summer's day and the call of the old circus lot must be in your blood! (*MOSHER glares at him, then goes to the door. MCGLOIN jumps up from his chair and starts moving toward the door. HICKEY claps him on the back as he passes*) That's the stuff, Mac.

MOSHER. Good-bye, Harry. (*He goes out, turning right outside.*)

MCGLOIN. (*glowering after him*) If that crooked grifter has the guts— (*He goes out, turning left outside. HICKEY glances at WILLIE who, before he can speak, jumps from his chair.*)

WILLIE. Good-bye, Harry, and thanks for all your kindness.

HICKEY. (*claps him on the back*) That's the way, Willie! The D.A.'s a busy man. He can't wait all day for you, you know. (WILLIE *hurries to the door.*)

HOPE. (*dully*) Good luck, Willie. (WILLIE *goes out and turns right outside. While he is doing so,* JIMMY, *in a sick panic, sneaks to the bar and furtively reaches for* LARRY's *glass of whiskey.*)

HICKEY. And now it's your turn, Jimmy, old pal. (*He sees what* JIMMY *is at and grabs his arm just as he is about to down the drink*) Now, now, Jimmy! You can't do that to yourself. One drink on top of your hangover and an empty stomach and you'll be oreyeyed. Then you'll tell yourself you wouldn't stand a chance if you went up soused to get your old job back.

JIMMY. (*pleads abjectly*) Tomorrow! I will tomorrow! I'll be in good shape tomorrow! (*Abruptly getting control of himself—with shaken firmness*) All right. I'm going. Take your hands off me.

HICKEY. That's the ticket! You'll thank me when it's all over.

JIMMY. (*in a burst of futile fury*) You dirty swine! (*He tries to throw the drink in* HICKEY's *face, but his aim is poor and it lands on* HICKEY's *coat.* JIMMY *turns and dashes through the door, disappearing outside the window at right of door.*)

HICKEY. (*brushing the whiskey off his coat—humorously*) All set for an alcohol rub! But no hard feelings. I know how he feels. I wrote the book. I've seen the day when if anyone forced me to face the truth about my pipe dreams, I'd have shot them dead. (*He turns to* HOPE—*encouragingly*) Well, Governor, Jimmy made the grade. It's up to you. If he's got the guts to go through with the test, then certainly you—

LARRY. (*bursts out*) Leave Harry alone, damn you!

HICKEY. (*grins at him*) I'd make up my mind about myself if I was you, Larry, and not bother over Harry. He'll come through all right. I've promised him that. He doesn't need anyone's bum pity. Do you, Governor?

HOPE. (*with a pathetic attempt at his old fuming assertiveness*) No,

686

bejees! Keep your nose out of this, Larry. What's Hickey got to do with it? I've always been going to take this walk, ain't I? Bejees, you bums want to keep me locked up in here 's if I was in jail! I've stood it long enough! I'm free, white and twenty-one, and I'll do as I damned please, bejees! You keep your nose out, too, Hickey! You'd think you was boss of this dump, not me. Sure, I'm all right! Why shouldn't I be? What the hell's to be scared of, just taking a stroll around my own yard? (*As he talks he has been moving toward the door. Now he reaches it*) What's the weather like outside, Rocky?

ROCKY. Fine day, Boss.

HOPE. What's that? Can't hear you. Don't look fine to me. Looks 's if it'd pour down cats and dogs any minute. My rheumatism— (*He catches himself*) No, must be my eyes. Half blind, bejees. Makes things look black. I see now it's a fine day. Too damned hot for a walk, though, if you ask me. Well, do me good to sweat the booze out of me. But I'll have to° watch out for the damned automobiles. Wasn't none of them around the last time, twenty years ago. From what I've seen of 'em through the window, they'd run over you as soon as look at you. Not that I'm scared of 'em. I can take care of myself. (*He puts a reluctant hand on the swinging door*) Well, so long— (*He stops and looks back—with frightened irascibility*) Bejees, where are you, Hickey? It's time we got started.

HICKEY. (*grins and shakes his head*) No, Harry. Can't be done. You've got to keep a date with yourself alone.

HOPE. (*with forced fuming*) Hell of a guy, you are! Thought you'd be willing to help me across the street, knowing I'm half blind. Half deaf, too. Can't bear those damned automobiles. Hell with you! Bejees, I've never needed no one's help and I don't now! (*Egging himself on*) I'll take a good long walk now I've started. See all my old friends. Bejees, they must have given me up for dead. Twenty years is a long time. But they know it was grief over Bessie's death that made me— (*He puts his hand on the door*) Well, the sooner I get started— (*Then he drops his hand—with sentimental melancholy*) You know, Hickey, that's what gets me. Can't help thinking the last time I went out was to Bessie's funeral. After she'd gone, I didn't feel life was worth living. Swore I'd never go out again. (*Pathetically*) Somehow, I can't feel it's right for me to go, Hickey, even now. It's like I was doing wrong to her memory.

HICKEY. Now, Governor, you can't let yourself get away with that one any more!

HOPE. (*cupping his hand to his ear*) What's that? Can't hear you. (*Sentimentally again but with desperation*) I remember now clear as day the last time before she— It was a fine Sunday morning. We went out to church together. (*His voice breaks on a sob.*)

HICKEY. (*amused*) It's a great act, Governor. But I know better, and so do you. You never did want to go to church or any place else with her. She was always on your neck, making you have ambition and go out and do things, when all you wanted was to get drunk in peace.

HOPE. (*falteringly*) Can't hear a word you're saying. You're a God-damned liar, anyway! (*Then in a sudden fury, his voice trembling with hatred*) Bejees, you son of a bitch, if there was a mad dog outside I'd go and shake hands with it rather than stay here with you! (*The momentum of his fit of rage does it. He pushes the door open and strides blindly out into the street and as blindly past the window behind the free-lunch counter.*)

ROCKY. (*in amazement*) Jees, he made it! I'd a give yuh fifty to one he'd never— (*He goes to the end of the bar to look through the window —disgustedly*) Aw, he's stopped. I'll bet yuh he's comin' back.

HICKEY. Of course, he's coming back. So are all the others. By to-night they'll all be here again. You dumbbell, that's the whole point.

ROCKY. (*excitedly*) No, he ain't neider! He's gone to de coib. He's lookin' up and down. Scared stiff of automobiles. Jees, dey ain't more'n two an hour comes down dis street, de old boob! (*He watches excitedly, as if it were a race he had a bet on, oblivious to what happens in the bar.*)

LARRY. (*turns on HICKEY with bitter defiance*) And now it's my turn, I suppose? What is it I'm to do to achieve this blessed peace of yours?

HICKEY. (*grins at him*) Why, we've discussed all that, Larry. Just stop lying to yourself—

LARRY. You think when I say I'm finished with life, and tired of watching the stupid greed of the human circus, and I'll welcome closing my eyes in the long sleep of death—you think that's a coward's lie?

HICKEY. (*chuckling*) Well, what do you think, Larry?

LARRY. (*with increasing bitter intensity, more as if he were fighting with himself than with* HICKEY) I'm afraid to live, am I?—and even more afraid to die! So I sit here, with my pride drowned on the bottom of a bottle, keeping drunk so I won't see myself shaking in my britches with fright, or hear myself whining and praying: Beloved Christ, let me live a little longer at any price! If it's only for a few days more, or a few hours even, have mercy, Almighty God, and let me still clutch greedily to my yellow heart this sweet treasure, this jewel beyond price, the dirty, stinking bit of withered old flesh which is my beautiful little life! (*He laughs with a sneering, vindictive self-loathing, staring inward at himself with contempt and hatred. Then abruptly he makes* HICKEY *again the antagonist*) You think you'll make me admit that to myself?

HICKEY. (*chuckling*) But you just did admit it, didn't you?

PARRITT. (*lifts his head from his hands to glare at* LARRY—*jeeringly*) That's the stuff, Hickey! Show the old yellow faker up! He can't play dead on me like this! He's got to help me!

HICKEY. Yes, Larry, you've got to settle with him. I'm leaving you entirely in his hands. He'll do as good a job as I could at making you give up that old grandstand bluff.

LARRY. (*angrily*) I'll see the two of you in hell first!

ROCKY. (*calls excitedly from the end of the bar*) Jees, Harry's startin' across de street! He's goin' to fool yuh, Hickey, yuh bastard! (*He pauses, watching—then worriedly*) What de hell's he stoppin' for? Right in de middle of de street! Yuh'd tink he was paralyzed or somethin'! (*Disgustedly*) Aw, he's quittin'! He's turned back! Jees, look at de old bastard travel! Here he comes! (HOPE *passes the window outside the free-lunch counter in a shambling, panic-stricken run. He comes lurching*

689

blindly through the swinging doors and stumbles to the bar at LARRY's *right.*)

HOPE. Bejees, give me a drink quick! Scared me out of a year's growth! Bejees, that guy ought to be pinched! Bejees, it ain't safe to walk in the streets! Bejees, that ends me! Never again! Give me that bottle! (*He slops a glass full and drains it and pours another— To* ROCKY, *who is regarding him with scorn—appealingly*) You seen it, didn't you, Rocky?

ROCKY. Seen what?

HOPE. That automobile, you dumb Wop! Feller driving it must be drunk or crazy. He'd run right over me if I hadn't jumped. (*Ingratiatingly*) Come on, Larry, have a drink. Everybody have a drink. Have a cigar, Rocky. I know you hardly ever touch it.

ROCKY. (*resentfully*) Well, dis is de time I do touch it! (*Pouring a drink*) I'm goin' to get stinko, see! And if yuh don't like it, yuh know what yuh can do! I gotta good mind to chuck my job, anyways. (*Disgustedly*) Jees, Harry, I thought yuh had some guts! I was bettin' yuh'd make it and show dat four-flusher up. (*He nods at* HICKEY—*then snorts*) Automobile, hell! Who d'yuh tink yuh're kiddin'! Dey wasn' no automobile! Yuh just quit cold!

HOPE. (*feebly*) Guess I ought to know! Bejees, it almost killed me!

HICKEY. (*comes to the bar between him and* LARRY, *and puts a hand on his shoulder—kindly*) Now, now, Governor. Don't be foolish. You've faced the test and come through. You're rid of all that nagging dream stuff now. You know you can't believe it any more.

HOPE. (*appeals pleadingly to* LARRY) Larry, you saw it, didn't you? Drink up! Have another! Have all you want! Bejees, we'll go on a grand old souse together! You saw that automobile, didn't you?

LARRY. (*compassionately, avoiding his eyes*) Sure, I saw it, Harry. You had a narrow escape. Be God, I thought you were a goner!

HICKEY. (*turns on him with a flash of sincere indignation*) What the hell's the matter with you, Larry? You know what I told you about the wrong kind of pity. Leave Harry alone! You'd think I was trying to harm him, the fool way you act! My oldest friend! What kind of a louse do you think I am? There isn't anything I wouldn't do for Harry, and he knows it! All I've wanted to do is fix it so he'll be finally at peace with himself for the rest of his days! And if you'll only wait until the final returns are in, you'll find that's exactly what I've accomplished! (*He turns to* HOPE *and pats his shoulder—coaxingly*) Come now, Governor. What's the use of being stubborn, now when it's all over and dead? Give up that ghost automobile.

HOPE. (*beginning to collapse within himself—dully*) Yes, what's the use—now? All a lie! No automobile. But, bejees, something ran over me! Must have been myself, I guess. (*He forces a feeble smile—then wearily*) Guess I'll sit down. Feel all in. Like a corpse, bejees. (*He picks a bottle and glass from the bar and walks to the first table and slumps down in the chair, facing left-front. His shaking hand misjudges the distance and he sets the bottle on the table with a jar that rouses* HUGO, *who lifts his head from his arms and blinks at him through his thick spectacles.* HOPE *speaks to him in a flat, dead voice*) Hello, Hugo. Coming up for air? Stay passed out, that's the right dope. There ain't any cool willow trees— except you grow your own in a bottle. (*He pours a drink and gulps it down.*)

HUGO. (*with his silly giggle*) Hello, Harry, stupid proletarian monkey-face! I vill trink champagne beneath the villow— (*With a change to aristocratic fastidiousness*) But the slaves must ice it properly! (*With guttural rage*) Gottamned Hickey! Peddler pimp for nouveau-riche capitalism! Vhen I lead the jackass mob to the sack of Babylon, I vill make them hang him to a lamppost the first one!

HOPE. (*spiritlessly*) Good work. I'll help pull on the rope. Have a drink, Hugo.

HUGO. (*frightenedly*) No, thank you. I am too trunk now. I hear myself say crazy things. Do not listen, please. Larry vill tell you I haf never been so crazy trunk. I must sleep it off. (*He starts to put his head on his arms but stops and stares at* HOPE *with growing uneasiness*) Vhat's matter, Harry? You look funny. You look dead. Vhat's happened? I

691

don't know you. Listen, I feel I am dying, too. Because I am so crazy trunk! It is very necessary I sleep. But I can't sleep here vith you. You look dead. (*He scrambles to his feet in a confused panic, turns his back on* HOPE *and settles into the chair at the next table which faces left. He thrusts his head down on his arms like an ostrich hiding its head in the sand. He does not notice* PARRITT, *nor* PARRITT *him.*)

LARRY. (*to* HICKEY *with bitter condemnation*) Another one who's begun to enjoy your peace!

HICKEY. Oh, I know it's tough on him right now, the same as it is on Harry. But that's only the first shock. I promise you they'll both come through all right.

LARRY. And you believe that! I see you do! You mad fool!

HICKEY. Of course, I believe it! I tell you I know from my own experience!

HOPE. (*spiritlessly*) Close that big clam of yours, Hickey. Bejees, you're a worse gabber than that nagging bitch, Bessie, was. (*He drinks his drink mechanically and pours another.*)

ROCKY. (*in amazement*) Jees, did yuh hear dat?

HOPE. (*dully*) What's wrong with this booze? There's no kick in it.

ROCKY. (*worriedly*) Jees, Larry, Hugo had it right. He does look like he'd croaked.

HICKEY. (*annoyed*) Don't be a damned fool! Give him time. He's coming along all right. (*He calls to* HOPE *with a first trace of underlying uneasiness*) You're all right, aren't you, Harry?

HOPE. (*dully*) I want to pass out like Hugo.

LARRY. (*turns to* HICKEY—*with bitter anger*) It's the peace of death you've brought him.

HICKEY. (*for the first time loses his temper*) That's a lie! (*But he controls this instantly and grins*) Well, well, you did manage to get a rise out of me that time. I think such a hell of a lot of Harry— (*Impatiently*) You know that's damned foolishness. Look at me. I've been through it. Do I look dead? Just leave Harry alone and wait until the shock wears off and you'll see. He'll be a new man. Like I am. (*He calls to* HOPE *coaxingly*) How's it coming, Governor? Beginning to feel free, aren't you? Relieved and not guilty any more?

HOPE. (*grumbles spiritlessly*) Bejees, you must have been monkeying with the booze, too, you interfering bastard! There's no life in it now. I want to get drunk and pass out. Let's all pass out. Who the hell cares?

HICKEY. (*lowering his voice—worriedly to* LARRY) I admit I didn't think he'd be hit so hard. He's always been a happy-go-lucky slob. Like I was. Of course, it hit me hard, too. But only for a minute. Then I felt as if a ton of guilt had been lifted off my mind. I saw what had happened was the only possible way for the peace of all concerned.

LARRY. (*sharply*) What was it happened? Tell us that! And don't try to get out of it! I want a straight answer! (*Vindictively*) I think it was something you drove someone else to do!

HICKEY. (*puzzled*) Someone else?

LARRY. (*accusingly*) What did your wife die of? You've kept that a deep secret, I notice—for some reason!

HICKEY. (*reproachfully*) You're not very considerate, Larry. But, if you insist on knowing now, there's no reason you shouldn't. It was a bullet through the head that killed Evelyn. (*There is a second's tense silence.*)

HOPE. (*dully*) Who the hell cares? To hell with her and that nagging old hag, Bessie.

ROCKY. Christ. You had de right dope, Larry.

LARRY. (*revengefully*) You drove your poor wife to suicide? I knew it! Be God, I don't blame her! I'd almost do as much myself to be rid of you! It's what you'd like to drive us all to— (*Abruptly he is ashamed of himself and pitying*) I'm sorry, Hickey. I'm a rotten louse to throw that in your face.

HICKEY. (*quietly*) Oh, that's all right, Larry. But don't jump at conclusions. I didn't say poor Evelyn committed suicide. It's the last thing she'd ever have done, as long as I was alive for her to take care of and forgive. If you'd known her at all, you'd never get such a crazy suspicion. (*He pauses—then slowly*) No, I'm sorry to have to tell you my

693

poor wife was killed. (LARRY *stares at him with growing horror and shrinks back along the bar away from him.* PARRITT *jerks his head up from his hands and looks around frightenedly, not at* HICKEY, *but at* LARRY. ROCKY'S *round eyes are popping.* HOPE *stares dully at the table top.* HUGO, *his head hidden in his arms, gives no sign of life.*)

LARRY. (*shakenly*) Then she—was murdered.

PARRITT. (*springs to his feet—stammers defensively*) You're a liar, Larry! You must be crazy to say that to me! You know she's still alive! (*But no one pays any attention to him.*)

ROCKY. (*blurts out*) Moidered? Who done it?

LARRY. (*his eyes fixed with fascinated horror on* HICKEY—*frightenedly*) Don't ask questions, you dumb Wop! It's none of our damned business! Leave Hickey alone!

HICKEY. (*smiles at him with affectionate amusement*) Still the old grandstand bluff, Larry? Or is it some more bum pity? (*He turns to* ROCKY—*matter-of-factly*) The police don't know who killed her yet, Rocky. But I expect they will before very long. (*As if that finished the subject, he comes forward to* HOPE *and sits beside him, with an arm around his shoulder—affectionately coaxing*) Coming along fine now, aren't you, Governor? Getting over the first shock? Beginning to feel free from guilt and lying hopes and at peace with yourself?

HOPE. (*with a dull callousness*) Somebody croaked your Evelyn, eh? Bejees, my bets are on the iceman! But who the hell cares? Let's get drunk and pass out. (*He tosses down his drink with a lifeless, automatic movement—complainingly*) Bejees, what did you do to the booze, Hickey? There's no damned life left in it.

PARRITT. (*stammers, his eyes on* LARRY, *whose eyes in turn remain fixed on* HICKEY) Don't look like that, Larry! You've got to believe what I told you! It had nothing to do with her! It was just to get a few lousy dollars!

HUGO. (*suddenly raises his head from his arms and, looking straight in front of him, pounds on the table frightenedly with his small fists*) Don't be a fool! Buy me a trink! But no more vine! It is not properly

iced! (*With guttural rage*) Gottamned stupid proletarian slaves! Buy me
a trink or I vill have you shot! (*He collapses into abject begging*) Please
for Gott's sake! I am not trunk enough! I cannot sleep! Life is a crazy
monkey-face! Always there is blood beneath the villow trees! I hate it
and I am afraid! (*He hides his face on his arms, sobbing muffledly*)
Please, I am crazy trunk! I say crazy things! For Gott's sake, do not listen
to me! (*But no one pays any attention to him.* LARRY *stands shrunk back
against the bar.* ROCKY *is leaning over it. They stare at* HICKEY. PARRITT
stands looking pleadingly at LARRY.)

HICKEY. (*gazes with worried kindliness at* HOPE) You're beginning to
worry me, Governor. Something's holding you up somewhere. I don't
see why— You've faced the truth about yourself. You've done what you
had to do to kill your nagging pipe dreams. Oh, I know it knocks you
cold. But only for a minute. Then you see it was the only possible way
to peace. And you feel happy. Like I did. That's what worries me about
you, Governor. It's time you began to feel happy—

CURTAIN

ACT FOUR

SCENE—*Same as Act One—the back room with the curtain separating
it from the section of the barroom with its single table at right of
curtain, front. It is around half past one in the morning of the following
day.*

*The tables in the back room have a new arrangement. The one at
left, front, before the window to the yard, is in the same position. So is
the one at the right, rear, of it in the second row. But this table now has
only one chair. This chair is at right of it, facing directly front. The two
tables on either side of the door at rear are unchanged. But the table
which was at center, front, has been pushed toward right so that it and*

the table at right, rear, of it in the second row, and the last table at right in the front row, are now jammed so closely together that they form one group.

LARRY, HUGO *and* PARRITT *are at the table at left, front.* LARRY *is at left of it, beside the window, facing front.* HUGO *sits at rear, facing front, his head on his arms in his habitual position, but he is not asleep. On* HUGO's *left is* PARRITT, *his chair facing left, front. At right of table, an empty chair, facing left.* LARRY's *chin is on his chest, his eyes fixed on the floor. He will not look at* PARRITT, *who keeps staring at him with a sneering, pleading challenge.*

Two bottles of whiskey are on each table, whiskey and chaser glasses, a pitcher of water.

The one chair by the table at right, rear, of them is vacant.

At the first table at right of center, CORA *sits at left, front, of it, facing front. Around the rear of this table are four empty chairs. Opposite* CORA, *in a sixth chair, is* CAPTAIN LEWIS, *also facing front. On his left,* MCGLOIN *is facing front in a chair before the middle table of his group. At right, rear, of him, also at this table,* GENERAL WETJOEN *sits facing front. In back of this table are three empty chairs.*

At right, rear, of WETJOEN, *but beside the last table of the group, sits* WILLIE. *On* WILLIE's *left, at rear of table, is* HOPE. *On* HOPE's *left, at right, rear, of table, is* MOSHER. *Finally, at right of table is* JIMMY TOMORROW. *All of the four sit facing front.*

There is an atmosphere of oppressive stagnation in the room, and a quality of insensibility about all the people in this group at right. They are like wax figures, set stiffly on their chairs, carrying out mechanically the motions of getting drunk but sunk in a numb stupor which is impervious to stimulation.

In the bar section, JOE *is sprawled in the chair at right of table, facing left. His head rolls forward in a sodden slumber.* ROCKY *is standing behind his chair, regarding him with dull hostility.* ROCKY's *face is set in an expression of tired, callous toughness. He looks now like a minor Wop gangster.*

ROCKY. (*shakes* JOE *by the shoulder*) Come on, yuh damned nigger! Beat it in de back room! It's after hours. (*But* JOE *remains inert.* ROCKY *gives up*) Aw, to hell wid it. Let de dump get pinched. I'm through wid dis lousy job, anyway! (*He hears someone at rear and calls*) Who's dat? (CHUCK *appears from rear. He has been drinking heavily, but there is no lift to his jag; his manner is grouchy and sullen. He has evidently been brawling. His knuckles are raw and there is a mouse under one eye. He has lost his straw hat, his tie is awry, and his blue suit is dirty.* ROCKY *eyes him indifferently*) Been scrappin', huh? Started off on your periodical, ain't yuh? (*For a second there is a gleam of satisfaction in his eyes.*)

CHUCK. Yeah, ain't yuh glad? (*Truculently*) What's it to yuh?

ROCKY. Not a damned ting. But dis is someting to me. I'm out on my feet holdin' down your job. Yuh said if I'd take your day, yuh'd relieve me at six, and here it's half past one A.M. Well, yuh're takin' over now, get me, no matter how plastered yuh are!

CHUCK. Plastered, hell! I wisht I was. I've lapped up a gallon, but it don't hit me right. And to hell wid de job. I'm goin' to tell Harry I'm quittin'.

ROCKY. Yeah? Well, I'm quittin', too.

CHUCK. I've played sucker for dat crummy blonde long enough, lettin' her kid me into woikin'. From now on I take it easy.

ROCKY. I'm glad yuh're gettin' some sense.

CHUCK. And I hope yuh're gettin' some. What a prize sap you been, tendin' bar when yuh got two good hustlers in your stable!

ROCKY. Yeah, but I ain't no sap now. I'll loin dem, when dey get back from Coney. (*Sneeringly*) Jees, dat Cora sure played you for a dope, feedin' yuh dat marriage-on-de-farm hop!

CHUCK. (*dully*) Yeah. Hickey got it right. A lousy pipe dream. It was her pulling sherry flips on me woke me up. All de way walkin' to de ferry, every ginmill we come to she'd drag me in to blow her. I got tinkin', Christ, what won't she want when she gets de ring on her finger and I'm hooked? So I tells her at de ferry, "Kiddo, yuh can go to Joisey, or to hell, but count me out."

ROCKY. She says it was her told you to go to hell, because yuh'd started hittin' de booze.

CHUCK. (*ignoring this*) I got tinkin', too, Jees, won't I look sweet wid a wife dat if yuh put all de guys she's stayed wid side by side, dey'd reach to Chicago. (*He sighs gloomily*) Dat kind of dame, yuh can't trust 'em. De minute your back is toined, dey're cheatin' wid de iceman or someone. Hickey done me a favor, makin' me wake up. (*He pauses— then adds pathetically*) On'y it was fun, kinda, me and Cora kiddin' ourselves— (*Suddenly his face hardens with hatred*) Where is dat son of a bitch, Hickey? I want one good sock at dat guy—just one!—and de next buttin' in he'll do will be in de morgue! I'll take a chance on goin' to de Chair—!

ROCKY. (*starts—in a low warning voice*) Piano! Keep away from him, Chuck! He ain't here now, anyway. He went out to phone, he said. He wouldn't call from here. I got a hunch he's beat it. But if he does come back, yuh don't know him, if anyone asks yuh, get me? (*As* CHUCK *looks at him with dull surprise he lowers his voice to a whisper*) De Chair, maybe dat's where he's goin'. I don't know nuttin', see, but it looks like he croaked his wife.

CHUCK. (*with a flash of interest*) Yuh mean she really was cheatin' on him? Den I don't blame de guy—

ROCKY. Who's blamin' him? When a dame asks for it— But I don't know nuttin' about it, see?

CHUCK. Is any of de gang wise?

ROCKY. Larry is. And de boss ought to be. I tried to wise de rest of dem up to stay clear of him, but dey're all so licked I don't know if dey got it. (*He pauses—vindictively*) I don't give a damn what he done to his wife, but if he gets de Hot Seat I won't go into no mournin'!

CHUCK. Me, neider!

ROCKY. Not after his trowin' it in my face I'm a pimp. What if I am? Why de hell not? And what he's done to Harry. Jees, de poor old slob is so licked he can't even get drunk. And all de gang. Dey're all licked. I couldn't help feelin' sorry for de poor bums when dey showed up tonight, one by one, lookin' like pooches wid deir tails between deir legs, dat everyone'd been kickin' till dey was too punch-drunk to feel it no more. Jimmy Tomorrow was de last. Schwartz, de copper, brung him in. Seen him sittin' on de dock on West Street, lookin' at de water and cryin'! Schwartz thought he was drunk and I let him tink it. But he was cold sober. He was tryin' to jump in and didn't have de noive, I figgered it. Noive! Jees, dere ain't enough guts left in de whole gang to battle a mosquito!

CHUCK. Aw, to hell wid 'em! Who cares? Gimme a drink. (ROCKY *pushes the bottle toward him apathetically*) I see you been hittin' de redeye, too.

ROCKY. Yeah. But it don't do no good. I can't get drunk right. (CHUCK *drinks.* JOE *mumbles in his sleep.* CHUCK *regards him resentfully*) Dis doity dinge was able to get his snootful and pass out. Jees, even Hickey can't faze a nigger! Yuh'd tink he was fazed if yuh'd seen him come in. Stinko, and he pulled a gat and said he'd plug Hickey for insultin' him. Den he dropped it and begun to cry and said he wasn't a gamblin' man or a tough guy no more; he was yellow. He'd borrowed de gat to stick up someone, and den didn't have de guts. He got drunk pan-handlin' drinks in nigger joints, I s'pose. I guess dey felt sorry for him.

CHUCK. He ain't got no business in de bar after hours. Why don't yuh chuck him out?

ROCKY. (*apathetically*) Aw, to hell wid it. Who cares?

CHUCK. (*lapsing into the same mood*) Yeah. I don't.

JOE. (*suddenly lunges to his feet dazedly—mumbles in humbled apology*) Scuse me, White Boys. Scuse me for livin'. I don't want to be where I's not wanted. (*He makes his way swayingly to the opening in the curtain at rear and tacks down to the middle table of the three at right, front. He feels his way around it to the table at its left and gets to the chair in back of* CAPTAIN LEWIS.)

CHUCK. (*gets up—in a callous, brutal tone*) My pig's in de back room, ain't she? I wanna collect de dough I wouldn't take dis mornin', like a sucker, before she blows it. (*He goes rear.*)

699

ROCKY. (*getting up*) I'm comin', too. I'm trough woikin'. I ain't no lousy bartender. (CHUCK *comes through the curtain and looks for* CORA *as* JOE *flops down in the chair in back of* CAPTAIN LEWIS.)

JOE. (*taps* LEWIS *on the shoulder—servilely apologetic*) If you objeats to my sittin' here, Captain, just tell me and I pulls my freight.

LEWIS. No apology required, old chap. Anybody could tell you I should feel honored a bloody Kaffir would lower himself to sit beside me. (JOE *stares at him with sodden perplexity—then closes his eyes.* CHUCK *comes forward to take the chair behind* CORA'S, *as* ROCKY *enters the back room and starts over toward* LARRY'S *table.*)

CHUCK. (*his voice hard*) I'm waitin', Baby. Dig!

CORA. (*with apathetic obedience*) Sure. I been expectin' yuh. I got it all ready. Here. (*She passes a small roll of bills she has in her hand over her shoulder, without looking at him. He takes it, glances at it suspiciously, then shoves it in his pocket without a word of acknowledgment.* CORA *speaks with a tired wonder at herself rather than resentment toward him*) Jees, imagine me kiddin' myself I wanted to marry a drunken pimp.

CHUCK. Dat's nuttin', Baby. Imagine de sap I'da been, when I can get your dough just as easy widout it!

ROCKY. (*takes the chair on* PARRITT'S *left, facing* LARRY—*dully*) Hello, Old Cemetery. (LARRY *doesn't seem to hear. To* PARRITT) Hello, Tightwad. You still around?

PARRITT. (*keeps his eyes on* LARRY—*in a jeeringly challenging tone*) Ask Larry! He knows I'm here, all right, although he's pretending not to! He'd like to forget I'm alive! He's trying to kid himself with that grandstand philosopher stuff! But he knows he can't get away with it now! He kept himself locked in his room until a while ago, alone with a bottle of booze, but he couldn't make it work! He couldn't even get drunk! He had to come out! There must have been something there he was even more scared to face than he is Hickey and me! I guess he got looking at the fire escape and thinking how handy it was, if he was really sick of life and only had the nerve to die! (*He pauses sneeringly.*

LARRY's *face has tautened, but he pretends he doesn't hear.* ROCKY *pays no attention. His head has sunk forward, and he stares at the table top, sunk in the same stupor as the other occupants of the room.* PARRITT *goes on, his tone becoming more insistent*) He's been thinking of me, too, Rocky. Trying to figure a way to get out of helping me! He doesn't want to be bothered understanding. But he does understand all right! He used to love her, too. So he thinks I ought to take a hop off the fire escape! (*He pauses.* LARRY's *hands on the table have clinched into fists, as his nails dig into his palms, but he remains silent.* PARRITT *breaks and starts pleading*) For God's sake, Larry, can't you say something? Hickey's got me all balled up. Thinking of what he must have done has got me so I don't know any more what I did or why. I can't go on like this! I've got to know what I ought to do—

LARRY. (*in a stifled tone*) God damn you! Are you trying to make me your executioner?

PARRITT. (*starts frightenedly*) Execution? Then you do think—?

LARRY. I don't think anything!

PARRITT. (*with forced jeering*) I suppose you think I ought to die because I sold out a lot of loud-mouthed fakers, who were cheating suckers with a phony pipe dream, and put them where they ought to be, in jail? (*He forces a laugh*) Don't make me laugh! I ought to get a medal! What a damned old sap you are! You must still believe in the Movement! (*He nudges* ROCKY *with his elbow*) Hickey's right about him, isn't he, Rocky? An old no-good drunken tramp, as dumb as he is, ought to take a hop off the fire escape!

ROCKY. (*dully*) Sure. Why don't he? Or you? Or me? What de hell's de difference? Who cares? (*There is a faint stir from all the crowd, as if this sentiment struck a responsive chord in their numbed minds. They mumble almost in chorus as one voice, like sleepers talking out of a dully irritating dream, "The hell with it!" "Who cares?" Then the sodden silence descends again on the room.* ROCKY *looks from* PARRITT *to* LARRY *puzzledly. He mutters*) What am I doin' here wid youse two? I remember I had someting on my mind to tell yuh. What—? Oh, I got it now. (*He looks from one to the other of their oblivious faces with a strange, sly, calculating look—ingratiatingly*) I was tinking how you was bot' reg'lar guys. I tinks, ain't two guys like dem saps to be hangin' round like a coupla stew bums and wastin' demselves. Not dat I blame yuh for not woikin'. On'y suckers woik. But dere's no percentage in bein' broke when yuh can grab good jack for yourself and make someone else woik for yuh, is dere? I mean, like I do. So I tinks, Dey're my pals and I ought to wise up two good guys like dem to play my system, and not be lousy barflies, no good to demselves or nobody else. (*He addresses* PARRITT *now—persuasively*) What yuh tink, Parritt? Ain't I right? Sure, I am. So don't be a sucker, see? Yuh ain't a bad-lookin' guy. Yuh could easy make some gal who's a good hustler, an' start a stable. I'd help yuh and wise yuh up to de inside dope on de game. (*He pauses inquiringly.* PARRITT *gives no sign of having heard him.* ROCKY *asks impatiently*) Well, what about it? What if dey do call yuh a pimp? What de hell do you care—any more'n I do.

PARRITT. (*without looking at him—vindictively*) I'm through with whores. I wish they were all in jail—or dead!

ROCKY. (*ignores this—disappointedly*) So yuh won't touch it, huh? Aw right, stay a bum! (*He turns to* LARRY) Jees, Larry, he's sure one dumb boob, ain't he? Dead from de neck up! He don't know a good ting when he sees it. (*Oily, even persuasive again*) But how about you, Larry? You ain't dumb. So why not, huh? Sure, yuh're old, but dat don't matter. All de hustlers tink yuh're aces. Dey fall for yuh like yuh was deir uncle or old man or something. Dey'd like takin' care of yuh. And de cops 'round here, dey like yuh, too. It'd be a pipe for yuh, 'specially wid me to help yuh and wise yuh up. Yuh wouldn't have to worry where de next drink's comin' from, or wear doity clothes. (*Hopefully*) Well, don't it look good to yuh?

LARRY. (*glances at him—for a moment he is stirred to sardonic pity*) No, it doesn't look good, Rocky. I mean, the peace Hickey's brought you. It isn't contented enough, if you have to make everyone else a pimp, too.

ROCKY. (*stares at him stupidly—then pushes his chair back and gets up, grumbling*) I'm a sap to waste time on yuh. A stew bum is a stew bum and yuh can't change him. (*He turns away—then turns back for an afterthought*) Like I was sayin' to Chuck, yuh better keep away from Hickey. If anyone asks yuh, yuh don't know nuttin', get me? Yuh never even hoid he had a wife. (*His face hardens*) Jees, we all ought to git drunk and stage a celebration when dat bastard goes to de Chair.

LARRY. (*vindictively*) Be God, I'll celebrate with you and drink long life to him in hell! (*Then guiltily and pityingly*) No! The poor mad devil— (*Then with angry self-contempt*) Ah, pity again! The wrong kind! He'll welcome the Chair!

PARRITT. (*contemptuously*) Yes, what are you so damned scared of death for? I don't want your lousy pity.

ROCKY. Christ, I hope he don't come back, Larry. We don't know nuttin' now. We're on'y guessin', see? But if de bastard keeps on talkin'—

LARRY. (*grimly*) He'll come back. He'll keep on talking. He's got to. He's lost his confidence that the peace he's sold us is the real McCoy, and it's made him uneasy about his own. He'll have to prove to us— (*As he is speaking* HICKEY *appears silently in the doorway at rear. He has lost his beaming salesman's grin. His manner is no longer self-assured. His expression is uneasy, baffled and resentful. It has the stubborn set of an obsessed determination. His eyes are on* LARRY *as he comes in. As he speaks, there is a start from all the crowd, a shrinking away from him.*)

HICKEY. (*angrily*) That's a damned lie, Larry! I haven't lost confidence a damned bit! Why should I? (*Boastfully*) By God, whenever I made up my mind to sell someone something I knew they ought to want, I've sold 'em! (*He suddenly looks confused—haltingly*) I mean— It isn't kind of you, Larry, to make that kind of crack when I've been doing my best to help—

ROCKY. (*moving away from him toward right—sharply*) Keep away from me! I don't know nuttin' about yuh, see? (*His tone is threatening but his manner as he turns his back and ducks quickly across to the bar entrance is that of one in flight. In the bar he comes forward and slumps in a chair at the table, facing front.)*

HICKEY. (*comes to the table at right, rear, of* LARRY's *table and sits in the one chair there, facing front. He looks over the crowd at right, hopefully and then disappointedly. He speaks with a strained attempt at his old affectionate jollying manner*) Well, well! How are you coming along, everybody? Sorry I had to leave you for a while, but there was something I had to get finally settled. It's all fixed now.

HOPE. (*in the voice of one reiterating mechanically a hopeless complaint*) When are you going to do something about this booze, Hickey? Bejees, we all know you did something to take the life out of it. It's like drinking dishwater! We can't pass out! And you promised us peace. (*His group all join in in a dull, complaining chorus, "We can't pass out! You promised us peace!"*)

HICKEY. (*bursts into resentful exasperation*) For God's sake, Harry, are you still harping on that damned nonsense! You've kept it up all afternoon and night! And you've got everybody else singing the same crazy tune! I've had about all I can stand— That's why I phoned— (*He controls himself*) Excuse me, boys and girls. I don't mean that. I'm just worried about you, when you play dead on me like this. I was hoping by the time I got back you'd be like you ought to be! I thought you were deliberately holding back, while I was around, because you didn't want to give me the satisfaction of showing me I'd had the right dope. And I did have! I know from my own experience. (*Exasperatedly*) But I've explained that a million times! And you've all done what you needed to do! By rights you should be contented now, without a single damned hope or lying dream left to torment you! But here you are, acting like a lot of stiffs cheating the undertaker! (*He looks around accusingly*) I can't figure it—unless it's just your damned pigheaded stubbornness! (*He breaks—miserably*) Hell, you oughtn't to act this way with me! You're my old pals, the only friends I've got. You know the one thing I want is to see you all happy before I go— (*Rousing him-*

self to his old brisk, master-of-ceremonies manner) And there's damned little time left now. I've made a date for two o'clock. We've got to get busy right away and find out what's wrong. (*There is a sodden silence. He goes on exasperatedly*) Can't you appreciate what you've got, for God's sake? Don't you know you're free now to be yourselves, without having to feel remorse or guilt, or lie to yourselves about reforming tomorrow? Can't you see there is no tomorrow now? You're rid of it forever! You've killed it! You don't have to care a damn about anything any more! You've finally got the game of life licked, don't you see that? (*Angrily exhorting*) Then why the hell don't you get pie-eyed and celebrate? Why don't you laugh and sing "Sweet Adeline"? (*With bitterly hurt accusation*) The only reason I can think of is, you're putting on this rotten half-dead act just to get back at me! Because you hate my guts! (*He breaks again*) God, don't do that, gang! It makes me feel like hell to think you hate me. It makes me feel you suspect I must have hated you. But that's a lie! Oh, I know I used to hate everyone in the world who wasn't as rotten a bastard as I was! But that was when I was living in hell—before I faced the truth and saw the one possible way to free poor Evelyn and give her the peace she'd always dreamed about. (*He pauses. Everyone in the group stirs with awakening dread and they all begin to grow tense on their chairs.*)

CHUCK. (*without looking at* HICKEY—*with dull, resentful viciousness*) Aw, put a bag over it! To hell wid Evelyn! What if she was cheatin'? And who cares what yuh did to her? Dat's your funeral. We don't give a damn, see? (*There is a dull, resentful chorus of assent, "We don't give a damn."* CHUCK *adds dully*) All we want outa you is keep de hell away from us and give us a rest. (*A muttered chorus of assent.*)

HICKEY. (*as if he hadn't heard this—an obsessed look on his face*) The one possible way to make up to her for all I'd made her go through, and get her rid of me so I couldn't make her suffer any more, and she wouldn't have to forgive me again! I saw I couldn't do it by killing myself, like I wanted to for a long time. That would have been the last straw for her. She'd have died of a broken heart to think I could do that

705

to her. She'd have blamed herself for it, too. Or I couldn't just run away from her. She'd have died of grief and humiliation if I'd done that to her. She'd have thought I'd stopped loving her. (*He adds with a strange impressive simplicity*) You see, Evelyn loved me. And I loved her. That was the trouble. It would have been easy to find a way out if she hadn't loved me so much. Or if I hadn't loved her. But as it was, there was only one possible way. (*He pauses—then adds simply*) I had to kill her. (*There is second's dead silence as he finishes—then a tense indrawn breath like a gasp from the crowd, and a general shrinking movement.*)

LARRY. (*bursts out*) You mad fool, can't you keep your mouth shut! We may hate you for what you've done here this time, but we remember the old times, too, when you brought kindness and laughter with you instead of death! We don't want to know things that will make us help send you to the Chair!

PARRITT. (*with angry scorn*) Ah, shut up, you yellow faker! Can't you face anything? Wouldn't I deserve the Chair, too, if I'd— It's worse if you kill someone and they have to go on living. I'd be glad of the Chair! It'd wipe it out! It'd square me with myself!

HICKEY. (*disturbed—with a movement of repulsion*) I wish you'd get rid of that bastard, Larry. I can't have him pretending there's something in common between him and me. It's what's in your heart that counts. There was love in my heart, not hate.

PARRITT. (*glares at him in angry terror*) You're a liar! I don't hate her! I couldn't! And it had nothing to do with her, anyway! You ask Larry!

LARRY. (*grabs his shoulder and shakes him furiously*) God damn you, stop shoving your rotten soul in my lap! (PARRITT *subsides, hiding his face in his hands and shuddering.*)

HICKEY. (*goes on quietly now*) Don't worry about the Chair, Larry. I know it's still hard for you not to be terrified by death, but when you've made peace with yourself, like I have, you won't give a damn. (*He addresses the group at right again—earnestly*) Listen, everybody. I've made up my mind the only way I can clear things up for you, so you'll realize how contented and carefree you ought to feel, now I've made you get rid of your pipe dreams, is to show you what a pipe dream did to me and Evelyn. I'm certain if I tell you about it from the beginning, you'll appreciate what I've done for you and why I did it, and how damned grateful you ought to be—instead of hating me. (*He begins eagerly in a strange running narrative manner*) You see, even when we were kids, Evelyn and me—

HOPE. (*bursts out, pounding with his glass on the table*) No! Who the hell cares? We don't want to hear it. All we want is to pass out and get drunk and a little peace! (*They are all, except* LARRY *and* PARRITT, *seized by the same fit and pound with their glasses, even* HUGO, *and* ROCKY *in the bar, and shout in chorus, "Who the hell cares? We want to pass out!"*)

HICKEY. (*with an expression of wounded hurt*) All right, if that's the way you feel. I don't want to cram it down your throats. I don't need to tell anyone. I don't feel guilty. I'm only worried about you.

HOPE. What did you do to this booze? That's what we'd like to hear. Bejecs, you done something. There's no life or kick in it now. (*He appeals mechanically to* JIMMY TOMORROW) Ain't that right, Jimmy?

JIMMY. (*more than any of them, his face has a wax-figure blankness that makes it look embalmed. He answers in a precise, completely lifeless voice, but his reply is not to* HARRY's *question, and he does not look at him or anyone else*) Yes. Quite right. It was all a stupid lie—my nonsense about tomorrow. Naturally, they would never give me my position back. I would never dream of asking them. It would be hopeless. I didn't resign. I was fired for drunkenness. And that was years ago. I'm much worse now. And it was absurd of me to excuse my drunkenness by pretending it was my wife's adultery that ruined my life. As Hickey guessed, I was a drunkard before that. Long before. I discovered early in life that living frightened me when I was sober. I have forgotten why I married Marjorie. I can't even remember now if she was pretty. She was a blonde, I think, but I couldn't swear to it. I had some idea of wanting a home, perhaps. But, of course, I much preferred the nearest pub. Why Marjorie married me, God knows. It's impossible to believe she loved me. She soon found I much preferred drinking all night with my pals to being in bed with her. So, naturally, she was unfaithful. I didn't blame her. I really didn't care. I was glad to be free—even grateful to her, I think, for giving me such a good tragic excuse to drink as much as I damned well pleased. (*He stops like a mechanical doll that has run down. No one gives any sign of having heard him. There is a heavy silence. Then* ROCKY, *at the table in the bar, turns grouchily as he hears a noise behind him. Two men come quietly forward. One,* MORAN, *is middle-aged. The other,* LIEB, *is in his twenties. They look ordinary in every way, without anything distinctive to indicate what they do for a living.*)

ROCKY. (*grumpily*) In de back room if yuh wanta drink. (MORAN *makes a peremptory sign to be quiet. All of a sudden* ROCKY *senses they are detectives and springs up to face them, his expression freezing into a wary blankness.* MORAN *pulls back his coat to show his badge.*)

MORAN. (*in a low voice*) Guy named Hickman in the back room?

ROCKY. Tink I know de names of all de guys—?

MORAN. Listen, you! This is murder. And don't be a sap. It was Hickman himself phoned in and said we'd find him here around two.

ROCKY. (*dully*) So dat's who he phoned to. (*He shrugs his shoulders*) Aw right, if he asked for it. He's de fat guy sittin' alone. (*He slumps down in his chair again*) And if yuh want a confession all yuh got to do is listen. He'll be tellin' all about it soon. Yuh can't stop de bastard talkin'. (MORAN *gives him a curious look, then whispers to* LIEB, *who disappears rear and a moment later appears in the hall doorway of the back room. He spots* HICKEY *and slides into a chair at the left of the doorway, cutting off escape by the hall.* MORAN *goes back and stands in the opening in the curtain leading to the back room. He sees* HICKEY *and stands watching him and listening.*)

HICKEY. (*suddenly bursts out*) I've got to tell you! Your being the way you are now gets my goat! It's all wrong! It puts things in my mind—

about myself. It makes me think, if I got balled up about you, how do I know I wasn't balled up about myself? And that's plain damned foolishness. When you know the story of me and Evelyn, you'll see there wasn't any other possible way out of it, for her sake. Only I've got to start way back at the beginning or you won't understand. (*He starts his story, his tone again becoming musingly reminiscent*) You see, even as a kid I was always restless. I had to keep on the go. You've heard the old saying, "Ministers' sons are sons of guns." Well, that was me, and then some. Home was like a jail. I didn't fall for the religious bunk. Listening to my old man whooping up hell fire and scaring those Hoosier suckers into shelling out their dough only handed me a laugh, although I had to hand it to him, the way he sold them nothing for something. I guess I take after him, and that's what made me a good salesman. Well, anyway, as I said, home was like jail, and so was school, and so was that damned hick town. The only place I liked was the pool rooms, where I could smoke Sweet Caporals, and mop up a couple of beers, thinking I was a hell-on-wheels sport. We had one hooker shop in town, and, of course, I liked that, too. Not that I hardly ever had entrance money. My old man was a tight old bastard. But I liked to sit around in the parlor and joke with the girls, and they liked me because I could kid 'em along and make 'em laugh. Well, you know what a small town is. Everyone got wise to me. They all said I was a no-good tramp. I didn't give a damn what they said. I hated everybody in the place. That is, except Evelyn. I loved Evelyn. Even as a kid. And Evelyn loved me. (*He pauses. No one moves or gives any sign except by the dread in their eyes that they have heard him. Except* PARRITT, *who takes his hands from his face to look at* LARRY *pleadingly.*)

PARRITT. I loved Mother, Larry! No matter what she did! I still do! Even though I know she wishes now I was dead! You believe that, don't you? Christ, why can't you say something?

HICKEY. (*too absorbed in his story now to notice this—goes on in a tone of fond, sentimental reminiscence*) Yes, sir, as far back as I can remember, Evelyn and I loved each other. She always stuck up for me.

She wouldn't believe the gossip—or she'd pretend she didn't. No one could convince her I was no good. Evelyn was stubborn as all hell once she'd made up her mind. Even when I'd admit things and ask her forgiveness, she'd make excuses for me and defend me against myself. She'd kiss me and say she knew I didn't mean it and I wouldn't do it again. So I'd promise I wouldn't. I'd have to promise, she was so sweet and good, though I knew darned well— (*A touch of strange bitterness comes into his voice for a moment*) No, sir, you couldn't stop Evelyn. Nothing on earth could shake her faith in me. Even I couldn't. She was a sucker for a pipe dream. (*Then quickly*) Well, naturally, her family forbid her seeing me. They were one of the town's best, rich for that hick burg, owned the trolley line and lumber company. Strict Methodists, too. They hated my guts. But they couldn't stop Evelyn. She'd sneak notes to me and meet me on the sly. I was getting more restless. The town was getting more like a jail. I made up my mind to beat it. I knew exactly what I wanted to be by that time. I'd met a lot of drummers around the hotel and liked 'em. They were always telling jokes. They were sports. They kept moving. I liked their life. And I knew I could kid people and sell things. The hitch was how to get the railroad fare to the Big Town. I told Mollie Arlington my trouble. She was the madame of the cathouse. She liked me. She laughed and said, "Hell, I'll stake you, Kid! I'll bet on you. With that grin of yours and that line of bull, you ought to be able to sell skunks for good ratters!" (*He chuckles*) Mollie was all right. She gave me confidence in myself. I paid her back, the first money I earned. Wrote her a kidding letter, I remember, saying I was peddling baby carriages and she and the girls had better take advantage of our bargain offer. (*He chuckles*) But that's ahead of my story. The night before I left town, I had a date with Evelyn. I got all worked up, she was so pretty and sweet and good. I told her straight, "You better forget me, Evelyn, for your own sake. I'm no good and never will be. I'm not worthy to wipe your shoes." I broke down and cried. She just said, looking white and scared, "Why, Teddy? Don't you still love me?" I said, "Love you? God, Evelyn, I love you more than anything in the world. And I always will!" She said, "Then nothing else matters, Teddy, because nothing but death could stop my loving you. So I'll wait, and when you're ready you send for me and we'll be married. I know I can make you happy, Teddy, and once you're happy you won't want to do any of the bad things you've done any more." And I said, "Of course, I won't, Evelyn!" I meant it, too. I believed it. I loved her so much she could make me believe anything. (*He sighs. There is a suspended, waiting silence. Even the two detectives are drawn into it. Then* HOPE *breaks into dully exasperated, brutally callous protest.*)

HOPE. Get it over, you long-winded bastard! You married her, and you caught her cheating with the iceman, and you croaked her, and who the hell cares? What's she to us? All we want is to pass out in peace, bejees! (*A chorus of dull, resentful protest from all the group. They mumble, like sleepers who curse a person who keeps awakening them, "What's it to us? We want to pass out in peace!"* HOPE *drinks and they mechanically follow his example. He pours another and they do the same. He complains with a stupid, nagging insistence*) No life in the booze! No kick! Dishwater. Bejees, I'll never pass out!

HICKEY. (*goes on as if there had been no interruption*) So I beat it to the Big Town. I got a job easy, and it was a cinch for me to make good. I had the knack. It was like a game, sizing people up quick, spotting what their pet pipe dreams were, and then kidding 'em along that line, pretending you believed what they wanted to believe about themselves. Then they liked you, they trusted you, they wanted to buy something to show their gratitude. It was fun. But still, all the while I felt guilty, as if I had no right to be having such a good time away from Evelyn. In each letter I'd tell her how I missed her, but I'd keep warning her, too. I'd tell her all my faults, how I liked my booze every once in a while, and so on. But there was no shaking Evelyn's belief in me, or her dreams about the future. After each letter of hers, I'd be as full of faith as she was. So as soon as I got enough saved to start us off, I sent for her and we got married. Christ, wasn't I happy for a while! And wasn't she happy! I don't care what anyone says, I'll bet there never was two people who loved each other more than me and Evelyn. Not only then but always after, in spite of everything I did— (*He pauses—then sadly*) Well, it's all there, at the start, everything that happened afterwards. I never could learn to handle temptation. I'd want to reform and mean it. I'd promise Evelyn, and I'd promise myself, and I'd believe it. I'd tell her, it's the last time. And she'd say, "I know it's the last time, Teddy. You'll never do it again." That's what made it so hard. That's what made me feel such a rotten skunk—her always forgiving me. My playing around with women, for instance. It was only a harmless good time to me. Didn't mean anything. But I'd know what it meant to Evelyn. So I'd say to myself, never again. But you know how it is, traveling around. The damned hotel rooms. I'd get seeing things in the wall paper. I'd get bored as hell. Lonely and homesick. But at the same time sick of home. I'd feel free and I'd want to celebrate a little. I never drank on the job, so it had to be dames. Any tart. What I'd want was some tramp I could be myself with without being ashamed—someone I could tell a dirty joke to and she'd laugh.

CORA. (*with a dull, weary bitterness*) Jees, all de lousy jokes I've had to listen to and pretend was funny!

HICKEY. (*goes on obliviously*) Sometimes I'd try some joke I thought was a corker on Evelyn. She'd always make herself laugh. But I could tell she thought it was dirty, not funny. And Evelyn always knew about the tarts I'd been with when I came home from a trip. She'd kiss me and look in my eyes, and she'd know. I'd see in her eyes how she was trying not to know, and then telling herself even if it was true, he couldn't help it, they tempt him, and he's lonely, he hasn't got me, it's only his body, anyway, he doesn't love them, I'm the only one he loves. She was right, too. I never loved anyone else. Couldn't if I wanted to. (*He pauses*) She forgave me even when it all had to come out in the open. You know how it is when you keep taking chances. You may be lucky for a long time, but you get nicked in the end. I picked up a nail from some tart in Altoona.

CORA. (*dully, without resentment*) Yeah. And she picked it up from some guy. It's all in de game. What de hell of it?

HICKEY. I had to do a lot of lying and stalling when I got home. It didn't do any good. The quack I went to got all my dough and then told me I was cured and I took his word. But I wasn't, and poor Evelyn— But she did her best to make me believe she fell for my lie about how traveling men get things from drinking cups on trains. Anyway, she forgave me. The same way she forgave me every time I'd turn up after a periodical drunk. You all know what I'd be like at the end of one. You've seen me. Like something lying in the gutter that no alley cat would lower itself to drag in—something they threw out of the D.T. ward in Bellevue along with the garbage, something that ought to be dead and isn't! (*His face is convulsed with self-loathing*) Evelyn wouldn't have heard from me in a month or more. She'd have been waiting there alone, with the neighbors shaking their heads and feeling sorry for her out loud. That was before she got me to move to the outskirts, where there weren't any next-door neighbors. And then the door would open and in I'd stumble—looking like what I've said—into her home, where she kept everything so spotless and clean. And I'd sworn it would never happen again, and now I'd have to start swearing again this was the last time. I could see disgust having a battle in her eyes with love. Love always won. She'd make herself kiss me, as if nothing had happened, as if I'd just come home from a business trip. She'd never complain or bawl me out. (*He bursts out in a tone of anguish that has anger and hatred beneath it*) Christ, can you imagine what a guilty skunk she made me feel! If she'd only admitted once she didn't believe any more in her pipe dream that some day I'd behave! But she never would. Evelyn was stubborn as hell. Once she'd set her heart on anything, you couldn't shake her faith that it had to come true—tomorrow! It was the same old story, over and over, for years and years. It kept piling up, inside her and inside me. God, can you picture all I made her suffer, and all the guilt she made me feel, and how I hated myself! If she only hadn't been so damned good—if she'd been the same kind of wife I was a husband. God, I used to pray sometimes she'd—I'd even say to her, "Go on, why don't you, Evelyn? It'd serve me right. I wouldn't mind. I'd forgive you." Of course, I'd pretend I was kidding—the same way I used to joke here about her being in the hay with the iceman. She'd have been so hurt if I'd said it seriously. She'd have thought I'd stopped loving her. (*He pauses—then looking around at them*) I suppose you think I'm a liar, that no woman could have stood all she stood and still loved me so much—that it isn't human for any woman to be so pitying and forgiving. Well, I'm not lying, and if you'd ever seen her, you'd realize I wasn't. It was written all over her face, sweetness and love and pity and forgiveness. (*He reaches mechanically for the inside pocket of his coat*) Wait! I'll show you. I always carry her picture. (*Suddenly he looks startled. He stares before him, his hand falling back—quietly*) No, I'm forgetting I tore it up—afterwards. I didn't need it any more. (*He pauses. The silence is like that in the room of a dying man where people hold their breath, waiting for him to die.*)

CORA. (*with a muffled sob*) Jees, Hickey! Jees! (*She shivers and puts her hands over her face.*)

PARRITT. (*to* LARRY *in a low insistent tone*) I burnt up Mother's picture, Larry. Her eyes followed me all the time. They seemed to be wishing I was dead!

HICKEY. It kept piling up, like I've said. I got so I thought of it all the time. I hated myself more and more, thinking of all the wrong I'd done to the sweetest woman in the world who loved me so much. I got so I'd curse myself for a lousy bastard every time I saw myself in the mirror. I felt such pity for her it drove me crazy. You wouldn't believe a guy like me, that's knocked around so much, could feel such pity. It got so every night I'd wind up hiding my face in her lap, bawling and begging her forgiveness. And, of course, she'd always comfort me and say, "Never mind, Teddy, I know you won't ever again." Christ, I loved her so, but I began to hate that pipe dream! I began to be afraid I was going bughouse, because sometimes I couldn't forgive her for forgiving me. I even caught myself hating her for making me hate myself so much.

There's a limit to the guilt you can feel and the forgiveness and the pity you can take! You have to begin blaming someone else, too. I got so sometimes when she'd kiss me it was like she did it on purpose to humiliate me, as if she'd spit in my face! But all the time I saw how crazy and rotten of me that was, and it made me hate myself all the more. You'd never believe I could hate so much, a good-natured, happy-go-lucky slob like me. And as the time got nearer to when I was due to come here for my drunk around Harry's birthday, I got nearly crazy. I kept swearing to her every night that this time I really wouldn't, until I'd made it a real final test to myself—and to her. And she kept encouraging me and saying, "I can see you really mean it now, Teddy. I know you'll conquer it this time, and we'll be so happy, dear." When she'd say that and kiss me, I'd believe it, too. Then she'd go to bed, and I'd stay up alone because I couldn't sleep and I didn't want to disturb her, tossing and rolling around. I'd get so damned lonely. I'd get thinking how peaceful it was here, sitting around with the old gang, getting drunk and forgetting love, joking and laughing and singing and swapping lies. And finally I knew I'd have to come. And I knew if I came this time, it was the finish. I'd never have the guts to go back and be forgiven again, and that would break Evelyn's heart because to her it would mean I didn't love her any more. (*He pauses*) That last night I'd driven myself crazy trying to figure some way out for her. I went in the bedroom. I was going to tell her it was the end. But I couldn't do that to her. She was sound asleep. I thought, God, if she'd only never wake up, she'd never know! And then it came to me—the only possible way out, for her sake. I remembered I'd given her a gun for protection while I was away and it was in the bureau drawer. She'd never feel any pain, never wake up from her dream. So I—

HOPE. (*tries to ward this off by pounding with his glass on the table— with brutal, callous exasperation*) Give us a rest, for the love of Christ! Who the hell cares? We want to pass out in peace! (*They all, except* PARRITT *and* LARRY, *pound with their glasses and grumble in chorus:* "*Who the hell cares? We want to pass out in peace!*" MORAN, *the de-*

tective, moves quietly from the entrance in the curtain across the back of the room to the table where his companion, LIEB, *is sitting.* ROCKY *notices his leaving and gets up from the table in the rear and goes back to stand and watch in the entrance.* MORAN *exchanges a glance with* LIEB, *motioning him to get up. The latter does so. No one notices them. The clamor of banging glasses dies out as abruptly as it started.* HICKEY *hasn't appeared to hear it.*)

HICKEY. (*simply*) So I killed her. (*There is a moment of dead silence. Even the detectives are caught in it and stand motionless.*)

PARRITT. (*suddenly gives up and relaxes limply in his chair—in a low voice in which there is a strange exhausted relief*) I may as well confess, Larry. There's no use lying any more. You know, anyway. I didn't give a damn about the money. It was because I hated her.

HICKEY. (*obliviously*) And then I saw I'd always known that was the only possible way to give her peace and free her from the misery of loving me. I saw it meant peace for me, too, knowing she was at peace. I felt as though a ton of guilt was lifted off my mind. I remember I stood by the bed and suddenly I had to laugh. I couldn't help it, and I knew Evelyn would forgive me. I remember I heard myself speaking to her, as if it was something I'd always wanted to say: "Well, you know what you can do with your pipe dream now, you damned bitch!" (*He stops with a horrified start, as if shocked out of a nightmare, as if he couldn't believe he heard what he had just said. He stammers*) No! I never—!

PARRITT. (*to* LARRY—*sneeringly*) Yes, that's it! Her and the damned old Movement pipe dream! Eh, Larry?

HICKEY. (*bursts into frantic denial*) No! That's a lie! I never said—! Good God, I couldn't have said that! If I did, I'd gone insane! Why, I loved Evelyn better than anything in life! (*He appeals brokenly to the crowd*) Boys, you're all my old pals! You've known old Hickey for years! You know I'd never— (*His eyes fix on* HOPE) You've known me longer than anyone, Harry. You know I must have been insane, don't you, Governor?

HOPE. (*at first with the same defensive callousness—without looking at him*) Who the hell cares? (*Then suddenly he looks at* HICKEY *and there is an extraordinary change in his expression. His face lights up, as if he were grasping at some dawning hope in his mind. He speaks with a groping eagerness*) Insane? You mean—you went really insane? (*At the tone of his voice, all the group at the tables by him start and stare at him as if they caught his thought. Then they all look at* HICKEY *eagerly, too.*)

HICKEY. Yes! Or I couldn't have laughed! I couldn't have said that to her! (MORAN *walks up behind him on one side, while the second detective,* LIEB, *closes in on him from the other.*)

MORAN. (*taps* HICKEY *on the shoulder*) That's enough, Hickman. You know who we are. You're under arrest. (*He nods to* LIEB, *who slips a pair of handcuffs on* HICKEY's *wrists.* HICKEY *stares at them with stupid incomprehension.* MORAN *takes his arm*) Come along and spill your guts where we can get it on paper.

HICKEY. No, wait, Officer! You owe me a break! I phoned and made it easy for you, didn't I? Just a few minutes! (*To* HOPE—*pleadingly*) You know I couldn't say that to Evelyn, don't you, Harry—unless ·

HOPE. (*eagerly*) And you've been crazy ever since? Everything you've said and done here—

HICKEY. (*for a moment forgets his own obsession and his face takes on its familiar expression of affectionate amusement and he chuckles*) Now, Governor! Up to your old tricks, eh? I see what you're driving at, but I can't let you get away with— (*Then, as* HOPE's *expression turns to resentful callousness again and he looks away, he adds hastily with pleading desperation*) Yes, Harry, of course, I've been out of my mind ever since! All the time I've been here! You saw I was insane, didn't you?

MORAN (*with cynical disgust*) Can it! I've had enough of your act. Save it for the jury. (*Addressing the crowd, sharply*) Listen, you guys. Don't fall for his lies. He's starting to get foxy now and thinks he'll plead insanity. But he can't get away with it. (*The crowd at the grouped tables are grasping at* hope *now. They glare at him resentfully.*)

HOPE. (*begins to bristle in his old-time manner*) Bejees, you dumb dick, you've got a crust trying to tell us about Hickey! We've known him for years, and every one of us noticed he was nutty the minute he showed up here! Bejees, if you'd heard all the crazy bull he was pulling about bringing us peace—like a bughouse preacher escaped from an asylum! If you'd seen all the damned-fool things he made us do! We only did them because— (*He hesitates—then defiantly*) Because we hoped he'd come out of it if we kidded him along and humored him. (*He looks around at the others*) Ain't that right, fellers? (*They burst into a chorus of eager assent: "Yes, Harry!" "That's it, Harry!" "That's why!" "We knew he was crazy!" "Just to humor him!"*)

MORAN. A fine bunch of rats! Covering up for a dirty, cold-blooded murderer.

HOPE. (*stung into recovering all his old fuming truculence*) Is that so? Bejees, you know the old story, when Saint Patrick drove the snakes out of Ireland they swam to New York and joined the police force! Ha! (*He cackles insultingly*) Bejees, we can believe it now when we look at you, can't we, fellers? (*They all growl assent, glowering defiantly at* MORAN. MORAN *glares at them, looking as if he'd like to forget his prisoner and start cleaning out the place.* HOPE *goes on pugnaciously*) You stand up for your rights, bejees, Hickey! Don't let this smart-aleck dick get funny with you. If he pulls any rubber-hose tricks, you let me know! I've still got friends at the Hall! Bejees, I'll have him back in uniform pounding a beat where the only graft he'll get will be stealing tin cans from the goats!

MORAN. (*furiously*) Listen, you cockeyed old bum, for a plugged nickel I'd— (*Controlling himself, turns to* HICKEY, *who is oblivious to all this, and yanks his arm*) Come on, you!

HICKEY. (*with a strange mad earnestness*) Oh, I want to go, Officer. I can hardly wait now. I should have phoned you from the house right afterwards. It was a waste of time coming here. I've got to explain to Evelyn. But I know she's forgiven me. She knows I was insane. You've got me all wrong, Officer. I want to go to the Chair.

MORAN. Crap!

718

HICKEY. (*exasperatedly*) God, you're a dumb dick! Do you suppose I give a damn about life now? Why, you bonehead, I haven't got a single damned lying hope or pipe dream left!

MORAN. (*jerks him around to face the door to the hall*) Get a move on!

HICKEY. (*as they start walking toward rear—insistently*) All I want you to see is I was out of my mind afterwards, when I laughed at her! I was a raving rotten lunatic or I couldn't have said— Why, Evelyn was the only thing on God's earth I ever loved! I'd have killed myself before I'd ever hurt her! (*They disappear in the hall.* HICKEY's *voice keeps on protesting.*)

HOPE. (*calls after him*) Don't worry, Hickey! They can't give you the Chair! We'll testify you was crazy! Won't we, fellers? (*They all assent. Two or three echo* HOPE's *"Don't worry, Hickey." Then from the hall comes the slam of the street door.* HOPE's *face falls—with genuine sorrow*) He's gone. Poor crazy son of a bitch! (*All the group around him are sad and sympathetic, too.* HOPE *reaches for his drink*) Bejees, I need a drink. (*They grab their glasses.* HOPE *says hopefully*) Bejees, maybe it'll have the old kick, now he's gone. (*He drinks and they follow suit.*)

ROCKY. (*comes forward from where he has stood in the bar entrance— hopefully*) Yeah, Boss, maybe we can get drunk now. (*He sits in the chair by* CHUCK *and pours a drink and tosses it down. Then they all sit still, waiting for the effect, as if this drink were a crucial test, so absorbed in hopeful expectancy that they remain oblivious to what happens at* LARRY's *table.*)

LARRY. (*his eyes full of pain and pity—in a whisper, aloud to himself*) May the Chair bring him peace at last, the poor tortured bastard!

PARRITT. (*leans toward him—in a strange low insistent voice*) Yes, but he isn't the only one who needs peace, Larry. I can't feel sorry for him. He's lucky. He's through, now. It's all decided for him. I wish it was decided for me. I've never been any good at deciding things. Even about selling out, it was the tart the detective agency got after me who put it in my mind. You remember what Mother's like, Larry. She makes all the decisions. She's always decided what I must do. She doesn't like anyone to be free but herself. (*He pauses, as if waiting for comment, but* LARRY *ignores him*) I suppose you think I ought to have made those dicks take me away with Hickey. But how could I prove it, Larry? They'd think I was nutty. Because she's still alive. You're the only one who can understand how guilty I am. Because you know her and what I've done to her. You know I'm really much guiltier than he is. You know what I did is a much worse murder. Because she is dead and yet she has to live. For a while. But she can't live long in jail. She loves freedom too much. And I can't kid myself like Hickey, that she's at peace. As long as she lives, she'll never be able to forget what I've done to her even in her sleep. She'll never have a second's peace. (*He pauses—then bursts out*) Jesus, Larry, can't you say something? (LARRY *is at the breaking point.* PARRITT *goes on*) And I'm not putting up any bluff, either, that I was crazy afterwards when I laughed to myself and thought, "You know what you can do with your freedom pipe dream now, don't you, you damned old bitch!"

LARRY. (*snaps and turns on him, his face convulsed with detestation. His quivering voice has a condemning command in it*) Go! Get the hell out of life, God damn you, before I choke it out of you! Go up—!

PARRITT. (*his manner is at once transformed. He seems suddenly at peace with himself. He speaks simply and gratefully*) Thanks, Larry. I just wanted to be sure. I can see now it's the only possible way I can ever get free from her. I guess I've really known that all my life. (*He pauses—then with a derisive smile*) It ought to comfort Mother a little, too. It'll give her the chance to play the great incorruptible Mother of the Revolution, whose only child is the Proletariat. She'll be able to say: "Justice is done! So may all traitors die!" She'll be able to say: "I am glad he's dead! Long live the Revolution!" (*He adds with a final implacable jeer*) You know her, Larry! Always a ham!

LARRY. (*pleads distractedly*) Go, for the love of Christ, you mad tortured bastard, for your own sake! (HUGO *is roused by this. He lifts his head and peers uncomprehendingly at* LARRY. *Neither* LARRY *nor* PARRITT *notices him.*)

PARRITT. (*stares at* LARRY. *His face begins to crumble as if he were going to break down and sob. He turns his head away, but reaches out fumblingly and pats* LARRY's *arm and stammers*) Jesus, Larry, thanks. That's kind. I knew you were the only one who could understand my side of it. (*He gets to his feet and turns toward the door.*)

HUGO. (*looks at* PARRITT *and bursts into his silly giggle*) Hello, leedle Don, leedle monkey-face! Don't be a fool! Buy me a trink!

PARRITT. (*Puts on an act of dramatic bravado—forcing a grin*) Sure, I will, Hugo! Tomorrow! Beneath the willow trees! (*He walks to the door with a careless swagger and disappears in the hall. From now on,* LARRY *waits, listening for the sound he knows is coming from the backyard outside the window, but trying not to listen, in an agony of horror and cracking nerve.*)

HUGO. (*stares after* PARRITT *stupidly*) Stupid fool! Hickey make you crazy, too. (*He turns to the oblivious* LARRY—*with a timid eagerness*) I'm glad, Larry, they take that crazy Hickey avay to asylum. He makes me have bad dreams. He makes me tell lies about myself. He makes me want to spit on all I have ever dreamed. Yes, I am glad they take him to asylum. I don't feel I am dying now. He vas selling death to me, that crazy salesman. I think I have a trink now, Larry. (*He pours a drink and gulps it down.*)

HOPE. (*jubilantly*) Bejees, fellers, I'm feeling the old kick, or I'm a liar! It's putting life back in me! Bejees, if all I've lapped up begins to hit me, I'll be paralyzed before I know it! It was Hickey kept it from— Bejees, I know that sounds crazy, but he was crazy, and he'd got all of us as bughouse as he was. Bejees, it does queer things to you, having to listen day and night to a lunatic's pipe dreams—pretending you believe them, to kid him along and doing any crazy thing he wants to humor him. It's dangerous, too. Look at me pretending to start for a walk just to keep him quiet. I knew damned well it wasn't the right day for it. The sun was broiling and the streets full of automobiles. Bejees, I could feel myself getting sunstroke, and an automobile damn

721

near ran over me. (*He appeals to* ROCKY, *afraid of the result, but daring it*) Ask Rocky. He was watching. Didn't it, Rocky?

ROCKY. (*a bit tipsily*) What's dat, Boss? Jees, all de booze I've mopped up is beginning to get me. (*Earnestly*) De automobile, Boss? Sure, I seen it! Just missed yuh! I thought yuh was a goner. (*He pauses —then looks around at the others, and assumes the old kidding tone of the inmates, but hesitantly, as if still a little afraid*) On de woid of a honest bartender! (*He tries a wink at the others. They all respond with smiles that are still a little forced and uneasy.*)

HOPE. (*flashes him a suspicious glance. Then he understands—with his natural testy manner*) You're a bartender, all right. No one can say different. (ROCKY *looks grateful*) But, bejees, don't pull that honest junk! You and Chuck ought to have cards in the Burglars' Union! (*This time there is an eager laugh from the group.* HOPE *is delighted*) Bejees, it's good to hear someone laugh again! All the time that bas—poor old Hickey was here, I didn't have the heart— Bejees, I'm getting drunk and glad of it! (*He cackles and reaches for the bottle*) Come on, fellers. It's on the house. (*They pour drinks. They begin rapidly to get drunk now.* HOPE *becomes sentimental*) Poor old Hickey! We mustn't hold him responsible for anything he's done. We'll forget that and only remember him the way we've always known him before—the kindest, biggest-hearted guy ever wore shoe leather. (*They all chorus hearty sentimental assent:* "That's right, Harry!" "That's all!" "Finest fellow!" "Best scout!" *etc.* (HOPE *goes on*) Good luck to him in Matteawan! Come on, bottoms up! (*They all drink. At the table by the window* LARRY's *hands grip the edge of the table. Unconsciously his head is inclined toward the window as he listens.*)

LARRY. (*cannot hold back an anguished exclamation*) Christ! Why don't he—!

HUGO. (*beginning to be drunk again—peers at him*) Vhy don't he what? Don't be a fool! Hickey's gone. He vas crazy. Have a trink. (*Then as he receives no reply—with vague uneasiness*) What's matter vith you, Larry? You look funny. What you listen to out in backyard, Larry? (CORA *begins to talk in the group at right.*)

CORA (*tipsily*) Well, I thank Gawd now me and Chuck did all we could to humor de poor nut. Jees, imagine us goin' off like we really meant to git married, when we ain't even picked out a farm yet!

CHUCK. (*eagerly*) Sure ting, Baby. We kidded him we was serious.

JIMMY. (*confidently—with a gentle, drunken unction*) I may as well say I detected his condition almost at once. All that talk of his about to-morrow, for example. He had the fixed idea of the insane. It only makes them worse to cross them.

WILLIE. (*eagerly*) Same with me, Jimmy. Only I spent the day in the park. I wasn't such a damned fool as to—

LEWIS. (*getting jauntily drunk*) Picture my predicament if I *had* gone to the Consulate. The pal of mine there is a humorous blighter. He would have got me a job out of pure spite. So I strolled about and finally came to roost in the park. (*He grins with affectionate kidding at* WET-JOEN) And lo and behold, who was on the neighboring bench but my old battlefield companion, the Boer that walks like a man who, if the British Government had taken my advice, would have been removed from his fetid kraal on the veldt straight to the baboon's cage at the London Zoo, and little children would now be asking their nurses: "Tell me, Nana, is that the Boer General, the one with the blue behind?" (*They all laugh uproariously.* LEWIS *leans over and slaps* WETJOEN *affectionately on the knee*) No offense meant, Piet, old chap.

WETJOEN. (*beaming at him*) No offense taken, you tamned Limey! (*WETJOEN goes on—grinningly*) About a job, I felt the same as you, Cecil. (*At the table by the window* HUGO *speaks to* LARRY *again.*)

HUGO. (*with uneasy insistence*) What's matter, Larry? You look scared. What you listen for out there? (*But* LARRY *doesn't hear, and* JOE *begins talking in the group at right.*)

JOE. (*with drunken self-assurance*) No, suh, I wasn't fool enough to git in no crap game. Not while Hickey's around. Crazy people puts a jinx on you.

(MCGLOIN *is now heard. He is leaning across in front of* WETJOEN *to talk to* ED MOSHER *on* HOPE's *left.*)

MCGLOIN. (*with drunken earnestness*) I know you saw how it was, Ed. There was no good trying to explain to a crazy guy, but it ain't the right time. You know how getting reinstated is.

MOSHER. (*decidedly*) Sure, Mac. The same way with the circus. The boys tell me the rubes are wasting all their money buying food and times never was so hard. And I never was one to cheat for chicken feed.

HOPE. (*looks around him in an ecstasy of bleery sentimental content*) Bejees, I'm cockeyed! Bejees, you're all cockeyed! Bejees, we're all all right! Let's have another! (*They pour out drinks. At the table by the window* LARRY *has unconsciously shut his eyes as he listens.* HUGO *is peering at him frightenedly now.*)

HUGO. (*reiterates stupidly*) What's matter, Larry? Why you keep eyes shut? You look dead. What you listen for in backyard? (*Then, as* LARRY *doesn't open his eyes or answer, he gets up hastily and moves away from the table, mumbling with frightened anger*) Crazy fool! You vas crazy like Hickey! You give me bad dreams, too. (*He shrinks quickly past the table where* HICKEY *had sat to the rear of the group at right.*)

ROCKY. (*greets him with boisterous affection*) Hello, dere, Hugo! Welcome to de party!

HOPE. Yes, bejees, Hugo! Sit down! Have a drink! Have ten drinks, bejees!

HUGO. (*forgetting* LARRY *and bad dreams, gives his familiar giggle*) Hello, leedle Harry! Hello, nice, leedle, funny monkey-faces. (*Warming up, changes abruptly to his usual declamatory denunciation*) Gottamned stupid bourgeois! Soon comes the Day of Judgment! (*They make derisive noises and tell him to sit down. He changes again, giggling good-naturedly, and sits at rear of the middle table*) Give me ten drinks, Harry. Don't be a fool. (*They laugh.* ROCKY *shoves a glass and bottle at him. The sound of* MARGIE's *and* PEARL's *voices is heard from the hall, drunkenly shrill. All of the group turn toward the door as the two*

*appear. They are drunk and look blowsy and disheveled. Their manner
as they enter hardens into a brazen defensive truculence.*)

MARGIE. (*stridently*) Gangway for two good whores!

PEARL. Yeah! And we want a drink quick!

MARGIE. (*glaring at* ROCKY) Shake de lead outa your pants, Pimp! A
little soivice!

ROCKY. (*his black bullet eyes sentimental, his round Wop face grinning
welcome*) Well, look who's here! (*He goes to them unsteadily, opening
his arms*) Hello, dere, Sweethearts! Jees, I was beginnin' to worry
about yuh, honest! (*He tries to embrace them. They push his arms
away, regarding him with amazed suspicion.*)

PEARL. What kind of a gag is dis?

HOPE. (*calls to them effusively*) Come on and join the party, you
broads! Bejees, I'm glad to see you! (*The girls exchange a bewildered
glance, taking in the party and the changed atmosphere.*)

MARGIE. Jees, what's come off here?

PEARL. Where's dat louse, Hickey?

ROCKY. De cops got him. He'd gone crazy and croaked his wife. (*The
girls exclaim, "Jees!" But there is more relief than horror in it.* ROCKY
goes on) He'll get Matteawan. He ain't responsible. What he's pulled
don't mean nuttin'. So forget dat whore stuff. I'll knock de block off
anyone calls you whores! I'll fill de bastard full of lead! Yuh're tarts, and
what de hell of it? Yuh're as good as anyone! So forget it, see? (*They
let him get his arms around them now. He gives them a hug. All the
truculence leaves their faces. They smile and exchange maternally
amused glances.*)

MARGIE. (*with a wink*) Our little bartender, aint he, Poil?

PEARL. Yeah, and a cute little Ginny at dat! (*They laugh.*)

MARGIE. And is he stinko!

PEARL. Stinko is right. But he ain't got nuttin' on us. Jees, Rocky, did
we have a big time at Coney!

HOPE. Bejees, sit down, you dumb broads! Welcome home! Have a
drink! Have ten drinks, bejees! (*They take the empty chairs on* CHUCK's

left, warmly welcomed by all. ROCKY *stands in back of them, a hand on each of their shoulders, grinning with proud proprietorship.* HOPE *beams over and under his crooked spectacles with the air of a host whose party is a huge success, and rambles on happily*) Bejees, this is all right! We'll makes this my birthday party, and forget the other. We'll get paralyzed! But who's missing? Where's the Old Wise Guy? Where's Larry?

ROCKY. Over by de window, Boss. Jees, he's got his eyes shut. De old bastard's asleep. (*They turn to look.* ROCKY *dismisses him*) Aw, to hell wid him. Let's have a drink. (*They turn away and forget him.*)

LARRY. (*torturedly arguing to himself in a shaken whisper*) It's the only way out for him! For the peace of all concerned, as Hickey said! (*Snapping*) God damn his yellow soul, if he doesn't soon, I'll go up and throw him off!—like a dog with its guts ripped out you'd put out of misery! (*He half rises from his chair just as from outside the window comes the sound of something hurtling down, followed by a muffled, crunching thud.* LARRY *gasps and drops back on his chair, shuddering, hiding his face in his hands. The group at right hear it but are too preoccupied with drinks to pay much attention.*)

HOPE. (*wonderingly*) What the hell was that?

ROCKY. Aw, nuttin'. Something fell off de fire escape. A mattress, I'll bet. Some of dese bums been sleepin' on de fire escapes.

HOPE. (*his interest diverted by this excuse to beef—testily*) They've got to cut it out! Bejees, this ain't a fresh-air cure. Mattresses cost money.

MOSHER. Now don't start crabbing at the party, Harry. Let's drink up. (HOPE *forgets it and grabs his glass, and they all drink.*)

LARRY. (*in a whisper of horrified pity*) Poor devil! (*A long-forgotten faith returns to him for a moment and he mumbles*) God rest his soul in peace. (*He opens his eyes—with a bitter self-derision*) Ah, the damned pity—the wrong kind, as Hickey said! Be God, there's no hope! I'll never be a success in the grandstand—or anywhere else! Life is too much for me! I'll be a weak fool looking with pity at the two sides of everything till the day I die! (*With an intense bitter sincerity*) May that day come soon! (*He pauses startledly, surprised at himself—then with a*

726

sardonic grin) Be God, I'm the only real convert to death Hickey made here. From the bottom of my coward's heart I mean that now!

HOPE. (*calls effusively*) Hey there, Larry! Come over and get paralyzed! What the hell you doing, sitting there? (*Then as* LARRY *doesn't reply he immediately forgets him and turns to the party. They are all very drunk now, just a few drinks ahead of the passing-out stage, and hilariously happy about it*) Bejees, let's sing! Let's celebrate! It's my birthday party! Bejees, I'm oreyeyed! I want to sing! (*He starts the chorus of "She's the Sunshine of Paradise Alley," and instantly they all burst into song. But not the same song. Each starts the chorus of his or her choice.* JIMMY TOMORROW'S *is "A Wee Dock and Doris";* ED MOSHER'S, *"Break the News to Mother";* WILLIE OBAN'S, *the Sailor Lad ditty he sang in Act One;* GENERAL WETJOEN'S, *"Waiting at the Church";* MCGLOIN'S, *"Tammany";* CAPTAIN LEWIS'S, *"The Old Kent Road";* JOE'S, *"All I Got Was Sympathy";* PEARL'S *and* MARGIE'S, *"Everybody's Doing it";* ROCKEY'S, *"You Great Big Beautiful Doll";* CHUCK'S, *"The Curse of an Aching Heart";* CORA'S, *"The Oceana Roll"; while* HUGO *jumps to his feet and, pounding on the table with his fist, bellows in his guttural basso the French Revolutionary "Carmagnole." A weird cacophony results from this mixture and they stop singing to roar with laughter. All but* HUGO, *who keeps on with drunken fervor.*)

HUGO.

> Dansons la Carmagnole!
> Vive le son! Vive le son!
> Dansons la Carmagnole!
> Vive le son des canons!

(*They all turn on him and howl him down with amused derision. He stops singing to denounce them in his most fiery style*) Capitalist svine! Stupid bourgeois monkeys! (*He declaims*) "The days grow hot, O Babylon!" (*They all take it up and shout in enthusiastic jeering chorus*) " 'Tis

727

cool beneath thy willow tree!" (*They pound their glasses on the table, roaring with laughter, and* HUGO *giggles with them. In his chair by the window,* LARRY *stares in front of him, oblivious to their racket.*)

CURTAIN